BETWEEN SILK AND CYANIDE

A CODEMAKER'S WAR
1941–1945

LEO MARKS

A TOUCHSTONE BOOK
PUBLISHED BY SIMON & SCHUSTER
NEW YORK LONDON TORONTO SYDNEY SINGAPORE

TOUCHSTONE
Rockefeller Center
1230 Avenue of the Americas
New York, NY 10020

Originally published in Great Britain in 1998 by HarperCollins Publishers
Published by arrangement with HarperCollins Publishers

First Touchstone Edition 2000

TOUCHSTONE and colophon are registered trademarks of Simon & Schuster, Inc.

Manufactured in the United States of America

10 9 8 7 6 5 4 3 2 1

The Library of Congress has cataloged the Free Press edition as follows:

Marks, Leo.
Between silk and cyanide: a codemaker's war, 1941–1945 / Leo Marks.
p.   cm.
Includes index.
1. Marks, Leo 2. World War, 1939–1945—Cryptography. 3. World War, 1939–1945—Secret
Service—Great Britain. 4. World War, 1939–1945—Personal narratives, British.
5. Cryptographers—Great Britain—Biography. I. Title.
D810.C88M375   1999   99–17581   CIP
940.54'8641—dc21

ISBN 0-684-86422-3
       0-684-86780-X (Pbk)

Contents

List of Illustrations

In December 1943 I wrote a poem which I gave to Violette Szabo to use as a code.

   This book is dedicated to all those who have shared it with her.

The life that I have
Is all that I have
And the life that I have
Is yours.

The love that I have
Of the life that I have
Is yours and yours and yours.

A sleep I shall have
A rest I shall have
Yet death will be but a pause.

For the peace of my years
In the long green grass
Will be yours and yours and yours.

ONE

A Hard Man to Place

In January 1942 I was escorted to the war by my parents in case I couldn't find it or met with an accident on the way. In one hand I clutched my railway warrant – the first prize I had ever won; in the other I held a carefully wrapped black-market chicken. My mother, who had begun to take God seriously the day I was called up, strode protectively beside me – praying that the train would never arrive, cursing the Führer when she saw that it had and blessing the porter who found me a seat. Mother would have taken my place if she could, and might have shortened the war if she had.

My father, who was scarcely larger than the suitcases he insisted on carrying, was an antiquarian bookseller whose reading was confined to the spines of books and the contents of the *Freemason's Chronicle*. His shop was called Marks & Co. and its address was 84 Charing Cross Road. He never read the gentle little myth by Helene Hanff;* long before it was published he'd become one himself.

My parents accompanied their only joint venture to the door of the train and, for the first time in twenty years, prepared to relinquish him. Mother's farewell to her only child was the public's first glimpse of open-heart surgery. Late-comers were offered a second. As I entered the carriage clutching my chicken and bowler hat, she called out at the top of her voice – if it had one – 'LOOK AFTER MY BOY.'

The captain in the seat opposite me accepted the brief. To distract me from the spectacle of Mother comforting Father and the station master comforting them both, he silently proffered his cigarette case. I indicated my virgin pipe.

* *84 Charing Cross Road* (André Deutsch, 1971).

1

'Going far, old son?'

My security-minded nod convinced him, if Mother's performance hadn't already, that I was being dispatched to some distant outpost of what remained of Empire. I was, in fact, going all the way to Bedford.

I had been accepted as a pupil at a school for cryptographers. Gaining admission hadn't been easy: I'd written to the War Office, the Foreign Office and the Admiralty, enclosing specimens of my home-made codes with a curriculum vitae based loosely on fact, but no more loosely than their formal replies stating that my letters were receiving attention. Since codes meant as much to me as Spitfires did to those who had guts, I resolved to make one last try and suddenly remembered that I had a godfather named Major Jack Dermot O'Reilly who worked in the Special Branch at Scotland Yard. I also remembered that Major Jack (like Father) was a Freemason, a branch of the Spiritual Secret Service for which I was still too young.

Arriving at the Special Branch unannounced, I called upon Major Jack carrying my codes in my gas-mask case, which he clearly considered was the most appropriate place for them. However, he must have put his 'Brother' before his country because a few prayers later I was invited by the War Office to attend an interview at Bedford 'to discuss my suitability for certain work of national importance'.

My audition took place at a large private house which tried to ramble but hadn't the vitality. A friendly sergeant told me the CO was expecting me – and I had my first meeting with Major Masters, the headmaster of the code-breaking school. He began the interview by asking what my hobbies were.

'Incunabula and intercourse, sir.'

It slipped out and wasn't even accurate; I'd had little experience of one and couldn't afford the other. I suspected that he wasn't sure what incunabula was and added: 'And chess too, sir – when there's time,' which proved a better gambit.

I answered the rest of his questions honestly – with one exception. He asked me how I first became interested in codes. There is only one person to whom I've ever told the truth about this and we hadn't yet met. The reply I concocted didn't impress him. I didn't think much else had either.

Three weeks later I received his letter of acceptance.

The school for code-breakers was the only one of its kind in England and its founding father, patron saint and principal customer was Britain's cryptographic supremo, John Tiltman. According to O'Reilly, Tiltman's talent had already received the ultimate Intelligence accolade: it had made him a bargaining counter with the Americans.

The course was due to last for eight weeks, at the end of which the students would be graded and sent to Bletchley Park, which was Tiltman's workshop and the headquarters of the cryptographic department, known in the trade as MI8.

Fifteen new pupils, including two young women, had been selected for the course and we sat at separate desks in a large, bright room, studying the mating habits of the alphabet, counting the frequency of letters and working our way through exercises which gradually became more difficult until we were ready to tackle codes of military and diplomatic level.

For a short while the whole class seemed to be moving in orderly mental convoy towards the promised land of Bletchley. But amongst those potential problem-masters there was one confirmed problem-pupil. I knew that if I didn't break behaviour patterns as well as codes, I would be lucky to last the term – a prospect which made me keep peace with my teachers for a personal best of about a week. The regression started when I felt a code of my own simmering inside me. This unwanted pregnancy was accompanied by morning sickness which took the form of questioning the quality of the exercises which were supposed to extend us. I was convinced that the school's methods of teaching would be better suited to a crash course in accountancy. The decline was irreversible when I tried to find quicker ways of breaking codes than the ones prescribed for us, and began to chase cryptographic mirages of my own making. Having somehow absorbed a few tricks of the trade, I spent hours trying to devise codes which would be proof against them. Although possibly not quite the waste of time it was then pronounced to be, this was still chronic indiscipline masquerading as creative impulse.

The chief instructor was a patient, conscientious lieutenant named Cheadle. He wandered round the classroom once a day, peering hopefully over the students' shoulders – urging us to 'dig out the root problems like a corn'. When he came to my desk, he found nothing to excise. He was like a chiropodist treating a wooden leg which insisted on kicking him.

By the time I was halfway through the course, all the others had reached the final exercise. Since I had no hope of closing the gap, I decided I had nothing to lose by vaulting it. It was strictly against the rules for any student to remove work from the premises; there was no law against memorizing it. By scanning the code until it became my favourite face, I was able to take all its key features home with me, slightly blemished by the spots before my eyes.

'Home' in Bedfordshire, a county which deserved its duke, was a boarding house – one of many in which the students were billeted. I had been instructed to tell the landlady that I was from the Ministry of Information. At supper time that night mine hostess, as usual, placed a piece of spam beside me and the code surrendered at the sight of it. It laid down its arms and said 'enough'. The rest was just hard work, a matter of gathering it in. Twenty-four hours later I was the proud possessor of a finished exercise.

Nobody had told me that it was intended to be a 'team effort' spread across a week. A bemused Lieutenant Cheadle showed my work to a highly suspicious Major Masters, who immediately tightened internal security. However, as so often happens in such matters, what is tightened at one end becomes loosened at the other and I was able to catch a glimpse of my confidential report.

It might have been written by the high master of St Paul's who would have expelled me had he not been a client of 84's: 'In his determination to find short cuts, he is apt to be slap-dash and erratic . . . though his approach shows some signs of originality, he is a very hard man to teach and will, I believe, be an even harder one to place . . .'

I wondered what arrangements Bedford made to dispose of its waste product.

The friendly sergeant was never friendlier than at mid-evening when he was prepared to reveal whatever he had heard on the grapevine in exchange for a little of the grape.

The rest of my course was going to Bletchley. As for its solitary failure, an interview had been arranged for me with 'some potty outfit in Baker Street, an open house for misfits'. If even they didn't want me, I would be regarded as unmarketable.

'It's called Inter Services Research Bureau,' said the sergeant. He lowered his voice. 'It's got another name, too. SOE or SOD or something.'

It had many names, Sergeant.

One of them was Bedlam.

The personnel officer who screened me at 64 Baker Street conducted the entire interview in the mistaken belief that I was closely related to Sir Simon Marks, the head of Marks & Spencer – an illusion which I was careful to encourage. It took me a little while to grasp what the 'potty outfit' was after from the great outfitters.

The answer was space.

The largest of the many buildings which SOE occupied in and around Baker Street was Michael House – which had been the head-quarters of Marks & Spencer. SOE badly needed extra canteen facilities in Michael House and only Marks & Spencer could grant them. The personnel officer made it clear that Sir Simon had already proved to be a most accommodating landlord and SOE was reluctant to impose upon him further.

If I was decoding the gist correctly, he was trying to assess whether I was suitably disposed to use my good offices to canvass even better ones. Unfortunately I had never met Sir Simon – but even more unfortunately, I *had* met, and couldn't stop meeting, his only son Michael, the heir-presumptive to the kingdom of M & S. We had had the incinerating experience of going to several schools together, including St Paul's, of being put in the same classes, and of being mistaken for brothers. We had finally tossed a coin (his) to decide which of us would change his name, an arrangement which he failed to honour. The princeling had not been a bit impressed when his father named Michael House after him, but he'd woken up sharply when Sir Simon offered him a cash bonus for every unwrapped orange he found in a Marks & Spencer store. I imparted these 'hot' family titbits to the enthralled personnel officer, and before he could enquire where Leo House was I assured him that I would nudge Sir Simon in the right direction the next time we dined together. A few days after this solemn undertaking 'Uncle Simon' volunteered the canteen facilities, which did no harm at all to my SOE scorecard. Marks & Spencer's greatest asset always was its timing.

I was also interviewed, skilfully and inscrutably, by Captain Dansey, the head of Codes, who indicated that he would think me over. A week later I signed the Official Secrets Act and was told to report to Dansey at nine in the morning.

On that last day of my innocence the personnel officer beamingly confirmed that I was to receive the equivalent of a second lieutenant's pay and then added, as tactfully as he was able, that my employment would be subject to review at the end of the month.

He was wrong again.

It was to be subject to review at the end of one day.

SOE's code department and teleprinter rooms occupied the whole of a mews building at the back of Michael House and I had my first glimpse of the wonders of Danseyland when an armed escort took me on an intensive route march to the captain's office, where I was handed over like a parcel of dubious content in exchange for an official receipt. This was standard SOE procedure for those who had yet to be issued with passes.

The sharp-eyed captain and his jovial deputy, Lieutenant Owen, explained that SOE's main function was dropping agents into Europe, and that my job would be to 'keep an eye on the security of their codes'. They then decided to test their new boy's ability. I was handed a message in code, put into an adjacent room and left there to break it. I knew from the little they had said about the code that it was one of the first Bedford had taught us to crack. If I risked no short cuts I should reach the code's jugular by the end of the day.

Dansey came in half an hour later to see if I'd finished but I was still taking a frequency count (this is the cryptographic equivalent of feeling a pulse). He looked at me with a hint of disappointment –

then smiled encouragingly and went out. It was then ten o'clock.

An hour later he was back again. The code's pulse was regular. Dansey's wasn't. 'Marks,' he said softly.

'Sir?'

'Do you know how long it took my girls to crack that code? . . . *twenty minutes*.'

'Sir, it takes me thirty just to clean my glasses.'

I hoped he was joking. He closed the door behind him and I knew that he wasn't.

At one o'clock Lieutenant Owen put his head round the door, watched the poor struggler as long as he could bear to, and said I was free to go to lunch if I wished. I didn't.

At four o'clock a bespectacled young lady put some tea on my desk. She departed hastily with each eye laughing at a different joke.

At a quarter to five I knocked on the door of Dansey's office and put the decoded message in front of him.

Dansey and Owen sat in silence. They were in mourning for their judgement. I knew I had failed and hoped it wouldn't prevent them from giving someone competent a chance. I thanked my ex-bosses for my tea and turned to go.

'Leave the code here, please.'

'What code, sir?'

Dansey closed his eyes but they continued glaring. 'The code you broke it with!'

'You didn't give me one, sir.'

'What the hell are you talking about? How did you decode that message if I didn't give you one?'

'You told me to break it, sir.'

He was one of the few people who could look efficient with his mouth open. 'You mean you broke it,' he said, as if referring to his heart, '*without* a code?'

I had always understood that was what breaking a code meant, but this was no time for semantics. 'How was I expected to do it, sir?'

'The way the girls do, with all the bumph in front of them. A straightforward job of decoding, that's all I was after! So we could test your speed. And compare it with theirs.'

'You mean, sir – that SOE is actually using this code?'

'We were,' said Owen. 'We have others now.'

They looked at each other. Something seemed to occur to them simultaneously. They operated like two ends of a teleprinter.

'Come with us, Marks.'

The three of us crowded into my workroom, which by now resembled an indoor tobacco plantation. Dansey didn't smoke. After a few moments of intensive rummaging he lifted a pyramid of papers and pointed to a blue card with a code typed on it in capital letters. He smiled as he held it up. His efficiency was vindicated.

I walked up to him till I was level with the pips on his shoulder. I had a request to make and, for the first time in far too long, it wasn't wholly self-interested. 'May I see those other codes, sir?'

The Baker Street code room, which Dansey and Owen ran with an efficiency and precision 'Uncle Simon' would have envied, was essentially a main-line code room. Its function was to communicate with embassies and base stations around the world using code-books and one-time pads which provided the highest possible level of security and were cryptographically unbreakable even by Tiltman. It was the luxury end of the business.

The agents in the field had to use their codes in conditions of difficulty and danger which were unique in the history of coding. Their traffic was handled in that main-line code room by anyone available to do it. The volume of main-line traffic allowed no specialization. Each girl had to be a multi-purpose coder, able in theory to switch from main-line traffic to agents' at a moment's notice, though the system called for very different aptitudes, attitudes and disciplines.

The responsibility for both main-line and agents' codes was vested in Dansey and Owen. Each of them had an asset which was rare in SOE – the ability to know what he was best at doing. They had repeatedly tried to persuade SOE that agents' traffic needed a cryptographer to supervise it – and permission had finally been given to add one to the staff. His brief, as SOE conceived it, was a simple one. All he would be required to do was 'keep an eye on the security of agents' traffic' – and perhaps break one or two of the indecipherable messages which poured in from the field.

The agents were using poems for their codes. Or famous quotations. Or anything they could easily remember. This concept of clandestine coding had been adopted by SOE because of a theory, traditional in Intelligence, that if an agent were caught and searched it was better security if his code were in his head. I had a gut feeling right from the start that this theory was wrong, and hoped that whoever advised SOE that the poem-code was suitable for agents would try performing its paper-gymnastics in the field.

The slightest mistake in the coding, a second's lapse of concentration, would render the entire message indecipherable. Frequently as much as 20 per cent of SOE's traffic could not be decoded due to agents' errors.

Whenever SOE received an indecipherable the agent responsible was instructed to re-encode it and have it ready for his next transmission.

I was prepared to fight this malpractice by whatever means I could.

If some shit-scared wireless operator, surrounded by direction-finding cars which were after him like sniffer dogs, who lacked electric light to code by or squared paper to code on – if that agent hadn't the right to make mistakes in his coding without being ordered to do the whole job again at the risk of his life, then we hadn't the right to call ourselves a coding department.

Surely the answer was simple? Squads of girls must be specially trained to break agents' indecipherables. Records must be kept of the mistakes agents made in training – they might be repeating them in the field. SOE would need more coders – and would have to compete for them in the far from open market. *There must be no such thing as an agent's indecipherable.*

Dansey didn't disagree with any of this. He simply pointed out a major obstacle of which I knew nothing. The name of that obstacle was Chain of Command.

All SOE's communications were under the control of the Signals directorate. Since these communications were worldwide, this empire-builder's paradise embraced main-line and agents' codes, all wireless stations, all wireless training schools, all wireless equipment – and one or two research establishments which no one had found time to visit.

The head of the Signals conglomerate, Colonel Ozanne, was a

problem to which no solution compatible with law was remotely in sight. A one-man obstacle course, the colonel was opposed to any kind of change except in his rank. He elected to concentrate on main-line communications whilst taking an 'overall view' of everything else, though he often had difficulty in focusing his viewfinder, especially after lunch. His second in command, Colonel George Pollock, controlled the wireless stations, the training schools and agents' communications generally. This hierarchical structure put Dansey in the delicate position of being answerable to Ozanne for main-line codes and to Pollock for agents'.

Pollock's peacetime occupation posed problems of a special kind. He was a highly successful barrister who'd been well on his way to becoming a judge, and he used the Signals directorate as an extension of his chambers. All Dansey's requests were subjected to litigation and the verdict invariably went against him. Though Dansey never hesitated to stand up and be frequency-counted, he was in every respect outranked. The colonel disliked the untidy conveyancing which placed Dansey under his command but not under his control and had made several attempts to take agents' codes away from him, the last of which had almost succeeded.

Dansey warned me that I must do nothing which would give him an excuse to try again. 'In fact,' he said, 'you must go very carefully until your appointment is confirmed. And, after that, old boy – you must go more carefully still.'

I managed to comply for two whole weeks.

Even SOE knew that for security reasons all messages to and from the field had to be at least 200 letters long – one more dangerous disadvantage of the poem-code. The country section officers who originated messages had acquired the appalling habit of sending the same text to as many as a dozen different agents with only marginal changes of phrasing.

The poem-code simply couldn't stand up to these mass-produced texts. If the enemy broke one agent's messages they would know what to look for in their other intercepts – it would be an anagrammer's delight.

I made my first contact with Buckmaster of the French section,

Hardy Amies of the Belgian, Hollingsworth of the Danish, Blizzard of the Dutch, Wilson of the Norwegian and Piquet-Wicks of another French section, though I wasn't yet sure why there had to be two. I asked them to paraphrase their messages and free their language whenever possible, and mistook their acquiescence for security-mindedness instead of the quickest way to get me off the telephone.

The next time I held out the begging-bowl on behalf of the infirm poem-code was for a very different ailment, and the remedy was even less to their liking.

To encode a message an agent had to choose five words at random from his poem and give each letter of these words a number. He then used these numbers to jumble and juxtapose his clear text. To let his Home Station know which five words he had chosen, he inserted an indicator-group at the beginning of his message. But if one message was broken – just one – the enemy cryptographers could mathematically reconstruct those five words and would at once try to identify their source.

Amongst SOE's best-sellers were Shakespeare, Keats, Tennyson, Molière, Racine, Rabelais, Poe and the Bible.

One agent had been allowed to use the National Anthem, the only verses which he claimed to remember: suppose the enemy broke one of his messages and the five words he'd encoded it on were 'our', 'gracious', 'him', 'victorious', 'send', then God save the agent. They could sing the rest of the code themselves and read all his future traffic without breaking another message.

Even works less familiar to the Germans than the National Anthem – the Lord's Prayer perhaps – would cause them no problems. Reference books are jackboots when used by cryptographers. But if our future poem-codes were original compositions written by members of SOE, no reference books would be of the slightest help in tracing them. Not even Marks & Co.'s.

It would make it slightly more difficult for SOE's messages to be read like daily newspapers if we started a Baker Street poets' corner.

I hadn't thought that writing poetry would be my contribution to Hitler's downfall, but it would at least prevent the Germans from using our traffic for their higher education. Striding up and down the corridors like the Poet Laureate of Signals, I did what I could to make my poems easy to memorize, less easy to anticipate, but I was obliged to turn to the country sections for help with their respective languages. I again telephoned Messrs Buckmaster, Amies, Hollingsworth, Blizzard, Wilson and Piquet-Wicks and asked if they would kindly write some poetry for me in their respective languages.

Rumour began to spread that there was an outbreak of insanity in the Signals directorate.

It was well founded. Agents were making so many mistakes in their coding that breaking their indecipherables single-handed against the clock was like being the only doctor in a hospital full of terminal patients. And the biggest indecipherable of all was SOE itself.

Formal acceptance into the organization had brought me no closer to understanding it. All it had produced was a pass of my own which I could rarely find, and a desk in Owen's office which I rarely left. Although the code room was only a few yards away, I seldom visited it as main-line codes were none of my business. All maimed agents' messages were brought in to me as the girls had neither the time nor the training to mend the fractures.

The prospect of ever being able to form a code-breaking team seemed even more remote when Dansey's foreboding hardened into fact. Ozanne transferred all agents' traffic to the wireless station at Grendon Underwood. The coding was to be done by groups of FANYs (First Aid Nursing Yeomanry). The takeover was to be in August, only a few weeks away. Dansey would still be in charge of agents' codes – but this could be changed at the flick of a mood-swing. He warned me not to visit Station 53 without the approval of the Gauleiter of Signals.

While grim power-struggles were raging throughout every directorate in SOE, I was engaged in a still grimmer one with Edgar Allan Poe.

He was the favourite author of an officer on Buckmaster's staff named Nick Bodington, who went backwards and forwards to France as if he had a private ferry. For this trip's traffic he'd chosen an extract from 'The Raven'. Bodington's message was indecipherable and I'd been impaled on the bloody bird's beak for six consecutive hours.

The passage Bodington had chosen was:

While I nodded, nearly napping, suddenly there came a tapping,
As of someone gently rapping, rapping on my chamber door . . .

If the indicator-group were correct, the five words he'd encoded the message on were: 'came', 'chamber', 'my', 'rapping', 'door'. When I tried decoding it on these five, all that emerged was the Raven's cackle.

Some 3,000 attempts later I discovered that the indicator was correct and the coding perfect. All Bodington had done was omit a 'p' from 'rapping', which turned it into 'raping' and screwed the lot of us.

The worst part of these indecipherables was the time element. If an agent had a schedule for six o'clock, his message would have to be broken by then or his section head would insist that he repeated it. I didn't always manage to beat the clock, but only once gave up trying.

I had been working for two days on an indecipherable from Norway contributed by an agent called Einar Skinnarland. There was something very peculiar about Skinnarland's traffic. He gave some of his messages to a wireless operator to be transmitted in the normal way (SOE was blasé enough to regard wireless traffic as normal) – but, for reasons which the Norwegian section refused to divulge, at any rate to me, most of his traffic was smuggled into Sweden by courier and re-routed to London by cable or diplomatic bag. He had already sent one indecipherable, and the usually imperturbable Wilson had stressed to me that he *must* know its contents within the hour. An hour in coding terms is only a paranoid minute. I needed to know what was so special about Skinnarland's traffic – but Wilson rang off abruptly to take another call.

That first indecipherable of Skinnarland's had been a warming-up present from him to me and had proved no more troublesome than an undone shoelace. Wilson expected the new one to be cracked as easily. But Skinnarland had had the better of our two-day duel, and five minutes before his operator's schedule I just had to get away from the thousands of failed attempts which littered my desk. I strolled upstairs to the teleprinter room to listen to the healthy chatter of Dansey's main-line codes. Suddenly I knew what Skinnarland had done and saw that, if I took a short cut and drew together several columns of his message, I would get the word 'sentries' in one line with the word 'Vermok' immediately beneath it. Taking an even shorter cut to the code room by falling down the stairs, I contacted Station 53 on the direct line.

The operator was still on the air, about to be asked to repeat the message. I told the signalmaster to cancel the instruction and send the Morse equivalent of 'Piss off fast.'

Breaking that indecipherable to the applause of my public meant far more to me at the time than that factory in remotest Vermok which Skinnarland had described in minutest detail. The rest of SOE remained equally remote.

The most distinguished visitors to our mews stronghold were the night duty officers who collected the confidential waste and the ladies who pushed around the teatrolley twice a day like sisters of mercy. But one afternoon I was struggling with yet another indecipherable from Skinnarland, who was rapidly becoming my least favourite agent, when I heard an uncommonly authoritative, disconcertingly purposeful barrage of footsteps coming our way. A moment later an RAF officer strode into the room and commandeered it without a word being spoken. I had never seen anger of such quality and substance, power and purpose as this man projected. It should have been weighed by the pound and sold as an example.

I forgot about Skinnarland as he advanced on my startled superior, making no attempt to conceal his repugnance at a pink slip (an internal message to Station 53) which was clutched in his outstretched hand.

'Who's responsible for sending this?'

'He is.'

The flight lieutenant transferred his attention to me, and his first question set the tone of our encounter: 'Who the devil are you?'

Every officer in SOE was allocated a symbol for use in correspondence; Dansey's was DYC, Owen's DYC/O. At last I had a chance to use mine. 'DYC/M,' I said, quoting it with relish.

'Tony had a sked at nine tonight. You've bloody cancelled it.! Why?'

14

Tony was an agent stranded in France with the Gestapo searching for him. A Lysander was standing by to pick him up, but his message giving map references had been indecipherable. He was due to repeat it.

'I cancelled it,' I said, 'because an hour ago we broke it after three thousand, one hundred and fifty-four attempts.'

Skinnarland's indecipherable whispered something to me in its coding sleep.

'How did you break it?'

A word was forming which could be 'mountain'.

'HOW DID YOU BREAK IT?'

It was 'mountain'.

'By guess and by God,' I said without looking up.

'Really, DYC/M? And which were you?'

'Barren mountain' – I hoped it would make sense to Wilson.

'Flight Lieutenant, if you come back in a year's time I may have finished this bugger, and I'll be glad to answer all your questions.'

'Very well, DYC/M. I'll look in again the Christmas after next, if you haven't won the war by then.'

He closed the hangar door behind him. I could still feel him looking at me.

'Who was that sod?'

'Didn't you know? That's Yeo-Thomas. Our Tommy! . . . he's quite a character.'

I didn't realize it at the time but 'quite a character' was even more of an understatement than 84's tax returns.

TWO

The Pilot Light

SOE's security checks were so insecure that I thought the real ones were being withheld from me. Their function was to tell us whether an agent was coding under duress. To convey this to us without the enemy being aware of it, he was required to insert various dummy letters in the body of each message – and their absence or alteration in any way was supposed to alert us immediately to his capture. As an additional 'precaution' he was instructed to make deliberate spelling mistakes at prearranged spots. The whole concept had all the validity of a child's excuses for staying up late, with none of the imagination. It took no account of the possibility of an agent's code being broken or tortured out of him, when the Gestapo would be in a position to work out the security checks for themselves. Nor did it make any allowances for Morse mutilation, which frequently garbled so much of the text that it was impossible to tell whether the security checks – for what little they were worth – were present.

I had already been puzzled by the traffic of a Dutch agent named Abor who'd been dropped into Holland in March. He'd sent a string of properly encoded messages – yet all of them were marked SECURITY CHECKS OMITTED, and he'd clearly made no attempt to use them from the moment he'd arrived. When I raised this with N (the Dutch) section I was told there was nothing to worry about – 'The whole thing has been looked into; the agent's all right.' There was so much else to worry about that I put this enigma on one side.

I had discovered that through no fault of anyone's (a rare situation in SOE) an agent could have a long period of waiting between leaving his training school and being dispatched to the field. His 'refresher course in coding' was left to his original training officer, if he wasn't too busy, or to his country section briefing officer, if he knew how to code. In case this accounted for the high rate of indecipherables, I raised a mortgage on my confidence and offered to brief agents myself.

Word spread quickly that someone in SOE was volunteering for extra labour, and my panel practice came of age when Buckmaster asked me to brief two F section agents named, respectively, Peter and Paul. Feeling like a pill-pusher with Messianic pretensions, I reported to F section's Orchard Court flat to meet my first pupils.

Peter's surname was Churchill – and thanks to a briefing from Owen I knew far more about him than he about me. This slender man, coiled in his chair like an exclamation mark with a moustache, had got into the habit of slipping across to the South of France, usually by submarine and canoe, and staying there as long as Buckmaster and circumstances would permit. I had no idea what Peter's new mission was but he seemed no more concerned about it than a day-tripper with some business on the side. The prospect of the South of France had put him in a holiday mood and it was with some reluctance that he interrupted it for a 'spot of coding'.

Within the next five minutes he made as many mistakes. I asked him to stop, which he did with alacrity. I knew that Peter had left Cambridge with a degree in modern languages and the reputation of being one of the finest ice-hockey blues the university had produced. Hoping to establish common ground, I discussed the 'language of coding', the rules of its 'grammar', the nature of its 'syntax'. I told him that he 'spoke coding' with a bloody awful accent which would give him away, and then switched metaphors. We chose five words of his poem and lined them up as if they were members of his hockey team, and I asked him for both our sakes to remember where the goal was. He skated through two messages without one false pass and was about to try a third when he received a phone call from Buckmaster.

'Yes, Maurice? . . . meet who? . . . his name's what? . . . (I was sure he could hear but being difficult was a sport for which he'd also won a blue) but Maurice, I'm still having a hockey lesson from Marks . . . all right then, if I must.'

17

He apologised for having to leave at half-time, promised not to get sent off for foul coding, and hurried away.

I went next door and met my first frightened agent.

When Paul and I shook hands they needed galoshes. He seemed even more of a refugee from the civil war of adolescence than I was. He was English but spoke French like a native and was due to be dropped into France in a few nights' time. He showed me a message he'd been working on. He'd found a way to go wrong which not even Skinnarland had thought of. He'd started by encoding his message quite normally, then switched to the process reserved for decoding it – which was like straddling two escalators going in opposite directions. This was after eight weeks of training. I took him through the whole system from beginning to end and he understood it perfectly, which was even more worrying.

He suddenly asked what would happen if he made 'a bit of a mistake' and sent us a message which we couldn't decode.

I didn't want him to know that he'd be dependent on me. I improvised a little and told him that we had a team of girls who'd been specially trained to break indecipherable messages. Each girl, I said, 'adopted' an agent so that if he made a mistake or two in his messages, she'd be familiar with his coding style. I then asked him to run through his poem for me and took out his code-card to check the wording. He shyly admitted that Tennyson's 'In Memoriam' was his favourite poem, and that he was grateful to his instructor for allowing him to use it. He added that he was afraid someone else might have picked it first.

He was silent for a few moments and then whispered the words – I wasn't sure to whom:

> Be near me when my light is low,
> When the blood creeps, and the nerves prick
> And tingle; and the heart is sick,
> And all the wheels of being slow.
>
> Be near me when the sensuous frame
> Is rack'd with pangs that conquer trust;
> And time, a maniac scattering dust,
> And life, a fury slinging flame.

Be near me when my faith is dry,
And men the flies of latter spring,
That lay their eggs, and sting and sing
And weave their petty cells and die.

Be near me when I fade away,
To point the term of human strife,
And on the low dark verge of life
The twilight of eternal day.

I was careful to keep looking at the code-card. There was nothing more that I could say to him. But there was one thing that I could do.

Without telling anyone, I ordered a car and went to meet the coders of Grendon.

Every girl in the code room at Station 53 could have walked out of her job at a month's notice. They were all in the FANY, a volunteer organization whose members could resign at will. The average age of these girls was twenty, though there was a sprinkling amongst them of watchful matriarchs, and most of them had been selected as coders on an arbitrary basis because they happened to be available when coders were wanted. After the briefest training they were dispatched to one of the most secret establishments in England and left to get on with it. They were never allowed to meet the agents whose traffic they handled and who were only code-names to them. The Gestapo had no more reality for these girls than when they'd joined the FANY.

As I opened the door of the lecture room, forty of them stood to attention. I wasn't sure how to get them to sit down again and made a vaguely royal gesture which had no immediate effect. I walked up to the blackboard at the far end of the room, wrote out a message in code which I hoped was legible and turned to face them.

It was the first time I'd ever given a lecture except to the one or two girls I'd taken out. I wasn't prepared for their impact *en masse*.

I spotted two gigglers at the back of the room and talked only to them for the first five minutes – about agents in the field and the risks they took to send messages to us. I quoted verbatim from a telegram Dansey had shown me only two nights ago about a Yugoslav partisan, eighteen years old, who had been caught with a wireless transmitter, had refused to betray the organizer whose messages he was sending and was eventually taken to the mortuary 'no longer recognizable as a human being'. They didn't handle Yugoslav traffic. There was a sudden urgency in that room to handle the Gestapo.

I asked them to help break the message on the blackboard as if they were the Gestapo; I showed them what enemy cryptographers would look for if they had intercepted the message. I began to anagram and asked them to join in. They were shy at first – but soon suggestions were being called out from all round the room and those from 'the gigglers' were amongst the brightest. I reserved them for Paul.

It was oversimplified, of course, but it gave them the 'feel' of codebreaking, and the principles they were shown were absolutely valid.

I let them finish the message themselves. The clear-text read: 'From the coders of Grendon to the agents of SOE. THERE SHALL BE NO SUCH THING AS AN INDECIPHERABLE MESSAGE.'

I knew I would be overloading the girls if I continued but I couldn't resist it. I wanted them to see how the enemy would now mathematically reconstruct the five words on which the message had been encoded.

It took them twenty minutes to recover those words but no one could identify the rest of the poem. I spoke it to them in full: ' "Be near me when my light is low . . ." '

Two days later they sent me a message on the teleprinter: 'WE HAVE BROKEN OUR FIRST INDECIPHERABLE. THE CODERS OF GRENDON.'

I sent them a message of congratulations on behalf of all agents. The pilot light in SOE's code room had started to burn.

THREE

A Collector's Item

By July '42 I felt sufficiently at home to rummage through the Top Secret documents on Dansey's desk while he and Owen were conferring with Ozanne. Remembering that 'You mustn't judge a book by its cover' was not only an agent's code-phrase but a Marks and Co. house rule, I ignored all the Top Secret documents, and selected for my further education an innocuous-looking folder which was lying in an in-tray.

It contained a prime collector's item: a Situation Report on the Free French, 'For Most Limited Distribution Only'. It soon became apparent even to my racing eyes that SOE and de Gaulle were too busy belittling each other's achievements to learn from each other's mistakes. The report also made clear that the in-fighting between de Gaulle and SOE had infected our policy-makers. They were unanimous that France was the life's blood of SOE but couldn't decide whether the formidable Frenchman should be treated as a valued ally or an internal haemorrhage. The sound of Dansey's footsteps stopped the rush of de Gaulle's blood to my head.

The report made no reference to a concession which SOE had made to de Gaulle in the interests of Anglo-French relations. It was a concession which amounted to a licence to lose agents and in the midnight privacy of my cubbyhole I referred to it as 'the Free French fuck-up'.

It was otherwise known as General de Gaulle's secret code.

Although de Gaulle, when he first occupied London in 1940, had had nothing he could call his own except France, and badly needed wireless facilities to tell her so, he had insisted at the outset of his

21

negotiations with SOE that all Free French agents must be allowed to use a secret French code in addition to the one which SOE would provide.

Our embryonic organization, having to fight for its life in the Cabinet as well as in the field, didn't wish to risk losing the Free French forces without having had a chance to evaluate them, and agreed to the use of a secret French code on one condition: the clear-texts of all messages in this code were to be distributed at once to RF section which SOE had formed to deal exclusively with the Free French. General de Gaulle gave his undertaking, the principle was established and both sides agreed that there was to be no departure from it.

SOE then laid on a special drill to implement this decision which was sufficiently convoluted to keep all parties happy: whenever a message was received from the field with a prefix denoting that it was in secret French code, Station 53 teleprinted it to Dansey's distribution department – which then passed it to RF section, which then passed it to General de Gaulle's Duke Street headquarters, which then decoded it and passed it back *en clair* to RF section – which passed it back to DDD (Dansey's distribution department) for circulation.

Conversely, messages to the field were handed over in code to RF section, with the *en clair* texts, and RF section then passed them to DDD, which then transmitted the code messages to Station 53, which then transmitted them.

This had become accepted procedure and no one saw the slightest reason to disturb it. Nor had anyone in SOE raised the minor matter of what kind of code the Free French were using. I hoped that they kept it as secret from the Germans as they did from us.

I watched these messages passing through the code department like distinguished strangers. And what distinguished them more than anything else was that one out of every three was indecipherable. I wasn't allowed to break them, nudge Duke Street into breaking them, or provide any kind of first aid for them whatever.

They were de Gaulle's untouchables. And every one of them reduced our battle-cry 'There shall be no such thing as an indecipherable message' to the level of a good intention.

Nor did they promote mutual confidence at my briefing sessions with the Free French. It was hard to face the agents knowing that I could help them when they made mistakes in their British code, but must look the other way when they made them in their French.

But, as Dansey firmly and sympathetically pointed out, it *was* de Gaulle's code; SOE had agreed to cede all jurisdiction over it, and the decision was irreversible. He advised me, though it had the force of an order, 'to leave well enough alone'.

I enquired whether he meant 'sick enough alone' and turned to go. 'Keep up the good work,' he said.

The only good work I was party to was being done by the coders of Grendon, who regarded an agent's indecipherable as a personal affront and did their best to scratch its eyes out. They had begun performing with the precision of relay racers and, by passing the baton of indecipherables from one eager shift to another, had succeeded in breaking 80 per cent of them within a few hours.

The bloody-minded ones which didn't respond, such as Einar Skinnarland's, they grudgingly passed on to me.

I visited the coders as often as I could to suggest quicker ways to the finishing post, to brief them about new agents, and because I enjoyed the illusion of their undivided attention. Unfortunately during one of these visits I was in the middle of explaining that the Free French were the only agents burdened with a secret code of which de Gaulle allowed us to know nothing, and that the strain of having to use two systems caused the agents to send an inordinate number of indecipherables in their British codes when Ozanne waddled in on a state visit. I immediately stopped referring to a forbidden subject but His Signals Majesty summoned me to his office to declare my interest.

I explained that indecipherables in secret French code had shot up by an alarming 12 per cent, and that Duke Street seemed to make no effort to break them. I then broke off on compassionate grounds as Ozanne's complexion had suddenly begun to match the colour of his tabs and I suspected that his blood pressure had shot up by an alarming 100 per cent. He left me in no doubt whatever that if I wished to keep my job I was never again to discuss, question or even think about the secret French code. It was entirely de Gaulle's business and anyone who didn't understand this had no place in the Signals directorate. He reminded me that I was there 'simply to keep an eye on agents' traffic', and was kind enough to add that he had heard good reports about me from Pollock and Dansey. He then assured me that if I had any important problems, I could always bring them direct to him.

A week later a Free French wireless operator was captured by the Gestapo while he was still on the air. He had begun to sign off after transmitting a message 250 letters long with a prefix denoting that it was in secret French code. Duke Street released the text of this message early next morning. It was a repeat of an indecipherable he had sent a week earlier and ended with an apology from the agent for his mistake in coding.

I waited until Dansey and Owen had left, then locked the door of my office and set about unlocking de Gaulle's secret code.

My first step was to select a dozen outgoing messages in secret code, a dozen incoming, and compare them with the *en clair* texts which Duke Street had sent us.

This was not an exercise in cryptography. With the facilities at my disposal it was a game of Scrabble played with General de Gaulle's counters.

I gave the secret French code the nudge it needed.

I couldn't, or wouldn't, believe the result.

There was no secret French code. The Free French were passing *all* their traffic in the British poem-code and disguising it from us by using a secret indicator system.

Whenever Duke Street and an agent communicated with each other in 'secret' French code, they chose five words from their British poem-code and encoded their message in the usual way. The difference was that they used their secret indicator system to inform each other – but conceal from SOE – which words they had chosen.

Technically it meant that SOE's fragile poem-codes were being used for two sets of traffic, when they could scarcely stand the strain of one. As an additional side-effect, every time an indecipherable was re-encoded in 'secret' French code it would be so easy for the interception service to identify that the operator was virtually advertising his whereabouts in neon-lit Morse.

I could see only one answer to this and set about providing it. I worked out the secret indicator system of every Free French agent, and got a timetable from Grendon of their wireless schedules so that I could be ready to decode the secret French traffic the moment it arrived.

I now had to lay on a special procedure sufficiently simple to avoid arousing suspicion. This was the high-risk part of the operation.

The teleprinter operators were used to my wandering into their office brooding over indecipherables, thinking up poems or cadging tea. I told the supervisor that Duke Street had been complaining about mutilations in traffic from the field and that, in future, I had to check all incoming messages in secret French code before they were sent to Duke Street. She didn't question this at all and handed me a message in secret French code which had just come in from Salmon's operator. I reeled Salmon's code-conventions into the lavatory for maximum privacy, looked up his secret French indicator, applied it – found that the message was perfectly encoded, remembered to pull the chain and returned it to the distribution department within ten minutes.

It was the start of an interception service which I expected to be blown at any moment, but once the drill was established the girls never questioned it.

As soon as a message was received from the field in 'secret' French code, I collected it for 'checking' and deciphered it before Duke Street had a chance to see it. If it was properly encoded, it was sent round to them at once. If it turned out to be indecipherable, I broke it as quickly as I could and then re-encoded it accurately in secret French code so that Free French headquarters could read their own traffic. It was at worst only a fringe infringement of de Gaulle's privacy.

Fortunately for the resources of a one-man code room the proportion of messages sent in secret French code was small (a little over 5 per cent) and my main problem in handling the traffic was that I was far too careless ever to have offered myself a job. On one humiliating occasion I broke an indecipherable, made a mistake in re-encoding it, and sent Duke Street an indecipherable of my own. None of the messages in 'secret' French code were operational: they were always confined to political or administrative matters. Why de Gaulle had made such an issue of using this code was none of my business. Being accurate was.

One night I was engaged in this particular labour of hate when, without any warning, the head of SOE walked in. He was known to his organization as 'CD', a tiny symbol to embrace so vast a man. Despite his size, Sir Charles Hambro could move very quietly and was prone to prowl corridors. His tours of inspection were always unexpected. He had seen a light on in my office and had come to investigate.

Sir Charles looked at me intently, as if trying to recall where he had seen me before. I willed him one of my blockages.

CD didn't know it, but we were neighbours. He had taken a flat in Park West, a Hambro-sized block in Edgware Road, which for him was only a stride away from Baker Street. My parents and I had lived there since the building had first opened, a comment on its durability. Our flat overlooked Sir Charles's and we had an excellent view of his bathroom window. CD was very security-minded when the black-out was on but relaxed his vigilance the moment it wasn't. We frequently had the privilege of watching the oversized banker wedged in his undersized bath, and Father suggested that he farted his way out.

It was in a very much larger bath that CD had watched a gymkhana of my own.

Park West had a swimming pool with a special facility for those requiring even more rigorous exercise than that on offer in their one-room flats. It consisted of thirty or so ropes suspended from the ceiling with steel rings attached to the ends of them. These ropes stretched across the entire length of the pool, a few feet above the water. To cultivate the muscles necessary for my dealings with the Signals directorate, I swung across these ropes forty or fifty times a morning with obsessive regularity. To vary the monotony, and because it was the only physical risk I had yet taken in the war, I frequently performed this exercise fully clothed. One particular morning I was swinging happily from ring to ring like a trainee gorilla, with my gas mask dangling from my shoulder and my bowler hat jammed firmly over my eyes, when I peered up at the balcony to see the head of SOE staring down at me with riveted astonishment. I was taught manners at St Paul's, if nothing else, tried to raise my hat, and seconds later gazed respectfully up at him from the bottom of the pool.

Now, as he filled the doorway of my office, I was once again in the deep end. There were one or two items on my desk which CD must on no account see. I stood up, which made no appreciable difference to the view, and introduced myself. CD's bald head hovered over my desk like a barrage balloon over suspect territory. I believed that most merchant bankers were bent and hoped that this one couldn't read backwards. He sat down and enquired what I was doing.

'Breaking an indecipherable, sir.'

'Oh? An indecipherable. Oh. Whose?'

'His code-name's Asparagus, sir. He's one of Major Buckmaster's agents.'

The broken indecipherable lying in front of me contained several references to 'mon général' which CD was unlikely to mistake for Maurice Buckmaster of F section even at the end of his longest day. CD expressed interest in seeing the message and held out a giant hand. There was nothing I could do but shake it. Prompt diversionary action was necessary. I grabbed a sheet of paper covered in figures and ash, told him that these were my calculations for breaking the message and proceeded to improvise a mathematical explanation. The figures were, in fact, my attempts to work out my monthly salary after the finance department had deducted tax. Fortunately CD was quite prepared to believe that codes were beyond him. A few moments later he professed himself very impressed by what he had seen and got up to go. I had no wish to delay him.

'I was under the impression,' CD said quietly, 'that Asparagus was Dutch.'

I felt like melted butter.

He was right, of course. Vegetables such as Cucumber, Broccoli and Kale were code-names for Dutch agents, who had been very much on my mind that day.

The ineptitude of this lie to CD was the moment of truth for the shape of codes to come. It convinced me, and I could never go back on it, that the traditional theory that all agents must memorize their codes was totally wrong.

27

If a healthy 'swinging' young man, in no danger at all except from himself, could allow his unconscious to express its tensions in a lie which even his dear old dad would have seen through, then how much worse must it be for agents under duress struggling to remember their false names, their imaginary families and the hundreds of other detailed lies on which their survival depended. I was determined to give them a code which would protect them instead of their having to protect it, or I would leave SOE.

I cleared what remained of my throat. 'Do the country sections ever admit if their agents are caught?'

That held him, and he asked me what I meant. Unsure of how much of this would be filtered back to Ozanne, I said that the security checks SOE was using seemed to be very unreliable; and it was curious that although certain agents, particularly the Dutch, consistently omitted their security checks their country sections ignored the implication that they might have been caught.

Looking at me intently, Hambro asked how long I had been with SOE. When I told him two months, he instructed me to continue asking questions until I found the right answers, his tone suggesting that he knew this would not be easy. He then said that it was time I went home, and strode down the corridor like an elephant in slippers.

An hour later he was running his bath.

SOE regarded the Signals directorate as a benign post office which delivered the mail more or less on time, could be given a kick in the transmitters if it didn't, but never caused anyone the slightest bother. The last thing the country sections expected was that a junior member of that inoffensive directorate would call on them – on the absurd pretext that the new codes he was devising must be shaped to meet their long-term requirements. Many times during that fact-finding tour I felt as if I were travelling across Europe in a carry-cot with a suspect visa.

No matter which country section I visited, everything was in short supply except confusion, and it was easy to mis-assess country section officers because the constant need for improvisation made it difficult to distinguish the few who understood their jobs from the majority who didn't.

That was the marvellous and the terrifying part of SOE in its adolescence: it was pitted and pockmarked with improbable people doing implausible things for imponderable purposes and succeeding by coincidence. One thing alone made it worth the price of the ticket. It was at the low levels at which I mixed – amongst the people SOE didn't really know it had – that the excitement of discovery really lay. It peaked and stayed there whenever I met the proud holder of the title 'Chairman of the Awkward Squad' – Flight Lieutenant Yeo-Thomas, who was one day to change his name by Resistance Movement deed poll to 'the White Rabbit'.

'Our Tommy' certainly wasn't everyone's Tommy. Many people in SOE disliked him intensely but that wasn't his only recommendation. He spoke bilingual French and had spent most of his life in France amongst Frenchmen. In 1939 he was general manager of one of the world's most famous fashion houses – Molyneux of Paris, then at the *haute* of its *couture*. He 'persuaded' the RAF to let him enlist as a ranker at the age of thirty-eight. Three years later it was SOE's turn and he joined RF section as pilot-officer.

Not even SOE could miss his immediate impact on the Duke Street intransigents. To his superior's astonishment he was able to criticize the Free French to their faces without causing a national temper tantrum and was the only Englishman actually welcomed into Duke Street by de Gaulle's fearsome right fist, young Colonel Passy. After Churchill, the man Tommy most admired was de Gaulle, and the Free French respected him for it even if Baker Street didn't. But there was one aspect of Tommy's conduct which worried SOE's hierarchy even more than his loyalty to Duke Street. He had earned his coveted title because he refused to obey SOE's house rule forbidding officers of different country sections from exchanging information. Tommy was always prepared to compare notes on the Gestapo, and similar obscenities, with anyone in SOE of whatever nationality; in the insularity which passed for security, few responded.

He hadn't waited till the Christmas after next to see for himself how indecipherables were broken. He'd looked in a few nights after our first meeting and ever since then we'd indulged in a series of late-night chat-shows during which we exchanged grievances, and shared the Havana cigars which I'd stolen from my father.

There were only two subjects which we never referred to. I didn't tell him that I was keeping a 'watching brief' on de Gaulle's secret code, and Tommy for his part never tried to involve me in a discussion about the rival French section run by Buckmaster, which recruited from those who owed no allegiance to de Gaulle. He disapproved of the principle of there being two French sections to win one war and left it at that.

One smoky midnight, when I hadn't seen him for about a week and was almost missing him, I was struggling with an indecipherable from a Norwegian wireless operator named Gunwald Tomstad. Wilson had told me that the Admiralty was anxiously waiting to read Tomstad's message, and wanted to pass its contents to 'a former naval person'. And then, as if reference to Churchill was not sufficient incentive, Wilson proceeded to warn me that if we hadn't broken the message before Tomstad's next schedule – which was only a few hours away – he would order him to re-encode and repeat it no matter what the consequences.

I thought of all the things Tomstad had done right as I tried to rectify what he hadn't.

He was a farmer who lived near a sea-port and regularly reported the movements of U-boats. He seemed to regard submarines as an extension of his livestock and his reports had already dispatched six to market, with two 'possibles'. But U-boat spotting was only the fringe of farmer Tomstad's war effort.

In 1941 he had been wireless operator for Odd Starheim (code-name Cheese) and had sent a message from Starheim reporting that four German warships were hiding in a fjord. The Admiralty immediately despatched the *Prince of Wales* and the *Hood*, and the subsequent sinking of the *Bismarck* and the crippling of the *Prinz Eugen* were directly attributable to Starheim's messages and Tomstad's operating.

Starheim was now back in London giving Wilson no peace until he was allowed to join Tomstad, and demanding to know the content of his latest message.

I tried my thousandth key without success. There was little time left. I didn't hear the door open but knew who was standing there.

Tommy recognized the symptoms of 'indecipherabilititis' and asked if he could help. I told him the bastard indecipherable wasn't from France. He shot me a tommy-gun look of utter contempt, then took off his tunic and sat down at the desk.

He spent the next two hours doing the dull, routine job of checking my work-sheets without really understanding them, but it was help beyond price to Tomstad and me. We pierced the indecipherable's hull at three in the morning ('cruiser in harbour disguised as island with tree in the middle'). Tommy didn't even glance at the clear-text. I'd have liked to tell him that it might soon be on its way to the man he most admired, a 'former naval person' – but I couldn't. I went into Dansey's office, closed the door and read the clear-text on the 'scrambler' to the Norwegian duty officer.

I returned to my office to finish the job.

The coders of Grendon had done all they could to break that message, and they deserved the satisfaction of succeeding. I telephoned the night supervisor and told her that I hadn't broken the message and was on my way home. I suggested twenty or so keys, including the correct one, and asked her to pass them to the night squad. I reminded her that if they did have any success, the message must be teleprinted to London marked 'Absolute Priority'. I wished them better luck than I'd had.

Tommy studied me thoughtfully as I gave him his cigar. 'How old are you?' he asked.

'Twenty-three.' I was tempted to be more specific and add 'next month'; I enjoyed presents.

He gave me one: 'Would you like', he asked, 'to tell me what's worrying you?'

I memorized the way he said it so that I could try it on the coders.

'Thanks, Tommy. But it would take all night.'

'I've got all night.'

'It's the poem-code! It has to go.'

'Tell me why. And then tell me what you think should replace it.'

I spared him nothing. My worry had a technical name: transposition-keys. They were the code equivalent of an anxiety neurosis.

Every agent had to work out his transposition-keys before he could either send a message or decode one from us. I wanted Tommy to

31

see for himself the kind of effort this involved in the soothing atmosphere of occupied Europe.

I asked him if there were any particular poem or phrase he would like to use; he left it to me. I wrote one out and told him it was based on an SOE opinion poll:

Y E O   T H O M A S   I S   A   P A I N   I N   T H E   A R S E

The lowest letter in that phrase is A. I asked him to put the figure 1 beneath it.

Y E O   T H O M A S   I S   A   P A I N   I N   T H E   A R S E
          1.

Then the figure 2 beneath the second A, a 3 beneath the third, a 4 beneath the fourth:

Y E O   T H O M A S   I S   A   P A I N   I N   T H E   A R S E
          1.   2. 3.   4.

The next letter is E. I asked him to put a 5 beneath it. Then 6 and 7 beneath the remaining Es.

Y E O   T H O M A S   I S   A   P A I N   I N   T H E   A R S E
5.   1.   2. 3.   6. 4.   7.

Without waiting to be asked, Tommy continued numbering the rest of the letters in alphabetical order until we were looking at:

Y E O   T H O M A S   I S   A   P A I N   I N   T H E   A R S E
25. 5. 16. 23. 8. 17.13. 1.20. 10.21. 2.   18.3.11.14. 12.15. 24.9. 6.   4.19.22.7.

That numbered phrase was called a transposition-key. I broke the good news that all messages were encoded on a pair of transposition-keys – so the agent now had to start numbering another one using, for security reasons, a different five words of his poem. An interesting repeat performance with an uninvited audience on the prowl outside.

The slightest mistake in the numbering would render the entire message indecipherable. The smallest error in the spelling would also produce gibberish. The permutations of mistakes an agent could make ran into hundreds of millions – and he still hadn't started to encode his message.

To do so, the agent used his transposition-keys to put his clear text through a series of complex convolutions not unlike Ozanne's mind, so that the message arrived in London in jumbled form where we (hopefully) could unscramble it because we (hopefully) were the only ones who knew what his poem was.

Unless the Germans had tortured it out of him.

Or unless their cryptographers had broken one of his messages – and mathematically reconstructed the words of his poem.

I told Tommy that the poem-code must go and be replaced by one *which the agents could not possibly remember*. Their transposition-keys must never again be based on words, poetic or otherwise. They must be mass-produced by hand by specially trained groups of coders shuffling numbered counters at random.

We would give each agent a series of transposition keys already worked out for him – and printed on silk. To encode a message, he would simply have to copy out the keys we had prepared for him – and *immediately* cut them away from the silk and burn them. There would be no way that he could possibly remember the figures he had used. They would all have been selected at random – and would be different for every single agent in the field.

Each silk would contain sufficient keys for 200 messages – 100 from the agent to us, 100 from us to him. The greatly increased security of these 'worked-out' keys would allow the messages to be shorter. One hundred letters could be sent instead of the existing minimum of 200.

The cryptographic parlour-game would be closed for the season. Enemy cryptographers would no longer have poems to reconstruct and would have to tackle every single message individually – an undertaking which was anathema to all cryptographers. Every message to and from the field would confront them with a new code, and to sustain an 'absolute priority' attack on this kind of traffic would mean that the bulk of Germany's cryptographic manpower would have to be deflected on to SOE – which would in itself be a major contribution to the war effort.

Indecipherables would be reduced to a minimum because we would no longer have to play the guessing-game, 'Which word has he misspelt?' The worked-out keys would also be proof against Morse mutilation, which frequently rendered perfectly encoded messages indecipherable because the indicator-groups (telling us which words the agent had chosen) were so badly garbled.

Silk itself was easy to cut, easy to burn and easy to camouflage. If the Gestapo or Vichy police ran their hands over an agent's clothing during a random street search, silk sewn into the lining could not be detected.

All the resources of the Gestapo would not force an agent to reveal a code he could not possibly remember. Destroying his worked-out keys as soon as he had used them must become as reflex to an agent as pulling the ripcord of his parachute.

But there was one thing for which he could still be tortured. His security check. And this to me was the most haunting and daunting issue of all. If we couldn't solve this problem, we had solved nothing.

For the first time I found myself wondering how best to put something to that silent, motionless figure with his unlit cigar. 'I need two minutes, Tommy.'

I grabbed a sheet of paper and started scribbling. Tommy would know if what followed was right, and I would be bound by his judgement.

When I'd finished, I wrote something on the blotter in front of me and covered it with an ashtray. I then showed him my scribbling. It was intended to be an artist's impression of how a silk code would look. All it lacked was the artist:

OUTSTATION TO HOME

14.2.13.4.6.13.1.5.7.15.3.9.11.16.10.8.	6.10.13.2.4.11.7.9.12.3.5.8.1.	CEDQT
9.10.1.7.11.4.12.8.5.2.6.13.3.	11.5.7.12.2.6.3.8.9.1.10.4.	PKBDO
2.9.5.10.14.1.6.11.4.15.8.3.12.12.7.	4.6.1.5.7.9.2.1.13.8.12.10.	RYTGE
6.3.7.4. 8.9.2.10.5.11.13. 1.14.12.	3.1.10.4.6.2.7. 8. 5. 9.11.	UVHJG
4.7.8.1. 9.2.10.11.3.5. 6. 12.13.14.	4.6.7.8. 5.1.9.10. 2.11.12.3.	ZAUBA

The explanation came out in a rush and a jumble:

'I'm an agent, Tommy, and I've been caught with my silk code on me. I've destroyed all the previous keys I've used but the Gestapo know bloody well that if they can torture my security check out of me they can use the rest of these keys to transmit messages to London and pretend they're from me.

'You'll see that opposite each pair of keys there are five letters printed. These are indicator-groups to tell London which pair of keys I've used to encode my message. The next pair I'm due to use are the ones at the top – starting 14.2.13.4. The indicator group is CEDQT. After this I'm due to use the next pair of keys – starting 9.10.1.7. The indicator-group is PKBDO. *But I never use these indicator-groups exactly as they are printed.* I have prearranged with London always to add 3 to the first letter and 2 to the fourth. Take the indicator CEDQT. C plus 3 is F, and Q plus 2 is S. So, instead of sending CEDQT I send FEDST. Instead of sending PKBDO I send SKBFO. At least, that's what I'm telling you because you're the Gestapo. All my previous indicator-groups have been destroyed; how can you know if I'm telling you the truth? Rough me up and I'll change it once again. When do you stop? Now I've written on this blotter what my *real* secret numbers are. If you can guess 'em, these Havanas are yours – and you'll be the only cigar-smoking Kraut in Baker Street.'

Herr Forest Frederick von Yeo-Thomas sat in silence for a very long time. I didn't interrupt him – except to say, somewhat nervously, that this was only one of the codes I hoped to introduce.

By the time the security-vetted cleaning women arrived to claim the office, his mind was made up. 'You're going to have a hell of a fight to get this accepted. I'm with you all the way. Let me know how I can help.'

I nodded.

'If it were done,' he said, misquoting a phrase then being used as a code by an F section agent, ' 't were well it were done on the bloody double!'

I agreed. The pails in the corridor sounded like church bells.

He got up to go. Then turned by the door and looked hard at me.

He must have had a strong stomach. 'Merde alors with your new codes'

He then added – almost as an afterthought – 'I may soon be needing one myself.'

FOUR

'Merde Alors!'

Scrambler telephones were in great demand in SOE because they were not only proof against crossed lines and wire-tapping but implied that those who possessed them had something to say which was worth overhearing. It hadn't occurred to me to ask for one of my own but early in September I found that a green telephone with three buttons on it had been installed on my desk, so I must have been doing something right. Pasted across it was a memo from Dansey emphasizing that it was to be used for Top Secret conversations only.

I pressed the right buttons to tell Tommy that I had a fresh stock of Havanas, and then contacted the Grendon supervisor to ask what progress the girls were making in the task I had set them of writing poems for agents. I'd made the suggestion a fortnight ago but the girls still hadn't produced a single stanza. Their supervisor assured me, with the hint of a chuckle, that I would not have long to wait.

I was still pondering the significance of that chuckle when I received an incoming call on the new toy from the commanding officer of Station 53, a benign major named Phillips who presided over his clandestine estate like a country squire.

Dispensing with the normal courtesies, he broke some bad news in a voice so strained that I considered asking him for proof of identity. 'Gammel's here.'

Brigadier Gammel was the commanding officer of the FANY Corps and I knew from a five-minute interview with her that she could cause grievous bodily harm with a glance. The whole of SOE was in awe of her. She was the embodiment of her famous pronouncement: 'Members of the FANY Corps must at all times conduct themselves like ladies.'

I asked the distraught major if Gammel were causing him any problems.

'Almost as many as you,' he snapped. And told me why.

The FANY supremo had arrived at Station 53 on a tour of inspection. After examining the remotest corners of Grendon for signs of impropriety, the bellicose brigadier had walked into the FANY mess, which was normally only marginally quieter than the last few minutes of a Cup Final. But today the acute Gammel ear was greeted by absolute silence. Even more unexpected to the piercing Gammel eye was the spectacle of a dozen or so FANYs clustered round a table totally absorbed in the ladylike pursuit of composing poems. She asked Phillips who had thought of this admirable idea. Mr Marks of Baker Street was given due credit. Gammel then advanced to the table to inspect the quality of her charges' writings.

She was now on the telephone complaining to Ozanne. Those dear girls, who knew damn well that Gammel was visiting them, had produced samples of hard-core pornography which Marks & Co. would have hidden in a glass case on the fourth floor, surrounded by Bibles.

Phillips read to me the first (and mildest) of the stanzas Gammel had examined:

> Is de Gaulle's prick
> Twelve inches thick
> Can it rise
> To the size
> Of a proud flag-pole
> And does the sun shine
> From his arse-hole?

He invited my comments.

I told him that the imagery was unusual, the words easy to memorize and the content not at all what the enemy would be expecting. I asked him to tell the girls that I was absolutely delighted with it and looked forward to receiving the rest.

He put down the receiver.

An hour later Ozanne sent for me and accused me of attempting to corrupt the FANY coders. It wasn't the moment to tell him that almost overnight his open city of a poem-code had taken on a new dimension of menace.

I'd learned from Dansey that there were soon to be operations, infiltrations and campaigns by the dozen in all the occupied territories, and that an unprecedented event was due to take place by the end of '42: General de Gaulle had given his permission for an Anglo-Free French mission (the first of its kind) to be sent into France to prepare for the Allied landings in '43, and 'our Tommy' was to be the Anglo.

Then there was the invasion of North Africa, code-name Torch, which General Eisenhower was planning for November/December '42. SOE had somehow persuaded Ike to allow an SOE mission to accompany the invading forces with its own communications direct to London and France.

There was also a mysterious operation into Norway referred to in whispers by its code-name, Grouse. Whatever Grouse was, it was scheduled to take place any time from the end of September, which was only a few weeks away.

All this new business was a major breakthrough for Baker Street head office but it was potentially an even bigger one for the German cryptographers. The moment they realized that our traffic was becoming important enough to warrant a full-scale blanket attack, the poem-code would provide them with a catalogue of wide-ranging war efforts at bargain prices.

I hurried off to consult the only friend I had yet made in the Signals hierarchy.

His name was Eric Heffer and he was our in-house expert on Ozanne. He was a civilian like myself but had been a captain in the First World War and preferred to be addressed as such. No one was quite sure exactly what his duties were. Occasionally he would leave his office in Norgeby House to wander at his leisure round Ozanne's kingdom, having the effect upon all of us of a walking tranquillizer.

Despite the daily crisis which surrounded him, Heffer remained permanently imperturbable. There was no known example of anyone or anything being able to hurry him. The one thing he could do with quite exceptional speed was think – a practice he recommended to me.

Producing each syllable as if it were a cigarette he had just carefully rolled, he explained that Ozanne's real weakness was not so much stupidity as respect for the Establishment. He simply couldn't bring himself to question their judgement. If the Establishment had decided that chamber pots made first-class transmitters, he'd have had SOE peeing in Morse. Almost doing so myself, I asked a) what the Establishment specialized in and b) whether it had a name.

No longer surprised by anything I didn't know, he accelerated to a crawl which served to remind me of my progress. The Establishment was officially called SIS (Secret Intelligence Service) though old hands in SOE invariably referred to the rival organization as 'C' (its Chief's code-name), and its speciality was thwarting SOE.

C had been running the British Secret Service (with emphasis on the Secret) since 1911 and were appalled when SOE received a mandate from Churchill in 1940 to Set Europe Ablaze. Their agents were intelligence-gatherers: ours were saboteurs, and C were convinced that the only thing they'd set ablaze was their agents' cover. SOE was convinced that C resented any organization which threatened its monopoly, and the mutual antipathy had the growth potential of an obsession.

In 1941 control of SOE's communications became a major issue. Our wireless station at Grendon was still being constructed, and we were forced to allow C to handle our early traffic. The station opened in June '42 (the month I joined SOE) and we withdrew the traffic immediately, much to C's annoyance as they could no longer monitor it.

Painstakingly Heffer finally turned to the subject which most concerned me. To C, giving codes to their peacetime agents had been a minor problem: there were so many channels of communication open to agents that poem-codes could safely be used, and this in itself was a definition of peace. But setting up two-way wireless traffic for circuits of agents in enemy-occupied territories was a wholly new event for which there were no precedents or guidelines, and by 1940 they had lost most of the agents they had put into Europe. This did not deter them from making a suggestion which threatened the existence of ours.

Ozanne was advised by his friend and mentor Brigadier Gambier-

Parry, C's director of Signals, that their agents were going to continue using the poem-code (or some minor variation of it) as he had no doubt whatever that agents' codes should be carried in their heads. This was all Ozanne needed to hear. What was good enough for the agents of the British Secret Service *must* be good enough for SOE's.

I waited for Heffer to tell me how we were going to transfer codes from aching heads to cuttable silk. But he chose this of all moments to indulge his knack of switching on silence as if it were air-conditioning. The captain emerged from his trance freshly recommissioned to announce that even in wartime few battles were won by direct confrontation – and even fewer if they were fought inside SOE. He had several ideas for outflanking Ozanne but would need time to consider them. Drawing on the last of the day's reserves, he agreed that worked-out keys (which we christened 'WOKs' to save breath) should be introduced as soon as possible – but there were 'one or two other things wrong' in the Signals directorate which had also to be put right. He recommended me to be patient for a little while longer.

He was too exhausted to tell me the formula.

The 'one or two other things wrong' were agents' sets, signal-plans and call-signs.

A signal-plan was a WT operator's timetable and he had to adjust his life to it. He *had* to be beside his set at certain specified times or risk losing contact with London. If he missed a fixed schedule, he had to wait for the next. But a radio operator was usually responsible for the traffic of other agents, including his own organizer, all of whom had poem-codes but no training in wireless transmission. This multiplied the pressures on him to keep his inflexible schedules irrespective of risk.

Call-signs identified an operator's traffic to the Home Station and the Home Station's traffic to him. They were the equivalent of Morse visiting cards and were an open invitation to the Gestapo's social services.

Signal-plans, call-signs and codes were the fundamentals of clandestine communication. But the Signals Directorate allowed no liaison between the officers who produced them. The Gauleiter of Signals preferred to keep us apart.

I took a surreptitious trip to the suburbs of Signalsland and it was worth every Ozanne-fraught minute of it. Many resourceful and imaginative technicians had ideas for improving the wireless side of agents' traffic but, apart from a few minor changes which had slipped through unnoticed, Ozanne had overruled them. I was prepared to leave if he vetoed WOKs.

The whole of SOE was suddenly a department store preparing for the Christmas rush, but all I found in my order book was an indecipherable from Einar Skinnarland. There were four messages from Colonel Wilson demanding that I break it.

A work-out with Skinnarland in our private gym would be a welcome respite from the prospect of going fifteen rounds with Ozanne. But the chronic invalid of coding had let me off lightly this time with a minor rupture of his key-phrase, and I found the right truss for it in a matter of minutes. The message was written in his usual mixture of Norwegian and English, which was excellent security and the one thing Skinnarland could be relied upon to do properly.

It was only when I spotted two words tucked away in the last line that I realized which of us was the chronic invalid. The words were 'heavy water'.

They had been distilled by Morse mutilation into 'heaxy woter'.

I wondered what heavy water was.

There were half a dozen files in Dansey's safe reserved for the special Skinnarland traffic which had been smuggled into Sweden and then re-routed to London by courier or diplomatic bag. I was allowed access to these files to help me break Skinnarland's indecipherables but until now the only one I'd studied was the file which contained his early messages. I soon realized why they were locked in a safe.

There were main-line telegrams from CD to Washington; main-line telegrams to CD from neutral Sweden (our men in Oslo were Munthe, Mitchelson and Binney); and main-line telegrams from Sweden to Wilson and from Wilson to Sweden; there was also a ten-page report from Munthe to Wilson (decoded by Dansey) and an even longer one (encoded by Dansey) from Wilson to Munthe.

All of them were Top Secret. All of them dealt with the same subject: the heavy-water plant, the Norsk Hydro, at Rjukan.

SOE's Norwegian directorate had been mounting a massive Intelligence-gathering operation which was astonishing in its breadth and detail:

They knew that in 1941 the Germans had ordered the plant to step up production of heavy water to 10,000 pounds within the next year; they knew how the Germans were planning to transport the heavy water from Norway to Germany; they knew the structure of the plant and its fortifications better than the layout of their own offices; they even knew where the guards were billeted, how many were on duty at any one time and the disposition of the sentries on the suspension bridge between Vermok and Rjukan. All this information had been passed by SOE to the Chiefs of Staff, who put it before Churchill.

The PM immediately asked Professor Lindemann, his chief scientific adviser, for a technical assessment. Professor Lindemann had no doubt at all (he seldom had) that the Germans required this heavy water to produce atomic bombs, atomic rockets and other atomic weapons as yet unknown.

The whole of SOE's information about heavy water flowed from one source: Einar Skinnarland. He was an engineer at the heavy-water plant. He had helped the Norwegians to build it and he was now committed to its destruction.

Sorry Mr Skinnarland, sir. Code with both eyes closed, if you aren't already.

The last document – in many ways the most revealing of all – summarized the history of the plant and the extraordinary way in which Skinnarland had been recruited.

The plant and its laboratories had been built before the war on the most isolated spot which the Norwegians could find – the Barren Mountain between Vermok and Rjukan, in the precipice- and glacier-bound wilderness of Hardanger Vidda. The Germans invaded Norway in 1940 and at once took over the plant – forcing its Norwegian technicians (including Skinnarland) to continue working there under supervision.

To find out more about the plant and if possible to recruit some

43

of the technicians, SOE dropped Odd Starheim on to a snow-covered field in Norway in December 1941 and left him to find his own way to the Barren Mountain. It was the same Odd Starheim (code-name Cheese) whose previous messages had helped the navy to sink the *Bismarck* and cripple the *Prinz Eugen*.

In March 1942 Starheim was introduced to Mr Skinnarland by a mutual friend – and it was sabotage at first sight. Skinnarland agreed to come to London with Starheim, bringing all the information he could about the plant and its fortifications.

Since SOE couldn't provide the transport, Starheim hijacked a coastal steamer, ordering the captain at pistol-point to change course for Aberdeen. Starheim had also invited a number of other Norwegians to join him on the 'trip' so that they could be trained by SOE as saboteurs and WT operators. Tomstad sent a message alerting Wilson that Starheim's boat was heading for Scotland and would welcome air cover. The RAF, as ever, obliged.

So did Skinnarland. As soon as he arrived in London he gave Wilson the fullest possible briefing about the plant – and in return was given a *twelve-day* crash course in the craft of sabotage and the agony of coding. In March '42 he was dropped back into Norway – his first ever jump – and landed on ice near his home in Hardanger Vidda. He reported to the plant, explained that he'd been ill and resumed his job as if he'd never left it. He was now awaiting the arrival of a sabotage team from London.

The four agents who'd been selected to blow up the plant had been waiting since mid-April to be dropped into Norway. The operation had already been postponed three times due to exceptionally bad weather, and they were still in London expecting the next attempt to be made in late September. The code-name of the operation was Grouse.

I closed the Grouse files.

Was it coincidence that in three days' time I had an appointment to brief four Norwegian agents who 'were standing by to go into the field after one or two delays'? Wilson had arranged this appointment personally (unusual) and confirmed it to me in writing (unprecedented). They *had* to be the Grouse team.

And when they made their bid to deny the Germans the use of

atomic power they would be sending their messages in the poem-code.

I telephoned Ozanne's secretary and said that I needed to see the colonel on an urgent matter, that it would take about an hour and that I would be grateful if Colonel Pollock could be present. I also requested the use of a blackboard.

She asked me to hold on and a few moments later told me that Colonel Ozanne would see me at ten in the morning. She sounded as surprised as I felt. She then added that Colonel Pollock could not be present; he was away at a training school. That was a setback because barristers have been known to take kindly to silk.

I spent half the night preparing for the appointment, the other half wishing I hadn't made it. I needed a booster from Tommy and I tried to phone him but he was still at Duke Street in conference with Passy. I left a message for him to ring me if he possibly could. It was essential to be prepared for a total rejection from Ozanne and I tried to work out a contingency plan.

At one in the morning Tommy phoned. I told him of my appointment with Ozanne.

He instructed me to keep my voice up, not to smoke cigars, under no circumstances to make a joke – and above all to cut off my temper like a silk code and burn it before I went in. I promised to comply.

He then wished me 'Merde alors!' – the ultimate SOE benediction.

I'd need it with the ultimate SOE merde.

FIVE

All Things Bright and Beautiful

Hoping Ozanne had cancelled our appointment, I knocked on the door of his Norgeby House office and aged five minutes (the wartime equivalent of as many years) when I was instructed to enter. He was seated behind a large desk covered with what I imagined were unread signals. The blackboard I'd asked for was a few feet away.

I imparted the good news that I'd come to show him how I believed the enemy would attack the poem-code, and he invited me to take all the time I needed; he had no other appointments for fifteen minutes.

I wrote out two coded messages, one on top of the other. Each message was fifty-five letters long, and by the time I'd given every pair of letters a number he was already consulting his watch.

	1.	2.	3.	4.	5.	6.	7.	8.	9.	10.	11.	12.	13.	14.
Message 1:	C	N	A	E	R	S	S	N	G	E	O	O	N	N
Message 2:	T	H	I	S	T	E	P	F	N	D	S	L	O	A
	15.	6.	17.	18.	19.	20.	21.	22.	23.	24.	25.	26.	27.	28.
Message 1 (cont.):	R	O	S	E	E	E	I	S	O	A	O	L	N	G
Message 2 (cont.):	O	Y	E	N	W	S	N	M	H	A	E	G	D	I
	29.	30.	31.	32.	33.	34.	35.	36.	37.	38.	39.	40.	41.	42.
Message 1 (cont.):	C	E	E	E	E	R	E	T	D	L	S	Z	E	
Message 2 (cont.):	E	P	B	E	K	S	T	K	U	G	I	G	D	S
	43.	44.	45.	46.	47.	48.	49.	50.	51.	52.	53.	54.	55.	
Message 1 (cont.):	L	T	H	S	S	N	A	V	A	N	T	E	M	
Message 2 (cont.):	U	U	S	E	E	A	T	R	N	C	C	O	E	

I explained that the messages were mini-examples of our agents' traffic. They'd been encoded on the same poem using the same five words, and were of equal length. This all too frequent occurrence was every cryptographer's wish-fulfilment as it gave him what was known in the trade as a 'depth of two'.

I glanced round at him. He was reading a newspaper. 'Quite,' he said, peering over the top of it.

I asked him what words he thought a cryptographer would look for when he tackled an average SOE message, and he picked up one of his signals.

'Dropping grounds,' he said, 'and containers and moon periods. That sort of bumph.'

'Yes, sir,' I said encouragingly. 'And "message begins" and "message ends" and "sorry about my indecipherable", and that sort of bumph.'

I then suggested that the messages contained the names of some of SOE's key figures, and that the enemy would try to anagram them. Whose names would they be most likely to start looking for?

After a modest pause he conjectured that his own might be one of them.

Thank God we'd got that far. I asked him if he considered rank to be important. He looked hard at me and agreed that it was. I wrote the words COLONEL OZEANNE on the blackboard.

'*You've spelled my name wrong, damn it.*'

I apologized and tried to make capital out of it. 'It's an uncommon one, sir – but its letters aren't, except for the z. That's the first letter they'd try to pinpoint. Is there a z in either message?'

'*No.*'

'Sorry, sir. It must be my bad writing. What's that letter in the top message under number 41?'

'*That's supposed to be a z is it?*'

'Yes, sir, and that's a D beneath it, in the bottom message. Those two letters must be tackled together. And that's true of all the other pairs of letters in the messages, sir. That's because both texts have been encoded on the same transposition-keys and put through the same poem-code mangler. That makes our stint much easier because instead of having to anagram each message separately, we can anagram them together. If we find a word in the top message, the letters in the bottom message should also make sense. If we find a word in the bottom message, the letters in the top message should also form

47

one. So if "Colonel Ozeanne" is on top, we shall soon discover what you've got underneath you!'

I showed him what I meant before he had me arrested.

41.

	C O L O N E L O Z E A N N E
Top message:	C O L O N E L O Z E A N N E
Bottom message:	(D beneath Z)

The only z in either message was at number 41 in the code-groups and D was beneath it. So whatever word lay beneath 'Ozeanne', the letter D had to be part of it.

The first step in the anagramming was to write out his name with all the letters from the bottom message which fell beneath it:

Top message:	C	O	L	O	N	E	L	O	Z	E	A	N	N	E
Bottom message:	T^1	S^{11}	G^{26}	S^{11}	H^2	S^4	G^{26}	S^{11}	D^{41}	S^4	I^3	H^2	H^2	S^4
„	E^{29}	L^{12}	I^{39}	L^{12}	F^8	D^{10}	I^{39}	L^{12}		D^{10}	A^{24}	F^8	F^8	D^{10}
„	Y^{16}	U^{43}	Y^{16}	O^{13}	N^{18}	U^{43}	Y^{16}			N^{18}	T^{49}	O^{13}	O^{13}	N^{18}
„	H^{23}	H^{23}	A^{14}	W^{19}	H^{23}					W^{19}	N^{51}	A^{14}	A^{14}	W^{19}
„	E^{25}	E^{25}	D^{27}	S^{20}	E^{25}					S^{20}		D^{27}	D^{27}	S^{20}
„		A^{48}	P^{30}							P^{30}		A^{48}	A^{48}	P^{30}
„		C^{52}	B^{31}							B^{31}		C^{52}	C^{52}	B^{31}
„		E^{32}								E^{32}				E^{32}
„		K^{33}								K^{33}				K^{33}
„		S^{34}								S^{34}				S^{34}
„		K^{36}								K^{36}				K^{36}
„		S^{42}								S^{42}				S^{42}
„		O^{54}								O^{54}				O^{54}

Cryptographers on a diet of alphabet soup would quickly recognize familiar ingredients, but Ozanne's appetites lay in other directions and I asked him to look first at the letters beneath the word COLONEL. Were there any words forming? Or familiar combinations of letters? TH, for example, or ER or ON or AN or RE? Was there anything promising under COLON? He told me what he usually found there and finally volunteered that he could see the word THIS. The coders of Grendon would have spotted THUS as well, but at least we'd begun.

Top message: C O L O N E L O Z E A N N E

Bottom message:

C	O	L	O	N	E	L	O	Z	E	A	N	N	E
T^1	S^{11}	G^{26}	S^{11}	H^2	S^4	G^{26}	S^{11}	D^{41}	S^4	I^3	H^2	H^2	S^4
E^{29}	L^{12}	I^{39}	L^{12}	F^8	D^{10}	I^{39}	L^{12}		D^{10}	A^{24}	F^8	F^8	D^{10}
Y^{16}	U^{43}	Y^{16}	O^{13}	N^{18}	U^{43}	Y^{16}	N^{18}		T^{49}		O^{13}	O^{13}	N^{18}
H^{23}	H^{23}	A^{14}	W^{19}	H^{23}			W^{19}	N^{51}			A^{14}	A^{14}	W^{19}
E^{25}	E^{25}	D^{27}	S^{20}	E^{25}			S^{20}				D^{27}	D^{27}	S^{20}
	A^{48}		P^{30}				P^{30}				A^{48}	A^{48}	P^{30}
	C^{52}		B^{31}				B^{31}				C^{52}	C^{52}	B^{31}
			E^{32}				E^{32}						E^{32}
			K^{33}				K^{33}						K^{33}
			S^{34}				S^{34}						S^{34}
			K^{36}				K^{36}						K^{36}
			S^{42}				S^{42}						S^{42}
			O^{54}				O^{54}						O^{54}

Couldn't we find what followed this? *Couldn't* we, sir? *Couldn't* we? After more subliminal prodding he eventually concluded that the word COULDN'T could be in the bottom message.

Top message: C O L O N E L O Z E A N N E

Bottom message:

C	O	L	O	N	E	L	O	Z	E	A	N	N	E
T^1	S^{11}	G^{26}	S^{11}	H^2	S^4	G^{26}	S^{11}	$\underline{D}^{41}$	S^4	I^3	H^2	H^2	S^4
E^{29}	L^{12}	I^{39}	L^{12}	F^8	D^{10}	I^{39}	$\underline{L}^{12}$		D^{10}	A^{24}	F^8	F^8	D^{10}
Y^{16}	U^{43}	Y^{16}	O^{13}	N^{18}	$\underline{U}^{43}$	Y^{16}	N^{18}		$\underline{T}^{49}$		O^{13}	O^{13}	N^{18}
$\underline{H}^{23}$	H^{23}	A^{14}	W^{19}	H^{23}			W^{19}	N^{51}			A^{14}	A^{14}	W^{19}
E^{25}	E^{25}	D^{27}	S^{20}	E^{25}			S^{20}				D^{27}	D^{27}	S^{20}
	A^{48}		P^{30}				P^{30}				A^{48}	A^{48}	P^{30}
	$\underline{C}^{52}$		B^{31}				B^{31}				C^{52}	C^{52}	B^{31}
			E^{32}				E^{32}						E^{32}
			K^{33}				K^{33}						K^{33}
			S^{34}				S^{34}						S^{34}
			K^{36}				K^{36}						K^{36}
			S^{42}				S^{42}						S^{42}
			$\underline{O}^{54}$				O^{54}						O^{54}

Progress to date:

Top message: C O L O N E L O Z E A N N E
Bottom message: T H I S C O U L D N T

This couldn't what?
The letters under NNE were aching to tell us.

Top message:	N	N	E
Bottom message:	H	H	S
	F	F	D
	O	O	N
	A	A	W
	D	D	S
	A	A	P
	C	C	B
			E
			K
			S
			K
			S
			O

Ozanne considered H O P was a promising combination. 'This couldn't hop?' I guided him on to H A P. 'This couldn't hap—'? What did hap— suggest? 'H A P P Y,' he said. I told him this word hadn't yet manifested itself in SOE's traffic. Nor did I expect it to *happen*. He got there.

Top message:	C O L O N E L O Z E A N N E
Bottom message:	T H I S C O U L D N T H A P P E N

The letters above P E N would tell us what Colonel Ozanne was up to. Letters above P E N (printed downwards for convenience):

P	E	N
E	S	E
S	S	I
	E	A
	C	C
	S	
	O	
	M	
	S	

I pointed to the five s s, and asked if he had any suggestions. None were forthcoming.

'There is one word beginning with s that everyone associates with you, sir!'

He looked at me suspiciously and demanded to know which word I meant.

'Signals'.

'Of course,' he said.

I chalked it up.

Top message: C O L O N E L O Z E A N N E S S I G N A L S
Bottom message: T H I S C O U L D N T H A P P E N

There was a real eye-catcher, though Ozanne's were half-closed, in the letters beneath GNALS:

```
I  H  I  G  E
N  F  A  I  P
   O  T  U  E
   A  N     M
   D        G
   A        E
   C        E
```

I put to my comatose colonel that the word IF was a natural to follow 'this couldn't happen', and that AGE could be the start of the most important word in our joint vocabularies: AGENTS.

C O L O N E L O Z E A N N E S S I G N A L S - - -
T H I S C O U L D N T H A P P E N I F A G E N T S

The letters above NTS offered us mercifully little choice (printed downwards for convenience):

```
N  T  S
H  C  E
F  R  O
O  R  E
A  A  E
D     E
A     H
C     F
```

FROM was a likely starter; there was an M waiting to oblige at number 22 in the code-groups. But ARE was also a possibility.

I asked which of them he fancied.

I can see a B up there,' he announced, 'and an F—'

51

And I could see a BF in the room.

'Let's leave Signals, sir,' I said, knowing that I might have to shortly. 'What else should we be looking for?'

'SOE,' he said. 'Everyone else is.'

A bullseye for Ozanne. SOE would take us in sight of the finish!

Letters beneath SOE (assuming it was in the top message):

```
S   O   E
E   S   S
P   L   D
E   Y   N
M   H   W
G   E   S
E       P
E       B
        E
        K
        S
        K
        S
        O
```

We didn't need to look further than MES. Nor would the Germans. MES-SAGE begins, MESSAGE ends, MESSAGE indecipherable, were part of the standard litany at the poem-code's funeral service. The orisons were:

Top message: S O E
Bottom message: M E S S A G E

The principal mourners may approach the grave and scatter handfuls of SAGE. Letters above SAGE (printed downwards for convenience):

```
O   N   L   S
E   A   D   S
H   N       E
F           C
E           O
E           M
E
```

The 'END' was nigh.

I needed one more guess from him. I pointed to the last letter in the E column of SAGE: the letter M.

'That M comes immediately after the word END. So what word is it likely to be the start of?'

'Marks, I should think. I can't believe you haven't signed it.'

'It's the agent who has! They usually sign off in the same way, no matter what we tell them. It starts with an M, sir . . .'

The word was message, and the letters beneath ESSAGE completed the internment.

Top message:	S	O	E		E	N	D	M	E		S	S		A	G	E	
Bottom message:	M	E	S	S	A	G	E	S	E	E	I	N	S
								D	P	P	A	I	D
								N	E	E	I		N
								W	M	M	N		W
								S	G	G			S
								P	E	E			P
								B	E	E			B
								E					E
								K					K
								S					S
								O					O

The messages now shared a common grave.

Top message:	S	O	E		E	N	D	M	E	S	S	A	G	E
Bottom message:	M	E	S	S	A	G	E	B	E	G	I	N	S

A few seconds later we had the full texts of both messages:

Top message:	COLONEL OZEANNES SIGNALS ARE THE NERVE CENTRES OF SOE END MESSAGE.
Bottom message:	THIS COULDN'T HAPPEN IF AGENTS USED WORKED OUT KEYS MESSAGE ENDS.

They appeared on the blackboard like this:

	1.	2.	3.	4.	5.	6.	7.	8.	9.	10.	11.	12.	13.	14.	15.	16.	17.	18.	19.
Top message:	C	O	L	O	N	E	L/	O	Z	E	A	N	N	E	S/	S	I	G	N
Bottom message:	T	H	I	S/	C	O	U	L	D	N	T/	H	A	P	P	E	N/	I	F/

	20.	21.	22.	23.	24.	25.	26.	27.	28.	29.	30.	31.	32.	33.	34.	35.
Top message (cont.):	A	L	S/	A	R	E/	T	H	E/	N	E	R	V	E/	C	E
Bottom message (cont.):	A	G	E	N	T	S/	U	S	E	D/	W	O	R	K	E	D/

	36.	37.	38.	39.	40.	41.	42.	43.	44.	45.	46.	47.	48.	49.	50.	51.
Top message (cont.):	N	T	R	E	S/	O	F/	S	O	E/	E	N	D/	M	E	S
Bottom message (cont.):	O	U	T/	K	E	Y	S/	M	E	S	S	A	G	E/	B	E

	52.	53.	54.	55.
Top message (cont.):	S	A	G	E/
Bottom message (cont.):	G	I	N	S/

Ozanne smiled, clearly believing that the demonstration was over. I had some bad news for him.

A code isn't broken merely because an individual message is. We had now to establish the words of the poem. Only then would we have broken the code itself. That was why every pair of letters had been given a number, though Ozanne hadn't once asked me their purpose. It was time to enlighten him.

To keep the mathematics of anagramming down to the level of my mother's housekeeping, I wrote up the first fifteen pairs of letters of each message and drew the last shards of his attention to them:

	1.	2.	3.	4.	5.	6.	7.	8.	9.	10.	11.	12.	13.	14.	15.
Top message:	C	O	L	O	N	E	L	O	Z	E	A	N	N	E	S
Bottom message:	T	H	I	S	C	O	U	L	D	N	T	H	A	P	P

I now invited him to join me in a game of cryptographic hide and seek. Each of these pairs of letters would be found lurking amongst the code-groups:

The first pair $\frac{C}{T}$ of $\frac{Colonel}{Thiscou}$ was number 1 in the code-groups.

But the second pair $\frac{O}{H}$ was number 23 in the code-groups.

Pair 3 $_{I}^{L}$ was number 39 in the code-groups.

Pair 4 $_{S}^{O}$ was number 11 in the code-groups.

Pair 5 $_{C}^{N}$ was number 52 in the code-groups.

Pair 6 $_{O}^{E}$ was number 54 in the code-groups.

Pair 7 $_{U}^{L}$ was number 43 in the code-groups.

Pair 8 $_{L}^{O}$ was number 12 in the code-groups.

Pair 9 $_{D}^{Z}$ was number 41 in the code-groups.

Pair 10 $_{N}^{E}$ was number 18 in the code-groups.

Pair 11 $_{T}^{A}$ was number 49 in the code-groups.

Pair 12 $_{H}^{N}$ was number 2 in the code-groups.

Pair 13 $_{A}^{N}$ was number 14 in the code-groups.

Pair 14 $_{P}^{E}$ was number 30 in the code-groups.

Pair 15 $_{P}^{S}$ was number 7 in the code-groups.

The remaining pairs of letters, numbers 16 to 55, had also changed their positions. If we could discover the process which had caused these changes, the game of hide and seek would be finished and the life of the code over, because we would be in possession of the transposition-key on which both messages had been encoded.

The mathematics involved would be basic but fiddling and I asked Ozanne which he would prefer: to see the process for himself or accept my word that within a very short time we could mathematically reconstruct the entire transposition-key on which both messages had been encoded.

My word was instantly accepted.

I wrote the transposition-key on the blackboard:

1.16.17.23.11.13.19.9.22.4.21.14.10.12.24.2.20.6.5.7.3.26.25.15.8.27.18.

I told Ozanne that it would take the coders of Grendon twenty minutes or so to convert those figures into the original words from which they came. Did he wish to see the process for himself? Or would he accept my assurance?

He accepted it.

George Washington Marks wrote the code-phrase 'ALL THINGS BRIGHT AND BEAUTIFUL' on the blackboard:

ALL THINGS BRIGHT AND BEAUTIFUL
1. 16.17.23.11.13.19. 9. 22. 4. 21.14.10.12.24. 2. 20. 7. 5. 6. 3. 26.25.15. 8. 27.18.

I suggested that German cryptographers might know the words too and that they would now be able to read the rest of the agent's traffic at will.

'You have five more minutes,' he said, 'in which to come to the point.'

It was there on the blackboard, glaring at him. He hadn't bothered to ask what 'worked-out keys' were. He probably thought they were iron-based laxatives. He wouldn't need one by the time I'd finished.

I pointed out the overwhelming advantages of a code which could be destroyed message by message, which could not be remembered, which could not be tortured out of an agent, which would allow him to get off the air in half the time it took him at present, which could easily be camouflaged because it would be printed on silk, which would put a stop to the blackboard follies we had just indulged in, and which would be the start of a programme to change the entire face of agents' coding. I then shoved a sample of a WOK at him like a door-to-door salesman and showed him how to use it.

His expression conveyed what he was considering using it for. Even his blackheads seemed to underline in porous italics his silent rejection of everything I'd said. I shaped my wares to suit Ozanne the expansionist and I told him that the Signals directorate would need fifty girls to produce WOKs by hand and another dozen to check their work. The keys would then have to be printed on silk and subsequently camouflaged. Perhaps the colonel would consider starting his own printing and camouflage sections? We would also need teams of girls at the briefing end of the assembly line to keep every agent practising his WOK ('use it and destroy it, use it and destroy it') right up to the moment that he left for the field. We must also make provision for some mistakes of our own and would need a small team of girls to monitor them.

'Very interesting,' he said, 'for a number of reasons.' He told me that any idiot could stand in front of a blackboard and break a message he'd composed himself. As far as he was aware, the Germans were not in that happy position. Nor was there any evidence that SOE's traffic was being intercepted, let alone broken. Furthermore, I had grossly exaggerated the poem-code's insecurity. Properly used, it was perfectly suitable for SOE's purposes. Moreover, after considerable discussion with experts in such matters he was firmly convinced that an agent's code *should* be carried in his head and any suggestion to the contrary was dangerous nonsense.

He added that my idea of a WOK-thing or whatever I called it was impractical, preposterous and he hadn't heard the like of it. Nor was he prepared to hear the like of it again, least of all from me. 'What you need is a dose of the army.'

He didn't actually call me a shirker but asked why the chosen people were so reluctant to get into uniform. I replied that being a member of the chosen people *was* a uniform but we did not depend for our promotion on the Army Council.

I knew by now that I'd wrecked the WOK campaign and ruined Heffer's chances of reviving it. I'd also blown my cover with Ozanne, and with nothing to lose I attacked that shuttered mind with the only key left to me.

I told him that I would write to CD stating in full my reasons for resigning. With this letter I would enclose a detailed report on agents' codes. Since much of the report would be technical, I summarized its punchier contents. Part One would demonstrate the effect of a cryptographic attack on a cross-section of SOE's traffic. The attack would be based on the assumption that agents' messages had not yet become important enough to the enemy to warrant a full-scale attack by their top cryptographers. Part Two would show the same cross-section of messages being attacked 'with absolute priority'. Part Three would set out the reasons why such a blanket attack was inevitable, if it hadn't already begun. Traffic such as Torch (I refrained from mentioning Grouse) could provide the enemy with a microcosm of the whole war effort and a breakthrough would have repercussions far beyond the confines of SOE. Part Four would be devoted entirely to security checks and the total inadequacy of the present system. The fifth and final part would deal with the archaic misthinking behind the poem-code and the new concepts which should immediately replace it. I undertook to send one copy of the report to CD and another to the War Office in case there was someone in *their* Signals directorate technically capable of understanding it.

Ozanne had a smile like a wartime *hors d'oeuvre*: small, confected and promising far worse to come. He produced a trayful of it. He informed me very quietly indeed that people did not resign from SOE; they were dismissed. He then telephoned his secretary and dictated a memo addressed to DYC/M (my symbol) from MS (his). The memo instructed me to prepare a detailed report on agents' codes which I was to deliver to MS personally within seven days. Under no circumstances was I to show this report to *anyone at all* or discuss its contents without his written consent. He ordered me to wait while the memo was typed and to sign an acknowledgement of it on my way out.

That memo was Ozanne at his tactical best. He had commanded the report, made it his own and could consider it in his own time. Above all, he had pre-empted its distribution.

It was good thinking because on the barren mountain of SOE's ethics there was one unforgivable sin. It was probably the oldest on record. The sin of *being caught* disobeying a superior's orders. The penalty was instant dismissal or permanent retention, whichever was the heavier.

I had tried a fool's mate on a grand master. But at least I could replace the pieces in the box with a hint of dignity.

Ozanne had flicked seven days' grace at me to complete my report. I didn't need seven days. Or even seven seconds. I'd written it the night before and had it with me in my pocket.

I pulled it out and served it on him personally, as instructed. He put it beneath the pile of unread signals. He then told me to find a duster and clear all the rubbish off the blackboard.

I was looking for an excuse to return to the blackboard. I rubbed out all the letters except for twelve. I dusted these precious letters lightly so that they stayed on the blackboard as a memento of my visit. They spelled a most unusual word. Ozanne wouldn't understand its meaning unless his real name was Ozeannavitch. But 'the chosen', if there were any others in SOE, would recognize it at once.

Just as 'merde alors' was the ultimate SOE benediction, this twelve-letter word was the ultimate Hebrew curse: Mother wished it to Hitler on his birthday; Disraeli may have wished it to Gladstone; my father wished it to tax inspectors, provided they weren't in the craft.

Its twelve deadly letters were positioned at numbers 55.4.6. 10.15.22.3.7.45.21.2.24. in the code-groups.*

I turned round to find Ozanne watching me. He told me I was to continue my normal duties until I heard from him again.

Part of those duties would be to continue spelling his name with an 'e' too many.

Hurrying to the door, I couldn't resist taking what was likely to be my last look at him. He was staring at the blackboard with mounting interest.

Perhaps his name was Ozeanneavitch after all . . .

---

* Warning from the author. The curse should be used only in emergencies, and in the hands of the inexperienced has been known to backfire.

SIX

The Fifth Grouse

Every agent was given the opportunity of carrying a cyanide pill as an optional extra. Some refused the facility on moral or religious grounds, but the majority regarded it as forward planning and a lethal tablet was as much a part of an agent's survival kit as the poem-code, which so often contributed to its use. I didn't envy the country section officers who had to issue the poison:

'By the way, old man, here's your L-tablet. Not that you'll need it, of course, but you might just as well keep it handy. In your tie perhaps? Oh, I've a little tip for you. Don't go confusing it with your booster tablets, there's a good lad.'

It took the good lads (and lassies) a good minute to die, though SOE's technicians were doing their best to improve the facility.

I was about to meet four exceptionally good lads who'd be lucky if they had the chance to use L-tablets. Blowing up a heavy-water plant was a full-time job. They were now waiting in Chiltern Court for what was likely to be our only session.

I wanted to give these Grouse agents one-to-one briefings but Wilson had warned me that they always turned up together no matter what the arrangements. 'What difference does it make, anyway?' he asked. 'There are only four of them.'

And they were only going to carry one corner of the free world in each of their knapsacks, but Wilson didn't know that I'd found out what their mission was, and I had to be careful not to think about it at the briefing. An agent's inner ear could pick up anxieties more quickly than instructions. Agents also had a flair for infecting one another. I'd twice known sadness to be wafted round a briefing room as if someone were smoking it.

A good briefing officer knew how to insulate himself against his pupils, if only with ignorance – and he'd arrive at Chiltern Court untroubled by the cost to the Allies if Operation Grouse failed, and the cost to the inseparables if it succeeded. A good briefing officer would confront the Grouse with his own togetherness, service their needs with the detachment of a maintenance man, and be in awe of nothing but his own limitations. And at three minutes to coding countdown, even the shell of a briefing officer would *make* himself believe that the poem-code was the best damn code there is.

I said it aloud: '*The poem-code is the best damn –*'

Chiltern Court was only a sandbag away. A maintenance man mustn't keep his customers waiting.

The Norwegian section's flat was less impersonal than most, and it was just possible to believe that it had once been lived in.

Colonel Wilson was not only waiting in the hall, he actually said hello to me instead of his customary, 'You again.' When he escorted me to the briefing room his comments were even less in character: 'My lads are completely at your disposal. See them as often as you consider necessary. Once a day if you like. Arrange it through me.'

Such generosity could only mean that Operation Grouse had again been postponed because of weather and that, as his lads had nothing better to do, they might as well practise their coding.

'I don't expect them to send much traffic,' he said casually, 'but what they do send may be pretty important. I don't want one indecipherable! Not one. Even if I have to send you in with 'em.' He pushed me into the briefing room and walked off chuckling.

Messrs Poulson, Helberg, Kjelstrup and Haugland sprang to attention as one Grouse and remained sprung until I'd carried my impedimenta to the briefing officer's desk. I'd brought a special prop with me to give me some confidence. It was a self-important briefcase which I'd purloined from the stationery department and nicknamed Ozanne. The tools of my trade were inside its gullet: some practice poems for the Grouse, some squared paper and a copy of Marks & Co.'s latest catalogue.

If a briefing officer had any special talent, he should demonstrate it in the first five minutes. Afterwards he might have lost his audience.

My special talent was distributing squared paper. The one obstacle in the way of my proving it was a briefcase named Ozanne. I'd forgotten the combination of the secret lock and was in no position to consult the stationery department. Growing sallower by the moment, I twiddled, reasoned and wrestled with it but my repository was closed for the duration.

'We could perhaps be of some helping?' enquired Poulson, the leader of the quartet.

I ceded the problem to them, hoping they'd think it was an aptitude test. They solved it inside a minute, then sat back to await the next conundrum.

They'd done no coding for six weeks and it was essential to establish how much they remembered and whether they were as accident-prone as their briefing officer. I'd devised a hard time for them which fell into three parts: exercise, checking and briefing officer's summary.

I handed them some squared paper and a poem apiece and asked each of them to encode an improvised message in Norwegian and English at least 250 letters long as quickly as they could. They started work as if they expected nothing less.

The agents were now in an exam situation and for the next thirty to fifty minutes I was redundant.

All briefing officers shared the problem of how best to pass the time while surreptitiously monitoring the progress of their pupils. Some prepared for their next briefings, others began reports on their last. I wrote poems for the agents, and since I did so strictly from Signals necessity, and my readership consisted of agents, coders and enemy cryptographers, I had no writer's block. I had not foreseen that in the presence of a courteous quartet dedicated to saving us from an atomic New Year I would be rendered wordless, wingless and grounded.

I gave up trying to swell the contents of the agents' ditty-box and turned for inspiration to Father's catalogue, Marks & Co.'s equivalent of a WOK. He was offering a first edition of Burton's *Anatomy of Melancholy* at a price which would have cheered its author, and a set of Gould's *Birds of Europe* in crushed levant at a few hundred a crush. The choicest item of all – a seventh-century illuminated bestiary – had been given an entire page to itself despite the national paper shortage. Those most likely to prevent the beast Goering from acquiring it were far too engrossed in their coding to know that their maintenance man was watching them.

It was like studying a compendium of sabotage talents. Haugland was the wireless operator. His WT instructor, who was convinced that praise was synonymous with careless talk, had said of him, 'He's the best man I've ever trained. He should be teaching me.' Helberg was an expert at silent killing. Poulson and Kjelstrup could map-read without maps. For months they'd all been on toughening-up courses which I wouldn't even wish on our director of Signals. The rigours of coding might well be a bore to them but could scarcely be a hardship.

I realized too late that all four had begun to slow down as if they'd been caught at the same traffic light. Worse still, they were looking across the room at me as if I were the improvised message they were supposed to be working on.

Improbable though it seemed that the Grouse could be put off by a mouse-glare, that's what had happened. It always did when agents caught me monitoring them but I'd hoped that just this once I'd be able to mount a benevolent surveillance without inducing the indecipherables I was there to prevent.

First the briefcase, and now this. What mistake was I going to make next?

I picked up my pencil. It felt like a spade; and a poem for the ditty-box dug itself out of me:

> Have you never known
> A glass-bottomed day
> When your minutes can be seen
> Flowing beneath you
> In every direction
> But the one you mean?
>
> Have you never known
> A winterproof night
> When wrong feels right
> When the heart's chill
> Is a matter of will

And mother's pride
Is safe inside
An envelope of ice
And doesn't even hear
A cock crow thrice?

Whichever agent used this as his poem-code (it was ultimately Bodington) would be told to spell glass-bottomed as two words. If he were caught, he could try spelling it as one. Until WOKs were introduced.

One of the Grouse coughed – a snippet of sound which broke through every defence I had.

I made the greatest mistake a briefing officer can. I thought about their mission instead of their coding: 'How bloody how,' I wondered, 'were the five of us going to drop into the middle of Hardanger Vidda, with no reception committee to guide us down, where visibility was nil because the fog was as thick as General de Gaulle's pr—, and where hundreds of precipices waited to impale us?' And if the four of them did survive the drop (the fifth Grouse hadn't survived the thought of it) then how bloody how could they survive what followed? How could they drag explosives and containers across minefields of ice till they reached the Barren Mountain and somehow contacted Einar Skinnarland and somehow crossed the guarded bridge at Vermok and somehow blew the plant up and themselves with it, after sending us an indecipherable to remember them by?

The how bloody hows of the future were replaced by a most immediate why:

Why was Knut Haugland still numbering his key-phrase while the others were a quarter way through their first transpositions? Nothing in Haugland's report had indicated that he was a slow coder.

I finally realized that I was a slow observer. Haugland wasn't using squared paper! He was encoding his message on a plain sheet of paper which he was carefully ruling for himself. He wasn't even using a ruler. He was drawing the lines against the edge of a pencil. I realized why. There were no stationery shops on the Barren Mountain and Haugland was 'coding for real'. Nobody, least of all me, had prompted him to do this. I wrote a memo on Father's catalogue, next to an offer to make valuations for probate, instructing the training schools that in future all agents must practise their coding on plain paper without rulers. I then continued to watch my instructor at work. He'd almost caught up with the other three but it was his style which impressed me even more than his speed. He attacked his code-groups as if each letter he disposed of were a limb on a sentry at Vermok. It was a formidable display of silent code-killing.

I won a flicker of surprise from them when I collected their poems and messages and distributed Helberg's to Poulson, Poulson's to Haugland, Haugland's to Kjelstrup and Kjelstrup's to Helberg, and asked them to decipher each other's traffic.

The sharp adjustment from one coding process to another usually caused agents to make their worst mistakes. Encoding and decoding were not the Signals equivalent of breathing out and breathing in and few FANYs and even fewer agents were equally good at both. At least one Grouse might find himself limping.

The atmosphere was suddenly as full of unspoken frustration as group therapy in the hands of an amateur. This was the time when coding character was shaped. In the next few minutes all the agents were likely to display habits or weaknesses which would be an invaluable help in our long struggle against their field indecipherables. But it would be the worst possible time to be caught monitoring them.

I gave up the luxury of watching and tried to make do with another sense, one with which only children like myself are especially familiar: I listened to the sounds of a pencil breaking, of a rubber being used with venom (I'd check up afterwards to see who'd erased what), of Poulson saying something sharply in Norwegian, and of the others laughing. He'd used an expletive which Wilson uttered whenever I asked him to write poems for his agents, a chore which he had so far declined.

According to my stop-watch, which I'd managed to set without the assistance of the Grouse, they were five minutes ahead of average swearing time. That was good. And the only sound now was of pencils claiming paper and that was good too. But it sounded more like three pencils than four. I glanced up to see which Grouse had fallen by the coding wayside.

Kjelstrup was showing all the symptoms of coding paralysis. Perhaps the fault lay with Haugland, whose message he was decoding.

Perhaps Haugland wasn't as good as I thought. I wanted to say, 'Go back to the beginning if you've lost your way. It's quicker in the end.' But Kjelstrup had to find his own way back.

An organ-grinder struck up a tune in the street outside. None of them seemed to hear it. There is a special loneliness in unshared music, even if it was 'The White Cliffs of Dover'. I reached for my pencil.

Kjelstrup glanced reproachfully in my direction as if I were personally responsible for his ordeal and was leaving him to flounder.

I know what loneliness is, old chap:

> I danced two waltzes
> One fox-trot
> And the polka
> With no partner
> That they could see
> And hope I did not tire you.
>
> I glided round
> The other ballroom
> The one called life
> Just as alone
> And have to thank you
> For giving me
> The sprinkling of moments
> Which are my place at table
> In a winner's world.
>
> Keep a space for me
> On your card
> If you are dancing still.

Whichever agent used this as his poem-code (it was ultimately Peter Churchill) would be told to spell fox-trot as one word. If he were caught, he could try spelling it as two. Until WOKs, etcetera . . .

Glancing again at the clock I saw that Kjelstrup had a long way to go but that the others had completely finished. What happened next was so surprising that I found myself breathing backwards. Without a word being spoken or a look being exchanged Poulson, Helberg and Haugland pretended that they were still dividing their messages into groups of five. It was as if they'd reached an agreement in silent Morse to give Kjelstrup a chance to catch up with them. It was a gala performance designed to ensure that if I reported one of them to Wilson for slow coding I would also have to report the rest.

I allowed Poulson to catch me watching him. He sighed as he resumed his labours, and the others sighed with him. I envied their togetherness almost as much as I marvelled at their shorthand.

> The fingers of feeling
> Be they gloved by the shy
> Or pointed bare and bold
> By the shyer still
> Seek to find
> By fumbling or by fate
> Another hand to clutch . . .*

I left it at that, not only because it contained the mandatory minimum of twenty-six words but because it had left me. When I looked up they had finished.

I collected their poems and messages and spread them in front of me for checking. I hoped there'd be no failures. If there were, I wouldn't tell Wilson. Their failure would be mine and there would be time to put it right.

I made several errors myself in the next few minutes and wished they'd stop watching me. But it soon became a square-papered world and some twenty minutes later I knew the Grouse the only way I was supposed to. With one exception, they were first-class coders: Haugland wasn't first class. He was in a class of his own.

The others had made a few minor mistakes and were merely terrific. In Haugland's case there wasn't a single letter wrong or a coding hair out of place – but it wasn't his accuracy which won me for life. He'd elected to encode a message 350 letters long instead of the 250

* Ultimately used as a reserve code by an American wireless operator.

67

minimum which the others had accepted. It was those extra letters, his golden century, which had delayed Kjelstrup. Haugland had performed another coding miracle. Unlike most agents he'd chosen the five longest words in his poem instead of the five shortest.

Haugland's work was an illuminated manuscript. Haugland himself was even rarer. He was a coder's man.

Careful not to single anyone out, I congratulated them on their exercises and spared them the usual summary. All they needed was a few basic tips.

I stood up to give them, hoping they'd carry more weight: 'Free your language, vary your transposition-keys, don't fall into set patterns. Code as if you're making love.'

The latter slipped out. The Grouse's inner and outer ears pricked up. They listened to the rest of what I had to tell them as if I were delivering a bulletin and they were starved of coding news. Their attention was so riveting that I was the captive audience and forgot that I had an appointment with the Free French in ten minutes' time.

I declared the Grouse season closed for the day. They stood to attention and thanked me for arriving to them.

I thanked them for opening my briefcase.

One of them held open the door for the fifth Grouse to leave.

The next time he arrived to them he hoped to give them a safe code instead of a snare.

SEVEN

SOE-minded

The RF section, our de Gaulle connection, occupied a house in Dorset Square which had formerly belonged to the directors of Bertram Mills Circus. This inspired continuity was one of SOE's favourite in-jokes, though it was no joke having to visit RF section, the most troubled and troublesome in the whole of SOE.

A new director of RF had just been appointed. His name was Colonel Hutchison and he'd been brought in at short notice in the hope that, as Tommy put it, 'he'd have the balls for the job'.

It took me five minutes to reach 1 Dorset Square from Chiltern Court and I was still too immersed in Norwegian waters to adjust so rapidly to a change of briny. I entered the house like a reluctant ringmaster to put the Free French through the hoops of their coding.

There would be no free flow between us. The agents were under strict orders from Duke Street not to discuss the secret French code with me and I was under strict orders from myself not to tell them to use it as seldom as possible. It would have been easier for all of us if I'd been able to brief them individually but they usually turned up in clusters of six, and today I was expecting eight.

I reminded myself at the door of the briefing room that the secret French code was the best damn code there wasn't. '*The secret French code is the best damn –*'

The briefing room was empty – as empty, that is, as any room can be which has a poster of de Gaulle in it. His eyes seemed to be reading my private traffic.

The Free French were punctilious about their appointments and I wondered what had happened to my missing eight. I waited fifteen

69

minutes, could produce nothing for the agents' ditty-box, and prepared to leave.

A hare of a colonel bounded into the room and sat down beside me. He introduced himself as Colonel Hutchison and started speaking French as if he'd invented it. If I interpreted his every other sentence correctly, he'd introduced a rule that everyone on the premises must speak only French. He also recommended that they *thought* in French. He relaxed his principles when he heard my accent. He had cancelled the agents' briefings in order to be briefed himself.

I asked if he wanted me to teach him to code.

'Good God, no,' he said. 'I'll set ten minutes aside for that some other time. I just want to discuss a point or two with you. Now, Marks, tell me what you know about the secret French code.'

I thought in French, *Get me out of here, mon Dieu, and I won't eat bacon for a fortnight*. This was the most dangerous question I'd yet been asked in SOE.

'The secret French code?' I echoed. 'I'm afraid I'm in no position to tell you anything about it.'

'Why not? Why all this secrecy? Tell me what you do know.'

I gave him a potted history of the code without specifying which pot it should be consigned to.

'Yes, yes,' he said impatiently, 'but what actually happens when they want to pass one?'

I presumed he meant a message in secret French code and described the mechanics of distribution as SOE believed them to be.

'So my directorate is just a clearing-house?'

I'd heard Tommy describe it as another kind of house, but nodded.

'Good. Tommy told me you were the man I should talk to!'

Thanks, Tommy.

'Now then. Who's your opposite number in Duke Street? And what can you tell me about him?'

I had no idea where this was leading, apart from the guillotine. I told him that my opposite number's name was Druot, that we'd met once, spoken twice and that he was brilliant at forged currency, forged documents and photography.

'What about codes?'

'I understand they're one of his many commitments.'

The hare-turned-ferret may have smiled. I could certainly see his moustache more clearly. 'Tell me. How do you contact this Druot? Through RF or directly?'

'Directly, when I can. Through Tommy if it's urgent.'

'Ah yes,' he said. 'Tommy.' There was a distinct frown in his voice and I wondered if he'd had any trouble from the Chairman of the Awkward Squad.

'I want to go back to that secret code. Why –'

The phone rang. He answered at once and I listened to the most informative conversation I had yet heard in the RF directorate. 'Right, right, right, right, right, right away.'

He bounded up – 'I have to see the director of Operations. But you and I will talk again! Very soon.' – and bounded out!

The length and line of his questions promised well for his directorate but badly for me. Given a little time, he was bound to notice that some incoming messages in secret French code weren't being delivered to Duke Street as promptly as they should have been, and he'd demand an explanation from Ozanne.

A phone call from Dansey – very rare when I was at a briefing session – instructed me to return to the office as quickly as I could.

It was equally rare for him to slam down the receiver.

Major offences in SOE – such as leakages to C, which were considered almost as treasonable as leakages to the enemy – were dealt with by the Executive Council. Minor offences, such as being right, were disciplined by the directorate in which they occurred.

Heffer, Dansey and Owen were waiting for me in Dansey's office. Heffer had just had a meeting with Ozanne and informed me with no apparent regret that the Signals directorate and I were soon to part company. I was not going to be sacked for technical incompetence ('That can sometimes backfire,' said Heffer) but on the far deadlier grounds of 'temperamental unsuitability for SOE-type work'.

Thanks to Heffer, it was a suspended sentence. He'd persuaded Ozanne that a stay of execution would give him and Dansey time to look for a suitable replacement; Heffer had even suggested that the shock might produce a marked improvement in me. 'Start looking today!' Ozanne had instructed. The reprieve was subject to one condition. If I showed my coding report to *anyone*, I was to be dismissed forthwith.

On the issue of WOKs Ozanne remained inflexible. They would leave when I did.

I suggested whoever succeeded me should come from Bletchley and have the experience which I knew I lacked.

They glanced at each other. Then Heffer announced that he had something to say to me on behalf of them all: 'Now and again you've shown a certain promise. But your greatest failing amongst a host of others is that you are not – and are now most unlikely ever to become' – I expected him to say 'adult' – '*SOE-minded*.'

I knew that I had just heard the most important phrase anyone had ever spoken to me – with the possible exception of 'help yourself'. I also knew that for the rest of my SOE life, however short, I would go in search of 'SOE-mindedness'. It was the vitamin deficiency I didn't know I lacked.

Eagerly, gratefully, I asked what it meant. Each waited for the other to define it.

'It's a state of disgrace which you must discover for yourself.' Heffer.

'If he's here long enough.' Dansey.

'Which I doubt.' Owen.

I realized that it meant something different to each of them, a sign of its reality. I asked whom they considered to be 'SOE-minded', present company excepted, of course.

Each waited for the other to commit himself. Nobody would.

I suggested some candidates.

'Hambro?'

'If he can forget he's a gentleman.' Heffer.

'Gubbins?'

'If he can forget he's a soldier.' Dansey.

'Tommy?'

'If he can forget the Free French.' Owen.

'Colonel Ozanne?'

'I prefer to forget him altogether.' Heffer.

He then rose by inches from his chair. 'It wasn't very SOE-minded of you to leave that word on the blackboard.' he said.

He waited for my mouth to reach half-mast. 'Before you took for granted Ozanne wouldn't know what it meant you should have found out where he played golf on Sundays.'

He told me the name of the club – and all was clear. I'd walked the course with Father and knew that the eighteenth hole was circumcision.

'Heff . . . you mean he went to the trouble of anagramming it out?'

'No,' he said, 'but I did.'

He enjoyed his exit lines almost as much as he did his exits.

'SM' ('SOE-mindedness', not sado-masochism, though they might be synonymous) was a cruel dish to set before a starving man. It might explain why SOE was sending missions to Mihailovič *and* Tito in Yugoslavia when the two leaders were virtually at civil war, why we were backing Communists *and* anti-Communists in Greece, why there was so little co-operation between the rival French sections that their agents had shot each other up in the dark after mistaking each other for Germans, and why the Dutch weren't concerned about incorrect security checks. It might even explain what a man like Ozanne was doing in SOE.

I wondered how to apply 'SM' to the Signals Gauleiter, and decided to make a start by taking his orders literally. Since Ozanne insisted that agents should have poem-codes, I would give them poem-codes – not one but dozens! Clusters of poems printed on soluble paper could be issued to each agent. They would be instructed by London to switch from one poem to another at the first sign of their traffic becoming overloaded. Nor must they attempt to memorize the poems. They must be destroyed as soon as they were finished with. I checked with the stationery department that the printing was within their competence and they foresaw no problems. I would make a start with the Grouse. The principle could then be applied to other agents and since it conformed strictly with Ozanne's coding convictions, I would not waste his time by mentioning it to him.

The concept was in every way the WOK's poor relation but it was a start. If this were a form of 'SM', it didn't hurt at all.

*   *   *

73

Expecting my successor at any moment, I settled down to what might be my last indecipherable from Bodington, which was based (of course) on a piece by Poe.

He'd returned from the field since using 'The Raven', had gone back to France with Peter Churchill – and his latest Poe choice was 'Annabel Lee':

> I was a child and she was a child
>> In this kingdom by the sea
> But we loved with a love that was more than love
>> I and my Annabel Lee
> With a love that the winged seraphs of heaven
>> Coveted her and me
>
> And neither the angels in heaven above
>> Nor the demons down under the sea
> Can ever dissever my soul from the soul
>> Of the beautiful Annabel Lee

I was determined to dissever Bodington's soul next time we met if this indecipherable was as tough as his last.

The five words he'd chosen were: 'child', 'under', 'I', 'can', 'heaven'. I knew that spelling was Bodington's weakness, possibly due to his peacetime stint as Paris correspondent of the *Daily Express* – and rapidly discovered that his version of heaven was 'heav*an*', and hoped he'd get to both one day.

I phoned Buckmaster to tell him the message was out. To my astonishment he appeared in person a few minutes later. First Hutchison, now Buckmaster – it was like meeting the stars of a play which was still being written.

Buckmaster and I knew each other by sight and had shaken hands on the telephone. I'd met him once at Chiltern Court under unfortunate circumstances.

I'd been briefing a wireless operator named Alec Rabinovitch, a vast young man of Russian-Egyptian origin who could (and did) swear in four languages. We both knew at a glance that we shared the Esperanto of being Jewish. From the way he clenched his huge

74

fists with the thumbs protecting his fingers, and from his ethnic background, I suspected that he'd done some boxing and, between exercises (he was a good coder), taxed him with it. It was the end of the coding session. I'd boxed for St Paul's in the days when self was the only thing worth protecting and we discovered a mutual admiration for the greatest boxer (and gentleman) our sport had yet produced, Joe Louis. I was very disappointed that Rabinovitch knew that Louis's real name was Barrow. I thought only Joe and I did. My pupil and I then had a serious disagreement. He was convinced that the Brown Bomber's best punch was a short right to the head whereas I knew for positive fact that it was a left jab to the chin. To put it beyond doubt, Rabinovitch swung his giant fist at my jaw and pulled it up a microdot away just as Buckmaster walked in. Buckmaster expressed the hope that Rabinovitch was here for coding practice and not unarmed combat and asked to see him as soon as we'd finished.

Rabinovitch was now shadow-boxing in France with great success (and at great risk) as the wireless operator for Peter Churchill's Spindle group. And here was Buckmaster, himself no stranger to fifteen-rounders with the RF section, looking at me thoughtfully. I was used to being thoroughly towelled down in the ring between rounds but not by blue eyes of such extraordinary penetration.

I didn't begin to understand the politics he was obliged to play to compete with de Gaulle and had no desire to. But I'd noticed that no matter how late I phoned to tell him that an indecipherable was broken, he was always waiting in his office, and his first concern was for the safety of the agent. Not all country section directors shared that attitude. To some of them, agents in the field were heads to be counted, a tally they could show CD. But Maurice Buckmaster was a family man.

He thanked me for breaking Boddington's indecipherable but he'd already done that on the telephone and Buckmaster never said anything twice. RF complained that he never said anything once. I suspected he'd come for some other reason.

'How reliable are our security checks?' he asked sharply.

He was the first country section head to ask that question. It deserved to be answered with the same directness.

'They're no more than a gesture to give the agents confidence.' I told him why in some detail.

'Can they *ever* be relied upon?'

I told him that if an agent was caught before he was sent any messages he could get away with giving them the wrong security check because they'd have no back traffic to compare it with. But not otherwise.

'What's being done about it?'

'We're working on a wholly new concept of agents' codes.'

He nodded. He understood the battles to get anything changed in SOE. 'Can't anything be done in the meantime?'

I told him that as long as the poem-code was in use there were only two things the country sections could do: a) they should ask their agents personal questions to which they alone would know the answers, and b) they should use prearranged phrases in their messages to which the agents must reply in a prearranged way. I warned him that these phrases must be used only once in case the agent's traffic was being read.

'We already do something of the sort. I'll make sure it's done on a regular basis.'

'Colonel Buckmaster' – he'd just been promoted – 'is there anyone in particular you're worried about?'

A microdot of hesitation. 'It was a general question. I'll consult you if I am.'

I knew that part of Peter Churchill's and Bodington's mission was to check up on the security of a circuit run by Carte (André Girard), which was causing F section great concern. That night I went through the back traffic of all the F section agents. It contained the usual mixture of Morse mutilation, wrong checks, right checks, no checks. If I were Buckmaster, I'd be worried about all of them and I was convinced that he was.

I wondered why he and the Free French refused to pool their anxieties.

It was time to say goodbye to the Grouse. They were on their final standby and were to parachute into Norway no matter what the weather.

I'd already phoned Wilson to discuss the clusters of poems on soluble paper which I wanted to give them. His reply was explosive, even by his standards: 'I've told you they'll be passing hardly any traffic. They're to use the poems they've learned and nothing else. Is that clear? Or do you want me to confirm it to Ozanne?'

I told him that would not be necessary.

'Very well then. Just make certain they send no indecipherables. Thank you.'

This time he wasn't waiting at Chiltern Court to greet me. Halfway down the corridor I could hear the Grouse laughing. They stopped as soon as I entered the room. An only child worries more than most about laughter stopping and I asked if I could share the joke. They showed me a poem in Norwegian and English contributed by Wilson. It was untranslatable in both languages.

I took each of them to one side to discuss their security checks and run through their poems with them. The one thing the Grouse couldn't share was their coding conventions.

The session was only a formality but towards the end they produced another example of their silent Morse. A feeling more than a look seemed to pass between Poulson, Helberg and Kjelstrup. Poulson then said they had to leave to have some special skis fitted but Haugland asked if he could stay behind to talk to me – his skis had already been fitted.

Since it was time to say goodbye to his companions and I didn't know the Norwegian for 'merde alors', I had to rely on my handshake to say it for me. From their slight looks of surprise the message was received and understood.

I wondered what Haugland wanted to talk about. This extraordinary man, as slender as the steel skis which he said had been fitted, foresaw the time when he'd have to brief agents in the field on their coding – Norwegian patriots who hadn't his good fortune to be brought to London for training. He wanted to make absolutely certain that he'd absorbed everything I'd tried to teach him. I was to be allowed my one-to-one briefing after all.

I was sure that, if Haugland encoded a message as he jumped from his aeroplane, he'd have double-checked it by the time he reached ground but I took him through the entire process from beginning to end.

I was also sure that his need to see something new was almost as great as mine to provide it so I opened my briefcase, which I'd had the foresight not to lock, and produced a mocked-up version of a WOK. He was only the second agent to have seen one (Tommy was the first) and, with a great deal of practise, spread over a great many years, I might conceivably handle a WOK half as well as Haugland did.

He asked a little shyly when these 'worked-out codes keys' would be ready, and I promised that it would be soon, and that they'd be printed on silk. I knew then that somehow I was going to make it happen. 'This would be very good code for us' he said quietly, and listened patiently while I stressed the importance of destroying the keys as soon as they'd been used.

He then spent another half an hour making sure he understood the security checks.

We shook hands until we nearly exchanged them and I walked to the door.

'Mr Marks . . .'

I turned back.

He made scissors of his fingers – and carefully went through the motions of cutting his silk.

EIGHT

The Plumber and His Mate

Many of Baker Street's major crises occurred long after those equipped to deal with them had gone home and it was a strictly enforced rule that everyone of officer status (including civilians) had to be available at short notice to act as night duty officers. The only exceptions to this rule were members of the Executive Council, which I had not yet been invited to join.

If an NDO were unfortunate enough to be given an entire building to look after, he had to sit in a minute office from six in the evening till eight the next morning with a Top Secret list of private telephone numbers in front of him, a camp bed behind him and potential chaos all round him. In emergencies he had authority to contact anyone from CD downwards but it was tacitly agreed that anything short of calamity could wait until morning. The definition of calamity was a matter for the NDO. But his duties were not wholly sedentary.

Escorted by an armed escort, he had to inspect every office in the building to ensure that the desks and safes were securely locked and that all documents had been put away. He had also to retrieve any scraps of paper left lying around which should have been disposed of in the confidential waste. He had strict orders to put these unburied treasures in a special satchel and deliver them to the security department when he handed in his report. All breaches of security, however small, had to be specified in this report with the names of the culprits, irrespective of rank.

Despite my imminent dismissal, or perhaps because of it, I was given two days' notice to act as night duty officer for Michael House. It was an ominous prospect for the building and me.

*   *   *

My parents did not need an NDO for the subversive activities they were in the habit of conducting from their Park West base. Every night, including Sundays, they engaged in a series of clandestine operations which were half black comedy and wholly black market, and they conducted their drops and pick-ups with a security-mindedness which outdid C's and SOE's combined.

Since my impossible pair were in the habit of boasting of their only child's slightest achievement, I'd convinced them that I worked at the Marylebone branch of the Ministry of Labour and National Service. Anxious that I should stay there, they loaded me up every day with enough illicit provisions to start a four-star hotel which I was ordered to distribute to colleagues in need. Amongst those qualifying for relief – and getting it – were the main-line coders, the coders of Grendon, Dansey, Heffer and Owen, and a growing number of country section officers who'd heard that the code department at teatime had a direct line to the Almighty. I gave credit for the largesse to my revered Uncle Simon, whose premises I was shortly going to safeguard.

I reported to the security department at precisely six o'clock for a briefing on an NDO's duties. It proved to be an object lesson in non-communication. The captain who instructed me was so full of himself that I spent the entire session trying to determine the reason for his self-esteem and failed to take in a single word of his instructions, except for 'Any questions? Right. Get on with it.'

I'd been assured by Owen that my armed escort would 'know the drill backwards' and would give me whatever guidance I needed. A young corporal, fully equipped for a march on Berlin, was waiting for me outside the NDO's office. An instruction seemed to be called for. 'At ease?' I suggested.

He substituted one hostile stance for another and mounted guard while I went into the NDO's office to assume control of my building.

The NDO's desk was so small, it was like keeping vigil on a splinter. The camp bed creaked with the disturbed nights of my countless predecessors. I put my lovingly wrapped dinner on it. The only redeeming feature anywhere was a poster on the wall of Churchill, the nation's NDO.

I phoned Grendon to see if there were any indecipherables. They'd just broken one from Julien (Isidore Newman, one of Buckmaster's

best operators) after 1,100 attempts. I congratulated them, then identified myself to the Michael House switchboard and announced that
the NDO's patrol was about to begin.

'Have the rules changed, sir?' she asked. 'They don't usually start
till twenty hundred hours.'

'My watch must be fast. Thank you.'

I wondered if I should ask the corporal to come in and sit down
but was uncomfortable in the presence of his artillery.

The phone rang. It was someone anxious to warn me that Hitler
had just been seen parachuting in the direction of Baker Street. I
thanked Tommy for the information and invited him to call in later
for a cigar. He said he was going home early.

I believed that home to Tommy was a fair-haired WAAF called
Barbara. I'd twice glimpsed them walking down Baker Street, which
they brightened considerably. He was trying to get her a job in Duke
Street and undoubtedly would. His own job prospects (the only one
he wanted was in the field) were in the balance. His mission to France
with Passy was still in the planning stage so Tommy had improvised
one of his own. Captain Molyneux (his former employer) kept a
powerful motor yacht in Monte Carlo and Tommy proposed to hijack
it, take it to Gibraltar, and hand it over to the navy, who badly
needed small craft of this class. Tommy was to be infiltrated by felucca
or dropped in by Lysander. The mission had been officially sanctioned
by SOE and welcomed by the navy. Tommy had been given the
code-name Sea-horse. I hoped he'd have better stables for the night
than I had.

The phone rang again. I answered it with relish:

'This is an official announcement. If Hitler's been sighted in the
Norgeby House bog he can bloody well stay there.'

Unfortunately it wasn't Tommy this time. It was Hutchison with
an enquiry about one of his messages. I told him what he needed to
know.

'That's Marks, isn't it?'

I was obliged to confirm that it was.

'I might look in and see you.'

Hoping to be out if he did, I picked up my NDO's satchel and
assumed command of my forces. 'Right, Corporal! Lead the way.'

He looked at me in bewilderment.

'What way, sir?'

'What do you mean "What way, sir"? Where do we start?'

'No idea, sir. I've never done this before, sir.'

I nearly fell over his sten-gun, if that's what it was, and requested an explanation.

'I'm standing in for the sergeant, sir. He's hurt his foot, sir.'

'But surely he gave you *some* instructions.'

'Yes, sir. He said I'm here to protect you, sir. And you'd tell me what to do, sir.'

'Of course,' I said. 'Quick march then.'

The plumber and his mate went walkabout in Michael House. I knew nothing about the geography of the place and very little about its natives. The third floor, I believed, was where merchant bankers in profusion practised their daily diabolicals and I suspected that members of the Executive Council weren't far away. I knew that amongst the giants who had offices in my building were CD himself, his deputy, Brigadier Gubbins, and his other right hand, Colonel Sporborg – who was principal private secretary to SOE's minister, Lord Selborne, on all matters concerned with SOE. It was rumoured that between these two right hands CD could afford the luxury of knowing what his left was doing.

I decided to start the paper-chase in the one office I *did* know and halted the patrol outside the door of the narcissistic captain who'd tried to brief me. There was no light on inside. 'Corporal, if I'm not out in five minutes, come in shooting.'

Something clicked behind me. I couldn't get inside fast enough. (Official procedure, subsequently discovered, was for the armed escort to go in first, search behind the curtains and anywhere else intruders might be lurking, and for the NDO then to enter.)

The captain's office had more scraps of paper in it than a royal park. I put them gleefully into my NDO satchel. I wouldn't report him, but first thing in the morning I'd paper his ego. The rest of the security department's offices were almost as insecure. One officer had left a blotter full of ink-marks on his desk. I removed it and made a note to hold up a mirror to the culprit in the morning.

The next six offices I went into were all empty and I wondered if it was early closing. One desk was full of rotten apples, a mirror-image of its occupant? Another contained a personal letter which didn't seem to be in code. (SOE used a code called Playfair for concealing secret messages in innocent letters. It was an innocent's code, and offered little more security than invisible ink when the right kind of heat was applied).

One door at the end of a small ante-room had a light on inside. Perhaps it had been left on by accident. I knocked.

'*Come.*'

A brigadier and a colonel with an eye-patch sat side by side at a desk. Gubbins and Sporborg. They glanced up from a document they were studying.

I was tempted to say that I'd looked in for a chat about the poem-code. I announced myself instead. 'Night duty officer. Is this room exempt from inspection, sir?'

They stared at me. Gubbins's eyes made de Gaulle's seem placid. Sporborg saw more from his single orb than most people with two.

Gubbins answered. 'The whole floor is exempt.'

'Thank you, sir.'

'Start from the top and work downwards.'

The story of my career.

'Thank you sir.'

'Who *are* you?'

'The night duty officer, sir.'

I had an instinct that I should withhold my name if I could get away with it. Gubbins gave Sporborg a look which said: 'Is this what we've come down to?' and Sporborg smiled. They returned to their document.

The intelligence in that room was like a vibro-massage and an iota of their combined brain-power seemed to have infected my corporal. He stopped outside a door which I hadn't even noticed and put his fingers to his lips. 'There's something funny going on in there, sir. Noise, but no lights.'

I couldn't hear a sound but didn't want to discourage him and went inside.

He was wrong about the lights. There was a candle burning on the desk and it flickered on to a pair of khaki trousers. But he was right about the sounds. They were coming from the far side of the room where a major and his lady were locked together in what I believed to be position number 69 in the sexual code-groups.

'Just checking the confidential waste,' I said, and left them to dispose of their own.

I supposed I should report them for not locking the door. Was the danger of official discovery more exciting than the prospect of mutual? It was worthy of personal research.

Five minutes later I lost my escort. I searched up and down the corridors but there wasn't a corporal in sight. Two minutes later I lost myself. Like the major and his lady, I no longer knew what floor I was on. I found myself outside Gubbins's office. I could hardly ask him the way to the NDO's room.

An antelope of a colonel named Dodds-Parker strode down the corridor and was kind enough to point me in the right direction – which turned out to be one of his specialities. He knocked on Gubbins's door and went in. Dodds-Parker was deeply involved in Operation Torch. From the demands that he was making for Signals equipment and personnel, we knew that the invasion of Algiers was imminent.

My long-lost corporal was waiting for me outside the NDO's office. His complexion was the colour of his uniform. 'Very sorry, sir. I was taken short.'

I knew how he felt. I was born short. I thanked him for his help, but he continued standing there. I wondered if he'd been taken short again. 'Dismiss?' I suggested tentatively.

He saluted, turned to go.

'By the way, Corporal, what was wrong with your sergeant's foot?'

'He dropped his wife on it, sir.'

'Give them my regards.'

I went inside to face my night.

For the first half an hour there was nothing much to face. Just a few routine calls which I did my best to answer. The atmosphere was as cheerful as an interview room in an under-privileged police station. I was doing my bit for the agents' ditty-box when a special messenger brought in an envelope from the code department marked FOR CD PERSONALLY.

I assumed it was my job to evaluate its contents and then telephone CD if I thought necessary. I opened it anyway. It contained a long Situation Report 'FOR CD'S EYES ONLY' from the head of SOE's Cairo Station, Lord Glenconner. The Sitrep dealt with the latest developments of Operation Bullseye, in which the Signals directorate had a vested interest.

The purpose of Bullseye was to persuade Mihailovič to concentrate his Yugoslav guerrillas against the occupying German forces instead of trying to kill his rival Tito, the leader of the Communist partisans. Like most of SOE's Balkans operations, Bullseye consisted of myriad complex details amounting to a horrific simplicity.

The mission had been entrusted to a resourceful, highly experienced SOE officer named Hudson who'd been put ashore by submarine on the coast of Montenegro in 1941 with three Yugoslavs, one of them a wireless operator. Julian Amery took time off from his duties in Belgrade to act as conducting officer and report that the mission had landed safely.

Hudson's first priority was to contact Mihailovič – which he eventually did – and set up wireless communications between Bullseye and London and Bullseye and Cairo. This proved even more difficult. The poem-code had spread its disease to the Balkans but instead of a poem the *Reader's Digest* was used for Bullseye's traffic, presumably because someone had paid his subscription. The first message received from Bullseye was indecipherable and remained so until it was discovered that Outstation and Home were using different editions of the *Reader's Digest*. The mistake was remedied by Cairo – one of the few that were.

Since SOE in London didn't yet have a wireless station it was forced to rely on C's to transmit and receive agents' traffic (including Bullseye's). Unbeknown to Glenconner (and to everyone outside the Signals directorate), two enterprising signals officers named Wing Commander Pyle and Captain Ward decided to check on C's efficiency, and they did so by erecting their own improvised monitoring station on the roof of Baker Street. They intercepted two Bullseye messages which C had missed. In a rare spasm of co-operation, C and SOE finally ensured that the right frequencies were used, the right equipment issued and the same code employed by Home Station and Out.

Glenconner's Sitrep was concerned with SOE's relationship with Tito, which was about as stable as mine with Ozanne. Glenconner was convinced that Tito was actively collaborating with the Germans to bring about the capture and execution of Mihailović and the disbandment of his forces. He reminded CD of a previous Sitrep he had sent and synopsized its astonishing contents:

The Germans had captured a group of Mihailović's guerrillas with the help (Glenconner believed) of information provided by Tito. They had told the prisoners that they would all be shot unless they revealed where Mihailović and his Chief of Staff were hiding. One prisoner jumped up and identified himself as Mihailović, another jumped up and said he was his Chief of Staff. Both men were shot. Mihailović and his Chief of Staff were hiding in the mountains.

Like the master diplomat he was, Glenconner had an eye for a punch-line, even in a Sitrep. He stressed that General Donovan (the head of OSS) was extremely concerned about the SOE–Tito relationship and was prepared to meet CD in London to confirm that he *totally endorsed* Glenconner's reservations about Tito.

Anything of concern to the Americans was of even greater concern to SOE. OSS had still not decided whether to do the bulk of its growing European business with C or with us.

Glenconner ended by urging CD to clarify SOE's policies towards Mihailović and Tito and asked for an immediate reply.

I was reluctant to disturb CD in his bath but it occurred to me that he might still be prowling the building. And that Gubbins and Sporborg might still be in conference. And here was I, only a floor away from them, taking no advantage of it. Why didn't I walk upstairs with my coding report and face the consequences?

Because I hadn't the guts.

What would an 'SOE-minded' NDO do to get a document into CD's hands as if by accident?

Suddenly I knew.

I went back to my office and did it.

*   *   *

Not even SOE allowed NDOs to desert their sentry boxes without good reason. I phoned the Norgeby House NDO and asked if he would take all my calls for the next thirty minutes as an urgent indecipherable had just come in.

'Have a drink on me,' he said.

I'd need one if my plan failed and several more if it succeeded. I christened it 'Operation NDO'. It had one objective: to get my report into the hands of CD no later than tomorrow without my appearing to know that he had it. Since I was forbidden by Ozanne to show it to him, I would have to rely upon the security department to act as my special messenger.

The first step in Operation NDO was to have my report read by the security department. I took a copy of it from its locked oasis and garnished it with a tomato-red label, a coloration reserved for highly sensitive documents.

The next step was to ensure that the security department became aware that a major security offence had been committed in the night.

I wrote in my NDO's report that in the course of my patrol duties I had discovered a Top Secret document, the contents of which I had not perused, in an unlocked drawer of a desk normally occupied, so I understood upon enquiry, by Marks of Codes.

My final act of self-immolation was to empty the NDO's satchel of everyone else's scraps of paper and put my code report in their place.

Security took every opportunity to bring its efficiency to the attention of the All Highest, and would make the most of an offence of this magnitude. Hopefully my report would be in CD's hands the following day. Technically, *I* would not have shown it to him. The security department would be responsible, and if Ozanne attempted to use my gross carelessness as grounds for instant dismissal, it would be cheap at the price. Before leaving SOE I would ask CD one question: 'If a report on agents' codes was such a breach of security, how much greater a breach was the continued use of them?'

There was one major flaw in Operation NDO: the security department might realize that the author of the report and the NDO who found it were one and the same person. But if they realized if *after* CD had read it, it would no longer matter.

I took good care when signing the NDO's report that my signature was as indecipherable as a Skinnarland message. Was there anything I had overlooked? What about the NDO who inspected the code department's premises? He *was the one who should discover that report on my desk.*

I realized that he would cause me no more problems than he usually did.

I was he.

The code department was always inspected by the Michael House NDO – and then most cursorily. We were the only department in SOE fully staffed at night and NDOs were never allowed to see the work in progress.

There were probably plenty of flaws I hadn't spotted but it was too late to worry about them. Operation NDO would be mounted in the morning, no matter what.

I returned to the NDO's cubbyhole. The corporal was dozing in a chair outside. I phoned my Norgeby House colleague.

He told me there hadn't been a single call for me. 'Nothing's happened in Michael House tonight,' he said wistfully.

But I suspected that a great deal was going to happen tomorrow – most of it to me.

NINE

The Godfather

The morning after my NDO experience I found an envelope addressed to 'Mr Marx' waiting on my desk. It contained a present from Rabinovitch which he'd left at Chiltern Court before taking off for the field. It was a photograph of Joe Louis knocking out Max Schmeling with a short left jab.

Ten minutes later I was instructed by telephone to report immediately to the security department. I'd gladly have changed places with Schmeling. I knew that the head of Security was a brilliancy of Gubbins/Sporborg calibre, and that he'd surrounded himself with a highly professional staff, most of them barristers like himself or peacetime Intelligence officers. His secretary silently pointed to a nearby office, and told me to go straight in.

I opened the door – and had to lean against it for support.

Seated behind a desk was my godfather, Major O'Reilly of the Special Branch at Scotland Yard, who'd been responsible for introducing me to Bedford.

He was studying my code report, and silently pointed to a chair without looking up. He turned back a few pages to re-read something, disliked it as much the second time, and finally closed the report.

I learned from his opening remarks that he'd been a member of SOE since its inception. He'd seen my name several months ago when it was being put through the cards* but had done nothing whatsoever to ease my way into SOE. I told him that I was glad for his sake.

The courtesies then ended.

He informed me that I was the first NDO in the history of SOE

* Security-jargon for screening.

89

who had failed to report a single one of the scraps of paper which the security department deliberately left lying around as a trap for indolent young watchpuppies like me! He then read me a list of the items which his department had planted on the night I was on duty, not one of which I had even mentioned. The rotten apples in the desk included one which had been hollowed out for an explosive charge and I hadn't even troubled to examine it. My respect for his directorate increased by the second.

'Before I deal with far and away the worst offence of its kind that I can recall,' he said, 'perhaps you'd care to explain what this is.' He held out a sheet of paper with which I was only too familiar.

'It's only a poem-code I wrote last night. It hasn't been issued to an agent.' Nor was it ever going to be! I'd spent most of my time on the NDO's bed thinking about a lady 'night duty officer' who was permanently on call in her Park West flat, and I'd jotted down the principal recommendations I would make to her for passing what remained of the night to our mutual benefit:

> Tickle my wallypad
> Tongue my zonker
> And make an oaktree
> Out of a conker . . .

He retrieved it from me in silence. It was part of the evidence. The more the better.

The next five minutes were riveting. His invective had been incubated in Ireland and honed in Whitehall and he could have written some interesting poems for the ditty-box. I had never seen anyone quite as angry, with the exception of Tommy when we'd first met and my boyhood CD (the high master of St Paul's) whenever we'd met. I should be hauled up in front of the real CD very soon.

A cryptographer's mind never stops counting frequencies, even in moments of extreme duress, and mine registered that the major was repeating himself. He had twice told me that he had several times read my report and now he was saying it again. I wondered what Freud would have made out of this, apart from a fortune. I began thinking about a Belgian indecipherable which had just come in until I

90

heard myself being accused of 'playing silly buggers'. It was then that I noticed certain personality changes in the major which alarmed me. The lilt had crept back into his voice, his manner had mellowed and he was softening into granite. Before I could do a thing to prevent it, the room became oppressive with imminent forgiveness. Since it *was* my first offence, and *was* my first stint of night duty, and I *did* seem to care about my job, he was going to exercise his discretion and let me off with a warning. *Just this once.* He pointed firmly to the door.

So much for my concept of SOE-mindedness. I couldn't even get myself reported!

Determined to try again, I wondered how I could reach Lord Selborne or go even higher, to Colonel Tiltman of Bletchley Park.

He called me back in mid-speculation, and, as casually as any Irishman can, said that he didn't wish me to misconstrue his leniency. It had nothing to do with his friendship with Father. There was another reason for it.

He finally said that a lady whose judgement he respected had spoken quite highly of me, and that if I had any problems I could do a lot worse than talk them over with her.

I casually asked for the lady's name as I'd like us to become better acquainted but it was the wrong question to have asked him.

'I'll tickle your zonker for you, you cheeky little bugger,' he roared.

He then threw my report at me, and pointed to the door.

On 18 October the Grouse boarded a Halifax, took off for Hardanger – and plummeted towards their icy plateau.

SOE didn't know if they had landed safely and didn't expect to hear from them until they reached the Barren Mountain. From now on round-the-clock listening posts would be maintained. One of them in my head.

The head of SOE's stationery department sat opposite me and waited for me to say something, though I hadn't asked her to call. Least of all at eleven o'clock at night.

Her name was Joan Dodd, and I was convinced that she was the lady who'd praised me to Major Jack. Unless Mother was working under cover in Baker Street.

Yet it seemed unlikely that she was my benefactress. At our only previous meeting she'd come storming into my office demanding to know why the code department had quadrupled its demands for squared paper, which was in very short supply and was needed by other departments just as important as ours.

I was then in the middle of trying to break one of Skinnarland's nastiest. I'd shown her why we wanted squared paper, but not content with that I'd kept her there till she knew enough about indecipherables to help me with Skinnarland's. The first key she tried was the one which broke it. Then I put her to work on another. This time she wasn't so lucky. By the time I let her go she could hardly find the door.

The next day squared paper arrived by the ream and I'd had no trouble from her since.

But why would the head of the stationery department have Jack O'Reilly's ear? And what would he respect her judgement about? Paper clips?

I asked her if she knew the Major.

'Slightly,' she said. 'He's my godfather.'

I enquired how this extreme good fortune had come about.

'My father was assistant commissioner of police,' she said.

Of course! Sir John Dodd. O'Reilly's peacetime boss.

'Well now, Miss Dodd,' I said, wondering if I had any illicit provisions left. 'What exactly have you come to see me about?'

'You phoned my department to ask if we could do some printing for you on soluble paper. You were told that we could. And we haven't heard from you since.'

This was very efficient of her. I hadn't followed up the enquiry. Nor had I referred it to her personally. I preferred dealing with one of her assistants with a view to long-term research into position number sixty-nine (and others) in my favourite code-groups.

I told her that my enquiry was only part of a much larger printing problem we had. She asked if I would care to discuss it with her. I didn't see the point but for the sake of good relations showed her a mocked-up version of a WOK. I told her that we would need large numbers of them, that no two would be alike, and that they'd all have to be printed on silk.

I showed her the purpose of the WOK.

She was very thoughtful. 'When do you want them?' she asked.

'Miss Dodd . . . do you mean you could help?'

'With the printing? I believe so. I know whom to ask.'

'And the silk?'

'I don't think that's a problem. I know whom to ask.'

She held up the mocked-up WOK to the light. 'Will they all be as illegible as this?'

'Why, Miss Dodd?'

She looked at me with an expert's contempt for a stupid question. 'Because if the copy were better they could be photographed straight on to silk. It would be quicker than printing.'

'You know a photographer?'

'Yes,' she said. 'The head of my directorate.'

'Miss Dodd,' I said, 'there's another problem.'

'I rather thought there was.' She said it like a mother who knew where the pain was. I was sure she'd realized that I had no authority to proceed with WOKs.

I told her that we hadn't got enough staff to make them – and that we'd need a team of girls who'd shuffle numbered counters at random. I wasn't sure how to go about getting them.

'Don't you know anyone in the personnel department?'

'Do you, Miss Dodd?'

'Yes,' she said. 'The head of it used to work for me!'

'Space might be a problem.'

'That's for the admin department.'

I asked if she knew anyone in the admin department.

'Yes,' she said. 'The head of it's a friend of mine.'

'Miss Dodd . . . this whole subject of WOKs is still a matter of internal discussion.'

'Isn't that what we're having, Mr Marks? An internal discussion?'

'May I ask you a personal question then?'

It was clear that I did so at my peril.

'Miss Dodd . . . is there anyone in SOE you don't know?'

'Yes,' she said. 'You.'

She produced a slip of paper from her handbag and handed it to me. There were seven numbers on it. The combination of the briefcase I had stolen from her office.

I returned it to her in silence.

'Thank you,' she said. 'Perhaps you'll let me know when you're ready to talk detail. Good night, Mr Marks.'

'Good night, Miss Dodd.'

I sat in a silence so deep that I could feel it inside me.

WOKS could happen. Whether in my time or my successor's didn't matter. They *could happen.*

I put the slip of paper she'd given me in the only place I wouldn't lose it – inside a drawer next to the photograph of Louis and Schmeling.

There was still no news of the Grouse.

A message arrived from Einar Skinnarland. He had encoded it perfectly, a phenomenon which allowed us no respite from its contents:

The Germans had ordered the entire stock of heavy water to be shipped to Berlin. The present quantity was believed to be sufficient for their High Command's purposes. The shipments were to take place at the earliest possible moment.

Skinnarland's message was passed to the British High Command, who at once sent it to Churchill. It was decided in Cabinet, with the Chiefs of Staff, Lindemann and Mountbatten present, that the RAF was to help SOE to mount a major new operation into Norway. In Churchill's opinion the situation was now far too serious to rely only on the Grouse.*

Wilson at once began planning for a commando of thirty men to be landed from gliders to attack the plant and link up with the Grouse if they arrived at Rjukan in time.

I pretended to myself that the FANY lieutenant I was briefing was not one of Buckmaster's agents but a candidate for Grendon's code room, that her supervisor would look after her if she had any troubles, and that I was simply there to provide her with basic essentials.

I tried not to think about what she was going to do or what might be done to her, and if she sensed that she was the first woman agent I'd briefed she showed no signs of it.

---

* Information known at the time only to CD, Gubbins and Wilson.

She was a steady coder, managing somehow to control the vitality that was the essence of her as she slowly and methodically checked her work before passing it to me.

It was perfectly encoded but I noticed that she'd spelled Vienna with one 'n' and had corrected it herself. She would have less time in the field and I made a note of the mistake.

We went through the shell of her security checks and I tried to forget the circumstances under which they'd be demanded of her.

She had a most beguiling accent, especially when she laughed. She even smiled in French.

I asked her to come through the coding process once more and she responded immediately.

There was no more I could teach her. I was too shy to wish her 'merde alors' and shook hands. She had a very firm grip, especially with her eyes.

I glanced at her code-card. She hadn't yet been given a code-name or, if she had, I hadn't been told of it.

I wrote on her code conventions the name by which everyone else seemed to call her.

Odette.

On 9 November a message arrived from the Barren Mountain from the Grouse.

It was a great day for SOE, our greatest so far.

Only one thing spoiled it.

The message was indecipherable.

I could not, would not, believe that Haugland had made a mistake in his coding. Not in his first message. Nor did I believe that he would in any. It now had to be broken with *absolute priority*. It was all indecipherables in one.

I allotted 5,000 keys to the coders of Grendon and sat back to think before I started work myself.

There were two likely possibilities. The indicator-group might be mutilated due to poor reception, but the signalmaster assured me that they'd had a clear strong signal and that the message had been monitored by three different operators. He thought Morse mutilation most unlikely.

The other possibility was that the Grouse had been captured and that Haugland had given the Germans the wrong poem. This didn't seem likely either. He knew that with his very first message his security check could safely be used. It was in any subsequent messages that it couldn't be trusted.

I decided that while the girls were making their blanket attack I would try to break it cryptographically.

Wilson had told me (though hardly able to speak with tension and frustration) that the Grouse's first message would contain the phrase 'three pink elephants' to indicate that they had arrived at Rjukan.

There was a 'k' in the code-groups, two 'p's and several 'l's. I had asked the Grouse to 'free' their language and this would now work against me, but 'three pink elephants' would be an enormous help. Its eighteen letters would straddle eighteen adjacent columns and words would start forming if I aligned them properly.

I stopped after five minutes.

I owed it to Haugland.

If he hadn't made a mistake – and I knew he couldn't, he simply *couldn't* – then there must be some other explanation, however improbable.

Ten minutes later I telephoned Wilson to tell him that the message was decoded. 'Three pink elephants, Colonel. And it's on its way over to you.'

'God bless you,' he said – which made it even worse.

It was an hour before I had the courage to phone him again.

He was in a teasing mood. 'Do you still think Haugland's the best coder you've ever met?'

'I know he is.'

'So why did he make a mistake? Nerves?'

'Haugland didn't make a mistake, sir. We did. I'm very, very sorry.'

A long pause.

'What mistake, Marks?'

'We copied a word of his poem wrongly. It was a typing error – I didn't spot it. I'm very, very sorry.'

There was a small sound the other end of the line which I couldn't decipher. 'Would it help to prevent this if a member of my staff checked the Norwegian words for you?' he asked.

'Enormously.'

'I'll lay it on at once. You can count on it from tomorrow.'

'Thank you, Colonel Wilson. I'm very, very sorry.'

I couldn't believe that the sound I was hearing was laughter. 'So it was all your fault, was it? You can't decode a perfect message? I can't wait to tell old Einar. He'll laugh his bloody head off after all you've said about him. And by the way, thank you for letting me know.' He strode off the phone chuckling.

I didn't mind if he told 'old Einar'. He'd have to be alive to be able to laugh his bloody head off.

But I rather hoped he wouldn't tell my pupil on the Barren Mountain.

I valued his respect.

TEN

The Sixth Sense

I had a gut feeling about the Dutch but it was a bride unwilling to be carried over the threshold of consciousness, and I couldn't pinpoint it.

'Why are you so concerned about them?' asked Heffer.

'I don't know.'

'In that case,' he said, 'it is serious,' and left me to pursue my missing Dutch something.

There was a cataract over my mind's eye and I didn't know how to remove it. There were so many conscious reasons for worrying about the Dutch traffic that this elusive anxiety could have been triggered by any or all of them. The obvious worries fell into three main areas:

1 Abor's and Ebenezer's security checks
2 A traffic snarl-up between Boni, Parsnip and London
3 The Dutch section itself.

Abor's and Ebenezer's Security Checks

The elementary system in which Ozanne had such confidence required Abor to make a deliberate spelling mistake *every* eighteenth letter of his *every* message. He was also required to insert three dummy letters at the end of his messages. Since he'd been dropped into Holland in March of this year he hadn't used either check once.

Ebenezer (who'd been dropped in November '41) was required to make a spelling mistake every sixteenth letter. He was also required to insert three dummy letters at the end of each message. He'd done

98

so correctly until April of this year but suddenly began introducing variations of his own, such as spelling 'stop' as 'stip', 'stap' and 'step' in places which were not multiples of sixteen. He'd also stopped using his second check altogether.

In the considered opinion of N section, these (and other anomalies) were entirely due to Morse mutilation and bad training.

The Boni–Parsnip Traffic Snarl-up

Boni (formerly known as Spinach) was a WT operator who transmitted and received all the traffic of Parsnip, his organizer. He was also responsible for the traffic of other key agents. The snarl-up, into which I could as easily read too much as the Dutch section too little, lasted from 3 August until 12 November. Throughout this period the Dutch section was planning to carry out several important operations, and relied on Boni, Parsnip and Potato for information about safe dropping grounds, changes in sentry patrols, and all the other bread-and-butter ingredients of sabotage and infiltration.

On 3 August they informed Parsnip that his friend Cabbage was ready to link up with him. Could they safely make contact via Potato? They also asked him several operational questions which required urgent answers.

No reply was received to these questions during Boni's next four skeds though he transmitted three messages from Parsnip in the course of them. The Dutch section then pressed for replies and were informed by Boni that *Parsnip had been unable to decipher London's message of 3 August*. Boni suggested that Parsnip's future traffic should be enciphered in his (Boni's) code. Boni then transmitted five messages from Parsnip, *none of which we could decipher despite a blanket attack of 5,000 attempts*.

On 9 September the Dutch section's message of 3 August was repeated to Parsnip in Boni's code. In a separate message to Boni the Dutch section informed him that five of Parsnip's messages could not be deciphered and that a sixth was missing and asked Boni to retransmit all of them in his own code (an appalling breach of cipher security but Ozanne was not prepared to intervene).

On 12 September Boni transmitted a message in Parsnip's code which did not answer one of London's questions of 3 August. The Dutch section acknowledged this message the next day and reminded Parsnip that five of his previous messages could not be deciphered and that a sixth was missing. They repeated their urgent enquiries of 3 August.

On 15 September Boni informed the Dutch section that *Parsnip had been unable to decipher London's message of the 13th.* Boni again suggested that all Parsnip's traffic should be encoded in his (Boni's) code. At the end of this dangerously long transmission he retransmitted Parsnip's five indecipherables in his own code. I noticed that they dealt exclusively with Intelligence matters.

On 19 September the Dutch section alerted Potato that his operation had to be postponed until the night of 7/8 October and urgently instructed him to re-check the details and confirm that there was no change. Potato made no reply at all to this message and on 2 October the Dutch section reminded Boni that they still hadn't heard from Potato.

On 3 October Boni transmitted two messages in Parsnip's code which we were unable to decipher despite a blanket attack of 5,000 attempts. From this point onwards approximately 70 per cent of Parsnip's traffic was passed in Boni's code, the remainder in his own.

On 7 October Boni retransmitted the sixth and seventh of Parsnip's indecipherables as well as Parsnip's two indecipherables of 3 October. He had re-enciphered them accurately in his own code. They all dealt with Intelligence matters.

On 12 October Boni informed the Dutch section that *Potato had been unable to decipher London's message of 19 September and asked them to repeat it. On the same day – after Heffer had personally intervened with Ozanne – the Dutch section paraphrased their message of the 19th and it was transmitted to Potato in Boni's code.*

On 13 October Potato confirmed that conditions had not changed and that everything was ready for the operation.

On 24 October Boni sent two messages in his own code from Parsnip. Both dealt exclusively with Intelligence matters.

On 31 October the Dutch section informed Parsnip that the time had come for him to contact Carrot. The message was enciphered in Parsnip's code.

On 7 November Boni informed the Dutch section that *Parsnip had been unable to decipher London's message of the 31st and asked for it to be re-enciphered in his own code.*

On 12 November a paraphrased version of this message was transmitted to Parsnip in Boni's code.

From 12 November onwards traffic proceeded to flow smoothly in both directions and the dropping operation took place on the nights of 28 /29 November to the complete satisfaction of the Dutch section.

The snarl-up had caused the following casualties:

Nine indecipherables from Holland to London
Four indecipherables from London to Holland
Nine repeated messages from Holland to London
Four repeated messages from London to Holland.

These repeated messages had totally compromised the security of Boni's and Parsnip's codes, such as it was in the first place.

The Dutch section attributed the entire snarl-up to the natural hazards of clandestine communication. The unnatural hazards were themselves and Ozanne.

The Dutch Section

I found the Dutch more difficult to approach than any other country section. The head of the Directorate was Major Blizzard; his deputy was Captain Bingham, and they were assisted by Captain Killick, whose real name was Kypers. They had a stock answer to every enquiry I made about the security of their agents: 'They're perfectly all right; we have our own ways of checking on them,' and I wasn't in a position to ask what they were.

Killick was the most open-minded and co-operative, though he was Foreign Office trained, but I discovered from reading the back traffic that he'd committed the worst breach of security I'd come across since joining SOE.

I taxed him with it on the telephone. 'Captain Killick, is it true that in April this year you authorized Trumpet to recruit and train a local wireless operator?'

'Yes.'

'And is it also true that you instructed him to make this operator transmit a test message?'

'Yes.'

'And when that message arrived, the operator hadn't used any security checks?'

'No, he hadn't.'

'Did you then instruct Trumpet to teach the operator how to use security checks? – and in the same message, did you tell him *exactly* what those checks were to be?'

'I did.'

'Do you consider that was good security, Captain Killick?'

'You weren't here in April,' he said, buying a little time.

'I've been reading your back traffic. Was it good security, Captain Killick?'

'Of course it wasn't. And I'll see nothing like it happens again.'

At least I'd achieved something but I still couldn't pinpoint that elusive worry. All I could say to anyone – with my hand on a WOK or any other Bible – was that there was something wrong with the Dutch traffic.

It was a relief to turn from the mysteries of Holland to the wonders of Denmark.

The Danish directorate was the least troublesome (though often the most troubled) in the whole of Baker Street. Ever since 1940, when King Christian had ordered his people to accept the German occupation with dignified demeanour – 'And God help you all, and God help Denmark!' – Churchill and the Chiefs of Staff had discounted the Danes as a fighting force. But this hadn't deterred the head of the Danish section (Commander Hollingsworth) and his deputy (Reginald Spink) from proceeding with dignified demeanour to prove that the tiny country had a contribution to make which was out of all proportion to its size.

The first Danish agents were dropped blind in December '41 – Dr Carl Bruhn to recruit partisans, and Mogens Hammer to set up wireless links with London. Bruhn's parachute didn't open and Hammer, who'd landed safely, couldn't find his body. Nor could he find the transmitter which Bruhn was carrying. The Germans found both. They also found Hammer's parachute and issued a warning that the first British agents had arrived in Denmark and that one of them was still at large. It was extremely dangerous for Hammer to move around Copenhagen but he dressed himself as a Protestant parson and became so at home in the part that he frequently preached at German military services.

His greatest problem was not divine communication but how to find a new transmitter and to solve it he contacted Ebbe Muncke, head of the Danish patriotic group in Sweden, who ran a weekly courier service to London. Muncke provided Hammer with the equipment he needed and in April '42 Hammer transmitted his first message to London. The signal was so weak that it was barely decipherable and Hammer persuaded a brilliant Danish engineer, Duus Hansen, to build a new one for him in his Copenhagen laboratory. Duus Hansen's set worked even better than SOE's own and Hammer made one of the most far-sighted decisions ever taken on SOE's behalf. He recruited Duus Hansen into SOE.

Something equally significant had taken place in neglected little Denmark in June '41 which neither Hammer nor SOE knew about at the time. Three young men, anxious to join what they believed to be an active Danish Resistance in London, had acquired the frame of a two-seater sports plane and, using the best of Danish inspiration and a motor-car engine, had built an aeroplane which they assembled in a barn outside Copenhagen. The three would-be aviators were Sneum, Petersen and Rottbøll. Since their plane would hold only two (if as many), Rottbøll decided to go by sea. In June '41 Sneum and Petersen flew to Britain in their contraption, bringing with them films of the latest German radar systems.

Astonished British scientists confirmed that the films contained the most valuable information yet received from any source about German radar – and C asked the two young men to return home and set up a wireless link with England. In September '41 Sneum and a wireless operator were dropped back into Denmark. They were friendly with a Danish police officer and with his help sent C a series of messages about the daily activities of the German security police. C did not inform SOE of this vital wireless link. Nor did C disclose to SOE the information about the movements of the German police. Even in a country the size of Denmark the sister organizations would not collaborate.

The third young man, Rottbøll, reached London with the help of Ebbe Muncke and so impressed Commander Hollingsworth that he was invited to take command of all SOE agents in Denmark. The young man accepted and in April parachuted with two wireless operators on to a dropping ground in Denmark prepared by Mogens Hammer.

In May 1942 there were only seven SOE agents in Denmark and Rottbøll's first priority was to recruit new ones and to find a distinguished Danish citizen to come to London to head up a Free Danish Council. He contacted Christmas Moller, a prominent politician, who arrived in London in May to form the Danish government-in-exile.

With little help from SOE (though Hollingsworth provided all he could) Rottbøll co-ordinated the various Resistance groups in Denmark and persuaded them to pool their resources under SOE. His chief wireless operator, Johannesen, was in regular contact with London, Stockholm and Gothenburg. Early in September German direction-finding units located the house from which he was operating and burst into it. Johannesen held them off with a pistol just long enough to swallow his L-tablet.

On 25 September the German police located the house where Rottbøll was living and surrounded it. They called on the young man to surrender. He died with twelve bullets in him.

On both these raids the Germans had insisted that Danish police should accompany them.

The raids continued, and by the end of September London was completely out of wireless contact with the Danish Resistance, though many messages were smuggled into our embassy in Sweden and relayed to London.

In the middle of October Hollingsworth asked to see me 'as soon as convenient'.

I was with him ten minutes later. His entire directorate was squeezed into three small offices in Chiltern Court, and he shared one with his deputy, Spink, an expert on Denmark's economy.

Hollingsworth was the only country section head I'd met who was prepared to discuss his problems with me as if I were a member of his directorate. He confided that Mogens Hammer had arrived in London, and was prepared to return to Denmark within the next ten days despite the dangers. It was essential that he took new codes with him. He must also have a stock in reserve to hand to new agents. He was waiting next door to be briefed.

I asked if he and Spink would write some original poems in Danish, and they at once agreed. I then suggested that, to make the reserve poems easier for Hammer to conceal, and if necessary to dispose of, they should be microfilmed on soluble paper. Hollingsworth liked the principle but asked if they could be produced on waterproof paper. It was an unusual request and I asked the reason for it.

Hammer was to be dropped into the sea.

It would be the first time this form of parachuting had been attempted by an SOE agent. After a great deal of research a special waterproof suit had been produced for Hammer which fitted over his ordinary clothing. It was still in the experimental stage and there was a great danger that, if the fabric were torn, water would saturate the suit and its sheer weight would cause the wearer to drown.

Hammer's reaction had been typical: 'If it doesn't work for me you will learn from it and it will work for the next man.'

I went next door to brief the sea-going parson.

It was likely to be a difficult session. I knew from his traffic that he was an excellent coder and WT operator, but instructing agents in the use of the poem-code would be a new experience for him, and it was a hard enough task in the safety of training schools, let alone in occupied Denmark.

He greeted me as if I were a member of his congregation who hadn't put enough in the plate, and was clearly in no mood to be taught how to teach. Like all agents who'd formed coding habits, he had some difficulty absorbing new security rules and showed flashes of temper which were mainly directed against himself. But at the end of an hour he'd made his peace with his coding and smiled from the pulpit when I wished him good luck.

On 20 October he dropped into the sea and arrived in Copenhagen a day or two later to resume his sermons to his German flock.

SOE had a massive success in November and an even more massive disaster.

The success was our contribution to the invasion of North Africa which had helped to secure Algiers for the Allies.

SOE's base had been set up at Guyotville and given the code-name Massingham. It was to be our communications centre in North Africa for main-line and agents' traffic. London was to provide most of the coders and Dansey told me to pick some of the best from Station 53. The girls were delighted but it meant breaking up a team. Dispersing them was like tearing out pages from an illuminated manuscript and selling them separately, one of 84's less desirable habits.

The disaster was Norway.

On 19 November thirty-four officers and men in two gliders were towed by two Halifaxes towards something approximating a flat strip of country near Rjukan. They were to be met on landing by the Grouse.

The clouds that night were so dense that the pilots decided to turn back thirty or so miles away from the dropping ground. One of the tow ropes snapped and the gliders crashed to the ground. The other Halifax crashed into a hill. Of the seventeen men in the first glider, nine survived. Four of them were taken to a hospital in Stavanger. Air bubbles were injected into their veins by a Quisling doctor and they died at once. The other five were taken to a concentration camp and executed, their hands tied behind their backs with barbed wire.

Only fourteen men survived the other plane crash and many of them were badly injured. They were rounded up by German security police and shot by a firing squad. The wounded were executed first, leaning against a wall.

Every one of the executed men was wearing a British army uniform. The Grouse were still safe.

At the beginning of December a new figure had begun prowling the corridors of Baker Street. He was a tall colonel, and Heffer was usually beside him.

Then the stranger began prowling alone.

He spent a long time in Dansey's office.

He did not come into mine.

In mid-December two signals officers were dismissed for inefficiency. Three more were posted back to their units. There were rumours that other dismissals were on the way.

Then the prowler disappeared for a while . . .

The gut feeling about Holland was now lodged in the abdomen, where it kept better company.

On 16 December the Dutch section informed Boni that in the following moon period were dropping six (it turned out to be seven) containers, and that new poems for Boni, Parsnip and Cabbage would be found in a small wooden box marked with a white cross. (Why did I keep seeing the agents in a large wooden box with no cross to mark it?) The containers were dropped on the night of the 22nd/23rd, and Boni acknowledged their safe arrival. He also acknowledged receipt of the poems.

I hadn't asked for them to be original compositions. It might alert the Germans in Holland that we were aware of the dangers of using famous quotations, and cause them to revise their opinion of any organization stupid enough to use the poem-code.

SOE had somehow heard that Christmas was imminent, and the coders of Grendon were anxious for some leave. I volunteered to stand in on Christmas Day for whichever coder won me in a raffle. I didn't envy the supervisor who'd have to check the results. My handwriting was as illegible as the gut feeling.

On 22 December the stranger resumed his prowling.

I knew by now that his name was Colonel Nicholls. I also knew what he was doing here.

He was to take over the Signals directorate.

Heffer had promised Ozanne that he'd look for a suitable replacement for me. Instead he'd found one for Ozanne. If this wasn't an example of SOE-mindedness, I wondered what was. I also wondered why Nicholls hadn't come anywhere near me, if only to say, 'Good riddance.'

I was convinced that the bad rubbish wouldn't have long to wait.

*   *   *

On Christmas Eve Joan Dodd presented me with a trial version of a silk WOK. The printing was too small and the silk would have to be chemically treated to make it easy to cut but it was the most beautiful sight I'd seen. My first impulse was to share it with Dansey and Heff, but with my job in the balance I knew that I daren't, and wore it as a pocket handkerchief instead.

The Xmas traffic was light and I was preparing to go home when Colonel Nicholls walked in and sat opposite me in silence.

He was very tall, very thin, with a nose like a snooker ball which had been potted once too often. A red one. 'Right, Marks,' he said. 'Tell me all about it.'

Obeying him immediately I told him all that was wrong with the codes and right with the coders, and kept only one thing back: the breaking of the secret French code.

He closed his eyes after twenty minutes or so and seemed to be asleep, but something warned me that it was his way of listening. He looked up the moment I stopped talking.

I gave him my WOK to examine and thought for a moment that he was going to blow his nose on it. I then explained how it worked.

He was silent for an agent's lifetime.

He spent ten minutes re-examining it and closed his eyes for five of them. He asked me to show him again how the security checks would operate and tried one for himself. 'Who advised you about this?' he asked quietly.

I told him that I'd discussed it with Dansey and Heffer.

'Yes, yes. But which cryptographer advised you?'

'Nobody has, sir.'

'Have you ever felt in need of expert advice?'

'Every minute of every day, sir.'

He asked whose advice I'd like if I could get it.

'If I could get it, sir, Colonel Tiltman's. He works at Bletchley Park.'

'Does he indeed? Have you met him?'

'No, sir. But I saw him once in a corridor at the code-breaking school.'

'Why didn't you meet him?'

'I wasn't considered promising enough, sir.'

He blew his snooker ball with his own pocket handkerchief. 'I'm afraid poor old John's got himself tied up in admin. It's a great waste of his cryptographic talent.'

Poor old John? – Does he actually know him?

He stood up suddenly, and became a very full colonel indeed. 'Colonel Ozanne's shown me your coding report.'

Goodbye, SOE. It's been nice not knowing you.

'I completely endorse it, though it would have been better without your occasional flippancies.'

He cut me short in mid-apology.

'Colonel Tiltman endorses it too – he read it last week – you'll be meeting him shortly.'

He had a smile which could lift the black-out. 'I suggest you go home now. Happy Christmas, Marks.'

'Happy Christmas, Colonel Nicholls.'

ELEVEN

The High-Pitched Bleep

All of us in SOE were as certain as we could be of anything that 1943 was going to be our make-or-break year. The make was likely to be the country sections' new operations; the break the poem-code which carried their traffic. I still had no authority to replace it with WOKs.

Nor did I have authority to install two girls on the top floor of Norgeby House to make WOK-keys by hand, but I'd done it with the help of Joan Dodd's circuit and hoped that it would be condoned.

Acute shortage of aircraft and equipment were the main obstacles to SOE's Happy New Year, and the country sections' rivalry for the wherewithal to take the war to the enemy was a war in itself. The piece of equipment which indicated a country section's priority was a brilliant device called a Eureka which enabled an agent to guide an aircraft to a dropping ground without the use of lights or flares, no matter how dark the night.

The Eureka was simple to work. Its built-in transmitter was tuned to the wavelength of the aircraft's receiver, and by emitting a continuous high-frequency signal it provided a radio beam down which the aircraft could fly. Several of them had been dropped into Holland.

I badly needed a Eureka of my own to help me resolve the niggling feeling that the Dutch traffic was continuing to emit a high-pitched bleep which I was still failing to pick up.

I had many reasons, some of which I knew, for being interested in an altogether more complex Eureka – the mind of Sigmund Freud.

The great decoder of unconscious signals had left Austria in 1938 to seek sanctuary in England and he'd found some for himself amongst the bookshelves of 84. Freud was seldom well enough to leave his Hampstead home and couldn't climb the stairs to the third floor of 84, where rare religious and occult books were housed. Frank Doel, the shop's anchor-man, had gladly carried down to him every-thing that he'd wanted to see. He was particularly interested in anything which had a bearing on the life of Moses.* He was too ill to visit Marks & Co. again and died in 1939. As compensation for arriving five minutes too late to see him sitting there (J. B. Priestley had pulled out a chair for him), I was given signed copies of *The Interpretation of Dreams* and *The Psychopathology of Everyday Life*. They were addictive and should have been issued on prescription only.

I tried with uninformed enthusiasm to apply their principles to the psychopathology of SOE life. According to my understanding of Sigmund, I was in the market for Joan Dodd's sexual stationery, felt that my parents should be starving instead of the Grouse, and knew in my unconscious exactly what was wrong with the Dutch traffic.

It must be a very dark night down there. The knowledge still refused to surface.

From all that I'd heard about SOE's director of Finance, he was as good at causing nightmares as Freud at decoding them. Group Cap-tain Venner had been in SOE long enough to believe that he knew every fiddle there was. He was convinced that I'd worked a new one and was determined to find out how I'd managed it.

I had forgotten that my two WOK-makers could not live by codes alone and that someone would have to pay them a salary. That someone was Group Captain Venner.

The unauthorized employment of two lowly paid civilians hardly seemed to warrant the personal attention of a member of the Execu-tive Council but I was duly summoned to Venner's office for a full accounting.

He wanted no time in skirmishing. 'I want to know how those girls got here.'

---

* Freud completed *Moses and Monotheism* (1937–9) in London.

111

I began to explain the importance to SOE of the work they were doing.

'I don't give a damn if they're planning the invasion of Europe. I want to know how they got here.'

'They *are* planning the invasion of Europe, sir.'

'*What?*'

I explained that we were going to invade it with a new code, which the girls were making by hand, and that to vary the drudgery they helped Grendon to break indecipherables.

The office was filled with that most despairing of sounds, a finance director's sigh. 'Will you *please* tell me how they got here?'

'By bus, sir.'

I was afraid he was about to send for the fraud squad. Its SOE equivalent was Major O'Reilly.

'What are indecipherables?' he suddenly asked.

He hardly had time to cover up his secret documents before I was seated by his side giving him a potted version of how indecipherables were broken. I showed him why the permutations could run into tens of millions. He did a quick calculation on his pad and nodded. 'Do we get many?' he asked.

Anyone who'd say 'we' in circumstances like this must be a good man to work for.

'Some weeks we get none, sir. But most of the time they come at us from all over Europe. We get them from the Free French, the normal French, the Danes, the Norwegians, the . . . you've been an absolute Godsend, sir. May I go now?'

I rushed back to my own office before he could answer.

The unconscious signal had finally reached its Home Station and only God and Freud would know how I'd missed it.

With the exception of Parsnip's traffic, which was passed by Boni, *we had never received an indecipherable from Holland which had been caused by coding mistakes.*

It was then that I realized the implications.

There was an essential piece of homework I had to do before trying to convince SOE of what the absence of indecipherables from Holland really meant. It was vital to establish whether Parsnip's indecipherables had been caused by Morse mutilation or mistakes in his coding. If it proved to be the latter, he was the only Dutch agent who was behaving normally.

Putting the code-groups of his seven indecipherables side by side with Boni's clear texts, I was about to start on a cryptographic jamboree to reconstruct whatever mistakes in coding Parsnip might have made when I remembered that his indecipherables had all been concerned with Intelligence matters. I also remembered that the Dutch section's traffic had twice referred to a special code (Playfair) which Potato used for passwords and addresses. Supposing Parsnip were using a special code for his Intelligence messages and for some reason we had no knowledge of it?

I telephoned Bingham and demanded that he talk to me. Yes, of course he'd given Parsnip a reserve poem for his Top Secret Intelligence messages. Yes, of course he'd informed Dansey which poem he'd selected, and yes of course he'd confirmed it in writing, there must be a memo on file. What was all the fuss about anyway? I told him that it was just a routine check.

And of course there was no such memo on Dansey's meticulous file, and of course Dansey had not been told by Bingham which reserve poem Parsnip was to use for Intelligence messages. We had tried a blanket attack on the wrong code.

Every one of Parsnip's messages came out perfectly on his reserve poem, and I was ashamed that I was glad. I could now say without any qualification to whoever would listen to me that *no Dutch agent had made a mistake in his coding . . .*

It was time to consult Heffer, the only man in SOE with whom it was safe to think aloud.

Why were the Dutch agents the only ones who never made mistakes in their coding? Were they all Knut Hauglands? Or were their working conditions so secure that they had as much time as they needed to encode their messages and didn't have to worry about Germans on the prowl?

And could the Abor/Ebenezer security check anomalies still be attributed to bad training and forgetfulness when that same bad training, that same forgetfulness, made them into flawless coders?

How much reliance could really be placed on the Dutch section's assurances that they regularly monitored their agents' safety? Were they relying on the reports of agents who might themselves be captured?

And was the traffic snarl-up no more than a natural hazard of clandestine communication? What about the four messages from London which Parsnip and Potato had been unable to decode? I'd checked and double-checked every one of them and they'd been encoded perfectly. Were Parsnip and Potato pretending they couldn't decipher them to postpone answering difficult questions and to avoid meetings which they couldn't possibly attend?

Heffer blinked, which was his way of holding up his hand, and asked what my conclusions were.

I put to him that indecipherables were a black plague and that there was only one feasible explanation for the Dutch agents' immunity from it. They were operating under duress.

He warned me that I was basing my conclusions on a negative inference. The Dutch section and others were likely to say that the 'discovery' was no more than coincidence or a specialist juggling with statistics. He advised me to look into it more deeply and prepare a written report for Nicholls, who'd be back in a week's time. I knew then that he took it as seriously as I did.

Showing signs of duress himself, he stressed the importance of finding supporting evidence that the agents had been caught. Inspired guesses only produced inspired excuses. He warned me against saying anything to the Dutch section prematurely. They might send a message to the field asking *why* there'd been no indecipherables.

He expressed, if the term were applicable to his tempo, interest in knowing what had pointed me in this direction.

I didn't tell him that it was a combination of Group Captain Venner and Air Commodore Freud.

The first thing to establish was who was actually encoding the messages. Was it the agents under supervision? Or were the Germans doing it themselves? The only way to determine this was to study the coding habits of every Dutch agent.

I took the clear-texts of all the messages which had been received from Holland since June '42 and encoded them as the agents had. It was a long and exhausting process and I found that by the end of it I'd made many mistakes, and that two of my messages were completely indecipherable. According to Freud, this was likely to be deliberate.

A pattern emerged which was not quite distinctive enough to be called a style. It was based upon a freedom of choice. Every agent could pick any five words of his poem for his transposition keys. Agents tended to have favourite words and often used the same combination for a number of messages. These words either had an emotive value for them or they were the easiest to spell. But above all, agents favoured the shortest words they could find because they minimized the tortuous process of numbering the key-phrases.

The Dutch agents were perfectly normal in their ratio of favourite words to new ones. I noticed that Boni never chose a key-phrase without the word 'wish' in it. They were also normal in their choice of the shortest words – with one exception: Ebenezer regularly used at least two of the longest words at his disposal. For one message he'd even used three, making his transposition-key over twenty letters long. Done by Haugland, it was an example of a first-class coder. Done by Ebenezer, it could mean that he had plenty of time for his coding and showed a marked departure from an agent's norm. The question was, was it the norm for Ebenezer?

I contacted his training school to check the length of the key-phrases he'd used in his student days, but his training messages had long since been destroyed. The instructor reminded me that it wasn't until July '42 that London had ordered the training schools to retain every agent's practice messages. I was familiar with this instruction. I'd sent it myself in the name of Ozanne.

It didn't help with Ebenezer but I was now able to examine the coding exercises of every Dutch agent who'd been sent into the field since July '42. They'd been average to good coders and each of them had sent a trainee's normal quota of indecipherables. Yet not one Dutch agent had repeated his early training mistakes when he reached the field.

This put the Dutch in a class apart.

So did their wireless habits.

Reports from the Grendon signalmasters showed that the Dutch

WT operators made as many procedural errors as other agents and that their traffic was as prone to Morse mutilation. *But with the exception of Boni, not a single Dutch WT operator had asked the Home Station to repeat a message on the grounds that it had been garbled in transmission and couldn't be deciphered.* This was an important discovery but it had to be kept in perspective.

Grendon's transmitters were powerful and the operators highly trained and the incidence of agents asking for repeats of messages was small. But it had happened several times in every country section except the Dutch.

The agent who'd come closest to it was Ebenezer. In April '42 he'd suddenly terminated a sked because of interference. Even so, he had never asked for London's messages to be repeated.

Why was it, then, that this same interference, which so troubled other countries' agents, hadn't caused the Dutch to send or receive a single indecipherable, with the possible exceptions of Parsnip and Potato?

I broke off at this stage to summarize for Nicholls my findings to date. I reported that, on balance, I thought that the Dutch agents were doing their own coding and that their messages were being checked by the Germans before transmission. I couldn't yet specify how many agents had been caught or who they were, but at least a large question mark had to be put against the names of Abor, Ebenezer, Boni, Trumpet and Potato.

The next phase would determine whether I could produce any substantive proof. It would be the first time that I had studied a country section's traffic for its content alone.

I read through every message which the Dutch section had sent to the field and compared each one with the agent's replies. It needed a trained Intelligence officer to do this job properly. The traffic contained so many disturbing implications that halfway through a second reading I went back to the beginning to make a précis of the principal exchanges. It was like trying to synopsize the Domesday Book.

When the précis was finished I listed the dropping operations in chronological order with the names of the agents involved. Remembering that Nicholls was a professional soldier, I refrained from adding a layman's comments. That was the most difficult part.

Ebenezer and Thijs Taconis (referred to in messages as 'Tall Thijs') were dropped into Holland in November '41. Their early traffic was mainly concerned with bread-and-butter Intelligence and the problems of setting up communications. Ebenezer's first message was received on 3 January and his skeds, which he kept regularly, were on alternate Fridays.

On 28 February two more agents Jordaan (Trumpet) and Ras (Lettuce) were dropped near Holten. Trumpet was referred to in messages by his field-name, Jeffers.

On 15 March the Dutch section instructed Ebenezer to find a dropping ground for a new agent and a number of containers. The operation was code-named Watercress and would take place in the next moon period. Ebenezer replied that he was looking for a dropping ground and would prepare a reception committee.

On 17 March London informed Ebenezer that Taconis had found a dropping ground near the banks of the Reitdeip canal. Ebenezer was instructed to prepare it for Watercress. Ebenezer replied that the Reitdeip dropping ground was too isolated and suggested that the drop should take place on the moorlands near Steenwijk.

It was in this message that he began his peculiar spelling of 'stop' as 'stip', 'step' and 'stap', and omitting his secondary security check.

On 25 March the Dutch section agreed to accept Steenwijk and informed Ebenezer that Abor would be dropped there within forty-eight hours. He was instructed to arrange the ground lights in the form of a triangle; the reception committee should identify itself to Abor by using the name Ebenezer.

On 28 March Ebenezer reported that Abor had been dropped safely with four containers.

On 29 March Lieutenant Andringa (referred to in messages as Akkie) and Jan Molenaar (Turnip, field-name Martens) were dropped near Holten.

Also on 29 March Ebenezer was instructed to find out what had happened to two agents who'd been dropped on 10 March and had failed to contact London.

On 4 April Ebenezer replied that one of the agents had been killed on landing and he was trying to establish contact with the other.

On 5 April Kloos (Leek) and Sebes (Heck) were dropped into Holland. They arrival coincided with a series of messages from the

Dutch section of Ebenezer asking him to find out what had happened to Akkie and Martens, who had been out of touch with London since their arrival. Ebenezer reported that he'd had no success in tracing them.

On 9 April Trumpet informed London that he had just met Akkie at a safe-house in Haarlem. Akkie wanted London to know that his WT operator Martens (Turnip) had been killed on landing. Akkie still had Turnip's signal-plan and he wanted Trumpet to use it and be his WT operator until London could send a replacement.

The Dutch section at once agreed that Trumpet should handle Akkie's traffic and promised to send a new WT operator during the next moon period.

Lieutenant de Haas (Potato, field-name Pijl) was landed by motor torpedo boat on the Dutch coast on 19 April. He was the first Dutch agent to be equipped with a Eureka. He was to link up with Akkie. His messages were to be passed by Ebenezer.

On 24 April Trumpet sent London an urgent message over 300 letters long. It was so disturbing that I put an asterisk against it and against the messages it gave rise to, and then erased them. It was better for Nicholls to insert his own.

Trumpet informed the Dutch section that Leek and Heck could not communicate with London as their WT sets had been lost on landing. They had contacted the Lettuce group to ask for WT facilities. (Trumpet was Lettuce's WT operator.)

Trumpet went on to say that Pijl (Potato) had also been in touch with him. Pijl had been unable to communicate with London because he couldn't contact either Thijs (Taconis) or Ebenezer, who were to send his messages for him. Trumpet had agreed to pass Pijl's traffic until Thijs or Ebenezer could be reached.

The Dutch section at once sent a message to Thijs via Ebenezer informing him that Pijl had been trying to contact him. Thijs was told to make arrangements through the safe-house at Haarlem to meet Pijl. Taconis replied via Ebenezer that he would contact Pijl immediately.

This was the start of independent circuits of agents being put in direct touch with each other, all of them dependent on Ebenezer, Boni or Trumpet for their traffic.

On 20 April Trumpet informed London that Akkie had found a

reliable local WT operator. Trumpet wanted London's authority to recruit him and teach him SOE's WT procedures. The Dutch section agreed to this request but stipulated that the new operator must send a test signal to London.

On 30 April the Dutch section informed Trumpet that the new operator's test signal was satisfactory but that he'd omitted his security checks. Trumpet was given specific details of these checks in the same message.

I put six asterisks against this one, then erased five of them.

On 2 May the Dutch section instructed Ebenezer to prepare a dropping ground on the Steenwijk moors for a large number of containers. Ebenezer confirmed that the dropping ground was ready. The drop took place without enemy interference.

On 11 May the Dutch section sent Pijl a message via Ebenezer's set instructing him to find suitable points along the coast where agents and equipment could be landed at night. He was to use his 'special equipment' for the first time.

This 'special equipment' was a lamp which emitted an invisible infra-red beam which signalled its position to a receiver on board a ship. The landing party would thus be able to pinpoint the spot where Pijl and his reception committee were waiting.

Pijl replied via Ebenezer suggesting several suitable landing points on the coast and the Dutch section selected Katwijk.

On 17 May Pijl sent a message that he and a reception committee had waited at Katwijk all night but that the ship had not appeared.

On 19 May London informed Pijl that the operation was to be repeated in two nights' time.

On 22 May Pijl reported that shortly after midnight there had been gunfire at sea and that he had again waited several hours but had still not made contact with the ship.

On 25 May the Dutch section informed Pijl that the operation had been abandoned for the time being. Pijl was now to concentrate on helping Ebenezer's group. He was also to investigate the possibilities of sabotaging German ships in Dutch harbours.

All this traffic was passed on Ebenezer's set.

On 28 May Ebenezer was warned by London to prepare for the arrival of Beetroot and Swede.

On 29 May Beetroot (Parlevliet) and Swede (van Steen) were dropped to a reception committee on the Steenwijk moors. They were equipped with Eurekas and S-phones. The latter enabled agents to have ground-to-aircraft conversations. Beetroot and Swede were to mount an attack on the Juliana canal locks.

On 12 June Trumpet was instructed by London to prepare dropping grounds for the arrival of Parsnip and Spinach.

On 22 June Parsnip and Spinach parachuted to the Assen dropping grounds suggested by Trumpet. Parsnip was to link up with Potato, who was well known to Ebenezer. Parsnip and Spinach were to organize a sabotage group in Overijssel.

On 23 June Ebenezer and Trumpet were alerted to the imminent arrival of Marrow, the most important mission of all. Marrow was Professor Louis Jambroes. He was to be accompanied by a WT operator, Joseph Bukkens.

On 26 June Jambroes and Bukkens were dropped to Ebenezer's reception committee at Apeldoorn with the help of a Eureka. Bukkens was equipped with the prototype of a small, highly selective WT transmitter, the first of its kind to be issued.

The Dutch section was so concerned for Marrow's safety that it had suggested five different dropping grounds to Ebenezer before finally agreeing to Apeldoorn.

Ebenezer and Trumpet were amongst the many agents who knew why this mission was so important to the liberation of Holland. Jambroes was the official representative of the Dutch government-in-exile and a member of the National Resistance Council in London. He was to take command of the Dutch secret army and prepare it for 'Plan Holland' – the code-name for the Chiefs of Staff's invasion plan to liberate the Low Countries. Jambroes was also to meet the leaders of the various Dutch Resistance groups and co-ordinate them under a National Committee of Resistance. His mission had the full support of the Allied High Command.

Shortly after he arrived Jambroes began sending London a spate of messages describing the poor morale amongst the various groups he had contacted and stressing the dangers of infiltration by German informers. He emphasized to the Dutch section that it was essential for his security that he travelled from place to place and that he would no longer be contactable on a day-to-day basis. He would also be unable to keep in regular touch with his WT operators but would send messages whenever he could. The Dutch section agreed to his proposals and warned him to take extreme care.

It was now Ebenezer's turn to send a request asking permission to recruit a local WT operator to help with his traffic. The Dutch section agreed to it.

On 5 July Ebenezer was instructed to investigate the possibilities of blowing up the Kootwijk wireless transmitter. The attack was to be led by Taconis, assisted by a team of demolition experts.

Between 8 and 20 July Ebenezer sent a number of messages giving full details of the layout of the Kootwijk transmitter and saying that it was lightly guarded. He suggested that it could be destroyed by small charges placed amongst the mast anchors.

On 28 July Ebenezer reported to London that the attack had been a disaster as some of Taconis's men had run into a minefield. The explosions had alerted the guards and the operation had been abandoned. Three of the attacking party had been killed; five men were still missing. Taconis himself was safe and unwounded. Ebenezer stressed that the Kootwijk wireless transmitter and all similar installations were now heavily guarded.

The Dutch section sent a message to Ebenezer regretting the loss of life and warning him to suspend all operational activities for the time being.

Two weeks later a further message was sent to Ebenezer congratulating all members of the raiding party on their heroic attempt and stating that Taconis would receive a British military decoration for his leadership.

In the middle of August the Dutch section's messages began to show increasing unease about Jambroes's long silences and his apparent lack of progress and he was sent repeated messages urging him to return to London for consultations.

Jambroes replied to these invitations explaining that he was too busy to come, that a pick-up by sea or air would be far too dangerous and that it wasn't the right moment for him to leave Holland.

On 25 August the Dutch section suggested to him that he should use SOE's Spanish escape route and offered to put him in touch with a group of agents in Paris who operated the escape line. Jambroes accepted the Spanish escape route as the safest plan yet and promised to use it at the earliest moment.

By mid-September that moment had still not arrived. Jambroes began reporting the excellent progress he was making with the sixteen new groups he was forming.

On 15 September the Dutch section warned Ebenezer to expect the arrival of an important new mission, code-named Erica.

Erica was dropped into Holland on 25 September to a reception committee arranged by Ebenezer. The mission was under the command of Christian Jongelie, whose field-name was Arie. He was the personal emissary of the Dutch Prime Minister and carried a message from him to the leaders of the political parties urging them to form a coalition under a National Council of Resistance. Arie was accompanied by Captain Beukema-toe-Water, who was to become his deputy in the field. The other members of the party were Cornelius Fortuyn and Adrian Mooy.

On 27 September Ebenezer reported that an accident had occurred during the drop and that Arie was suffering from severe concussion and was still unconscious. His three companions were uninjured. The Dutch section made repeated enquiries about Arie's recovery. Each time Ebenezer assured London that he was making good progress.

On 4 October Ebenezer reported that Arie had died suddenly and would be buried on the Steenwijk moor. He added that Arie would be given a worthy memorial after victory was won.

Between October and November the Dutch section received a number of messages from Captain Beukema, who had taken over the Erica mission. Beukema extolled the progress which Jambroes was making.

On 16 October the Dutch section instructed Beukema to return to London for consultations and arranged with Ebenezer that he should be picked up by motor torpedo boat.

On 30 October Ebenezer reported that Beukema had been drowned while waiting for a pick-up on the coast.

On 1 November the Dutch section sent a message appointing Cornelius Fortuyn, one of the two remaining survivors of the Erica mission, as Beukema's replacement. He was to act as political co-ordinator in the field.

A tally at this point showed that between September and November seventeen agents had been sent into Holland, most of them to help the build-up of the Secret Army. These included three agents (one of them a WT operator, Tomato) sent in on 22 October, followed two nights later by four more (including WT operators Chive, Celery and Broccoli). They were reinforced on 28 October by two more agents (including WT operator Cucumber). Containers full of arms and explosives were dropped with each of these missions.

Jambroes now had more than six WT operators at his disposal, including Chive, Broccoli, Tomato, Celery and Cucumber.

Towards the end of November the Dutch section decided to give an important new mission to Akkie. (At this point the messages became so convoluted that I had to make a précis of the précis.)

On 29 November the Dutch section instructed Trumpet to tell Akkie that he must contact Vinus (Levinus van Looe) at an address in Amsterdam. Akkie was to ask Vinus to introduce him to members of the Dutch Resistance Committee so that they could establish a wireless link with London. The message also referred to a small photograph which Akkie must produce to Vinus as evidence of his credentials. Trumpet confirmed to London that he had passed these instructions to Akkie.

On 6 December Trumpet sent a message stating that Akkie had shown the photograph to Vinus but that Vinus had refused to introduce him to the Resistance Committee until he was given further proof of Akkie's credentials. The proof he required was for the BBC to broadcast over its Radio Oranje programme the name with which Vinus had signed his last but one letter to London. The broadcast must take place within the next forty-eight hours. The Dutch replied that the broadcast would take place as Vinus had requested.

I made a note in the précis asking Nicholls whether the Signals directorate had any jurisdiction over the messages broadcast *en clair* over Radio Oranje.

On 4 December a long message was received from Jambroes reporting that more than 1,500 men were under training in his various Marrow groups. He asked for supplies to be sent urgently, including underwear, boots, tobacco, tea and bicycle tyres.

In the middle of December the Dutch section answered this request by dropping in thirty-two containers in a single night.

Shortly before Christmas the Dutch section informed Ebenezer and Trumpet that a special team was being assembled in London to assist Jambroes to leave Holland. It would be dropped into the field early in the New Year. Ebenezer and Trumpet duly acknowledged the messages.

That marked the end of the 1942 traffic.

And of my last vestige of belief in the security of the Dutch.

I could have confined my report to four words: '*God help these agents.*'

Instead I wrote twelve pages and then drained them of feeling and reduced them to four.

Some of my anxieties I could develop orally. A lot would depend on Nicholls's responses to negative inferences and the content of the Dutch traffic.

My own were unequivocal. I found the extent to which the Dutch section relied on its anchor-men a total negation of field security. Ebenezer, Boni and Trumpet had virtually become a clearing-house for the Dutch traffic. They not only knew all the principal operations; in many instances they had helped to arrange them. There didn't seem to be one wholly independent WT operator in Holland.

Nor was the potential damage confined to WT operators.

Groups of agents such as Marrow, Beetroot, Cucumber, Chive, Celery, Turnip and Potato had become so interlocked that, if any one of them were caught, there could be repercussions all the way up to the Committee of Resistance and Plan Holland.

And if all this were conjectural, one thing was not. The pressure under which the Dutch agents were working was there in black and black for all to see.

Yet despite deaths by drowning, by exploding minefields, by dropping accidents, despite every kind of difficulty, setback and frustration, not a single Dutch agent had been so overwrought that he'd made a mistake in his coding.

It seemed to me unarguable that the bulk of the messages had been sent by the Germans and that the main question was no longer which agents were caught, but which were free. I ended my report by saying as much.

There was nothing more that I could do about Holland until Nicholls returned.

I renounced my Dutch citizenship.

During my four days and nights of total immersion, eight indecipherables had come in from the rest of SOE.

TWELVE

A Shock Discovery

The ladies of the First Aid Nursing Yeomanry, otherwise known as the coders of Grendon, had force-fed their eight indecipherables with a diet of transposition-keys, and all but one of the invalids had responded to treatment. The malingerer was waiting on my desk with a curt note from the Grendon supervisor acknowledging defeat.

It was Peter Churchill who had thwarted them. By now irretrievably set in his coding ways, Peter had become a classic example of an agent in the field repeating mainly the same mistakes which he'd made in training. He'd transposed three columns in the wrong order at our Orchard Court session and had twice repeated the process when he'd reached the field.

Unscrambling Peter's 'hatted'* columns required minor mathematical surgery which Grendon was not yet equipped to administer. I made a few calculations based on Peter's past performances and plunged the knife in. The clear-text bubbled up like the man himself. He was complaining to Buckmaster about his difficulties with Carte (André Girard), who was promising SOE far more than he could possibly deliver. Peter also reported that he was arranging new safe-houses for Odette and Rabinovitch. I telephoned Buckmaster to tell him the message was out.

It was then that I got a Dutch buzz. Something warned me that I wasn't finished with Peter's message; it had a relevance to Holland. The idea was ridiculous and I attributed it to the Dutch incarceration I'd only just left. Yet it niggled away as I tried to catch up with the rest of the traffic.

* Trade jargon for misaligned.

126

A glance at the new symbols list increased my anxieties. It showed that Ozanne (MS) was still director of signals and that Nicholls (MS/A) was still only his deputy.

A typical SOE power-struggle was now inevitable and I spotted the first signs of it when I visited Norgeby House. The whole building had been invaded by Grendon Signals officers. They were wandering round its alien corridors in small bewildered groups – segments of Morse lost in the ether.

On the ground floor two rooms were being knocked into one like a schizoid in treatment. No one knew why. Some more Grendon technicians were holding a conference in room 52. Heffer emerged from it. I asked him what was happening. He didn't seem to hear me.

Ozanne came down the passage, looking more bemused than anyone, though it wasn't yet lunchtime. He took about as much notice of me as a tank would of a pebble and disappeared into room 52.

Clutching a box of Mother's provisions, I rushed up three flights of stairs to my WOK-makers' garret in case they'd been dispossessed or had begun to feel neglected. They were happily shuffling counters and had missed Mother's cream cakes far more than they had me. They said that a 'nice group captain called Venison' had called in to see how they were getting on! He'd helped them make two WOK-keys and they hoped he'd call again. I left them before my growing unease about Nicholls spoiled their appetite.

He'd been away from Baker Street for almost a week now and I was missing him badly. It was like being deprived of a night-light.

I decided that if I needed security symbols in order to function I'd better return to the source of them.

I went home early.

An envelope addressed to me had been put through the letter-box and Mother had opened it, thinking it was personal. It contained a white feather and a typed card with one word on it: '*Shirker*'.

My distraught parents were convinced that our next-door neighbours had sent it. Only Ozanne deserved what was shortly to be put through their letter-box.

I assured my two inconsolables that a white feather was a marvellous tribute to security and that their friend Jack O'Reilly would thoroughly approve of it. I then disclosed to them what I was really doing at the 'Ministry of Labour', that I was trying to prove to SOE that the Dutch agents were caught, and that with Nicholls's support I was hoping shortly to introduce a code called a WOK.

(I disclosed all this to them in my mind. But I'd been only a pride's kick away from saying it aloud.)

I went to the swimming pool and swung fully-clothed across the rings. My near lapse had given me a great deal to think about.

The need to justify and its sister frailty, the need to boast, were lethal weaknesses in SOE, and the shock discovery that I was prone to both started me worrying about the coders of Grendon.

The 'old hands' were by now as security-minded as they were ever likely to be, but many of them would soon be posted to Massingham and Cairo, and would be replaced by apprentices. I'd done all I could to convince the newcomers that the duty of care which they owed to all agents mustn't be relaxed on weekend passes or extended leaves, but I knew that fledgling FANYs took a lot of persuading and were unlikely to remember a word of what I'd said beyond the coach ride to Grendon, if as far.

Heffer had once asked me to define a good security risk and I'd replied, 'Someone who knows whom it's safe to be indiscreet to.' If there was slightly more truth in this than in most pat responses, then a bad security risk was somebody likely to confide in the wrong 'safe someone'. None of us knew whom the coders talked to in their off-duty hours.

An idea occurred to me in mid-swing: there was something which might remind them for the rest of their coding lives that they must talk to no one, and the more I considered it, the more promising it seemed.

I realized that my next-door neighbours were watching me from the balcony, and that if they were the feather-donors I owed the idea to them. I waved my gratitude without falling in.

The Dutch section was more determined than ever to bring Jambroes back to London for consultations.

Four agents now in the final stages of training were going to parachute into Holland in the February moon period to help him to cross the Spanish escape route into France and Belgium. Their code-name was to be Golf, N section having exhausted its supply of vegetables. I was due to brief the Golf team within the next fortnight.

Messages continued to arrive from Holland reporting the steady progress of Jambroes's organization and the build-up of the Secret Army. The encoding was perfect.

The Signals directorate's night-light returned to Baker Street and Heffer put me at the head of the long queue waiting to be guided by it.

Nicholls occupied a small office in Norgeby House which I hoped was temporary. He took my report from me before I could say good morning and at once began reading it. He was interrupted a few minutes later by a call from CD asking to see him immediately. He promised to finish the report by the end of the day and to send for me as soon as he had considered it.

Three days later I still hadn't heard from him. It seemed a very long time for the jury to be out. When he finally sent for me on the morning of the fourth day Heffer was sitting opposite him in watchful attendance. My report, now covered in red-ink annotations, was open on the desk. There was a large grey folder beside it with MOST SECRET printed on its cover in block capitals. I couldn't remember seeing one like it in SOE. Next to the folder was a map (which I took to be of Holland) with coloured pins stuck all over it.

Nicholls was studying this map with his eyes closed. Heffer was studying Nicholls. I edged forward and tried to read the red-ink annotations. They looked like a spider bleeding to death. I had an instant rapport with it. It was hard to believe that I was watching a highly trained Signals mind at work, but I knew that this stylistic somnolence was Nicholls at his most productive.

He opened his eyes and shot his first question at me:

Had I established whether the Dutch WT operators were transmitting from their usual operating posts or were they sending their messages from new sites? If so, which were they?

It hadn't even occurred to me to make direction-finding enquiries and I undertook never again to criticize my Signals colleagues for their insularity. Heffer nodded his approval.

Nicholls picked up the grey folder without comment and read out

a list of the WT operators who'd previously been transmitting from
The Hague, Rotterdam and Amsterdam but who were now sending
their messages from Eindhoven, Utrecht and Arnhem. He quoted the
districts in these towns from which the traffic was being sent as well
as the date of each transmission.

These precise readings could not possibly have come from Grendon,
whose direction-finding facilities were rudimentary, and I was even
more curious about the source of that folder.

Nicholls now proceeded to minimize the significance of his discovery.

He had read all the Dutch traffic and was satisfied that the transmissions from Eindhoven, Utrecht and Arnhem coincided with the
agents' accounts of their movements around Holland. The new transmission sites were not therefore grounds for suspicion. He would
confirm this with the Dutch section at a general discussion on the
WT situation in Holland.

It almost cost me a lip not to interject that the 'accounts of movements' around Holland might be coming from the Germans and that
the new operating sites strongly reinforced the grounds for suspicion,
but a glance from Heffer warned me to let Nicholls finish.

He agreed that the linking together of three circuits of agents was
appalling security, especially in WT terms, but doubted if this practice
was confined to the Dutch section. However, the Signals directorate
had no jurisdiction over the way that a country section dispersed its
agents as decisions of this kind were essentially operational. But he
was going to warn the country sections of the dangers of WT operators being in a position to compromise the Signals security of other
WT circuits. He would make particular reference to Ebenezer, Boni
and Trumpet when he had his general discussion with the Dutch.

This was the second time he'd spoken about a 'general discussion',
and it worried me. There was nothing more specific than a lack of
indecipherables, yet it hadn't once been mentioned. A glance from
Heffer warned me to be patient.

Nicholls next fastened with a technician's relish on the plain language messages broadcast to Holland over the BBC's Radio Oranje.
How and why did SOE use these messages? Was there a standard
procedure?

I said that all country sections had 'Voice of Freedom' facilities from the BBC to broadcast plain language code-phrases to their respective territories. The rival French sections were the most prolific broadcasters and shared a BBC programme called 'Les Français Parlent aux Français', which was about all that they did share. Other country sections used similar programmes for the same purposes. If an agent such as Peter Churchill, for example, wanted to borrow a large sum of money in the field and the prospective lender doubted whether the debt would be honoured by the British government when the war was over, Peter could invite the prospective lender to make up a sentence known only to the two of them, which the BBC would subsequently broadcast on 'Les Français Parlent aux Français'. This was usually the only verification which the lender required. Plain language phrases were also used by the country sections for last-minute confirmations or cancellations of impending operations. My anxiety about these phrases was that their wording was arranged in poem-codes. If the Germans recorded them and matched them with the code-groups which they intercepted, it would make the poem-code even easier to break.

Nicholls pointed out that there were a great many plain language phrases and that the Germans would have to be very skilful indeed to pinpoint which messages to anagram. I asked if there were any reason to suppose that they lacked this skill. He replied that he wasn't, but there was every reason to suppose that they lacked the manpower. He conceded the security risk and I said that the real answer was to change the poem-code.

He reminded me sharply that this was not the object of the present discussion and I apologized for its irrelevance.

He then glanced at my report and, with the persistence of a steam-roller capable of flight, asked why I had put an asterisk against the Dutch section's *en clair* message to Vinus (I had forgotten to erase it).

I explained that this message was intended to confirm to Vinus that he could introduce Akkie to the Committee of Resistance. If the Germans were reading the traffic and Akkie was taken to the Committee of Resistance, how far behind him would the Germans be?

Nicholls stressed that these were operational matters for the Dutch

131

section to decide upon and begged the question as to whether the traffic was being read. The Signals directorate couldn't interfere with any country section's right to broadcast messages to its agents via the BBC.

I replied that I wasn't concerned with the country sections' right to broadcast but with the agents' to survive.

He looked at me thoughtfully and I tried to make a draw of it. We both knew that the moment had come for the main event and I was fascinated by the way he prepared for it.

He read and then re-read the last page of my report, which included the statistics of other country sections' indecipherables. He looked at the pins spread across the map and seemed to be searching for one in particular. He referred to his folder and then looked again at the map.

He wasn't playing for time. To all of us in Signals, he *was* time. But from the very start of the meeting I'd sensed a private conflict of some kind in Nicholls. I also sensed that Heffer knew what it was. I glanced at Heffer. He was deep in Nicholls's thoughts.

Nicholls closed the report, the folder and his eyes. His next question opened mine: *When an agent in the field sent an indecipherable message, did I regard this as proof that he* wasn't *caught?*

I assure him that I didn't.

'In that case, why are you trying to prove the converse?'

I respectfully suggested that this question was a soriticism.

'A *what*?'

I quoted the classic example of a *reductio ad absurdum*: 'If a man with one hair is bald, then a man with ten thousand hairs must be ten thousand times as bald.'

'You haven't answered the colonel's question,' said Heffer, his first contribution to date.

Before answering it, I tried to imagine how it felt to be in a prison cell in Holland hoping that someone in London was awake. I put to Nicholls that, when an agent sent an indecipherable, I didn't take it to mean that he was in good health but that his coding temperature was normal. But the Dutch were behaving abnormally by any known standards of code conduct, and I'd left it very late in the day to spot it. If Nicholls had lost confidence in me, then I must accept the consequences. But if he still retained some, then he must accept that there was something grievously wrong in Holland for not one Dutch agent to have made a mistake in his coding. So wrong that only the subnormal or the purblind could continue to ignore its implications. I was not begging the question as to whether the Germans were reading the Dutch traffic. I was begging for answers which would satisfy me that they weren't. Until those answers were forthcoming, I would continue to believe that the Germans were sending at least some of the traffic and nothing was going to budge me from that position, least of all a polemic.

I couldn't tell from Nicholls's expression whether I had said too much or too little. Heffer was studying the map.

Nicholls lifted his telephone so sharply that I wondered if I was about to leave SOE the way I'd arrived, under armed escort. He ordered tea for three. It would be undrinkable but it didn't seem opportune to offer him Mother's.

Heffer decided that it was time to join the party and (typically) asked the most perceptive question yet: if the Germans were running the traffic, they were doing it very skilfully – so surely it would have occurred to them that they must send us some indecipherables to allay any suspicions which London might have?

I replied that perhaps we weren't the only ones who made mistakes. Nor did I know the calibre of the Germans we were up against in Holland or even who they were.

As casually as if he were telling us the date, Nicholls said that we were likely to be up against Giskes, a most experienced Intelligence officer. I asked whether Herr Giskes was experienced in the ways of the poem-code. Nicholls assured me that he was, and invited me to explain why he hadn't sent us any indecipherables.

I said that Herr Giskes and his assistants must have decided that any Signals organization which was stupid enough to use the poem-code wasn't likely to be bright enough to notice the absence of indecipherables and was even less likely to draw the proper conclusions from it.

That put a stop to what was becoming a chat. Clasping both hands behind his head and looking like a radio mast about to earn its keep, Nicholls delivered his summation.

My report had drawn his attention to what was potentially a disastrous WT situation in Holland, if it weren't one already, and had given him a great deal to think about. He was most concerned about the lack of indecipherables and could offer no explanation for it – but still couldn't decide if I were lending too much weight to it. However, it certainly could not be ignored and he was most concerned about what practical steps could now be taken. We still had no *positive* proof that any agents had been caught. Nor could I even say how many agents I believed were caught or specify their names. I could only put question marks against some of them, and question marks were not enough for an organization which hadn't been educated in WT security, a deficiency which he would shortly remedy.

The immediate problem was that if my theory had substance, all the Dutch agents might be caught. What was he to recommend to the Dutch section? That it should cancel all its operations or only some of them? And which ones? And for how long? Until more tangible evidence could be found by the Signals directorate? It just wasn't on. The most he could do until this evidence was found was stress the Signals directorate's concern about the general WT situation in Holland and the overloading of operators such as Trumpet, Boni and Ebenezer. We would also press the Dutch section to explain what steps they took to confirm that their agents weren't blown. But if I or anyone else in Signals found anything which could be regarded as proof positive, he would raise it at the highest level.

To me he was the highest level, but it wasn't getting me very far.

I told him that I very much wanted to examine the early codegroups which had been received and decoded by C's wireless station before June '42 so that I could establish the length of the keys the agents had chosen and see if there'd been any significant changes in their coding style.

He promised to do his best and made a long note on his pad which seemed out of proportion to the request. He then proceeded to develop his ideas about educating the country section in Signals security but I was no longer listening.

Nicholls had paid us the compliment of thinking aloud and I responded to it by thinking about him. The breadth of his knowledge was extraordinary. He knew where to get information about the location of WT sites, he knew the latest direction-finding techniques, he knew Giskes's name. I admired him more than ever and he probably knew that too. Yet almost all his observations had been slanted from the viewpoint of a wireless expert, with codes a poor second. And I was convinced that there was some problem to do with the Dutch which was greatly worrying him but which he wasn't going to mention in front of me.

And perhaps he had to become controller of Signals before he could stop worrying about his directorate's jurisdiction. Tommy ignored the proprieties when the safety of agents was at stake and I wished that he were in the Dutch section. But then I wished that the Chairman of the Awkward Squad were in every section, especially Signals.

Nick exchanged a long glance with Heffer and told me that he had one more thing to say. I was to report back to him at four o'clock this afternoon for a very important meeting.

I tried to explain that this afternoon was my last chance to talk to some new coders before they were sent to Grendon.

'Then it's their lucky day because you'll have to cut it short. Four o'clock sharp, please.'

He then ordered me to say nothing to the Dutch about my suspicions until the grounds for them were firmer. The burden of proof was once again on me. I carried it to the door.

I couldn't conjecture what SOE wouldn't consider conjectural. A receipt from Giskes for the Dutch agents perhaps?

I left just in time to avoid the tea.

THIRTEEN

The Biter Bitten

The fledgling FANYs who were waiting for me in Norgeby House had arrived when SOE was at its busiest.

Although the country sections had only two squadrons of aircraft to share between the lot of them, they were determined to make next month's moon their fullest yet. According to Tommy, even the mice in Duke Street's basement were increasing their dropping operations. He was going to descend on France in February, no matter what. He was to accompany his Free French friends Commandant Passy (the head of de Gaulle's secret service) and Pierre Brossolette on an important mission into the Northern zone which was code-named Arquebus.

SOE's other main event (it was wrong to think in these terms; there was no such thing as a supporting bout) was Operation Gunnerside. This was the code-name for the Norwegian section's second attempt to blow up the heavy-water plant at Vermok. Six agents were to be dropped into Hardangar Vidda to reinforce the Grouse. They were to be led by Joachim Ronneberg. The Grouse meanwhile were sheltering in an eyrie in the Barren Mountain.

The Dutch were contributing Operation Golf, and Major Hardy Amies was doing his dapper best on behalf of the Belgian section. Buckmaster was sending in four more missions and even neglected little Denmark wasn't completely out of it. Hollingsworth was trying to mount a new team to help Hammer ('the preacher') to explain to Danish patriots aching for action why neither London nor Stockholm was yet in a position to send them arms and equipment.

The country sections had every right to take for granted that the code department would be ready to cope with the sharp increase in agents' traffic. None of them knew that in mid-February many of Grendon's most reliable coders were being posted abroad. This would place an even greater strain on the new recruits who'd be expected to lighten Grendon's work-load as soon as they entered the coderoom. They'd also be expected to provide the nucleus of a coding staff for Station 53b, which was now being built at Poundon. We could rapidly assess their coding potential but would have no time to discover whether they were good at keeping secrets, and I was determined to try out the noxious idea which had occurred to me whilst swinging on the rings.

The experiment was too difficult to carry out alone, and I'd asked a bright young signals sergeant named Tom Blossom to help me conduct it.

To give it the best chance of working, the girls had been kept waiting for over an hour in a freezing basement without a chair between them, a window to jump out of, or any other creature comforts. The room was Norgeby House's equivalent of the Barren Mountain.

All conversation ceased as I opened the door. I walked unmolested to the far end of the room and pressed a switch. The immediate result was an electric thunderstorm which startled the lot of us. It was followed by a replay of the last hour's dialogue which bright Sergeant Blossom had recorded.

The girls took a little while to realize that it was their own voices they were listening to, and I put this down to the quality of the recording rather than poor reaction-time. The ill-lit room was rapidly illuminated by a corporate blush.

As the recording progressed, it became clear that we had a most promising intake. Their free-flowing language, scatological humour and picturesque imagery promised well for the agents' ditty-box.

They looked everywhere but at me, which was in every way understandable – and suddenly seemed reluctant to look at each other. Sensing that their embarrassment was about to peak I turned the volume up.

We then listened to a lengthy debate concerning the nature of the commitments which had made me late. The consensus was that I'd been 'having it off' with the FANY supremo in a variety of positions (specified) though they were by no means unanimous as to whether she had kept her brigadier's hat on. They would decide when they saw me whether the transpositions had been single or double.

They next dealt with the state of the 'piss-house' in which they found themselves waiting. They blamed the lack of chairs on my failure to realize that FANYs had fannies – which one of them proposed to remedy in a time-honoured way. If it were the beefy one against the wall it could prove a terminal experience.

I switched off halfway through because we had limited facilities for coping with seizures, but I noticed as I did so that one young blusher sighed with relief. I switched it on again briefly.

Someone (I presumed it was she who had sighed) was going to ask her father to put down a question in the House of Commons. There were some interesting suggestions as to how he should phrase it. I switched off and prepared to address a hostile house.

I could see from their bemused expressions that the shock of being recorded, a process still new to most of us, had done much of my work for me and I had to be careful to avoid an anticlimax.

I moved cautiously towards them to give myself time to think of what to say. I was suddenly aware that the room smelled of talcum powder and dry rot, the basic ingredients of my average address.

I spoke to them for twenty minutes, which seemed twice as long as the forty I usually allowed, and then asked if they had any questions. They stared at me in silence, far too bright to give me a chance to identify their voices. I left the Barren Mountain with no external injuries.

The girls were then taken upstairs to a small ante-room and were recorded again while they waited for their transport. Their tones were muted, their dialogue vivid. 'What a little bastard.' was the mildest comment.

I intended to play this second recording to them until I suddenly found myself listening to the sound of what, until this moment, had been my favourite voice. The girls hadn't been the only victims of the Signals directorate's toy. I had also been recorded. The biter was not only bitten, he was savaged by his own words. I was convinced that what I'd said had been a model of disciplined persuasiveness. I couldn't believe what I now heard, courtesy of Sergeant Blossom:

'You've been kept waiting in a cold room to make you tired and irritable because when you're tired and irritable you grow careless, and when you're careless you're talkative. I promise you that, before you've been with us long, you'll be limp – but next time you feel like talking, remember that the Germans have recorders too – where even you wouldn't think of putting them.

'Each of you has a crowd of admirers you've never met. Don't get excited – they're Gestapo admirers and they welcome you today just as much as I do. They hope you're green enough to want to boast. You'll have plenty to boast about. You're important people. You're going to be told about things you shouldn't know – but we can't help ourselves, we have to trust you.

'Every department has its secrets – you in Codes will read all the secrets of all the departments. If you talk about any of them, a man will die. It's as simple as that. Now, I'm never going to mention security to you again.

'You think you're tired, don't you? Then imagine how tired an agent feels who's had no sleep for three nights and has to encode a message. The Germans are all around her so-called safe-house. She has no supervisor to check her coding. All she has is a vital message which she must transmit. Now, I'm going to put a question to this house. Hasn't that agent a right to make a mistake in her coding? And, if she does, must she pay for it with her life? Must she come on the air again to repeat her message, whilst German direction-finding cars get her bearings?

'You look puzzled. Is there something you want to ask? No? Perhaps no one's told you that many of our agents are women? Members of your corps and about your age. I'm thinking of one in particular. Last week the FANYs at Grendon tried four thousand keys to break one of her messages and succeeded on the four thousandth and second. You'll find that double-transposition is easier to joke about than to crack.

'There's an indecipherable down there with your names on it. It's from a Belgian agent who's completely blown. He's sent us a message telling us his co-ordinates – that is, where he can be picked up. A Lysander is standing by to get him out. The message won't budge. At ten o'clock this evening he's due to come on the air and repeat it.

If he does those cars will close in. We will lose that man – just as a few weeks ago we lost a young Norwegian named Arne Vaerum, code-name Penguin. The SS shot him while he was retransmitting an indecipherable message.

'Must that happen tonight if there's any chance that you can help us to prevent it? Well you're going to have that chance! You will be told what to do by your colleagues. You will find that they are tired, tense, sulky – and the salt of the earth. None of them is quite sane – but don't worry, you'll soon be like them. Sleep in the train going down – sleep in the coach that waits at the station – sleep when you shake hands with your commanding officer – but don't sleep in the code room.

'If any of you finds the key that breaks this message, you all will have broken it. You're part of a team now, an indispensable part. Sorry about the recording – if you can think of a better way of reminding you never to talk about your work please tell me now.

'I'd like to end with a word of advice. Don't grow old too quickly and don't stay young too long! Good luck – good coding, and remember . . . you're the only hope that agent's got!'

I erased my speech from the tape – or believed that I had but should have known my Signals colleagues better. Much talcum powder and dry rot later I discovered that the boys in Signals had not only made a separate recording of it; one of them had kept a copy.*

The Grendon supervisor phoned to say that the Belgian indecipherable had been broken after 4,000 attempts. The new coders had not yet arrived.

There would be some compensation awaiting them. They would cut their baby teeth, if they had any left, on an indecipherable from

---

* A few years after the war ended (I shan't give away who won it – for those who may not know) the BBC asked Sir Colin Gubbins, as he had then become, and me, to broadcast a tribute to the FANYs on a programme called 'Now It Can Be Told'. Tom Waldron, the producer of this programme, wanted me to contribute one of the talks I'd given to the FANYs, using as nearly as possible the same words. A signals technician who'd seen an announcement of the broadcast sent me a copy of the original tape. I'm sure he meant it kindly. Not to include it in this book would justify today's equivalent of a white feather, if there is one, so out of obligation to my former colleagues and as a further tribute to all that the FANYs had to endure, it has been quoted in full.

Mr Einar Skinnarland. He was the greatest ager of coders in the business.

The Signals directorate had more departments than most directorates had members, and was by far the largest group in SOE. The 'important meeting' convened by Nicholls was attended by representatives of its principal branches. The only person missing from it was the night-light himself. He was in conference with the Executive Council. I hoped he wouldn't burn himself out.

Everyone at this Signals convention was an expert in some branch of communication, a fact which the small-talk brilliantly concealed. The most senior officers were in the front row. They were the commanding officers of Station 52 (the training school for agents), Station 53 (Grendon) and Station 54 (the training school for Signals personnel). They were all majors.

The next row was full of captains, representing the Research and Supply stations. I sat behind Dansey and Owen on the government back benches.

Nick strode in five minutes later, and addressed us with the sureness of touch which he displayed to everything but codes. He made clear that the meeting had two objectives. The first was to weld us together into one unit, which the size of the room had almost achieved. The second was to ensure that all of us understood the reasons behind the major changes which were about to take place. He then outlined what these changes were to be.

I noticed that several of the military acquired a special kind of pallor, a shade of promotion-grey. I just about survived the first announcement.

As of February, agents' messages were no longer to be received and circulated by Dansey's distribution department. They were to be distributed by a newly formed HQ Signals Office in room 52 at Norgeby House.

Dansey seemed relieved that his distribution room could concentrate on main-line traffic. But I was rigid with anxiety. A new distribution department might make it impossible for me to intercept incoming messages in secret French code.

Nicholls went on to describe in detail the workings and function

141

of this new Signals Office. It would be staffed day and night by signal masters and FANYs, and would act as a clearing-house for all agents' traffic. It would be open at all times to the country sections, who would be encouraged to visit it. The senior supervisor would deal with their queries and liaise on their behalf with the appropriate Signals departments.

The front row of the stalls nodded its approval. The next major change affected Grendon. It was to hand over the Dutch traffic to Station 53b when it opened in March.

This should not cause Herr Giskes any inconvenience.

As if he'd picked up the thought, Nicholls announced that new direction-finding equipment was to be installed which would enable Grendon and Poundon to take precise readings of WT operators' transmitting sites. As a further precaution all new WT operators were to be 'fingerprinted', which would provide us with an accurate record of their operating styles.*

What had started as a talk had become a proclamation. He now introduced a series of non sequiturs which he expected to be followed.

A new kind of WT set was to be produced by Station 9. It had a powerful generator which would allow an operator to transmit without having to use current from the mains, which the enemy could detect.

The signal-planning department had been instructed to produce new signal-plans which would allow operators to stagger their frequencies and transmission times. The BBC's *en clair* broadcasts could in future be monitored by Major Buxton, who was to be appointed SOE's liaison officer with the BBC. He then made an announcement which got less audience response than any so far.

The OSS was planning to start its own WT station under the auspices of SOE and we would have to give the Americans every possible co-operation.

A gadget called a 'squirt transmitter' was now in production. It would enable agents to transmit messages at very high speed. The enemy would find it difficult to intercept 'squirt traffic' unless they had similar equipment.

---

* The outcome of 'fingerprinting' is dealt with in the appendix, and is my sole justification for having one.

I glanced at Heffer, who had engineered the arrival of this Signals Messiah. He had the proprietorial look of a satisfied sponsor.

Nicholls now dealt lovingly and at length with the technical changes which were to be introduced to improve the quality of the Home Station's transmissions. The congregation started taking notes, anxious not to miss a single miracle.

I made one too: '*How long, oh Lord, before he talks about codes?*' Perhaps the new equipment was so efficient we could dispense with them.

I tried to project the thought of WOKs to the man on the mountain but he was imparting his vision of a new kind of wireless mast.

Insular as ever, I drifted off – and landed in Holland. None of these innovations, excellent though they were, would help me to prove that a single Dutch agent had been caught. Even the early Dutch code-groups, if Bletchley ever produced them, were unlikely to prove that Herr Giskes was SOE's most regular penfriend. I wished I could put a face to him. I imagined him as an Ozanne with brains. The thought of Ozanne brought me sharply out of the Dutch clouds.

Nicholls had changed the subject and the audience was fidgeting slightly so it might be important.

A Security and Planning Office was to be started in Norgeby House. Its principal function would be to monitor the security of agents' traffic.

I hoped that whoever did the monitoring would be able to spare a moment for the Dutch because I was about as much use to them as a squirt-transmitter which had run out of squirt. The answer did not lie in further research, it lay in making something happen. But what? Could we set a trap for the Germans? Could we give them a chance to make a mistake without alerting them to our suspicions? Could *we* take the code war to *them*?

I fell into the trap of trying to devise a 'Plan Giskes' while Nicholls droned on, and suddenly realized that there was something different about the room.

It was completely silent.

The proclamation was over and everyone was looking at me! Had I been thinking aloud?

I risked a glance at the Messiah. He wasn't exactly angry but his sigh was a gust of wind which I felt in my marrow-bone. 'For the benefit of those at the back who may not have heard me,' he said, 'I will repeat what I have just announced.'

As of February agents' codes were to be split *entirely* from main-line codes. The two departments would function as separate entities. Main-line codes would remain under the control of Captain Dansey, assisted by Lieutenant Owen. Agents' codes would be under the control of DYC/M, who would be answerable directly to the head of Signals. DYC/M would move to Norgeby House in February. One of his functions would be to act as field-cipher representative in the Security and Planning Office. DYC/M's symbol would remain unchanged when he took up his appointment as head of agents' codes.

I realized that I was DYC/M.

That February was only a few weeks away.

That I was scared out of what remained of my wits.

And that Nicholls, Dansey and Owen were smiling at me.

FOURTEEN

The Last-Chance Month

The Signals directorate invaded Norgeby House in the first week of February despite sporadic resistance from the sitting tenants. To everyone's surprise (except Nicholls's) the new distribution department took over from the old without one message being delayed and only two going to the wrong country sections, and the new Signals Office was a great social success as country section officers, who rarely had a chance to meet each other, found it an excellent place for a quiet chat. Occasionally they came to it for Signals enquiries.

I'd been allotted a room on the first floor and awarded custody of a secretary with sunset-red hair. Her name was Muriel Eddy and she was the equivalent of a typing pool.

I learned on my first day that there was a drawback to my new accommodation. I had to share it with two formidable ladies who'd been brought into SOE by Nicholls, presumably as part of his unlisted improvements.

Mrs Charlotte Denman was a short grey-haired chain-smoker who spoke fluent French and whose job was to liaise with the French, Free French and Belgian sections.

Mrs Molly Brewis was a large red-faced chain-smoker who spoke fluent Italian and Dutch and whose job was to liaise with the country sections in preparing signal-plans.

This enforced intimacy became a serious risk when I discovered that both ladies had had a longstanding professional and personal relationship with Nicholls and that they were his close confidantes. They spent most of their time filing his secret reports and conferring alone with him in his office. They always took their confidential files with them.

The ladies and I were rapidly bonded into a unit by SOE's most common denominator – ignorance. The subject we knew least about was the newly formed Security and Planning Office. None of us understood its function until a memo from Nicholls informed us that we *were* the Security and Planning Office and would shortly be sent our terms of reference.

Our security to date consisted of the ladies' attempts to hide from me what they were filing and mine to hide from them that I was breaking secret French messages. There were few signs of any planning and still less of any progress. But our terms of reference as room-mates were clearly established: they pretended to take no notice at all of what I was doing and I did my best to reciprocate.

We were not the only ones playing charades.

A spate of perfectly encoded messages arrived from Ebenezer, Trumpet and Boni, telling the Dutch section what it most wanted to hear.

The build-up of the Secret Army was steadily progressing. Akkie was in contact with the Council of Resistance and reception committees were being prepared to receive the Golf team which was to guide Jambroes into Spain via the French and Belgian escape routes.

These escape routes, particularly the Belgian ones, were life-lines not only for SOE's agents but for Allied airmen stranded in enemy territory. If the Dutch agents were blown, it could lead to the escape routes themselves being penetrated and the damage could be incalculable, but I still couldn't provide what SOE would consider proof that a single Dutch agent had been caught. Nor could I think of a way to entrap Herr Giskes.

Over a month had elapsed since Nick had dangled the possibility of introducing me to Tiltman of Bletchley to discuss my idea of giving every agent an individual WOK printed on silk, but the miracle still hadn't happened and I no longer believed that it would.

Nor had Nick allowed me to recruit more WOK-makers until 'an all-clear had been given for the system to be adopted'. When I'd asked him how much longer we had to wait for the siren to be sounded, he'd assured me that a decision would be reached within a week.

I didn't point out that a week was seven days longer than most agents' life expectancy if we continued to give them poem-codes.

I had four more days to wait.

A new menace emerged in the first week of February which threatened SOE with extinction. Since there had been only eighteen months' advance notice of it, it took Baker Street as a whole (which occasionally it was) completely by surprise. That menace was C's determination to expunge SOE from the Intelligence alphabet.

Although the state of the civil war between our two organizations was supposed to be known only to CD, Gubbins and the Executive Council, I was briefed on it by Heffer, from whom nothing was secret except how to hurry.

According to the Guru, C's latest campaign to close SOE down, take us over or restrict our activities until we were operationally neutered had come to Downing Street's attention, and was soon to be fought out in Cabinet by our respective ministers. Our chief cornerman in this sacrosanct arena was Lord Selborne, the Minister of Economic Warfare. 'The Bastards of Broadway' (which was what we called C in rare moments of understatement)* were represented by the Foreign Secretary, Anthony Eden. The key issue was SOE's role in the invasion of Europe, and the timing of the Bs of B's attack was inspired.

After two years of sustained effort but sporadic achievement SOE's credibility with the War Cabinet, the Chiefs of Staff and itself was little higher than 84's with the tax inspector. Our political manoeuvres, forward planning and operational techniques were all suspect, and the scale of our D-Day participation would be determined by the Chiefs of Staff. This formidable body – accustomed to losing its battles by orthodox means – didn't share Churchill's enthusiasm for irregular warfare, and had refused to give SOE an official directive setting out its terms of reference and operational responsibilities. Without this Intelligence equivalent of a banker's reference, SOE would have no chance of getting its proper quota of aircraft

---

* C's headquarters were in a street called Broadway, which to our regret was in the borough of Westminster instead of New York.

147

and equipment and would be unable to fulfil its growing commitments to the agents in the field or to their governments-in-exile.

If SOE was ever to get that long-awaited directive instead of a winding-up order, it had above all to convince Lord Selborne – and through him the War Cabinet and the Chiefs of Staff – that the Secret Armies and Resistance groups it claimed to be forming not only existed, but would be ready by D-Day to fulfil Churchill's mandate to 'Set Europe Ablaze'. The Executive Council's hopes of obtaining this proof centred on the prospects of thirteen men. The Golf quartet was expected to bring Jambroes out of Holland; the Arquebus trio to establish de Gaulle's leadership in France; and the six Gunnersides to blow up a heavy-water plant in Norway. The vital thirteen were now in the final stages of their training.

But there was one more major problem in this last-chance month. The outcome of the battle with C was likely to depend on the responses of the Americans.

C and SOE were competing for their custom and, in an effort to acquire the bulk of it, CD had sent a telegram in main-line cipher to Bill Stevenson, our man in Washington, and asked him to show it to Bill Donovan, the head of OSS: 'SOE WILL BE READY BY FEBRU-ARY AT THE LATEST TO MOUNT OPERATIONS INTO FRANCE, SCANDINAVIA AND THE LOW COUNTRIES AND I AM CONFI-DENT THAT THE FEBRUARY MOON, WHICH STARTS ON THE 14TH OF THE MONTH, WILL MARK THE TURNING POINT IN EUROPEAN RESISTANCE.'

I did my best not to shout. 'Doesn't CD realize that the Low Countries' security *couldn't be lower*?'

He left without comment.

Until my appointment as head of agents' codes I'd been head of nothing except a queue for a sweet shop, and the main advantage of my promotion (apart from acquiring Muriel) was the ease with which I was able to intercept secret French messages before they were sent to Duke Street. The supervisor of the new distribution room, a FANY sergeant I intended to head-hunt, had been told by her predecessor that all incoming code-groups had to be checked by me as soon as they arrived, and she usually had them waiting.

Returning to my office clutching Salmon's latest, I was dismayed to find Nick seated at my desk. He was also clutching a document which he held out to me in silence.

It was a curt note from Gambier-Parry, C's head of Signals, stating that the early Dutch code-groups which I wanted to examine were no longer in his possession as all such material had been sent to Captain Dansey in June of last year. We knew this was a lie because Dansey had meticulously listed every item he'd received from C and there'd been no record of any Dutch code-groups.

Nick said with a hint of sadness that it would be pointless to press Gambier-Parry further – the reply would be the same.

He and the ladies then went home early, presumably to their separate destinations, and I stared round the empty office like a small boy in detention who's forgotten his offence. There were no indecipherables to break, no agents to brief, no coders to interview, and Nick's records were locked up. My only company was Giskes, and I could no longer bear his smirk.

I hurried upstairs to give the WOK-makers their cream-cake tea, and spent ten minutes trying to relieve their monotony, which probably made it worse.

I then had to cope with my own, and faced the shock discovery that I was stale.

I hadn't taken a day off since June '42, and wanted to escape from escape routes, blown agents and everything to do with SOE for the rest of the afternoon.

The nearest bolt-hole was a flat in Park West to which daytime visitors were always welcome, but Major O'Reilly's flat was in the same corridor, far too close for the peace of mind essential to that particular comfort.

A film perhaps? If it didn't deal with the war. Fred Astaire and his other foot, Ginger Rogers, were doing their nimble best to *Follow the Fleet* at the local cinema. But it wouldn't be much of a respite to hear:

> We joined the Navy
> To C the world
> And what did we C?
> We saw the C.

Besides, two agents in training were using Irving Berlin's lyrics for their poem-codes and we probably owed him royalties.

I knew all the time that I was going to the only haven which had never failed me in times of distress, where the answers to everything were to be found if one knew where to look for them, and where agnostics like me could safely say their silent prayers . . .

84 Charing Cross Road.

FIFTEEN

The Bolt Hole

'Giving a small boy the unsupervised run of a rare bookshop can put the future of both at risk. In my case, it also jeopardised SOE's.'

Author to himself en route to 84, February '43

The tortuous road which led from childhood to Baker Street had begun at 84 Charing Cross Road.

Every Saturday morning from the age of 8 onwards I was taken to Father's shop (which was doing too well to open on Saturdays) so that he could start teaching me the profit margins of rare books, and a few elementary tricks of the trade. As compensation, every Saturday afternoon Mother took me up the road to the Astoria cinema which occasionally showed films we both understood.

But one Saturday morning when I was 8 and a half my higher education began. Father proudly showed me a signed 1st edition of *The Gold Bug* by Edgar Allan Poe which he had just acquired. It had cost £6 10 shillings and was to be priced at £850 as the Americans were certain to want it. Although I wasn't supposed to waste time reading the merchandise, the moment he left to attend to the overnight mail I riffled through *The Gold Bug* hoping that at that price it might contain a few interesting pictures. Instead I found myself reading about a message in code which had to be broken because it contained the secrets of a buried treasure. Poe used dozens of words which I didn't understand including cryptograph but I knew what a crypt was as I'd learned at school that Crippen had once crept into one, crapped, and crept out again.

An hour later I needed no cinema. All I wanted was a code of my

151

own to break. I remembered Father telling me that every book worth over £5 had its cost written in code at the back so that his staff could tell at a glance how much discount to allow awkward customers but he hadn't explained how the code worked. 'Time enough for that,' he said. For me that time had now come.

At the back of *The Gold Bug* C/MN was written in pencil. Since it had cost £6.10/- – father never lied about anything except his consumption of whisky – then surely C must be 6 and MN 10. But Poe would want to know how Marks & Co. dealt with the rest of the figures.

I examined the backs of 20 other books, and found that the only letters written in pencil were A C E H K M N O R S.

Whatever the code was, it couldn't be as difficult as Poe's or Father and his partner Mark Cohen couldn't have used it. Could it have come from a word? The letters C E H N O spelt C O H E N. That left A K M R S – M A R K S. 84's code was M A R K S C O H E N
                                                        1 2 3 4 5 6 7 8 9 0

But could I have solved it if I hadn't known that C was 6 and MN 10? It was time to find out.

My grandfather had a rare bookshop (E. and M. Joseph) at Leicester Square and my cousins an even rarer one (Myers and Co.) in Bond Street, and as I was usually welcome at both premises the next time I visited them I took the opportunity of inspecting their codes. They were far harder to work out than father's but I was eventually able to tell him that their profit margins were even greater than his.

From that moment onwards, I had two ambitions: to know as much about codes as Edgar Allan Poe, and one day to become a writer, probably of horror-stories, possibly of films.

The shop stood on four floors at the corner of Cambridge Circus, and one of its regular patrons stood on four paws outside the Palace Theatre opposite. He was a benign bulldog who was the constant companion of a lady named Doris. Doris was a short-term companion for those who could afford her prices. She was an avid collector of Rudyard Kipling as well as passing clients. Whenever she left her beat to enter Marks & Co. she insisted on being served by the most physically prepossessing member of Father's staff, who was also its best salesman, Frank Doel.*

On the rare occasions when Doris hadn't enough cash on her to acquire the Kipling she coveted she would ask Frank to reserve it for her and return sometimes a few minutes later, sometimes a few hours (it depended on the weather) to complete her transaction.

Although 84 was respected by book-collectors around the world – and numbered amongst its other distinguished clients a member of the royal family (who liked his pornography bound in vellum), Charles Chaplin, Bernard Shaw, Field Marshal Lord Alanbrooke, Michael Foot, MP (who later saved 84 from demolition by having a preservation order placed on it), the British Museum, scores of universities and (most important of all to Marks & Co.) the booktrade itself – the firm indulged in one activity of which its loyal customers knew nothing.

Marks & Co. were kings of the book ring. They were one of the five leading firms of antiquarian booksellers who never bid against each other in the auction rooms. One member of the ring would be allowed to buy a book for a nominal sum, say £100. As soon as the auction was over the five conspirators would hurry to their nearest safe-house – usually a Lyons tea shop – and conduct a private auction. If one of them bought the book in question for £500, the £400 profit would be divided in cash amongst the other four. This process was called a 'knock-out', and Frank Doel once blew an entire operation.

A famous heart specialist named Evan Bedford instructed him to bid up to £300 for an edition of Harvey's *De Motu Cordis*, the earliest printed book on the circulation of the blood, which was coming up for auction at Hodgson's. Too busy with his own Harley Street salesroom to attend the auction himself, he telephoned Frank at home late at night demanding to know why the book had been sold to another dealer for £200 when he'd authorized Frank to bid three. Frank confided that it had been sold in the knock-out for £650. The irate physician immediately undertook to have the whole question of

* Frank's concept of personal service, which was altogether different from Doris's, took on a new dimension when Helene Hanff discovered him in 1949.

the book ring raised in the House of Commons, which caused cardiac arrest amongst its five participants.

The then editor of *The Times Literary Supplement*, himself a collector of rare books, was anxious to avoid a scandal and invited the five leading firms of antiquarian booksellers to sign an undertaking that they would take whatever steps they thought necessary to put an immediate stop to the book ring – if such a thing existed. The Big Five arrived at the editor's office a quarter of an hour earlier than expected and, whilst waiting to sign the undertaking, held a knock-out in the ante-room. It was far better security for them than a Lyons tea shop and the tea was free.

I asked the normally discreet Frank why he'd told a client about the book ring.

'Well, you see,' he said, 'when the phone rang the wife and me were having a jolly good fuck in front of the fire.' He hesitated. 'And I don't think too well on my back.'

He seemed to be thinking well enough on his backside as he sat at his desk at the far end of the room totting up the day's takings. He was closely watched by Father's partner, Mark Cohen, who had reluctantly agreed when the firm first made its bid to enter the élite world of antiquarian booksellers that it should be called Marks & Co. rather than Marks & Cohen. The two men made one perfect bookseller, Mr Cohen providing the knowledge, Father the acumen. They'd worked together for twenty years without a written agreement because they understood what a partnership meant. Mr Cohen, who had two daughters but no son, regarded the war as a welcome postponement of his partnership with me and asked somewhat nervously if I had been given the day off by the Ministry of Labour. I was relieved that my domestic cover-story hadn't yet been blown.

Monitored all the way by Mr Cohen, I wandered along the densely packed shelves picking up a handful of peacetime whenever I stopped and reluctantly putting it back, going from *Jorrocks's Jaunts and Jollities* to Gibbon's *Decline and Fall*, from Johnson's *Rasselas* to Goldsmith's *Deserted Village*, and Baker Street didn't exist until I came to Macaulay's *Lays of Ancient Rome*.

I'd stood alone with Brave Horatius, the bloody Captain of the Gate, for twelve consecutive hours because a Belgian agent with an urgent message had spelt his name 'Horateous'. And that same agent with an even more urgent message had spelt the Etruscans who could scarce forbear to cheer with a 'k', and it had taken the girls and me 16,000 attempts spread over three cheerless days to discover it.

I decided to cede the ground floor to SOE and visit the rarities upstairs, which included Father.

As I passed the one part of the shop which was artificial – a door covered in the spines of books to conceal the fact that it led to the unmanned basement – Mr Cohen and Frank were engaged in some complex research. The till was two and sixpence short.

Only established clients – or newcomers who survived Frank's scrutiny, 84's equivalent of a pass – were allowed to climb the staircase which led to Father's office and the two floors above. The CD of Marks & Co. was seated at his desk with his back to Doris. He was absorbed in collating 84's latest acquisition – a first edition of *Vedute di Roma*, which included the rare volume of *Carceri*, the Italian prisons. According to Father, good booksellers never turned the pages of books, they strummed them, and he was strumming *Vedute* now to the glorious tune of its asking price.

I enquired about the state of 84's health, which was more important to him than his own, and he pointed to a pile of orders from dealers and private clients around the country and from America. He then proudly produced a letter on War Office notepaper from Field Marshal Lord Alanbrooke and whispered, as if it were a state secret, that he was Chief of the Imperial General Staff. The letter started 'Dear Ben' and was written as from one field marshal to another. I knew that Alanbrooke had a passion for books on ornithology and that the bulk of his library had come from 84. Now he wanted Father to find him a Gould's *Birds of Asia* in mint condition and was enquiring about the price.

Commenting that Alanbrooke was a real 'Mensch' with no side to him at all, Father retrieved the letter from me, picked up his pen (he could write more quickly than most people could type), and began composing his reply.

I tested the powers of thought transference:

Dear Alanbrooke,

My boy tells me that at C's behest your Chiefs of Staff committee is continuing to withhold an official directive from SOE and that if it doesn't deliver one soon in mint condition this splendid organization may be obliged to shut shop.

I am at a loss to understand why C has such animus towards SOE. Would I be wrong in conjecturing that there's an Intelligence ring in existence with a knock-out in Broadway?

Please accept Gould's *Birds of Asia* with the lad's compliments. Yours, etc.

Why was Father looking at me as if wondering whose son I was?

The second floor was the magic floor, the healing floor, my refuge from St Paul's School and my hope in years to come. It was called the Occult and Masonic department.*

It consisted of a large outer office, a small inner one, and George Plummer, whose specialized knowledge established the prices of occult and masonic books around the world.

Like most outstanding booksellers Plummer had little formal education and seldom read for pleasure. He had a particular flair for masonic books and was honorary adviser to the Grand Lodge library, yet he wasn't a Freemason himself because Catholics were forbidden to join secret societies other than their own. This didn't prevent him from taking Father into the inner office and rehearsing him in masonic ritual until he was word-perfect.

Of all the bizarre clients who'd visited Plummer's domain there were three who interested him most. One, an erudite mystic called Aleister Crowley, charged his devotees exorbitant prices to watch him perform a popular ceremony not in front of a fire but on top of an altar; the second was Edward Everett Horton, an American comedian who appeared in several Astaire–Rogers films, collected books on tintinnabulation, and confessed to Plummer that three Dominican bell-ringers were constantly at work in his head; and the last was his

---

* So was the Foreign Office from time to time.

employer's son who, as a small boy of eight, had perched on a stool at his desk and broken his first code.

I didn't want to be reminded of that episode but found myself glancing at the space which he'd cleared for me. It was occupied by a copy of Bourke's *Scatological Rites of Mankind* reserved for Mr Harry Edwardes, the president of the Society for Psychical Research, and I wondered why he was interested in excremental practices. I left a note for Plummer saying how sorry I was to have missed him and managed not to sign it DYC/M.

The third floor glowed like the face of a young FANY who's just broken her first indecipherable. It was full of books in exquisite bindings and they hardly seemed to have aged a wrinkle since they'd paraded like mannequins in their former salon, the palace of Versailles. Ten minutes in their company was a day in the sunshine.

The fourth floor was Marks & Co.'s war room. Everything in it was locked away in bookcases whose doors it was impossible to see through. Behind the dark glass were thousands of coloured plates, title-pages and frontispieces – spare parts which could be transplanted into any book which needed them, none of them more spare than I.

What the hell am I doing hiding from Giskes in a bookshop?

I said goodnight to Father, who inspected me thoughtfully to see what I'd borrowed. He warned me to make sure I closed the front door behind me as Cohen and Frank had already gone home. Presumably the two and sixpence had been accounted for.

I hadn't visited the basement but there wasn't much point; I was in one already. Turning to the front door, I realized that for the first time in my life I had the shop to myself.

I found myself sitting in the chair which Freud had once occupied hoping that we might make contact through anal osmosis. I'd welcome his concept of a Plan Giskes.

I looked at the table where he'd examined all that 84 could produce for him on the subject of Moses. There was a solitary book on it, and with the special conceit of those who roam bookshops in search of they know not what, I felt it was waiting for me.

It was a reproduction of the 1455 Gutenberg Bible, the first book printed in movable type. I was drawn to all incunabula and would proclaim early printed books my personal duchy if ever I ascended to the throne of 84. I leafed through the Bible, surely the most comprehensive Situation Report ever written.

Halfway through it I felt the beginnings of a Dutch buzz. Where was it coming from? – Gutenberg and Freud? What did the man who gave us movable type and the man who gave us immovable type-casting have to do with Herr Giskes?

The buzz was in the stomach now, and it was similar to the one I'd had when I'd finished breaking Peter Churchill's message.

Freud, Gutenberg and Peter Churchill. – What nonsense was this? . . . but for God's sake and the Golf team's cling on to whatever it is that's trying to break through to you in your old man's shop. . . .

The solution when it finally emerged was so obvious that the small boy who'd broken his first code on these premises would have spotted it at once and gone home for some pancakes.

I knew now how to give the Germans a chance to go wrong.

The idea was dangerous and could easily backfire. I would have to wait for exactly the right moment before launching it.

But at last I knew what the right moment was.

The benign bulldog was peeing on the pavement with stylish intensity. Doris was looking around as if to charge someone for the exhibition.

I was tempted to have a short talk with her about Rudyard Kipling and one or two more pressing matters but Father was watching from the window.

She examined me briefly then turned her attention to a better prospect.

I said a silent thank-you to the shop which hadn't yet failed me and hoped that Plan Giskes wouldn't fail it.

SIXTEEN

A Question of Y

The February moon was due on the 14th of the month, and not even C could postpone it.

Aware that the minister needed demonstrable results to put before the Cabinet, the whole of SOE was moonstruck – every country section, every service department setting out to prove that it could reach its stated targets. But there was one forlorn non-contributor to the frenetic countdown. As late as the morning of the 7th, I was still waiting to be told when the Arquebus, Gunnerside and Golf missions would spare time for their final code briefings; still waiting for Tiltman or some other expert to give his verdict on WOKs; and above all, still brooding over Plan Giskes – a brainchild with a missing chromosome.

I'd discovered a stunt in its growth for which there was only one remedy, and it wasn't likely to arrive in time to stop the Golf team from being dispatched to Herr Giskes. No matter how costly the delay, I had to wait for the Dutch section to cancel a message to one of its agents. Then, and only then, could a trap be set for the Germans which even SOE might regard as conclusive.

As the latest news arrived from the field, most of it bad, country sections often had to cancel messages which were already at the wireless station waiting to be transmitted. They then issued new ones, which were themselves subject to cancellation. But for a variety of reasons, some of them valid, they usually left it until the last possible moment to arrange these cancellations and twice in the past month overwrought country section officers had contacted overworked Grendon signalmasters and cancelled the wrong ones.

Determined to put a stop to this, Nicholls issued a memo to the country sections which was to have far wider repercussions than even he could foresee:

TO ALL COUNTRY SECTIONS FROM MS/A

Despite repeated requests to the contrary, when Country sections need to cancel messages which have been sent to the wireless station for transmission to the field they are continuing to contact Grendon directly, often when an agent's schedule has already begun. *This practice must cease forthwith.*

In future Country sections must notify *all* cancellations to the Headquarters Signals Office, and refer *all* requests for information to the Signals Office Supervisor or to a member of the Headquarters staff. I repeat *there must be no further direct contact between Country sections and the wireless station.* A.R. [Acknowledgement required]

This proclamation gave the station the seclusion it needed, ensured a better service for the country sections, and allowed the head of the code department to put it to uses for which it hadn't been designed.

I instructed the Signals Office supervisors that I was to be notified as soon as any country section cancelled a message to the field. I stressed any because I didn't want them to realize that I was concerned only with the Dutch. The sooner that cancelled message was in my hands the more quickly I could prove that the Dutch Resistance was in Giskes's.

At the start of a week which I'd built round the briefing of the vital thirteen, Mr Einar Skinnarland put me to the test for the first time on the present premises.

The great miscoder was still working in the Norsk Hydro at Vermok, still waiting for the Gunnerside and Grouse teams to mount their attack on it, still sending most of his messages (this was one of them) via the British legation in Stockholm. His latest indecipherable had travelled well and its bouquet filled the office for most of the morning. It was vintage Skinnarland and its text was as heady as its coding. Skinnarland warned London that unless the attack on the plant took place during the next moon period the Germans would be ready to start shipping large quantities of heavy water to Berlin.

I read the clear-text to Wilson over the scrambler and he shipped large quantities of appreciation. He then added something which mattered: the Gunnersides would be available for briefing in two days' time.

A few seconds later Duke Street telephoned: the Arquebus mission would be available for briefing in two days' time.

Killick was the next to telephone: the Dutch agents would be available for briefing in two days' time.

The verdict on WOKs was also expected in two ds'. t..

I decided to spend the next forty-eight hours thinking only about Holland.

Setting a trap for Giskes was in itself a trap; so much could go wrong. Convinced that while I was having buzzes in my head the Dutch agents were having buzz-saws put between their teeth. I found it hard to think dispassionately. Yet it was never more necessary. The greatest problem of all was my superiors' responses to Plan Giskes.

Although I still didn't understand SOE-mindedness, I would stake the future of WOKs that if I disclosed my intentions the plan would be aborted. This was more than a buzz; it was a total conviction. I had to decide whether to launch the plan without authority and risk the consequences or abandon it and try to think of another, and until I'd resolved the dilemma it would be unfair to brief a single agent, let alone thirteen.

And there was a moral issue. Did I have the right to risk the lives of captured agents who'd be no further use to Giskes if he saw through the plan and realized that we suspected they were blown?

In the absence of a coin I tossed my conscience, which weighed far less than the sixpence I lacked, and it produced a generalization – the most that could be expected from such a rarely used source: I must do whatever gave the greatest possible number of agents the best possible chances of survival.

This meant going it alone, which had one insuperable drawback. My inexperience.

I badly needed technical guidance from Nicholls and Heffer but daren't ask them for it because once they knew what the plan entailed they'd be duty bound to ask CD and Gubbins (and possibly the Dutch) for 'permission to proceed', and it would be safer to seek it from Giskes.

Yet there was certain information which I *had* to have, and if I couldn't get it by picking brains I might have to pick locks.

There was a document in Nick's desk which I was determined to see. During my critical debate with him about the perfection of the Dutch agents' coding he'd frequently glanced at a distinctive grey folder unlike any that I'd seen in SOE. By consulting this folder he'd been able to state quite categorically that the Dutch WT operators who'd previously been transmitting from The Hague, Rotterdam and Amsterdam were now sending their traffic from Eindhoven, Utrecht and Arnhem (as their messages proclaimed). He'd also been able to pinpoint the districts in these towns from which the traffic was being sent as well as the dates, times and frequencies of every transmission.

I'd wondered ever since where that folder had come from but now had to do much more than wonder. It was essential to find out not only the folder's origins but what other information it contained, and my one slender hope (apart from petty larceny) was the menaces whose office I was obliged to share.

I glanced across at them as they huddled together in menace territory preparing for a session with Nick. It would be useless to ask them outright as they'd never volunteer anything he didn't want me to know; I'd have to devise a 'Plan Menace'.

I escaped to the privacy of the loo with a message in secret French code, and a few minutes later was able to thank le bon Dieu that it had been properly encoded. Returning to the comparative civilization of the office, I saw not only one distinctive grey folder but a whole pile of them being carried towards me in the menaces' arms, the safest strong-boxes in Baker Street. I held open the door for them and took advantage of their astonishment to make my bid. Targeting Mrs Brewis, the more maternal of the two, I asked if the folders had come from the stationery department as they had pockets inside, and would be useful for carrying WOKs if the occasion should ever arise.

She said she hoped that it would, but no, they didn't come from the stationery department but they very soon might as Nick had got so used to them when he was working at Y. After a sharp glance from her sister menace she left the room in disgrace. She had given me the largest tip ever received by a doorman, but I'd have some difficulty in spending it as I hadn't even heard of Y, let alone the fact that Nick used to work there.

The person who could enlighten me about Y never appeared until the menaces had left, and his timing didn't fail him today.

As Heffer entered the room in his customary slow motion, I at once asked him what Y did. Like all gurus he could only be startled by other gurus but he did have to shelter for a moment behind his 'what have we here?' expression.

'Well, well,' he said. There was a long pause while he lit a cigarette and gazed out of the window at the nether regions of Norgeby House. It was impossible to tell whether he intended to answer. 'Well, well,' he repeated, and kept me in suspense for a puff or two longer.

Twenty minutes and as many surprises later I knew that I'd asked my first sensible question of 1943.

In the early thirties, when Top Secret meant what it said, Y was the pinnacle of the Top Secret list and, officially, didn't exist. Y specialized in logging diplomatic, military and other sensitive wireless traffic through its worldwide chain of listening posts, and in monitoring cable and wireless traffic from embassies. Because of the nature of its work, Y was staffed by technicians of exceptionally high calibre, many of whom were recruited from the Post Office engineers. Y worked closely with C but was an independent arm under the control of the chief signalmaster of the Royal Corps of Signals. Heffer said this with noticeable pride. Nick had been a member of Y since the mid-thirties and had been responsible for setting up Outstations in Palestine and India. In 1938 Y had been able to intercept high-speed Russian wireless traffic using special equipment which was still on the secret list. Heffer pointed out that because of Russia's vast size and poor communications, Moscow had to depend almost entirely on wireless for maintaining contact with its outlying territories. In the same year (1938) Y had monitored the wireless traffic of the German armed forces while Hitler was still declaring his peaceful intentions. Y's then head had privately briefed Churchill about the military build-up, but the great man wasn't yet in office and no one took him seriously but Hitler. Soon after the briefing Churchill thundered a warning to Parliament without disclosing his sources.

Y's impact on the war was immediate, massive and ongoing. Warning me that he knew only the fringes of its activities, Heffer said that Y was monitoring vast quantities of enemy and Allied traffic with equal dispassion, forecasting the battle-plans of Panzer divisions from the volume of traffic passing between units, and logging the wireless messages of German agents while they were still practising at their training schools in the fatherland.

Glancing at my littered desk, Heffer added that Y was also expert at detecting 'dummy traffic' used for deception purposes. Glancing at my waste-paper basket, he commented that Y logged *all* WT traffic and retained it for future reference, no matter how insignificant it might have appeared at the time.

Exhausted by his exposition, he sat down and studied my face too closely for comfort – his as well as mine.

Blowing a smoke ring, a warning that something especially important was about to emerge, he told me that Y sent most of its intercepted material to Bletchley for breaking or to C for information. Access to Y's archive was strictly limited to British organizations as it was logging Allied as well as enemy traffic. One smoke ring suppurated into another and there was a pause.

He was on the point of adding something when I made the mistake of saying, 'What, Heff?' He shook his head, retreated inside it, and could no longer be monitored even by Y.

I knew that the next few minutes could determine the outcome of Plan Giskes and that there must be no more involuntary 'What, Heff?'s. If it were Y's policy to log *all* WT traffic 'no matter how insignificant it might have appeared at the time', then somewhere in its massive archive there might be copies of the early Dutch code-groups which C claimed to have sent us.

There was no point in fencing with Heffer; he enjoyed it too much, knew me too well. I asked him outright how long it would take to set up a meeting with Y.

He looked at me with an expression which reminded me of Father's when a valued client once burned a hole in a sheet of Caxton, and rose from his chair as if it were scorching him. He told me that such a meeting was out of the question, that Y never dealt with polyglot organizations like SOE, and that for both our sakes I must immediately forget this entire conversation.

'Well, well,' I said. 'What have we here?' I certainly didn't have Heffer because he'd closed the door behind him.

But what did *we have here?*

Why had he told me about Y in such detail if I couldn't make the slightest use of it? Was there something he especially wanted me to know which he'd tucked away in guru fashion amongst his throw-away comments? If so, what was it?

And if so plus one, what was so wrong about wanting to ask a few questions of Y?

There were thirteen agents to be briefed tomorrow. How many of them would we lose because C, Y and SOE, for all their brilliancies, hadn't the common sense to make common cause?

Someone in the corridor gave a raucous laugh.

It was probably Herr Giskes.

SEVENTEEN

Arquebus, Gunnerside and Golf

One of the most difficult tasks in SOE was persuading country sections to arrange appointments with agents. It was even more difficult persuading them to change them.

But not for everyone.

While I'd been skirmishing with Heffer, my red-haired right hand, Muriel, had rescheduled my entire briefing programme with humiliating ease. I was to see Arquebus and the Gunnersides in the morning and their Golf team in the afternoon. The lunch hour was reserved for contingencies.

I had no idea what an arquebus was and looked it up in the dictionary. It was an early type of portable gun supported by a tripod. I knew that Tommy was the tripod, and that the two big guns he was supporting were Colonel Passy, the head of the Free French secret service, and Pierre Brossolette, a founder-member of the Conseil National de la Résistance. It was typical of Tommy not to have mentioned that he was the first British officer ever to be invited to take part in a Free French mission, the biggest compliment Duke Street could pay an Englishman, especially one belonging to SOE.

Since he was too modest or security-minded to discuss his role in Arquebus, I consulted Charlotte Denman for further and better particulars.

The testy little menace understood the complexities of our rival French sections even better than she understood Nick's, and went to great lengths to prove it to me.

According to the t.l.m. (testy little menace), Arquebus was to be dropped into the Northern zone of France, which was German occupied, the South being controlled by the puppet Vichy government.

166

The mission's first objective was to contact the growing number of independent Resistance groups whose political differences prevented them from working together, and weld them into the nucleus of a Secret Army. Arquebus then had to estimate this army's potential as a paramilitary force, and persuade its leaders to serve under one field commander who would receive his instructions from London. Once this was accomplished, Arquebus next had to establish under what circumstances (if any) the active but volatile Communist groups would be prepared to co-operate with the Secret Army.

The unexpected presence of a British officer at these vital negotiations would demonstrate to the French as well as to SOE that (in Tommy's words) 'both sides had finally noticed they were fighting the same war'.

From the moment that Passy, Brossolette and Tommy (code-name Sea-horse) landed in France they had a major PR job to do, and if ever a public figure needed one it was Tommy's idol, General *'Moi je suis la France'* de Gaulle.

This proud, arrogant self-proclaimed embodiment of the croix de Lorraine (the Free French symbol), disliked by Churchill, distrusted by Baker Street (the ultimate compliment), complained with all his Gallic fervour that the British were habitually discriminating against him and his followers. He was particularly incensed at having to get SOE's consent every time he wanted to dispatch a Frenchman back to France, knowing that no such strictures were placed on Buckmaster's agents except by the Germans. Barely tolerated in London, not yet established in France, he was engaged in a battle for survival of SOE vs. C dimensions with his formidable rival General Giraud. The prize was control of all French military, paramilitary and resistance forces. Giraud had the backing of the Americans while de Gaulle had to make do with SOE's, and the success of the Arquebus mission was as important to his future as a directive was to Baker Street's. He would have led the mission himself if he could, but he knew that it could safely be entrusted to Passy and Brossolette.

Passy was almost as difficult to handle as de Gaulle. He had a list of grievances against SOE as long as the Magna Carta, and I had one against him. He was the principal advocate of the secret French code.

One of Passy's justifiable complaints concerned French citizens who'd escaped to this country. He knew that if any of them volunteered to return to France they were sent to the Royal Victoria Patriotic School to be screened by the British. But once there, they were *never* offered to the Free French until Buckmaster had had first refusal of them, and his head-hunters invariably selected the most promising.

His even more serious grievance was harder to substantiate. He was convinced that British agents in France were persuading French citizens that they were being recruited to serve under de Gaulle when in reality they were being enlisted for F section or for other British interests (C). He wanted a British officer to accompany him to France to witness the scale of this deception, discover who was responsible for it and make a full report in writing, no matter what his findings. Who better for this than the Chairman of the Awkward Squad?

De Gaulle knew very little about Tommy but was prepared to accept Passy's judgement that he was the only person in SOE who could be trusted to tell the truth as he saw it.

I'd begun to understand why de Gaulle needed a code the British couldn't read and wished I could oblige him.

I thanked Charlotte for the trouble she'd taken and offered to teach her how to break indecipherables any time she wanted.

As a courtesy to Passy I'd offered to conduct the Arquebus briefing on Free French territory instead of in Dorset Square, and Tommy had readily accepted. With shoes shined, curls disciplined and larynx sprayed to give body to a voice which Mother referred to as my 'deep brown melter', I set out for Duke Street – often called Puke Street by members of F section.

I had only two legs of Arquebus to brief because Pierre Brossolette had already left for France. I was sorry to have missed him as he owned a bookshop on the rue de la Pompe and we could have compared notes on le knock-out.

I checked the most important item I was carrying – a Churchill-sized Havana which I'd stolen from Father's humidor ('they breathe more easily inside there, my son'). I hoped it would help Sea-horse to breathe more easily inside occupied France. I'd also written a code-poem for him but suspected that he'd find the cigar more acceptable.

A Free French sergeant examined my pass as if I'd just printed it, spoke briefly into a telephone (my name sounded better floating in garlic), and then reluctantly allowed me to proceed upstairs.

Tommy was in a small ante-room surrounded by half a dozen Free French officers. General 'Moi je suis' stared down at them from the wall looking slightly less censorious than he did at Dorset Square. Tommy introduced me to Capitaine Manuel, Passy's second in command, and then led me down a short passage to Passy's office.

Charlotte Denman had spoken of Passy with awe, all the more awe-inspiring because she so rarely had any, and I'd learnt from her that his real name was Dewavrin and that he'd taken his *nom de guerre* from the tube station at Passy. Nick had once described him as a 'cold fish' without disclosing where he'd sampled him.

My first impression of him as he rose from behind his desk was that he had the energy of an express train out to break a record, and the mental quality of a barracuda with a high IQ. Tommy introduced me as SOE's 'chef de codage', which impressed me more than it did Passy. We locked eyes for a moment and I was relieved when he looked away that a stye hadn't formed. I suspected that he was trying to be cordial.

There was an incoming message on his blotter which looked like the one in secret French code which I'd broken in the toilet. He studied it, then rose to his feet, frowning from his engine to his luggage compartment. He announced he had to leave and offered to come to Dorset Square for briefing if I wasn't here when he returned.

It took me a little while to realize that Tommy and I were alone.

'My God, Tommy, what a powerhouse.'

'You should see him on a good day,' he said proudly.

I was seeing Tommy on a good day. He was so relaxed it was unnerving. Puffing away at his cigar, he asked for WOK news, and I told him I was expecting a verdict within twenty-four hours, though I didn't know from whom.

He instructed me to stop worrying as you couldn't keep a good code down, that progress of any kind took twice as long in SOE as anywhere else, and that I must push on with all my other codes which were on the boil. I'd not said a word to him about the codes which were incubating, but then, that was Tommy.

He waited patiently for the chef de codage to get on with his job.

I showed him a WOK which had been produced on waterproof paper. He examined it as if he had nothing else on his mind, then gave a brief nod which was his seal of approval. I told him that as he was the first person to have seen a WOK, I wanted him to be the first agent to use one, and nobody but the coders of Grendon need know if he did.

He thanked me for the offer but declined it. He wouldn't accept anything which wasn't available to all agents. Nor did he think he should use an original poem for his code even if I'd brought one with me. He felt sure he'd send fewer indecipherables in some verses by Verlaine which he knew by heart.

I told him that if Sea-horse sent any indecipherables I'd ask Buckmaster to break them.

'Good,' he said. 'It's time he learned French.'

He reached for a pencil and paper to show that he wasn't claiming exemption from coding exercises. I asked him to encode a message at least 300 letters long and he nodded approvingly.

His coding instructor at Beaulieu had said in his report that Tommy had arrived at the school 'already a first-class coder', and I knew that the exercise was academic. He numbered his transposition-key as if he were climbing a ladder to Barbara's window.

The next time he did any coding he'd be in occupied France. That was his goal, his ambition, his WOK, and I was glad for his sake that he was in sight of achieving it.

I had never met anyone I trusted so completely or whose trust I valued more. I remembered the long nights when he'd helped me to break indecipherables without even asking who'd sent them, and the encouragement he'd given me to stand up to Ozanne. It was hard to believe that he would no longer be on call and I wished that bright Sergeant Blossom could arrange for me to ring him in France.

He finished his exercises without a single mishap, and when he gave me his work for checking, I found that I was the one who'd made a mistake. He'd referred to Arquebus twice in the body of the message and each time he'd spelled it Arquebuse. I'd looked up the wrong word.

The former tripod listened patiently while I ran through the precautions he'd heard so often at other agents' briefings: use long key-phrases, try not to repeat them, free your language, send messages in a mixture of English and French. Double-check your security checks.

Nod and nod and nod.

I told him that we would soon be recruiting a bevy of FANYs licensed to use all their resources to make code-briefings as memorable as possible.

Nod and nod and nod.

I realized that I was impinging on precious Barbara time, that the briefing was over, and that I must say goodbye to the Chairman of the Awkward Squad. We shook hands in silence. I was the first to disengage because my fingernails were sweating.

He put his hand firmly on my shoulder.* 'Well, Chef de codage,' he said quietly, 'congratulations on your new appointment.'

'And on yours. Merde alors, Tommy.'

'Your French is improving.'

'You should hear it on a good day. Merde alors, Tommy!' I wasn't sure if two 'merde alors' were as good as one 'mazzeltov' so I wished him that as well.

Under my breath, of course. What there was left of it.

London had had no contact with the Grouse since their abortive attempt to destroy the heavy-water plant. According to Skinnarland, a kindly man when he wasn't coding, they'd been hiding in the mountains for the past four months and were thought to be starving. Two weeks ago their code-name had been changed to Swallow.

The new attempt to blow up the Norsk Hydro was even more dangerous than the first because the Germans had had time to prepare for it, and its outcome was even more important as they were known to be stockpiling heavy water. SOE's attacking force consisted of the Gunnersides, the Grouse and Mr Skinnarland himself, who was prepared to blow his cover.

* It's still there, Tommy. Hope you know it.

171

Wilson was waiting for me in the hallway of his Chiltern Court flat. He was looking more harassed than I'd yet seen him and asked me to stand by for a quarter of an hour as the Gunnersides were in the final stages of a briefing which he now had to attend himself. He told me to make myself comfortable in his office – a technical impossibility – and hurried into the briefing room.

I was convinced I knew who was conducting that briefing and preferred to stay in the hall to see who emerged.

Over the past two months a spate of Top Secret telegrams in main-line cipher had been exchanged between Wilson and Major Malcolm Munthe, SOE's man in the Stockholm legation. The messages concerned the chief engineer at the Norsk Hydro, Professor Jomar Brun, who was uniquely placed to advise on the new attack and was fully prepared to do so.

With Munthe's help, Brun was smuggled across the Swedish frontier a few weeks ago and arrived in Stockholm bringing with him hundreds of photographs of the Germans' latest fortifications, charts of their patrol systems and a detailed layout of the plant itself. Munthe immediately arranged for the RAF to fly him to London, and Wilson at once dispatched him and his invaluable data to SOE's camouflage and special devices section, the Thatched Barn at Barnet. With all the station's facilities at his disposal, Brun rapidly constructed a large working model of the Norsk Hydro, and the Gunnersides had been practising on it ever since at their Southampton training school under his personal supervision. Brun's presence in England was the greatest asset, apart from courage and Skinnarland, which the Grouse/Gunnersides had.

The fifteen-minute wait slouched into thirty and the thirty into forty-five. I was well into contingency time and began to worry about the Golf briefing, an appointment I was so reluctant to keep that I was determined to be early for it.

Wilson finally emerged from the briefing room accompanied by two men. I recognized one of them as Colonel Bjarne Oen, chief Intelligence officer on the Norwegian General Staff, a key member of Wilson's brains-trust. The other was a bushy-haired civilian who was talking in undertones which he appeared to have difficulty in hearing himself, and if he wasn't the professor I was Ozanne.

Wilson apologized for the delay and said that the Gunnersides were now ready for me.

I tried to look as if I were ready for them, and hurried towards the room where four months ago I had briefed the Grouse.

The six Gunnersides were Joachim Ronneberg, the team leader, Birger Strømsheim, Fredrik Kayser, Knut Haukelid, Hans Storhaus and Kasper Idland. They sprang to attention with the same immediacy as the Grouse, projected the same aura of indivisibility, and might just as well have been called Haugland, Helberg, Kjelstrup and Poulson.

I wanted to present them with a working model of a briefing officer but felt too pedestrian to conduct any traffic – a private joke which caused me to laugh out loud. I realized that the tension of my next briefing was building up on the Gunnersides' time.

They responded to their coding exercises as readily as the Grouse had, and I focused on Knut Haukelid's bowed head, unable to believe that I was in the same room with him.

He'd been an active member of the Norwegian Resistance since 1940, and was one of the audacious trio which had blown up the submarine base at Trondheim. This same trio had helped to create the shuttle service of fishing smacks known as the 'Shetland bus' which ferried agents between Scotland and Norway. After the Trondheim raid Haukelid had escaped to the safe harbour of the British legation in Stockholm, and SOE's harbour-master, Major Munthe, had helped him to reach London. But the other members of his trio – Sverre Midskau and Max Manus – had been captured. Midskau was feared dead, but Max Manus threw himself off a train which was taking him to concentration camp, found his way to Stockholm, and with Munthe's help would be arriving in London in a few weeks.

That man Munthe was an invisible presence at every Norwegian briefing, and at every operation. Nor were his activities confined to Scandinavia. He'd transformed the Stockholm legation into a centrepoint for SOE's finances and communications, and its apparently limitless resources were at the disposal of agents in Eastern Europe, the Low Countries and France. He'd also started a training school in Sweden so that would-be Resistance fighters who'd been

173

smuggled across the frontier could return to their own countries to act as wireless operators and saboteurs.

The Swedish authorities were aware of his extra-curricular activities (he was assistant military attaché) and showed their country's strict neutrality by allowing anyone in Sweden with the inclination to do so to sing the German National Anthem in public. Occasionally Munthe was one of them.

I'd met him when he'd called at Dansey's office to discuss main-line and agents' codes. He was younger than his traffic suggested, in his middle to late twenties, a Scots fusilier whose appearance in a well-cut kilt caused the main-line coders to flash messages at him he couldn't fail to decipher. After the meeting I asked him if he were related to Axel Munthe, author of *The Story of San Michele*. Our Malcolm was his son. I'd offered to smuggle him across the frontier of 84, where a first edition of his father's masterpiece had pride of place in my father's legation. One day, perhaps.

The Gunnersides were proving to be slow, methodical and unadventurous coders, with Haukelid in the lead by half a message. At this rate of progress there was a real danger that I would be late for the Golf team's briefing, but I wasn't prepared to hurry the Gunnersides. Time was all I could give them.

A limpet on the hull of Haukelid's message seemed to have come unstuck and he was checking it carefully. That was the sign of a good coder. The others were labouring on.

So was I. My confidence was seeping away like sixpences in a fairground, and I knew the reason that made it even worse.

I'd caught myself committing the briefing officer's worst crime: I'd thought about my next briefing in the middle of my present one, and still couldn't stop it.

Nor could I stop worrying about Plan Giskes. The operation would be so much safer if I could have access to Y's records, followed by a technical session with Nicholls and Heff.

The Gunnersides were ready, and I heard myself telling them to check each other's messages. Returning to the present, I then checked their checking, and suddenly was on my feet talking security.

I would have kept them there all day if I could. Anything to postpone the next briefing.

I realized that they were looking at me with the courteous resignation which was the Norwegian equivalent of a fidget. They had let me off lightly. Any officer who briefs entirely by reflex should be blown up at the Norsk Hydro.

My job here was done. Shoddily. Perfunctorily. But done.

I left Chiltern Court for my final briefing of the day, no longer sure if I were right about anything except the cost of being wrong.

EIGHTEEN

The Coding Cabaret

Unless I'd misread the situation in Holland, I was on my way to meet four Dutch agents who were already blown.

Over the past two months eleven messages about their impending drop had been exchanged between London and Trumpet and Boni, who were at the very top of my list of suspect operators. Trumpet's circuit was now organizing their landing grounds and reception committees. The elusive Jambroes was said to be eagerly awaiting them, but the elusive Giskes was just as likely to be.

Nick had strong views (which I'd canvassed) on the best way to handle the Golf team: it must be a normal briefing in every way and on no account must the agents suspect that we had any special anxieties about them. Nor must I give them code-conventions or security checks which weren't already in use in Holland because if the agents were caught and forced to disclose them, the Germans might be alerted to our suspicions about Dutch agents generally.

He agreed that each member of the Golf team could safely be given a set of questions with prearranged answers and he would ask the Dutch section to prepare them at once so that the agents had time to learn them by heart. He would make clear that the same request was being made to all country sections in case the Dutch felt singled out. I suggested he made sure that the Golf team were not told each other's questions.

I'd had such a rare feeling of security when he'd referred to '*our* anxieties . . . *our* suspicions' that I'd nearly disclosed Plan Giskes to him but the Executive Council had summoned him just in time and it was still a secret between me and 84.

The briefing was to be held in Bickenhall Mansions, which was a few regrets away from Chiltern Court. Major Blizzard and Captains Bingham and Killick, the three people I most wanted to avoid, emerged from the briefing room just as I arrived. They were escorting, or were being escorted by, Colonel Elder Wills, who topped the bill at any briefing. He was commanding officer of the Thatched Barn at Barnet, where he and his gifted technicians, some of them ex-convicts, forged huge quantities of currency, travel passes and work permits so that agents like the Golf team could survive in occupied Europe until they perished by the poem-code. He and I knew each other by eye-flicks but had never spoken – an achievement we saw no reason to diminish. After a whispered conversation in which I heard him utter the magic word 'Guilders', he left.

Captain Killick was the first to notice me, and signalled the glad tidings to his colleagues. This was the first time that I'd faced them as a group, and togetherness was what they projected. Nothing could persuade them that their traffic was blown, and if I'd told them that none of their agents had ever made a mistake in his coding, they'd have sent a message to the field asking why not.

Blizzard thanked me for coming at such short notice, and Bingham asked if I'd like some coffee – a substantial improvement on the impenetrable obstinacy with which he'd responded to my countless phone calls about Ebenezer's security checks.

Declining the coffee as I'd sampled it before, I enquired how long they could allow me with the four Golfers. Blizzard and Killick exchanged puzzled glances, and Bingham finally explained that there weren't four Golfers, as I'd put it. Golf was the code-name for Broadbean's W.T. operator, and the other two agents I was going to brief were Hockey and Tennis. They had common objectives but would operate independantly.

I apologised for my mistake and continued to think of them as the Golf team. But it was Bingham who'd misled me in the first place, and not for the first time.

Without pausing for breath (for which I couldn't blame him as it was highly unpleasant) he rattled off the code-names, field-names and real names of the four agents, and said that they were waiting for me in the briefing room.

This was the moment I'd been dreading. I'd prepared a special performance for the Golf team and wasn't sure that I could carry it off. I was even less sure that I had the right to try.

Blizzard asked if I would like Bingham or Killick to attend the briefing.

If I accepted his offer I couldn't proceed with my act, and nearly said, 'Yes please'. But instead I said that providing the four of them spoke English I thought I'd be better off alone with them and he agreed.

I hurried to the briefing room before either of us changed our minds, but paused outside the door to review what I was letting myself in for . . .

The target of today's proceedings was not the four agents. It was Giskes himself.

Until now we'd given our longstanding pen-friend no cause whatever to credit anyone in the Signals directorate with the competence to set a trap for him. We were still using the poem-code, still relying on its security checks, still sending him top secret information. It was essential to Plan Giskes that he continued to believe that he was dealing with incompetents, and one way of giving him the necessary reassurance was through the four agents waiting to be briefed.

I could do nothing to prevent their capture. But if they were interrogated by Giskes about their final code-briefing, my conduct in the next hour could do a great deal to allay whatever suspicions he might have when Plan Giskes was launched.

In basic terms, the ideal impression they would convey to him was that I seemed inexperienced, uninspired, and whatever the Dutch was for a bit of a cunt.

The high master of St Paul's had frequently expressed this in Latin in my end-of-term reports, and I was about to demonstrate just how right he had been.

I strode in, said, 'Good morning, gentlemen, or should it be good afternoon, nice weather for coding,' or some such inanity, then strolled to the briefing officer's desk, brushed some dust off the chair, some more off the desk, announced that I was allergic to dust and sneezed three times to confirm it. The mopping-up operations took a few moments to complete, then I straddled a chair and faced them.

Their names were Captain Jan Kist (Hockey), Lieutenant Gerard van Os (Broadbean), Lieutenant Willem van der Wilden (Golf) and Lieutenant Peter Wouters (Tennis). But for the next hour, which I would try to ensure that they didn't forget, their activities in the field had no relevance. They had their missions; I had mine. All four seemed very relaxed and had obviously enjoyed their session with Wills. They had no idea what was in store for them.

Breaking them in gently, I made great play of unlocking my brief-case and searching inside it for something of utmost importance. They seemed slightly surprised when all I produced was a copy of *The Times*, which I spread on the desk with great decorum. It was a valuable prop which I intended shortly to use.

I began the coding cabaret by enquiring if they had enough squared paper, though there were reams of it in evidence; whether their pencils were properly sharpened, which they clearly were; and whether the light was good enough, which it obviously was. I then asked them to encode a message 250 letters long – no, let's make it 300, why not? – waited until they'd started and then told them *not* to use squared paper as they might not have any in the field, might they? They glanced at each other as they ruled their own.

I was already familiar with their coding as I'd sent to the training school for their practice messages. These showed that all four were above-average coders, and that William van der Wilden usually started his key-phrases with a word from the beginning of his poem and Peter Wouters with a word from the end. Kisk and van Os had not developed any pattern I could spot. One in twelve of their mes-sages had been an indecipherable and I uttered a silent briefing-room prayer that they would continue to send indecipherables when they reached the field.

They glanced at me with a hint of amusement as I grimaced my way through *The Times* crossword, and were only slightly distracted when I started doing it aloud. I asked for their help with one across, 'just to get me started', but none was forthcoming. I then enquired if they were any good at anagrams as I was hopeless at them myself. Van Os muttered something which sounded like 'Anna who?' and started his transposition again. I apologized for interrupting them, 'But you'll have to get used to it in the field, you know,' and resumed my struggle with one across. I wasn't quite as stuck as I hoped to

179

appear because I'd set the puzzle myself, a paying hobby I'd indulged in at St Paul's as a substitute for homework.

With my incompetence at anagrams hopefully established for Giskes's benefit (a cryptographer who can't anagram is a motorist who can't steer), I rose from the desk and broke a fundamental rule of briefing by peering over their shoulders, making clucking noises of approval and encouragement, while they were still involved in the coding process.

These noises, so alien to me, were interrupted by the telephone. It was the Signals Office supervisor to tell me that two messages had just been cancelled, one to a Belgian agent, the other to a Dane.

William van der Wilden was the first Golfer to reach the eighteenth hole, followed shortly afterwards by van Os, Jan Kisk and Peter Wouters.

I collected their work, told them to check each other's messages because if I checked them myself, we'd be here all night, and carefully redistributed them. Remembering that the great Spencer Tracy always under-acted, I showed no surprise at all when we discovered that I'd 'accidentally' given each agent his own message to check! When this was finally resolved, one message was found to be missing. I'd 'accidentally' dropped it on the floor.

I apologized, saying that I hadn't got the hang of things yet as I'd only been head of codes for a week or two (vital for Giskes to know he was dealing with a new boy) but was sure that I'd soon catch on.

Finding that I had a few clucks left, I walked behind them checking their checking. They'd have been good coders, given the chance.

All that remained was the grand finale, which was unlikely to leave the audience wanting more.

I announced that I was going to read them a list of security rules, though they would have to be patient as some of them were new to me. I then produced two sheets of foolscap paper from my briefcase, and proceeded to inflict on them an elongated version of the normal security patter, apologizing now and again for the difficulty I had in deciphering my handwriting.

As soon as I'd finished I offered to read the list again and, before they could refuse, was racing through it. This time I stressed all the points they'd need to know if they were free to do their own coding when they landed in Holland – pausing at an appropriate moment to say that I'd solved one across.

I'd already kept them there an hour and ten minutes and said how quickly the time had passed.

I finally enquired if they had any questions. Looking at me in silence, they shook their heads, but their expressions showed what they were longing to ask. It was the oldest question known to man. 'Whose arse did you kiss to get this job?'

I said a cheerful goodbye to them and walked to the door.

It may have been my most successful briefing.

A fairly full day was not quite over.

I was determined to find that bastard Nicholls and legitimize him. On behalf of every agent using a poem-code I was going to demand a WOK-decision, and if the Messiah still refused to tell me who was going to make it he could prepare himself for the Second Going.

But when I returned to my office I found a message on my desk instructing me to report to him immediately.

He was seated behind his desk studying a grey folder. His complexion matched it. He at once asked how I had got on with the Golf team's briefing, and I assured him it had been as normal as I knew how to make it.

He looked at me quizzically and told me to sit down. It was as well that he did because I couldn't believe what I now heard him saying.

Tomorrow I was to discuss the future of WOKs with Colonel Tiltman of Bletchley Park.

The Colonel Tiltman of *the* Bletchley Park. The cryptographic supremo.

I was to keep the whole morning free for him.

No problem! – I'd keep my whole coding life free for him if he had any use for it.

I tried to thank Nick for what he'd achieved but the deep brown melter wouldn't function and all that emerged was the last of my clucks.

He pointed to the door and ordered me to go home immediately. I was in for the longest night of my life in repayment for what I'd done to the Golf team.

NINETEEN

Summit Meeting

'Dear Bletchley wizard

On this of all nights
You must not become
One of sleep's walking wounded
Trapped between the day's achievements
And tomorrow's bereavements
And if a wet dream
Would help you
To awake fair-minded
To judge the merits
Of the codes you will see
Then with all my fearful WOK-filled heart
I wish you one!
Or two!
Or three!
With the compliments, dear Bletchley wizard
Of the whole of SOE.'

(Written on the eve of the Supremo's visit)

On the morning of Tiltman day an event took place which silenced everything in Norgeby House but the teleprinters, caused Nick to believe that Hitler was using hallucinogenic chemicals, and gave our stunned work-force an even greater shock than a kind word from a country section. Heffer arrived early.

Having demolished the one stable factor in our Morse-bound world by appearing before noon, he drifted into my office like an ominous

183

sea-mist – caught me in the act of concealing secret French messages, Mother's illicit provisions and whatever else might detract from Tiltman's WOK-benediction – and made history twice in one morning by coming straight to the point.

There were certain aspects of Tiltman's visit which he felt he should discuss with me. But before doing so, was there anything about the meeting which I would like to ask him?

I admitted that three things puzzled me. Why had it taken Nick since December to set the meeting up? Why had he told me at Xmas that Tiltman had read my coding report and approved it in principle, and remained silent ever since? Had Tiltman changed his mind for some reason?

He patted me with a smile and said that nobody could anticipate Tiltman's mind, including Tiltman, and that the reasons for the delay would become all too clear to me when I understood Nick's relationship with Tiltman and Tiltman's with C. There were also one or two other matters which he felt I should be aware of.

The one-man education board began his disclosures over a shared breakfast, and by the time he'd asked me to present his compliments to the chef I'd lost my appetite altogether.

Listening to Heffer's account of the Nick–Tiltman relationship was like turning the pages of a wedding album.

They'd first met when they were subalterns in the Signals Corps. Nick specialized in wireless, Tiltman in codes. Their careers advanced in parallel with equal distinction, and their combined talents helped to make MI8 the force that it was.

When Nick gave up gainful employment to join SOE his first major decision was to get Tiltman's reactions to my coding report. His second was to repeat them to CD and Gubbins. But although they were impressed by what Tiltman had said, his verbal approval wasn't enough for them. They needed his official endorsement of such radical changes in case C attacked them as a matter of principle. Moreover, because of my age and inexperience they felt that an expert of Tiltman's standing should supervise any other innovations I might try to introduce, and had formally invited him to be SOE's adviser on codes.

'Then, by God, Heff, we're safe.!'

'I'm afraid,' he said quietly, 'that it isn't quite as simple as that.'

Of course not! Why else would he be here at eight in the morning?

Choosing his words as carefully as a chancellor with a shaky budget, he explained to the now hushed house why the conflict between C and SOE placed Tiltman ('a very decent chap by all accounts') in a most awkward position.

Bletchley was controlled by C and before committing himself to helping SOE Tiltman decided to discuss his position with Brigadier Gambier-Parry, C's head of Signals. Gambier-Parry was convinced that he'd already given SOE all the advice that it needed (he'd recommended the poem-code) but after a great deal of reflection (presumably his own in a mirror) he'd agreed that it would be in everyone's interests if Tiltman did what he could to keep SOE's codes on the right lines so long as it didn't interfere with his more important commitments. Tiltman had then notified CD and Gubbins that he was prepared to act as SOE's code adviser.

I let out a whoop of delight that could have been heard in Bletchley but suddenly noticed Heffer's expression. He was looking at me as if I'd mistaken a condemned man's breakfast for a mid-morning snack and, after a thought-pause which broke the existing record, asked for another cup of tea. There was something he was clearly reluctant to say, and I was careful not to prompt him.

Eventually he pointed out that though Nick and Tiltman were experts in their own field, like all professional soldiers they were hopeless at Intelligence politics. But Gambier-Parry was a past master, and was certain to question Tiltman about *everything* he learned here. It wouldn't matter what Tiltman reported about codes but it could do untold damage to SOE's chances of a directive if he told Gambier-Parry about the muddles we'd got into in Greece and Yugoslavia, and the operational problems we were encountering elsewhere. It was essential therefore that I limited my conversation with Tiltman strictly to codes, without referring to any particular country section's traffic or indeed to any particular country section.

It took a long time dawning. 'You mean I mustn't tell him about the Dutch?'

He confirmed that this was precisely what he meant, then looked at me suspiciously. 'You've kept very quiet lately about Holland. – that either means that you're no further forward or that you're up to something. Which is it?'

I assured him that I still hadn't thought of a way of setting a trap for Giskes, and realized that the temptation to tell the truth to Tiltman would be more than I could cope with. 'If I can't discuss Holland of all countries with Tiltman of all people I'd rather not meet him.'

He stared intently at my desk. 'I was under the impression,' he said quietly, 'that the future of WOKs was your top priority.' I'd placed one in the centre of the desk where Tiltman couldn't possibly miss it, and surrounded it with poems to point up the contrast. It was the first table I'd ever laid.

Gently now, because his point was made and he knew I was impaled on it, he told me that Tiltman's schedule had been rearranged. He would be arriving at ten for a short session with Dansey on main-line codes, and after that he was mine. And since he'd expressed a preference for seeing me alone, my two room-mates would be spending the whole day in the Signals Office – a fringe benefit Heffer was sure I would welcome. He urged me not to forget for a single moment that whatever I said to Tiltman I would also be saying to Gambier-Parry.

'I suppose they both work closely with Y?' I said, hoping to shake him right down to his privies, though he probably kept them in his head.

'Who's Y?' he asked blandly. He then wished me the best of luck (he wasn't a 'merde alors' man), announced that it was time he had a haircut, and went in search of a barber who wouldn't charge him by the lock.

The quickest way to divert the protest march forming up inside me was to skim through the overnight traffic waiting in my in-tray. Messages had come in from Duus Hansen in Denmark, Peter Churchill in France and Boni in Holland.

Duus Hansen was pinpointing targets for the RAF to bomb – which meant that neglected little Denmark was at last considered important enough to be attacked by air, a triumph for Hollingsworth as well as for the Danes.

Peter Churchill's message contained a warning that German troops now occupying the Southern zone of France were causing his circuit great difficulties, and that he, Lise (Odette) and Anton (Rabinovitch, the Joe Louis fan) were looking for new bases.

Boni was his usual informative self. He confirmed that he was recruiting new agents for the Parsnip/Cabbage organization, that Cabbage would be standing by from the 11th onwards to receive a drop of seven containers, and that he and Cabbage were finding safe-houses for Broadbean and Golf. Boni ended his message with a plea for more money as his group would be completely out of funds within the next two months.

Skinnarland had also made an overnight contribution – indecipherable, of course – which was being attended to by the day squad.

I put all the traffic in a drawer where even my unconscious couldn't produce it by accident, and spent the next five minutes trying to draw the Almighty's attention to the conflict of interests I was involved in. But I had a strong feeling that his line was engaged, and that C was already on the scrambler.

I now had the two greatest luxuries SOE could offer – time on my hands and the office to myself. But I had a penance to perform, and could postpone it no longer.

Three weeks ago I'd stumbled on to a method of tackling indecipherables which cut the time it took to break them by half. I'd made the discovery whilst being broken in half myself by an indecipherable in secret French code which had to be broken and re-encoded before Duke Street started asking what had happened to it.

The new method, which I should have discovered long ago, worked equally well on *all* indecipherables, and although it was only minor league cryptography, it could be developed further. Even in its present form, it helped us to win the race to break messages before country sections ordered the agents to repeat them.

The average indecipherable was 200 letters long but every time a new key was tried, all 200 letters had to be transposed to see if the message was broken. This cumbersome process was no longer necessary because of some charts I'd devised which did the bulk of the work.

It was now possible to select a key and allow the charts to calculate which of the 200 letters would appear in the first line of the message if that key had been used. If the letters formed words, then the rest of the message would also make sense and the right key had been chosen. If the result was gibberish, then the wrong key had been tried and it was 'on with the next'.

'Scanning,' the code-groups instead of having to transpose the whole lot of them would be invaluable to the coders of Grendon. But I'd hesitated to show it to them in case they were put off by its apparent complexity (the charts were in fact very easy to use; the difficulty lay in preparing them). I'd finally decided to give Grendon a trial demonstration.

The FANYs once again proved me wrong, and the more adventurous of them now used the charts on all indecipherables and ostentatiously teleprinted at the foot of the messages 'broken on your chart system'. One young FANY, as bright as she was cheeky, had asked why I hadn't also calculated the *last* lines of messages because surely they would be just as useful as the first? I didn't tell her that there were two reasons. One that I hadn't thought of it, the other that it was extremely hard and time-consuming work. But she was right, of course, and Tiltman day was the ideal occasion for making a start. I reached for a mountain of squared paper, gritted my arithmetic and began the calculations.

Like all acts of minor expertise, it was wholly absorbing and some hours or weeks later I glanced up and found two men watching me from the doorway. One was Nick, the other was a large teddy bear of a colonel with amused eyes.

I'd seen those eyes before when they'd had nothing to amuse them. They'd aged a thousand ciphers since then.

The supremo had called at the code-breaking school in Bedford to interview candidates for Bletchley. Of the twenty-five pupils on the course, I was the only one not sent in to him for fear of wasting his time. But by standing on tiptoe and peering over the other pupils' shoulders I'd managed to gaze at him across the great divide called talent. That was ten months ago.

The divide seemed even greater as I shook his hand. I then shook Nick's for producing him.

Slightly puzzled by these SOE formalities, the supremo said that my face seemed familiar. I explained that we'd once been at opposite ends of the same corridor but didn't add how certain I was that we always would be.

There was a short pause as the two master signallers discussed a mutual acquaintance who apparently had last been seen entering a public toilet and hadn't been heard of since. It sounded like shorthand for joining C. Glancing at his watch, Nick reminded Tiltman that he had another appointment as soon as he'd finished with me. He then left the room rapidly before I could shake his hand again.

I was alone with my coding godfather.

And Gambier-Parry.

TWENTY

The Findings of the Court

Tiltman sat opposite me with the WOK at right angles to his navel, and wasted no time on preliminaries. Opening his briefcase, which had more locks on it than leather, he produced a document which I finally recognized as my coding report. He then read it from cover to cover while I did my best to remember what I'd written.

Gazing for a moment into the middle distance – my middle, his distance – he then delivered his verdict like a magistrate anxious to proceed with his next case. He endorsed the report's view that the poem-code was unsuitable for SOE's traffic, and agreed that 'its security checks were valueless except as a means of giving agents confidence'.

There was nothing he wished to add to the list of security precautions already in use (most of them had come from him anyway). The idea of giving agents original composition was sound, though he sympathized with those who preferred famous quotations which they already knew by heart. But he was puzzled by the report's reference to 'compromise poems'. Would I please explain what they were?

I told him that some agents allowed me to alter a few words of their famous quotations, which I thought was better security than making no changes at all. He asked to see an example.

I produced one which I'd given to Peter Churchill to use as a reserve:

> The boy stood on the burning deck
> His feet were full of blisters
> He hadn't got them from the fire
> But from screwing both his sisters.

I didn't repeat Peter's comment that he hardly ever screwed with his feet because he had ingrowing toe-nails but I couldn't resist adding that this agent's indecipherables were particularly tricky as he regularly 'hatted' his columns. I wanted to establish that I knew the jargon.

Tiltman's eyes became sheets of calculus at the mention of inde-cipherables but he said that we'd come to those shortly.

Having established which of us was setting the pace of the meeting, he thoroughly endorsed the concept of giving agents a supply of poems on microfilm. But this brought him to another point which the report hadn't made clear.

His question seemed harmless enough at first hearing. When WT operators were at training school, did they transmit their practice messages in the poems which they were going to use when they reached the field?

I said that I'd stopped them from doing this as trainee operators worked together in teams and could get to know each other's poems. Did he think I was right?

He nodded, and seemed relieved at my answer.

I was convinced that there was something behind his question which I hadn't spotted and registered it for a future brood.

He was silent for a moment and looked restlessly round the office as if wondering what he was doing here. His mind was clearly on other matters and I felt the weight in the room of some terrible responsibility.

Then the sheets of calculus returned and he was ready to talk about indecipherables.

He found that this part of the report was written for laymen and gave no indication of the techniques we used to break indecipherables. Nor did it explain how girls with no previous cipher experience and whose average age was twenty had been turned into a team of code-breakers. So would I cast my mind back to June '42, when SOE took over its traffic from C, and explain in detail what our techniques were, how the girls had been trained, and anything else that might be relevant to a subject which was new to him?

I dried up completely – not because I didn't want to discuss the only coding corner I could call my own but because by Bletchley's standards we had no techniques. The deep brown melter managed to provide a few statistics:

When I joined SOE in '42 approximately a quarter of all incoming messages were indecipherable due to careless coding or acute Morse mutilation. In July '42 I gave my first lecture on code-breaking, and in the following week the percentage of indecipherables broken by the Home Station rose from 3 per cent to 28 per cent, to 35 per cent the next week, then six weeks later to 62 per cent, then to 88 per cent, then rose to a peak of 92 per cent, and steadied itself at an average of 80 per cent: The number of indecipherables broken to date was 930, and the number of keys tried approximately 800,000.

The sheets of calculus awaited the techniques.

Since the subject was new to him (or so he said) I reminded him that if a message hadn't been broken by the time an agent's next schedule was due, the certain knowledge that he'd be ordered to repeat it forced us to use rudimentary methods designed to beat the clock.

'Regard me as the clock,' he said. 'What are the methods?'

I described the 'blanket attacks' of 1,000 keys at a time undertaken by successive shifts of coders, the anagramming based on a message's probable contents and the agent's language patterns, the analysis of the agent's previous mistakes both in training and in the field, and the tests for 'hatted columns', misnumbered code-keys and Morse mutilation of the indicator-groups.

'How did you teach this to them? I'd like the details, please.'

I described my first visit to Grendon when I'd written a coded message on the blackboard and shown the girls how enemy crypto-graphers would break it. I told him how eagerly they'd joined in until clear-text emerged: 'THERE SHALL BE NO SUCH THING AS AN INDECIPHERABLE MESSAGE', which had become their motto. They'd then helped me to reconstruct the poem on which the message had been based: 'BE NEAR ME WHEN MY LIGHT IS LOW', which I thought about whenever I briefed agents. I then poured out all the reasons why we had to change the face of agents' coding, and described SOE's resistance to anything new until the miracle of Nicholls, which resulted in today, and many tummy rumbles later (mine) I realized that I'd delivered a lecture without any idea of how long I'd been speaking, and hoped it was still February.

He was silent for a full minute after I'd finished. The sheets of calculus had gone but I couldn't read what had taken their place and waited to be told to go back to Bedford for a refresher course.

Instead he quietly asked if the charts he'd seen me using when he and Nick arrived had any connection with breaking indecipherables. I confirmed that they had. He at once asked me to explain how they worked.

I forgot that I was talking to Tiltman and began explaining how to read off the first line of a message as if the cryptographic supremo were a Grendon coder. When I tried to change style he shook his head impatiently, so I continued my exposition in FANY language. He waited for me to finish, then demanded to know who had devised these charts.

'You, sir.'

He looked at me in astonishment.

Since surprised bears need careful handling I hastily explained that the charts were only an extension of a method we'd been taught at Bedford called 'reading the heads of columns'.

'An extension, you say? I see! And how long ago did you extend it?'

I told him that the charts had been in use for roughly three weeks.

It was my turn to be astonished when he said he'd like me to demonstrate the charts on an unbroken indecipherable. When I most needed an indecipherable, there wasn't one in the office, even from the Free French! I wondered if he'd believe me.

I was rescued by my red-haired typing pool, Muriel, who quietly brought with her Skinnarland's latest indecipherable which the day squad had been unable to budge. She knew his traffic had absolute priority and hoped the colonel would forgive the interruption. The colonel not only forgave with a subaltern's smile but accepted her offer of a cup of tea. It was Heffer who'd told me that red was a professional soldier's favourite colour.

I realized what a poor host I'd been. Tiltman hadn't broken a code for several hours and might be suffering from withdrawal symptoms. I invited him to help us with this urgent indecipherable and perhaps he'd like to try the charts for himself. Less than ten seconds later the thinking man's teddy bear was sitting beside me waiting to be briefed.

193

I gave him a break-down of one of our most regular customers' coding habits, warning him that the villain always started his messages with five dummy letters, the only security rule he never forgot. I then kitted him out with charts and squared paper, and even pushed the WOK on one side to give him more room. He asked me to suggest the best line of attack and I gave him the list of keys waiting to be tried. He began work at once, numbering his transposition-keys in less time than it took Tommy and me to light our cigars. Wishing I had a camera because I certainly wouldn't believe this tomorrow, and doubted if I would tonight, I watched him demolishing the keys with astonishing agility. It took me a little while to realize that there was something not quite right about the way he was doing it. Although he was executing the four mandatory movements – number transposition-key, consult chart, select the letters it indicates, see if they make sense – his speed was the equivalent of a one-minute mile, and there could be only one explanation for it: the Tiltman method was to number the transposition-key, glance cursorily at the charts, *and calculate in his head which letters would appear in the first line of the message* – an awesome achievement even for a cryptographic supremo. This suspicion was confirmed when I 'accidentally' handed him the wrong chart and he still produced the right set of letters.

He seemed suddenly to realize that this was becoming a spectator sport, and pointed out the list of keys. 'Can't manage all of 'em.'

I took over the bottom half of the list and hobbled along behind him.

Skinnarland continued to defy the pair of us like the champ that he was until I suddenly noticed that there was neither sound nor movement coming from my left. I glanced up and found that our newest recruit was holding a sheet of squared paper towards me as proudly as any FANY with her first success.

Skinnarland's first line read: 'TGOHL [dummy letters] THE GERMANS ARE INCREAS—'*

I remembered that I wasn't supposed to let Tiltman see any of our traffic, nor could I read the clear-text to Wilson while he was still in the room. He seemed to be preoccupied with studying the charts, and

* The letters ING were the start of Skinnarland's next line.

194

I scrambled the right key to the Grendon supervisor, instructing her to teleprint the clear-text to London with absolute priority. I accepted her congratulations guiltily.

Giving me no chance to thank him, Tiltman asked if he could have a set of charts to take back to Bletchley, and if I'd calculated the last lines he'd like those as well. I handed him a spare set, which disappeared at once into his jewel-box, and promised him the last lines as soon as they were ready.

He was still sitting companionably beside me and I made the novice's mistake of basking in the moment. A sidesweep from the bear's paw took me completely off guard. 'Do you suspect that any agents are blown and sending their messages under duress?'

Hoping to learn from his timing, I said that I stood by what I'd written in the report. No reliance could be placed on the poem-code's security checks as they were little more than a gesture to give the agents confidence, or on the poem-code itself, and there was nothing I could add to this.

'But what about irregularities in their coding or their WT transmissions? Are you saying there haven't been any?'

I had to stop myself from showing him the file of an agent called Kergolay whom even SOE realized was blown. He'd gone into France in 1941, and was the first WT operator to send London an indecipherable.*

He was a Skinnarland-class coder and an equally inept operator, but in mid-'42 he began transmitting on another circuit's set and his coding and WT craftsmanship were suddenly transformed. No indecipherables, little or no Morse mutilation, scarcely any procedural irregularities. The whole of Signals – including Ozanne – was convinced that he was caught and so was Buckmaster, who was still keeping up the pretence of exchanging messages with him in a brilliant attempt to prolong his life. This was a rare example of country section and Signals directorate working as one.

What possible harm could there be in showing him the file? What use could C make of it?

---

* He transmitted it in December '41 and when I joined SOE in June '42 I broke it as a matter of interest.

But I knew that I wouldn't, and heard myself telling him that the best person to address his questions to was Nick.

He looked at me with such understanding that I knocked the thing I most believed in on to the floor.

He picked up the WOK and smiled. 'Excellent,' he said.

I was barely able to listen as he delivered his formal verdict on WOKs, which he referred to by their proper title, Worked-out Keys. As far as I could gather I'd made an important contribution to agents' coding ... *But none at all to Kergolay, Plan Giskes, or any of the other matters I should have discussed with him.*

He listed the WOK's assets, which far outweighed my own. It had the great merit of being a one-time code which agents could destroy message by message and could not possibly remember. It saved them the wearisome business of numbering transposition-keys, and would virtually end indecipherables as the indicators were proof against Morse mutilation. The number of letters passed in a WOK could safely be reduced to 100 and its security checks were high grade. However, he had two reservations, though they were not about the system itself. He had my full attention now.

He doubted whether shuffling counters by hand would produce transposition-keys which were truly random as the girls would inevitably grow bored or careless. It would be far safer if Bletchley produced the keys by machine and he would ask Commander Dudley-Smith, one of his principal assistants, to contact me to discuss the quantity of keys required.

His more important reservation concerned the destruction of the keys as soon as they'd been used. How would an agent do this in field conditions? He regretted that he had no suggestions to offer. I told him that I'd ask our Research Station to produce a specially sensitized silk which would make the keys easy to cut away and burn. I caught him looking at me with a specially sensitized face – a one-time expression which he quickly put away before his traffic could be read. But I had no difficulty in interpreting the tummy-rumbles (his) which suddenly filled the office, and realized that it was well past lunchtime.

He did as much justice to Mother's provisions as any three coders, and chatted about a visit he'd once made to 84. But over his last cream bun he said that there was something he'd been meaning to ask me.

I hadn't relaxed over lunch and was ready for anything – *absolutely* anything. Except for his question.

He wanted to know how I'd managed to avoid being sent to Bletchley.

I told him that I'd had no need to avoid it because the question had never arisen. Bedford had done everything possible to help me but I was a hopeless pupil and was glad to accept the first job offered. He said that if ever I wrote a paper about unteachable pupils he'd like to read it. And perhaps I'd be interested in visiting Bletchley? He had no need to ask twice, and told me to arrange it with his secretary. And when I did come, perhaps I'd bring the last lines of the charts with me?

He glanced at his watch, and said he must go. He held out his hand and repeated his invitation to visit Bletchley, though he couldn't provide me with this kind of lunch.

I wanted to thank him for the banquet which he'd given me, but a question popped out before I could even begin. 'Colonel Tiltman, sir, is there any reason why agents shouldn't use one-time pads?'

Colonel Tiltman sir didn't so much change colour as rank and I caught a glimpse of Lieutenant Tiltman as he must have looked to Lieutenant Nick. 'One-time pads, did you say? For agents?'

He quickly resumed his rank, which was peerless. 'You can discuss it with Commander Dudley-Smith when he comes here. Please thank your secretary for the tea.' He hurried away as rapidly as Nick had.

What was wrong with giving agents one-time pads?

Depression set in the moment he left, and I was alone again with my own flashy talent.

Although he'd praised WOKs, I'd lacked the courage to disobey orders and discuss the Dutch traffic with him. He'd know better than anyone if Plan Giskes would work.

I felt like a rat who'd produced an anti-toxin. It was the kind of loneliness that made school days seem companionable.

There was only one thing I could do about it, though I never thought I'd need to. I asked to be put through to the Signals Office with top priority, and told the menaces that it was time to come home.

TWENTY-ONE

Repercussions

A stickler for established procedure, especially when it was he who'd established it, Sir Charles Hambro never communicated with the lower orders except through the heads of their directorates. But the morning after Tiltman's visit he sent a personal message 'from CD to the coders of Grendon' congratulating them on breaking over 900 indecipherables, urging them to maintain their great efforts, and assuring them that a new code called Works (sic) would make their task much easier. He also undertook to visit the station shortly to congratulate them in person.

The testimonial remained on the Grendon notice board until an anonymous FANY spelled out in capital letters the four-letter word which she believed the C of CD stood for.

It was typical of Tiltman to have put in a word for the low levels when dealing with the highest, and although Nick wouldn't disclose what else he'd told CD after he'd left me, its repercussions were immediate. I was transformed overnight from WOK-pedlar into licensed code-maker, with authority to recruit six WOK-makers, six WOK-briefers, and the staff of the Thatched Barn to do the camouflage. I also had authority to launch Plan Giskes.

My licence to be a trap-setter hadn't come from SOE but from an authority with wider terms of reference: my own free mind. Now that Tiltman was SOE's adviser, I need no longer worry about the future of agents' codes if Plan Giskes cost me my job.

But I was beginning to run out of excuses for visiting the Signals Office in case the Dutch section cancelled a message to the field and I wasn't on hand to make improper use of it.

*   *   *

To briefing offices, every agent was a problem. But Francis Cammaerts was a problem agent. Officially I knew nothing about him. Nothing, that is, except for the few mandatory details every country section supplied with a 'body for briefing'.

He was a Buckmaster agent, would be known in the field as Roger, and was due to go into France in the March moon. Further information would be irrelevant to the teaching of double-transposition. If it hadn't been for the grapevine operated by the Brotherhood of Briefing Officers I would never have known about Francis Cammaerts's extraordinary past which set him apart from any agent in our combined experience.

None of us quite understood what he was doing in SOE. He was an ardent pacifist who refused to join the armed forces as all human life was sacrosanct, and it was wrong to take it under any circumstances. He registered as a conscientious objector and was summoned to appear before the tribunal set up to judge the sincerity of 'conchies'. After cross-examining him about his principles, the tribunal ordered him to take up agricultural work for the duration of the war. After a year as a farm labourer he volunteered to be dropped behind enemy lines. Some thought it was the death of his brother in the RAF which had convulsed his thinking, others that he was sickened by what he'd read about Nazi atrocities. Whatever the truth of it, he'd convinced Selwyn Jepson, SOE's chief head-hunter, and Maurice Buckmaster, a tribunal of one, that he was an excellent prospect as both saboteur and organizer, and they'd recruited him into SOE.

The Brotherhood of Briefing Officers (BOBO for short) unanimously disagreed with his acceptance. Although they reluctantly conceded that he was highly intelligent, in the opinion of the BOBO he had no flair for sabotage or leadership, and was in conflict about reversing his attitudes. The kindest comments about him came (as they so often did) from his coding instructor at Beaulieu, who said in his report that he was 'a plodder who does his best to follow instructions but seems unable to grasp the basic principles'. A schoolmaster by profession, and apparently a gifted one, he'd proved a problem pupil on every course he'd so far attended.

Reluctant to leave my desk in case N section cancelled a message to the field, I resolved to spend as little time briefing Cammaerts as

I conscientiously could. There would be ample time between now and March to re-brief him if I made the plodding progress I anticipated.

I was quite unprepared for his physical impact. Buckmaster had cornered the market in giant agents, and this one dwarfed even Rabinovitch, whose Orchard Court chair he was straddling with equal discomfort.

There was nothing plodding about his eyes as they assessed the merits of his briefing officer. Nothing plodding about the way he wrote out the text of the message he was about to encode. It was when he started to encode it that he began living up to his reputation.

He paused after every five letters as if counting heads in a classroom. Eventually satisfied that all were present and correct, he appeared to form the letters into a crocodile, which he led in slow procession across the courtyard of his paper. There was another pause while he took a roll-call. And yet another while he seemed to rebuke some letters he'd caught pulling faces at each other. And that was only the first transposition.

By the time he'd reached the second I could have strolled to the nearest church, said a prayer for Tiltman's preservation, and waited for an official acknowledgement. Instead I glanced at his code-card.

His poem was in French, and I remembered that his uncle was a famous Belgian poet. If he'd chosen one of his, I hoped he'd do justice to it.

The BOBO's explanation that Cammaerts was a plodder wouldn't help me to unplod him. Yet the longer I watched him at work, the more I began to suspect that he wasn't plodding at all. I asked him to stop encoding for a moment. I was going to take a gamble with Cammaerts which might bring him to a permanent standstill.

I showed him the mathematics of double-transposition.

If I'd been teaching him to drive (which God forbid, for both our sakes) I'd have assessed him as someone who needed to understand the mechanics of his car because he suspected that it wasn't roadworthy, and that he'd have to be his own breakdown service on this particular journey.

Feeling like a spiritual AA, I did my best not to talk down to him. Sensing that maths wasn't his subject (it turned out to be history), I explained as simply as I could what happened to the letters as they were shuffled through their 'cages', and showed him the relationship between the code-groups when the transposition was complete. His questions showed that he'd understood every word of it, and I didn't lose him at all until I forgot that I wasn't trying to turn him into a cryptographer.

As if to confirm that he'd seen enough, the man with a need to know resumed his encoding. He didn't spurt or do anything spectacular but cruised towards the traffic lights, waited till they changed, and proceeded quietly and steadily to pass his driving test.

There was a lesson in all this. The more intelligent the agent, the less likely he was to respond if he were taught the mechanics of coding mechanically.

I'd been slow to realize that what Cammaerts had really been doing was coding with character, testing the logic of it all, trying to satisfy himself that these alien procedures were soundly based, taking nothing and no one for granted, least of all his various instructors.

It was going to need a special calibre of WOK-briefer to deal with agents like this one. I couldn't recruit FANYs for their looks alone. I decided to be selfish and show him a WOK myself. There would be plenty of time between now and March to make sure that he understood the thinking behind it.

I realized that he was asking me a question. He wanted to know if maths were my subject, and I told him that I didn't have one.

He looked hard at me and smiled.

It may have been the quality of that smile or the penetration of that look, but I found myself feeling very sorry for anyone who made the mistake of writing this man off.

Unless he happened to be German.

On 15 February I had a better excuse than usual for visiting the Signals Office. The night squad had broken an indecipherable from Rabinovitch after 1,500 attempts, and I wanted to teleprint my congratulations.

Bingham of the Dutch section slithered towards me and asked if we could have a quick word, though we rarely had any other kind. He was a verbal weight-watcher. He said that he wanted to cancel a message to Holland but didn't know the new procedure. Who should he talk to?

It took me a moment to realize what he'd said. *He wanted to cancel a message to Holland*. It was the first time I'd been tempted to kiss a fox.

I told him that he was talking to the right person, and that I'd be delighted to cancel it for him. He said that it was message number 60 to Boni, and thanked me for my help as he had a meeting in five minutes. Lowering his lisp, he added that if it was too late to cancel the message, it wouldn't really matter as he was sending a message to Boni tomorrow changing his instructions. He thanked me again and hurried off to keep his appointment.

I hurried into the supervisor to keep mine with Giskes.

Number 60 to Boni was on top of a pile of messages waiting to be teleprinted to Grendon. I told the supervisor that there was a query on it which the country section wanted to discuss with me, and that if she'd give me her copy I'd return it as soon as I could. She handed it over at once.

An empty office. A cancelled message. A panic attack.

The entire concept could be wrong.

I picked up the receiver to speak to Tiltman. It put itself back.

I wished I knew what moral courage was, but it was too late to ask Cammaerts to define it, though those who have it seldom can. I remembered his smile, picked up my pen, and with an unsteady hand prepared the cancelled message for transmission to the field.

Plan Giskes had begun.

TWENTY-TWO

The Launching of Plan Giskes

Locked in my desk in readiness for this moment were brief notes on the background and performance of every Dutch agent, and a detailed blueprint of Plan Giskes.

At arm's length with the plan at last, I reviewed the elements likeliest to determine its outcome:

1 Boni's record (no detail could be considered irrelevant)
2 The message to be sent to him
3 The concept itself.

Boni's Record

Boni (formerly known as Spinach; real name Cornelis Buizer) was dropped near Assen on 23 June 1942 with his organizer Parsnip. He had been transmitting regularly ever since and had become one of the busiest operators in Holland, handling not only Parsnip's traffic but that of Potato and other key members of the Parsnip/Cabbage organization.

A radio operator in peacetime, his 'touch' at the keyboard and knowledge of wireless procedures made him, in the words of a Grendon signalmaster, 'as good if not better than anyone here'. His coding was equally efficient and his security checks were invariably correct, though he had twice omitted them.

The volume of traffic which other agents entrusted to him allowed him to straddle most of the bizarre events which had taken place in Holland in the past six months.

It was Boni who had been at the heart of the traffic snarl-up between

London and Holland which lasted from 3 August to 12 November last year.

It was Boni who suggested that all Parsnip's traffic should be in his (Boni's) code. He subsequently made the same suggestion for all Potato's traffic. N section acceded to both requests, Ozanne refusing to intervene.

It was Boni who claimed that two key messages from London to Potato had been indecipherable. These messages had been checked and rechecked and had been perfectly encoded. Nor had there been any atmospheric problems which might have caused Morse mutilation to the indicator-groups. It was far likelier that the Germans had been unable to answer London's questions satisfactorily and had been playing for time.

The Cancelled Message

Message number 60 to Boni of 15 February was in reply to his number 58 of the 9th, in which he'd confirmed that a reception committee would be standing by for Broadbean and Golf. He'd also stated that he would run completely out of funds within the next two months and asked London to send money urgently. He'd added that he was recruiting new agents for the Parsnip/Cabbage organization.

The message which Bingham wanted to cancel promised Boni that 10,000 florins would be dispatched with Broadbean and Golf, and confirmed that the reception committee should stand by for a dropping operation on the 16th. It also confirmed the arrangement of the lights, and asked for details of the new recruits he was enlisting. It ended with a sentence in Dutch which I took to be a message to be broadcast over Radio Oranje or a password to be used in the field.

This was an excellent message for the purpose of Plan Giskes. It was long (over 300 letters), had substance and, above all, called for a reply. The nature of that reply would determine whether Boni, and the agents for whom he operated, were in enemy hands.

The trap was basically so simple that its best chance of success lay in the Germans not believing that it could have been devised by simpletons.

204

The Concept

I intended to send Boni an indecipherable message which he could not possibly decode without the help of a cryptographer.

But it would be no ordinary indecipherable. These can sometimes be broken by luck. This indecipherable would be encoded in such a way that if Boni replied to it other than by stating that it was indecipherable then an expert must have helped him to unscramble it. And that expert had to be German.

The incentives for the German to reply to it were very great indeed (and will be dealt with under 'possible German reactions').

But there was one imponderable factor which was more important than any of these. What if Boni were NOT in enemy hands?

However remote the possibility, it had to be catered for.

Special Precautions

If Boni were free but couldn't decode his instructions an entire operation could be jeopardized.

But if Boni couldn't decipher a message that he wasn't supposed to receive anyway because its contents were obsolete, no harm would have been done to him apart from the tedium of trying to decode it. That was why I'd delayed Plan Giskes until the Dutch cancelled a message to the field.

And if he made the mistake of replying to it, he'd tell us what we needed to know.

Method of Encoding

Boni's poem was:

> I sometimes wish
> I was a fish
> A-swimming in the sea
> A starling on a chimney pot

205

A blackbird on a tree
Or anyone but me.

I chose five words and numbered the letters sequentially, wishing I had the dexterity of the Grendon coders:

```
T   R   E   E   C   H   I   M   N   E   Y   F   I   S   H   W   A   S   S   E   A
19. 15. 4.  5.  3.  9.  11. 13. 14. 6.  21. 8.  12. 16. 10. 20. 1.  17. 18. 7.  2.
```

I began by encoding the message in the normal way but deliberately misspelt several words of the text to give the impression it was the work of a tired and careless coder.

Then came the point of no return. I transposed two columns in the wrong order – a favourite pastime of Peter Churchill's (known in the trade as 'hatting').

The effect of 'hatting' was to throw the letters out of alignment so that some of the clear-text would read normally, and the rest (to the untrained eye) would be gibberish. A cryptographer could tell at a glance what had happened and would calculate how to 'unhat' the columns to bring the letters into proper alignment – a process which would tax his patience more than his mathematics. But agents like Peter Churchill also 'hatted' columns in the *second* transposition.

A double dose of 'hatting' would be an altogether different matter. It would throw the letters much further out of alignment and make the cryptographer's task at least twice as onerous. This posed a (to me) unanswerable problem:

Swamped by important military traffic, how much time could the Germans devote to unravelling dropped stitches in an agent's message? What priority did they give to SOE's traffic?

These were the questions I'd wanted to ask Tiltman. Without his guidance, I took no chances on the Germans being overloaded and encoded the second transposition normally. It was essential that they didn't take long to unravel 'London's mistake', but possession of Boni's poem would cut the time by half, and after a few 'Gott in Himmels' they'd be certain to spot some key-words amongst the surrounding gibberish:

FLORINS would appear as FLOR with INS in the line beneath it.

THOUSAND would appear as THO with USA and ND in the same line.

MESSAGE (a word which all cryptographers looked for) would appear as MGE with ESSA in the line above it.

A few nudges later and the rest of the message would fall into place for them.

Problem Areas

At this late stage the only one worth a final ponder was Giskes's reactions to an indecipherable from London.

He'd pretended that two of our messages to Potato were indecipherable. When confronted by a genuine one, why wouldn't he tell us that it was indecipherable instead of attempting to reply to it?

Because he was playing for time with Potato. But time was against him now. With a dropping operation one night away – with agents, florins, containers, the lot, about to descend on him – why should he risk causing even a few hours' delay by asking London to repeat a message when he already knew its contents?

I was convinced that we had everything to gain and nothing to lose by trying to catch Giskes in an off moment.

It was time to find out.

Praying that Bingham wouldn't suddenly appear, I handed message number 60 to the Signals Office supervisor, and told her that I'd encoded it myself to save time. I then instructed her to teleprint it to Grendon with top priority in time for Boni's next sked.

As I hurried back to my office, my spine began tingling. Why did I have a feeling in the mind of my back that somewhere in all this I'd made a mistake?

It wasn't until I received a panic-stricken call from the supervisor of the Grendon night shift that I realized what was wrong.

The coders had discovered that the message to Boni was indecipherable. Knowing that I'd encoded it, they hadn't checked it until it had already been transmitted. I'd forgotten my standing instruction that all messages to the field must be double-checked and initialled by the supervisor.

I assured her that no harm had been done because message 60 had just been cancelled, and its replacement would be sent on Boni's next sked.

She asked if she should notify the Dutch section, which was the last thing I wanted, and I undertook to contact N section immediately and accept full responsibility.

An idea then occurred for turning the mistake to advantage, a prerequisite for survival in SOE. If I could tell the sceptics in SOE that a squad of coders had made a blanket attack on the indecipherable and failed to break it, they could hardly maintain (as some undoubtedly would) that Boni could have decoded it himself.

I informed the remorseful supervisor that I'd carefully checked my encoding and thought the mistake was in the teleprinting. To prevent this happening again I'd like the night squad to do their best to break it so that we could determine whose fault it was. I added that I was very anxious to know the result, and that if the girls hadn't broken it by the time I left the office I'd be grateful if she'd telephone me at home, no matter how late it was.

She promised that the night squad would start a blanket attack at once.

I waited another hour, and then went home.

Boni stretched out a hand which had only one finger on it and screamed into my face, 'What have you done to me, what have you done to me?'

It was Mother trying to awaken me at six in the morning. She'd had a message from some girl whom she'd refused to put through to me. The message was to tell Mr Leo Marks that she and her friends couldn't do it.

Mother demanded to know what it was that she and her friends couldn't do that I had to be told about at six in the morning.

'Their duty,' I said.

Boni was still screaming when I tried to do justice to her black-market breakfast.

TWENTY-THREE

Special Devices

On the morning of 16 February there was a sound rarely heard in the code department – a sigh of relief – when a car called to take me to the Thatched Barn at Barnet. I'd forgotten that I was to spend the whole day with its commanding officer, Colonel Elder Wills.

Boni's next sked would be over by the time I returned.

The Thatched Barn was a famous inn on the Barnet bypass which Wills had skilfully converted into a camouflage and special devices station. The gifted colonel had offered me a conducted tour of his bizarre establishment not because he wanted to meet me but because he'd been offered a contra-account he couldn't resist: a conducted tour by Nick of an equally inaccessible workshop, the wireless station at Grendon.

It was my job to persuade him to give absolute priority to the camouflaging of WOKs.

I stood at a respectful distance as he proudly displayed a huge assortment of horse manure, camel dung, and mule, cow and elephant droppings, which had been delivered to him by the London Zoo at the personal request of Sir Charles Hambro.

It was a huge dollop of 'merde alors' for Wills that Hambro was not only a friend of Churchill's, *and* the youngest director yet appointed by the Bank of England, *and* a former chairman of Great Western Railways, but was also a fellow of the Royal Zoological Society, and it was in this capacity that he'd persuaded the head of the zoo that his waste product could make a valuable contribution to the war effort.

I thought at first that this exotic collection of excreta was a present for C but he gleefully explained that it was in the process of being

209

reproduced in plastic, and would then be hand-painted and filled with explosives. The horse manure was destined for Western and Northern Europe, the camel dung for North Africa, and the mule, cow and elephant droppings for the Far East. Once trodden on or driven over (hopefully by the enemy) the whole lot would go off with a series of explosions even more violent than the ones which had produced it.

Amongst Wills's more civilized creations were milk bottles which exploded when the caps were removed, fountain pens guaranteed to write off whoever unscrewed them, and loaves of bread it would be unwise to regard as the staff of life. He had a stock of cigarettes guaranteed to cure people of smoking as they were packed with incendiary and explosive materials, and they'd done no good at all to German stores, fuel tanks and armament dumps in France, Belgium, Holland and Norway. He also had on offer a variety of nuts and bolts which had been hollowed out and filled with explosives; these he warmly recommended for railway engines and shunting yards.

Since agents often hid their WT sets in lavatory cisterns, he'd devised a lavatory chain which could act as an aerial. He also had a stock of lethal toilet paper which he hadn't yet issued because he couldn't be sure it would be used by the right behinds.

He took me into a shed which was packed with innocuous-looking suitcases specially made for carrying WT sets. Each suitcase had been artificially aged and designed to fit into the territory in which it would be used. Every suitcase was equipped with secret compartments and a false bottom.

Agents' clothing was the only problem which had come close to defeating him. He had to reproduce continental tailoring and stitching, which was very distinctive and varied greatly from territory to territory. He'd finally recruited a Jewish tailor, a refugee from Austria, who'd visited synagogues all round the country to borrow old clothes and labels from his fellow refugees. These labels were reproduced in Wills's workshop and sewn into the clothes, which the tailor had copied and which Wills had carefully aged. Boots and shoes (also carefully aged) were provided by a firm in Northampton, and Wills added sliding heels to them to provide cavities for microfilms and other small objects. In fact, everything in sight was 'suitably aged' but me.

I found myself thinking about the ageing process, an undignified business which both sides in the war were doing their best to spare us:

> When your words
> Become distant relatives
> Who seldom visit you
> When all dates are one
> And all times the same
> And what you put down
> You can no longer pick up
> Remember that you
> Now helpless
> Who used to be a fighter
> Make fools
> Feel brighter.

Another one for the ditty-box perhaps?

Keeping the best till the last like the Supersalesman that he was, Wills took me into the 'special documents' department where most of the forgeries were done, and showed me what he'd provided for the Golf team.

They were to be issued with forged Dutch, Belgian and French identity cards, frontier passes, dyes for forging German passes, rubber stamps with Swastikas on them, and everything else that would be needed to guide Jambroes through France and Belgium to the Spanish escape-line. Some of the printing had been done by Professor Newitt of the Imperial College of Science where Wills had his own office. He also had the use of a workshop in the Natural History Museum – where Julian Huxley was his technical advisor on urgent problems such as the reproduction of excreta.

Glancing at his watch, which concealed god knows what, he finally asked what he could do for the agents' code department.

I had to be careful how I answered him. I'd been warned by Joan Dodd, who knew him well, that he had a propensity for taking instant

---

* *Subsequently included in a batch of microfilmed poems sent to Jugoslavia.*

dislikes to people, and that his receptivity was an excellent example of his own camouflage. She'd also told me that he used to be an art director at Elstree Studios, that he'd graduated to making films (including *Song of Freedom* with Paul Robeson), and that his present production at the Thatched Barn was running well over budget. To get the best out of Wills, he had to be confronted by a major challenge, and there weren't many which were new to him.

Wishing I could sing like Paul Robeson, I began the *Song of the WOK* by stressing that agents would resist carrying them because of the number of random street searches. The decisive factor would be the quality of the camouflage.

Clearly disappointed that he couldn't see a problem, he said that silk codes could easily be camouflaged in toothpaste tubes with special compartments, in shoelaces with soft tubes inside, and in an infinite number of conventional objects which would certainly stand up to random street searches, and might even be safe under close examination.

Having disposed of the WOK problem, he picked up two lumps of coal which were packed with high explosives and began to describe their glowing future. WOK were obviously just another job to him.

Determined to raise their status, I shot some questions at him: Could code-keys be invisibly printed? – on handkerchiefs perhaps? How could agents read them? – and when they'd used them, how could they erase them? They couldn't cut them away and walk around with their handkerchiefs in tatters!

In his excitement he dropped both lumps of coal, and I said goodbye to my parents.

But they must have been defective (the coals, not my parents) because the only explosion came from Wills himself: 'Y-E-S! – *we can do it*.'

Of course it was practical for WOKs to be invisibly printed! And of course the agents could read them. He'd invented a new invisible ink which could be detected only when exposed to infra-red lighting. All the agent needed to do was switch on a torch with infra-red discs inside it and he could read the WOK-keys without difficulty. Nor did the torches need to be camouflaged. Everyone in occupied Europe carried one to cope with the black-out.

My suggestion about handkerchiefs was good but there were other possibilities. WOKs could be invisibly printed on men's shirt-tails and pants and on women's knickers and petticoats. As for erasing each key chemically, it was a fascinating problem and would have his immediate attention.

The Tiltman of camouflage now galvanized everyone within earshot at his Barnet Bletchley. WOKs could be microfilmed and carried in tiny containers which could be hidden in various parts of the body such as the navel or rectum. A matchstick could accommodate 200 WOK-keys. It would be hidden in an ordinary box of matches and the agent could identify it by a tiny indentation which only he knew about. As for reading the microfilm, he was working on a small powerful microscope with detachable parts which could easily be assembled and which would be no problem to camouflage.

He then began a long technical discussion with his assistants, many of whom he'd recruited from Elstree Studios.

They rapidly lost me. Nor was I any longer necessary. I was a little disturbed about codes being concealed in the rectum, and intended to be missing when the coders of Grendon announced: 'We have received our first indecipherable due to anal interference beyond the agent's control.'

But everything else I'd heard and seen had removed my last anxiety about the future of silk codes. If Wills could devise a lavatory chain which acted as an aerial, he was capable of camouflaging anything. He might even be able to return me to Baker Street camouflaged as an adult.

I decided to leave before he had the chance.

TWENTY-FOUR

Judgement Day

There were only three things which SOE's agents could anticipate with confidence. That their parachutes would open, that their L-tablets would kill them, and that their messages from London would be accurately encoded.

The Signals directorate could be sure of only one thing. That any WT operator who received a message which he couldn't decipher would ask the Home Station to 'check and repeat' it at his next sked. This elementary procedure was a fundamental act of self-preservation, and as reflex to an operator of Boni's calibre as switching on his set.

His indecipherable had been transmitted to him on 15 February, and he'd acknowledged receipt of it by sending AK/R in Morse. He'd also acknowledged receipt of Bingham's new number 60, which amplified several parts of his (as he believed) cancelled text.

That was twenty-four hours ago, and from his next sked onwards it was essential to play the devil's (Giskes's) advocate and assume that Boni was free until his responses proved otherwise.

On 16 February London and Boni exchanged messages. London's message (number 16) informed Boni of a change of plan. The money he'd asked for would not be delivered to him by the Golf team but by the two other agents (Tennis and Hockey), who were waiting to be dropped. The message confirmed that a stores operation would take place that night.

Boni's message (number 59) broke new ground. It contained an urgent request from Koos Vorrink (code-named Victory). Vorrink wanted the BBC to broadcast messages twice daily warning Dutchmen against a Gestapo agent named Johnny, who claimed to have arrived from London with important instructions from the Dutch government. The message ended with a short account of Mik's (Cabbage's) recruiting activities in The Hague and Leiden.

This was Boni's first chance to report that he'd received an indecipherable from London, but it wasn't necessarily significant that he hadn't. He could easily have encoded his number 59 before receiving the message he couldn't decipher. He must be given the benefit of such doubt as there was.

On the 17th Boni missed a sked. He'd missed remarkably few (eight in all) since he'd begun transmitting in June of last year, but missing this one wasn't necessarily significant. Circumstances didn't always permit WT operators to be at their sets when their signal-plans demanded it, and their surest way of keeping their inflexible schedules was to be in enemy hands.

Yet it was now forty-eight hours since he'd received the indecipherable. He couldn't know that it was a cancelled message any more than he could know what instructions it contained, and if he didn't ask for it to be 'checked and repeated' at his next sked Plan Giskes would have to be disclosed to SOE at once.

He had a second sked on the 17th, and this one he kept.

London's 62 was transmitted to him. It asked for a detailed description of Johnny (the Gestapo agent) and promised that Vorrinck's request for warnings to be broadcast was being taken up immediately with the authorities concerned. The message ended with further questions about new recruits.

Boni acknowledged receipt of the message. He then transmitted 'QR/U', which signified that *he had no traffic of his own to pass*.

To me, this was the most significant message he had ever passed but SOE didn't respond well to negative inferences and I decided to wait for one more sked in case he referred to the indecipherable. Perhaps it was taking the Germans longer to break than I'd thought.

On the 18th Boni transmitted his 60th message. In it he confirmed that the first batch of containers had been successfully dropped, and that he was waiting for the rest, together with the agents and the 10,000 florins. He also confirmed that London's messages had been received and understood and passed on to Victory and Cabbage, and that he would send further details about Johnny. He would also send information about the new recruits.

He didn't once refer to the indecipherable, and there was even a phrase in the message which made me wonder if he were trying to tell us he was caught. It went all the way back to his days as a trainee operator.

Although it was appalling security, when Boni was at training school (spring '42) all agents were instructed to use stock phrases like 'Your message received and understood'. Boni had used this particular phrase only three times in the whole of his traffic. Was it coincidence that he was using it now? How could he (the most experienced operator in the field) say to London, 'Your messages received and understood' when he'd had one for three days which was completely indecipherable?

I now realized that his missed sked was not insignificant. Nor were the gaps in his traffic. They were examples of Giskes's timing. He'd waited until the first part of the stores operation was complete, and the containers safely in his hands, before replying to London's messages.

And with four more agents, six more containers and 10,000 florins yet to come, he had nothing to gain and invaluable time to lose if he asked the amateurs he was playing with to 'check and repeat' an indecipherable message they were clearly unaware of sending.

But his contempt for London (though justified) left me in no doubt whatever that Boni was caught.

And who else? What about Parsnip, Cabbage and Potato – and other agents whose traffic he handled?

What about Ebenezer and his gallant attempts to stip, step and stap?

What about the links these agents had with the Committee of Liberation? And the Secret Army? And Jambroes himself? How complete was Giskes's victory? Surely to God not total?

Balanced minds must decide the next step.

'Christ,' exploded Heffer when I owned up to Plan Giskes. 'Now you've done it.'

He accompanied me to Nick's office and stood beside me while I tried to prove that Giskes was head of N section.

Nick listened to me with his eyes half closed, then glanced despairingly at Heffer, and examined the indecipherable like a coroner with a putrescent corpse. A few moments later he put it in his briefcase, and rose abruptly from the desk.

Ignoring me completely, he hurried to the door, addressing Heffer over his shoulder. 'See that he stays in his office. And stay there with him till I get back.'

The Guru and I had the office to ourselves.

He refused to discuss Boni's traffic. His immediate concern was the harm I had done to the Signals directorate.

With a final puff of his cigarette, and probably of me, he said that Nick was about to be appointed head of Signals, that he'd spoken highly of me to CD and Gubbins, and that my unauthorized actions would reflect on his judgement in the worst possible way. They might even result in Ozanne continuing in office, which would be the greatest disservice anyone could render SOE

I tried to assure him that I would take full responsibility but he shook his head. My conduct would still cast doubts on Nick's judgement of people.

And on his. He had been my greatest supporter till now.

Stubbing out his cigarette as if it were an errant coding officer, he warned me that when Gubbins returned from North Africa (he'd been away since 21 January) my unauthorized action would be reported to him. He also warned me that if there were any other irregularities I ought to own up to, now was the time to do so. It would be fatal to let Gubbins discover them for himself. Did Heffer suspect what I'd been doing with de Gaulle's secret code? I'd sometimes wondered.

Nick hurried back without saying where he'd been and proceeded to prove the Guru's prescience. My report on Plan Giskes would be shown to Gubbins when he returned in March and the General would decide what action – if any – was called for. In the meantime, under no circumstances must I discuss Plan Giskes with N section or with anyone else in SOE. If the country sections found out that their traffic had been tampered with by someone in Signals, they'd lose confidence in the whole damn lot of us. Was this clear?

'Yes, sir.'

It was even clearer that he and Heffer had lost it in me.

217

TWENTY-FIVE

Permission to Proceed?

By the end of February, SOE's bid to convince the Chiefs of Staff and other sceptics of its D-day potential had been launched with last-chance urgency.

The six Gunnersides had dropped into Norway; Passy and Tommy had landed in France; and for those who believed the collected works of Herr Giskes (otherwise known as the Dutch traffic) the Golf team had arrived safely in Holland, and were staying with their reception committee. I was still waiting to hear when Tiltman's assistant was arriving from Bletchley to discuss the production of WOKs but I now had another reason for wanting to see him. I was determined to introduce one-time pads for agents' traffic but couldn't do so without Bletchley's help.

Although Tiltman had pronounced WOKs 'an excellent system as the keys could be destroyed after every message', they had two drawbacks. They obliged agents in the field to use double-transposition, a cumbersome process in any conditions, and for security reasons every WOK message had to contain at least 100 letters, which was often far more than the agents needed to send.

But one-time pads were unbreakable even by Bletchley, and if they were issued to agents their traffic would have a diplomatic level of security, which was what it deserved. They could send as few as ten letters and get off the air, and I wanted them to keep their WOKs in reserve, and have poems in their heads in case they lost their silks or couldn't get to them in time.

But there was one obstacle in this cipher Utopia, and I was counting on the Bletchley expert to help me surmount it. In its present form, one-time pad traffic was passed entirely in figures, which would increase the dangers of clandestine communication.

The one-time pad (which had been invented by the Germans in the First World War, and adopted by all those with anything worth hiding) required the use of a code-book with figures printed opposite every phrase.

The coder looked up the requisite phrases, copied out the figures beside them, and wrote them underneath the figures of a one-time pad. The two groups were then added together *without* carrying the tens:

one-time pad:	8209
code-book:	0796
	8995

'8995' would be followed by the rest of the message, which would remain unbreakable for as many years.

But it would be a very different matter if agents tried to use the same procedure. Figures took longer to transmit than letters, and would lengthen their skeds (every figure consisted of five dots or dashes instead of the one dot or dash to a maximum of four dots or dashes, which letters required). Figure traffic would also increase the likelihood of mistakes in transmission and (most serious of all) would stand out from the rest of the clandestine traffic in the occupied territories.

There must be a way of adapting the principle by substituting letters for figures and abandoning the code-books. But what was it?

I decided I had nothing to lose but sanity by trying to find out.

Seventy-two hours later I was no closer to the solution.

A batch of telegrams from Stockholm in main-line cipher made the long nights bearable.

On 16 February the six Gunnersides marched across the Hardanger mountains, and on 23 February linked up with the four starving frost-bitten Grouse (now code-named Swallow).

They decided to attack the heavy-water plant wearing British battle-dress so that in the event of capture they had the right under the

Geneva Conventions to be treated as soldiers. Each man agreed to take his L-tablet if capture seemed inevitable.

Carrying heavy explosives, they reached Rjukan, which was heavily patrolled by SS reinforcements, and at thirty minutes past midnight launched their attack. Less than an hour later the plant was virtually demolished.* Even more incredibly, the ten agents suffered no casualties.

Poulson, Helberg, Strømsheim, Storhaus and Idland made their way to the frontier and crossed into Sweden, still wearing British battle-dress. Knut Haugland, Haukelid and Kjelstrup stayed in Hardanger to monitor the damage and were joined there by Einar Skinnarland.

His file of indecipherables was just about ready for its second volume, and he more than anyone would benefit from a simple system such as a one-time pad consisting entirely of letters.

If only for his sake, I tried once again to find the formula. 5,000 attempts later I was still looking for it.

---

* It took the Germans six months to restore the plant to even partial capacity.

TWENTY-SIX

Court Martial

By the beginning of March, SOE was still operating without an official directive, and every department seemed to be holding its breath in case it was its last. While C pushed ahead in all directions, we were dress-rehearsing for a show which couldn't find backers.

I was luckier than most because I had one pleasurable experience. I was given the opportunity to service the Danes, if providing them with poem-codes could be considered a service.

I was asked by Hollingsworth to brief nine agents, including the new head of the Danish Resistance.

The Danish traffic made clear (and Stockholm's messages confirmed) that a new organization had been formed in Denmark. Its code-name was Table, and Mogens Hammer (the present head of Danish Resistance) was now called Table Top and his chief of Communications (Duus Hansen) was now Table Napkin. Hammer was unaware that he was about to be replaced by Flemming Muus, who would be known as Table Talk.

In the first week of March I gave a final code-briefing to Muus, Table Salt, Pepper, Mustard and five other condiments.

The new head of Danish Resistance was a large and exceedingly jovial zealot with the knowing eyes and infectious self-confidence of a stand-up comedian booked to play Hamlet in his home town. He and his supporting cast of eight were to be dropped into Denmark on 12 March.

I also inflicted poem-codes on three Dutch agents – Peter Dourlein, Peter Arendse and Peter Bogaart, who were code-named Sprout, Seakale and Kohlrabi respectively. The three Peters were dropped into Holland on 9 March. I regarded their chances of survival as nil as Boni had arranged their reception committee.

221

On 10 March Heffer warned me that Gubbins was back in his office, and that to help him evaluate the results of Plan Giskes Nick had given him the report on the absence of Dutch indecipherables which I'd written in January. He added that Gubbins would be far too busy to see me in the day, and that I must stand by for a late call during the next few nights.

Realizing that my stay in SOE might soon be coming to an end, I renewed my attempts to devise a letter one-time pad but with no more success than before, and it was a relief when I received a phone call from Nick well after midnight instructing me to report to the General's office at once.

Six months ago a novice night duty officer and an armed lance corporal, who was supposed to be his escort, had patrolled the whole of Michael House searching for scraps of paper, enemy agents and each other.

Was it really only six months since that evening of havoc when I'd knocked on the general's door to enquire if I should inspect his credentials?

His terse '*come!*' hadn't changed.

Nick was seated to his left and avoided looking at me, but the general's scrutiny more than made up for it.

Pointing to a chair Gubbins then immersed himself in my Dutch report, and within a minute had reached the third of its closely packed pages. Colin Gubbins was a closely packed man.

Described by Tommy as 'a real Highland toughie, bloody brilliant, should be the next CD', he was short enough to make me feel average, with a moustache which was as clipped as his delivery and eyes which didn't mirror his soul or any other such trivia. The general's eyes reflected the crossed swords on his shoulders, warning all comers not to cross them with him. It was a shock to realize that they were focused on me.

'What's this word?' he demanded, pointing at a scribbled annotation.

' "Bollocks", sir.' It was a reference to Boni's claim that London had sent indecipherables to Potato.

He turned the page in silence.

At his rate of reading he'd soon reach another annotation – 'Is this

222

bit too technical for some of the pricks who may have to read it?'

From the sudden anger on his face I thought that he might already have reached it. He turned sharply to Nick. 'This breakdown of communication between Signals and N section when, according to Marks, the wrong codes were used. I want to know who was responsible. A full report.'

Nick nodded eagerly as if glad to be of use.

The Mighty Atom resumed his reading but stopped suddenly in the middle of a page and glanced at Nick. Nothing was said but Nick gave the slightest of nods, as if he understood what was worrying the general. It was the kind of look I'd seen my parents exchange.

The general levelled it at me. 'This report – how many copies did you make?'

'One, sir. Colonel Nicholls has it.'

'How many people have read it? The complete list.'

'Colonel Nicholls and Captain Heffer, sir.'

'The Dutch know nothing about it?'

'No, sir. They think the message was cancelled.'

'Who typed this report?'

'I did, sir. Sorry about the mistakes.'

'Your secretary hasn't seen it?'

'No, sir. She wasn't with me at the time.'

There was a warning gleam in those forbidding eyes. 'What did you tell Colonel Tiltman about the Dutch situation?'

'Nothing, sir. I was instructed not to discuss the country sections.'

'And you always obey your instructions?'

'No, sir. But in this instance I did.'

There was silence as Celt met Jew on the frontier of instinct. We then went our separate ways.

A minute later he reached the last page and re-read the closing paragraph, which was probably a reflection on my style of writing. It had been hard to find the right finish at four in the morning:

... yet despite the pressure under which they've been working, despite deaths by drowning, by exploding minefields, and by dropping accidents, despite every kind of difficulty, danger, setback and frustration, not a single Dutch agent has been so overwrought that he's made a mistake in his coding ... It seems to me unarguable that the bulk of their messages have been sent by the Germans and the main question is no longer which agents are caught but which are free.

The general closed the report and, without pausing for breath, proved that he was a field-marshaller of facts: 'According to you, twenty per cent of all indecipherables are caused by Morse mutilation to the indicator-groups, and seventy per cent by mistakes in the agents' coding. Of these mistakes, twenty-five per cent are caused by wrongly encoded indicator-groups.'

An excellent example of total recall, but what was his point?

'Now then – the Dutch traffic. According to you, the *only* indecipherables received from Holland were due to Morse-mutilated indicator-groups – but you don't explain how you people distinguish between an indicator-group that's been Morse-mutilated, one that's been mistransmitted, and one that's been misencoded. Explain now.'

He'd expect a lightning synopsis, which wasn't possible.

'Answer fully.'

Was the bloody man telepathic?

In any event, he should have addressed his question to Nick. He was the expert on Morse technicalities. But Nick's eyes were still averted.

Tap tap ...

And his face a forbidden war zone.

Tap tap ... It was the general's fingers drumming on the desk.

I decided to answer him in kind.

Resting my elbow on one end of the Dutch report and my fingertips on the other, I demonstrated to the glowering general that WT operators fell into two main categories: those who waggled their wrists and those who waggled their elbows. The elbow-wagglers were more consistent but if any operator were exceptionally tense or had an attack of 'Morse-cramp', the slightest deviation in his touch could butcher the indicator groups. The letter N (-.) could be transmitted as A (.-), the letter L (.-..) as Y (-.--), and the commonest letter of all, E (.), could easily become the next commonest letter, T (-).

Tap tap from the general's fingers. Too much detail?

224

Speeding up my crawling commentary, I explained that monitoring a WT operator's traffic was like listening to a foreigner with a broken accent, and signalmasters could always distinguish between mistransmitted groups and Morse-mutilated ones for a very simple reason: poor atmospheric conditions affected all the code-groups, often making the clear-text impossible to read, whereas an operator's mistakes affected only individual letters.

The warning gleam was back. 'That's all very well as far as it goes. – but what if an indicator-group had been wrongly encoded, then wrongly transmitted, and atmospheric conditions were bad? How could you detect the original mistake?'

How indeed?

'It would be quite beyond us, sir – and it's about as likely as C giving SOE a vote of confidence . . .'

The atmosphere deteriorated sharply but for once my courage didn't.

'. . . and, sir . . . if the point of your questions is to suggest that we *have* had indecipherables from Holland due to coding mistakes but wrongly attributed them to other causes, could you please explain why no Dutch agent has ever misnumbered a transposition-key, "hatted" a column, misspelt a word in his poem, or made any of the other coding mistakes which free agents will continue to make until WOKs are introduced?'

'Sit down, Marks,' he said quietly.

I didn't realize I wasn't, and complied forthwith.

He looked at me like a marksman reassessing his target. Then a new thought marched into his eyes, and he began rummaging through the 'Giskes evidence' which was stacked in front of him. 'Where's that damned indecipherable? I want another look at how it looked to Boni.'

Two looks in one sentence? – Had something disturbed him?

He spent several minutes (the equivalent of hours by normal standards) studying the jumble of malformed words which Boni had received.

'Marks. Are you telling me you don't know of a single agent who might be able to decode this message?'

'Knut Haugland, sir – if he had the time.'

'Did you brief him?'

'Yes, sir.'

'Did you brief Boni?'

'No, sir.'

'Then how do you know he's not another Knut Haugland.?'

Opening my briefcase, I handed him Boni's training-school reports. These showed that he was a first-class WT operator but only an average coder who was frequently careless and took short cuts which seldom worked. The instructor strongly recommended more coding practice for Boni before he left for the field.

The general immediately asked if I'd read Knut Haugland's report. 'Yes, sir.'

'How did his instructor assess him?'

'Below average, sir.'

'Then why do you trust the judgement of Boni's instructor if you can't trust Haugland's?'

'It might save time, sir, if I showed you the only thing I have any faith in at all . . .' Delving once more into my briefcase, I handed him a complete list of the keys the girls had tried in their blanket attack on Boni's indecipherable. There were 6,000 of them.

He seemed astonished when I explained what they were. 'Do you always go to these lengths to break an indecipherable?' It was the first time his tone had been muted.

'That's only phase one, sir. Some indecipherables take days to break. The girls never give up.'

'And WOKs would put a stop to these indecipherables?'

'And to a lot of other things, sir. Including meaningless security checks.'

The gleam again. 'Did you tell the coders this was a deliberate indecipherable?'

'No, sir! They all think it was caused by a teleprinting mistake.'

He brusquely conceded that Boni had little or no chance of breaking the indecipherable but before I could say 'Hallelujah.' - or Marks & Co.'s equivalent, 'He's paid in cash.' – he'd begun demolishing the whole concept of Plan Giskes.

Why should Boni risk coming on the air to ask for the indecipherable to be repeated when he had all the operational instructions he needed from his other messages?. And why was I so convinced that he'd do so 'by reflex'? In his experience agents were unpredictable at the best of times, let alone in the middle of dropping operations (as my stomach now was).

H then targeted my 'Potato theory'. Just because Boni had informed London of Potato's indecipherables, it didn't follow that he'd notify us the moment he received one himself. 'And if my memory serves me right, it took him the best part of a week to report Potato's indecipherables. He's only had yours for three days.'

Nor could he accept that Boni's missed skeds were evidence of Giskes's timing as my anxieties about Holland were based on pre-misses which could easily be wrong! – Incidentally, how did I know so much about Giskes?

I had to admit that the little I did know had come from Nick.

He shot his next question at me as quietly as a machine-gun can. Did I have similar anxieties about any other country section's agents?

Wary now of saying anything, I brusquely informed him that *all* messages in the poem-code were suspect, and I had no doubt at all that the Germans were running some French and Belgian agents just as skilfully as they were the Dutch. The only difference was that we now had proof that Boni was caught.

He reminded me sharply that he was still far from convinced that my ingenious little trick had proved anything at all except that I was capable of heinous misconduct. He then proceeded to make three things clear:

1 There was a place in SOE for the unorthodox but not for the wholly undisciplined
2 My unauthorized actions were *absolutely* inexcusable
3 If the country sections found out that their traffic had been tampered with they'd lose all confidence in the Signals director-ate, and ideas like WOKs wouldn't even get a hearing.

He added that he'd dismiss me on the spot if Nick hadn't urged him to give me one more chance. As it was, he was still in two minds as to what should be done about me.

Death by drowning, by exploding minefields, by –

227

'But before discussing your future, if any, in SOE I must make one thing *absolutely* clear to you.'

He then made a statement which caused a drop of perspiration to parachute from the end of my nose and land on the edge of his desk.

He was satisfied that my report raised enough questions to warrant an independent investigation into the Dutch agents' security, and he would institute one immediately. He was particularly disturbed about the interlocking of so many WT circuits, which was potentially extremely dangerous. He got a quick nod from my saviour.

Before I could begin to absorb the miracle he produced his caveats.

If I wished to stay in SOE, under no circumstances must I discuss Holland with *anyone* but Nick and himself. And if I had any further anxieties about the Dutch I must consult Nick immediately. 'And if for any reason he's not available, you will telephone Miss Jackson and come direct to me. Is that understood?'

'Yes, sir.'

He looked harder at me than at any time since the meeting began. 'If you've been up to anything else without Colonel Nicholls's permission you'd better stop it at once. I don't want to curb your initiative but this sort of thing must never happen again. *Is that understood?*'

'Yes, sir.'

I must have used the wrong tone because I got his blackest look yet. 'You're not the only one who's concerned about our agents' safety. Certain steps are taken that you know nothing about, and you will no longer question the decisions we make or ask questions about them. *Is that also understood?*'

'Yes, sir.'

Once again Celt met Jew on their favourite frontier, and I could tell from his expression that my passport was in order. He signalled my dismissal and I stood up to go.

'For your information, there's one more thing. I am not one of those pricks who found the report too technical. As far as I'm concerned, it wasn't technical enough.'

Is that a twinkle that I see before me, the handle towards my throat?

*   *   *

228

I didn't discuss the meeting with Heffer when I reeled into his office next morning, nor did he expect me to. But I did tell him that Nick had intervened to help me keep my job.

'You sound surprised,' he said. 'What else would you expect? But I think you should know what really saved your bacon – no insult intended to the pig.' He kept me waiting for a puff. 'It was Tiltman.'

I was beyond surprise by this time.

'Can you guess what he said about you to CD and Gubbins?'

'That I serve the best black-market lunch in London?'

'Something a bit more unexpected. He said that as far as Bletchley was concerned you were the one that got away!'

He added an afterthought: 'It wouldn't suit SOE if you got away to Bletchley.'

But I still couldn't get away from my failure to devise a letter one-time pad . . .

TWENTY-SEVEN

Criminal Negligence

I had a feeling I couldn't define that there was something in Boni's traffic which I'd completely overlooked, and that some action was called for that I'd neglected to take.

More convinced than ever that every message he sent was some Dutch agent's obituary notice, I decided to become Boni-immersed, and divided his traffic into two categories:

1   His normal traffic, if the term could be applied to it
2   His 'special messages' from Victory and Vinus, which he'd begun transmitting last December.

His Normal Traffic

The March moon-period (which began on the 11th) was a bumper one for him. He was alerted on the 10th that seven containers would be dropped any time from tomorrow night onwards, and that the 10,000 florins he'd been waiting for since January would be inside a cell marked with a white cross. He must tell London at once if Parsnip and the reception committee could handle the containers in two separate deliveries.

Boni confirmed on the 13th that separate containers would present no problems, and asked for two sets of bicycle tyres to be included for the reception-committee.

Could anything be more persuasive than this last-moment request for bicycle tyres? Giskes deserved the 10,000 florins for his attention to detail.

But respect for him brought me no closer to my elusive mistake, and I reluctantly turned to the traffic where I was likeliest to find it.

Every time I read the messages which Boni transmitted on behalf of Victory and Vinus my waxy inner ear started to throb. Desperate to dredge up whatever was worrying me, I made a précis in longhand of the Victory–Vinus–Boni relationship in the hope that the tedium of trying to decipher my own handwriting would force me to acknowledge what I'd overlooked.

The Victory–Vinus–Boni Relationship

Victory (real name Koos Vorrinck) was a senior member of the National Committee, and one of Holland's leading politicians. A dedicated partisan, he worked independently of SOE but badly needed to communicate with the Dutch government-in-exile, and asked his friend Vinus (real name Levinus van Looe) to provide him with a WT operator.

Vinus, a member of the Cabbage/Parsnip group, asked London if Boni could handle Victory's traffic until new operators could be sent in, and with N section's consent he began transmitting it last December, and had continued ever since.

All the messages were long, and most of them contained information which London already knew, but N section regularly replied to them and sent copies (some of them accurate) to the government-in-exile, who also replied to them. Via Boni.

One of these messages (number 60 of 16 February) had puzzled me when I first read it, and caused me to ask questions which had nothing to do with my role as a cryptographer.

It reported that a Gestapo agent named Johnny was telling Dutch citizens that he'd returned from London with important instructions for them from the Dutch government, and Victory wanted the BBC to start broadcasting messages twice daily warning the Dutch public to have no dealings with him. The broadcasts should begin at once, 'before Johnny did more damage'.

London replied on 17 February asking for a detailed description of Johnny as without one the warnings would have little effect! The broadcasts would begin as soon as they received it.

Johnny's vital statistics didn't arrive for another three weeks. On 12 March Boni transmitted a detailed description of the alleged agent (he sounded remarkably like Father's partner Mark Cohen whose movements I'd check) but the message made no attempt to explain the delay.

Surely experienced agents like Vinus didn't need to be told that a detailed description was vital? And surely someone of Victory's calibre would have provided it in the first place? So why had it taken three weeks to arrive?

Because Johnny didn't exist?

In which case, I envied him.

The feeling that I'd not only been careless with the Dutch traffic but criminally negligent was now a conviction. My last chance of pinpointing it lay in a segment of Boni's traffic which had raised his transmissions to a different level.

On 28 December he reported that Vinus had asked him to transmit an important communication from Victory to Queen Wilhelmina. The communication would consist of twelve separate messages which would add up to one long telegram. He asked London's permission to proceed.

On 1 January he was authorized to send the twelve messages on two conditions:

1 That they didn't endanger his other transmissions.
2 That they weren't of a purely political nature.

On 14 January Boni agreed to send the messages if their importance warranted it, but admitted for the first time that Victory's traffic had begun to interfere with his other transmissions (another master-touch?). He left the final decision about future Victory messages to London.

On 15 January (number 54) he was authorized to start transmitting the queen's messages, and told to await instructions regarding further Victory messages.

On 17 January he transmitted the first of the twelve messages, and the last of them was received on 30 January.

Far from being purely political (a contradiction in terms?), Victory's messages were highly militant. They cited many examples of German brutality, and urged immediate reprisals. German cities should be bombed, leading Nazis in Holland targeted, and Dutch citizens told that they would have the full support of the queen if they engaged in acts of sabotage and resistance against their German oppressors.

It took the government-in-exile the best part of a month to reply to Victory, which was either an insult to his judgement or a tribute to his eloquence.

Finally, on 2 March, they sent him a message via Boni (number 64) thanking him on the queen's behalf for his 12 messages. But their reply made clear that although they were aware of the Germans' brutality, they feared that the measures which he advocated would result in even greater oppression, and urged him to use his considerable influence to discourage any form of retaliation at the present time.

Victory made no direct response to this. But on 5 March Boni informed London that he'd received a further batch of 'Victory messages' from Vinus, and that in the absence of instructions to the contrary he would begin transmitting them, which he proceeded to do with his customary skill on 5 and 11 March. One message in particular redefined 'Dutch courage'. It stated that in readiness for the German collapse, the National Committee was attempting to form a caretaker Government which would remain in office until Queen Wilhelmina and the Dutch Government returned to Holland. All six members of the National Committee including Vorrinck were referred to by name in this message which had been transmitted in a poem-code.

A cryptographer-in-exile realized that if he spent any more time searching for a mistake which might be illusory instead of producing new codes, Giskes's victory would be even more complete. I put the Dutch traffic aside, and resumed my attempts to devise a letter one-time pad. Three hours later I realized what I'd overlooked. A doctor would have been struck off for it, a soldier court-martialled, an accountant promoted. I'd been so busy trying to prove that Boni was

233

captured that I'd given no thought whatever to prolonging his life.

I remembered Buckmaster's dictum 'the best way to help a captured agent is to pretend that he's free'. I'd taken no such steps to help Boni. Instead I'd sent him a deliberate indecipherable.

Giskes may not have realized it was a trap as he had no reason to credit Baker Street's poem-bound amateurs with the ability to set one. But surely he'd expect even SOE's code department to issue some elementary precautions when a WT operator transmitted messages to a head of State, *and* received her replies, *and* disclosed the existence of the National Committee, *and* named its members? Yet all I'd done was ask N section to warn Vinus to use different prefixes for his and Victory's messages, (number 48 of 28 December), and issued new poems for the Cabbage group.

When I realized what I *should* have done I hit my forehead so hard I improved its shape.

As per my instructions from Gubbins, I took the problem to Nick. He listened sympathetically while I admitted my negligence but I hadn't come for forgiveness. There might still be time to produce some bicycle tyres of our own, and I told him what I thought they should be.

He undertook to consult Gubbins immediately.

An hour later he authorized me to make an appointment with N section to explain the security precautions I wanted to take. But on no account must I discuss Plan Giskes, or disclose why I believed that Boni and most other Dutch agents were blown. He added that the independent enquiry into the situation in Holland had already begun.

I asked for an appointment with Killick and got one with Bingham. He listened so attentively that I had to double-lock my thoughts as I explained that I was a *bit* worried about the number of Victory messages which Boni was transmitting, especially in view of their importance. I was also worried that Victory might discuss the contents of his messages with some of his colleagues.

Bingham agreed that this was likely, and asked what I had in mind. I suggested that Vinus should be warned that it was bad security for Victory's traffic to be transmitted verbatim, and that in future he must paraphrase each Victory message by putting it into his own words before it was encoded. I also suggested that he should insert 8 random letters at the beginning and end of each message, and be reminded to use transposition-keys at least 18 letters long.

Bingham agreed to this at once for which I could happily have stroked his pelt.

The message was transmitted to Boni on 18 March, and on the 20th he sent another Victory message. It didn't seem to have been paraphrased but it might well have been encoded before London's instructions were received.

The seven containers and the 10,000 florins (but no bicycle tyres) were dropped on the night of the 24th, and on the 25th Boni acknowledged their receipt. During this sked he received a message promising that the tyres would be despatched in the next moon-period beginning 9 April. Golf surfaced for the first time on the 24th, and announced that he was ready to start his regular skeds. London congratulated him and Broadbean on their safe arrival, and advised them to take things quietly until they were sent further instructions.

On 30 March Ebenezer (who'd given up inserting slip-step-slap in his messages probably in despair) was instructed to investigate the possibilities of sabotaging submarines with the help of the Catarrh group (number 173). An almost identical message had been sent to Boni on 25 March (number 68). And so everything in Holland seemed to be under control, and I didn't doubt whose.

Without any warning an idea for a letter one-time pad fell into place, and two hours later I produced a working model which I christened a LOP.

I wanted Nick to be the first person to see it.

Racing to his office, I learned from the typing pool (the best informed body in SOE) that he'd been summoned to a meeting of the Executive Council, and that his secretary was out walking her Pekinese, a permanent fixture we'd gladly have dispensed with.

I decided to leave the LOP on his desk with a note attached to it: 'To MS/A from DYC/M. Permission to proceed?'

I was so elated that for the first time in years my handwriting was legible.

Nick's desk was cluttered by his standards, immaculate by mine.

I placed the LOP in the centre of his blotter, where it might have a chance of jumping the queue, and wished I could have been there when he realized what it was.

I was about to tiptoe away when I spotted a grey folder on the top of his in-tray. There was a sheet of paper protruding from it. It was covered in green ink, which Nick invariably used when compiling *aides-mémoire* of particular importance.

I considered writing another note 'To MS/A from DYC/M. Permission to read your *aide-mémoire*?' Hoping that his meeting would last all morning, and that the Pekinese would pee the length and breadth of Baker Street, I opened the folder. It contained sheaves of notes in Nick's flowing longhand.

One glance was enough.

They were headed 'The Role of the Dutch Resistance on D-Day', and I was as green as Nick's ink by the end of page one.

TWENTY-EIGHT

Green Ink

Under the heading 'Secret Army' Nick made some astonishing disclosures. The Chiefs of Staff expected the Secret Army to be ready on D-Day to disrupt German communications with Holland, France and Belgium. They also expected it to delay the passage of German troops from Holland into France, to block the Rhine passages, *and* to attack the Wehrmacht from the rear on a signal from the High Command.

And then the real shocks began.

Alanbrooke had become one of the principal supporters of SOE's Plan Holland. In his view, 'if the Dutch uprising could even partially paralyse the German forces on D-Day it would be a major contribution to Overlord'. He'd therefore instructed SOE to give Holland's requirements priority over all other country sections, including France. He'd also insisted that the Secret Army should stay completely under cover until D-Day began, 'to preserve its security'.

Nick didn't refer to the possibility that Giskes had become an honorary colonel in the Secret Army. Nor was he even mentioned by name. But I found Churchill's name instead, and what Nick said about him increased my rising panic:

Churchill continues to have faith in SOE despite the efforts of Eden [the Foreign Secretary] to undermine it. The PM has given Plan Holland his full backing, and is relying on Morton to keep him informed of the Secret Army's progress. Morton is well disposed to SOE but could be turned. Essential to retain his goodwill.

Morton's name was new to me. I subsequently discovered that he was one of the PM's most trusted advisers and chairman of the Committee on Allied Resistance.

The first welcome surprise was Churchill's attitude to the Intelligence services:

Churchill suspects the Intelligence services of carefully doctoring any reports from the field which cast doubts on their efficiency and insists that they show them to Morton in their original form before he submits the important ones to him. SOE included in this.

A note in the margin read: 'What show Morton re the Secret Army?' I had to restrain myself from adding, 'Why not my coding report?'

I realized how much Nick knew about Holland which he hadn't told me, and how little I'd found out for myself.

The next page provided further confirmation.

The Chiefs are becoming increasingly anxious about Jambroes [Marrow]. Having approved his appointment as Commander in Chief of the Secret Army when he was dropped into Holland in July '42 [June actually] they now want him recalled for urgent consultations, and are pressing to know the reasons for the delay. Morton equally anxious to see him in London. Their constant enquiries re news of Jambroes difficult for CD and Colin . . .

The next three lines were so heavily crossed out that they looked as if they'd been covered in green wallpaper. But what followed them was all too legible.

Colin has now informed the Chiefs that a support team has been dropped into Holland to expedite Jambroes' return via French and Belgian escape-lines. Confirmation received that agents arrived safely and being sheltered for next few days by reception committee.

The underlining was Nick's, the reassurance about the Golf team was Boni's.

All the best horror stories have tranquil patches, and after making a rough estimate of the number of sets, signal-plans and codes the Secret Army would need for internal communication and for traffic with London, Nick resorted to some cryptic one-liners:

Blizzard to be replaced as head of N section? Who suitable take over ... ? Should reception-committees be allowed in Holland? Surely blind-drops safer? Same applies other territories! Has MVD (Dutch Intelligence Service) been penetrated? How London personnel recruited? C also concerned. Is Dutch Government in exile communicating directly with Holland? Possibly via fleet? Major breach regulations if happening. How best looked into? C also suspicious but no help.

I dropped blind on to the last page. It was less than half full but the handwriting warned me that I'd landed on a minefield. Nick's sloping letters were suddenly tense as if the vowels had back-ache.

The Chiefs of Staff have still not issued an official directive to SOE and, unless they do so within next few weeks, fear C will have a field-day. The importance of our terms of reference being formally defined is to be raised yet again at Cabinet level but much will depend on Plan Holland's progress ...

The final paragraph was in block capitals.

SELBORNE [SOE's Minister] DOING WHAT HE CAN TO LOBBY MORTON BUT MORTON SEEMS TO REGARD HIM AS LIGHTWEIGHT. SITUATION NOW CRITICAL, AND UNTIL IT IS RESOLVED IT IS IMPERATIVE THAT SOE CONTINUES ITS EFFORTS TO ...

And that's where it ended.

Its efforts to what, Nick? – to conceal from the Chiefs and Morton that Boni's traffic is blown, that the Secret Amy might no longer be a secret, and that Plan Holland might have to be aborted?

Is that why four Boni-linked agents were despatched last week?

239

And why three more are being sent in next? – Because if the drops were cancelled the Chiefs and Morton would demand to know the reasons?

All this for the sake of a directive they might never issue? – and which they'd withhold till 84 gave its books away if we failed them in Holland?

Of all the territories on which the mandate depended, why in God's name did it have to be the Netherlands?

No wonder my Dutch report got the reception it did.

No wonder Tiltman must know nothing of it.

But this kind of wondering was the equivalent of thinking with a stammer . . .

I told myself to hold on a minute, though I wasn't sure to what.

Nick was the only prop I had, and I'd begun to lose confidence in him. He was fighting what was surely his last war (if it weren't we were engaged in a farce), and was hoping to be appointed head of the Signals directorate. No one deserved promotion more but how far would he go to secure it? Would he abuse his knack of making authoritative statements which brooked no contradiction (an ability rare amongst Signals Officers unless very junior)? Would he say what he was told to about Holland to help SOE retain the tenuous confidence of the Chiefs of Staff? – would he condone a burial-day for the Dutch to avert a field-day for C?

Not the Nick I knew, and I was ready to stake Tommy's survival on it. But what about the Gubbins I didn't know?

Everything I'd sensed about him at our meeting, and had learned about him since, convinced me that he wouldn't either – not the spiky little bastard with an MC on his tunic and an Intelligence department in his head which Tommy regarded as the greatest asset our agents had.

Then why were Boni-linked operations still being mounted? – had the enquiry into Dutch security already taken place and made nonsense of my 'proof'? – or did SOE have a Dutch master-plan I couldn't even guess at? Remembering Gubbins's words 'a lot goes on in SOE you know nothing about' I realized that the time had come for me to issue myself with a directive which I'd be bound by for as long as I was in charge of agents' codes.

I would stop trying to understand SOE-mindedness, it was an indecipherable to which I'd never find the key. I would give up questioning SOE's plans, policies and operations, they too were beyond me. I would stick to what I did least badly. I would give SOE's agents the safest possible codes, the most efficient coders, and a team of FANY officers they would find it a pleasure to be briefed by.

But in my own dealings with agents I would substitute technique for involvement. I would attack their indecipherables, watch their security checks, and do whatever was necessary to safeguard their traffic. But the content of that traffic must be left to those who understood it.

I replaced the *aide-mémoire* in its folder, and left the desk exactly as I'd found it. But I couldn't bring myself to leave the LOP where it rightfully belonged.

I had nothing else to cling to in a green-ink world.

TWENTY-NINE

Best Read at Night

Throughout March we were Morse-stunned by the traffic which poured into the wireless station at Grendon (now called 53a) and to our new station at Poundon (53b)

Tommy had sent three messages. The first two described the efforts he, Passy and Brossolette were making to weld dissident Resistance groups into a Secret Army under one Field Commander, but it was his third which earned him a box of the finest.

He'd discovered that under a compulsory service order all Frenchmen were required to register their dates of birth, and those aged between nineteen and thirty-two were sent to Germany to work in factories, or were despatched to the Russian front. Those who failed to register were hunted by the French and German police working in unison, and he estimated that every week at least 20,000 Frenchmen were picked up on the streets of Paris, put into lorries, and sent to Germany. He was convinced that the age-limit would soon be raised to forty-two, and then to the middle fifties, and that when this happened there'd be little or no hope of forming a Secret Army.

He suggested to London that all Frenchmen should be encouraged by radio broadcasts, underground newspapers and every conceivable form of propaganda to avoid conscription by leaving France or by living clandestinely. Few would be able to manage the former but the latter course should be open to all if they were given sufficient help. He urged London to send large quantities of francs and forged ration cards so that all who deserted could buy food. He was convinced that if London responded quickly Frenchmen would desert in their tens of thousands, perhaps to the hills, where they could be provisioned by London, trained and formed into the nucleus of a Secret Army.

The concept of the Maquis had effectively been born.

But much of the March traffic was best read at night, when wincing could be more private. Messages from Norway and Stockholm described the atrocities carried out by the Gestapo and the Quisling government on Norwegian citizens in the Hardangar area as retribution for the successful attack on the heavy-water plant. Homes had been burnt, women and children arrested, and hundreds of innocent people taken hostage and sent to concentration camps. The nine saboteurs were still safe.

Flemming Muus had replaced Mogens Hammer as head of Danish Resistance, and Hammer had been recalled to London and promised an important new post when he returned to Denmark – though Hollingsworth had no intention of sending him back. Ola Lippmann, a young Dane who'd worked for the Resistance since its inception, and set up the first clandestine newspapers as well as the escape lines to Sweden, and was now in charge of political intelligence, would not only be Muus's principal assistant, he could take over for him at a moment's notice. (He eventually did.)

On the night of the 22nd Cammaerts the plodder (code-named Roger) lumbered into a Lysander with his fellow agent Dubourdin and they were deposited in France a few hours later. Their places in the Lysander were at once taken by Peter Churchill and Henri Frager, who were shuttled back to London to have breakfast with Buckmaster!

While all this was happening the code department was a Maquis no one wanted to supply.

The transposition-keys which Tiltman had offered to produce by machine at Bletchley had finally arrived and were a great disappointment. There were long spaces between each pair of keys which would make them difficult to photograph, and I'd found mistakes in several where numbers had been duplicated. Nor were the key-lengths sufficiently varied. The six WOK-makers were doing a better job by hand.

An even greater disappointment was the non-arrival of Tiltman's assistant who'd be responsible for mass-producing the keys. I was anxious to get his reactions to letter one-time pads, which I regarded as my bid for legitimacy in a world full of bastards. It was now essential for my concept of substituting letters for figures to be vetted by an expert. Without Bletchley's approval, I couldn't proceed with it.

The system would also need Nick's support. I'd explained it to him a week ago and he'd promised to think it over, but I hadn't heard from him since. I was about to break his door down when his secretary phoned me. Nick wanted to see me immediately. Tiltman's assistant would be arriving in an hour, and it was essential that we discussed the agenda.

A Lysander couldn't have got me there more quickly.

THIRTY

The War Dance

The moment I crossed Nick's sacrosanct threshold I knew that I'd been summoned to a *conférence extraordinaire*.

He and Heffer were so immersed in a letter one-time pad that its proud daddy had been obliged to knock twice to gain admittance. They were examining the fledgling code as if unable to decide whether to christen or circumcize it.

Pointing to a chair without looking up, Nicky brusquely informed me that he'd explained the system to CD and Gubbins, who were very impressed by its simplicity. However, they insisted that it mustn't be used without Bletchley's blessing. '. . . which you mustn't count on getting. They may have reservations about one-time pads for agents.'

I didn't need to ask why. If the Germans copied the idea, Bletchley could no longer break the codes of their trainee agents when they transmitted practice messages which Y intercepted. (The agents used the same codes when they landed in England as they did at training school.)

'*Marks, are you listening to me?* We must settle what you're going to say to Commander Dudley-Smith.' He pointed out that the commander couldn't spend long with me as he had another appointment, and that he was expecting to discuss the volume of machine-made keys we'd need from Bletchley over the next few months. He then warned me that the commander was 'exceptionally bright', and was likely to ask me some awkward questions. On no account must I disclose the code requirements of individual country sections, or allow myself to be drawn into discussing SOE's future commitments. 'Is that understood?'

'Yes, sir.' I nearly said 'only too well'.

Bletchley worked closely with C, and the less the 'bastards of Broadway' knew about our plans for expansion the better our chances of survival.

'And there's one other thing. Heffer and I don't insist on this but neither of us think you should discuss one-time pads with him –' He turned to Heffer for confirmation.

The Guru looked at me thoughtfully. 'The timing's wrong,' he said.

He then explained between puffs that letter one-time pads were an important new concept but their use by SOE might involve Bletchley in a conflict of interests, and I'd be well advised not to refer to them until a special meeting could be arranged with Tiltman present.

The wizard of Bletchley had been present ever since I'd met him, but Heffer misread my expression. 'I need hardly remind you,' he said, doing just that, 'that *he* is SOE's coding adviser, that he *did* support your concept of WOKs, and that if letter-pads make Bletchley's task more difficult, then the least we can do is . . .'

I switched off at this point because I'd prefer to see German agents sitting in the War Cabinet or even running 84 than allow SOE's agents to be deprived of LOPs for a day longer than was absolutely necessary, providing that the system had no flaws.

Nick pointed his finger at me as if he didn't want it back. 'You must learn to concentrate on one code at a time, and WOKs are more than good enough to be going on with.'

But good enough wasn't good enough if we could produce something better, though I had the sense not to say so.

Thirty minutes later my visitor arrived.

Nick was right in saying that Commander Dudley Smith was 'exceptionally bright'. His gold braid glistened, his eyes sparkled and his mind was a torpedo looking for a target.

Firing practice began at once. He regretted he couldn't lunch with me, as he'd heard 'excellent accounts of Baker Street cuisine', but he'd be glad of some coffee if we had any going (it was already on its way). He congratulated me on the charts for breaking indecipherables which I'd shown Tiltman, and was then kind enough to explain the various uses to which Bletchley put them, none of which had even occurred to me, though I nodded knowingly. It was a subtle way of reminding me that amateurs don't belong in the same ring as professionals. His round on points.

I returned the compliment by thanking him for Bletchley's machine-made keys, and he at once asked what was wrong with them.

I decided not to dissimulate until it was absolutely necessary, and pointed out that the long spaces between the keys would make them difficult to reproduce. I also pointed out some mistakes in them, including duplicated numbers. He thanked me for bringing them to his attention and assured me that the mistakes wouldn't occur again, at which point I began to suspect that they were deliberate.

He asked whether country sections shared their forward-planning with the Signals directorate, and I replied that as far as I could see they had none to share.

I was saved from further questions by the arrival of the coffee and black-market sandwiches.

I waited until he was involved with the problem of selection before presenting the bill: 'Commander, I've a favour to ask.'

'Go ahead,' he said with smoked-salmon-induced euphoria.

I told him that I'd been working on a new code which I hadn't thought of when Tiltman was here. Could he possibly spare the time to discuss it with me?

He said that he'd be glad to help in any way he could, though it might be better if I waited for Tiltman's next visit.

'I'd value your opinion, Commander.'

'What sort of code is it?' he enquired with ill-concealed reluctance.

He stopped chewing when I said it was a new form of one-time pad which used letters instead of figures and required no code-book.

I produced a LOP which Joan Dodd had managed to have printed on silk as a very special favour.

'Brief me as if I were an agent,' he said, 'or a country section head.' He sat next to me just as Tiltman had when we broke Skinnarland's indecipherable.

I asked him to choose a message but he preferred to leave it to me. '"Long live Tiltman"?' I suggested.

'I second that,' he said.

I'd have preferred 'Vivat Tiltman' to show off my Latin, but I wanted a phrase at least fifteen letters long.

I asked him to copy out the first fifteen letters of his one-time pad, and write our benediction beneath them.

His handwriting was a flotilla of small ships setting out for Dunkirk. Twelve seconds later (it was important to time him) he completed the first part of his message.

One-time pad: OPXCA PLZDR BHTEJ

Message: LONGL IVETI LTMAN

'You now have to encode each pair of letters in turn, starting with the first pair O over L, and ending with the last J over N . . .'

'How do I do that.?' he asked, as if his future depended on it.

'With the help of a substitution square, which may look complicated but couldn't be simpler.'

I produced one for him.

A	B	C	D	E	F	G	H	I	J	K	L	M	N	O	P	Q	R	S	T	U	V	W	X	Y	Z
A^p	A^b	A^l	A^d	A^f	A^q	A^k	A^s	A^r	A^x	A^a	A^i	A^j	A^c	A^g	A^n	A^o	A^y	A^t	A^v	A^u	A^w	A^m	A^z	A^c	A^h
B^e	B^a	B^w	B^z	B^x	B^f	B^x	B^i	B^m	B^d	B^y	B^t	B^h	B^q	B^r	B^c	B^g	B^k	B^o	B^b	B^l	B^p	B^v	B^i	B^u	B^n
C^s	C^n	C^k	C^g	C^w	C^t	C^l	C^p	C^z	C^o	C^c	C^e	C^m	C^i	C^d	C^b	C^x	C^u	C^q	C^h	C^y	C^f	C^j	C^r	C^a	C^v
D^r	D^p	D^o	D^a	D^d	D^v	D^x	D^z	D^u	D^b	D^e	D^i	D^k	D^m	D^c	D^s	D^n	D^q	D^h	D^w	D^t	D^g	D^l	D^y	D^i	D^f
E^b	E^x	E^m	E^f	E^h	E^y	E^i	E^n	E^p	E^k	E^d	E^c	E^i	E^a	E^w	E^o	E^l	E^z	E^u	E^q	E^r	E^v	E^e	E^s	E^g	E^t
F^u	F^r	F^n	F^e	F^a	F^w	F^b	F^y	F^t	F^p	F^m	F^k	F^x	F^l	F^i	F^z	F^s	F^v	F^g	F^h	F^c	F^o	F^q	F^a	F^d	F^d
G^z	G^s	G^x	G^c	G^g	G^h	G^o	G^r	G^y	G^n	G^i	G^m	G^l	G^j	G^a	G^p	G^b	G^t	G^v	G^f	G^q	G^d	G^k	G^u	G^e	G^w
H^t	H^u	H^s	H^m	H^c	H^g	H^p	H^q	H^h	H^r	H^l	H^x	H^b	H^o	H^j	H^y	H^z	H^w	H^d	H^c	H^i	H^n	H^v	H^k	H^a	
I^n	I^o	I^j	I^w	I^v	I^u	I^m	I^b	I^s	I^l	I^g	I^a	I^e	I^c	I^f	I^x	I^k	I^r	I^y	I^t	I^z	I^h	I^i	I^p	I^d	I^q
J^o	J^l	J^i	J^v	J^q	J^r	J^e	J^x	J^n	J^m	J^w	J^d	J^a	J^g	J^h	J^k	J^j	J^p	J^z	J^u	J^s	J^t	J^c	J^b	J^f	J^y
K^l	K^m	K^c	K^q	K^y	K^p	K^a	K^k	K^o	K^e	K^v	K^f	K^d	K^w	K^t	K^i	K^i	K^b	K^s	K^r	K^n	K^u	K^g	K^x	K^h	K^z
L^k	L^i	L^a	L^t	L^u	L^s	L^c	L^l	L^x	L^i	L^h	L^w	L^g	L^f	L^q	L^m	L^e	L^n	L^p	L^z	L^b	L^y	L^d	L^o	L^v	L^r
M^x	M^k	M^e	M^h	M^t	M^z	M^i	M^o	M^b	M^i	M^f	M^g	M^c	M^d	M^y	M^l	M^m	M^s	M^r	M^y	M^p	M^q	M^a	M^n	M^w	M^u
N^i	N^c	N^f	N^r	N^p	N^o	N^w	N^e	N^i	N^g	N^u	N^q	N^v	N^t	N^z	N^a	N^d	N^l	N^x	N^n	N^k	N^s	N^h	N^m	N^y	N^b
O^j	O^i	O^d	O^u	O^r	O^n	O^g	O^m	O^k	O^c	O^t	O^v	O^w	O^h	O^y	O^e	O^a	O^o	O^b	O^s	O^x	O^z	O^f	O^l	O^q	O^p
P^a	P^d	P^v	P^s	P^n	P^k	P^h	P^c	P^e	P^f	P^z	P^u	P^t	P^y	P^p	P^g	P^w	P^i	P^l	P^x	P^m	P^b	P^q	P^i	P^r	P^o
Q^v	Q^q	Q^r	Q^k	Q^i	Q^a	Q^z	Q^h	Q^w	Q^y	Q^x	Q^n	Q^s	Q^b	Q^l	Q^t	Q^u	Q^d	Q^c	Q^e	Q^g	Q^m	Q^p	Q^f	Q^o	Q^i
R^d	R^f	R^q	R^n	R^o	R^i	R^t	R^g	R^a	R^h	R^s	R^r	R^u	R^z	R^b	R^w	R^v	R^i	R^m	R^k	R^e	R^x	R^y	R^c	R^p	R^l
S^c	S^g	S^h	S^p	S^b	S^l	S^v	S^a	S^i	S^w	S^r	S^y	S^q	S^u	S^s	S^d	S^f	S^m	S^k	S^o	S^i	S^n	S^t	S^e	S^z	S^x
T^h	T^t	T^z	T^l	T^m	T^c	T^r	T^v	T^f	T^u	T^o	T^b	T^p	T^n	T^k	T^q	T^y	T^g	T^a	T^i	T^d	T^i	T^s	T^w	T^x	T^e
U^f	U^h	U^y	U^o	U^l	U^i	U^u	U^w	U^d	U^t	U^n	U^p	U^r	U^s	U^x	U^v	U^q	U^c	U^e	U^i	U^a	U^k	U^z	U^s	U^b	U^m
V^q	V^y	V^p	V^i	V^i	V^d	V^s	V^t	V^v	V^z	V^k	V^o	V^n	V^x	V^m	V^u	V^r	V^f	V^g	V^a	V^w	V^c	V^b	V^h	V^l	V^c
W^y	W^z	W^b	W^i	W^c	W^f	W^n	W^u	W^q	W^s	W^i	W^l	W^o	W^k	W^e	W^r	W^p	W^h	W^w	W^d	W^v	W^x	W^a	W^t	W^m	W^g
X^m	X^e	X^g	X^y	X^z	X^b	X^d	X^i	X^l	X^a	X^q	X^h	X^f	X^v	X^u	X^i	X^c	X^x	X^n	X^p	X^o	X^r	X^w	X^k	X^t	X^s
Y^w	Y^v	Y^u	Y^x	Y^k	Y^e	Y^y	Y^f	Y^g	Y^q	Y^b	Y^s	Y^z	Y^r	Y^o	Y^h	Y^t	Y^a	Y^i	Y^m	Y^c	Y^l	Y^r	Y^d	Y^n	Y^i
Z^g	Z^w	Z^t	Z^b	Z^x	Z^m	Z^q	Z^d	Z^c	Z^p	Z^v	Z^z	Z^y	Z^r	Z^n	Z^f	Z^h	Z^e	Z^i	Z^l	Z^i	Z^o	Z^u	Z^a	Z^s	Z^k

'You see the alphabet which runs along the top? Glance down the
O column until you come to the L. What does O over L give you?'

'Q.'

'Then that's your first pair of letters encoded. Your next pair is P
over O. What does P over O give you?'

'E,' he replied.

'Then that's your next code-group. No great hardship, is it? The
third pair is X over N . . . what does X over N give you?'

'M.'

Eighteen seconds later his task was complete.

One-time pad:	OPXCA	PLZOR	BHTEJ
Message:	LONGL	IVETI	LTMAN
Code-groups:	QEMXK	XOTKR	JVYFG

In the absence of any comment, such as 'Rise, Sir Leo', I explained
that the decoding process was just as simple. All he had to do was
write the code groups under the one-time pad groups and the substitution square would decode each pair in turn.

Pretending that he really was an agent, I pointed out that O over L had
produced Q, and that in the decoding process O over Q would produce L,
and the same principle applied to all the other pairs of letters.

He accepted my word for it without bothering to check, which
made me uneasy.

But his frown worried me even more. It was clear that something
was puzzling him.

Wondering what I'd overlooked, I explained that agents would use
LOPs as their main code, have WOKs in reserve, and fall back on
poems if they lost both. I then pointed out that the pads and substitution squares would be different for each agent, and that they'd be
given high-grade security checks. I started to describe them.

'Hold on a minute.'

I did – to the desk.

'I agree that the pads must be different, but why the substitution
squares? Surely it wouldn't matter a damn how many of them were
captured? What use would they be without the pads? Or have I missed
something?'

'No, Commander – I have. Of course they can be the same – you've saved us an enormous amount of work.'

But he was still frowning.

What other idiocy had he spotted?

'Look here, Marks . . .'

I prepared for the worst.

'. . . did I understand you to say that you didn't think of this code until after Tiltman had left?'

'Yes! What's wrong with it?'

'Nothing at all . . . As a matter of fact letter one-time pads have been working very successfully for quite a long time."

I'd forgotten how to handle relief, and he was closer to being hugged than he'd ever know. It was the equivalent to hearing that Hitler had choked to death on a piece of gefilte fish.

'My God, sir [I'd decided to promote him], that's the best news you could possibly have given me.'

And so it was – but why was he looking at me in such an extraordinary way? Surely he didn't think I was disappointed because I couldn't take the credit for LOPs? Surely to God it couldn't be that?*

'What's the problem, Commander?'

He hesitated for fully ten seconds.

I prepared for the worst.

'The problem is knowing the best way to put this to you . . .'

Put what, for Christ's sake?

His smile was as unexpected as a self-peeling banana. 'It's quite an achievement thinking up LOPs without any help.'

I was as embarrassed as he was but returned to full alert when his expression hardened.

'I must also say this – and let me emphasize it's just my personal opinion because you've rather sprung this on me . . . I don't believe SOE needs letter one-time pads – WOKs are far better suited for agents' traffic.'

I asked him to explain why.

---

* Even in 1998, when so much has been written about SOE that only its secrets remain, I am still credited with inventing the letter one-time pad. WOKs, yes – but with LOPs I was pre-empted, and I wish I knew by whom! Whoever you are, and wherever you may be, my apologies and thanks. L.M.

250

His assessment of the codes' relative merits was brusque, informative and apparently impartial. In his view, WOKs had one great advantage: They allowed 200 messages to be passed on only two sheets of silk, whereas for 200 to be passed in LOPs would require at least a dozen sheets of one-time pad.

As for WOKs' security, provided that they were used once only every message would have to be attacked separately, which would place as great a strain on the enemy's resources as it would on Bletchley's. For all practical purposes, we need look no further than WOKs.

He paused for breath but I had none to offer him.

It was true (he continued) that LOP-users could send as few as ten letters, but how many agents could take advantage of this? Surely many of them had to transmit lengthy reports? In which case, wouldn't their dozen sheets of pad be harder to camouflage and more dangerous to carry than two sheets of silk? Warning me by eye-glint not to interrupt, he compared the coding demands which each system made.

WOK-users had only to copy out one line of figures before starting the process of double-transposition. But LOP-users had to copy out at least fifty letters of their one-time pads, then write their messages beneath them, and start using their substitution square. Although the system was simpler than double-transposition, the effort involved was just as great, and was likely to take longer.

I pointed out that it had taken him eighteen seconds to copy out his one-time pad groups and write his message beneath them, and another fifty seconds to encipher LONG LIVE TILTMAN. Assuming that agents were twice as slow, they could still encode or decode the average message in under twenty minutes.

Straightening his cuffs, Dudley-Smith said he didn't realize that I'd been testing him for a job in SOE or he'd have put up a better performance. He then made what was clearly his closing statement.

He appreciated that agents had to keep the messages as short as possible because of the efficiency of the Funk-Horchdienst (the German interception service). But it was equally important that they destroyed the used portions of their codes, and surely it would be easier for them to cut away one line of a WOK than a dozen lines of a one-time pad? Given the choice between WOKs and LOPs, he felt that most agents would opt for WOKs.

'Which system would Bletchley opt for if it were faced with breaking it?'

'You know damn well that letter-pads are unbreakable on a depth of one.' (Used once only.)

'Are they produced at Bletchley, Commander? And could you help us to get some?'

In the silence that followed I knew that I must leave nothing unsaid. I told him that I agreed with most of his reservations but the fact remained that 90 per cent of SOE's messages could be far shorter than the minimum of 100 letters required by WOKs, and that if Bletchley couldn't help us we'd recruit a special team of girls and produce the pads by hand.

'You realize how much work that would involve?'

'Yes, Commander.'

'And you'd be prepared to take it on?'

'Yes, Commander.'

He took a deep breath. The ozone was comparatively clear as my cigar was unlit. 'They're produced at Oxford by Commander Hogg. He supplies SOE's figure pads – Dansey knows the details.'

'Thank you, Commander.'

'You'll have to make an appointment with him through the head of SOE – and Nick should have a word with him in advance.'

'Thank you, Commander.'

He glanced at his watch. 'God – I must go.'

To forewarn Hogg?

We both stood up. In his case it showed.

He thanked me for the sandwiches, and reminded me of Tiltman's invitation to visit Bletchley. He then held out his hand as if I were no longer a stowaway on a coding flagship. 'I agree with you that the poem-code is shit, and I want to help you to replace it if I possibly can! I hope you know that.'

'Thank you, Commander. I do.'

And meant it . . .

And to help me continue meaning it if he were forced to be obstructive, I encoded a reminder to myself on a letter one-time pad: VIVAT DUDLEY-SMITH.

It took me two minutes and twenty seconds.

THIRTY-ONE

Accidents Will Happen

Oxford had a variety of irresistible attractions. It was sixty-five miles from Baker Street, every one of them a continent. It had yet to be troubled by air raids (I was one of the few sandbags in sight), and it had managed to retain so much of its awesome presence that the GI visitors who swarmed across the cobblestones allowed the spires to do the strutting. Above all, it was the home of the Bodleian Library, which was not only the shire's soul, and one of the main reasons for resisting invasion, but was allowed six months' credit by 84.

Yet the feature of Oxford which transformed it into an English Lourdes was unknown to all but a privileged few.

It produced letter one-time pads.

Commander Hogg's office was on the first floor of a large country house which had been taken over for official purposes with no obvious signs of desecration.

There were no obvious signs of a welcome either.

The commander rose from his desk, took my pass from me and examined it as if it were written in code. He was middle-aged, grey-haired, with none of Dudley-Smith's elegance but all of his authority. The quality of his product was reflected in his face, which was impossible to read on a depth of one.

Something about my pass seemed to be troubling him, and he put on his glasses for a second reading.

It was an uncomfortable start to a critical meeting for which I was inadequately briefed. I knew nothing about this inscrutable man except that he was a purveyor of one-time pads to the nation of which SOE believed itself a part.

The first words he addressed to me weren't so much clipped as stapled together.

'Is it Marks with an "x".?'

Dear God, one of those. 'Not according to my birth certificate or my great-grandfather's! May I ask if it's Hogg with one "g"!?'

There was a short pause during which the room was filled with the stimulating throb of mutual antipathy. He then invited me to sit down, and brusquely informed me that he'd been asked by the head of S.O.E. to supply us with letter one-time pads, and to discuss the details in the course of our meeting.

He looked at me with a 'torpedoes away' expression. 'I'm still not sure what you people do.'

'The Germans, sir. In every way we can.'

I was absolutely certain that Captain Bligh didn't need a briefing from Fletcher unChristian about SOE or any other wartime anomaly. But I needed one about him. There must be some reason for his hostility other than good taste.

'Who recommended letter-pads to SOE?'

I admitted responsibility.

'What experience have you had with them?'

'None, sir.'

He said 'Good God' so softly that unless the Almighty were in the room with us, of which there was increasingly little sign, he couldn't expect much feed-back from the supreme crow's nest.

'Can I assume you know how they work?'

I said that I believed I did; and he pounced at once: 'Who explained them to you?'

I daren't admit that until very recently I thought I'd invented them. 'Dansey, sir. He used to be in charge of agents' codes.'

His expression said, 'It's a pity he still isn't.'

'Do you usually recommend coding systems you know nothing about?'

'No, Commander. But I rarely hear of any as good as LOPs.'

He winced at the word. And continued wincing while I explained why letter-pads were ideally suited for agents' traffic.

255

He waited until I'd finished the litany, then looked at me as if my bilges were leaking. (One of them was.) 'Tell me Marks, what other codes have you recommended to SOE?'

I gave him a thorough WOK-ing, and he suddenly brightened. 'That idea sounds secure and practical. Who devised it?'

I admitted paternity, which seemed to surprise him.

'Commander, may I give you two examples of why letter-pads would be better?'

Without waiting for permission, I told him about the Norwegians who reported the movements of German battleships to London while surrounded by the enemy, and about the agents who attacked submarines with limpets, who also reported to London. *The information the Admiralty was waiting for could have been transmitted in less than fifty letters, had the codes been safe enough.*

Hogg couldn't quite hide a smile at these nautical disclosures and assured me that he'd taken my point that agents must get off the air in the shortest possible time. But he was afraid that letter-pads were unlikely to be the answer.

'*Why not, Commander?*'

I was disconcerted by his softly spoken reply. 'I think you'd better see one.'

He lifted the receiver, issued a quiet instruction, and asked if I'd like some tea. Scarcely able to breathe, let alone swallow, I declined with thanks.

A door which I hadn't noticed because it was right in front of me opened almost immediately and his Muriel (if there were another such) brought in the first letter one-time pad I'd seen. It was accompanied by a large substitution square.

She put them in front of him, gave me the kind of encouraging smile Muriel bestowed on my long-suffering visitors, and left us alone.

The letter-pad was the most important person in the room. The commander watched me while I paid my respects to it. 'It won't bite you if you pick it up,' he said encouragingly.

But it did.

Home Station to Out was a Caxton first edition, and *Outstation to Home* was the Gutenberg Bible.

'My God, Commander, they're beautifully produced.'

That was as close to an understatement as I had ever come. The letters were clear and would be easy to read at half their present size.

I was already back in Baker Street giving my first LOP briefing, and wished the commander would stop asking questions.

'I take it you wouldn't issue them to agents just as they are?'

I shook my head firmly.

'You'd photograph them down and have them reproduced on silk?'

On silk myself, I hardly bothered to nod.

'Then tell me, Marks . . . *where do you propose to get all the silk? And who's going to undertake all that photography?* – you must have better sources than I have . . .'

Oxford's first bomb had just been exploded.

The shock-waves forced me to realize that I hadn't done my homework. He'd been expecting me to provide him with details of SOE's production facilities and not my opinion of the merits of his codes. But what could I say to him?

Joan Dodd's enthusiasm and Elder Wills's inventiveness hardly constituted a production programme, and I'd made no attempt to approach anyone else.

Like an amateur entrepreneur, I'd proceeded on the precarious premiss that what an agent needs an agent must have, and that ways would be found to provide it.

The commander knew that he'd landed on target, and that this was the moment to demolish it completely. 'Don't you realize how many other organizations with greater priority than SOE also need silk? Have you people never heard of parachutes? *Has no one told you that there's an acute shortage of silk – and of printing facilities – and of skilled photographers?*'

I mumbled something about being able to manage with sensitized paper.

'I suppose you're not aware that there's an acute shortage of paper as well?'

And of goodwill to SOE., you supercilious bastard.

'It seems to me you've done no homework whatever and wasted a lot of people's time.'

I looked him in the eye and grudgingly recognized the tiny tic of extreme tiredness. 'Commander, I think there's something you should see.'

257

I twiddled the knobs on my briefcase (I still didn't know how to open it) and finally produced SOE's version of a letter one-time pad. But in my eagerness to show him what our technicians could produce, I allowed my briefcase to spill out the remainder of its Top Secret contents. They consisted of six bananas, a selection of Mother's sandwiches and a contraceptive in a plastic container.

Although a bunch of bananas was one of England's rarest sights, the commander's expression as he gazed at the contraceptive was rarer still, and I hastily explained that it had arrived on my desk earlier that morning with a note from the head of special devices suggesting that 'a contraceptive made of local rubber would be excellent camouflage for a microfilmed code'.

The now rigid commander murmured 'Dear God', and once again received no noticeable response. He then gave his considered opinion of Elder Wills's special device. It was an example of inventiveness for the sake of it, had no practical application to clandestine communications as he understood them, and was a waste of manpower and material – amateurishness at its worst.

Quite wrong. Out of all this amateurishness came Elder Wills's magic.

The commander's hand strayed towards the buzzer.

I pushed the home-made pad towards him.

He glanced at it perfunctorily, realized what it was and started examining it with growing interest.

I slid the contraceptive back into my briefcase as I had no immediate use for it.

The commander looked at me sharply. 'Where did you get this pad?'

I owned up to my fantasy that I'd invented the system and told him that this mocked-up pad was the product of our service departments.

'How long did it take them?'

I admitted that it had taken a fortnight, including Sundays.

'But it's only three pages long. Still, it's a good effort considering it's not machine-made – but I doubt if these letters are truly random.'

They were as random as three bored FANY counter-shufflers could make them.

'Now then, Marks –' His next volley of questions, his deadliest yet, concerned the statistics I should have prepared.

How many letter pads would be needed over the next few months . . . ? What were their dimensions . . . ? How much silk would be required . . . ? How much paper . . . ? Had I told the service departments the size of the commitment they would be faced with . . . ? Did I know it myself . . . ? Had I worked out my time-scale . . . ? Had I made allowances for the service departments' mistakes – they didn't always get things right the first time . . . ! And had I . . . ? And had I . . . ? . . . And had I . . . ? . . .

The answer to everything was that I hadn't.

He said that he often reminded his own young people that enthusiasm was no substitute for homework – and this was particularly true in my case if I wanted letter pads for agents.

He glanced at his watch, and I stood up at once. 'Thanks for your advice, Commander, I promise it won't be wasted. And I apologize for coming to you prematurely. Do I need that pass to get out?'

He was examining our letter pad again and didn't seem to hear me. He looked up and saw me standing there with my hand out. 'Sit down and listen to me.'

I was back in place before he could blink.

'We simply can't afford to waste a single letter pad. Nor can we afford to change their format to suit SOE. But I'll tell you what I am prepared to do . . . Tomorrow I'm sending figure pads to Dansey and I'll include some letter pads with 'em – use them sensibly. Show them only to those people who might be able to reproduce them – never rely on their imagination; they must see what you're talking about – and make sure they're security-vetted. Contact me at once if you have any success – and I'll see what I can do. Will that be a help to you?'

'More than that, Commander.'

'Very well then, we'll leave it at that.' He stood up, and returned the pass to me. 'I doubt if you've got a hope in hell's chance of getting sufficient silk – but good luck to you.'

He shook my hand, signed my pass, and a few lifetimes later Marks with a 'k' and his briefcase with a condom landed in Baker Street to start a crusade.

THIRTY-TWO

Pilgrim's Progress

The difficulties of supplying silk codes to all our Signals dependencies were greater than even Hogg had foreseen.

The poem-code had become a worldwide malignancy, and to send WOKs and LOPs to Cairo, India and Burma – whose agents needed them just as badly as their European counterparts – enough silk would be needed for at least 40 million code-groups.

It was my job to find it, and not for the first time since joining SOE I wished that there were some substance in the most enduring of all myths: that the chosen people have direct access to everything in short supply with the possible exception of tolerance. As it was I had no ideas, no contacts, and no option but to join the long queue of mendicants waiting for SOE's Supply directorate to live up to its job description.

I was luckier than most because my rejection was immediate. None of the Supply departments (there were four main ones) could undertake a commitment of this size, even if its priority was as high as I maintained. Nor did they know of anyone who could.

Once again I turned to Joan Dodd, whose official position as head of the stationery department was the biggest misnomer in Baker Street. But this time she called in the head of her directorate, Major Ince, to help me get my thinking right. As they saw it, the solution to mass-producing silk codes, each of which had to be different, lay in a combination of printing and photography, and much would depend on the inventiveness of the technicians involved.

They then produced a list of six printing firms and as many photographers, but warned me that they were already 'working their balls off'. Ince, an expert photographer himself, offered to help out to a limited extent but couldn't possibly accept the entire commitment. Nor must I count on Elder Wills, who turned down nothing that interested him but couldn't always deliver.

But these were minor problems compared to the shortage of silk. He knew of only two people in Baker Street with sufficient clout to obtain it in large quantities, and my forebodings escalated like SOE's traffic when he disclosed their names: George Courtauld and Tommy Davies, otherwise known as the 'hard men'.

He warned me that if I were to have the slightest chance of success with them, there was one obstacle I must first overcome. It would be useless to approach them for even a yard of silk unless I could satisfy them that the printing and photographic problems had already been solved. But the printers and photographers wouldn't even consider the commitment unless they were assured that the silk was available.

He described it as a 'chicken and egg situation', and it was clear that I was the one about to get laid.

My campaign managers agreed to arrange all my appointments and 'put in a word or two' before I arrived, but warned me that I mustn't blow SOE's cover by referring to agents. They also warned me that most commercial firms didn't consider the Inter Services Research Bureau (one of SOE's cover-names) to be much of a calling-card – 'so don't be disappointed if they turn you down flat'.

They picked up their telephones and began mass-producing my appointments before I'd even reached the door.

Before taking off to meet my first printers I authorized a Belgian agent in training to use the Twenty-third Psalm as his poem-code – he was convinced it would bring him good luck.*

I then picked up my rod and my staff (a WOK and a LOP) to comfort me, and trusting that the Lord would be my shepherd and that the agents I must not mention would not want, set out on my pilgrimage.

No one in the first five firms I visited actually said, 'Don't you know there's a war on?' – a non-combatant's favourite question – but they were clearly indignant that anyone should consider that they weren't

---

* He broke his leg in a practice jump and never left for the field.

fully employed. None of them could undertake any further printing for at least three months, and the most I could extract from them was an invitation to try again later. I thanked them on behalf of Caxton and Gutenberg, whom they seemed to think were directors of ISRB.

The last firm on my list was in the heart of the City of London, assuming that it had one.

I was warmly received by two elderly brothers (the joint proprietors) who thought that ISRB was a liaison department with the War Office. They examined a WOK with great interest and asked several technical questions which Ince had primed me to answer. But when I told them of the quantities we'd require they turned me down flat as they'd just taken on 'a major job for another branch of the war effort'.

Seeing my disappointment, and apparently disturbed by it, they suggested I should try two other printers – 'rivals of ours but excellent just the same.' – and took the trouble to give me their addresses and phone numbers. They then insisted that I had some tea.

There was something about this gentle and courteous couple which was strangely evocative, but I couldn't pinpoint it until I went through the familiar motions of replacing the WOK in my briefcase.

They'd printed several of Marks & Co.'s catalogues.

I said that my father sent his best wishes to them, told them who he was, and the premises were suddenly floodlit.

They took it in turns to ask to be remembered to him, *and* to Mr Cohen, *and* to Mr Doel, *and* to Mr Plummer – 'such nice people to deal with and such a beautiful shop.'

After a brief conference, which they conducted in undertones, they asked if they could borrow the samples to show to their foreman.

'You needn't tell us what it's for, it's better we don't know,' said the saint with slightly more hair.

'Much better,' agreed his brother. 'You can meet our foreman if you like; he's only next door.'

I was certain that they'd prefer to talk to him alone, and handed over the WOK, which was a difficult operation as my fingers were crossed.

Alone in their office, I wished I'd told them that the printer's ink in their veins could be turned into life's blood for SOE's agents. I recited the Twenty-third Psalm, and a few other biblical quotations agents had selected, until the brothers strode back.

One look at their smiling faces and I knew we'd found a home. They gleefully informed me that six more printers would be joining them in two weeks' time, and they'd be able to do *all* our printing if we still wanted them to.

I didn't know which to thank first – the brothers, the Bible or 84.

But there was a snag. They'd have enough silk to start the job, but when their reserves ran out, they'd have to ask ISRB to help them.

I assured them that there'd be no problem, that Ince would immediately confirm the commitment, and their work would be put to good use.

But they were far more concerned with the damage Hitler might do to 'those beautiful books in 84.'

The next stage in the code safari was finding photographers to reproduce LOPs, but the six firms I visited proved to have one thing in common: an anxiety to get rid of me as quickly as possible. Their responses were wholly negative, and between the lot of them they couldn't have produced a passport photograph till the end of '43.

I asked Ince to suggest another source.

He avoided looking at me, a luxury which he hadn't yet allowed himself, and for the first time seemed to be holding something back. Goaded by Joan Dodd, he finally admitted that he had a 'special relationship' with an RAF photographic unit which had helped him out from time to time, and which he knew had some silk in reserve. But if they were asked to take on a commitment of this size it would have to go through official channels, and he wanted his name to be kept right out of it.

I promised to think up a cover-story which wouldn't involve him if he'd give me the details.

It took all Joan Dodd's skill to persuade him to part with them, and I wondered what she'd have to do in return.

The photographic unit was only a few spools away from the Houses of Parliament, but had a view of St James's Park as compensation. A young squadron leader rose from his cockpit in a small office, taxied towards me with outstretched hand, and said that Air Commodore Boyle's secretary 'made it sound very urgent.'

It hadn't been easy persuading Muriel to make the call.

He waited until I was seated, then asked in a confidential whisper if I knew anyone in ISRB called Ince.

After due consideration I replied that I had met a major of that name but wasn't quite sure what department he was in, which appeared to satisfy him.

His desk was bare except for a notebook and a telephone, and there was no indication that any work was done in this office – a sure sign that a great deal was.

I realized that it was time I added to it.

Dumping six LOPs on to his desk, I asked if he could photograph the whole lot on to silk within the next three days. Before he could react, I informed him that we were hoping he'd photograph far larger quantities for us on a regular basis if this first batch turned out satisfactorily.

For a moment I thought he was going to air-lift me out of the window, and St James's wasn't my favourite park. It was too full of itself to need people.

There was a precarious pause.

Is it wishful thinking on my part or is he trying to conceal a hint of amusement?

'Let's have a look-see,' he finally said.

He examined the LOPs through the private lens every skilled photographer carries in his head. He then casually asked what size we'd require them to be (a hopeful sign?) and I gave him the dimensions Ince had worked out for me.

He then stared out of the window, but his look-see was now directed within, and I knew that his decision was still in the balance. I was certain that he realized it was codes he'd been examining, and decided to go as far as I could. 'They have to be used in rather trying circumstances, Squadron Leader.'

He turned round, and though I didn't mean to insult him I thought I detected a kindred spirit. 'I imagined they served a special purpose. And I don't suppose there are many photographers who can take the job on?'

'There aren't any.'

He looked at me as if I were an aircraft trying to limp home, then glanced at the notepad on his desk. 'We can cope with this first batch, but not in three days. We'd need a week from tomorrow to do the job properly.'

The limping aircraft tried to stutter its thanks.

'Now, about the rest,' he said, cutting me short. 'What quantities?'

'Two hundred a month.'

'That's a hell of a lot.' He made some rapid calculations on his notepad and frowned at the result, unaware that he'd been using a heart as his pencil.

'Now, Mr Marks . . .'

It didn't feel right being called 'Mr' by an officer in the RAF.

'I'd better tell you a bit about our set-up . . .'

'A bit' was a considerable overstatement, and he disclosed as little about his unit as I had about ISRB. But he did admit that he was allowed a fairly free hand in running it.

'However, Mr Marks . . . there are limits to what I can do on my own authority.' He couldn't even consider photographing 200 a month unless he had a formal request from someone high in ISRB – Air Commodore Boyle perhaps?

'Would it be a help if the request came from someone higher?'

'The higher the better.'

I explained that the person I had in mind was named Heffer, and he was responsible for certain policy matters I wouldn't want to weary him with.

He nodded gravely, and said that '*If*, repeat *if*' he was allowed to take on 200 a month he hoped that Mr Heffer would provide the silk.

'He will, Squadron Leader.'

Please, Lord – start softening up the 'hard men'.

He softened up the squadron leader instead. 'Look here,' he announced, 'let's stop iffing-about. You said this stuff might have to be used in "rather trying circumstances!" – message received! So get me that letter to protect my back and one way or another we'll photograph 200 a month starting three weeks from now – good enough?'

265

'Thank you, Squadron Leader. Good enough.'

We shook hands on the deal.

He then signed my pass, though I was no longer the same person.

I was a civilian when I entered his office.

I was a code-group captain when I left it.

I was demoted to corporal when I gave Heffer a verbatim account of the historic conversation.

He upbraided me for taking his name in vain, but agreed to sign the request on condition that I obtained a few yards of silk for his wife. He then asked who was going to supply it.

'I'm going to talk to the hard men.'

He looked at me as if we mightn't meet again. 'God help you,' he finally said, 'if you try iffing them about.'

And God help the agents if I didn't.

THIRTY-THREE

The 'Hard Men'

SOE's special strength, and one of the few edges it had over C, came from the bankers and industrialists Sir Charles Hambro had introduced into Baker Street. They were the sanitized section of the dirty tricks brigade, and most of them drew on their experiences as City moguls to implement Churchill's concept of 'ungentlemanly warfare'.

None of them did so with greater relish than two tycoons-turned-soldiers named George Courtauld and Tommy Davies, otherwise known as the 'hard men'. Courtauld was a major, Davies a colonel, which in no way reflected their real status.

Courtauld was a director of the giant textile concern his family had founded, and a shipping magnate in his spare time. He'd intro-duced many of his former colleagues (including Tommy Davies) into SOE, and was one of Baker Street's senior head-hunters. Davies, allegedly the softer of the 'hard men' (which meant he was made of granite), was a member of the Executive Council, head of the Research, Development and Supply directorates, and monitored the Camouflage Station in his spare time.

Such protocol as existed in SOE required Nick to arrange my appointment with them and preferably accompany me to it. But after a few searching questions he decided that I should 'go it alone' as he was certain I'd been up to something he preferred not to know about – a well-founded suspicion which didn't prevent him from assuring Courtauld and Davies that I had his full backing.

I was summoned to Courtauld's office at ten minutes' notice, but due to a combination of April showers and perspiration I arrived at the royal enclosure looking like a puddle of dubious content.

Courtauld was a gaunt, pale and exceedingly fragile-looking 'hard man' who seemed to have barely enough energy to muster a nod. But his eyes sparked more warnings than a smoker's cough.

Tommy Davies, who sat a few feet away from him, was a large florid Welshman – but not a Dylan Thomas/Emlyn Williams pit-boy Welshman. I sensed that the only pits on this boyo's mind were the ones he'd dug for his opponents.

The 'hard men' made a concerted effort to put me at their ease.

'Colonel Nicholls says you have an interesting problem for us,' said Courtauld in a resonant voice.

'Take your time,' said Davies, glancing at his watch.

They listened with the incomparable receptivity of trained minds hearing something new while I explained the importance of WOKs and LOPs, keeping the technical details to a minimum. There wasn't a problem in sight until I tried to skirt over the arrangements I'd made with the squadron leader and the brothers.

'Hold on a minute,' said Courtauld. 'You say they've agreed to use their own silk?'

'Yes, sir – but only until their stocks run out.'

'Which will be – ?'

'In about three weeks' time, sir.'

He considered this carefully. 'Then what happens?'

'That's what I'm here to discuss, sir.'

'What exactly did you say to them?' asked Davies suspiciously.

'That ISRB would supply the rest of the silk, sir.'

'Did you, by God?' said Courtauld.

'Who gave you the authority to say anything of the sort?!' thundered Davies.

'No one, sir.'

'Does Colonel Nicholls know what you've promised these people on SOE's behalf?'

'ISRB's behalf, sir; SOE wasn't mentioned.'

'*Does he know?*'

'No, sir.'

'*You acted entirely off your own bat?*'

It was hard to imagine Davies on a cricket pitch unless he was the roller.

'Entirely, sir.' (With a little help from low-levels like Joan Dodd, Ince and Heffer.)

'Preposterous,' said Courtauld. 'There's no other word for it.'

Davies nodded so hard he almost lost a jowl.

The only sounds were Courtauld's breathing and April cleaning the windows.

'Since you're here,' Courtauld said wearily, 'you'd better explain why these lollipops or whatever they're called have to be on silk.'

If I'd had a lollipop I knew precisely where I'd stick it. In lieu of such a luxury, I leaned forward and, before Courtauld could stop me, or I could stop myself, ran my hands rapidly over his tunic, beneath his armpits, and as far down his abdomen as propriety permitted. In case he took this personally, I hastily explained that the Gestapo and the Vichy policy cordoned off entire streets without warning and searched everyone in sight. If he were a Frenchman carrying a code, wouldn't he prefer it to be on silk which groping hands couldn't feel rather than on sheets of paper hidden inside a portable object which they might have time to examine?

His mouth was so wide open that I feared he'd have a stroke. There was an extraordinary sound from somewhere on my right.

It was Tommy Davies laughing. 'Point taken,' he said before I could offer him the same facility. 'It's clear that silk has its advantages.'

I returned hastily to my still-damp chair and awaited reprisals.

Courtauld cleared his tunic of all traces of trespass. 'How long have you been in SOE?' he asked quietly.

'Since June forty-two, sir.'

'As long as that? And before then?'

'Code-breaking school.'

Two specks of red appeared on his cheeks. *'You came here straight from school?'*

'Yes, sir.' I didn't add that I was straight when I arrived but was now bent as a corkscrew.

Davies finally broke the silence. 'I presume, Marks, that you've brought some figures with you?'

This was the moment I'd been dreading. I'd prepared some estimates for them but Hitler's fortune-teller could have done a better job.

269

'Well? Have you brought them or haven't you?' demanded Courtauld.

'Yes, sir.'

I lifted the estimates from their rain-sodden envelope. They'd been typed by Muriel as if they were a royal proclamation but each page was covered in manuscript corrections and the ink had run. Wishing I could join it, I gave the drier copy to the Gestapo (Courtauld), and surrendered the other to the Vichy police.

Watching them cordon off the rest of the world while they searched the pages for concealed common sense was a lesson in concentration I wished I could have shared with all coders.

They reached the last page without complaining about the ink-blots (there were enough for a Rorschach test), then exchanged glances like Gauleiters at the door of a torture chamber.

The Cairo/India/Burma estimates were the first to be stomped on. Glaring at them with jackboot eyes, Courtauld said they were based on the extraordinary assumption that paramilitary operations in the Middle and Far East faced the same obstacles as our clandestine operations in Europe, which was nonsense.

He then gleefully pointed out that Special Forces in jungles and deserts didn't have to fear random street searches like their European counterparts or executives in Baker Street, and that the only use they'd have for silk codes would be to swat tsetse flies with them.

Exchanging smiles with Davies, he announced that the estimates for these theatres must be cut by 90 per cent, and drew two heavy lines through them.

Until he did this, SOE had been the only jungle I'd known. But the finality of those heavy lines gave faces to the figures, and for the sake of the paramilitaries, who were no longer remote, I had to challenge his judgement before it was too late: 'There's something you've overlooked, sir.'

He glared at me like the captain of one of his liners whose concentration had been interrupted by the hooting of a tug while I reminded him that paramilitary traffic was just as liable to be intercepted as clandestine, that the codes it was being passed in were highly insecure, and that if paramilitaries didn't need WOKs and LOPs on silk then they must have them on waterproof paper which could be destroyed after each message to protect the back traffic.

'We're here to discuss silk,' snapped Davies, 'not waterproof paper.'

'But you'll be able to get that as well, won't you, sir?'

'*As well as what?*' thundered Courtauld. 'We're still trying to make sense of these figures.'

They ploughed through the European estimates with growing despair. Courtauld then gave me a brief lecture on how they should have been prepared which was probably priceless and which I pretended to understand.

Then Davies took over. 'What the devil's this?' he enquired. '"Contingencies, various", with none of them stipulated.'

'Perhaps they're too confidential to share with us?' suggested Courtauld.

Another mistake. In attempting to keep the document to containable length, I hadn't considered what would be important to them. I rattled off a few of the 'contingencies, various' – How many agents would lose their codes? . . . How many replacements would go astray? . . . How many WOKs and LOPs would Secret Armies need?

Davies interrupted sharply. 'Have the country sections agreed to use the bloody things?' he asked.

'They will, sir. Colonel Nicholls is going to talk to them himself.'

'And you'll have a word or so to say, I don't doubt,' commented Courtauld.

'Only to fill in the details, sir.' I began explaining why the 'bloody things' would make so much difference to our agents.

'We're not questioning their merits,' said Davies, 'but the reality of getting silk. There's a queue a mile long for it.'

'You have an excellent case,' said Courtauld quietly, 'but so have all the others.'

How many people with excellent cases have sat in this chair asking them to use their influence to produce the unobtainable?

Davies glanced impatiently at his watch. Courtauld gave a barely perceptible nod. 'Well now,' said Davies, 'if you'd like to leave these figures with us . . .'

I tried to spot the waste-paper basket, but I was the only one in sight.

'Unless you feel there's something you should add,' said Courtauld.

'Yes, sir. There is.' I wondered how to convince them that silk codes were more than just another 'excellent case'.

The 'hard men' – whom I finally recognized as responsible men seeking hard facts – waited expectantly. *What would jolt them into jumping the queue for the sake of the agents queuing to jump?*

I decided to stake the future of our codes on a loaded question. 'Will SOE be allowed to know the date of D-Day?'

They looked at me in astonishment. 'Why the devil do you ask that?'

'Because at some stage in the invasion the agents will have to be sent instructions from London.'

'What of it?' demanded Courtauld.

'It would be safer for SOE to use Courtauld's code than the present system.'

Courtauld sat motionless. Davies rose from his chair. '*What do you know about Courtauld's code?*' he thundered.

'That it's a variant of the commercial code, and you use it to minimize the high cost of international cables.'

'*Who told you about it?*' he persisted.

I'd seen a copy in Dad's shop. 'Do I have to answer that, sir?'

'No,' said Courtauld heavily. 'We've more important matters to dispose of.' His other half continued to glare at me.

I waited to be disposed of.

'We'll help you all we can,' said Courtauld, 'though the final decision won't rest with us.'

'Far from it,' said Davies.

'It will be made by a certain person who has very little time to spare.'

'Very little indeed,' confirmed Davies.

'It would be a great help to him – and to us – if you could put down on *half a sheet of paper* the difference silk codes would make to our agents.'

'*Half a sheet at most!*' echoed Davies.

'I think it could be done in a phrase, sir!' *But what?*

'Oh?' said Courtauld. 'We'd be interested to hear it.'

'It's between silk and cyanide.'

There was a pause.

'Is it now?' said Courtauld softly.

Davies stared at me in silence for the best part of a fortnight. 'How old are you?' he finally asked.

'I'll be twenty-three in five months, six days and a quarter of an hour, sir.' It was a chance to test his arithmetic.

'What did you do in peacetime?'

'I didn't have enough of it to find out, sir.'

Courtauld smiled as if he understood his colleague's drift, and then addressed me in his brusquest tones yet. 'That's all for now,' he said. 'You'll hear from us shortly through Colonel Nicholls.'

'Thank you, sir. And thank you for seeing me . . .' I turned to the door.

'*Marks* . . .' It was Tommy Davies, determined (like any true Welshman) to have the last word. 'Shortly doesn't mean five minutes from now! Or even five hours! Nor does it mean September the 24th [he'd worked out my birthday.] You'll have to wait for at least a week. So forget about us and push on with your work . . .'

It was exactly a week before Nicholls sent for me. Heffer, at his most inscrutable, was standing beside him.

Nick shook hands in silence, then showed me a memo from the 'hard men'.

Ten minutes later I telephoned Commander Hogg and told him that SOE was assured of sufficient silk to reproduce 200 LOPs a month, and a further fifty on waterproof paper. I added (though it wasn't strictly his business) that we were also in a position to produce 200 WOKs a month.

Long pauses from quick thinkers should be prohibited by law.

'I'll require confirmation of this from General Gubbins,' he finally announced.

'It's on its way to you by dispatch rider.'

'Then you can expect your first pads within forty-eight hours.'

I may have been mistaken but just before he replaced the receiver I thought I heard him chuckle.

THIRTY-FOUR

Judicial Review

Distrustful though most of us were of anything in Baker Street which looked like progress, some events had taken place while I'd been importuning printers and photographers which even the most cynical of us recognized as landmarks. I'd been privy to most of them, made a contribution to some of them, and properly absorbed not a single one.

It was essential to look back at them without being distracted by the rigours of code-birth.

On 1 March the Dutch directorate was drastically reorganized. Bingham became head of N section, and his predecessor Blizzard (described by Heffer as 'the lesser of two weevils') was transferred to the Italian section. Killick continued to be communications officer, and on 8 March wrote a long letter to the Signals directorate which had the distinction of requiring an answer.

Ozanne (still in charge of Signals, though seldom of himself) passed the screed to Nick, and it was waiting on my desk when I dropped back from the City.

At a reluctant first reading it seemed a pristine example of a new regime testing its strength on a directorate renowned for not having any. But even to City-glazed eyes it soon became apparent that there was much more to it than that:

FROM NT [KILLICK] TO MS [OZANNE]
8TH MARCH 1943

A Dutch wireless operator [Netball] will be going to the field to a reception committee in about a week's time. On the WT forms

274

which I submitted in respect of this agent I requested that sufficient spare plans and code poems should be given to him to cover his needs for six months. The choice of the period of six months is, of course, purely arbitrary. I was informed by DYC/M [me] this morning that OC Station 52 [Major Byrne] objected to providing this man with spare poems on the grounds of security. I would now like to confirm my conversation with MS/A [Nick] on this subject in which I pointed out:

(a) That the agent in question is going to a reception committee, and can, if necessary, leave any written matter which he does not care to carry about with him with this committee.
(b) That if spare plans and poems are not taken by the agent himself they will have to be sent with a container operation to the same reception committee and passed to him by hand through various intermediaries. This is an undertaking which we naturally wish to avoid.

I ventured to suggest to MS/A that the question of whether an agent should take spare plans and poems with him, or whether these should be sent to him afterwards, was a matter for the Country section to decide after consideration of the circumstances of the agent's work in the field and the requirements of MS section.

I understand that MS/A agrees that in this case at least the operations should go on as requested in our W/T form, and would respectfully ask you to take the necessary action.

Nick had added a footnote, 'Contact me immediately', with the last word underlined.

We had an unusually open debate considering that the subject was Holland. He was reluctant to leave the distribution of codes to the discretion of any country section, least of all the Dutch. And we agreed that Byrne's objections to giving Netball a supply of spare poems were valid. Yet we both saw hidden advantages in allowing him to have them. To Nick, it was a chance to reassure the Dutch that we trusted their judgement and were merely observing routine Signals precautions. To me it was a chance to send a message to

Giskes – the kind that could only be delivered by a captured agent.

Killick's letter clearly stated that Netball could leave any written matter which he didn't care to carry about with him with his reception committee. But the reception committee in which Killick had such confidence was being organized by Cucumber, who was high on my list of suspect agents. Moreover, Cucumber had close links with Boni, the one agent about whose capture I was absolutely certain, with Ebenezer a close second.

If my convictions about Holland were right (and they were so intense that I sometimes doubted them), Netball's chances of survival were virtually non-existent, and he was likely to be picked up on landing. In which event he'd have no chance to dispose of his codes, and if his journey to Holland achieved nothing else, he might unwittingly help us to mislead Giskes.

If the Master discovered that Netball had been given a six months' supply of poems he might reasonably conclude that we weren't about to change his favourite coding system, and were likely to remain wedded to poem-codes till the death of our agents did us part. Either misconception would help the surprise element of WOKs and LOPs, and might even prolong the lives of his prisoners.

Nick didn't comment on any of this. Nor did his eyebrows dissent from it.

Netball was issued with twenty-five spare poems photographed on soluble paper and carefully camouflaged. Three of the poems had been written by Killick after I'd explained to him that original compositions offered far better security. Such was the convoluted thinking which had become second nature to us when dealing with N section.

On 15 March I gave Netball his final code-briefing. It lasted the whole morning, and the stem of my pipe snapped in two (I smoked cigars in front of no agent but Tommy) when he thanked me for all the trouble I'd taken. I blamed the mishap on the manufacturers, and nearly snapped in two myself when he promised to bring me a meerschaum from Holland when his mission was over.

I gave printers and photographers a hard time for the rest of the week.

*   *   *

Although few of us believed in miracles unless we were responsible for them, two occurred on 20 March:

1 Heffer was still at his desk at six o'clock.
2 The Chiefs of Staff issued an official directive to SOE.

The latter was a forceps delivery after two years of acute labour pains, and the Guru proceeded to summarize its wondrous implications.

The parameters between C and SOE were now clearly defined. We'd become the first organization in the history of British warfare with a licence to commit sabotage, with the possible exception of the Houses of Parliament.

We were henceforth responsible for conducting all forms of clandestine warfare, for building up Secret Armies in occupied territories, and for securing maximum co-operation from governments-in-exile. SOE's quota of aircraft, arms and essential supplies would be substantially increased, which would lead to a sharp rise in dropping operations, and every department in SOE would at last have a chance to fulfil its potential.

Above all, the directive was explicit enough to be C-proof.

'So God bless the Chiefs of Staff,' said Heffer, 'even if no one else does.'

I made a note to remind Father to give Alanbrooke a discount on his bird books.

And suddenly heard myself shouting three questions at Heffer, who seemed in a hurry to leave: *Was SOE at last in a position to discuss the Dutch situation openly with the Chiefs of Staff? ... Could the Dutch traffic be shown to Tiltman of Bletchley instead of to some anonymous investigators called in by Gubbins? ... Was it too late for us to prevent Netball and two other agents (Lacrosse and Gherkin) from being dropped?*

His expression warned me that for all the good the directive was going to do Holland, it might as well have been drafted by Giskes. He gently explained that the Chiefs were counting on the Dutch Secret Army to implement 'Plan Holland' (the D-Day uprising), that its success was one of their main reasons for granting the directive, and that far from Dutch operations being cancelled he'd understood from Nick that they were going to be increased.

He then urged me to concentrate on producing WOKs and LOPs, and escaped while he could.

On 23 March I gave Lacrosse and Gherkin their final code-briefing. They were to be dropped into Holland the same night as Netball. And to the same reception committee.

That was the end of the March retrospective.

Devoid of prescience except when it wasn't needed, I had no inkling of the catastrophes to follow.

THIRTY-FIVE

The Masterstroke

Home Station wireless operators were closer to agents in the field yet further removed from them than anyone else in Signals.

They transmitted and received all their messages yet never read their contents.

They knew agents by their touch but never saw their faces.

They worried if they were late for their skeds but were never told the reasons.

It was a new experience for them to have an agent being captured while he was still transmitting . . .

On 2 April Boni came on the air at his prearranged sked, signalled QTC2 ('I have two messages'), and began transmitting them with his customary skill. But a few seconds later he stopped operating normally and sent a series of unintelligible letters. He then broke off altogether, 'and his transmission ended with a sharp emission as if the operator's hand was resting on the keyboard'.

This description was sent to London by Ken Howell, our most experienced signalmaster. It was rare for Ken to express himself strongly but he ended his report with a definitive statement: 'I have no doubt whatever that this agent has been caught at his set after sending the first five groups of his 67th message.'

I listened to a recording of these five groups, and said 'fuck' 100 times under my breath, each one a tribute to Giskes's craftsmanship.

Boni had been caught long before 2 April.

But who in SOE was going to believe it?

*   *   *

While high-level conferences were taking place between Gubbins, Nick and Bingham, and between Gubbins, Nick and the Executive Council, I tried to grasp the implications of Giskes's masterstroke, the most baffling indecipherable I'd yet encountered.

Why had he suddenly decided to dispense with the services of Boni – a one-man Signals directorate who handled the traffic of Parsnip, Potato, Cucumber, Trumpet and Tomato (amongst others)? And why had he done it in such a way that SOE couldn't fail to realize that Boni was blown? What new trap was the cunning bastard setting for us?

'The hand resting on the keyboard' might mean that Boni himself was finally at rest.

But there'd be none for me until I understood Giskes's motivation, and could convince SOE of it.

Nick sent for me as soon as his conferences were over. Clearly not wanting another, he gave me as brief a situation report as he thought he could get away with.

All Boni-related operations had been cancelled in case he'd been taken alive, and the three new agents (Netball, Lacrosse and Gherkin) wouldn't be dropped before 16 April. As a further precaution, all Boni's contacts were going under cover, and London wouldn't know the details of his capture until they resumed transmitting.

Pre-empting my bombardment, he added that Gubbins had never been convinced by Plan Giskes (the indecipherable to Boni) that he'd been caught months ago, and accepted Ken Howell's report as conclusive.

He made the mistake of pausing for breath, and I shot my first question: 'If other agents confirm that Boni's been caught, will this be regarded as proof that they aren't blown themselves?'

He snapped that decisions of this kind must be left to those qualified to make them, and that our job was to report irregularities and breaches of security, and not pass judgement on the contents of agents' messages.

I pointed out that I'd been forbidden to discuss the biggest irregularity of all with anyone but himself and Gubbins, and reminded him that since June '42 not a single Dutch agent had made a mistake in his coding, and whether or not he and Gubbins chose to believe it, the few indecipherables they'd sent us were due to Morse-mutilated indicator-groups, and I was beginning to think that the whole damn lot of them must have been caught on landing.

Our fatigue made equals of us for the next ten seconds, and he wearily admitted that he was as concerned about the Dutch traffic as I was, but there was no point in rehashing reports which had already been considered. However, if anything new aroused my suspicions, I was to bring it to him at once, and he'd take it to the general. He reminded me to keep my anxieties about Holland to myself, and eyebrowed me from the office before I could unload the other million of them.

On 7 April Ebenezer broke cover to transmit a long message from Potato, and a short one of his own.

Potato regretted to inform London that at the beginning of April Boni had been caught in a surprise raid on his flat in The Hague, and that Cabbage believed he'd been betrayed by a traitor in the Victory group. Potato shared this suspicion, and contact had been broken off with all members of the Victory group. Potato assured London that Parsnip and Cabbage were both safe but had suspended all activities for the time being.

Ebenezer reported that during the recent bombing raid on Amsterdam three members of the Catarrh group had been killed, and he warned London that the damage caused by such raids was out of all proportion to the harm which they did to the civilian population. *(A caring Giskes?)*

Two-way traffic was then resumed.

On 8 April N section informed Ebenezer that they'd lost contact with Boni since he'd faded out completely during his 2 April sked, and asked him to authenticate Potato's account of his capture.

He replied almost by return that Boni had been picked up on 2 April by three police agents, who seemed to know when and where to find him, and that everything had happened very quickly. He added that according to Parsnip, Vinus had also disappeared and was feared to be in German custody.

N section's confidence in Ebenezer, Parsnip, Potato and Co. was now greater than ever, but even they had become anxious about Kale.

This key figure had taken over command of the Secret Army last November but had consistently found excuses not to return to London to give a first-hand account of his progress.

I began to sense the dimension of Giskes's problems, and made a list of questions which only he could answer.

Had he decided to sacrifice Boni not only to cast doubts about the Victory group's loyalties, but also because he was running out of excuses to explain Kale's failure to return? And surely he must have had similar difficulties explaining why Professor Jambroes (Marrow) had also failed to return despite N section's repeated requests? (After months of inspired prevarication Jambroes had finally agreed to return in November, but on the day he was due to leave he was killed 'in a shoot-out with German soldiers', a 'tragedy' first reported by Kale and subsequently confirmed by N section's favourite team of investigative reporters, Messrs Cucumber, Potato, Parsnip and Co.)

On 13 April Kale sent a lengthy message via Cucumber stating that because of the unavoidable delays in returning he proposed to send a full report on the Secret Army's progress in a number of separate messages. He would use his own code and spread the transmissions between Cucumber, Broccoli and Tomato.

With Nick's permission, I warned N section that Kale was in danger of overloading his code, and that it would be safer to send all his reports in Cucumber's reserve poem number three, which he must use exclusively for his Secret Army traffic. Another reason for suggesting a change of code was that if Kale had been caught it might prevent Giskes from realizing that London suspected it.

On 14 April N section instructed Kale to use Cucumber's reserve poem number 3 for his Secret Army reports, but stressed that continued efforts must be made to assist Broadbean to reach Paris to organize new escape lines.

N section then instructed Tomato to inform Kale that Netball would bring an envelope with him containing spare poems for Kale, Cucumber, Tomato and Broccoli, and that if Netball's drop were delayed until 16 April, Gherkin, a first-class organizer, would accompany him.

*   *   *

While these arrangements were being finalized without any objections from Holland's leading travel agent, the April moon was also being used (not always to better advantage) by SOE's rival French sections.

On 15 April Peter Churchill was once again dispatched to the South of France. This time he was dropped into the Haute Savoie, where Odette, Sanson and Rabinovitch were waiting to receive him. He almost succeeded in dropping into Odette's arms, and Rabinovitch transmitted a message from him that he'd arrived safely, and that his reception committee was 'absolutely perfect'.

Two days later Rabinovitch reported that Peter and Odette had been captured the previous night in the Hôtel de la Poste in St Jérioz. He would send a detailed report as soon as he could.

On 18 April he sent a message which was far too long for his own security explaining that, after leaving Peter and Odette at the hotel, he'd returned to his set to report to London. The hotel had been raided in the early hours of the morning by a group of Carabinieri led by a German who he believed was a senior member of the secret police. Peter and Odette, posing as husband and wife, had been found in an upstairs bedroom and arrested. He thought they'd been taken to an Italian prison.

On 19 April Buckmaster urged Rabinovitch to return to London via the Spanish escape routes but Rabinovitch refused. He knew that Roger (Cammaerts the plodder) had gone to Cannes and wanted to warn him of Peter's and Odette's arrest. Only when this had been accomplished would he return to London. In the meantime he would keep his messages as short as possible and would stay out of touch for the next week.

Three days later two more of Buckmaster's agents were arrested. They were Germaine Tambour and her sister Madeleine, whose contacts had been invaluable to F section and whose house had been used by a group of key agents (including Peter) as a letter-box and meeting place.

It was a major setback for Buckmaster, and I pretended not to see him when I passed him in the corridor on his way to the Signals Office. He was deeply involved with all his agents, but Peter was in a special category. He was not only Buckmaster's friend but a member of his headquarters staff with a detailed knowledge of his forward planning, and Maurice now had to face the likelihood that two of his principal circuits (Prosper and Carte) had collapsed. He sent a batch of messages to the field warning his agents not to use safe-houses frequented by Peter, Odette and the Tambour sisters, and gave them a list of new ones which they must start using immediately.

It was left to Duke Street to provide April's only good news.

On 16 April de Gaulle recalled Passy, Brossolette and Tommy from France. They were picked up by Lysander close to midnight, and resumed their duties in London early next morning.

I checked that Tommy's cigar lay in state next to the photo of the Louis–Schmeling fight which Rabinovitch had given me. They were still the only objects in my desk I could be sure of finding.

On 18 April Kale's first report on the Dutch Secret Army was transmitted by Cucumber. It was perfectly encoded in Cucumber's reserve poem number 3 and gave a detailed analysis of the progress being made in the sixteen provinces where the main recruitment was taking place.

On 21 April Netball, Gherkin and Lacrosse were dropped into Holland with twenty-eight containers and seven packages.

On 22 April Ebenezer confirmed Lacrosse's safe arrival. He added that more supply operations would be very welcome in the near future and that eight tommy-guns should be included. He also needed a large quantity of abrasives (my comments on supplying them were open to offer).

On the same night Cucumber reported the safe arrival of Netball and Gherkin, and asked when the next shipment of containers could be expected.

Compliant as ever, London assured him that dropping operations would continue until the end of the moon period on 25 April but would be cancelled during the dark period and resumed when the new moon started on 9 May.

Later the same day (23 April) London assured Ebenezer that six containers would be dispatched to him in the next moon period but warned him that the address in Switzerland used by Potato for his innocent letters was no longer safe.*

---

* 'Innocent letters' were usually sent to neutral territories for onward transmission to SOE. The only innocent thing about them was the code they used, which was a form of Playfair at its most vulnerable.

284

April's biggest shock (if not the war's) came on 24 April, and although I'd been taught by Father that anyone who complained that the bottom had dropped out of his world was an arse-hole, I joined that distinguished company.

I was informed by the supervisor at 53b that Cucumber had transmitted an indecipherable from Kale, and that all routine attempts to break it had failed. The code-groups were being teleprinted to London.

I immediately contacted the signalmaster, who assured me that atmospheric conditions had been excellent, that Cucumber's operating had been flawless, and that there was no question of Morse mutilation.

This negated every theory I had about the Germans double-checking Dutch agents' coding.

Lacking the self-confidence to give up a conviction, I decided that only two inferences could be drawn from this unique indecipherable. Either Kale *had* made a mistake in his coding, which meant that he was free. Or Giskes had produced another masterstroke!

Perhaps he had broken my deliberate indecipherable, and was repaying me in kind.

I prayed in Hebrew and in Latin that this wasn't the case because God only knew what he'd think up next.

I was still praying when Muriel put the code-groups in front of me.

THIRTY-SIX

Desperate Measures

Despite Nick's perceptive advice to 'treat Kale's indecipherable like any other' I was unable to respond to it with the necessary detachment. But after wasting ten minutes searching for new approaches, I realized that speculation about Giskes would hold up the breaking, and that I must proceed on the assumption that Kale was free.

The most important question was whether he'd encoded the message himself or allowed his WT operator (Cucumber) to do it for him. It was a hard one to resolve because, despite strict orders to the contrary, organizers often handed their codes to their WT operators and asked them to encode their messages for them; Kale might not regard this as much of an infringement as he was using one of Cucumber's poems.

I referred to the notes I'd made on their respective briefings.

Kale's had taken place on 18 September '42, and he'd been dropped into Holland on the 24th (my birthday, since no essential information should be withheld). Cucumber's had taken place on 25 October, and he'd been dropped on the 27th. Both had an excellent grasp of double-transposition, but agents tended to put on special performances at their final briefings, if only to get rid of me, and it was essential to see what kind of mistakes they'd made at their training schools.

Muriel produced their training files without having to be asked.

Kale had encoded four indecipherables in fifteen messages, all due to misnumbered key-phrases. Cucumber had encoded twelve indecipherables in thirty messages – six due to 'hatted' columns, five to misnumbered key-phrases, and one to a misspelt word in his poem.

286

If Kale had done his own encoding, we'd concentrate on misnumbered key-phrases. If Cucumber had done it for him, we'd have to broaden the attack.

I decided that commanders of Secret Armies were occasionally known to set good examples and that Kale had encoded the message himself.

1,500 attempts later there was no sign of a misnumbered key-phrase. I instructed the girls to try another 1,000, and tackled 100 myself. None of them succeeded, and the message's 300 letters began to feel like 3,000.

Staring at the code-groups, I suddenly realized that there was an important factor which I'd completely overlooked.

This was only the second time that Kale had used Cucumber's poem, and its unfamiliarity might have caused him to misspell a word. The poem was in Dutch, and I'd need someone to advise me on common misspellings.

I tried to contact Bingham and Killick but was told that they were on their way to a training school, and left a message for them to ring me as soon as they could.

I then enquired if there was anyone in the Signals directorate who had even a smattering of the language.

A coder admitted that she'd spent a week in Amsterdam and knew the Dutch for 'kiss my arse', and a signalmaster had been able to order a Dutch cap in The Hague, but that was the limit of their fluency.

I was wondering whether to contact the Dutch government-in-exile when rescue arrived from a source far closer to home.

The menaces who shared the office with me (Charlotte Denman and Molly Brewis) knew that I was in dire straits and hadn't once interrupted me. Then, without any warning, Molly Menace cleared her throat and blushed like a schoolgirl admitting her first crush. 'I know a word or two of Dutch,' she said.

The three of us occasionally surprised each other (a major asset to involuntary intimacy), and I thanked her for the best news of the day. I waited until the great frame was seated beside me, and explained that agents not only misspelled the words of their poems but frequently replaced them with similar-sounding words ('piece' for 'peace', 'mite' for 'might, 'soul' for 'sole'). Hoping to promote some rivalry, I added

287

that Vera Atkins of F section excelled at suggesting similar-sounding words, and had helped us with many a French indecipherable (some of them Duke Street's, though I hadn't admitted it).

'Oh God,' she exclaimed. 'I'm awful at guessing games.' And then proceeded to prove it.

Her first dozen guesses produced gibberish, and she tried a dozen more, watching anxiously while I tested them.

To make her feel part of the operation, I explained that the charts I was using showed how the first line of the message would be read if her guesses were correct. But unfortunately none of them were.

By now she was beginning to enjoy it, and made another twenty suggestions. Twenty more fiascos.

Unaccustomed to being a silent spectator, Mrs Denman announced that she'd like to ask a question.

'Please do,' I said, hoping she wanted to know when Molly could return to her desk.

'Do you still think that the message was either encoded by a German or checked by one before it was transmitted?' It was my first intimation that Nick had told her of my suspicions.

'Yes – what of it?' was my courteous response.

'Then shouldn't you be trying to misspell the poem as a *German* might instead of a Dutchman?'

The idea hadn't even occurred to me.

'Will you marry me, Charlotte? – and we'll adopt Molly?'

A team by now, we held a brief conference and agreed that the obvious solution was to consult X section (the German directorate), though there was so much secrecy about anything to do with the Dutch that we mightn't be allowed to approach them.

Charlotte suggested that by the time we got official permission we could have learned the language ourselves.

Blushing again, Molly admitted that she spoke a word or two of German.

Our adopted daughter then went into action.

Her first dozen suggestions produced nothing but *Kauderwelsch*, which according to her was the German for gibberish.

Her next dozen produced more of the same but, encouraged by Charlotte, she Kauderwelsched on.

288

I'd decided by now that it would be quicker if I tried to anagram the message out using Kale's first message for probable content. I was wondering how to break the news without hurting everyone's feelings when they came to the next word of the poem: 'Prijs'.

'I suppose it would be "preis" in German," said Molly, without much conviction.

'No doubt of it,' said Charlotte, 'no doubt at all.'

Having no faith in it whatsoever, I substituted 'Preis' for 'Prijs' and numbered the transposition-key accordingly, making two mistakes in the process.

'Can't Molly help?' enquired Charlotte. 'She's good at maths too.'

Glad that one of us was, I numbered the phrase correctly, and then applied the charts, warning them that there was very little chance of clear-text emerging.

The letters UTR appeared, followed by ECHT . . .

'*Utrecht*' yelled the ladies in case I missed it.

Ten minutes later Kale's second report on the Secret Army was ready for distribution. Nick, N section and Gubbins were notified, and I told the coders at 53b that their colleagues in London had broken it to make them feel less excluded.

Bingham telephoned and instructed me to read the message to him over the scrambler. He rang off without comment the moment I'd finished.

'Some people', said Charlotte, 'know the Preis of everything and the value of nothing.'

An hour later I learned that I was one of them.

Nick called in to offer his congratulations, and I asked if Charlotte and Molly could be transferred to the code department.

The three of them then had a personal conversation which they made no attempt to conduct in undertones – an event without precedent. It concerned two of their friends who'd been married for fifty years without being separated for more than a day. The wife had died recently, and although her husband had nothing physically wrong with him, he took to his bed and willed himself to follow her. Two days ago he had succeeded, and tomorrow they were to be buried side by side.

289

I wondered how it must feel to be buried next to one's other half for ever, bombs and property developers permitting:

> It will feel strange
> Not to nudge you
> Or to talk to you
> Or keep you warm
> When you're lying there
> Only a few feet away
> Or perhaps even less
> But we shall get used to it in time
> Of which we'll have plenty
>
> We always treasured silences
> In which we said everything
> We shall continue to treasure them
> And to say everything
> Throughout the longest silence of all.

It had no place in the ditty-box but I'd found that occasional dollops of sentiment cleared my head for facts, and there were three which I had to live with:

1   I was never going to convince SOE of the extent of Giskes's penetration.
2   I was too close to the corpse of Kale's indecipherable to conduct a proper autopsy.
3   My talent as a cryptographer was the longest silence of all.

THIRTY-SEVEN

Punitive Expedition

It was rare for anyone outside the Signals directorate to show the slightest interest in how indecipherables were broken, but when I least welcomed it Gubbins and Bingham displayed too much.

The general required a full report on the significance (if any) of 'Prijs'/'Preis', and Bingham wanted to know if we'd made the mistake ourselves.

After a cooling-off period of one morning (a millennium by SOE's standards) I returned to 'Prijs'/'Preis', and rapidly decided that Giskes hadn't sent London a deliberate indecipherable. If he'd wanted to return the compliment, he'd have taken at least as much trouble as I had, and wouldn't have used a Germanicized misspelling. But this still didn't mean that Kale wasn't caught.

It was unlikely that Giskes would undertake the manual labour of double-transposition in addition to his own creative writing, and a negligent subordinate might have encoded the message, or failed to check Kale's encoding if he'd been permitted to do it himself. Perhaps the Germans had their off moments too.

I said as much in my report to Nick, emphasizing that 'the hitherto perfect encoding of all Dutch agents despite the circumstances in which they operated' must surely lead to only one conclusion: that most of them had been caught on landing, or shortly afterwards.

I was instructed by return to keep a 'special watch' on Kale's future traffic.

His next batch of messages were perfectly encoded, and on 29 April he sent his final Secret Army report. He ended by stressing that if the battle to liberate Holland didn't take place soon even his most resolute supporters would be influenced by German propaganda (vintage Giskes?).

The traffic of Ebenezer, Heck, Hockey and Co. was equally disturbing as they'd never been more active in the Allied cause. Between the lot of them, they were going to evacuate Broadbean to Paris, locate the headquarters of the 65th Marine Infantry division, and verify a report that the Germans were preparing to re-inundate the old Dutch water defences in case of invasion.

I wondered how much longer Giskes could keep it up.

At the beginning of May the Executive Council made an announcement which was so long overdue that all but agnostics had given up praying for it. The symbols list proclaimed that Colonel F. W. Nicholls had replaced Colonel G. D. Ozanne as director of Signals.

Heffer, who'd been lobbying for months to bring this about, confided that Ozanne had been sent on leave prior to being outposted on 1 June, and had been allowed a few hours' grace in which to clear out his belongings. SOE had no use for empty bottles.

I congratulated the Guru on his part in our liberation, and asked the key question: Was Nick now in a position to insist on showing the Dutch traffic to Tiltman?

Edging towards the door, he reminded me that Nick had been MS (director of Signals) for less than half an hour and that I mustn't expect miracles. He then quietly informed me that Nick was now in the running to become a member of the Executive Council and that it would be a great help to all of us if he were elected.

He escaped without answering my question about Tiltman.

En route to the Signals Office for a punitive purpose, I spotted the deposed Ozanne waddling down the corridor. He stopped outside his office as if he wondered whether to knock, then disappeared inside, perhaps for the last time.

A few seconds later I found myself knocking on his door.

His Gubbins-like 'Come' was now a fledgling FANY's quaver. He was as astonished to see me as I was to be there.

I knew I daren't smile in case he thought I'd come to gloat.

'What the devil do you want?'

As I tried to work it out, the drowning man's life flashed before me.

He'd been appointed MS in February '42 and immediately imposed C's concept of clandestine communications on SOE. Despite the protests of his subordinates his confidence in C's judgement remained purblind, and by the time Nick arrived to take control of agents' traffic he'd successfully crushed all efforts to scrap the poem-code and replace it with WOKs. He'd also supported all the other Signals deathtraps recommended by C. A professional Signals officer, he'd suffered the ultimate ignominy of being found inadequate by amateurs but at least his convictions were genuine, unlike those of some senior figures in SOE.

'I need a bit of advice, sir.'

He clearly thought he'd misheard me. *'You need a bit of what?'*

I was tempted to say 'nookie' but, true though this was, it was hardly likely to concern him. 'A bit of advice, sir.'

He examined me from head to toe (a regrettably short distance) as a silent reminder that I'd thwarted his efforts to make a second lieutenant in the Royal Corps of Signals. 'If you've got a problem, take it to Colonel Nicholls or Captain Heffer — it's what they're here for.'

I explained that they were on their way to Station 53b and that I didn't think it could wait.

He eyed me suspiciously as I struggled to think of a problem to present to him. 'What is it then?' he finally asked. 'I haven't much time.'

I remembered that I was clutching a telegram which I'd been on my way to dispatch when I'd spotted him in the corridor. It was addressed to the coders of Massingham, who'd received an indecipherable from an agent in Italy which they'd made no attempt to break, though it had been in the code room for almost a week. My reprimand included the motto, 'There shall be no such thing as an indecipherable message', and contained a number of other pertinent comments. 'It's about this message I want to send Massingham, sir.' I informed him of the girls' dereliction, and that I wanted to send them a suitably worded reprimand.

'What the devil's that to do with me?'

I explained that the first thing I wanted him to do was initial the telegram so that it could be sent out at once.

293

He reminded me sharply that ever since I'd been appointed head of agents' codes I'd been allowed to originate main-line telegrams, and he wasn't aware that my authority had been rescinded, though he suspected that it should have been.

'I have the authority, sir, but I was hoping for your comments on the message itself. I'm not sure if it's strong enough.'

He examined the telegram as if it too were wearing civilian clothing which had been manufactured by a Jewish tailor who was far from bespoke. A sound escaped him which might have been a belch, or an even less sociable intestinal call-sign. 'I don't know what you're up to, Marks! But if you *really* want my opinion of this . . .'

I assured him that I did, and found that I meant it.

He gave me a brief lecture on the art of reprimanding subordinates, his chins waddling as he warmed to his particular sphere of expertise. He then said that in his opinion the motto was the only reminder the girls needed, that the phrase 'get off your arses' was not in SOE's code-book, though he often felt it should be, and that the best of us can make mistakes.

He ended by running his pencil through everything which he considered redundant, and contemplated the result with an editor's satisfaction. It had lost twenty words and was all the better for it.

I thanked him for improving the message and repeated my request for him to initial it.

'Why do you need me to if you've got the authority?'

'So that I can blame it on you if it backfires, sir.'

He chuckled as he initialled his last telegram, and his next question took me completely by surprise.

'What's happened to your new codes which I didn't think much of?'

I told him that the first WOKs and LOPs would be delivered in a fortnight but would have to be checked and camouflaged and couldn't be issued until the June moon.

A small smile checked and camouflaged whatever he was thinking. 'Don't be impatient. June will be here all too soon, take it from me.' His outposting was due on 1 June.

He stared down at an in-tray which was as empty as his future, and I couldn't believe what I said to him next.

'I'm not sure they're going to work, sir.' It was the first time I'd admitted this to anyone, myself included.

'*Why not?*'

'I don't know, sir – I've a feeling I've missed something.'

'Nonsense. They'll do the job, that's one thing I *am* sure of. . . . What's more . . .' His voice trailed away like Boni's touch on the keyboard, and a moment later he reached for the drawer where his bottles were kept.

But he wasn't quite ready to relinquish command, and pointed a shaky finger at our joint telegram. 'You've marked that message "Top Priority" and it's high time you gave it some! Dispatch it at once.'

'Right, sir.'

I wanted to thank him and wish him good luck but he gave me a dismissive nod which might have been meant for both of us.

It was only when I'd closed the door that I realized why I'd opened it. I needed the company of another failure to make my own bearable.

SOE would never know how much it owed to a tube of French toothpaste and a Belgian labourer's cap.

They'd arrived last night from the Thatched Barn. The toothpaste was intended to camouflage a WOK, the cap a LOP, and I was happily examining the false bottom of one and the lining of the other when I heard what was usually my favourite sound (my own voice) telling Ozanne that I was afraid the new codes weren't going to work as I had a feeling that I'd missed something.

The feeling was now a conviction.

It had something to do with the camouflage, though I'd no idea what. To ease the growing tension and allow the cause of it to surface, I wore the Belgian cap LOPsided and gave the French toothpaste a hearty squeeze. A white blob emerged but gave no warning of the dark truth which accompanied it.

We'd paid endless attention to the camouflaging of codes but none whatever to the camouflaging of code-groups. If any of our code-groups stood out in isolation, wireless interception units could pinpoint them and track the movements of the operators who'd transmitted them. They could also detect the arrival of new agents, and build up a picture of impending operations.

WOK code-groups were exempt from this worry as they were the product of double-transposition and couldn't be distinguished from poem-code traffic. But LOP code-groups were the product of substitutions and would stand out from all our other messages because of the proportion of vowels to consonants, and the shortness of the messages (as few as ten letters).

Unless we found a way to remedy this deficiency, interception units would have a field day.

I hurried into Nick and showed him the same message encoded in both a WOK and a LOP:

WOK message: COFIH LADEO STESA LERTD NUSOT DRNIS
LOP message: XTZOM YVHJR ZDVGG TYPHL XVSTG DOZTE

He took one glance at the code-groups, and at once sent for Heffer.

The Guru was now MS/A (deputy director of Signals), but still saw no reason to hurry, and examined the messages like a tortoise reconnoitring a leaf. 'Right,' he finally said. *'What can we do about it?'*

We agreed that there was no way of making substitution code-groups resemble transposition-keys without a major re-encipherment process which agents couldn't undertake. Nor could we conceal the shortness of the messages. We also agreed that LOPs were far too valuable to be abandoned.

Nick said that he'd encountered similar problems with peacetime traffic, though they had little relevance to our present dilemma. After exchanging reminiscences with Heffer, he decided that the only way to prevent the enemy from pinpointing individual messages would be to wait until large numbers of agents had been issued with LOPs so that they opened up simultaneously right across Europe.

Heffer suggested that the best time would be August, when dropping operations were likely to expand. Nick favoured November, and they compromised on September, subject to what might happen in the meantime.

Nick then congratulated me on spotting the problem in time, and I hurried from the office before I exploded.

I should have spotted it from the outset. But so should Nick and

296

Heffer! And what about Tiltman and Dudley-Smith, the experts from Bletchley? Did they neglect to mention it because it was so elementary that they felt they didn't need to?

What else was so obvious that the head of agents' codes had completely overlooked it?

After wasting an hour brooding about Holland, and the dangers of Dutch agents using Belgian escape lines, I heard the sound of my favourite footsteps.

I hadn't seen Tommy since he'd called in to claim the cigar which made his return from France official. That was over a fortnight ago and I'd missed being part of his dawn patrol.

However, I'd kept track of his progress, and knew that he'd been sent for by his idol de Gaulle, who'd thanked him for all that he was doing for France, and asked for his impressions of the French will to resist.

I hoped that he hadn't come to evaluate mine.

He sat opposite me, which made the office complete, studied my face instead of the contents of my desk, and asked if he were interrupting.

'No more than usual.'

He accepted a new cigar and continued to watch me in silence as he lit it. 'Now then,' he said. 'Bring me up to date.'

I produced a silk for his inspection, and he examined it as if he were wearing gloves. Pronouncing it excellent, he reminded me that the first time he'd seen a WOK it was still an idea on paper.

I was about to say that without his encouragement it probably still would be when he caught sight of a LOP. 'That looks interesting. Are you allowed to tell me what it is?'

'No,' I said, and proceeded to show him how it worked.

He listened in silence, then asked if he could try it for himself. He wrote a message in French fifty letters long 'to give it a proper test', and I watched him become the first agent to encode a message in a LOP.

It was a ponderous performance as he double-checked each letter he enciphered. 'This is bloody slow going,' he complained. But halfway through the message he began to find his rhythm, and he finished the last twenty-five letters more quickly than I could.

'What do you call this code?'

'A LOP!'

'Short for "Leo's an old pisspot"?'

'Letter one-time pad.'

'Available to Duke Street?'

'If they'll accept it.'

'Why the hell shouldn't they? – I'll help you all I can . . . remind me about the checks.'

I took him through them again, though I knew he understood them and was simply making sure that he'd done his correctly.

'Do we have to make a choice between WOKs and LOPs?'

I said that I hoped that LOPs would become the main code, with WOKs in reserve, and poems in emergencies.

'There'll be plenty of those . . . but I can promise you this. These codes are going to make a lot of difference to a hell of a lot of agents and I hope to be one of them. I'll use both of them next time I go in. Agreed?'

'Yes, Tommy.'

I hoped that if he had to go in again, it wouldn't be before September.

He glanced at his watch as if it were September already, then rose abruptly, and I wished him goodnight.

He didn't reply till he reached the door. He then turned back, and spoke very quietly. 'Next time, perhaps you'd care to tell me what's worrying you – something bloody well is, and it's about time it stopped.'

'Old pisspot' spent the rest of the night wondering how he knew.

THIRTY-EIGHT

The Secret Weapon

Country sections approved of poem-codes because they couldn't be detected if agents were searched. The fact that they could be tortured out of them and were easy to break were secondary considerations. If they opposed the introduction of silks and we had to ask Gubbins to over-rule them (as he'd assured Nick he would), we'd get their reluctant co-operation but forfeit their goodwill.

Knowing this, on 2 June Nick took the unprecedented step of sending a memo to all country section heads requesting them to see me in the presence of their respective signals officers, so that I could explain on MS/A's behalf why a radically new system of agents' traffic would shortly be introduced. We agreed that there was no point in mentioning LOPs: if WOKs didn't convince them of the value of tangible codes, nothing would.

On 3 June I embarked on the sales campaign, knowing that Frank Doel would make a far better job of it.

Maurice Buckmaster was the first country section head to be shown a WOK. Normally responsive to everything which would enhance the welfare of his agents, he was facing the collapse of his two principal circuits, and suggesting new codes to him was like taking a drowning man's hand and offering to manicure it.

He gave a cursory glance at the WOK which I put in front of him, muttered that he didn't want his agents to carry another damn thing, and left the rest to Captain Noble, his signals officer.

He couldn't have submitted the code to a better qualified judge. Noble (real name George Bégué) was a self-effacing Frenchman with the added distinction of being the first SOE agent to parachute into the field. He'd been dropped blind into France in May '41, taking

299

with him a rudimentary wireless set and a poem-code. He transmitted more than forty vital messages but had such contempt for his security checks that he'd ignored them altogether, and relied on prearranged questions and answers. He'd been arrested by the Vichy police in October '41, and F section didn't expect to hear from him again. But in July '42 he'd escaped from a Vichy-run prison in the heart of the Dordogne, taking nine of his fellow-agents with him. He made his way to Lyons, crossed the frontier into Spain, and was taken on to Buckmaster's HQ staff as soon as he returned to London.

He'd be a major asset to the Signals directorate as a briefing officer. But at this moment he could also be an insuperable obstacle.

I explained the advantages of silk codes to him but didn't mention their security checks. I wanted to see if he'd refer to them himself, and with a cynical little smile he eventually did.

Although he grasped the principle at once, I gave him a detailed exposition in case Maurice was tuning in. Noble waited impatiently till I'd finished, then copied out a pair of WOK-keys, rapidly encoded a message, and changed the indicator by secret numbers known only to him. As if to prove Nick's maxim, 'once an agent always an agent', he checked his handiwork carefully while his fingers drummed out the code-groups in Morse. Satisfied that he hadn't forgotten how to doubly-transpose, he produced a razor blade and without asking permission (which I'd gladly have given) cut the keys off the silk and watched them smoulder. I knew just how they felt.

He then turned to Buckmaster, who was somewhere in France. 'If I'd been given such a silk to take in,' he said, 'I'd have troubled to use my security checks.'

Maurice reluctantly conceded that WOKs might be suitable for WT operators because they could hide them with their sets, but he was damned if he'd force organizers to carry codes as they moved around France, no matter how well the bloody things were camouflaged. He glared at me with his 'My decision is final' expression.

Noble was silent when I needed him most.

I confided to Maurice that WOKs were in very short supply and that it was most unlikely that we'd be able to spare them for all his organizers as the Free French demands were likely to be heavy.

At this point I had my first order.

An outraged Maurice accused me of not realizing how important his organizers were, and he absolutely insisted that all F section agents were given silk codes or I'd damn soon hear from him. And so would Nicholls.

And if the WOKs weren't forthcoming he'd go straight to Gubbins. Noble winked at me as I left.

My next potential client was Colonel Hutchison.

I could hardly tell the head of RF section that I was ten minutes late for our appointment because I'd stopped off en route to break an indecipherable in de Gaulle's secret code and sent it round to Duke Street properly enciphered.

The autocratic colonel glanced at his watch as soon as I entered his office, and I apologized for the unavoidable delay. His signals officer (tiny Kay Moore) was perched beside him, notebook at the ready.

I noticed that he had Nick's memo in front of him with several words underlined.

He announced that although French was the only language permitted on the premises, he'd make an exception in my case. I made an exception in his by giving him a simplistic WOK-briefing, and he commented on the quality of the *soie*.

He then said that although he was expecting 'radical changes' he hadn't anticipated such a complete volte-face, and was by no means convinced it was for the better. He then insisted on encoding a message himself.

It took him five minutes to decide on a suitable text, another five to copy out his transposition-keys, and five more to remember what to do with them.

Kay and I studied each other in silence. I was surprised that she could bear to look at me. It was largely my fault that she had the most unrewarding job in the whole of SOE.

It was her responsibility to liaise between me and an enemy I'd made at Duke Street named Lieutenant Valois, who was in charge of all Free French radio and Signals planning. She also had to act as our interpreter (his English was on a par with my French) and we both knew that she edited our exchanges.

301

The main cause of our dissension was the prefixes he needed for de Gaulle's secret code. In order to show each other when they were using this abomination, Duke Street and its agents added special prefixes to their messages, and it was up to me to provide them. At present I owed Valois twenty, every one of them a potential L-tablet.

I'd repeatedly told him that these prefixes made it easy for the Germans to identify the secret French code and, though I had no idea what sort of code it was, it would be safer if the agents stopped using it as it was overloading their traffic.

He angrily reminded me that SOE had agreed to the use of this code, that the Free French had no intention of abandoning it, and that he was in no position to meddle with high-level policy. He suggested that I might care to raise the matter with General de Gaulle.

'Who?' I'd said.

At which point Kay had remembered another appointment.

I returned sharply to 3 June when Hutchison announced that he'd finished his message, and allowed me the privilege of inspecting it.

He'd 'hatted' three columns and omitted five code-groups, but I congratulated him on his excellent coding.

'It's simple enough,' he said, 'and has a number of advantages, but the problem is Duke Street . . .' He explained that the Free French were being more than usually obstructive over a number of issues, and might not agree to the poem-code being scrapped.

I pointed out that it was our responsibility to provide them with safe codes, and that Duke Street's autonomy applied only to de Gaulle's secret code, whatever that might be.

'That's all very well,' he said, 'but they mightn't see it that way. I'll have to think the whole thing over.'

I urged him not to take too long as I'd just come from a meeting with F section, whose requirements could exhaust our limited supplies.

However, he was too experienced an in-fighter to respond with order number two, and said he'd deal with the question of priorities if and when it arose. He then asked for Kay's opinion of silks.

The canny little lady made the most of her opportunity. Smiling sweetly, she said she thought they were an enormous improvement, and that Duke Street was far likelier to agree to them if Leo would send Valois the list of prefixes he was waiting for.

He looked at her in astonishment. 'What list? What prefixes? First I've heard of this.'

They then had a rapid exchange in French, and the only word I recognized was Leo.

The look which the colonel shot at me needed no translation. 'It's your job to provide prefixes as soon as Valois asks for them. Why haven't you?'

I explained that it was due to an oversight for which I accepted full responsibility.

'Then remedy it at once.'

I agreed that I would.

'*When?* Be precise.'

I told him that I was on my way to some appointments which were almost as important as this one, and would attend to the list by the end of the day.

'I want them on my desk first thing tomorrow and I'll send them to Duke Street with a covering note.'

I realized that he wanted the kudos of breaking the deadlock.

'Do I have your word that they'll be here?'

Sensing that a deal was in the offing, I promised that my secretary would deliver them to him personally.

'In that case you can count on my full support. Do I make myself clear?'

'*Mais oui, mon colonel – absolument – je vous remercie mille fois.*'

Kay didn't translate it.

Two down, and four to go.

Although the Norwegian, Danish and Belgian sections were having as hard a time as the French they gave me an easy one. Their questions were pertinent, their estimates sensible, and they hoped the system would be working by August.

Which left only the Dutch.

Bingham and his signals officer, Killick, had coffee waiting but were kind enough not to offer me a Dutch cigar. Bingham congratulated me on breaking Kale's indecipherable, and asked if I'd come to any further conclusions about 'Preis'/'Prijs'.

I told him that I hadn't, and plunged into the briefing.

They listened to my recitative as if it were a personal message from Queen Wilhelmina, and Bingham asked his few questions with a hint of apology.

I still didn't trust the man but he'd done a good job since he'd become head of N section, abandoning reception committees and insisting that new Dutch agents should be dropped blind.

I enquired how many WOKs they were likely to need over the next few months.

They exchanged glances. Bingham then explained that the loss of Boni had forced them to rethink their plans and they'd be sending in very few agents during the next two moon periods. He added that he and Killick were confident that fullscale operations would be resumed in August.

Without any warning Killick asked if I thought that the Germans were reading any of their messages.

I was still under instructions not to disclose my suspicions, and Killick's timing warned me to treat him with respect. I replied that the poem-code wasn't secure enough for the level of traffic SOE was passing, but we had no evidence that the Germans had cracked it or were reading Dutch or any other country section's messages.

Refilling my cup, which I'd made the supreme sacrifice of emptying, Bingham asked if I were suspicious of any Dutch agent's security checks.

I admitted that I was suspicious of *all* security checks in the poem-code except for prearranged questions and answers, and that this applied to *all* country sections. I then assured them that WOK-checks would enable agents to alert London the moment they were caught, and offered to run through the system again.

They declined politely. 'What we really want to know,' said Bingham, 'is whether you suspect any particular agent's security checks.'

The atmosphere was as fraught as a gynaecologist's ante-room.

'I've told you what I think of security checks,' I said, sinking to the occasion. 'I distrust the lot of 'em. But can't we pinpoint this? Are there any agents you're especially worried about?'

Bingham transfixed me with a stare, then shook his head.

I was wondering whether history would ever credit our follies, let alone learn from them, and whether Ebenezer would ever stip, step, and stap us in the balls, when I realized that Bingham was holding out his hand.

He thanked me for coming, apologized for taking up so much time, and said that silks would be a great help to Dutch agents.

I didn't tell him that one reason they were having them was that Giskes would be suspicious if they didn't.

I gave Nick and Heffer a verbatim account of each meeting, stressing that the Dutch were worried about their traffic, and that they'd tried hard to get me to confirm their suspicions. I didn't mention how close they'd come to succeeding.

Nick patted my shoulder as if conferring a knighthood and said that I'd handled their questions very tactfully.

'But why's tact necessary? Surely it's time we talked to them openly?' Perhaps I'd done one sales-pitch too many and my voice was inaudible because he didn't seem to hear me. I raised it an octave, and asked if we could discuss Boni's capture with them.

It was clear from his expression that a mutiny was about to be crushed. Rising like a cathedral in the course of construction, he reminded me that the general's orders hadn't changed, that it wasn't my business to question them, and that having won the battle for silks I should concentrate on producing them.

I realized that the internal Dutch game was completely beyond me, thanked him for his clarification, and turned to go.

Looking at me suspiciously, Heffer said he was certain I'd been up to something which I hadn't disclosed, that the experience had shaken me in a way that nothing else had, and he'd like to know what it was.

I told him that I would too, and that I'd let him know if I ever found out, and left it at that.

But he was right.

There'd been reports in the press, which didn't necessarily mean they were without foundation, that a Whitehall department was investigating rumours that Hitler had finally given in to his mystical impulses and was trying to use telepathy as a secret weapon. In which case, the Führer and I had something in common.

Lacking his resources, I'd developed a home-made technique for which the patent was pending. It consisted of a switching-off process with a tuning-in appendage, and I'd tried it on the country section heads.

Although I couldn't sustain it for more than a minute at a time, I was convinced that it had enabled me to pick up some vital signals from them. I was then appalled to discover that I couldn't decipher a single one. It was as if their unspoken thoughts had been transmitted in LOPs. The harder I tried to understand what I knew I knew, the more remote it became.

Exhausted by my efforts to dabble in unconscious communication, I went home early, and awoke with such heightened awareness that I heard the sun come out.

It was then that I realized the nature of the special traffic which had passed between us. Without knowing it, the section heads had made a present to me which I'd been slow to unwrap. It was an unsolicited gift of a kind which I had never expected to receive from them, but it couldn't have arrived at a more inopportune moment.

They'd given me a wholly new idea for agents' codes.

THIRTY-NINE

Appointment with Royalty

'The road to hell is paved with good intentions' caused forty-eight hours of purgatory when an F-section agent spelt hell with three 'l's. But that was a year ago, which meant it was ancient history, and I'd long since discovered a quicker road to hell.

It led from my black-market flat to the abattoir which employed me, and every inch of it was paved with discarded ideas for winning the code war. But last night's arrival reached Baker Street intact. It was far more than just another coding system. It was a wholly new approach to the job.

Credit for it (an important consideration even in wartime) belonged to the country section heads.

The experience of seeing six of them in situ at a time when nothing was going right for them had been as great a revelation to me as WOKs had been to them. The bloody-minded resilience with which they responded to disasters, especially those of their own making, and their determination to liberate their territories no matter what, had been my first glimpse of what would one day be known as the Spirit of Resistance.

I'd made another discovery about them which came as an even bigger surprise, if only because it was obvious.

Aggression was their common denominator, and each of them had as much in his make-up as a saint's unconscious. They taught me (without knowing it) that I was only half doing my job. It wasn't enough to give agents safe codes and reliable security checks. These were defensive measures.

We must mount a deception scheme to convince the enemy that they were confronting poem-codes, when in fact they were dealing with

WOKs. LOPs would be harder to counterfeit, but could be thought about later. I christened the offensive 'Operation Gift-horse', and decided to forget it for a week to give its flaws a chance to emerge.

But Gift-horse refused to canter away, and I spent several hours jotting down the clues which would most attract the enemy.

Late that night someone knocked on the door so I knew it couldn't be Tommy.

Maurice Buckmaster apologized for disturbing me, slumped into a chair, and was silent for thirty seconds, which may well have set a record.

I expected bad news about Peter and Odette.

'I wish that damn canteen was open' he finally said.

That at least I could remedy.

Between mouthfuls of mother's sandwiches, he again apologised for disturbing me, then blurted out a name.

'Noor Inayat Khan!'

Getting no response, he explained that she was a W.T. operator who'd finished her course at Beaulieu, and was due to be dropped into France in ten days' time.

He stressed that although Beaulieu hadn't had to teach her a damn thing about operating a set as she'd previously been trained by the R.A.F. ('who were damn sorry to lose her'), the problem was that 'that bastard Spooner' (Beaulieu's C.O.) had 'taken against her', and had written a report saying that she was 'temperamentally unsuitable' to be an agent, and would be a major security risk if she were sent to the field. 'Which is absolute balls' said Buckmaster, returning somewhat to normal. He admitted that all her Instructors agreed with Spooner's reservations.

'What else could one expect from that mob of second-raters?'

He then confided that 'that damn busybody' had sent a copy of his report to Baker Street, and the question of whether Noor would be allowed to go to France was now in the balance.

Restoring his own equilibrium with the help of mother's cakes, he conceded that Noor's character needed more understanding than Spooner and Co could possibly provide.

His face betraying a hint of tenderness, he described her as a 'sensitive somewhat dreamy girl' who'd spent her childhood in Paris, and thought that her bi-lingual French would be far more useful to the Resistance in France than it could ever be to the R.A.F.

After a moment's pause, he said he thought I should know she'd been given a 'mystical upbringing' by her father, an Indian Prince! But despite his influence, she could be practical when necessary, and could think a damn sight more quickly than Spooner. He added with paternalistic pride that she'd even had a book published.

I asked him for its title and he thought it was 'the Tales of Jakarta', but couldn't remember its publishers.*

A blob of cream gave his face its only hint of colour.

Unaware of his moustache, he reminded me that she'd been given a 'stinking report' by her coding-Instructor, but had an appointment with me on June 7th for her final briefing.

He then looked at me with Gubbins-like penetration. 'I'm going to ask a favour of you,' he said, an unusual approach from Maurice, even at his most exhausted.

When I learned what the favour was I was disappointed that he considered it one. He wanted me to give Noor one of my 'extended briefings'. In his opinion, nothing less would ensure that she not only understood her code-conventions but wouldn't forget them when she arrived in France. But under no circumstances must I give her one of the new silk codes. It might thoroughly confuse her and she'd be just as likely to leave it lying around. 'I must admit,' he said, 'that Noor has a tendency to be absent-minded.'

'Haven't we all?' I replied, wondering if I should tell him about the cream on his nose. (He was always delighted when his rival de Gaulle had egg on his face, which was most of the time.)

He then reminded me that I'd given Roger (Cammaerts) an extended briefing, and that he'd turned out to be an excellent coder. 'And look at the rubbish they wrote about *him*.' he said. 'Now he's one of the best men I've got.' ('Plodder' Cammaerts, written off by his instructors, was now one of F section's most reliable organizers, though the competition was decreasing daily.)

Having vented his indignation, Maurice tried the effect of a whis-

---

* Twenty Jakarta Tales published by George G. Harrap 1939.

per. 'Will you do the same for Noor? And can you spare the time to send me a written report on her?'

I didn't answer him immediately because of what he'd withheld. I knew that Spooner had sent adverse reports on her to the controller of the French, Belgian and Dutch directorates (Robin Brook) and to SOE's liaison officer with the Chiefs of Staff (Brigadier Mockler-Ferryman), hoping that the latter would refer the dispute to Gubbins, with whom Maurice was temporarily out of favour.

I also knew that an attempt had been made to drop Noor in May but her plane had had to turn back as there was no reception committee waiting. (I hadn't given her a final code-briefing because F section had failed to notify us she was leaving.)

Nor had Maurice admitted that because of recent losses in the field he was desperate to send another WT operator to France, and that Noor was the only one available.

It was tempting to tell him that the Signals directorate picked up more gossip than the country sections did agents, and that he shouldn't try to involve us in high-level battles without a proper briefing. 'I'll spend as long with her as it takes,' I said.

'And send me a written report afterwards?' He was obviously counting on it being favourable. He might also be afraid that Noor had forgotten how to code.

'Certainly, Maurice.'

He said something in French which I took to be thanks, shook my hand, and de Gaulled out of the office.

I looked up 7 June in my diary. Muriel had pencilled in an hour-long appointment with Noor Inayat Khan. I extended it to three. Any longer than that and I might emerge as an Indian mystic.

On the morning of the 6th I contacted Noor's publishers, introduced myself as the son of 84, and asked if they had a copy of *The Jakarta Tales*.

Astonished to be asked for one, the manager agreed to make it available at once, and allowed me a trade discount. I sent a WOK-maker to pick it up, and re-read Noor's 'stinking report'.

Her instructor, a virile young lieutenant, had summarized her coding as 'completely unpredictable' but may have had something

The author at his
most mature.

A WT operator disguised as
a cow. He broadcast his
traffic from a field in France.
His antennae were housed at
the rear, without causing
morse mutilation.

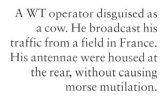

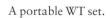

A portable WT set.

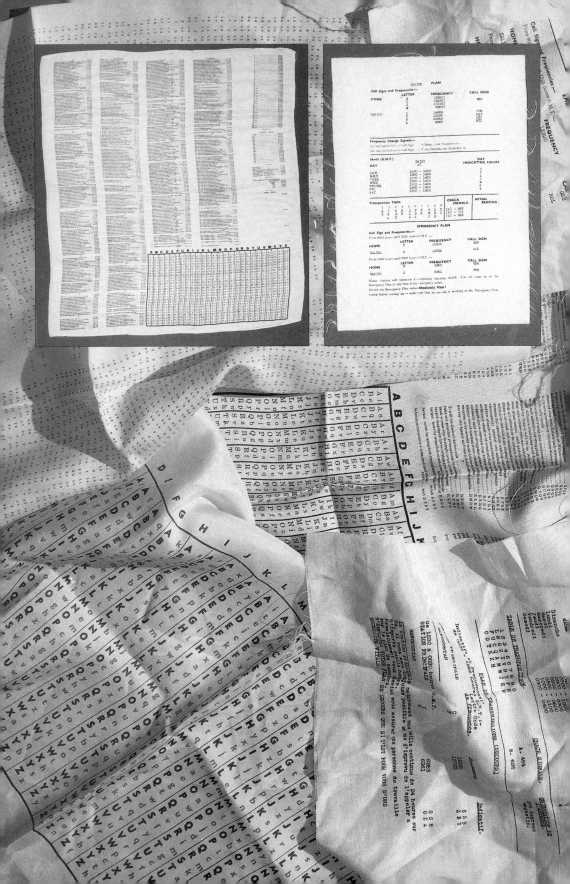

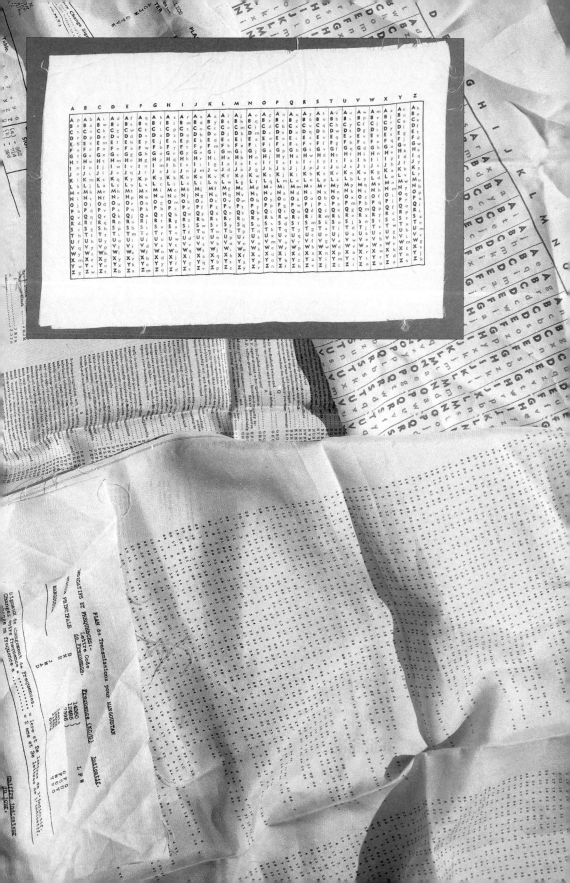

Previous page: Some of SOE's silks.

Portraits of Colonel Buckmaster
and Vera Atkins, and a sketch of
Violette Szabo (taken from a
wartime photograph), all by the
author's wife, the artist Elena
Gaussen Marks.

Noor Inayat Kahn.

Tommy. Photograph taken for
false identity papers, 1944.

The author at the Cannes film festival,
1968, taken by Michael Powell, director
of the film *Peeping Tom*.

Leo and his wife, Elena at a Special Forces Reunion dinner, 1982.

This article was published first in the *Daily Telegraph*'s Peterborough column, March 1995.

PETERBOROUGH   *by Quentin Letts*

The code master flies out to clear Ebenezer

WARTIME London's master cryptographer will today fly to Holland on a mission of great and heavy personal importance. Leo Marks, ace code breaker with the Special Operations Executive, intends to clear the name of an old Dutch resistance agent. Marks will also meet him for the first time, more than 50 years after the agent was tortured by the Gestapo.

Code master Marks long presumed that the man, codenamed Ebenezer, had died at the hands of his captors. Then, last month, came contact from a Dutch television station which alerted him to the fact that Ebenezer, real name Huib Lauwers and now aged 80, is in fact alive. Since the end of the war Lauwers has had to live with question marks over his reputation. Some people hold that, once caught in 1942, he made insufficient efforts to alert London to the fact that the messages he subsequently dispatched — with a Nazi at his shoulder — were done so under duress. Those messages were highly misleading.

SOE's records have been destroyed and Marks is perhaps the only person who knows the truth. The full story can not be told for the details are officially restricted. But Marks vows that Ebenezer *did*, via subtle and ingenious methods, try to show the Allies that he was in German hands. Some people in London were slow to understand, but there was no shortage of courage from the stranded agent.

For years Marks has been haunted by the thought that a brave man had gone to his grave without receiving due credit from his countrymen. The German occupation remains a source of bitter anguish in the Netherlands. Today he hopes to convince them Ebenezer was sound. He will make a declaration for Dutch television, then — accompanied by his artist wife Elena Gaussen — will visit Lauwers at his house. Miss Gaussen will sketch the extraordinary meeting in preparation for a portrait of Lauwers.

From his London home yesterday Marks said: "Ebenezer did everything he could. I do not want him to die without his reputation being cleared."

Rescue mission: Leo Marks and his artist wife Elena

Comparing notes with Huib
Lauwers, 'Ebenezer' in Holland,
March 1995.

Ebenezer, painted by Elena
Gaussen Marks, March 1995.

The famous book shop at 84 Charing Cross Road, where the author broke his first code.
Helen Hanff's 84 Charing Cross Road by Elena Gaussen Marks.

else on his mind as he'd spelt it 'unpredicktable'. My suspicions were confirmed when he was happy to spend his lunch-hour discussing her on the telephone.

According to young virile, the 'potty princess' had caused more dissension than any pupil in the history of Beaulieu. No two instructors could agree on quite how bad an agent she'd be. Yet none of them could deny that she was an excellent WT operator, though she tended to stay on the air as if she were part of it. They were also unanimous that her 'crackpot father' was responsible for her 'eccentric behaviour'.

I pressed him for details of Daddy and a formidable picture emerged. The 'crackpot' was head of a mystical sect (the Sufi), and had founded the 'House of Blessing' in Paris, where Noor had spent her childhood. He'd also founded Sufi lodges in most European capitals in order to spread the doctrine of love and forgiveness, but his 'Houses of Blessing' were a curse to Beaulieu.

'Do you know what the bastards taught her? That the worst sin she could commit was to lie about anything.'

As a result of this disastrous programming, she was unable to observe even the most elementary precautions. He was happy to provide a few examples.

Beaulieu had sent her on a WT exercise, and she was cycling towards her 'safe-house' to practise transmitting when a policeman stopped her and asked what she was doing.

'I'm training to be an agent,' she said, 'here's my radio – want me to show it to you?' She then removed it from its hiding place and invited him to try it.

Like all Beaulieu trainees, she was given a mock interrogation by the Bristol police, after which the superintendent in charge told Spooner not to waste his time with her 'because if this girl's an agent I'm Winston Churchill'.

She'd been so startled by an unexpected pistol shot that she'd gone into a Sufi-like trance for several hours, and finally emerged from it to consult a Bible.

He hoped this would be a help to me, and rang off to have his lunch.

I'd lost my appetite for food, crackpots and extended briefings.

*   *   *

On the morning of the 7th (the ordeal was at noon), I received a call from tiny Kay Moore to thank me for Valois's prefixes, and to solicit twenty more. As a contra-account, she gave me the latest news of Tommy.

Our mutual friend was in nearly as much trouble as he caused. On 19 May he'd been awarded the Croix de Guerre (with palm) for his services to France (which made him the first Englishman to be decorated by de Gaulle, other than with acid), but the Air Ministry refused to allow him to wear it on the grounds that no British officer can accept foreign decorations without official permission. Nor did the Air Ministry accept that de Gaulle had the right to bestow it, and it had taken several onslaughts by Hutchison to persuade 'the cretins' to allow Tommy to wear his Croix de Guerre. But this was only the start of his problems.

He'd also been awarded the Military Cross by the British, and his delighted French friends had given a party in his honour at Duke Street. He was then informed (without any reason being given) that the Air Ministry had refused to sanction his MC and that he must stop wearing it at once. This time even the combined wrath of Hutchison, CD and Gubbins couldn't persuade the Air Ministry to reverse its decision.

It was one insult too many for Tommy. Angry at having to find excuses to explain to his friends at Duke Street why it had taken him so long to wear his Croix de Guerre (his usual pretext was that it was on his other uniform), he was determined not to let them know that he was having even greater problems with his MC. His solution was vintage Tommy.

Whenever he was in Dorset Square he wore a tunic with only the Croix de Guerre on it. Whenever he visited Duke Street (which was several times a day) he changed into a spare tunic, on which Barbara had sewn both decorations. It was a delicate operation because if Hutchison caught him *in flagrante delicto*, he would have no alternative but to order him to remove the MC.

Tommy had repeatedly told Kay that he couldn't wait to return to the peace and quiet of occupied France.*

---

* It was almost a year before his MC was officially sanctioned.

I thanked Kay for her contra-account, and was reading the last few pages of *The Jakarta Tales* in a desperate attempt to become Noor-minded when I heard my favourite footsteps. Tommy hurried in wearing a tunic with the Croix de Guerre on it. He was carrying a briefcase and a parcel.

Stripping off his authorized tunic, he removed his Duke Street version from the parcel and quickly put it on. 'Malpractice makes perfect,' he muttered, followed by a string of French imprecations. He said that his normal changing room, the bog in Dorset Square, was occupied, probably by Hutch to judge from the noises, and that his next best safe-house was my office. Could he leave his tunic with me for the next few hours?

I promised not to use it as an ashtray, except in emergencies.

Glancing at my desk, which was fortunately devoid of de Gaulle's secret messages, he said he was delighted to learn from Kay that I'd stopped playing silly buggers with Valois. He then demanded to be told what I had against the Free French using their own code for their political messages.

I hesitated, always a mistake with Tommy, and he looked at me sharply. 'They send us the clear-texts so what's all the fuss about?'

Although it was more distasteful to prevaricate with Tommy than with anyone else in Baker Street, including myself, I hastily explained that I had no idea what code the Free French were using.

'I should bloody well hope not. A deal's a deal.'

He softened slightly. 'What's worrying you? Perhaps I can help.'

I almost told him the truth, but MCs and Croix de Guerre are never won by almosts, and I was no candidate for either. I said that having to memorize two coding systems was clearly overloading the agents because they sent so many indecipherables in their secret code.

'They've not sent a single one since I've been back. And, now I come to think of it, I don't remember any for the last six months.'

His 'now I come to think of it' worried me.

It was essential to change the subject before he put two and two together and came up with a Marks.

I was curious about his latest code-name, and asked how he'd come to be called the White Rabbit. 'I work for a fucking mad hatter's tea party,' he said. 'Can you think of a better reason?'

Without waiting for a reply, he pointed to a pile of WOKs on the desk. 'I'll be needing one of those before much longer. Why not give it to me now so I can get used to carrying it?'

He hurried off, suitably attired, to his appointment in Duke Street. I sensed an anger in him which had nothing to do with his decorations, and was worried by his impatience to return to France.

My intercom buzzed twice, a warning from Muriel that it was perilously close to Noor-time.

Even in SOE it simply wasn't done to keep a princess waiting.

FORTY

The Extended Briefing

The Jakarta Tales contained twenty stories of Buddha's former birth. I'd read each story twice, and knew one of them by heart.

It concerned a monkey who ruled over 80,000 other monkeys, and who loved them so much that he allowed them to use his body as a bridge so that they could cross it safely to avoid being shot by wicked King Brahmadatta, who coveted their mangoes. But one of the monkeys jumped on him too heavily and broke his back, and as he lay dying wicked King Brahmadatta stood beside him.

'You have given your life to save your followers,' he said. 'Who are you, blessed one? And who are they?'

'O King,' replied the dying monkey, 'I am their chief and their guide. They lived with me in this tree and I was their father and I loved them. I do not suffer in leaving this world because I have gained my subjects' freedom. And if my death may be a lesson to you, then I am more than happy. It is not your sword which makes you a king; it is love alone.'

And Brahmadatta ruled with love over his people and they were happy ever after.

O Noor. What the hell are you doing in SOE?

I longed to be able to walk into a briefing room and switch on the detached receptivity with which an analyst treats his patients – especially those who've paid his fees in advance.

But as soon as I glimpsed the slender figure seated at a desk in the Orchard Court briefing room I knew that the only thing likely to be detached was one (if not both) of my eyeballs. No one had mentioned Noor's extraordinary beauty.

I invited Her Highness to compose a message at least 250 letters long and encode it for transmission.

'Right.'

As if she'd been waiting all her life to obey this command she wrote out a message in French, but as soon as she'd finished it she spent five minutes changing it. She then contemplated the result with the special smile of a satisfied creator. I suspected that she'd written another Jakarta tale and had forgotten that she was supposed to encode it.

As gently as I could I reminded her that London was on the air and would like to receive her message.

She apologized profusely and produced her poem-code from her handbag. It was in French, and in answer to my question she said she'd written it herself. (If only other agents would copy her example, at least in this – but most of them insisted on using poems which they'd learned at school.)

She chose five words, and made a note of the indicator-group. She took a little time to recover from this effort, and I had a feeling that she'd left the room. Returning suddenly from a better place, she glanced shyly at the nearby lecher and began numbering her key-phrase as if she were a small child trying to prove that she could count to ten.

Without any warning she changed gear and completed her first transposition more rapidly than any agent I'd briefed. Apparently believing that the job was now finished, she picked up the sheet of paper on which she'd written her clear-text and became absorbed in re-reading it. She even altered a word but made no attempt to correct what she'd so far encoded. Finally satisfied that it was ready for publication, she looked up at me as if wondering what came next. She was astonished when I pointed out that the encoding was only half-finished.

Apologizing profusely, she dug the pencil (and me) into the paper, and finished transposing the message in under ten minutes (an in-house record). Looking at the code-groups as if wondering where they'd come from, she submitted her message for official approval.

I asked her to decode it herself.

Twenty minutes later she was still trying.

Disliking cruelty to children with the fervour of one who's never been subjected to it, I picked up her work-sheets and started to examine them. Princess Einar Skinnarland had indeed set a record: she'd hatted two columns, made a mistake in her indicator-group, and misnumbered her transposition-key.

I sat as close to her as I dared, and took her through her encoding line by line. There was no response from her. I glanced up to make sure she was still there, and saw that she was nearly in tears, which made two of us.

'You've made fewer mistakes than most,' I said, 'but those you have made are very inventive.'

This seemed to please her. But I knew that a wrong note now would lose the battle of the briefing.

'Coded messages have one thing in common with monkeys,' I said. 'If you jump too hard on them you'll break their backs – and that's what you've done to this one. I doubt if Brahmadatta himself could decipher it, I know my monkeys in the code room couldn't.'

It didn't seem possible but her eyes grew larger. 'You've read my book?'

The intensity of her look reduced me to chutney. 'Yes. And I greatly enjoyed it. It also taught me a lot.'

'What?'

I pointed to the indicator-group and took a calculated risk. 'You've told me a lie, Noor – and you've made the code tell a lie.'

I knew I'd used a loaded word but wasn't prepared for the loaded Noor, who sprang to her feet to confront her vilifier. *'I've what?'*

'Given the wrong indicator-group. What else is that but a lie?'

'I hadn't thought of it like that – really I hadn't.'

I waited for her to sit down, then I made her look at each of her mistakes before totting them up like a waiter with the bill. 'That makes a total of six lies and one half-truth. We'd have to try 100,000 attempts before Colonel Buckmaster could read this message – and even they mightn't be enough.'

I could barely hear her whispered 'Oh no'.

It was time to produce the only lifeline I could offer her: 'I believe your *Jakarta Tales* could help you to become a very good coder.'

She looked at me in astonishment. 'How?'

'Every time you encode a message think of the letters in it as monkeys trying to cross a bridge between Paris and London. If they fall off, they'll be caught and shot . . . but they can't cross by themselves, and if you don't help them by guiding them slowly and methodically, one step at a time, giving them all your thoughts and all your protection, they'll never reach the other side. When there's a truth to pass on, don't let your code tell lies.'

'May I try again, please?'

She encoded a new message at half her previous speed (but still more quickly than most), and copied out the code-groups carefully. But before surrendering them to me she closed her eyes and ran her fingers across them as if searching for injuries. Without being asked, she encoded another message, again running her fingers across the code-groups before giving them to me. Both messages were perfect, and she knew it before I said so.

'Thank you, thank you – but will it be all right if I think about pigs sometimes?' (One of her stories was about two piglets named Mahatundila and Cullatindila.)

I wondered if she'd asked my permission to introduce piglets because she sensed I was Jewish. 'You must do whatever helps you to cross that bridge – but Noor, will you be able to keep it up?'

'Mr Marks, I promise you I will.' It was the promise of an adult. But her maturity was about to be tested to the full.

'We must discuss your security checks.'

'May I ask you something first?'

'Of course.'

'What do you want to do when the war is over?'

This was extending the briefing to its outer limits but Sufi Marks owed her the truth. 'Write a play.'

'What about?'

'A girl who can't laugh.'

She wanted to know why she couldn't, what had been done to help her, and what the story was – the kind of questions authors indulge in when they don't envy one another's royalties.

Like all shy people she mistook hesitancy for reticence. 'Don't you want to tell me? – or shouldn't I have asked?'

I was afraid of disappointing her. 'She hasn't laughed since she was five, and she's now eighteen. Her parents have taken her to every doctor, psychiatrist and comedian in the country but she still can't laugh. Then one day she looks out of the window and sees a dirty old tramp, and bursts out laughing. They bring him into the house and she finds him even funnier. They persuade him to stay, but the one thing he won't stand for is being laughed at.

'However, he's no ordinary tramp, and he's determined to find out what stopped her from laughing. And when he discovers what some-one did to her she's cured. And that's when she sees him as he really is – a dirty old tramp. And he has to leave her.'

'It's very sad. And very funny. I suppose he leaves without letting her know how much she owes to him?'

What Sufi instinct told her that?

'He doesn't think she owes him anything.'

'Does it have a title?'

It hadn't until then. But her expression supplied it. 'It's called *The Girl Who Couldn't Quite!*'*

'Lots of people will come and see it, including me – if I can.'

Her ability to do so might depend on the next few minutes.

'Security checks, Noor.'

'I'm still wondering what stopped her from laughing. Sorry, security checks.' She returned reluctantly to less important business.

Like all agents using the poem-code, she had a 'bluff' check which she was allowed to disclose to the enemy, and a 'true' check which was supposed to be known only to London. The only circumstance in which the checks had any value was if the agent were caught *before* passing any messages, as the enemy had no back traffic to refer to. With the situation in France worsening daily this could well happen to Noor.

---

* Produced at St Martin's Theatre in 1948. Despite its press, it ran in the West End for several months. One benevolent reviewer, C.A. Darlington likened its climax to *The Turn of the Screw*. The others screwed it altogether, though a few were kind enough to suggest that the author try again. Possibly because of its suggestive title and its small cast (it had few other merits), it became an even greater success than *Charley's Aunt* in repertory and amateur companies. It was then inflicted on Australia and South Africa, who in those days had done nothing to deserve it. It still lingers on, as does this meeting with Noor, some fifty years later.

I glanced again at her work-sheet. She'd used her checks correctly but might not have realized that she had to lie about them.

'Lie about them?' she echoed. 'Why should I do that?'

'Because if you tell them what your "true" check is they'll pretend that their messages are coming from you, and we shan't know that you've been caught. That's why you must lie to them.'

'To stop them lying to you?'

'Yes.'

'But there's a better way. Suppose that I refused to tell them anything at all – no matter how often they ask?' It was a statement of intent.

I remembered how she'd ended her tale of the dying monkey: 'I do not suffer in leaving this world because I have gained my subjects' freedom. And if my death may be a lesson to you then I am more than happy.'

She'd let her back be broken rather than tell a lie.

'Noor, we've got to find a way round this . . .' I struggled desperately to think of one, and the dying monkey warned me that there was very little time.

'I'm going to give you a security check that's completely new, and you won't have to lie about it because no one but you and me will know that it exists.'

It had only just been born and I suspected that she sensed it.

'All you have to do is remember one thing. *Never* use a key-phrase with eighteen letters in it – any other number but not eighteen. If you use eighteen, I'll know you've been caught.'

'Eighteen's my lucky number. Yes, I could do that. and I promise you not to forget it. I promise you, Mr Marks.'

But her father had a twenty-year start on me, and I wasn't taking any chances. 'I want you to encode three messages at least two hundred letters long and have them ready for me at twelve o'clock tomorrow.'

'Right.'

'Include your true and bluff checks but remember –'

'I mustn't use a key-phrase eighteen letters long.'

'See you tomorrow then.'

She was reaching for her pencil as I left.

*   *   *

320

I prayed or my equivalent – went without a cigar – that she'd repeat all her old mistakes, and that I could write a bad report on her to prevent her from going in.

She'd encoded six new messages, and every one of her monkeys had crossed the bridge safely, including her security checks.

I asked how she'd let me know if she were caught.

She immediately numbered a key-phrase eighteen letters long, and handed it to me proudly.

On 10 June I sent Buckmaster the report that he needed.

On the night of 16 June Noor boarded a Lysander, and in the early hours of the 17th landed in France.

On 21 June Maurice telephoned me. He thought I'd like to know that she'd left the Loire valley and had arrived in Paris. He wasn't sure when she'd be able to start transmitting but hoped it would be soon. Throughout the conversation he referred to her by her field name, Madeleine.

She might be known as such to F section, to her fellow-agents and to the Germans. But to me she was, and would always remain, the Girl Who Couldn't Quite.

FORTY-ONE

Operation Gift-horse

In a disorganization like SOE, where a single mistake could cost an agent's life, all new ideas needed a cooling-off period, and Gift-horse had been confined to its stall for over a week.

Feeling sufficiently distanced from it, I took it from its paddock for a health check, confident that anything so innovative that had been conceived so painlessly would end in the confidential waste. Finding no flaw in it, which was extremely disturbing, I decided to submit it to Nick and Heffer for a dispassionate briefing. The Gurus would know instinctively whether Gift-horse was a turning point or a non-starter, which was what made them gurus.

At first the deception scheme amused them and they called it 'bloody sauce'. But when they realized that it was a serious attempt to confuse WOKs with poem-codes and waste the time of the enemy's cryptographers they found the sauce very much to their liking. They warned me not to overdo it, added a few kind words about its ingenuity, and prepared to resume more important business.

But they weren't rid of me yet.

I wasn't prepared to launch Gift-horse until I had the answer to a question which had been troubling me for months. I wanted to know what had gone wrong with Germany's cryptographers.

Having been taught by Father (who was also my boxing instructor) never to underestimate the opposition, I was convinced that the enemy's Tiltmans were as brilliant as their Bletchley counterparts. But if they were, why had we been allowed to blow up the Norsk Hydro, expand our Secret Armies, and earn ourselves a mandate from the Chiefs of Staff?

322

It couldn't be due to the quality of our Signals. Our traffic was easy to intercept, and the poem-code even easier to break. So why were we still in business, and on the point of expanding in all directions?

I sought enlightenment from Nick, and to my surprise he was delighted to provide it.

Speaking with all the authority of a Signals lifetime, he declared that our traffic hadn't been penetrated 'to a significant extent' because the enemy's cryptographers had been forced to concentrate on more important commitments. He cited as examples America's entry into the war, the Allied invasion of North Africa (Torch), and the Russian counter-attack at Stalingrad (surely the most effective eviction notice ever served on an invader).

But there were other reasons why we'd been allowed to get away with the 'cock-up of a code' we'd inherited from C.

According to 'a reliable source' (Tiltman himself?), for the past eighteen months German cryptographers had been unable to function at their best because of high-level interference of a kind which Bletchley 'simply wouldn't tolerate.' Although stretched to their limits by military, diplomatic and Intelligence intercepts, they were under orders from Hitler to break the traffic of his Japanese and Italian Allies, and knew that hell hath no fury like a Führer kept waiting. They also had to humour Goering, Goebbels and Himmler, whose relationships were comparable to ours with C, and who insisted on reading each other's messages. As a result of these and other pressures, SOE's traffic had been given little or no priority, and was usually attacked at local level by groups of German sergeants with a flair for cryptography.

However, our involvement with D-Day put us in an altogether different category. He was absolutely certain that SOE's traffic would soon be upgraded, and if Gift-horse could make it more trouble than it was worth and waste their 'bloody time', it might even help the war effort generally, and I must push ahead with it. 'Your attitude's right!'

'More power to its hoof.' added Heffer.

I almost neighed with relief.

Then the responsibility hit me.

*　　*　　*

323

In the absence of any advice about Gift-horse except 'don't overdo it', I reviewed the entire concept as if C had suggested it. That way I knew I'd be taking no chances.

The success of Gift-horse depended on a fact of cipher life on which I'd stake my own as I'd learned it from Tiltman. Even his experienced eye couldn't tell whether a message had been encoded in a WOK or a poem-code as both were the product of double-transposition.

Every WOK-message began with a five-letter group to show which pair of worked-out keys had been used. Every poem-code message began with a five-letter indicator-group to show which five words of the poem had been used. These indicator-groups were the quickest way of ending a poem-code's life if the agents used the same ones for different messages. And if the messages were of equal length (as they frequently were) a novice could break them in a matter of hours. I'd done so myself at Bedford. (And once broken, the five words of the poem could be reconstructed, and if they were part of a famous quotation, the rest of the traffic would be read automatically.)

But WOK-traffic offered no such facilities. Every key was made by hand, and no two were the same.

The ETs (enemy's Tiltmans) couldn't tell which system was in use, and it was up to us to point them in the wrong direction. To achieve this, we would sprinkle WOK-traffic with repeated indicator-groups, as if the agent were using a poem-code and had chosen the same five words of his poem for different messages, though the keys were completely unrelated.

This apparent duplication would stimulate the ETs' cryptographic taste buds for a meal which wasn't on the menu. And if by some lucky chance these repeated indicators were used on messages of identical length, the temptation to take appropriate action would be as hard to resist as a lady casually declaring that she'd forgotten to put on her knickers (an experience with which I was familiar only from hearsay).

I collected twenty sets of WOK-keys from the counter-shufflers, took them to my office, and inserted 200 duplicated indicators.

Three hours later they were on their way to the printers, and would soon be ready to lie with silken tongues.

It was a puny enough attempt to take the code war to the enemy, and I might never know if it achieved its objective, but it had one compensation: lacking the courage to take the slightest risk unless it were strictly mental, I imagined myself mounted on a charger leading my code-groups to the heart of Berlin.

If ever I had to write the history of agents' ciphers, I resolved that Gift-horse would have a chapter to itself.

FORTY-TWO

A Terrible Gaffe

By the end of June six WOKs had opened up in France, two in Norway, and eighteen others (seven of them Gift-horsed) had been issued to agents waiting to be dropped.

But the elation was negated by the worst breach of security any country section had yet committed.

It concerned Archambault (real name Gilbert Norman), who'd been dropped into France by F section in November '42 to transmit and receive traffic for the Prosper circuit and to act as deputy to Prosper himself. The twenty-seven-year-old Englishman hadn't made a single mistake at his final code-briefing (not always a good sign), but turned out to be one of those rare agents who encoded even better in the field than they did in practice, sending only three indecipherables in eight months' traffic and inserting his true and bluff checks in every message.

But on 27 June he sent a message with his true check omitted. I told Buckmaster that I was examining all Archambault's messages to make certain that he hadn't done this before, and was checking the original decodings in case any of the girls had made a mistake.

Giving me no hint of his intentions, Maurice immediately informed Archambault that he'd forgotten to insert his true check in his last message, and accused him of committing 'a serious breach of security which *must not*, repeat *must not* be allowed to happen again!'

Nor must blunders of this magnitude, though we'd done out damnedest, repeat our damnedest, to prevent them.

While Nick was still a new boy I'd shown him six messages about signals which country sections had sent to agents without consulting

326

any of us (including N section's to Trumpet concerning missing security checks).

He'd immediately issued a directive to all country section heads (copy to Gubbins) instructing them not to refer to codes, signal-plans or any matters relating to WT security without first consulting him or a member of his directorate. He'd then ordered me to bring any future lapses to his immediate attention so that he could report the culprits to Gubbins.

Reluctant to subject anyone I liked to the ultimate deterrent, I said nothing to Nick, and spoke to Maurice myself.

He accepted full responsibility for a 'terrible gaffe', and assured me it wouldn't happen again. He then asked if I thought Archambault had been caught.

I promised him my answer within an hour.

Archambault's back traffic confirmed that he'd always used his true check, and that he hadn't made a single mistake in his coding (his three indecipherables were due to Morse mutilation), but I needed a little longer with his traffic because several things puzzled me.

Assuming he was in enemy hands (he'd convinced me that he was), why had they allowed him to leave out his true check? Was it because they didn't want him to be late for his sked, but hadn't had time to read his back traffic and work out what his checks really were? Or was it because they might have had difficulty in identifying his messages as he'd used four different prefixes, and they hadn't had time to collate them?

Neither explanation satisfied me as it reflected on their efficiency, for which I still had the utmost respect, but this didn't change my conviction that Archambault was in their hands.

It was the first time that I'd been able to reach a definitive conclusion from a poem-code's security checks, and I called at Maurice's office in case he had any questions.

Still contrite from his gaffe, he said he'd reached the same conclusion, but intended to continue sending messages to Archambault in the hope of prolonging his life.

He was brilliant at doing this (he'd had plenty of practice), and I left him to get on with it.

*　　*　　*

Thinking about captured agents had become a June preoccupation. RF section had lost one of its giants a fortnight ago and the shock had yet to wear off (for some it never would). His name was Jean Moulin, and I'd heard so much about him from Tommy that I felt as if we'd met.

I had in fact caught a glimpse of the great Moulin when I'd called at Duke Street a few months ago to deliver overdue prefixes for the accursed French code. He'd been picked up by Lysander the previous night, and was striding side by side with Tommy towards Passy's office.

At first glance (there wasn't to be a second) the two agents could have been mistaken for brothers (which in all essential respects they were). Both in their early forties, they had the same chunky build, the same purposeful stride, the same aura of limitless chutzpah.

The main difference was that Moulin was already a legend. In an organization like ours reputations like his were hard to acquire, and recalling a few of his achievements was as close as I could get to a memorial service.

In 1940, the Vichy government dismissed him from his post for being anti-German and he became a freelance partisan, forming three separate Resistance groups in Vichy-controlled France.

Having achieved more without SOE's help than most freedom fighters with it, he decided that his only chance of getting arms, supplies and working capital would be to join forces with one of London's Big Battalions, and he escaped to England via Lisbon in 1941 to make a first-hand assessment of the relative merits of SOE and Duke Street.

His arrival in London was the start of a Dutch auction (without Giskes, thank God) between de Gaulle and Buckmaster, who interviewed him personally, each determined to recruit him on the spot. But in reality it was Moulin who interviewed them, and he kept them in suspense for several weeks before announcing his decision (he was an experienced politician). To Duke Street's delight he finally opted to join de Gaulle, who at once appointed him his personal representative in France (it takes a natural leader to know one). He was also appointed delegate-general to the Free French Committee, and at

Tommy's suggestion was code-named Rex in London and Max in the field.

Armed with excellent credentials but very little else, Rex/Max was dropped blind into France on 1 January '42 and landed in a ditch. He then faced the even greater quagmire of persuading the leaders of mutually antagonistic Resistance groups to unite under de Gaulle, and three weeks later reported to Duke Street that he'd had a 100 per cent success rate and was hoping to improve it.

In February he was joined by Passy, Brossolette and Tommy (the Arquebus mission) and numerous policy differences emerged which had not been apparent in Duke Street. Putting unity above all, he formed the MUR (Mouvement Uni de la Résistance), and continued welding his compatriots into the nucleus of a Secret Army until his arrest near Lyons on 20 June. (On the day Buckmaster heard of Moulin's capture he commiserated with his rival Jim Hutchison on the loss of 'one of the most valuable agents in the whole of France'.)

But memories of giants seldom came sequentially, and I also knew that in 1940 he'd been severely tortured by the Germans for refusing to sign a document which falsely accused the French of committing atrocities. When they finally released him, he tried to commit suicide for fear that he'd weaken if they tortured him again, and as a result of his self-inflicted injuries he was left with a badly scarred throat and husky voice and rarely appeared in public without a scarf or muffler (he was wearing both when I glimpsed him in Duke Street).

Now he was in their hands again.

I was wondering whether his capture would give Tommy yet another reason for returning to France when he put his head round the door and asked if he were disturbing me.

'No more than usual.'

He advanced towards me while I pressed the buzzer for sandwiches and coffee, which Muriel produced within seconds.

He congratulated her on running a first-class hotel, despite its proprietor, then slumped into a chair and announced that the personnel department was an absolute disgrace. 'There's not a person in it who can tell his pass from his elbow.'

He spent the next few minutes suggesting imaginative remedies but didn't tell me what they'd done to upset him, and I knew that he was venting his distress at the loss of Moulin. (To call it distress was as great an understatement as describing Moulin as a dedicated patriot or a hanged man as being out of breath.)

Speaking in a voice as husky as Rex/Max's, he said that Moulin wouldn't break no matter what they did to him, and was certain to be executed before much longer.* He then contrasted Moulin's achievements as a recruiting officer in occupied France with the personnel department's disastrous attempts to staff preoccupied Baker Street. 'I can find only one thing in the bastards' favour. They give jobs to large numbers of people who'd do even more damage elsewhere.'

He suddenly switched his attack to the Signals directorate. '. . . and you people let the bastards get away with it.' He cited as examples two new arrivals at the HQ Signals Office who treated every enquiry as if it were an intrusion on their privacy, and were more interested in distributing lipstick than messages.

I didn't tell him that the Signals directorate was responsible for its own recruitment, and we'd picked the two horrors ourselves. (I'd already taken steps to have them transferred, hopefully to C, from whence they probably came.)

He left shortly afterwards without realizing (though one could never be sure with him) that he'd touched on a problem which was causing the Signals directorate even more trouble than C and the Germans: the problem of keeping pace with SOE's expansion.

Agents' traffic, which had doubled since the Chiefs of Staff's mandate, was expected to reach a million groups a week in the run-up to D-Day, and SOE took it for granted that we'd have the resources to deal with it. SOE also took it for granted that we could continue to send fully trained coders, WT operators and briefing officers to Massingham, Cairo and the Far East. No matter how often we protested that we were so short-staffed ourselves that we were in difficulties with the daily traffic, we were expected to maintain the standards SOE hadn't wanted in the first place.

By the end of June the Signals directorate was the largest in SOE, and the code department the largest in the Signals directorate, and I

---

* He was beaten to death three weeks later on the orders of Klaus Barbie.

was under orders from Nick to ensure that every branch had an adequate intake of new 'bodies'.

I relied on the FANYs for coders, on the personnel department for WOK-makers, and on God for briefing officers. Anxious not to overload the Almighty (his blessing on LOPs was urgently required), I also relied on both the FANYs *and* the personnel department for briefing Officers, whom I collected as if they were rare first editions. (The ones I most coveted had to be in mint mental condition, preferably with their bindings intact.)

But other organizations were also scouring the market for incipient code-mindedness. Bletchley and C were constantly head-hunting, had Top Priority and were expert scavengers. We were also up against the Foreign Office and the Signals units of the armed forces.

Since competing with the opposition by orthodox means was getting us nowhere, I contacted two of SOE's most formidable ladies, Miss Furze and Captain Henderson, to discuss alternative measures. Miss Furze's function was to recruit female civilians for the whole of Baker Street, Captain Henderson's to supply the Signals directorate's FANYs. Although I was aware that both empresses preferred to be visited, I invited them to meet me in my office, and was amazed when they accepted.

My first step was to show them a pile of indecipherables waiting to be broken, a heap of WOKs waiting to be collated, and a long list of agents waiting to be briefed. I then asked them what they could do to strengthen our depleted work-force.

Miss Furze's expression said 'Fuck all', and Captain Henderson's confirmed it.

I pushed the exhibits aside and waited for the worst.

Miss Furze reminded me that the staff she provided 'didn't grow on trees', though I allowed them to walk about looking as they did. They came from the Ministry of Labour and National Service, which had fallen badly behind in its quota because of the huge demand for women to replace men.

Captain Henderson added that FANY recruitment had fallen off for much the same reasons, and because of competition from the WAAF and the WRNS (the Women's Auxiliary Air Force and the Women's Royal Naval Service).

They then looked at each other sympathetically, and took it in turns to emphasize that they couldn't see any prospect of the situation improving.

According them the deference due to experts, I suggested that the real reason why so few girls were coming our way was that the officials who interviewed them hadn't the slightest idea how to detect incipient code-mindedness.

Two explosions occurred in the immediate vicinity, one from anger, the other from natural causes.

Thundering from all points, Miss Furze accused me of being partly responsible for the shortage of applicants.

'But what have I done?' I asked in a rare burst of genuine innocence.

'It's what you haven't done,' she snapped. Waving an umbrella at me (on all too close inspection it turned out to be a finger), she pointed out that she'd twice asked me for a written analysis of the qualities I was looking for so that she could send a copy of it to the ministry but she might just as well have saved her breath. She also pointed out that I'd rejected fifteen of the candidates she'd sent me but hadn't troubled to explain why.

Captain Henderson then joined in the indictment, stressing that I'd turned down twenty FANYs without giving her my reasons, and still hadn't listed the attributes her interviewers should look out for.

The truth was, I didn't know myself.

I was wary of saying that if a girl admitted she loved music and crossword puzzles but was hopeless at arithmetic we could usually repair the damage a maths teacher had done, and turn her into a coder. They'd simply ask new candidates, 'Do you like music and crossword puzzles and are you bad at arithmetic?' and leave it at that. Nor did I relish the tedium of explaining how to measure a potential WOK-maker's threshold of boredom. I also shirked trying to define the instinct which said, 'This girl can do it.'

I promised to deliver a summary by the end of the week.

'Which week?' Miss Furze enquired sweetly.

The empresses then departed, leaving me no closer to the thousands of young hopefuls queuing round the country for a chance to help the war effort.

Determined to get our fair share of them, I sent the Ministry of Labour an *aide-mémoire*: 'Do not reject any girl on grounds of insanity without first offering her to SOE.'

The memo backfired.

The ministry sent a copy of it to Air Commodore Boyle (head of our personnel board), who passed it to Commander Senter (head of security), who instructed me to report to him at once.

Brandishing my memo as if it were scorching his fingers, he informed me that no one in his right mind would make any reference to SOE on a sheet of notepaper headed INTER SERVICES RESEARCH BUREAU, thereby blowing Baker Street's cover! I'd committed a major breach of security.

I apologized for my terrible gaffe, and assured him that it wouldn't happen again (I'd use toilet paper next time).

'That isn't all!' he thundered. He then castigated me for daring to communicate with the ministry 'without the prior knowledge and consent' of the personnel department, and warned me that I hadn't heard the last of it.

On my way out I had just enough sense not to head-hunt his secretary.

Although June and I were on the point of expiring, I came to life when Nick asked me to discuss the month's production figures with him as his continued support for WOKs and LOPs was their lifeline. It took me several hours to prepare them, and Muriel stayed past midnight to type them, but they were waiting on his desk when he arrived next morning.

Ten minutes later he sent for me.

I still didn't know if my gaffe had been reported to him, but nothing in his manner suggested that I was anything less than welcome.

The figures showed that we were ahead of schedule and had increased our reserves of silks by 100 a week. He said that, considering the difficulties, we were making excellent progress, and he intended to show the figures to Gubbins. He then asked if I foresaw any problems in July.

'Plenty. – and they're all to do with recruitment. We need more coders, more briefing officers, more WOK-makers . . .'

To my surprise, he closed his eyes the better to concentrate. 'I've an idea,' he said, as if it were a new experience.

I waited expectantly.

'SOE must instruct the ministry not to reject any girl on grounds of insanity if she's prepared to cut away and destroy Mr Marks.'

There was nothing left of me to cut away. I'd been given an object lesson in how to deal with subordinates.

Nick added that the only reason I hadn't got myself into very serious trouble was that my memo had amused Gubbins. He then said that the whole question of finding staff for the Signals directorate was now being looked into by the Executive Council, but under no circumstances must I dispatch any similar memos without consulting him first.

Wondering what mistakes I'd make next, and whether I had the resources to stay in SOE, and why I was suddenly depressed, depleted and devoid of all confidence, I returned to my desk and sought refuge in the ditty-box:

> There is a strength
> Beyond the one that is failing
> An added length
> To the time
> Now run out
>
> There is sight
> In the eyes now closing
> A light
> Which none others can see
>
> And it guides unbelievers
> And other self-deceivers
> To a place
> Where they had never thought to be.*

I then began describing the qualities which distinguished coders from briefing officers, and WOK-makers from the rest of mankind.

---

* Used by a Jedburgh on D-Day.

FORTY-THREE

Operation Sidetrack

July began with the most disconcerting of all experiences: SOE behaving rationally.

I was informed by Nick that no more Dutch agents were to be sent into the field for the next few months.

Heffer was present at the meeting, which suggested that I'd been told the good news first, and that Nick felt in need of support.

He added that supply drops into Holland would continue, though the RAF had cancelled their July ops. because of the losses they'd suffered in the last moon periods.

He then announced that Gubbins had ordered an internal enquiry into Dutch agents' security, and that I was to take part in it.

Better and better. So why was Heffer looking worried?

Nick disclosed that the enquiry was to be conducted by a member of the security department named Harvey, who was anxious to know more about Kale's indecipherable in which 'Prijs' had been misspelt 'Preis'. He then spelled out my part in the inquiry.

I was to show Harvey how the poem-code worked, explain how the indecipherables had been broken, and answer whatever questions he asked about coding procedures. But that was all that was required of me in the initial stages! Under no circumstances was I to refer to my Dutch reports, mention Plan Giskes, or disclose any of my other suspicions. Harvey must have a chance to make up his own mind about Holland without undue influence from anyone in Signals. He stressed that these instructions had come from Gubbins, and were irrevocable.

He then asked if I had any questions.

'Only one, sir. Is this to be a genuine enquiry or an in-house cover-up?'

Heffer blew a number of smoke rings in my direction which I suspected were the Apache equivalent of 'You stupid little shit', but it was Nick who scalped me.

Speaking very quietly (his deadliest tomahawk), he said that if I couldn't do my job without questioning Gubbins's instructions or SOE's policies then he might have to look for someone who could. As for the enquiry, if I wasn't prepared to give Harvey a chance to make up his own mind without trying to influence him from the outset, then other arrangements would have to be made.

I didn't believe my job was seriously in jeopardy because C or Bletchley might need a new office boy, and there were one or two matters which SOE would prefer me not to discuss with them, but this wasn't the moment to put it to the test. I assured Nick that I would answer Harvey's questions as if he were a member of N section.

'Which is how you answer mine,' he said.

He then instructed me to report back to his office in two hours' time 'in a suitable frame of mind'.

The in-house enquiry took place on the bite of 11 a.m., and I arrived early carrying a bulging briefcase to show how seriously I'd prepared for it.

Harvey was already there, and I realized that I'd met him before in unfortunate circumstances.

I'd bumped into him (literally) in the security department's corridor after being blasted by my godfather, Major O'Reilly, for being the worst NDO in the history of SOE.

He shook hands as if taking my fingerprints, and said he knew 'next to nothing about codes', and would be grateful if I'd explain the general principles before we got down to specifics at a later stage.

There were two ways of dealing with this. I could either spend an hour teaching him properly, or I could give him the simplified version which I used on FANY candidates to test their potential. Deciding on the latter, I showed him how to use his name as a key-phrase (which helped me to remember it), and explained the workings of the poem-code's gear-box.

At this point the good candidates asked questions about the areas which I'd deliberately omitted, but this FANY's mind was focused elsewhere. 'Is this the only code the Dutch agents are using?'

I replied that at present it was, though they sometimes used Playfair to encode addresses, and I'd gladly show it to him but doubted if it could have much relevance to his enquiries.

He brusquely informed me that anything to do with addresses was of the utmost importance, and he'd like me to explain Playfair at a later stage. Would I now show him the Dutch agents' security checks?

He absorbed them in silence, seemed surprised at their simplicity, and asked if I had much faith in them.

'None at all except in special circumstances, which is why the whole system is being changed and silk codes introduced.'

Frowning slightly, he said he'd want to discuss the security checks in detail. 'But first I want you to tell me all you can about Kale's indecipherable message when he spelled "Prijs" in the German way, "Preis".'

I wondered whether he were setting a trap, and bumped into him again, this time verbally. '*It wasn't Kale* who misspelt "Prijs". The message was encoded by Cucumber in his reserve poem number three.'

I could see that his surprise was genuine, and produced a copy of Cucumber's poem from my portable warehouse so that he could check it for himself. I also handed him Cucumber's code-groups, which I'd obtained from the station.

He examined them carefully, then asked how long it had taken us to break the message.

'Twelve hours.'

'How many goes did you need?'

'Five thousand, six hundred and eighty-one.'

'Good God.' He glanced at Nick and Heffer, who nodded confirmation.

'Whatever made you think of spelling "Prijs" "Preis"?' he finally asked with a hint of respect.

'It was suggested by two very bright colleagues, Mrs Denman and Mrs Brewis. They're very helpful with indecipherables.'

337

He made a note of their names while I caught a twinkle from Nick, their favourite indecipherable.

Harvey looked up in time to spot the three of us smiling, and seemed to sense a conspiracy. A few seconds later I had nothing to smile about.

'Do you get many indecipherables?'

It was the question I'd been dreading but he'd phrased it carelessly. He should have said 'from Holland', and its omission was a godsend as it enabled me to give him a generalized answer.

'About fifteen a day. It depends on atmospheric conditions.' I wondered what they were like in Giskes's prisons.

He then asked if I considered Cucumber a careless coder.

I was about to say that no Dutch agent was allowed to be, and that this was one of Giskes's few mistakes, when Heffer puffed a warning in my direction.

Heeding it in time, I said that Cucumber had sent five indecipherables since he'd first begun operating in October '42. I then produced a list of the 4,000 attempts it had cost us to break them but didn't add that they'd all been caused by Morse-mutilated indicator-groups and not by mistakes in coding.

He studied the list as if it were a roll of honour, then emitted his second 'Good God.' He was likely to need a third very shortly as I'd prepared a major diversion for him.

Opening my briefcase, I said that the best way to judge a coder like Cucumber was to examine the mistakes he'd made while he was still at training school. I then produced every practice message Cucumber had encoded, and dumped them in front of him. 'And there's something else you should look at which may help you even more . . .'

I then produced a nautical log-book in Cucumber's handwriting which his instructor had retained after I'd warned him what would happen to his balls if he destroyed anything personal which might be of use to us. My briefcase was now far lighter than my conscience. I could have saved Harvey a great deal of work by summarizing my own examination of the messages and the log-book, but this would have negated Operation Sidetrack.

He protested that he'd need a 'bit of time' to examine them properly. Could he take them to his office and keep them for the next few days?

Ignoring Nick's nod, I said I was very sorry but we had our own security rules, and under no circumstances could documents like these be allowed to leave the code department.

I decided that Heffer's new smoke ring meant 'bloody good tactics but don't go too far', and asked Harvey if he spoke Dutch.

He nodded abruptly and I realized that I'd insulted him. Switching on the brown-melter, I suggested that he should read the log-book now and tackle the message later so that we could at least make a start at discussing 'Prijs'/'Preis'.

He accepted the bait, but said he'd prefer to examine the lot here and now if we didn't mind giving him a 'bit of time'.

Nick told him to take as long as he needed, and not to hesitate to ask any questions.

The Gurus then had a whispered conversation about Bodington (neither of them trusted him) while I thought about his admiration for the poems of Edgar Allan Poe, which I shared when he spelt them properly. I wondered what masterpiece of a horror story Poe would have written if he'd witnessed SOE masturbating at its own cruci-fixion, and whether his prowess as a cryptographer would have earned him a place at Bletchley.

Still thinking about Poe, I felt the nudge of a theme which would one day be known as 'Peeping Tom', but dismissed it as surplus to requirements, and felt the ditty-box beckoning:

> Little lady
> With a long needle
> Seldom threaded
> Where is she headed?
>
> Little lady
> With a small box
> Which she always locks
> Why is she dreaded?

And why does she smile
When she orders
Cards with black borders?*

Harvey's bit of time turned out to be precisely that, and I wondered how thorough he'd been. Ten seconds later he left me in no doubt.

Holding up a page of notes, he announced that he'd found eight spelling mistakes in the practice messages and four in the log-book, including a word which Cucumber had spelt with an 'ij' on one page and an 'ei' on another.

He then declared that unless there was something he'd overlooked there couldn't be much doubt that 'Prijs'/'Preis' was no more than a mistake, and that Cucumber was an even worse speller than he was. There were in fact ten mistakes in the practice messages and six in the log-book, but it had taken me a lot longer than thirty minutes to find them and his concentration was to be envied.

Without the slightest warning or change of expression he asked if I had any reason to suspect that Kale and Cucumber had been caught, or that any other Dutch agents were blown.

Making my last effort to bite back the truth, I heard myself telling him I'd found it impossible to reach any reliable conclusions about Kale and Cucumber from the Germanicized spelling of 'Preis', and that there was little else in their traffic to go on. As for the other agents, their security checks could be tortured out of them and weren't reliable anyway, which was why we were introducing silk codes which could be destroyed after every message, plus security checks which –

Nick interrupted what had begun to sound like patter. 'I think our friend's got the point,' he interjected.

Our friend agreed that he had, and asked a few nebulous questions which I answered in kind.

He then said he'd absorbed as much as he could for one session, and thanked me for 'all the stuff' I'd prepared for him.

I assured him that I'd help him in any way I could.

He shook my hand before I could dry it, though he was probably used to slippery customers. He looked back at me apologetically as

* Issued in March '44 to a Belgian Agent named Pandarus.

340

he reached the door. 'I'd better warn you. I'll be coming back very shortly.'

So, I hoped, would my self-respect.

A few days after the meeting Nick was made a member of the Executive Council, with the rank of brigadier. He was the first director of Signals to acquire Cabinet status.

I didn't hear from Harvey again.

FORTY-FOUR

Beyond Belief

Giskes peaked in July.

Like all skilled fiction-writers from Graham Greene (whom SOE tried to head-hunt) to chancellors of the Exchequer, he had the knack of keeping his readers in suspense till the last chapter, and his handling of Jambroes and Kale was an example of his art.

Both were commanders-in-chief of the Dutch Secret Army. The former had agreed to return in November '42 after months of procrastination, but had been 'killed in a street fight' on the day he was ready to leave. The latter had been appointed his successor, and from February onwards London had been urging him to return. But his prevarications had been on a par with his predecessor's, and N section had finally lost patience with him.

He was informed on 15 June that he *must* return in July, and that details of his escape route would be sent to him via his operator, Broadbean.

Kale received his instructions a week later, and they must have taken his breath away, if Giskes hadn't already done so.

He was to make his way to Paris, where his escort would introduce him to a group of French agents who would guide him across the French and Belgian escape lines until he reached the Swiss frontier, and as soon as he'd crossed it London's contacts would do the rest.

This was the first time that SOE's escape lines had been put at the disposal of the Dutch, an achievement for which Giskes deserved an iron cross with N section nailed to it.

Forty-eight hours later London received Kale's reply. He accepted the plan in principle but continued to maintain that his commitments to the Secret Army prevented him from leaving himself, and urged

342

N section to allow Nicolas de Wilde, his second in command, to use the escape lines in his stead. He was also anxious for an important contact named Anton to be smuggled out of Holland as he had information which would be a great help to the government-in-exile as well as to the British.

In a rare display of security-mindedness N section insisted in knowing more about Anton before allowing him to use the escape lines, and continued to insist that Kale *must* report in person; in the first week in July he finally agreed.

I offered to wager Heffer a box of cigars against an early book on thimbles which his wife coveted (a pricey item, but 84 wouldn't miss it) that Kale would find a last-minute excuse for staying in Holland. But the Guru wasn't in a betting mood.

On 9 July Kale sent a message via Broccoli suggesting that it would be much quicker if he made the journey in a sea-going lifeboat fitted with the latest security devices which some friends in Zeeland had put at his disposal. He added that Mangold would take command in his absence.

On 10 July N section agreed that he could travel by sea, but urged him to take every possible precaution, and to send London full details of his departure.

Two days later he sent a message via Netball that he was leaving the mouth of the Schelde on the midnight high tide and would head for Broadstairs. His lifeboat was capable of doing seven knots in calm water, was painted grey and would show three flags. He estimated that it would reach Broadstairs the following afternoon.

At Gubbins's instigation planes of Fighter Command patrolled the mouth of the Schelde at high tide, and their controller reported that although visibility was excellent no craft of any kind had been spotted. Reconnaissance continued throughout the day and naval patrols were called in but there was still no sign of a sea-going lifeboat.

On 15 July Mangold sent a message via Netball that Kale had left the mouth of the river at high tide on the night of the 14th/15th.

Fighter Command again sent out patrols but were unable to find any trace of the lifeboat.

On the 17th all searches for Kale were abandoned.

On 18 July Netball sent a message which was the first of its kind to pass through the code room. *I was convinced it was personal from him to me.*

The message stated that Mangold had heard nothing from London, and was anxious to know if Kale had arrived safely, a persuasive enough text.

But Giskes had made one of his rare mistakes: the message was only eighty letters long.

I'd spent two and a half hours briefing Netball and knew the eyes, nose and broken teeth of his coding. He would never send a message with less than 150 letters in it unless he were trying to tell London he was caught.

I'd taken particular care with him because he was to carry a six months' supply of poems to distribute to other agents, and because he was dropping to a highly suspect reception committee organized by Cucumber.

Convinced that he was going to be caught, I'd used him as a messenger boy to persuade Giskes that London had no immediate intentions of changing the poem-code.

I regarded his eighty letters as an SOS which he knew I'd pick up. He'd also expect me to realize that Mangold had also been caught. I took out my report on Netball's briefing and hurried in to Nick with it.

Heffer was present, and they stopped their conversation as soon as I entered, which I tried to interpret as a compliment. I showed them Netball's message but they'd already seen it and found nothing wrong with it.

I then handed them my report.

They studied it at length, and each other for even longer, and something passed between them which was a generation away from me. They agreed that it was an extraordinary lapse on Netball's part, and might well have the significance I attached to it, but it would need careful consideration.

I suggested that we should respond to Kale's message normally, and ask N section to point out his mistake to him.

They again exchanged looks.

After a long pause Nick telephoned Bingham and asked him to remind Netball at his next sked never to send less than 150 letters.

I made a final effort to stress that this wasn't a lapse on Netball's part but a brilliant way of warning us that he was caught, and suggested that Harvey should be informed of it.

Reddening, Nick put my report in his briefcase, and repeated that he'd discuss it with Gubbins.

Just before Heffer and I went our occasionally separate ways, I asked him what he thought the outcome of their discussion would be.

'I suspect you'll have a meeting with Gubbins.' As usual, he was right.

In many ways mortal, Gubbins was unable to conceal his intense fatigue, but a single glance from him was still the equivalent of a brain-scan, and he subjected me to an exceptionally long one.

I sensed that I was going to be addressed as Marks and not Leo, and glanced at Nick to guess how much support I could expect. He was sitting motionless, as if breathing through his ears.

'Now then, Marks . . .' Speaking at a rate of nots (thinking in puns helped to lessen his impact), he said that Netball's eighty-letter message was disturbing but couldn't be regarded as conclusive proof that he was caught as there was another factor that could account for it. '. . . and it's one that you constantly overlook . . .'

He then pointed out that no matter how carefully I briefed agents, and he had no doubt that I did, they were under so much pressure in the field that they were likely to forget every word that I'd said to them, especially when they had to transmit urgent messages, and that Netball's unusual mistake had probably been caused by exceptional tension.

'Sir, that's about as likely as Giskes offering to return Kale to England on the back of a whale.'

Gubbins brusquely informed me that my understanding of agents was strictly limited to teaching them codes, and Netball was a case in point. I expected him to behave in the field as he did in the briefing room, a mistake which had caused me to overlook a vital question: *If Netball were blown, why had he been allowed to send only eighty letters?* If my theories about Giskes were right, the Germans knew our security rules even better than we did. That being said, I was right to have brought the message to Nick's attention but on no account must I bring it to Harvey's. It was his job to establish *facts*, and he mustn't be sidetracked by persuasive conjectures. '. . . is that clear?'

'Absolutely, sir.'

It was even clearer that there was something behind all this and that I was the one being sidetracked.

He then asked how many silk codes would be available by the beginning of August.

'Four hundred WOKs and three hundred LOPs, sir.' He disliked the word LOPs, and I hastily amended it to letter one-time pads.

'That may not be enough.' Glancing at Nick, he warned me to expect demands for the new codes from 'unexpected quarters', and urged me to concentrate on increasing production.

With a sudden twinkle, for which I'd have forgiven him anything except living, he asked if I were still having problems finding suitable women.

I assured him that the new intake had doubled, but we were always on the lookout for promising talent. I didn't add that his secretary, Margaret Jackson, had everything we sought for in a woman except availability.

After repeating his warning not to sidetrack Harvey, he gave me his customary nod of dismissal, but added a rider as I stood up to go. 'You're doing a good job, Leo. But you'd do a damn sight better one if you'd leave some things to other people . . .'

'Thank you, sir.'

I stormed into Heffer's office unannounced. 'Heff,' I said at my most deferential, 'what the fuck's going on in this abattoir?'

The Guru enjoyed dealing with technical questions. 'Do I take it you've been slaughtered?'

I blurted out what I hadn't fully thought through, a mark of my respect for him. 'Something's going on in Holland that Gub and Nick don't want me to know about. If they can't trust me, they must bloody well start looking for a new head of Codes, and the sooner the better. I mean it, Heff.'

He pointed to a chair, and a few smoke rings later he said that if I promised under the Official Secrets Act called friendship not to let him down, he'd tell me the 'sorry tale' they didn't want me to know about.

'Thanks. But I don't care any more.'

Having children of his own, he appeared not to hear this. 'C is trying to put us out of business.'

'Good luck to them,' I said, still smarting from not being trusted.

'But it's all to do with Holland.'

I shook his hand for the first time since I'd known him.

The 'sorry tale' emerged . . .

Towards the end of June C had informed Gubbins that they'd discovered from their own sources in Holland that eight of SOE's agents had been arrested. But being expert mixers, they hadn't left it at that! They'd sent the information to the Dutch authorities in London in the hope of shaking their already waning confidence in us. '. . . but that's nothing compared to what else the bastards have done.'

They were using the information to convince the Chiefs of Staff that SOE was incapable of organizing an uprising in Holland or anywhere else.

He then explained why Kale's disappearance was the biggest bonus C could have had.

The Chiefs had been promised a chance to question Jambroes when he returned to London, but Gubbins had had to tell them that he'd been killed in a street fight just as he was leaving. They'd been waiting since November to question his successor, and Gubbins had now had to tell them that Kale had also met with a 'fatal accident' at the last moment. Coming on top of C's news about the eight arrested agents, if the Chiefs had the slightest reason to suspect that the whole Dutch Resistance was in enemy hands, SOE could lose its mandate. '. . . and that would be the end of our role on D-Day.'

He paused to see what effect this was having.

I asked who the captured agents were.

Looking at me blandly, he professed not to know. As he was under no obligation to tell me anything, I pretended to believe him, and waited equally blandly for him to finish.

He added that no one had done more than Gubbins to secure our mandate, and that the only reason he didn't want me to disclose my anxieties to Harvey was that his report might be leaked to C, who'd pass it on to the Chiefs of Staff.

And the sooner the better.

The Guru then pointed out that Gubbins and Nick had been assessing security-mindedness for longer than I'd been born, and the question of them not trusting me didn't arise. They had great confidence in the way I ran the code department but somewhat less in the way I ran myself! They knew bloody well that I was prone to unpredictable responses, such as writing to the Ministry of Labour, and felt that the less I knew about C's skulduggery, the less likely I was to send a protest to Winston Churchill. But as soon as the present crisis was over, they'd brief me fully, and until that happy day I couldn't really blame them for proceeding on a 'need to know' basis.

At this point the telephone rang. He lifted the receiver reluctantly, and a few seconds later switched over to the scrambler.

His face growing greyer by the moment – a substantial achievement – he listened for several seconds, then finally said 'Christ!' and replaced the receiver. He lifted it again immediately, and asked to be put through to Gubbins's office because he had an urgent message for Nick.

I stood up to leave but he shook his head emphatically. I was all ears – a considerable improvement – as he informed Nick that there'd been a development concerning Netball which he must know about at once.

Major Adams (the CO of 53b) had told him that Ken Howell (the chief signalmaster) had been suspicious of Netball's operating since he'd begun transmitting two weeks ago, and at the end of today's sked he'd set a trap for him.

Knowing that German wireless operators often signalled 'HH' (Heil Hitler) when they were about to sign off, he'd signalled 'HH' to Netball at the end of his sked, and Netball had replied 'HH' without a moment's hesitation. The speed of Netball's response had convinced Ken that Netball's set was being operated by a German.

Adams was anxious to apologize to Nick for Howell's unauthorized action, for which he accepted responsibility.

I could hear Nick barking questions at him but couldn't tell from Heffer's answers what he was asking, one of the Guru's outstanding accomplishments. But it was his final response which interested me most.

'Right!' he said. 'I'll make sure Marks knows, if he doesn't already,' and replaced the receiver. 'So now you know.' he said. 'And you can get back to work.'

'Heil Howell.' I replied. And continued heiling him for the rest of the day.

But that wasn't the end of SOE's indebtedness to the single-minded signalmaster.

Nick went to the station on the 19th to listen to Netball's next sked. He was accompanied by a civilian whom no one could identify (Heffer conjectured that 'he was a trusted colleage from Y'). Each of them carried 'split-cans' (radio sets which enabled them to listen to both ends of the transmission simultaneously).

Netball was several minutes late for his sked (not significant) and signalled 'QRU' ('I have no traffic for London'). Howell replied 'QTC' ('We have a message for you'), and proceeded to transmit it (the message warned Netball never to send less than 150 letters). Howell then signalled 'HH', and Netball immediately replied 'HH'.

'Right,' Nick was heard to say to his companion, 'that's it then.'

I asked Heffer what he thought 'that's it' meant.

'You're the cryptographer,' he said. 'You decipher it.'

But understanding my peers was yesterday's dream. The only reality I could be sure of was that Heffer had put himself at risk for me.

I visited 84 when the shop was deserted, and the next day he was able to present his wife with her book on thimbles.

FORTY-FIVE

Parallel Action

Throughout July the traffic made clear (if confirmation were necessary) that Holland wasn't our only nightmare. Every country section had become a sea-going lifeboat which might not arrive.

The Prosper circuit had collapsed, and there'd been no further news of Peter and Odette. And Buckmaster had developed an attitude problem.

He accepted that Prosper had been caught but was trying to persuade himself, his colleagues and me that Archambault was free. Keeping his options open, he continued to exchange messages with Archambault in the hope that he wouldn't be executed. But there were limits to what he could say, and an idea for helping him had occurred to me.

It would lend conviction to Maurice's messages if we dropped a WOK to Archambault. The Germans were unlikely to suspect that we thought he was blown if we sent him a silk with instructions in its use, and urged him to cut it away and destroy it key by key, and limit his messages to 100 letters.

We'd also give him new security checks, and explain that if he changed his indicator-groups by his secret numbers the Germans could never work them out if he'd destroyed his previous keys.

Unable to find any flaws in the concept (always disturbing) I consulted Nick and Heffer.

They sympathized with my intention (always a bad sign) and agreed that the Germans were unlikely to kill Archambault if they thought we still trusted him. They also agreed that some silks were bound to be captured, and that making the Germans a present of one wouldn't affect their security. But both Gurus felt that the timing was wrong,

350

and that it would be in the interests of agents as a whole if we delayed the discovery of silks for as long as we could.

Heffer conceded that the idea would probably achieve its objective, but that in the hands of F section 'it would end by doing more harm than good'.

I didn't argue; out of deference to their experience, and because I was worried by Heffer's comment. It didn't occur to me until I'd left them that the idea could be helpful to other country sections, and might prolong the lives of captured Dutch agents.

I was about to turn back when I realized that like most amateur welfare officers I was in danger of becoming addled.

I'd given Netball a six months' supply of poems to persuade Giskes that we had no reason to doubt their security but he might ask himself why we hadn't given him silks instead. And even if the bastard concluded that they weren't available at the time (22 April) he was bound to ask himself two vital questions: What had prompted London to make such drastic changes? And was there any further point in keeping the agents alive?

It was time to think again.

Everything was eclipsed (including Giskes) by a telegram from Sweden in main-line cipher which arrived on the 15th. It was originated by Ronald Turnbull ('our man' in the Stockholm legation).

The telegram stated that German scientists at the research station at Peenemünde were under orders from Hitler to devise ways of mass-producing long-range rockets so that he could carry out his threat to 'plaster London with thousands of missiles a day till it was razed to the ground'.

Turnbull added that new radio apparatus for the rockets was being researched at Bornholm (a Danish island which the Germans had sealed off), and that the scientists were under great pressure from Hitler to complete their experiments.

Unsealing the secrets of Bornholm would be the Danish director-ate's responsibility, and Hollingsworth's response was immediate. On 16 July he asked me to call on him as soon as I could, and showed me a message which was to be transmitted to Duus Hansen in a few hours' time:

Can you report on activity at Peenemünde where enemy are producing and experimenting with long range rockets. It is believed that radio apparatus on Bornholm is connected with these experiments. We urgently need a description of the rockets and their emplacements, and as much information as possible about the scale of rocket and projector production at the research station.

Hollingsworth then disclosed his anxieties about the Peenemünde traffic.

Most of if would be passed by Duus Hansen, and he was anxious for him to stop using his poem-code and switch to a silk, which could either be dropped to him during the August moon or sent to Sweden and infiltrated. The difficulty was that the system would be new to him. Did I think he could learn to use it from written instructions? And did I foresee any other problems?

I replied that Hansen knew as much about WT as anyone in Signals, and I was certain he'd have no difficulty understanding how to use a WOK from written instructions and, at a later state, a one-time pad. The only problems I foresaw were his security checks, which mustn't be included with his silks and would have to be delivered to him separately.

Hollingsworth assured me that a trusted courier would hand the checks to him in a coded message, and that on reflection the safest course would be to send all his codes via Sweden. Would it take long to produce them?

He had a dozen WOKs on his desk an hour later with a set of instructions which I'd done my best to keep simple. When he telephoned to tell me that he'd tested the instructions and found them 'just the job' I felt like a guided missile.

The latest developments in Holland brought me sharply back to earth.

N section had ordered the Dutch agents to attack enemy installations, though the security of their WT links must at all costs be preserved. Their targets included U-boats, coal harbours and railway sidings, as well as goods trains, electrical repair shops and factories producing spare parts for night fighters.

N section also required information about the Luftwaffe divisions in Amsterdam, and urgently needed to know at what times night fighters were lined up on the tarmac at Venlo and Gilze in readiness for take-off.

The agents were quick to comply. According to a spate of messages from Ebenezer, Parsley, Catarrh, Cucumber and Co., freedom fighters had successfully attacked patrol boats, barges and railway carriages in Rotterdam, Amsterdam and Delft, as well as mine-sweepers, coach-building factories and storage depots, but had suffered very few casualties.

Other 'reliable' information continued to reach N section: Catarrh reported that the cut-out who delivered the Victory group's message was a traitor and gave a full description of him; Broadbean was arranging for two agents to be smuggled to England, and asked London to broadcast a contact phrase, 'A better world starts with yourself'; and Cucumber was continuing his efforts to establish what had happened to Kale and his boat.

He wasn't the only one to express concern about the missing commander. Mangold sent a message via Netball saying that although there'd been no news of Kale, he was still hoping that his old chief was safe. Meanwhile he'd continue to take Kale's place, and to carry out his instructions.

Yet despite all this traffic not a single agent had made a mistake in his coding. Nor could I see any signs in the outgoing messages that SOE had really accepted the extent of the collapse. Perhaps the new operations were part of an SOE master plan which I'd be told about when the C crisis was over. Perhaps with a capital pee . . .

I was about to close the books on July when I received the biggest shock of my SOE life.

Nick walked in accompanied by my former boss Dansey, who never left his main-line code department without very good reasons.

Mercifully unaware of what these were, I produced the special sandwiches reserved for welcome visitors, and won a short reprieve.

Nick then informed me that he and Gubbins were becoming increasingly concerned about our Middle East traffic, and had decided that Dansey should go to Cairo in August to improve the efficiency of their main-line code room, and to prevent further backlogs. I was to join him in Cairo a week later to deal with the agents' traffic, and to explain the importance of WOKs and LOPs.

I neither moved nor spoke, and they looked at me as if realizing rigor mortis had already set in. I managed to smile, a habit to which I understood corpses were prone, but was careful not to part my lips in case the reason for my panic slipped out.

Nick asked if I had any questions, but I was keeping them for the Almighty.

Puzzled by my silence, a rare event in his presence, Nick glanced at Dansey, who was equally perplexed. 'I'd better warn you,' Nick finally said, 'that the natives are likely to be hostile.'

Sod the natives, and *Gubbins,* and *Nick. None of them knew how lucky they were.*

They didn't have to deal with my parents.

FORTY-SIX

The Club Rules

Approaching twenty-three and frequently mistaken for an adult, I was reluctant to blow my cover by admitting to my colleagues that being a member of the JOCC (Jewish Only Child's Club) conferred many advantages, but leaving home for a week wasn't one of them – and as for leaving this country.

I remembered the heartache which had accompanied my only other trip abroad.

At the age of sixteen I'd been allowed to visit Paris escorted by an uncle, who'd been ordered to prepare me for the throne of 84 by confining our expeditions to libraries, museums and antiquarian bookshops. Ignoring his brief, my conducting officer introduced me to a brothel which specialized in beginners.

My parents had phoned Paris several times but didn't know the brothel's number, and the proceedings were uninterrupted except by my ineptitude.

I now had the problem of explaining to them why the Ministry of Labour required me to visit its Cairo branch. I decided to give them time to adjust to it, but not enough to attempt to accompany me.

On 5 August I waited till our black-market dinner was no more than a rumble, and announced that I was going to the Middle East for a week.

Hard of hearing at will, Mother convinced herself that I'd said the East End, and warned me that Whitechapel was a very rough district and that I mustn't stay there after dark.

I explained that I was going to Cairo.

'But that's abroad.' she said.

I was unable to dispute it.

She didn't keel over because she had Father to support.

I explained that I'd been temporarily transferred to a branch of Intelligence.

'They need to have their heads examined,' said Mother, 'sending a baby to that awful place.'

Father announced that he'd be back in an hour and left the room abruptly.

'Now look what you've done,' said Mother. 'He's gone to get pissed.'

But for once Benjamin Marks had another objective, and returned an hour later clutching a large solar topi, which he thrust into my hand.

'Swear on your mother's life you'll never be without it,' he said.

'And swear on your father's life that you'll never drink the water.'

'And swear on your mother's life that you'll never . . .'

I swore twelve oaths in all, each as unbreakable as a LOP.

'When do you leave?' Father finally asked.

'In about a fortnight.'

'A lot can happen in that time,' he said.

It was one of his rare understatements.

Dansey's departure was scheduled for the 15th, mine for the 23rd. SOE had arranged for me to spend a few hours in Lisbon *en route*, and all my papers were in order except for the visa known as courage. Always a nervous traveller even in a pram, I was convinced that my plane would crash, and that I'd perish cigarless in the desert.

I began thinking about my successor, and hoped he'd come from Bletchley. I also thought about the problems he'd inherit.

Determined to help him take over without losing momentum, I decided to leave him the fullest possible briefing, and set about preparing my last will and testament. If I spent my few remaining days doing nothing else, I'd have just enough time to finish the document, amend it and deposit it with Muriel – my most valuable bequest to him.

In the middle of my preparations a crisis occurred which few had foreseen, and which could have disastrous consequences if the code department failed to achieve the technically impossible. It was the most difficult problem I'd encountered since joining SOE.

Einstein (Father's favourite Yiddisher boy) might have known how to solve it. This one could only say his prayers.

FORTY-SEVEN

Lake Como's Bottom

'. . . this is the most important commitment SOE's
ever undertaken, and it can't succeed without Signals.
So you'd better get your thinking cap on.'
                            (Nick to author, August '43)

I was disappointed to learn that the commitment was Italy. Unable
to take seriously any country which was run by Mussolini, I continued
brooding about my successor while Nick explained that the Italians
were preparing to surrender to the Allies, and that the negotiations
were being conducted by SOE.

'. . . but what's more to the point, *we shall be handling the traffic.*'

Mistaking my frown for a thinking cap, he explained how vital it
was that the Germans didn't learn about the armistice attempt or
they'd probably occupy Rome and shoot the negotiators. His
summary of the Italian situation was like an excerpt from Dante's
Inferno.

Mussolini had been deposed in July after a meeting of the Fascist
Grand Council, and Marshal Badoglio had replaced him as premier.
A fervent anti-Nazi, he'd instructed his agents in Madrid to inform
their SOE counterparts that the new Italian government was prepared
to negotiate a surrender.

After preliminary talks in Lisbon with an Anglo-American team
(the British were represented by members of SOE) the marshal's
deputy, General Castellano, had flown to Massingham to finalize
surrender terms with Harold Macmillan and Lord Sheffield from
London, and two American generals (Bedell-Smith and Strong).

All the arrangements for this key conference had been made by our man at Massingham, Colonel Douglas Dodds-Parker, who was skilful enough to be our man anywhere. (Dodds-Parker was the 'giraffe in uniform' who'd shown me the way to Gubbins's office on my one and only stint as night duty officer.) The Italian delegates had used Dodds-Parker's bedroom for their private discussions but he'd had the foresight to bug it, which took much of the surprise out of the subsequent discussions.

Although the parties reached 'agreement in principle' after an all-night session, the surrender terms had to be ratified by Badoglio in Rome, and both sides realized that it was essential to establish a radio link between him and Massingham.

Helpful as ever, Dodds-Parker informed the Italians that one of SOE's most reliable WT operators was in prison in Verona. His name was Dick Mallaby and he'd been captured by the Italians when he'd dropped into Lake Como. Castellano undertook to secure Mallaby's release, and to smuggle him into the Quirinale in Rome with his captured WT set. Badoglio would then be in a position to communicate with Massingham.

The Allied commander, General Eisenhower, had been kept fully informed of these developments and had given them his blessing. The traffic had been code-named Monkey, and would start as soon as Mallaby was safely installed.

Monkey's real significance, apart from shortening the war, was that C had been entirely excluded from the negotiations, and it would be a major 'up-yours' if we succeeded without them. But there was one minor problem: Mallaby's code.

Hardly daring to ask, I enquired what it was and was shown his file. He'd been trained in Cairo and given a novel from which to extract phrases for his double-transposition. He'd then been sent to Algiers to prepare for his drop, and the chief signals officer had given him a poem to memorize in case he lost his novel, but he'd been captured by the Italians before passing any traffic.

Dodds-Parker suspected that the novel was at the bottom of Lake Como (the best place for it) but was convinced that Mallaby wouldn't forget his poem as 'Dick had a most retentive memory'.

It then emerged that it was considered impossible to get a new code to him, and that the armistice traffic was to be passed in his poem. I was ordered by Nick to drop everything and devise a way of making it more secure.

The first thing I dropped I'd have been happy to share with Mussolini. The only way of sending Mallaby security instructions would be to transmit them in an insecure code. But that was only the fringe of the problem.

We couldn't be sure the Germans didn't already know Mallaby's poem. He'd been tortured by the Italians and might have thought he could safely disclose his poem to them as he hadn't used it (they might even send a message with the wrong security checks), and they in turn might have passed it to the Germans as part of their efforts to impress them.

I asked Nick why letter one-time pads couldn't be smuggled into the Quirinale.

He replied that there wouldn't be enough time unless I dropped them in myself *en route* to Cairo. He was always frivolous when at his most worried, and telephoned Major Roseberry (head of the Italian directorate).

A few hours later a dozen LOPs were on their way to Massingham and another dozen to Lisbon, where two Italian generals might have an outside chance of smuggling them in. (LOPs were essential for this level of traffic and Mallaby should have no difficulty understanding the instructions.)

In the meantime his poem had to be strengthened, but my thinking cap was several sizes too small.

The problem seemed insoluble until I suddenly remembered Dodds-Parker's comment that 'Dick had a most retentive memory'. If it was as reliable as Douglas believed (his own was photographic), we might be in sight of a short-term solution: we could transmit a message to Mallaby in his blown poem, giving him the words of a new one. These would consist of intimate details of his private life which the Germans couldn't possibly know.

He'd be instructed to memorize the new words (there'd be twenty-six of them) in the order in which we'd encoded them, and to use five different ones for each message. He could show Massingham which five he'd selected by using his normal indicator system. He'd also be instructed that his messages must never contain less than 300 letters (which with the voluble Italians was hardly likely), and to ensure that his transposition-keys were at least twenty letters long.

I took the idea to Nick, and stressed that it was only a short-term answer but it might be better than none.

He took a long time considering it, then studied me in silence. 'Dodds-Parker was right to code-name the traffic Monkey,' he said finally.

He then asked Roseberry to examine Mallaby's records and consult his colleagues in J section (the Italian directorate) for the information we needed, and sent messages to Cairo and Massingham urging anyone who knew Mallaby well (instructors, briefing officers and friends) to provide London with personal details which must be absolutely accurate. He didn't disclose why they were needed.

Sifting the data until I knew his foibles by heart, I selected the twenty-six words which were to become his new poem. They included: his mother's maiden name, his father's Christian name, the brand-name of his favourite beer, the title of his favourite film (*Metropolis*), the surname of the actress he most wanted to sleep with (Jean Harlow) and the make of his first car. I then took the package to Nick and Heffer.

Nick's only reservation was the inclusion of Jean Harlow, but Heffer thought she'd be excellent security and asked me to let him know next time one of her films was shown in London. The blonde bombshell (as Miss Harlow was popularly known) was allowed a part in the armistice traffic.

Our next job was briefing the head of Signals at Massingham (Bill Corbett), and Nick sent a message to him in main-line cipher, which he was to decode personally. The message explained how the new code worked, and then instructed Corbett to lock it in his safe until it was required, and to allow no more than three coders to use it. Each of them must be warned that under no circumstances was she to discuss the code or the traffic with anyone but Corbett. The texts of the messages would not be subject to normal distribution procedures. Incoming messages would be collected by Colonel Dodds-Parker or by someone he'd appointed, and outgoing messages handed to Corbett personally. If Mallaby transmitted any indecipherable messages the code-groups must be sent to London in main-line cipher, and we would assist in breaking them. (It would be impossible for Massingham to mount a blanket attack when only three girls were allowed to know the code.)

Corbett confirmed that he fully understood Nick's telegram and would take the necessary steps.

I was still hoping that the Italians in Lisbon would find the Quirinale easier to penetrate than Gubbins's mind was to me, and that the silks would reach him in time. SOE's telepathic system was on red alert, and I received a call from the general within seconds of the thought.

'Damn good Monkey business,' he said, and replaced the receiver.

But I knew the truth. I'd produced a flashy idea with little merit because Mallaby's poem couldn't stand up to heavy traffic, and would have to be changed as frequently as possible.

I set about preparing the reserve poems. I had plenty of material left, including the age at which he'd lost his virginity (he'd repeatedly maintained that he was nine), but some details of his early life were contradictory, and I had to be careful which I selected.

Three hours later the new poems were on their way to Massingham. I said a silent prayer that they wouldn't be used, and retired to my own Quirinale to prepare my last will and testament.

FORTY-EIGHT

'I Hereby Bequeath . . .'

Most of the information my successor would need was fully documented, and my first task was to ensure that he knew where to find it without having to depend on third parties.

The records which I kept in my safe and updated weekly would give him a compendium of the strengths and weaknesses of every member of the code department except its present head, and provide him with the coding idiosyncrasies of every agent. They also dealt with the foibles of our country section clients, and the vulnerabilities (or otherwise) of our suppliers.

But none of these would give him the insights he needed and I'd have no peace (if the luxury existed where I was likely to be going) unless I disclosed certain malpractices I'd committed which were nowhere on record.

I confessed to intercepting all messages from the field in secret French code, breaking the indecipherables and re-encoding them accurately so that the agents wouldn't be instructed to repeat them, and hoped he'd continue the malpractice with the utmost caution. I also admitted to launching Plan Giskes without authority, and referred him to my Dutch and Belgian reports to help him evaluate the results.

The crime sheet was so long that I decided to leave it to the last as it was more important to brief him about two recent events which were likely to need immediate attention and which had complicated backgrounds.

On 12 August Bodington returned from France.

His request to be picked up by Lysander had been transmitted by Noor Inayat Khan, who'd been wandering around Paris with her set in a suitcase. Although he'd been reluctant to entrust his message to her, he'd found he had no option as the Prosper, Chestnut and Bricklayer circuits had completely collapsed, and 'Madeleine' was the only one of Buckmaster's WT operators still at liberty in Paris.

I learned from Maurice that she'd committed many indiscretions, including leaving her signal-plan and poem in the hallway of a flat, where they'd remained open for inspection for several hours. Bodington had urged her to 'lie low' till London instructed her otherwise, and she'd agreed to do so. But Maurice doubted if she would.

I warned my successor that 'lying low' was as close to lying as Noor could ever get, and that because of her attitude I'd given her a special security check which would be new to the Germans, and which she was to use only if she were caught. (Her transposition-key must be eighteen letters long.) I also warned him that there was no guarantee that she'd remember it (though I was convinced that she would), and I urged him to take special care with every message she encoded.

The other event concerned Hitler's intention of razing London to the ground. According to Duus Hansen, as reliable a source as any in the field, the rocket sites at Peenemünde had become a tug-of-war between C and SOE.

On 12 August he sent a message to Sweden asking which organization he was supposed to be working for. He was especially keen to know whether he should send information about the rocket sites to the Danish section of SOE or to Hannibal (a department in C he'd previously worked for and was still in touch with). He complained that both organizations were asking him to obtain the same information!

Turnbull sent him a long message (repeated to London in main-line code) stressing that operational matters were SOE's responsibility and that he should send his information to SOE's Stockholm office. It would then be forwarded to SOE's London HQ, which would be responsible for distributing it!

I reminded my successor that Hansen's silks and security checks were being delivered to him by courier, and that although the Stockholm office had so far proved reliable, no chances should be taken and Hansen must be asked a number of test questions when he began using his WOK.

I was in the middle of dealing with our techniques for breaking indecipherables when Tommy walked in wearing his Croix de Guerre uniform. He was standing by to mount a two-man mission with Brossolette, code-named Marie-Claire. Its function was to restore morale in the field following the capture of Moulin, and to establish a new chain of command. Tommy had been selected for the mission by de Gaulle and Passy – yet another sign of their confidence in him.

He looked at me sharply and asked what was wrong.

I told him that SOE was sending me to Cairo to convert the natives to Judaism.

He knew my domestic situation and it invariably amused him, but there was no humour in his face as he studied me thoughtfully. He asked me whether I'd like him to keep in touch with my parents while I was away. If so, he'd introduce himself as my Ministry of Labour supervisor.

I couldn't let him see how much his offer had affected me, and for the first time since I'd known him I averted my face from my favourite supervisor.

One half of Marie-Claire closed the door behind him.

I realized that I hadn't even asked him what he'd wanted.

I tried to define 'SOE-mindedness', but soon gave up in despair (perhaps I'd understand it from the other side), and gave the document to Muriel for typing, warning her to take no copies.

Unaware that she was my executor, she began work at once.

Alone in a way that was new, I made a contribution to the ditty-box, wondering if it would be my last:

> We have a little time left
> The wise doctor said
> Unless there's a miracle
> Which is another man's trade
>
> Selfish as always
> I've started missing you now

Want to say so
Don't know how
Want to hug you
Don't know if I should
Hope you understand
I'd take your place if could.*

I was in the middle of adding a codicil about Nick and Heffer when Muriel put her head round the door and, without a trace of regret, reminded me that I had a plane to catch.

* Issued in September '44 to a Jedburgh. He was killed a week after he'd landed in France.

FORTY-NINE

A Treat for the Natives

'You must forget all about Baker Street for the next seven days, and that includes Monkey. Keep everything for Cairo. God knows it needs it.'

(Nick's parting instructions)

On 24 August one of the war's lesser events took place outside the main entrance of Shephard's Hotel, Cairo, where a room had been reserved for me – probably by mistake.

My braces broke, and my trousers slid gracefully to the ground. The next to descend were the shimmering underpants which only yesterday my tearful mother had lovingly pressed.

She would have been proud of the interest they aroused in the open-mouthed natives. At the time of the involuntary exposure I was clutching a briefcase full of silks in one hand and my solar topi in the other. Reluctant to relinquish the former for security reasons, I put the latter between my knees to protect an indispensable appendage from sunstroke. I then bent down to retrieve my dignity, affording the fascinated drivers and pedestrians a view of kosher rump, which Nick may not have had in mind when he instructed me to keep everything for Cairo.

The honking of car-horns was followed by a round of applause from the direction of the hotel.

Looking up, I saw a world-famous American watching me from the veranda. He continued to watch me as I hobbled towards the entrance, clutching my trousers, then leaned across the veranda for a closer inspection. His voice was marginally less carrying than Chur-

367

chill's and almost as famous. 'Excuse me, sir. *What are you going to do for an encore?'*

Wishing he knew, Sir hobbled inside.

Next time we met, my fingers would be free to give him an appropriate answer.

SOE's HQ was in Rustom Buildings, a large grey-pillared block in the centre of an otherwise respectable residential area. Every taxi-driver in Cairo knew the address and charged double for reaching it.

Dansey, one of the few people whom khaki shorts aged, was waiting at the reception desk. Handing me my pass, he warned me not to lose it or I'd have to buy a new one from the head porter at Shephard's. He then led me into an ante-room and briefed me in undertones.

The situation as he saw it was 'pretty damn serious'. The main-line traffic had been allowed to pile up and more coders would have to be sent from London to deal with the backlog. I must make up my own mind about agents' traffic, but he thought he should warn me that the silks I'd sent from London 'hadn't caught on' and my visit was considered completely unnecessary.

He then outlined what he referred to as 'the drill'.

Cairo's Chief of Staff, Brigadier Keble, would send for me sometime this evening as he was far too busy to see me before, but I probably wouldn't meet the head of Signals (Ridley-Martin) at all as he was away for a week. Nor was I likely to meet his deputy (Jerry Parker), who was also away, but the third in command (Bill Chalk) would look in sometime this afternoon to say hello. He suggested that I should spend the whole day 'getting the feel of the code room' until Keble was ready to send for me.

He then looked at me appealingly. 'Don't rub him up the wrong way, old chap. He's a short-tempered little sod at the best of times!'

Picking up my solar topi (I'd sworn 'on Mother's life' *never* to be without it), I assured him I'd be careful and followed him upstairs.

To the untrained eye (as great a liability in wartime as the untrained heart) all code rooms looked alike. But to those afflicted with cipher awareness, every one had an aura of its own, and Cairo's was as bowed as the heads of its coders.

It was a multi-purpose code room, and the girls were required to switch from main-line traffic to agents' and back again, a malpractice which London had long since abandoned. (Dansey had been the first to agree that the systems needed different skills and temperaments, and that agents' traffic should be a separate entity.) Many of the girls on the present shift (including the supervisor) were veterans from Grendon, where they'd been trained to behave like mini-cryptographers rather than cipher clerks. They watched with growing apprehension as Dansey led me to an empty desk in the corner. He then explained the mechanics of the office, told me where to find him if I needed his help, and left me to get on with it.

The facts emerged slowly, like soldiers from a brothel.

The agents were given novels from which to obtain their transposition-keys, though several had been issued with magazines, and one appeared to be using a military manual. The volume of traffic was heavy, and at peak periods several hundred messages a day were exchanged with agents in Greece, Yugoslavia, Tehran, Istanbul, Crete and a number of Balkan towns and villages. There were also two-way exchanges with long-range desert groups.

Even the most rudimentary precautions were ignored, and I found eight examples of the same transposition-keys being used for messages of identical length (cryptographically fatal), and six examples of messages which contained fewer than fifty letters. (One was from the Home Station.) A file marked 'Indecipherables' disclosed that fifteen had been received in the past week, and that in each case the miscreants had been instructed to re-encode them.

I casually enquired if any attempts were made to break agents' indecipherables, and there was a bewildered shaking of heads. As one renegade put it, 'They have a lot more time than we have.' I barely recognized the Grendon coders as they plodded away at their desks.

But the biggest shock was reserved for midday, when I barely recognized the code room.

It was suddenly invaded by a succession of captains and lieutenants who weren't members of the Royal Corps of Signals (their only discernible asset). They were allowed to saunter into the code room, examine the novels and magazines which were being used as codes, then saunter out again carrying whichever took their fancy. A casual enquiry elicited that they read them on the roof during the lunch hour but always returned them.

Determined to repel the invaders, and equally anxious to pee, I followed a young lieutenant and his novel out of the code room, but instead of going upstairs, where I presumed the roof to be, he went in the opposite direction and headed for the exit.

Tapping him on the shoulder, which I was barely able to reach, I introduced myself as the head of Codes from London. I then informed him that on the instructions of General Gubbins the lending library was closed for the duration, and suggested that if he were short of reading matter he should write to an excellent bookshop in London whose address was 84 Charing Cross Road.

The bemused lieutenant surrendered the book without the slightest opposition. It turned out to be *The Four Just Men*, and I felt like the fifth.

I then asked if he'd be kind enough to show me the way to the gents.

Five minutes later I returned to a code room which was even more badly in need of a flush.

By mid-afternoon I'd broken my first Cairo indecipherable, and was embarking on my second when Major Chalk (number three in the Signals hierarchy) walked in 'just to say hello', as Dansey had predicted.

He was a professional signals officer and it soon became apparent that he knew more about wireless than he did about codes. He expressed the hope that I'd find nothing wrong with Cairo's. I didn't tell him that so far I'd found nothing right.

I was summoned to Keble's office at 7.30 p.m. Dansey and Chalk were already there.

The 'short-tempered little sod at the best of times' didn't look up for almost a minute while I stood in front of his desk clutching my briefcase and solar topi. He then shook hands perfunctorily and pointed to a chair.

He had a ginger moustache and eyes which complemented it. They informed me within seconds that he wasn't going to be taught his business by a young pup of a Jew-boy who, like most of his kind, had managed to avoid military service. He eyed my solar topi as if it were a Hasidic skull-cap.

I took my WOKs and LOPs from my briefcase, where they'd been refrigerating, and began explaining their function.

He interrupted me to say that it was time 'you people in London' realized that Cairo's clandestine communications had damn-all in common with Europe's. As for 'those silk knickers' I was trying to peddle, he'd been advised on good authority, including that of a naval cipher expert from Alexandria, that the codes issued to agents were secure enough for all practical purposes, and he saw no reason to interfere with them.

I agreed that Cairo's agents operated in different circumstances from ours but suggested that cryptographers were the same the world over. His eyes said 'so are Yids', and he ordered me to come to the point.

Desperate to rescue a joke which now couldn't possibly come off, I said that cryptographers would have far more to show for their efforts if they examined silk knickers for what they normally concealed than if they probed them for agents' traffic. I then hastily pointed out that silk codes would put an end to indecipherables, provide reliable security checks, and cut agents' air-time in half.

'Try not to make too much of a nuisance of yourself, old chap . . .'

Old chap stood up. 'Brigadier, if you don't believe that your agents' traffic is wide open to cryptographic attack, could you please provide me with a blackboard, risk wasting an hour of your valuable time, and allow me to prove to you how vulnerable it is.'

End of meeting.

Twenty-four hours later I was too tired, torpid and listless to care about anything. Nor did I need to worry any more about making a nuisance of myself. I simply didn't have the energy. I attributed the improvement to the change of climate, and to Cairo's infectious attitude, 'What happens will happen'.

It was only when I could no longer distinguish a WOK from a LOP or a coder from a code-book that I realized that I'd picked up a bug, and that it was making itself at home in its new accommodation.

I was given an injection by a medically qualified pig-sticker, and an even sharper one by a bespectacled lady who approached the desk as if about to claim alimony. She informed me that she was Brigadier Keble's secretary, and that I was to report to him in an hour to give a demonstration. She didn't say of what, but added without much enthusiasm that she would return and collect me.

I managed to encode two messages and must have dozed off because when I opened one eye the coders were tittering and the bespectacled lady was beckoning to me from the doorway.

Trying to keep pace with her as she strode down the corridors was like crossing the Gobi Desert carrying a camel. She escorted me into what she described as the 'lecture room', where twenty or so uniformed tribesmen were clustered around camp-fires which turned out to be desks. I glimpsed Keble's red tabs shining like traffic lights signalling STOP. A blue blur on one side of him crystallized into a naval commander, and a brown one on the other side into Dansey and Chalk. The haloes at the back were groups of coders flanked by their supervisors.

Mounting a mile-long platform an inch at a time, I confronted a large Nubian with crossed arms, which turned out to be a blackboard. He had coloured chalks on his person where lesser men had testicles, and I wrote my messages on his chest in block capitals which were twice their normal size as I had half my normal confidence.

I then left the room completely. I was in the Quirinale with Mallaby, in Peenemünde with Duus Hansen, in Duke Street with Tommy. And in Park West being cosseted.

I had no idea what I said. I heard the phrase 'You cairo-practitioners' and knew I was accusing them of something but wasn't sure what. I also heard someone who sounded like me saying, 'No agent must stay on the air a second longer than necessary,' and thoroughly agreed with him.

A few hundred bewilderments later I heard suggestions being called out from all around the room which either meant I was being told to fuck off or that I'd reached that point in the lecture where I invited the audience to become cryptographers.

I found myself replacing the chalk, and realized that the messages had been broken and that I must have given the congregants some help or they'd still be floundering. I knew that I was, but they were clearly waiting for me to build to a climax.

But with what?

Remembering past successes, a sure sign of ageing, I told them about the first agent I'd briefed who'd been as frightened of going into the field as I'd been of meeting him, who was convinced that he'd make mistakes in his coding, and who'd recited his poem to me as if it were a personal appeal to his Home Station.

I spoke on his behalf. It began:

> Be near me when my light is low,
> When the blood creeps, and the nerves prick
> And tingle and the heart is sick,
> And all the wheels of Being slow . . .

And ended:

> Be near me when I fade away,
> To point the term of human strife,
> And on the low dark verge of life
> The twilight of eternal day,
> Be near me.

The final 'Be near me' was mine, and I hoped that Tennyson would forgive me.

I stumbled off the platform, and suddenly found myself in Keble's office, wondering who'd carried me there.

Giving me no indication of whether the past hour had been a disaster, he instructed me to write a full report on agents' ciphers which must be presented to him no later than forty-eight hours before I left Cairo (my departure was set for 3 September, five days away). His secretary would type the report but I must allow her time to finish it as she was extremely busy with important correspondence. He then returned to his own.

When I staggered back to the code room expecting to be greeted with titters, the girls ignored me altogether.

They were far too busy trying to break an indecipherable.

The pig-sticking doctor must have been better than I thought because a third of the way through the report I understood what I was writing. It was finished on the 29th, and typed on the 30th by the bespectacled lady. Despite my conscientious attempts to cut it (if an author's ever are), it was thirty-five pages long.

It contained a list of security precautions which should be introduced immediately, and cited twenty examples of traffic which must be considered blown if the enemy cryptographers' commitments allowed them to attack it. The case for adopting WOKs and LOPs took up most of the space.

I'd made no attempt to criticize the coders or the Signals Office staff as I'd misassessed their lassitude, and what I'd diagnosed as 'gyppy-head' was really 'gyppy-tummy'. I'd also failed to understand the complexity of Cairo's traffic.

Keble's secretary instructed me to submit the report to him the following morning.

He was alone and offered me a lunchtime drink, which was a bit early for me so I imagined I was Father.

The atmosphere changed when he saw the length of the report. Weighing it in his hand, he said he'd hoped to discuss it with me before I left Cairo but there was little chance he could read 'a damn encyclopaedia' before the 3rd. However, he'd do his best.

I thanked him for his drink and stood up to go, but he called me back. 'There's something I've been meaning to ask you.' He pointed at my solar topi, which always seemed to magnetize him. 'What are you hiding in that damn thing? *A miniature recording machine?*'

'Yes, sir. My head.'

He seemed about to crown it with the 'damn encyclopaedia' but changed his mind at the last moment.

He was reading the report as I left.

Late that night I was pacing up and down a deserted lounge in Shephard's wondering whether I'd said too much in my report or not enough when someone fell into step behind me, and an unmistakable voice asked a question which was seldom addressed to me. 'Mind if I join you?'

It was the world-famous American who'd witnessed my striptease.

Without waiting for an answer, he kept pace with me for the next few miles. He then expressed concern for the carpet, and invited me to join him in a drink. Knowing his reputation for meanness, I checked that I had enough cash on me to pay for it, and sat down beside him wishing I could tell him that amongst his many admirers in London was one called Yeo-Thomas.

A group of American officers waved to him from the doorway and he waved back at them without inviting them to join us. They gave me the kind of look which said, 'What the hell's he doing with that little pisspot?'

It puzzled me too until I remembered he had a reputation for enjoying the company of oddballs.

By the time we were sharing a bottle of what was possibly wine he was calling me Leo but I insisted on addressing him by his surname (with a Mr attached), partly because I respected his talent but mainly because his surname was Mother's pet-name for Father. He'd probably charge her if he knew.

He elicited that I'd flown in from London, and I was certain he realized that I might expose a long list of things to him but not why I'd come to Cairo. He also elicited that my father had a bookshop called Marks & Co. in Charing Cross Road. 'I've heard about it from Charlie,' he said. 'He's the only friend I have who can read.'

'Charlie who?'

'Chaplin.' He looked at me apologetically as if he'd been caught boasting. It was one of his most famous expressions.

The fact that we were both Jews was no help in establishing a relationship between us (contrary to a widespread belief amongst those less fortunate), and as communication was his speciality I waited for him to explain what we had to share apart from a table.

With the timing that his 'friend Charlie' had publicly described as 'the best in the business' he told me that he'd be interested to hear from an Englishman what English Jews felt about the war, and what their main contribution was to the downfall of Hitler. His was making the troops laugh but I was being offered his serious side.

I told him that English Jews were well represented in the armed forces, though many of us had branched out in certain other directions.

He leaned forward expectantly as I produced two examples of our diversification.

We'd created the best black market in the whole of Europe, and those of us who were anxious to avoid military service, which I estimated to be not much more than 99 per cent, were responsible for a major scientific discovery. With the help of two Harley Street doctors we'd found a way to deceive our medical examiners by producing sugar in our urine when ordered to pass water. And when we were told to wait two hours in the presence of an orderly and then pass some more, our urine retained its sugar! This ensured a medical certificate which guaranteed exemption from military service.

Although incredulity was his speciality, his disbelief was genuine, and he said that a small proportion of draft-dodgers could give the rest a bad name. He was sure the majority of Jews realized that this was their chance to fight the greatest anti-Semite of all time.

I agreed that Jews certainly recognized a chance when they saw one but pointed out that centuries of persecution had given us an atavistic instinct for self-preservation which was never more in evidence than in the First World War, which was also against an anti-Semite known as 'Kaiser Bill'.

'But you weren't even born then. Or is the light bad in here?'

Sensing I had his interest, I told him about my uncle, a distinguished bookseller who pretended to be deaf to avoid military service. He managed to fool the doctors but was called before a military tribunal for his final examination. While he was busy saying, 'Eh?' to whatever he was asked, someone fired a revolver. But he'd been warned about this and didn't flinch. As he turned to go, someone dropped a coin. He still didn't flinch. But when he reached the main hall someone quietly said, 'Got the time on you, Guv?' and he looked at his watch!

He then ran for his life, chased by two military policemen, and rushed into a nearby delicatessen. Although the owner didn't know him, he must have been familiar with his plight because he raised the lid of a herring-barrel, and uncle jumped in. He hid there for several hours until it was safe to emerge, and managed to avoid conscription, but he stank for the rest of the war and on warm nights still did, according to my aunt.

There was a long silence while he looked at me with his famous dead-pan expression. 'What was that line your uncle fell for? – "Got the time on you, Guv?"'

I confirmed that he was word-perfect.

He then treated me to a display of mime thousands of his admirers would buy black-market tickets for. Appearing to stand up without moving from his chair, he recreated the entire proceedings for an invisible audience, giving uncle and the delicatessen owner lines they'd have been proud of. He was still in the herring-barrel when the door of the lounge opened and his wife walked in.

He introduced me to her as his friend Mr Marks, and she examined me closely. 'I'm his wife,' she said. 'Mind if I ask you something?'

I could only nod. She was far more attractive at close quarters than when she appeared in public as her husband's stooge.

'Are you Groucho in disguise? No one else makes him laugh like this!'

He held his nose as she pulled him from the herring-barrel, and I hoped she didn't take it personally.

I then witnessed a transformation which I found hard to believe. He began walking like Uncle as she led him away! But I hadn't told him that he affected a limp or that he leaned on a stick or that his right shoulder was lower than his left, though I'd seen it all in my mind when I'd described his examination.

I watched him stop suddenly in the middle of the room, though I couldn't see why, and heard her ask what he thought he was doing.

'Pissing sugar.'

He waved to me over his shoulder, and was still laughing as she took him away to perform elsewhere.

I knew he'd given me an experience which I could dine out on for the rest of my life if anyone would believe it. And if I had anyone to dine out with . . .

Thank you, Jack Benny, for giving me a month's holiday in the hour that we spent together. I shall be ready for Keble if he sends for me tomorrow.

Thank you for letting me be Groucho, though I'm a Marks without brothers, and for listening with an inner ear when I spoke about Uncle. It may help me with my briefings.

And thanks for not being ashamed of being proud of your race. I wish I had the courage to be one of the troops you're here to entertain but even you can't work miracles except on the stage.

Goodnight, Mr Benny. I hope we'll meet again, though I doubt if I shall know what to do for an encore.*

And just for the record, the drinks were on him.

* I didn't see him again until a few years after the war, when he was mesmerizing the London Palladium with his solo performance. I wanted to go backstage afterwards to say hello, but my forebodings had been right: I didn't know what to do for an encore.

FIFTY

Home-Coming

Brigadier Keble couldn't find time to discuss my report with me, and was unavailable when I called in to say goodbye to him (perhaps he didn't like breaking down in front of strangers). But as I left, the girls were tackling a batch of indecipherables, and presented me with some unsnappable braces, so my visit to Cairo wasn't a complete waste of time.

On the night of 3 September I returned to London and went straight to the IIQ Signals Office to find out what had happened to Mallaby.

By 29 August the silks still hadn't reached him, and he sent his first message in his old poem confirming that he was safely installed in the Quirinale, and was ready to start operating his old set, which the Italians had returned to him. Massingham replied giving him his new poem, and he began using it at once.

On 1 September Corbett reported that Mallaby was having no problems with his set or his skeds, and hadn't sent a single indecipherable He was allowed to come on the air whenever he wished and was about to start using LMT, a form of double transposition which he'd learned in Cairo, although every effort was being made to supply him with LOPs.

Six messages had been exchanged between Marshal Badoglio and Massingham, but they were repeated to London in main-line cipher and it was impossible to get the feel of Mallaby's coding.

On 3 September the Italians confirmed that they were ready to sign an unconditional surrender, and Massingham informed General Eisenhower that the negotiations were concluded.

The Germans seemed unaware of what was happening, but Mallaby's code was already overloaded, and there was still time for the

Germans to break it. If they did, according to Nick they'd occupy Rome and shoot the negotiators.

Hoping that I hadn't used up a lifetime's luck, and that there'd be a little left over for Mallaby's poem, I returned to Park West wearing my solar topi.

On the morning of the 4th I learned from Heffer that while I'd been 'on holiday' an 'almighty row' had broken out between SOE and Duke Street. Before he could explain why, CD's secretary telephoned. I was to report to him at once, and take my Cairo report with me.

Heffer assured me that the row would still be on by the time I got back.

It was the first time that I had been summoned to the sanctum sanctorum (Latin was compulsory at St Paul's), and the experience became even more harrowing when I saw that Gubbins was present.

He introduced me to CD, who looked at me with a twinkle. 'We know each other pretty well,' he said.

I'd hoped he'd forgotten me.

We'd met when he'd called in on one of his midnight prowls and caught me breaking a message in secret French code which I'd pretended was a Buckmaster indecipherable.

My other encounters with Sir Charles Hambro had been entirely domestic. We still lived opposite each other in Park West; he still left the curtains undrawn while he took his bath; and he still occasionally watched me as I took my early morning swings across the rings above the swimming pool fully-clothed and ready for Baker Street. 'I've received a message from Brigadier Keble . . .' he announced. He picked up a main-line telegram from the desk while I tried to stop my stomach from rumbling.

'He accepts almost everything your report recommended,' he said. 'But that's not all. He wants me to send "a cryptographer of Marks's calibre to Cairo as quickly as possible" Congratulations on an excellent job'

'Hear, hear,' said Gubbins – words I didn't think he knew.

They had a ring-side view of my epiglottis. Wary of praise unless I bestowed it on myself, I was bewildered by Keble's change of heart, and by the fact that SOE's powerhouses had taken the time to congratulate me personally instead of doing it through my guv'nor.

With an uneasy feeling that all was not quite what it seemed, I took my report from my briefcase. 'I believe you want a copy of this, sir?'

'Indeed I do,' said Sir Charles, glancing at the general.

Not sure which powerhouse I should hand it to, I placed it between them.

Their enthusiasm waned a little when they saw its size. 'We shan't read it now,' CD said, 'but we'd like you to sum it up for us.'

'You will also tell us what you *didn't* put in,' barked Gubbins.

I spent fifteen minutes describing Cairo's cipher situation, but although they listened attentively I sensed that their interest wasn't really in codes.

This feeling was confirmed when they questioned me closely about my impressions of the discipline in general, and then encouraged me to describe my meetings with Keble without actually inviting me to criticize a senior officer. But a coward of my calibre wasn't prepared to engage in sabotage – verbal or otherwise – and I praised the efforts of everyone I'd met.

CD thanked me with a hint of disappointment, while Gubbins glared at me in silence. He asked his next question without any warning. 'What do you know about the secret French code?'

Uncle would have feigned deafness at this pistol shot, but I shuddered at its impact and prayed it wasn't mortal. 'I'm not allowed to know anything about it, sir.'

'That's not what I asked you,' he snapped.

I was desperate for a cigar or any other prop. Even a herring-barrel would have helped.

'Speak up,' barked Gubbins. 'What *do* you know about it?'

I replied that I couldn't help noticing that large numbers of messages in secret French code were indecipherable.

'How do you know they're indecipherable?' asked CD.

'Duke Street makes the agents re-encode them, sir, which means they have to stay on the air for longer than necessary and could be de-effed.' Hoping he didn't think I was swearing, I explained that direction-finding units were a major hazard.

So was the speed of Gubbins's reaction. 'There haven't been any indecipherables for at least six months. Any idea why not?'

The little bastard's timing was on a par with Jack Benny's, but it gave me nothing to laugh about. 'I noticed they'd dropped off, sir – but I didn't realize there hadn't been *any*.'

'I repeat. How do you account for it?'

'Perhaps the briefing has improved, sir.'

'Any other possibilities?'

'Perhaps their coders have woken up, sir.'

'They aren't the only ones.' he snapped.

CD examined me as if I were one of Hambro's more suspect accounts. 'You've no idea what their code is?' he finally asked.

'It's obviously some kind of double-transposition, sir – at least I *hope* it's double – but beyond that I know nothing. My Free French opposite number refuses to discuss it.'

CD glanced at Gubbins with an unspoken question. The general glared at me, then nodded almost imperceptibly, like God on a Sunday.

'I don't suppose you know this,' CD said, 'but a serious dispute has arisen with Duke Street over two of their messages . . .' He then explained that if the contretemps weren't resolved quickly it could get completely out of hand, and that I might be called upon to take 'certain action'. He hoped it wouldn't prove necessary but if it were he knew I'd do my best. He added that there was no point in discussing the details now.

I was certain that Gubbins knew I'd been lying about De Gaulle's secret code through my cigar-stained teeth, and the only action I wanted to take was a quick visit to the gents.

'There's one more thing,' said CD, 'and then we can let you go.' He picked up Keble's telegram and looked at me with a hint of his old twinkle. 'I have to send Cairo a cryptographer of your calibre. Is there anyone you can recommend?'

'There's Ensign Hornung at Station 53b, sir, and General Gubbins. But Ensign Hornung can't be spared.' The remark slipped out before I could stop it, and I hurried to the door before I made matters worse.

Later that day I learned that they couldn't be.

FIFTY-ONE

Stranglehold

The Signals directorate was used to handling messages on which many lives depended, but SOE's involvement with the armistice negotiations caused the code department's nerves to prick and tingle, and its heart to be sick, to an extent that nothing else had.

By 3 September the end of Monkey was in sight with no signs of a mishap, which added to the tension.

On 4 September Massingham informed London that the only issue to be resolved with Badoglio was the formal announcement of Italy's surrender.

On 5 September the real nightmare began.

General Eisenhower sent a message to Badoglio which was transmitted in double transposition. The message informed him that Allied troops were standing by to occupy Salerno and urged him to time his announcement of the surrender with the news of the invasion so that it would have maximum effect on the Italian armed forces.

It backfired. Within hours of receiving the message Badoglio informed Massingham that the Germans had somehow learned of the armistice proceedings, and the announcement of the surrender would have to be postponed.

Eisenhower was notified and the news presented him with a major decision. Should he allow the invasion to proceed?

He telephoned Dodds-Parker at Massingham and asked if SOE's codes were secure.

Sticking his neck out, the Giraffe replied *Yes*.

Eisenhower immediately sent a message to Badoglio confirming that the invasion would proceed as planned, and urging him to postpone the announcement of Italy's surrender.

On 9 September 50,000 Americans occupied Salerno, the armistice was announced, and three days later Italy declared war on Germany. But Mallaby still had vital information to pass on to Allied forces HQ, and on 14 September London's LOPs and substitution squares finally reached him, and he began using them at once for the rest of his traffic.

Allied Forces HQ then took over his traffic, and on 21 September the round the clock listening watch on Monkey was cancelled.*

It may have been providential – it was certainly a huge slice of 'merde alors' – that my involvement with Monkey was reduced to a stranglehold by the contretemps with Duke Street which took place in parallel. Although by comparison with Monkey it was no more than a domestic dispute, according to Charlotte Denman (our French encyclopaedia), it was likely to cause a divorce between SOE and Duke Street.

Trying not to take sides, and almost succeeding, she explained that the capture of Jean Moulin in July, followed by the arrest of most Free French leaders, had forced de Gaulle to rethink his structure of command. The problem was that SOE disagreed with his conclusions.

The general was determined to divide France into two zones, each controlled by a commander appointed by Duke Street. But SOE was adamant that the Free French should decentralize, and that the new Conseil National de la Résistance should be based as far away from the Gestapo as possible, preferably in London.

'Neither side will give an inch, not that they have one to spare,' added Charlotte.

She then hurried off to meet Nick, leaving me to ponder two questions: What had CD meant when he referred to 'a serious dispute over two messages'? And what was the 'certain action' I might have to take? Divided into two zones myself, I returned to Mallaby.

On 6 September Robin Brook, the controller of Western Europe, instructed me to report to him. He was the only person (apart from Gubbins) whom the whole of Baker Street regarded as brilliant, which was one of the few majority verdicts he saw no reason to question.

Tall, slender, with the kind of eyes I'd sooner have than look into,

---

* Mallaby was subsequently awarded the MC, which in his case meant Master Coder.

he allowed me to settle down before saying that he had a question to ask me which I must regard as strictly confidential.

'Yes, sir.'

'If I give you the authority to do so, could you break a message in secret French code?'

Unaccustomed to senior officers making improper suggestions, I gaped at him in appropriate bewilderment. 'I'm afraid I know nothing about the secret French code, sir.' It was time to have it printed on my lapel.

'I didn't expect you to. But that won't prevent you from trying, will it?'

'I suppose not, sir.' I was beginning to enjoy this, which made it even more dangerous.

'There are two messages I want broken – both from Duke Street to Serreules in secret French code . . . you probably know him by his code-name Scapin.'

'Indeed I do, sir. I gave him his English code.'

He'd been dropped in July, and since then I'd broken three indecipherables from him in his secret French code, and re-encoded them accurately. I could have complied with Brook's request in a matter of minutes but dared not let him know it. 'I'll need some help from you before I can start, sir.'

It was the first time I'd seen the famous Brook frown, and once was enough. 'What sort of help? – I've given you my full authority.'

'That won't help me break it, sir. I'll need as much information as you can give me in case the messages need anagramming.'

The jargon seemed to reassure him. 'Very well. I'll fill you in on the background, and then show you the messages.'

'Thank you, sir.'

He then explained that in spite of knowing SOE's attitude, Duke Street had encoded a message to Scapin appointing Mangin and Morinaud as 'chefs de zone', each to control one half of France. They'd sent the code-groups to RF section with a copy of the clear-text 'as per standard procedure'. But Brook had refused to allow the code-groups to be sent to Signals for transmission until all references to the chefs de zone had been deleted. Duke Street had agreed to do this, and had sent a new set of code-groups to RF section with an assurance that the deletions had been made. Someone in RF section spotted that the second message contained the same number of code-groups as the first, and raised the question whether Duke Street was telling the truth.*

He then handed me both sets of code-groups and a copy of the original texts. 'I need to know if the deletions have been made. – I can't impress on you enough how important this is.' He proceeded to do so. '. . . SOE and Duke Street have lost all confidence in each other, and Anglo-French missions like Marie-Claire are likely to be cancelled. As it is, it's been postponed.'

I hadn't realized that Tommy was involved. 'I'll start right away, sir.'

He looked at me searchingly. 'I'm sorry if this is an impossible question, but how long will it take you?'

I indulged in a Jack Benny pause. 'It depends on what the damn code is, sir. It could take hours or days, and there's no guarantee I can do it at all – but your briefing will help . . .'

'Give it absolute priority, and contact me on the scrambler one way or another.'

'Of course, sir.'

I took Scapin's code to the gents, and decoded both messages while someone in the adjacent cubicle uttered a grateful 'that's better'. The texts were identical. It was only the code-groups which had changed. All that remained was my cover-story.

I returned to my desk, and with Charlotte as my witness pretended to launch a full-scale blanket attack on Scapin's messages. By teatime I'd accumulated enough evidence to convince everyone, myself included, that I'd broken the messages with the help of the charts, and announced to Charlotte that I'd found the right key. I then contacted Robin Brook on the scrambler and told him that his fears were well-founded.

He asked me to bring the proof to him at once.

It was a relief to return to Monkey.

*   *   *

---

* That someone turned out to be Captain O'Bryan-Tear, one of my class-mates at St Paul's. Old Paulines (General Montgomery was one of them) could usually be relied upon to spot other people's discrepancies.

On 7 September I learned from Heffer that officers of RF section and Duke Street were no longer allowed to speak to each other, and had to meet in 'safe-houses' as if they were in France.

'How about Tommy?' I asked. 'Where's it leave him?'

'In limbo. He's the one I feel sorriest for after all that he's done.'

I waited anxiously for the sound of my favourite footsteps. They reverberated down the corridor around 6 p.m., which was far earlier than usual.

I had never seen Tommy looking so tense. He invited me to tell him about Cairo in one sentence,

'Why waste words?' I asked, and blew a raspberry instead.

'I'm getting plenty of those from other quarters. I'd prefer a cigar.'

I waited until he was puffing away, and then invited him to tell me in one sentence what the row was all about.

He took a deep breath. 'I can tell you what it's not about. It's not about killing Germans or helping agents to survive or shortening the war, though that's what they all pretend it is.' His eyes were glowing like the tip of his cigar. 'Robin Brook accuses Duke Street of lying about the messages, and says he can prove it because he instructed you to break them. They say he's the liar, and that the only thing he's broken is SOE's agreement with de Gaulle.'

'What agreement's that?'

'You know bloody well what agreement . . .' He sat bolt upright. '. . . the agreement which says that copies of the secret French code must be lodged in D/R's safe [Robin Brook was D/R], and that D/R mustn't look at them without Duke Street's consent.'

The secret French code was the only subject (except Holland) that I'd never discussed freely with him, though I'd often longed to tell him the truth.

And the truth was that the agreement was a sham because there was no secret French code to deposit. The agents used their British code for both sets of traffic. All Duke Street gave them was a secret indicator to show which words of the British poem they'd used, and the most they'd deposit in D/R's safe would be a description of how the system worked.

I'd been silent for far too long because Tommy pounced. 'Have I got something wrong?'

'No more than usual.'

I was relieved when he didn't pursue it, but should have known better.

'So the question, my friend, is this. Did Brook instruct you to break Scapin's code, or did he take it from his safe without Duke Street's consent – they're convinced that he did? And if they're right, how many times has he done it before? I've got to know the truth . . .'

I'd glimpsed his distress at the death of Moulin. This was as great. 'I broke it on D/R's instructions . . .' I tried to say it matter-of-factly.

'You're feeling guilty about something. But no one's going to blame you for this, you have to obey orders sometimes. And Brook can't be blamed either because Duke Street shouldn't have lied to him. But then why did they feel they had to? – Christ, what a mess! . . .' He stood up slowly. 'My friend, we're all in the shit – SOE, Duke Street and Signals. – all because we haven't the guts to talk to each other openly.'

He turned to the door.

'I've something else to tell you.'

'Next time.'

I knew there wouldn't be one. 'I'd already broken Scapin's secret code. I've broken the secret code of every Free French agent since July '42. Nobody knows this but you.'

The White Rabbit turned round. Very white. 'You what?'

'How else could I stop the indecipherables? – Duke Street never tried to . . . and there's something else you should know . . .' I bombarded him with the reasons the Free French code was insecure but he cut me short.

'And you've only just told me after all this time?'

I did my best to meet his gaze but had no dark glasses.

'Do you think you're the only one who cares about agents, and that I wouldn't have helped you if I could? Or were you afraid I'd turn you in?' He clenched his fists but I didn't care because I was toothless anyway.

Instead he threw his cigar on the floor, and stamped on it until both of us were extinguished. He followed this with the ultimate rejection. 'Jesus Christ.' he whispered. 'Isn't there anyone in SOE who knows the meaning of trust?'

He closed the door so quietly I was almost deafened.

I'd lost a lifeline nothing could replace.

He was waiting outside my office when I returned the next morning. I asked him to come in but he shook his head. His contempt had matured overnight, and was now as entrenched as my parents' admiration.

He told me he'd been in touch with Brook, Nicholls and the Free French and that a decision had been reached. 'You're to report to Duke Street and show the Free French how you broke their code.'

'*I'm what?*'

'You're expected at two o'clock this afternoon – kindly be there!' He turned away abruptly.

'Kindly wait a sec,' I called out.

He halted in mid-stride but didn't turn round.

He hadn't told me what to say or who the Frenchmen were or what the objective was.

But I had a far more important question, and it popped out in a very small voice. 'Will you be there?'

He strode down the corridor in silence.

FIFTY-TWO

Man with a Mission

"You're going to Duke Street for one purpose.
To convince the Free French that they can trust
SOE. They'll try to trip you up so be careful what
you say! ... For God's sake don't make matters
worse.'
(Nick to the ambassador of goodwill, September '43)

On 8 September I insisted on being driven to Duke Street to deliver
my address. I didn't want to trip up before I arrived. Knowing the
quality of my French, Charlotte had offered to accompany me to act
as my interpreter, but I daren't let her in case she gave Nick a verbatim
report of everything I said.

Without an interpreter I could always claim to have been mis-
understood.

A young lieutenant who spoke excellent English escorted me into
a briefing room full of Free French officers, and I felt it being redecor-
ated in high-quality hatred. I spotted Valois in the front row, and
remembered I still owed him a dozen prefixes for his sacrosanct code.
The only face I wanted to see wasn't there.

I sensed them preparing to make moules of me as I followed the
lieutenant to my journey's end: a blackboard which had been
delivered to Duke Street to await my arrival. Its contents were concealed by a cloth.

Turning his back on the assembly, an example I was quick to
follow, my escort asked me in a garlic-flavoured whisper if I'd like
him to be my interpreter as not everyone present spoke good English
(Valois knew two words: 'no' and 'prefixes'), and as the atmosphere

needed no interpreting I replied, 'Merci mille fois', Father's favourite phrase when clients paid him in cash.

'It is now time for me to introduce you,' he whispered. 'Do I call you "chef de codage", or how shall I say?'

'Say nothing,' I replied. 'They know why I'm here.' And pulled the cloth from the blackboard.

It disclosed two encoded messages of equal length which I'd written one on top of the other. Each pair of letters had a number, a format I'd used at Cairo and at countless FANY lectures. At the foot of the blackboard there was a simple announcement in large block capitals: LE SECRET FRENCH CODE.

The room was filled with angry whispers. I glanced at my interpreter. His complexion was the colour of his garlic. I turned to face the Bastille.

Tommy was standing at the back of the room. His eyes were focused on a point far beyond the blackboard. He was the only person whose judgement I'd trust to evaluate the effect of a surprise I'd prepared for them which could have disastrous consequences if I'd misconceived it, but it was too late now. I was committed to building up to it.

'Alors, messieurs . . . the messages sur the blackboard are from one of your agents. Je suggest that we attackez votre code together.'

This did nothing to diminish the whispering.

'Messieurs,' I said, 'c'est the moment to have a go.'

With the help of the interpreter I explained that the messages would be easy to anagram as they'd been encoded on the same transposition-keys, and that if enemy cryptographers correctly guessed the words of one message the words in the other would also make sense.

Since my hosts clearly regarded me as an enemy cryptographer I couldn't be sure how much they were taking in and it was time to put them to the test. 'Je vous en prie to start calling out suggestions.'

One of them did, and the laughter which greeted it would have done credit to a Jack Benny one-liner. The interpreter refused to translate the suggestion on the grounds that he hadn't heard of it.

'Je vous en prie to call out another.'

Someone obliged, causing even more hilarity than his predecessor. Tommy was looking worried.

'Agents die because of this,' I said.

The lieutenant translated immediately, and there was complete silence. It was a beautiful sound.

Taking it as a licence to proceed, I asked whether the word 'stop' appeared in most agents' messages, and if so, why didn't they start with it?

They agreed that 'stop' did appear, and soon discovered that 'nuit' appeared beneath it, and one word led to another, as they invariably did in this deadliest of parlour games, and twenty minutes later they reluctantly contemplated two broken messages.

Whispering again broke out.

Wondering how best to time my surprise, I began explaining how the words of the poem could now be reconstructed, but an imperious voice interrupted.

'*Un moment, s'il vous plaît.*'

'One moment, if you please,' said the interpreter nervously.

A bemedalled officer had risen to his feet and was addressing me in rapid French.

My vocabulary simply wasn't up to it (though it was slightly larger than I wanted my hosts to realize), and I didn't understand a word of what he said. But there was no mistaking his confrères' reactions. Heads were nodded, hands were clapped, and they gave him a sitting ovation. His comments must have been devastating because Tommy seemed to be willing me both his decorations.

I turned to the interpreter. 'Translatez-vous, s'il vous plaît.'

He was clearly embarrassed.

'I want to know exactly what he said ... it's time Duke Street provided accurate transcripts.'

This didn't go down too well with those who spoke English.

He looked at me apologetically. 'The colonel accuses you of trying to deceive us. He says you cannot have broken Scapin's code in the way you have said.'

God bless the bastard. He's given me my cue.

'Pourquoi not?' I demanded indignantly.

'He says our messages to Scapin were enchiffré on different keys, and that the method you showed us does not apply. He says you didn't break his code at all, and that Colonel Brook took it from his safe.'

There was a chorus of approval at what they took to be my embarrassment.

'Please tell the colonel he is absolutely right. I have been trying to deceive you. It's a relief to admit it . . .'

There was a chorus of surprised approval. I avoided looking at Tommy.

'. . . but I haven't deceived you in the way you think . . .' I pointed to the blackboard. 'That isn't the French code you've broken, it's the British. Votre code is an even bigger fuck-up.'

Ignoring the gasps of astonishment, I turned the blackboard round. They found themselves looking at two more messages, one on top of the other like those they'd just dealt with.

I knew they were code-saturated but couldn't stop now. I explained that these messages really were in Scapin's code, and had been encoded on the same transposition keys, and made them an offer: 'Si vous voulez, I'll show you how to break them on different keys but I'd have to keep you here a week.'

They didn't seem to relish the prospect, and reluctantly agreed to call out some suggestions when I en-pried them to break their own code.

Anxious to save time, I told them that cryptographers always searched messages for well-known names, and asked if there were any famous Frenchmen they might find mentioned.

'General de Gaulle' was called out from all round the room, with 'Passy' a close second. Beneath GENERAL DE GAULLE some significant letters appeared:

GENERAL DE GAULLE
GIR

Someone called out 'Giraud' (de Gaulle's arch-rival in France who was favoured by the Americans) and a storm of booing broke out, accompanied by a few Gallic raspberries.

Ten minutes later they'd cracked both messages, and like most who played the parlour-game were unable to conceal their sense of accomplishment.

Knowing that I was about to risk far worse than booing, I

approached the real purpose of my visit. 'This is the code we now give your agents . . .' I whipped a WOK from my pocket.

'A good code too,' someone called out.

'Don't take my word for it. Talk to one of your own cryptographers – you've plenty of good ones. Ask him whether it wouldn't be safer for you to use the British code for your secret messages than the one you've just broken. Je vous en prie to talk to him quickly for the sake of your agents.'

This put the chat amongst the pigeons more than anything else I'd said. Excited conversations broke out all round the room, and I noticed Valois whispering to a naval captain sitting in judgement beside him. The captain nodded and held up his hand. 'I have a question, please . . .'

'Je vous en prie,' I replied, hoping it meant what I thought it did.

He seemed in no hurry to ask it, and his colleagues waited in respectful silence while I dangled from the yardarm.

'If we use the British code for our messages, could the British read them?'

'Oui, mon capitaine, at any time. *Mais jamais les Boches.*'

This was greeted by what sounded like applause, though it was so long since I'd heard any that I couldn't be sure, and questions started coming from all directions. I turned to the interpreter to help with the answers.

'Your English–French will do,' someone called out.

An authoritative voice then took over. 'I too have a question for Monsieur Marks, which I hope he will answer honestly.'

It was the colonel who'd tried to skewer me in whirlwind French. He renewed his efforts in excellent English. 'Have you been breaking indecipherable messages in our code to save the agents from repeating them? – And because you knew we hadn't staff to do it ourselves? The truth, please . . .'

I almost gave it but discovered I was human. 'I was hoping not to be asked this because I'm ashamed of the answer.'

They waited expectantly.

'I *should* have broken them and re-encoded them without you knowing if I'd been doing my job properly – but I shirked it! I was merde-scared of what SOE would do to me if they found out that I'd broken the agreement. Je apologize beaucoup.'

The colonel looked at me with a twinkle, then wrote rapidly on a notepad and showed it to the officers on either side of him. He then tore off the page and passed it to Valois, who nodded emphatically and passed it to mon capitaine, who also nodded and handed it to the interpreter.

A century or so later he translated. 'They wish you to know they are satisfied you broke Scapin's code, and that Colonel Brook did not take it from his safe.'

I should have said 'mille mercis' and left it there, but something popped out of my safe before I could stop it. 'I have a favour to ask. Could you please give me another five minutes?'

'Take as long as you wish,' someone called out.

'There's something about the code department I want you to know. We're not concerned with politics – yours or anybody else's – unless we're forced to be, which is what's happened today . . . but there's something you don't seem to realize . . .' I took a deep breath, which might well be my last. 'The Free French aren't the only ones involved in power struggles. SOE has its own Girauds, and tells as many lies as you do. It's unfortunate for you you've been caught out in a stupid one. Better luck next time.'

The interpreter was lagging behind but I couldn't wait for him.

'I have to tell you something personal. I'm too merde-scared to be an agent. I sit in the back room and do what I can to keep 'em safe. And next time I'm involved in a dispute with you, and there's bound to be one, please remember this.'

I looked at all of them and at none of them. *'I don't give a shit if after the war your agents vote for de Gaulle or against him as long as they're alive to vote.* So for God's sake change your secret code because the Boche can break it as easily as I can. Thanks for listening.'

I tried to reach the door but couldn't distinguish between the Free French and their furniture. They seemed to be standing up, probably to lynch me.

The colonel put his hand on my shoulder. 'Monsieur merde-scared,' he said, 'there is more than one kind of courage.'

I knew I'd reached the door because Tommy was holding it open.

He pressed a handkerchief into my hand. 'Wipe your forehead. It's worse than Niagara.'

He then gave a wicked impersonation of my accent. 'Le next time vous et moi meet je vous donnez un kick up the arse. Je shall aussi want mon mouchoir back, wrapped round a cigar si vous avez one. And now pissez-vous off, Monsieur Marksiavelli.'

I stumbled away like a drunken matelot.

I sobered up twelve hours later when Gubbins paid me a late-night visit. (He rarely wasted time on me during the day as he was even more of a midnight prowler than Hambro.) His face was medium ferocious. 'There's been an official request from the Free French which I find somewhat surprising.'

Marks's head on a plateau or we take our business elsewhere . . .

'They want you to have a meeting with one of their senior French cryptographers who's flying in from Algiers.' His mighty eyebrows arched. 'I want to know exactly what you said at Duke Street.'

'I wish I knew, sir.'

He laughed, and shook his head in despair. 'Merci bien, Leo.'

I envied his accent.

On the night of 23 September Brossolette and Tommy boarded a Lysander and landed in France to start mission Marie-Claire.

FIFTY-THREE

Breaking Point

SOE rarely received official congratulations, except from itself, but the success of Monkey and the information our Danish agents had obtained about the Peenemünde rocket sites earned plaudits from Churchill and the Chiefs of Staff which were all the sweeter because we'd excluded C from Monkey, and scooped them on Peenemünde. But the glow didn't last long, and between mid-September and the end of October a series of upheavals and reshuffles extended our in-built absorbers to breaking-point.

Sir Charles Hambro resigned as CD and was replaced by Gubbins.

Hutchison resigned as head of RF section to train as an agent at the age of fifty. His replacement (Sweet-Escott) was replaced at short notice by Colonel Dismore, who chose Tommy as his deputy, a move so wise few of us could credit it.

Captain Uren of the Balkans directorate was sent to prison for passing information to the Russians.

One effect of these developments was to turn Baker Street into a debating society and some believed it should remain one.

Hambro's Departure

The consensus of uninformed opinion was that Sir Charles resigned because of a disagreement with our minister over Greece, but that he'd still be with us if his senior colleagues hadn't been stricken with laryngitis when invited to support him.

The Arrest of Captain Uren

This was known to few people in Baker Street, and I was unlikely to have been one of them if Major O'Reilly (my godfather) hadn't found an entry in Uren's diary (in red ink?): 'Appointment with Marx [sic] to discuss codes.'

He sent for me and demanded to know what had taken place at the meeting with no details omitted.

I told him that Uren had called on 19 July to see the new codes which were being issued to Hungarian agents, and that I'd shown him a WOK and a letter one-time pad. He'd asked if he could borrow them for a day as it would help him and his colleagues to prepare suitable camouflage, and I'd readily agreed. He'd returned them to my office the following morning.

The major anxiously enquired what harm it would do if Uren had shown them to a Russian agent. I replied that it wouldn't matter if he'd shown them to Hitler as they were different for every agent. To reassure him still further, I added that if he showed them to Stalin as well it might even help the war effort because if the Russians copied them the Germans could no longer read their traffic.

Sharply reminding me that this was an extremely serious matter, he warned me that Soviet agents were trying to infiltrate SOE, and that they'd be particularly interested in Signals. He instructed me to bring anything suspicious to his immediate attention, but didn't tell me what symptoms to look for.

He also instructed me to give his best wishes to 'little Benny', which would have been bad security as Father still didn't know that his best friend and I worked for the same organization, but I agreed to do so to end the interview.

There was just time to change the security checks of every agent known to Uren.

The worst of the autumnal heart-stoppers concerned two old favourites (it was wrong to have any but impossible not to), who were causing great alarm.

Noor Inayat Khan (I rarely thought of her as Madeleine) had astonished all who believed they knew her by continuing to be the only WT operator in Paris on whom F section could rely. Still living in Paris (now almost as dangerous as Amsterdam), she'd sent a brief message in mid-September naming the few agents who'd survived the Prosper collapse. It was perfectly encoded with its security checks present. She resumed WT contact at the end of September and organized an arms drop.

Knowing the risks she was taking, Buckmaster ordered her to return to London but she refused to leave until she was satisfied that he'd found a replacement for her. He assured her that he had, and she finally agreed to be picked up by Lysander in mid-October. She then went off the air for ten days, and missed the moon period. She surfaced again on 18 October with a new batch of messages, and although their security checks were correct the first message had a transposition-key eighteen letters long.

I immediately informed Buckmaster that this was a special security check which she was to use only if she were caught. This confirmed his suspicions that she was in enemy hands as the style of her new messages had changed, but he intended to reply to them as if nothing were amiss, and to continue two-way traffic with her.

I said a silent prayer that Noor was having one of her lapses, but knew I was having one of my own not to accept the truth.

The other contributor to restless nights (which Mother attributed to malnutrition) was Tommy.

He and Brossolette had arrived in Paris on 21 September to make contact with Serreules, and on 26 September Tommy sent a message which his operator was unable to transmit until 14 October, by which time Tommy had sent another.

The first message reported that he and Brossolette were extremely concerned about Serreules's lack of security, that the number of arrests was increasing daily, and that Morinaud (who was about to be appointed one of the Secret Army's new leaders) had been arrested and had swallowed his L-tablet before he could be tortured.

The second message reported that Serreules had been arrested at the end of September, and had left a number of *en clair* messages in his flat as well as a list of his principal contacts, which the Germans were believed to have found. He added that the situation was even worse than he and Brossolette had feared, and that he would keep his future traffic to a minimum.

However, he wasn't completely out of touch with London. Barbara sent *en clair* messages to him every day via the BBC which were prefaced 'Du moineau au lapin' ('from the sparrow to the rabbit').

Another of Tommy's sparrows also had a message for him but there was no way I could send it. I wanted him to know that a senior French cryptographer had arrived from Algiers, and that I was about to have a meeting with him.

I'd been told by RF section that my visitor's name was Commandant Cassis, that he had to return to Algiers within twenty-four hours, and that he was now in Duke Street hoping I'd phone him as soon as possible. I contacted him immediately, and he enquired in serviceable English if I had a little time to spare. I told him that I'd be available for as long as he needed, and he at once asked if I would prefer to meet him at Duke Street or Dorset Square or perhaps would like him to call upon me.

Sensing from his tone what his real choice would be, I invited him to come to my office, and he accepted before I'd finished the sentence. He would be the first Free Frenchman who'd been allowed to visit my workshop, and I prepared a pass for him without asking permission. I then instructed Muriel to make no more appointments for the rest of the day, and to put no phone calls through once he'd arrived unless I gave her our private signal (two bleeps on the buzzer), in which case she was to come in immediately with an urgent summons to the Executive Council.

To do justice to this special occasion, I then went to sleep for fifteen minutes.

Commandant Cassis was slender, grey-haired and wore his uniform as if it were a fine French binding. He smiled at me from the doorway, took my outstretched hand in both of his, and thanked me for seeing him at such short notice. He then accepted a seat at my cluttered desk, and seemed instantly at home.

I had an unaccountable feeling that I was in the presence of a Gallic Tiltman.

He wasted no time on the secret French code except to say with a craftsman's sympathy, 'What suffering it must have caused you.' but he didn't enquire what steps I might have taken to alleviate it.

He then meticulously examined three WOKs and asked if the keys had been produced by machine or by hand.

When I described how the WOK-makers shuffled their counters he nodded his approval. 'Safer human tiredness than a machine's,' he said, which led us to a short discussion about the problem of producing figures which were genuinely random.

He then asked what we did to convince agents that they must destroy their keys as soon as they'd used them, and I told him about the briefing officers who instilled the necessity into them by every means at their disposal.

Again that nod of approval. 'They will not want to destroy such silks,' he said. 'Good to give to their ladies after the war.'

He examined the security checks as if his own life depended on them, and decided they couldn't be improved.

I then showed him a LOP. It was clear that he hadn't seen one before, and it took him all of ten seconds to grasp its significance. 'A one-time pad in letters,' he exclaimed.

He reminded me of father holding an original Caxton.

'Enough here for a hundred messages each of the ways?'

I nodded.

'And the least number of letters an agent need send is ten? – twenty?'

'Five if all he wants to say is merde.'

He looked at me as if he were an exile in sight of his long-lost land. 'For us?' he said quietly. 'You will be giving them to us?'

'If Duke Street will accept them.'

He pushed back his chair and stood up. But not to leave. He was in urgent need of pacing room, a feeling I knew well. 'Forgive me to ask this but time is short. Are you perhaps preparing other codes as well?'

'*Yes*' I said, delighted to be asked. Without telling him that no one else had seen it, I showed him a code-book I was preparing which had a 1,000-word vocabulary, and which was to be printed on silk and used in conjunction with a letter one-time pad. I explained that code-books would save valuable air-time in the run-up to D-Day and on D-Day itself as it would reduce the length of agents' messages, though I wasn't sure if they could be persuaded to use them.

Puzzled by his lack of response, I pointed out that the code-groups had been structured to minimize the effects of Morse mutilation, a major problem with all our traffic.

He spent a full five minutes examining this claim, and I wondered if he'd found a flaw in it.

When he finally turned to me his eyes were as hard as Tiltman's when he'd tried to persuade me that SOE didn't need LOPs. 'Monsieur Marks . . .' I almost bowed to myself. '. . . it would be a great help if we could now talk in absolute confidence . . . a very great help indeed.'

But I couldn't forget that momentary hardness, and suspected that I'd been softened up for this moment. 'I can't promise absolute confidentiality until I've some idea of what it concerns.'

He thanked me for my frankness, which he'd heard about from Duke Street, and said that he'd rely on my goodwill to the Free French 'as to how much I need repeat of the delicate matters he now wished to confide in me'.

He started with some minor secrets and slowly grew franker. He had a handful of assistants, some of whom had had very little training, who had been given the responsibility of providing codes for the Free French to use on and after D-Day. The function of these codes would be to provide internal communications with the Free French forces, and to maintain contact with the Allied High Command.

The problem was that General de Gaulle very much doubted if the Free French would be allowed to use their own codes.

Careful not to sound as if he were complaining, he said that Churchill's relationship with de Gaulle hadn't improved, that the Americans continued to support Giraud, and that the High Command had excluded the Free French from any discussions about the D-Day landings. But the general was determined to make a major contribution to the liberation of France, and one way in which he might achieve it was so dependent on communications that it was essential that I knew what it was.

He then studied the ceiling as if asking someone far beyond it to strike him dumb if it were in the interests of France. Having apparently received the divine all-clear, he said that shortly before D-Day the Committee of National Liberation in Algiers would announce the formation of a new organization which would unite *all* French freedom fighters under one command and make them members of the new French army. The organization would be known as the FFI (Forces Françaises de l'Intérieur), and would need codes which were suitable for a unique mixture of military, paramilitary and agents' messages. He confided that even if Churchill and the Americans allowed the Free French to use their own codes, they had no facilities for making them. But this was only part of the problem. His superiors didn't realize how long it took to prepare codes and to train instructors, especially those who had to do their teaching in the field.

I realized that he was having as hard a time in Algiers as I'd had in Baker Street, and asked what codes he had in mind for the FFI.

Clearly relieved to be asked, he said he'd decided on code-books and figure one-time pads, as many army signallers knew how to use them. But he now realized that letter one-time pads might be even better! He'd think it over when he returned to Algiers.

He then hesitated, and I was completely unprepared for what he'd been leading up to. 'If I send to you our code-book, could you make for us copies on silk? And could you also send to us the one-time pads we would need? I would the quantities estimate when I can so do so . . .' Before I could reply he stressed that he hadn't discussed this with any of his superiors, and was asking me informally if such a thing would be possible.

I should have pressed the buzzer there and then because this was a policy matter and I was well and truly out of my depth. Instead I stared at the ceiling for divine guidance and noticed a crack which hadn't been there before. 'I'll be glad to help you in every way I can,' I said.

'Will your superiors agree?'

'I've just consulted them. They say I'll need as much time as possible, and that it would be a great help if you'd make a formal request.'

This clearly troubled him, and he explained with an apologetic smile which I wished I could add to my armoury that some of his superiors might not like the idea of the British providing their codes. But if everything depended on it, he would do whatever he could.

Giving what I hoped was a Gallic shrug, I said that one way or another the codes would be ready when the Free French needed them, even if it meant we both had to take a risk.

He thanked me in the best way a cryptographer can – by becoming technical: 'You have found a way to protect letter-pad code-groups from Morse mutilation. Is there a similar way to protect figure-pad code-groups?'

I replied that I hadn't thought about it but didn't see why not, and we did some homework together (he was far quicker than I was).

Twenty minutes later we were able to reduce figure-pad mutilation by 40 per cent, and I promised to incorporate the idea if we hadn't improved on it by the time we started production.

He then did some homework on my face before addressing me quietly without appearing to lower his voice. 'We have an understand-ing?' he asked.

'More than that,' I said. 'We have an agreement.'

We shook hands on it, and I regarded Tommy as our witness.

We spent our last hour together discussing cryptography, and he proved to have something else in common with Tiltman: A healthy appreciation of Mother's black-market sandwiches.

I didn't tell him that I was twenty-three today, and that he was the only present I wanted.

FIFTY-FOUR

Who Stole Your Grace?

Two days after my visitor had returned to Algiers, Duke Street confirmed to SOE that they were abandoning the use of the secret French code. No reasons were given but thanks were expressed for the co-operation Commandant Cassis had received from the chef de codage.

I'd told no one about our private arrangement, which had begun to worry me as I'd entered into it before doing my homework. A glance at the monthly figures (which I'd neglected to examine since returning from Cairo) showed that code production had fallen by almost 50 per cent, and I immediately contacted our printers and photographers.

The two elderly brothers who printed WOKs on silk brusquely informed me that they'd fallen behind with their other commitments, that they were suffering from shortage of staff and defective machinery, and that they saw no prospect of the situation improving. It was clear that I'd taken them for granted for far too long, and allowed it to become 'just another job' to them.

But an even worse situation had arisen with the RAF unit which photographed one-time pads on to silk. A newly appointed wing commander had discovered that most of his staff were working for the Inter Services Research Bureau at the request of two senior officers named Heffer and Marks. He'd also discovered that the squadron leader who'd accepted the commitment six months ago 'to help us out of trouble' had been doing so ever since, and had exceeded his budget without authority. The wing commander allowed us until the end of November to make other arrangements.

Unless I could do so quickly we'd have to start dipping into the reserves we were building up for D-Day, but I had no idea where to start looking.

The situation (like so many others) needed a Gubbins to resolve it, but I'd left it too late to approach him. Within a few days of becoming CD the Mighty Atom had taken off on an extended tour of Massingham and Cairo, and his deputy, Colonel Sporborg, was now in temporary (we hoped) command.

I decided to seek Heffer's advice without disclosing my undertaking to Cassis.

The Guru wasn't surprised by the production problems, which he'd been anticipating for weeks, and advised me to consult the 'hard men' (Messrs Courtauld and Davies), who were continuing to supply all our silk. But he warned me not to approach them immediately as they were inundated with requests for help, and mightn't take kindly to a new one.

He then looked at me keenly. 'There's something you're not telling me, isn't there?'

Relieved that he was on form, I blurted out my undertaking to Cassis, which I regarded as binding but saw little chance of fulfilling.

He was used to my confessions by now, but this one produced more astonishment than all the rest combined. 'You've committed us to sup-plying them with unspecified quantities of code-books and one-time pads by an unknown date for traffic we know nothing about?'

I nodded miserably.

Lowering his eyes to heaven, he enquired why I'd left it until now to disclose the arrangement.

'Because SOE's so unpredictable. They'd either react prematurely and blow Cassis's cover or refuse to sanction it. – I'm not sure which.'

He looked at me pityingly. 'The trouble with villains like you is that you never know when you've done the right thing.'

He then explained as if to a cretin (an assessment I couldn't ques-tion) that supplying the Free French with code-books and one-time pads at their request would enable Gubbins to show the High Com-mand how much confidence they had in his Signals directorate! It would also enable us to read their traffic, and strengthen Nick's hand on the Executive Council.

'It might even help the Free French,' I said.

Ignoring irrelevancies, he said that it couldn't possibly have happened at a better time. He then stared out of the window, a sure sign
that he was considering a confidence of his own.

'Go on, Heff,' I urged, 'reward me.'

Warning me that if I repeated a word of what he said we'd both be
in trouble, he confided that SOE had recently obtained sight (possibly
legitimately) of a Top Secret document from de Gaulle to Duke Street
which had so astonished Gubbins and the Executive Council that
they'd sent a copy to Cossac.

'I don't think I know him . . .'

Another pitying look, this time tinged with exasperation. 'COSSAC
stands for Chief of Staff to the Supreme Allied Commander.'

'Who's the supremo going to be, Heff – an American?'

His tone ensured that this would be my last interruption. 'The post
of supreme commander is still being considered by Churchill and
Roosevelt,' he said, 'and I very much doubt if you're in the running for
it.'

He then disclosed that de Gaulle's document dealt at great length
with Overlord, which he'd correctly guessed was being planned for
next summer. 'In case there's no limit to your ignorance,' he said,
'Overlord is the code-name for the invasion of France.'

Glancing at his watch, he quickly explained that the extraordinary
part of de Gaulle's document was that his plans for Overlord were
almost identical with the Allied High Command's. He'd even worked
out what the tides would be, and had selected the same beaches as
the High Command. Cossac was convinced that someone in SOE
had broken the strict injunction not to discuss Overlord with the Free
French under any circumstances, and de Gaulle's document was now
being studied at Cabinet level. He added that nothing could do more
to enhance SOE's reputation than the ability to read de Gaulle's
post-D-Day traffic.

Escorting me from the office, he said was off to tell the good news
to Nick. He'd also try to explain why I'd kept it to myself.

I didn't point out how easy it would be for Cassis to reassemble
the one-time pads, and make it a merde of a job to decipher a single
message.

*   *   *

407

Nick sent for me the next morning, and I knew at once he had something unpleasant to convey.

He referred briefly to my arrangement with Cassis, which he'd reported to the Executive Council, and then said he had two 'comparatively minor matters to discuss'. But they weren't minor to me, and he knew it.

Impaling me with his eyebrows, he imparted the glad tidings that while I'd been in Cairo, Gubbins, Sporborg and several of his colleagues on the Executive Council had complained to him about the number of young women they'd seen parading up and down Baker Street at all hours, window-shopping and making bloody nuisances of themselves. The miscreants had all been identified as members of my department (coders, briefing officers and WOK-makers), and he'd decided that a supervisor must be appointed to put a stop to their chronic indiscipline.

Before I could protest, he added that he'd already interviewed someone whom he considered ideal for the post. her name was Audrey Saunders, and she'd be starting her duties within the next few days.

At the risk of rupturing a blood vessel, preferably his, I jumped up and protested that the girls' conduct wasn't indiscipline but an unwinding process essential to their jobs, and that what they needed was a 'mad room' where they could relax between spells of duty without risk of interruption. The problem was that suitable accommodation wasn't available unless they could use Gubbins's office while he was away.

Sharply instructing me to resume my seat, he said that there was no point in discussing the matter further as his decision was final, and he expected me to give Miss Saunders a fair chance to do her job however she saw fit.

'And there's something else you'll have to get used to . . .' He then disclosed that a Mr M. P. Murray had joined the Finance directorate as an assistant to D/FIN, and would shortly visit every department head in Baker Street, including myself, to determine our future requirements. Since my demands were increasing daily, he would spend at least a week in my office, and I must provide a desk for him, let him sit in on any meetings he might wish to attend, and answer all the questions he would undoubtedly ask on D/FIN's behalf. '. . . and I advise you not to even consider misleading him.'

He then indicated that that would be all for now, and lifted the receiver to speak to Sporborg.

The last thing I wanted was to be incarcerated for a week with a D/FIN investigator (ten seconds would be nine too many), and I was equally reluctant to spend any time at all with the disciplinarian Nick had appointed before I'd even met the cow. I resolved to give both intruders a lesson in garbage disposal they were unlikely to forget.

Murray came first, and I was disconcerted to find that I liked him on sight, a phenomenon which I attributed to the attraction of opposites.

He was unpretentious, had an orderly mind, and didn't need artificial techniques to be a good listener. Nor did he try to flaunt his intelligence.

I was convinced within minutes that he was the answer to our production problems, and that his closeness to D/FIN was a gift from on high. My first step in turning him into a coding ambassador must be to win his confidence, and I could only do this by being completely frank with him – a risk I was prepared to take. I welcomed His Excellency to the code department, and began work on him at once.

He said nothing about his background, but I learned that he'd been in SOE for less than a month, and was still 'feeling his way'. We quickly established that he'd had no experience of codes, and I asked if he'd like to take a crash course. He readily accepted, and I handed him over to a briefing officer who privately reported that he was the easiest agent she'd ever had to teach.

He looked a few years older when he returned (I placed him at forty when he left), and he said that 'instructresses of her calibre must take a bit of finding'.

'I'm glad you say that, Mr Murray. She's one of six I took on without your department's authority.'

From this admission onwards we were on Christian-name terms and I put him to work breaking indecipherables as part of his higher education. He seemed relieved to find himself gainfully employed and worked methodically through the long list of keys which I put in front of him, quickly falling into the rhythm which suited him best.

I knew that he'd broken his first indecipherable when he sat back and exclaimed, 'Good God.' (New coders frequently said, 'Well fuck me.' which to the best of my knowledge occurred outside the code room.)

'Well done, Michael – I'll inform the station that they can cross it off their list.'

He listened to my conversation with the supervisor as if it were the most important he'd ever heard, and for all I knew it was.

I immediately informed him that there were six girls in Norgeby House who broke indecipherables the stations couldn't cope with, but I'd been forced to pretend to D/FIN that they were WOK-makers as I'd exceeded my quota of coders. 'I've given up submitting honest estimates, Michael, because by the time they've been cut in half so has an agent's life expectancy.' I anxiously awaited his response.

'What are WOK-makers? – or did I mishear you?'

Delighted by his priorities, I immediately showed him a WOK and a LOP, stressing that amongst their other assets they'd put a stop to indecipherables. Supply problems came next, and Plan Murray was in sight of its first target.

Watching for signs of inattention (of which there were none), I informed him that LOP production was on the point of collapse due to a bloody-minded wing commander who'd given us till the end of November to take our business elsewhere. 'But I'd better admit it's not altogether his fault.'

I explained that the arrangement for his unit of work for ISRB had been 'somewhat irregular', though I wouldn't worry him with the details now, that he hadn't been told what ISRB did or why his photography was indispensable, and it was high time that someone put him in the picture.

Pausing for the smile that never came, I said that the ideal person to change his or anyone else's mind would be Gubbins, but in his absence the best spokesman would be senior RAF officers who out-ranked him such as Air Commodore Boyle or Group Captain Venner (D/FIN). 'The problem is, I'm the wrong person to approach them.'

I then admitted that they'd both caught me out in one or two misdemeanours, though I wouldn't worry him with the details now, and I was wondering whether he'd consider talking to Venner himself.

WHO STOLE YOUR GRACE?

It would flatter D/FIN to be asked, and show him how quickly he'd got on top of his job.

He thanked me for the opportunity I was giving him, but added that he thought he should know a little more about the code department before making recommendations to D/FIN. His training as an ambassador then began in earnest.

Despite his reluctance to attend a final code briefing in case his presence proved intrusive, but I insisted he come along as my assistant, and the quality of his silence gave the agent more confidence than anything I said.

He also sat in as my assistant when I interviewed six prospective briefing officers. I wrote down the names of the ones I'd selected, and asked him to do the same. We then compared notes. Our choices were identical, and I went up in my estimation.

By the end of the fourth day he knew what I thought of every country section head in Baker Street, and of most members of the hierarchy. He also knew the code department's every trick and subterfuge.

By the end of the fifth day I missed him whenever he was called away to a meeting. I had no idea where he went but he seemed as glad to return to his desk as I was to see him there. His absences became more frequent, and usually lasted an hour.

But he was present when the signalmaster at 53a telephoned to report for the second time that Noor's touch on the keyboard had changed, and he was convinced that the Germans were operating her set. He was watching my face while I took the call but looked away as soon as it was finished, and pretended to be immersed in an indecipherable which I knew he'd already broken.

He was also present when Nick hurried in, flushed with excitement, and informed us that the Free French had formally asked SOE to provide them with code-books and one-time pads, and that SOE had agreed provided that the High Command gave permission for de Gaulle to use his own codes. Nick was convinced that they would since the British had supplied them, and the code-book was already on its way to London. Murray nodded his approval.

Noor's capture made me forget that his time was also up, and that tomorrow he'd belong to D/FIN. I told him that as soon as he'd finished all his reports, especially the one about the code department, I'd like him to be my deputy. He would also be in sole charge of administration, at which he excelled and I was hopeless. The post would carry with it a G2 rating (the civilian equivalent of a major), which was certain to be upgraded if he continued breaking indecipherables at his present rate.

Looking away, much as he had when I'd taken the call about Noor, he said my offer both astonished and touched him, and he wished he could accept it because codes fascinated him, and the question of rank didn't arise. But he was certain that he wouldn't be released from his other duties, though at moments like this he wished he could be. He then thanked me for all the trouble I'd taken, and for giving him an experience he'd never forget.

As soon as he'd left I urged Nick to use his influence to have him transferred to Signals, and gave him my reasons, most of which I knew. He listened to them in silence, gave me a very odd look, and promised to think the matter over.

He then reminded me that I still hadn't found time to meet his protégée, Miss Saunders, and he was confident that I'd find her equally compatible. Remembering how wrong I'd been about Murray, I undertook to see her at once.

I disliked her at first sight and loathed her at second.

As the interview progressed I pretended to be taking notes to avoid looking at her, but her appearance drove me to the ditty-box:

> A long line of lips
> The eyes an eclipse
> Arteries hardened
> Nobody pardoned
> Who holds the key
> To that self-locking face
> Who stole your grace?

To which another was soon added:

> Nag nag niggle nag
> Spit your life away

412

Waggle your acid
In front of the placid
To establish your right of way
Then pick a point
Peck a point
Grind it on a nerve
Nag nag niggle nag
Till you get what you deserve

I was obliged to concede that she had one redeeming feature: she wore shoes instead of jackboots.

I discovered that her brother was Colonel Hugh Saunders, who was highly placed in SOE's admin department and was a close friend of Air Commodore Boyle's, which might well account for Nick's benevolent interest in her.

Over the next few days I did everything I could to make her life intolerable, but she was an ardent Christian Scientist and no matter what measures I took to persuade her to resign, she shimmered forgiveness at me and decided to stay. Tired of being regarded as part of the suffering she was put on earth to endure, I tried bribing her to leave by offering her a signed first edition of the works of Mary Baker Eddy (one of 84's lesser treasures), but she said that she had one already, and recommended that I should read it. Desperate to get rid of her, I was on the point of asking Nick which of us he preferred to keep on his strength when deliverance arrived from an unexpected quarter.

Robin Brook telephoned and the edge to his voice consigned Miss Saunders to the temporary oblivion I hoped to make permanent. He'd received a serious complaint about the code department from the Belgian section. An important message had been held up because the agent's WOK had been sent to the wrong station, and by the time it reached the right one the agent had gone off the air. He'd come up on his emergency sked and the message was transmitted to him twelve hours later.

Robin added that delays of this kind could have disastrous consequences and it was sheer luck that the agent had had time to carry out the vital instructions which the message contained.

413

I accepted full responsibility for the error, as a department head must, and thanked him for bringing it to my attention.

He would never know why I was so well and truly grateful. Nick in his wisdom had put his protégée in charge of the distribution department, and it was her responsibility to ensure that WOKs and LOPs were sent to the right stations. She was assisted in this by her deputy, Doris Lafosse (excellent), and two capable dispatchers.

I instructed Miss Saunders to report to my office immediately. In all our previous meetings I hadn't once invited her to sit down or called her by her Christian name before launching into the day's insults, but at least I'd acknowledged her presence with a frown. But on this occasion (my Overlord) I ignored her completely for the best part of a minute while she stood in front of me, preparing to forgive.

'Good morning, Miss Saunders,' I said cheerfully. 'I have a little news for you.' I then congratulated her on creating havoc in Belgium, and spent the next five minutes exaggerating her mistake out of all proportion until we both believed it had cost us an entire circuit of agents and very possibly the war.

'If you have an explanation to offer, I'd like to hear it,' I said.

She stared at the floor, then shook her head.

'No excuses at all?'

She shook it again, this time vehemently.

'I have to say, Miss Saunders, that I have no confidence in you whatsoever, and cannot risk this happening again.'

She took a quick look at me and seemed on the point of making an announcement.

'Yes, Miss Saunders?' I said encouragingly.

'You've been waiting for me to make a mistake like this ever since I came because you want me to go, and go I will! But you're a pig, Mr Marks – an absolute pig.'

I didn't mind being called one as I had no religious convictions except in emergencies. 'I'm sure your brother will find you a post for which you're better suited . . .'

She walked quickly to the door but in my moment of triumph a blob of memory spurted up like fat from a frying pan, and stung me into recalling her. 'One moment, please.'

Her hand was already on the door knob, and she didn't turn round. 'We have nothing further to discuss, Mr Marks.'

'I'm sorry, Miss Saunders, but I believe we have . . .' That damn blob had forced me to remember that on the day of the mistake I'd fancied roast Saunders for lunch but Muriel had told me that Nick had given her the whole day off.

She couldn't be held responsible for what happened in her absence but had accepted the blame for her subordinate's mistake as a department head must.

Better still, she'd managed to keep silent under duress. What more could I ask of her, other than forgiveness?

I told her I knew she wasn't responsible, and tried to apologize the only way I knew: 'Sit down, Audrey,' I said, 'and have a cream cake.'

Her eyes quivered and then her lips, and seconds later she burst into tears.

I couldn't understand why because the cakes were fresh.

I knew with the instinct of the lonely that this was the start of a lasting friendship.

But a shock was on its way about my other new friend.

Heffer walked in as grey as the ash on his cigarette and advised me to sit down while I heard what he had to say. He'd just learned from Nick that Murray hadn't the slightest intention of joining D/ FIN.

It was his cover-story to extract maximum information from every department head he visited! He was about to be appointed deputy head of SOE.

'He'll be closer to Gubbins than anyone,' said Heffer, 'and what's more he knows where all the bodies are buried. *And you'll be lucky if yours isn't one of them.*'

He swore me to secrecy until the announcement was formally made.

Murray's charade was the only example of SOE-mindedness I'd yet understood, and I decided to respond to it in kind.

I waited until the symbols list announced that M. P. Murray was appointed D/CD, and telephoned his secretary to ask if I could have a quick word with him. I was put through at once.

'Sorry to disturb you, Michael, but we've just received an urgent indecipherable! Can you come over and help us break it?'

To my astonishment, ten minutes later he sat at his old desk with an indecipherable in front of him, and without a word began working his way through the long list of keys.

I'd arranged for Muriel to telephone me two minutes later to say that the girls had just broken it. When I told him the good news, he stood up at once and turned to the door.

But we hadn't quite finished and I suspected that he knew it. 'Before you go, Michael, there's something I must ask you.'

He waited in silence.

'Now that you've been demoted, will you be able to spare time to deal with the wing commander?'

'I've already spoken to him . . . it was the first call I made from my new desk. You'll have no further problems with him. He's confirming it in writing to CD.'

'Thanks a lot, sir.'

He turned back at the door and looked at me severely. 'If I have further problems with you, I may have to pay you an unexpected visit – but I'll make sure that my secretary gives you plenty of warning.'

The second most powerful man in SOE closed the door behind him. I said a silent prayer on behalf of the first: *Please God, take special care of Colin Gubbins. It takes a good leader to pick a good deputy . . . and can anything be done to help Noor, who knows you by another name? I can feel her pain from here, and know how much worse it must be for you.*

The mush out of the way, I returned to work.

FIFTY-FIVE

The Forty-Eight Mistakes

On 2 November the Executive Council wrote formally to Nick praising the code department's 'outstanding achievements', and as their approval was often synonymous with incompetence I wondered what we were doing wrong.

Three factors may have contributed to our sudden popularity: our output of silk codes had increased by 50 per cent (due entirely to Murray); our briefing officers had learned discipline from Audrey without losing their allure; and our coders were breaking 90 per cent of their indecipherables in under twelve hours, at an average of 2,000 attempts per indecipherable. We'd also begun reproducing the Free French code-book, which had arrived from Algiers (it was to be used in conjunction with letter one-time pads), but I suspected that the real reason for the council's plaudits lay elsewhere.

I then learned from Heffer that they weren't a reward but a down payment for what the council hoped we'd achieve in the most important operation the code department had yet taken part in: we were expected to make a major contribution to the latest battle with C.

The civil war had broken out in a new direction. Both sides were competing for the patronage of some American VIPs who'd arrived in London on a shopping expedition.

They were all senior members of OSS, which had opened a thriving branch in Grosvenor Square halfway between Baker Street and C's HQ. One reason for their visit was to investigate the relative merits of C and SOE before deciding which contender should have the privilege of sharing their business, and their head (General 'Wild Bill' Donovan) had announced his intention of inspecting the whole of our Signals directorate when he had a minute or two to spare.

The OSS had many functions (some of which we understood, a few of which they did) and was divided into three main branches: one specialized in the gathering of secret intelligence, and was the equivalent of C; another was known as SO and was the American counterpart of SOE; and the third specialized in research and analysis, though no one seemed sure into what.

Having already co-operated with both organizations in the invasion of North Africa, the Americans distributed their favours evenly and a new joint venture with SOE was being planned for D-Day. It consisted of dropping three-man teams into France, each consisting of one American, one British and one French member who'd be wearing uniform (they were fully trained saboteurs, and uniform might save them from being shot). They were to be known as 'Jedburghs', and their function was to supervise local Resistance groups, liaise with the invading forces, and maintain wireless contact with London.

But there was one major snag in the Jedburgh concept. The Americans insisted on handling all the traffic themselves at their newly built wireless station at Poundon, which was to be known as 53c. They also insisted that an American signals officer must command the station, which would use only American wireless operators.

As soon as they'd got Nick's reluctant agreement (he was in no position to argue) they made what seemed to them a sensible request. Since they were 'kind of new' to clandestine traffic, as soon as 53c opened early next year they suggested taking over the Norwegian traffic from 53a 'to help them get their hand in', and after consulting the council (those well-known experts on Signals problems), Nick agreed.

The decision to entrust Norwegian and Jedburgh traffic to a station which hadn't yet passed a single message scared the Morse out of our signalmasters and the silk out of me. But the Americans were full of surprises (a few of them welcome) and they asked Nick to advise them on the setting-up of their code room, which they wanted us to staff with our most experienced coders.

Nick was delighted to agree, and instructed me to prepare to transfer 'the best of our FANYs' to the American station.

I tried to point out that our teams of coders had been depleted by transfers abroad but he cut me short in mid-splutter, and ordered me to produce a list of suitable candidates within a week at the latest. He stressed that of all the jobs I had in hand, this was 'by far the most important'.

I didn't tell him that it was the one I felt least equipped to do.

I'd lost all confidence in my ability to choose reliable coders. I'd also begun to wonder if I'd ever possessed it.

I'd discovered a flaw in the girls' functioning which I couldn't account for and which I was determined to keep to myself until I did.

I'd learned that 90 per cent of the girls made major mistakes which were wholly out of character, that experienced coders behaved like beginners when we least expected it, and that methodical plodders, the life's blood of a code room, were just as accident-prone as coders with flair.

I hadn't realized the extent of the carelessness (consciously, that is) until Noor's message to London with eighteen letters in her transposition-key. I'd left strict instructions with the station that, in the event of this happening, the supervisor was to notify me at once and teleprint the code-groups to London.

But the supervisor had taken no such action, and if it hadn't been for my unease about Noor I wouldn't have asked to examine the code-groups. I then discovered that she'd inserted her distress signal.

The supervisor in question whispered, 'Oh Christ.' when I pointed out her mistake, and I left it to the most successful briefing officer in history to take the matter further.

But although I'd let her off lightly in case she lost all her self-confidence, her lapse jolted me into making a complete list of every major mistake the coders had made over the past six months. It was like counting the bullet wounds in a much-loved body. They totalled twenty-three. – not half as many as I'd made myself but probably not the true figure as it took no account of the mistakes I was sure they'd covered up.

I then listed all the errors which the coders in London had made during the same six months. They totalled twenty-five (Londoners had a harder time concealing them as I was their next-door neighbour).

Comparing the two lists, I sensed a pattern to the lapses which I couldn't define.

I then discovered that the malfunctioning wasn't confined to the coders, and that every branch of the code department appeared to be flawed. Wrong codes had been taken to final briefings, WOK's had been incorrectly assembled, and LOPs intended for the training schools had been sent to Nick's office, where they'd languished for a week. Even Muriel had made mistakes when typing agents' code-cards, and had failed to correct them.

I again sensed a pattern to the lapses but it continued to elude me.

Determined to discover the unknown factor, and hoping its name wasn't Marks, I re-read *The Psychopathology of Everyday Life*. But according to Freud, an expert in off-moments, most carelessness was unconsciously motivated and triggered by sexual frustration, and if this were true of the girls I must put my country first and end their deprivation.

In the meantime I had twenty coders to select for 53c and had so far chosen only two, and one of these I had doubts about. With less than forty-eight hours of Nick's deadline remaining, I decided to pocket my pride with my other loose change and consult Captain Henderson, the personnel officer in charge of the Signals directorate's FANYs.

I hadn't seen the attractive Canadian since she visited me with Miss Furze to debate recruitment, but I'd done my homework on her. I'd learned that her several hundred charges called her 'Mother Hen' and knew that they could safely confide in her as she had a liberal interpretation of her CO's dictum, 'FANYs shall at all times conduct themselves like ladies'. When I arrived for my appointment the passage was thronged with FANYs waiting to be counselled, and half of them were coders.

She at once asked for a progress report on two corporals at 53a who'd been promoted sergeants. As both girls were high on my list of gifted 'unreliables', her question enabled me to come to the point immediately, the hallmark of a good personnel officer.

I explained the importance of the new code room, and said that, much as I wanted both sergeants to be part of it, I was extremely concerned about their unaccountable lapses. She nodded wisely, which encouraged me to disclose the full extent of the problem and admit that it was baffling me.

She suggested that it might have something to do with periods.

Thinking she meant moon periods, I sharply reminded her that we were discussing coders and not agents.

Permitting herself a glance of disbelief, she explained that girls had 'monthly problems' which could well upset their concentration, and that many of them suffered acute discomfort a few days before their periods began.

Having no sisters except my mother, I was obliged to ask 'Mother Hen' for further and better particulars and realized from the silence which followed that I'd blown my cover as a man-about-town.

Lifting the receiver, she informed her secretary that she wanted no calls put through for the next thirty minutes.

I wondered what could possibly take her so long to explain, and waited anxiously when she began, 'Well now, Mr Marks . . .' She then gave me a birds and bees description of the girls' monthly cycles, and I had the utmost difficulty in not blurting out that this was the pattern which had been eluding me.

I became even more convinced of it when she said that some girls sailed through their periods with hardly any ill-effects, but that in the majority of cases the onset of their periods made them tense, erratic and depressed, even under the best of circumstances, which SOE's most certainly weren't.

Warming to the over-heated subject, she pointed out that most of the girls had never worked before but suddenly found themselves in remote country stations where agents' lives depended on their skill, and that if their periods occurred when they were subjected to inordinate pressure it was a miracle that they were able to function at all. She was also most concerned about how the 'monthly disturbances' affected women agents, though she understood that in most cases their periods stopped altogether when they arrived in the field.

It was my turn to nod wisely. I thanked her for confirming what I'd long suspected and said how much I regretted not consulting her before as it was obvious that certain measures must be taken at once.

'Really, Mr Marks? I'd be interested to hear what they are.'

Once more the man-about-town, I outlined my programme for the alleviation of periods. She or someone she appointed must inform me of the relevant dates, and I would then arrange for the girls to be given tasks which wouldn't overtax them. This would apply particularly to coders engaged in blanket attacks, and to briefing officers giving agents their final exercises, when nothing less than their best would do. The sooner the information was available, the sooner we could give the Americans a model code room and ensure continuity of performance throughout the entire department.

Captain Henderson looked at me as if it were time to change my nappies, a task for which officers in the First Aid Nursing Yeomanry had received no training. 'Do you realize what you're asking?'

She then explained that periods were a 'most delicate matter' which none of the girls would be willing to discuss! The relevant dates didn't appear on their files, and the subject hadn't once cropped up at any of her interviews, nor did she think it was ever likely to. The regimental doctor might know a few of the dates but he wouldn't disclose them unless instructed to do so by the head of the FANY. It was essential to respect the girls' privacy, but if I absolutely insisted, she'd arrange for me to meet the corps commander, though she'd prefer not to be a fly on the wall as it was likely to come tumbling down.

I was forced to make a guarded admission of my total bemusement. 'It's clear to me that once a month even FANYs must conduct themselves like ladies – but I just don't understand why they're so shy about discussing it.'

'Few men do, Mr Marks.' She said it so forcefully that I wondered if she were married.

'What do you suggest, Captain Henderson?'

'Recruit more girls, increase their rest periods, and send them on leave every couple of months. And above all, respect their privacy.'

I aborted a poem:

> This woman in front of me
> Is making a complete . . .

'There's one thing you could do, Captain Henderson – tell me some of the problems they bring to you.'

But mother hens of her calibre were seldom taken off-guard, and she looked at me quizzically. 'If you're trying to find out whether your name crops up, it's fair to say that it does from time to time.

Sorry, Mr Marks, but that's all I'm prepared to tell you.' She smiled sympathetically and pressed the buzzer on her desk.

But she'd also pressed one in me and I was glad to be dismissed. She'd made me realize that by the time I'd discovered the dates of the girls' periods they'd be too old to have them, and that more practical measures were called for.

I decided to tackle the problem cryptographically and made a blanket attack on the girls' forty-eight mistakes to establish a pattern. But even with the inventory in front of me, pinpointing their 'trying times' was like breaking an indecipherable with a misnumbered key-phrase and a dozen hatted columns.

After several hours of total immersion I managed to establish that one thoroughly reliable girl made serious errors during the same four days of every month but at no other time. And that seven others who were equally dependable also made them at monthly intervals, though the dates varied by roughly a week. But in all cases the pattern was unmistakable.

I selected six of these girls for 53c, and completed the list with a mixture of plodders and supervisors whose cycles were predictable. Nick barely glanced at the names before nodding his approval. I was anxious to tell him how the list had been compiled, but this was clearly the wrong moment to discuss the intricacies of female signals.

I was equally anxious to compare notes on the subject with Tiltman of Bletchley, but decided to postpone convening a national period conference until I knew what I was talking about, should that time ever come.

I was mercifully unaware of the other 'curses' which would shortly become due, one of them known as Giskes.

FIFTY-SIX

Unique in SOE

On the night of 15 November the White Rabbit returned to England by Lysander with a female member of the French Resistance sitting on each knee (accommodation was strictly limited).

The three of them had already become closely acquainted as they'd travelled to their pick-up point in the back of a hearse. Unaccustomed to this form of transport, Tommy had prepared for all eventualities by arming himself with a sten-gun, hand-grenades and a bottle of brandy. The hearse had been stopped several times by German soldiers, who examined the undertaker's credentials but not the state of his corpses. Their final resting-place was a farm a few minutes from their airfield, and when they reached it they found that the entire area was being guarded by members of the local Resistance, none of whom had seen an Englishman since the fall of France. Their leader told Tommy that it was an honour to be able to protect a British officer who was such a good friend to their country.

This much, plus an explicit description of the drawbacks of travelling by hearse, I learned from my old schoolmate Lieutenant (now Captain) O'Bryan-Tear (the first to become suspicious of Duke Street's clear-texts). But he'd had to break off when Tommy walked in.

The details of Tommy's Marie-Claire mission came from little Kay Moore, deputy chairman of the White Rabbit fan club.

Making sure that he was out of earshot (never easy), she began by saying that although his code-name – Shelley – had become part of the language of French Resistance, and a high price had been put on his head, the RAF still hadn't confirmed the Military Cross he'd been put up for six months ago, which Duke Street believed he'd received.

This meant that he was still forced to wear two tunics, one displaying his Croix de Guerre, the other displaying both decorations to convince Duke Street that helping the Free French was considered worthy of recognition.

Having vented at least some of her wrath, she said that she believed he was about to be offered a DSO for his part in mission Marie-Claire. Although the mission was by no means over, he and his partner Brossolette had achieved some astonishing results.

With Brossolette's support, he'd 'done a Gubbins' on the Resistance movement leaders, uniting them, revitalizing them and giving them his word that he, Passy and Brossolette would ensure that London sent them everything they needed for their D-Day preparations. He'd also won the confidence of the rank-and-file freedom fighters (I wondered which girl was the rank and which the file), and the Committee of Resistance had asked for either him or Brossolette to remain in France when the other returned to London.

Having no authority to agree to this, they'd done so at once, and had promised to change places with each other at two-monthly intervals. Tommy was to be the first to leave to start fulfilling his assurances.

Kay warned me that he was already on the rampage for arms and supplies but without much success, and she'd never known him in a more difficult mood.

I hoped he'd rampage in my direction and spent several nights listening for his footsteps, but it was a week before he telephoned to say that he proposed to call round for a brief talk later that evening if I was likely to be there.

I replied equally formally that it would probably be convenient.

His footsteps had lost none of their thunder nor his eyes their lightning, though they reflected a backdrop I hadn't seen before. The darkness of that hearse, perhaps – or some other blackness which he found impenetrable?

I greeted his return in the time-honoured way by silently proffering the Corona Corona which I'd kept for the occasion.

He seemed to be debating his right to indulge in such luxuries while his friend Brossolette was still in the field, but he finally produced a French match-box and lit the cigar like the expert he'd become. The contentment which followed justified Havana's existence, if anything could. But it didn't last long.

'I'm here to talk about WOKs,' he thundered.

I remembered his enthusiasm the first time he'd seen them and awaited his verdict like an apprehensive parent whose child was in the dock.

He said that putting aside the security aspects, which he didn't question, the system was a great improvement on the poem-code as it shortened the messages and saved time and mistakes. But the silk was extremely difficult to cut without causing it to fray, and this often damaged the unused keys. He was convinced that many agents would give up trying to cut them and risk being caught with their silks intact. He then opened his briefcase and silently handed me the remains of his WOK.

The silk was as grey as he was, and was so badly frayed that several rows of figures were impossible to read.

I pointed to the WOKs on the desk. 'Pick one at random, and see if it's easier to cut.'

He chose a WOK from the middle of the pile, took a small pair of scissors from his pocket, and a few seconds later cut away the top key as if it were a fingernail. He had a similar success with the next two keys. He then chose another WOK and repeated the experiment. Again, nothing frayed apart from my nerves.

I explained that this was the first batch of WOKs on specially sensitised silk, and that they would be standard issue from now on. I apologized for the delay, and hoped he'd agree that we'd finally got it right.

He nodded and, to my great disappointment, held out his hand for the return of his WOK. The Tommy of old, who understood children, would have known that I was longing to keep it as a memento.

'You can have this if you like.' He offered me his French match-box, and I liked very much.

'Thanks. How about this in part-exchange?' I proudly handed him the first draft of the Free French code-book, but he barely glanced at it until I told him what it was.

He then examined it page by page, and asked how the system worked.

I explained that all the code-groups would be re-enciphered on letter one-time pads, and assured him that they'd be on specially sensitized silk.

He was silent for longer than I'd expected, then said in little more than a whisper that the Free French 'had every reason to be grateful for an excellent job'. He seemed to have forgotten that they had him to thank for it.

'You're its godfather, you stupid sod. If you hadn't made me talk to Duke Street, there'd be no code-book.'

He studied the tip of his cigar. 'If I'm in any way responsible for it,' he said, 'then I've helped to send the Free French at least one thing they need!' His face was grey with the weight of his unfulfilled promises.

Seeing no arms or supplies in the office, he nodded abruptly and turned to go.

'Can you spare a minute? I need your help with an urgent problem.'

He swung round at once.

'What can you tell me about periods?'

It was the first time I'd seen Tommy startled. 'Comment?' he said in reflex French. 'What did you say?'

I repeated the question.

'What periods are you talking about?'

'The monthly awkwards. Didn't the girls at Molyneux have them when you were managing director?'

The Rabbit leaned forward, sniffing the air in the immediate vicinity. 'Either you've been drinking or you've got some girl into trouble. Or am I being unfair to you and it's both?'

I told him it was neither, and that I was the one getting into trouble. It took me five minutes to explain the forty-eight mistakes which had led me to research periods, and another five to admit that I had no idea what to do with the results.

Glancing up to ensure he hadn't left, I noticed that at least one of his eyes held a glint of amusement, and that a Corona Corona didn't fit comfortably between twitching lips. He then sat at my desk like the Tommy of old, and helped himself to one of Mother's black-market finest. A crumb fell on his Croix de Guerre, which was as close to official recognition as mother was likely to get.

Removing the intruder, he quietly explained that he didn't think he was the right person to advise me, as he wasn't an authority on the 'monthly awkwards', as I'd so delicately described them.

I replied that I couldn't think of a better person: his long experience of Molyneux mannequins could surely help me use the information I'd discovered without embarrassing the girls.

He sighed with relief. 'I thought you were asking me for a medical diagnosis. If you want advice on man-management, that's quite a different matter . . .'

Recalling his days at Molyneux as if they were part of his childhood, he said that mannequins were more than capable of looking after themselves, and that the only signs he'd seen of the 'monthly awkwards' had come from the male dress designers. In any case, didn't I realize that his mannequins and mine worked under slightly different 'circumstances'? Or did I make the coders change costumes several times a day and parade round the code room holding up their indecipherables?

At this point I gave up hope of being taken seriously, but should have known that he never ignored an SOS from anyone in SOE.

'. . . your safest course, if there is such a thing, would be to ask a woman you can trust to talk to the supervisors in confidence without letting them know you've put her up to it. But you'd have to choose her carefully.' He then listed her qualifications.

She must be considerably older than they were. She must be in charge of girls doing comparable work. She must be in a position to give the supervisor a guarantee of confidentiality, and be prepared to keep it. Above all, she must have the discipline to stick to her brief, which was to convince them that she was there to ask advice and not to give it.

At that moment there was a knock on the door, and the woman he might have been talking about came in to say goodnight.

Miss Saunders knew Tommy was the White Rabbit but never expected to meet him, and when I formally introduced her she blushed like the scarlet woman I hoped to turn her into.

He chatted to her with the wide-eyed innocence reserved for those who didn't know him, and then said that he'd been away from London for a bit, and would she mind if he asked her which department she worked for?

She replied that she looked after some of Mr Marks's girls.

'But not Mr Marks himself?'

'Oh no, Wing Commander. I know my limitations.'

'In that case, Miss Saunders, you're unique in SOE, and I hope Mr Marks realizes it.' It was his way of telling me that I need look no further.

He shook hands with both of us, and I felt the remnants of his WOK pressed into my palm. 'For your bottom drawer.' he said.

I caught a glimpse of his Barbara-face as he hurried away.

'What an extraordinary man,' Audrey whispered.

'I suppose he is. Now, Miss Unique in SOE, I've a delicate job for you.'

She listened in silence while I explained what was required of her, and to my astonishment she not only accepted the mission without hesitation but appeared to understand it.

Miss Unique left for the stations early the next morning, and returned forty-eight hours later apparently intact. Seated at my desk with a large notebook in front of her, she announced that the 'problem in question' certainly existed, though I'd greatly exaggerated the scale of it, and that 'various steps' were being introduced which would help to alleviate it. However, since they were none of my business she wasn't prepared to discuss them.

I respected her attitude but pointed out that the balance of our teams was at stake, and I badly needed to know the 'dates' of four key coders to ensure that they weren't on duty together.

A long debate ensued, but Mary Baker Eddy must have been on my side because Audrey finally relented and consulted her notebook. Thirty seconds later I knew the relevant dates and enciphered them in a one-time pad the moment she'd left. In the interests of security and out of gratitude to Tommy I code-named the four girls Marie and Claire, White and Rabbit.

Eight hours later Nick summoned me to his office to discuss 'a critical development concerning Holland'. He added that if I had any of Mother's coffee left he'd be glad if I'd bring it with me.

I laced it with Father's brandy, and set out to hear the worst.

FIFTY-SEVEN

The Major Development

Nick was alone in his office except for the shadow of Giskes, and didn't look up as I hurried towards him (at one in the morning he couldn't be blamed for it).

He was studying a Top Secret folder, which he suddenly put face downwards on the desk as if tempted to join it. My Dutch reports were in front of him, and one of them was open, though I couldn't see at which page. I put the black coffee beside them.

Finally glancing up at me, he wasted no time on preliminaries. 'According to a report just in from Switzerland, the greater part of the Dutch Resistance is in enemy hands.'

Clearing his throat as if his career were lodged there, he instructed me not to interrupt him till he'd finished giving me the details. He then disclosed that Sprout (Pieter Dourlein) and Chive (Ben Ubbinck) had escaped from Haaren prison on 30 August, and had arrived in Switzerland two days ago. They'd at once reported to the Dutch military attaché, and informed him, and subsequently the British consul, that the Germans had been waiting to arrest them when they landed in Holland (Chive in November '42; Sprout in March '43). They'd then supplied details of the dozens of other SOE agents in Haaren prison.

Pausing to comment that the coffee was even better than he remembered it, he proceeded to disclose the consequences of their arrival in Switzerland.

The head of C's Berne Station at once sent a message to his London HQ stating that the Germans knew all about SOE's codes, WT procedures and passwords, and were regularly exchanging traffic with London over dozens of captured sets.

C's controllers in London then transmitted a warning to their chief agents in Holland, which Nick quoted verbatim from his Top Secret folder, a sure sign that it was well past his bedtime: ' "Sister service totally infiltrated by Germans. We therefore urge you to break off all contact with their agents and keep clear of them. Please warn OD [Dutch Intelligence] and other organizations." '

I thanked God for C's existence but kept the heresy private.

Nick's next comment was so unexpected that I had to ask him to repeat it.

'We must consider the possibility that the escape's been engineered by the Germans.'

He pointed out that Trumpet had sent two messages in September warning London that Sprout and Chive had been captured by the Gestapo, who'd turned them round and helped them to escape so that they could spread disinformation.

Before I could protest, he added that there was another reason for doubting their story. A cargo ship had recently been blown up in Amsterdam harbour, which could hardly have happened if the entire Dutch Resistance was in enemy hands.

At which point I also blew up. Pointing to my reports, I said that if they were worth anything at all then Trumpet was completely blown, and when I'd read his denunciation of Sprout and Chive I'd regarded it as a guarantee of their bona fides. As for the destruction of the cargo ship, surely this was yet another example of Giskes at his best? 'For God's sake, Nick ... surely SOE isn't still allowing itself to be taken in?'

I rarely called him Nick to his face but it wasn't that which caused him to go scarlet with annoyance.

He said that he didn't object to seeing Giskes's hand in the explosion: it was a sound basic principle. But he took the strongest objection to being interrupted before he'd finished explaining exactly why he'd sent for me.

I apologized and waited.

He then began building towards his climax, and I slowly understood his reluctance to reach it.

He said that C was using the situation to discredit SOE at the highest level, and the War Office was about to order us to discontinue all activities in Holland, Belgium and Denmark, and wherever poss-ible to withdraw our personnel. He thought that SOE would be able to resist these orders, but a far more serious threat was being posed by the Chief of Air Staff.

The RAF had been refusing to fly sorties over Holland since May, and had curtailed operations over Belgium, but as a result of the latest disaster the whole of SOE's air operations were being reviewed.

The crux of the review was the security of SOE's communications, and in particular its codes. The RAF needed to be satisfied that our communications wouldn't cause unnecessary loss of aircraft between now and D-Day, and on D-Day itself. For this purpose a senior RAF officer named Air Commodore Payne was to visit SOE. Nick would show him the latest wireless equipment and WT procedures. I was to show him the new codes.

Draining the last of his coffee, he stressed that the competence of the Signals directorate was the real issue at stake, and that the scale of SOE's future operations would depend on the air commodore's findings. He added that I'd be alone with him for as long as it took and that he was certain to ask me some searching questions, especially about Holland. 'You must answer them fully.'

He looked hard at me with an expression I couldn't fathom and seemed about to add something, but changed his mind at the last moment and yawned instead. 'You'd better get some sleep,' he said. 'He'll be here at ten o'clock.'

Halfway home I realized what had been missing from the briefing: I hadn't been instructed not to produce my Dutch reports. Had he forgotten to injunct me? Or was he relying on me to use my initiative, and show them without consent?

Was that why I was being allowed to see the air commodore by himself?

I fell asleep wondering.

FIFTY-EIGHT

'If I Should Die, Etcetera'

On the morning of 30 November Air Commodore Payne, Nick and Heffer held a conference in Nick's office. An hour later an unusually ruffled Heffer warned me on the telephone that our visitor had been 'got at' by C, and seemed already to have decided that SOE's air ops. must be cancelled. He instructed me to show him our new codes 'down to the last detail', and not to let him ruffle me.

Ten minutes later the air commodore taxied across the runway which led to my desk, and I found myself staring into eyes full of dead pilots.

Even while Nick was introducing us, he looked round the office as if annoyed that it was still functioning, and silently conveyed that in his opinion SOE's Signals directorate was solely responsible for the collapse of the Dutch Resistance and the loss of God knows how many aircrews and aircraft.

We were alone ten seconds later, and tacitly agreed to become old enemies.

'Coffee, sir?'

Shaking his head abruptly, he said he understood from Brigadier Nicholls that I knew the purpose of his visit.

To ground us, you bastard.

Without waiting for my reply, which was possibly just as well, he glared at the silks which I'd lovingly arrayed on the table beside him. 'I'm not here to be fobbed off with SOE's new codes. I want to see every system you've been using for the past two years! *In detail!'*

At this stage I stopped thinking of him as Air Commodore Payne and nicknamed him PITA (pain in the arse), a) because he was one,

433

and b) because it would help me to forget how much depended on the outcome of this meeting.

I began my PITA-patter with the poem-code, stressing that we'd inherited it from C, and that it was the greatest of their many disservices. 'It gives the agents no chance, sir. Their poems can be tortured out of them, and their back traffic read ... which is why we've introduced new codes which –'

'One system at a time, thank you.'

He then asked how much reliance the country sections placed on the poem-code's security checks.

'Far too much, sir. And so did the former head of Signals because he knew they came from C.'

This angered him. 'I'm not concerned with where the damn things came from but with the damage they do. There must be dozens of captured agents setting up dropping operations, and you people in London have no means of knowing they're in enemy hands.'

I replied that with the exception of certain territories this was undoubtedly true, which was why we'd introduced –

'*Stop there.*'

My heart nearly did.

'Which territories?'

I told him that I was referring to Norway and Denmark, where the circuits were so tightly structured that if an agent were caught it would be known at once to the rest of his group, who'd report it to London immediately.

'That's an operational matter, not cryptographic. Are you qualified to assess it?'

C had done a good job on PITA.

'There's only one thing I'm qualified to do, sir – and that's to show you how we try to protect agents and aircraft from C's concept of a safe code. It would take me twenty minutes, and it would be a great help if you'd point out anything we've neglected.'

He stared disdainfully at my ashtray, where last night's cigar was almost as stubbed out as I was, then pressed a button on his stopwatch. This was clearly a signal for the crash course to begin, though I'd had no chance to structure it.

'Would you mind telling me your favourite poem, sir?'

This took him aback, though not far enough. '*WHY?*'

'So that you can encode a short message as part of your crash course.'

'My favourite poem, eh?' He mused for a moment, then admitted he wasn't a 'poetry wallah' but believed his favourite was Rupert Brooke's 'If I should die, et cetera.'

I invited him to choose five words from it, and he asked me to remind him how the damn thing went.

Sensing that he knew it by heart, I declined to prompt him.

He then began reciting the poem like a schoolboy who hasn't done his homework:

> 'If I should die,
> Think only this of me:
> That there's some corner
> Of a foreign field
> That is for ever England.
> And there shall be
> In that rich something
> A richer something concealed . . .
> Washed by the something,
> And blest by the et cetera . . .'

He added that Brooke had also written, 'Stands the Church clock at ten to three? and is there honey still for tea?'

He'd apparently forgotten that I'd asked him to pick five words, and I had no intention of reminding him.

'Any five words?'

'Yes, sir; they don't have to be consecutive.'

' "Think only this of me",' he said promptly.

At this point I wondered how much PITA really understood about codes as he had been sent by the RAF to evaluate them, and decided to set a small trap for him. 'Please turn those five words into a transposition-key.'

I shoved some squared paper up his runway and awaited developments.

He at once whipped out his fountain pen and numbered his chosen phrase as if he were issuing a cheque which no one dared bounce. *I hadn't had to show him how to do it.*

But I did have to remind him to encode a short message.

'It'll be short all right.'

He set about the encoding without any help from me, and delivered the result with a flip of his forefinger.

His message consisted of five Latin words, and his expression made clear that a dead language reflected his opinion of SOE's traffic.

I resolved to look up the meaning of 'Ne supra crepidum suter judicaret' the moment he'd gone, and regretted spending my Latin lessons trying to devise codes.

He looked at me impatiently. 'If I understand you correctly, because you tend to mumble, my crash course will last twenty minutes. You've fourteen left.'

The telephone rang, although I'd given strict instructions that I wanted no calls until the RAF had taken off. It was from the supervisor at 53a with news she didn't think could wait. The station had received its first indecipherable in a WOK, and the girls couldn't break it.

It had been transmitted by Brossolette's WT in good atmospheric conditions so the fault must lie in the coding, but 100 'routine attempts' had failed to produce clear-text and the girls didn't know what to try next.

I called out a string of suggestions to the supervisor, and instructed her to teleprint the code-groups to London so that the Norgeby House coders could help with the blanket attack. I then telephoned Tommy and assured him that we were giving Brossolette's indecipherable absolute priority. I'd forgotten about PITA, and found him looking at me with slightly less than his usual disdain.

Adjusting his stop-watch, he magnanimously announced that since the call was obviously important, the five minutes twenty seconds I'd spent on it wouldn't be deducted from the rest of his course. He then made some rapid notes on the pad in front of him, and underlined them.

I was convinced they had something to do with indecipherables, and pointed out that if he had no faith in anything else he was told today, he could have it in the girls' ability to break them.

He didn't actually call me a bloody liar but his sceptical expression required immediate attention, and I remembered just in time that three months ago Nick had shown me an astringent memo from the Air Ministry to SOE which I'd done my best to forget as it was an insult to the coders. The memo reminded our RAF liaison officer that it was essential for pilots to be given last-minute information from the field before taking off, and that if they were deprived of it because of indecipherables they had to 'fly blind', which resulted in heavy casualties. The memo also warned SOE that if key information were delayed on D-Day the consequences to the RAF would be even more serious.

To stop PITA brooding when I needed his full attention, I explained how blanket attacks worked, and assured him that the girls' 90 per cent success rate would be even higher by D-Day, and that their round-the-clock dedication to breaking indecipherables was only the fringe of their achievements.

As a gesture of goodwill, I then made what he clearly regarded as an indecent proposal. 'Would you care to inspect our FANYs, sir?'

'God forbid.' he exclaimed.

At which point I realized that I had only twelve minutes in which to finish his course.

Snatching up his coded message, I blurted out that if the Germans broke it they'd reconstruct his key-phrase, 'Think only this of me.' They'd then identify its source, and be able to read the rest of his message without further effort. I added that, to make their task harder, we tried to persuade agents to use original compositions which couldn't be looked up in reference books as they'd been written in Baker Street.

He looked at me in astonishment. 'Original compositions? – *Do you mean to tell me that you people in SOE write poetry?*'

'We do other things as well, sir.'

'I'm well aware of them,' he snapped.

He then announced that he wanted to see some specimens. '. . . now, if you please.'

Since writing bad poetry could hardly be used as a reason for grounding us, I pointed to the ditty-box without disclosing that I was its sole contributor. 'They're all in there, sir, waiting for customers.'

He reached into the box, and chose two at random.

I recognized the first from its spacing, and remembered feeling that I'd lost my own at the time of writing it:

> I searched the pages
> Now blank
> The drawers
> Now empty
> The pictures
> Now faded
> The rooms
> Now rooms
> And nothing more
> But could not find my life
>
> I found only wood
> In the forest
> Only water
> In the sea
> Only sand
> On the beach
> I could not find me.*

PITA started his second poem without comment and read it with such total disbelief that I suspected he'd picked one of a dozen which were so pornographic that I'd typed them myself. He re-read it as if he now had the confirmation he needed that SOE was an obscenity.

I tried to convince him that the use of sexual imagery made a valuable contribution to the code war because it was hard for the Germans to anticipate and easy for the agents to memorize, and that we only issued erotica to those whose minds it wouldn't cause to wander. I added that anything which helped to delay the reconstruction of a poem increased an agent's life-span.

To my astonishment he replaced the poem and selected two more.

---

* Issued in May '44 to an agent of D/F section, which specialized in escape routes.

I realized too late that C had guided his hand to a batch of poems which I was equally reluctant for him to see.

I'd marked the poems UFA (unsuitable for agents). I used them once a fortnight to convince the girls that the Germans could reconstruct *any* code-poem provided they had sufficient specimens of it. I'd composed the UFA he was reading after listening to the traitor Lord Haw-Haw (William Joyce) extolling the virtues of the Führer on Berlin radio:

> His first few goose-steps
> Were no damn use steps
> And his opening Heils
> Gave his mother piles
> For he was still in her womb
> When he began campaigning
> For Lebensraum
>
> As she felt him growing
> His mum couldn't help knowing
> That she was housing
> A rabble-rousing
> Frenetic anti-Semitic peripatetic
> Not even the strongest emetic
> Could dislodge
>
> When he finally crossed the border
> In physical good order
> He could hardly have been littler
> But grew up to be Hitler.

I'd pencilled the last verse in the margin as it had occurred as an afterthought:

> Although the sperm
> Which created him
> Hated him
> It elated him.

A bemused PITA then turned to the second UFA as if it couldn't be worse than the first, and discovered how wrong he was:

> She spent her hours
> Breast-feeding flowers
> Fearful of rabies
> From the lips of babies
>
> Her terror of skin
> And what sheltered within
> Made her humour
> A tumour
> Malign and malignant
> A figment and fragment
> Of all that was stagnant
> In the refuse bin
> Of her unknown sin
>
> At the end of her life
> She ignored her food
> And swallowed her knife.

'Good God,' whispered PITA, clearly doubting His existence.

I hastened to assure him that we didn't inflict poems marked UFA on agents.

'I'm delighted to hear it. I suppose you chant them to each other?' He pushed the ditty-box aside as if it were SOE's future, and glanced at his watch.

Abandoning his course, I asked how many words he remembered of the UFAs he'd read.

'Piles.' he said with feeling. 'You seem to think that Hitler gave them to his mother.'

I informed him that indecipherables were the code department's haemorrhoids, and that UFAs were the best antidote we had. '. . . do you mind if I explain why, sir?' I then pointed out in less technical language:

a) That the speed with which the enemy could break a poem-code depended on the number of messages they'd managed to intercept (known in the trade as 'depth').

b) That the more 'depth' they accumulated, the easier it was for them to reconstruct the words of a poem.

c) That every time an agent had to re-encode an indecipherable, he was providing them with another sample of his poem.

'. . . now you see where UFAs come in?'

'If you use them as ointment for haemorrhoids, there's only one place . . .'

I explained that to ram home the dangers of 'depth' to the girls, and to give it to them as people, I wrote a dozen transposition keys on the blackboard, all based on the same UFA, and challenged them to reconstruct the entire poem.

I added that although this extended them to their outer limits (and taught me what they were), when they found that they could reconstruct even the most unexpected phrases they worked round the clock to keep agents off the air. I added that their 90 per cent success rate had already been increased by the introduction of charts, and that the RAF wouldn't be kept waiting on D-Day for the latest reports from the field.

'I'd now like to resume your crash course –'

'Thank you – your time is up, and I've heard enough.'

He then switched off his stop-watch and accused me of wasting the best part of an hour trying to blame all SOE's calamities on the poem-code we'd inherited from C, and of giving him a lot of waffle about the precautions C hadn't thought of taking, when all he was concerned about was hard fact and not inter-departmental rivalries, which frankly sickened him.

He seemed equally nauseated by the array of silks awaiting his inspection – 'I'd better look at the new codes your brigadier thinks so highly of. I see you've set them out to their best advantage.'

'Sorry! I'm not prepared to discuss them with you until I've answered your last remarks.'

I didn't mind being addressed by him as if I were an East End barrow-boy because that's how Father's career had started, but I could no longer stomach the contempt which blazed from his corneas, of which he appeared to have several.

I told him I was sorry if all he'd got out of the past hour was digs at C and waffle; I'd intended to convey to him the very hard fact that between now and D-Day scores of agents were likely to lose their silks, and would have to arrange their dropping operations in poems. This meant that the RAF would continue to be in danger from our traffic no matter what precautions we took, and I thought he should know it.

My frankness seemed to puzzle him and I decided to explain it. 'I was hoping that absolute honesty from me might be worth a Lysander or two from you.'

Without any warning he sprang to his feet and strode to the door.

I was convinced that I'd wrecked SOE's chances, and called out to him in despair. 'PITA.'

He swung round so angrily I suspected that his Christian name was Peter, and that he wouldn't tolerate familiarity from a barrow-boy.

'*What was that?*'

'I was about to tell you that "Peter Piper picked a peck of pickled pepper" was a code-poem – but the agent who used it spelled pickled with two 'k's, and it took us thirty-eight thousand attempts to break his message! I thought you should know we don't give up easily!'

He clearly considered that I was more pickled than the peppers. Backing towards the door, he gravely thanked me for my invaluable information and announced with some urgency that he had to have a pee!

'Second door on the left, sir. The chain needs a bit of a pulling.'

'So does my leg.'

He then went about his business, and I spent his loo-time (which was all too short) calling out suggestions for Brossolette's indecipherable. He resumed his seat not perceptibly relieved, and waited for the barrow-boy to explain the contents of his stall.

Forty minutes later I was convinced that he understood as much about WOKs and LOPs as anyone I'd briefed. Although he didn't ask a single question, I could feel his interest growing when I showed him the Jedburgh code-books, which were to be used on D-Day with letter one-time pads, and which the Americans had accepted.

He seemed even more interested when I told him that we'd mounted a deception scheme called Gift-horse to persuade the enemy that WOK-traffic had been passed in poem-codes 'in the hope of wasting their bloody time.'

He still appeared to be riveted when I showed him a Gift-horsed WOK, and pointed out the indicator groups which we'd deliberately duplicated.

He then asked a question which caught me completely off-guard: '*I assume you know about the two Dutch agents who've escaped to Switzerland?*'

His timing was brilliant, and I realized that I'd been handled by a master.

'Well, do you know about them or don't you?'

I admitted that I did.

'Do you accept their statements that almost the whole of the Dutch Resistance is in enemy hands, and that your codes and passwords are completely blown?'

'I haven't read their statements, sir.' It was true. Nick had read them to me, but I needed time to think.

'Marks, I'm going to cut this short . . .' He didn't specify which part of my anatomy he meant. 'What do you believe the position in Holland and Belgium really is?'

A fucking disaster, sir.

'Well?'

The honest way to answer him would be to show him my Dutch and Belgian reports but I still didn't know if I was supposed to let him see them. I knew that I was going to, and decided I'd need a cover-story to protect me from the charge of wilfully disobeying orders.

I'd maintain that he'd asked me for a report on security checks but the bastard had so flustered me that I'd shown him the wrong documents, and he was halfway through them before I'd realized my mistake, an explanation so improbable that SOE might believe it. But I'd need PITA's co-operation, and didn't know how to get it.

'Take your time, old chap. I want your considered opinion.'

His use of 'old chap' could only have come from the old chap upstairs as it was Father's way of comforting me from childhood

443

onwards. I started considering what Dad would do if he had PITA to deal with.

He had one trick for which he was infamous. Whenever he was ready to bid for a library he'd conceal two pieces of paper with a different offer written on each. He'd then invite the vendor to write down what he thought his library was worth while he pretended to do the same. As soon as he saw the vendor's estimate, he'd produce whichever piece of paper was closest to it, and the deal was done.

I decided to adopt his technique in a worthier cause.

'I'd better show you these, sir.' I unlocked my centre drawer and produced three folders. 'These will give you an analysis of every Dutch and Belgian agent's security checks from '42 onwards . . .'

They were in fact my Dutch reports, and I now had to persuade PITA to insist on seeing them.

'Oh Christ, sir! I've just realized I'm not allowed to show these to anyone! SOE has some very strict rules.'

He bridled at being considered anyone. 'I suspect Brigadier Nicholls would make an exception, but we needn't trouble him. You don't have to show them to me – you can summarize them.'

'I really think it would be better if you read them, sir.'

'I'll be the judge of that. Summarize them.'

I need a cover story, you prick. If I show you something I'm not supposed to it's because I made a mistake. Mea culpa, SOE, mea maxima culpa (another Latin phrase I had good reason to know).

'I wish you would accept my judgement, sir, if only on this. It really would be better if you read at least one of them.'

'I've already told you my decision. Now kindly get on with it.'

Although I outranked him, being a civilian, I couldn't force him to read what he didn't want to, and had only one hope left.

The folder I most wanted him to see 'slipped' from my fingers and fell open at page one, which was headed 'Plan Giskes' (I admitted in the first paragraph that I'd no authority to launch it).

He glanced at it perfunctorily, then stiffened slightly and picked the folder up. He read the whole of page one, then looked up at me with a glimmer of understanding. 'I must insist on reading your reports on Dutch and Belgian security checks. Shall I contact Brigadier Nicholls?'

'That won't be necessary, sir – but may I leave them with you while I go next door to help with that indecipherable?'

His abrupt nod concluded the deal.

'Would you like some coffee?'

'Black and strong, please.'

He put the folders face downwards on the desk when Muriel arrived with her tray. Staring at the selection of cream cakes she'd reserved for the occasion, he informed her that they'd help him to digest 'Mr Marks's reports on security checks.'

She knew at a glance what I'd given him to read but left without comment.

PITA picked up the folders and weighed them by the ounce. 'Come back in an hour.'

'Right, sir, but if you need me for any reason, just press that intercom.'

'I'll try to avoid it,' he said, and began sipping his coffee.

The indecipherable was waiting on Muriel's desk.

Dispossessing her, I completed two new sets of blanket attacks and dispatched them to the station and to the Norgeby House coders with instructions to the supervisors to monitor the girls' progress as the procedures would be new to them.

I made a dozen attempts myself, and by sheer luck discovered Brossolette's mistake. He'd chosen one key from the first line of his silk and the other from the third instead of using them in pairs the way they were printed. I telephoned Tommy to tell him the message was out and cancelled the blanket attacks.

The indecipherable forced me to accept that even with silks no mistake was so improbable that our agents wouldn't make it, and I began preparing a new series of blanket attacks for WOK malefactors.

I was startled when Muriel warned me that the air commodore's time was up.

I wondered if the same could be said of SOE's.

PITA was staring at my favourite patch of ceiling. The folders were as tightly closed as his face. He waited until I was seated before acknowledging my return.

'How's the indecipherable?'

'The girls broke it after 800 attempts.'

He made no comment and continued staring at the ceiling. 'I have only one question,' he finally announced.

He relapsed into silence he showed no signs of breaking.

A sliver of panic began crawling up my spine. He should have had a spate of questions. One sounded ominous.

To ease the tension, I laid odds on what it was: 2–1 it was about the results of Plan Giskes, 5–1 it was about the 'Heil Hitler' call-sign, 10–1 it was about the Dutch agents who'd been allowed access to the Belgian escape lines . . .

But PITA had something more important on his mind: '*Where did you get those incredible cream cakes?*'

I saw that two had disappeared, and was spared the embarrassment of answering him when he patted his stomach and said it would be a kindness to his tailor if I withheld the information.

Showing little benevolence himself, he brusquely announced that there was nothing in the reports I'd shown him that we needed to discuss. He then patted his stomach again, and I'd have liked to help him. 'I've seldom enjoyed a better cup of coffee – visiting SOE has some advantages.'

He glanced at his watch, and stood up abruptly. 'It's time I called on Brigadier Nicholls. Perhaps you'd point me in the right direction.'

What else have I been trying to do the whole bloody morning?

'I'll take you to his office, sir.'

We walked into silence down the longest corridor I'd known.

'I've another question for you,' he finally announced.

He was in no hurry to ask it, but I didn't reopen my betting-shop.

'Was it true what you told me about Peter Piper and his peck of pickled peppers?'

'Absolutely true, sir – but not the whole truth.'

'I thought as much. I can manage the rest of the way, thank you.'

He nodded abruptly and I began the long trek home but he at once called me back in a *coup de grâce* tone.

I turned to face the firing-squad, and perspiration was my blindfold.

'Leo, I've a bit of advice for you. No matter what happens to SOE in the short-term, keep your pickled pepper up and push on with your job. The code war, as you call it, isn't over yet. Oh, and while I think of it – that security check bumph was a great help to me but I don't propose to tell anyone I've seen it. Goodbye, old chap.'

Ten minutes later I discovered the meaning of 'Ne supra crepidum suter judicaret':

'A wise cobbler should not judge above his last'.

A far from wise head of Codes had to wait twelve hours before learning from Heffer what PITA had said to him and Nick at their second conference.

He'd been very impressed by our new codes and security checks, and by all that he'd heard about the quality of our FANYs! He'd also been impressed by our new WT sets and equipment. But above all, he was satisfied that we'd learned from our mistakes, and would be able to cope with the problems of the D-Day traffic, and intended to say so in his report to the ministry. He also intended to recommend that the ban on flights over Holland must continue, and that in the short term sorties over Belgium must be cancelled or curtailed.

'He's done all he can to let us off lightly,' said Heffer. 'The trouble is he's been overrruled.' He then disclosed that, without warning to SOE, the head of Bomber Command had cancelled all our air ops. over Western Europe. 'He's been got at by C, but grounding us isn't enough for them. They're trying to persuade the War Office to close us down completely, and if Gubbins doesn't catch the next plane home, they've a damn good chance of succeeding!'

I thanked him for the information and turned to go, but he called me back as sharply as PITA had.

'Payne made a comment about you which puzzled us. He said that to prove some point you were trying to make, you insisted on showing him some Top Secret documents.'

I vowed never to trust another cobbler. 'Top Secret documents, Heff?'

'He described them as UFAs, and we couldn't admit that we had no idea what he was talking about. Perhaps you'd care to enlighten us when you have a moment?'

I assured him that I would.

*   *   *

Two days later a first edition of *Peter Piper's Practical Principles of Plain and Perfect Pronunciation, 1819* was acquired by 84.

I tried to buy it from them at cost so that I could present it to a friend, but according to Father (the biggest cobbler of us all) the British Museum had stepped in first.

Convinced that my friend and I would never meet again, I wrote a short UFA in his memory:

> Think only this of me
> That there's some corner
> Of an SOE barrow-boy
> That is forever PITA.

The girls failed to break it.

FIFTY-NINE

The Invisible Presence

Gubbins had been in the Middle East for six weeks and SOE regretted every year of them. His deputy, Sporborg, had kept him fully informed about the crisis in London and expected him to fly back while we were still in business, but on 3 December Gubbins sent him a message:

. . . ESSENTIAL TO REMAIN CAIRO TILL CHURCHILL BACK FROM TEHERAN. AM CONFIDENT CRISIS CONTAINABLE ON LINES AGREED WITH SELBORNE OUR TELEGRAMS OF 2ND. ALSO CONFIDENT ATTLEE (DEPUTY PRIME MINISTER) WILL DEFER FURTHER MEASURES TILL ABLE CONSULT CHURCHILL. EXPECT RETURN LONDON MID-DECEMBER. FURTHER MESSAGE FOLLOWS.

Heffer, seldom a pessimist unless he was happy, was convinced that SOE would be disbanded if the Mighty Atom didn't catch the next plane home. Nor did he share his confidence in Lord Selborne's ability to defend us in Cabinet.

On 4 December the minister's personal assistant was dispatched to Baker Street on a fact-finding mission, and was escorted into my office by Sporborg and Nick.

She was a red-haired sledgehammer named Pat Hornsby-Smith. Her manner was brusque, her figure superb, and her voice had parquet flooring. She at once admitted that she knew nothing about codes, and spent the next thirty minutes asking highly perceptive questions about each silk she was shown. She then made several jokes at her own expense which convulsed Sporborg and Nick, a sure sign of the importance of her visit.

An hour later she enquired with a hint of provocation if there was anything else I'd like her to look at.

The wrong person to be asked such a question, I made the mistake of producing an artefact which even Nick hadn't seen as it had only arrived that morning from the Thatcher Barn.

It looked like an ordinary pocket handkerchief, and in case she was tempted to blow her nose on it I hastily handed her a torch which had been fitted with an ultra-violet beam, and invited her to switch it on. A few seconds later she was astonished to find herself staring at 100 WOK-keys which had been invisibly printed.

'. . . it would be useless without this, Miss Hornsby-Smith.'

I then picked up an ordinary-looking pencil which it had taken Elder Wills six months to produce. Praying it would work, I rubbed it across the handkerchief and a whole line of WOK-keys disappeared.

I then explained that the chemicals in the pencil ensured that the keys could be permanently erased the moment they'd been used, and her response was immediate.

'So if the handkerchief is captured the back messages are safe?'

Impressed by her perception but disturbed by her enthusiasm, I hastily added that invisible codes weren't for general issue as they could only be used in special circumstances.

This didn't deter my visitors from testing Wills's wizardry (ladies first), and Nick accidentally erased three lines of keys.

The sledgehammer then asked for a specimen of every silk she'd seen 'with instructions attached' so that she could explain them to the minister. She was particularly keen to show him the handkerchief and pencil, but I had to explain that they were the first examples of their kind the Thatched Barn had produced, and I'd promised Elder Wills not to part with them.

Giving me a look which she would one day bestow on the House of Lords when she was Baroness Hornsby-Smith, she declared that they'd be far more use in the minister's hands than languishing on my desk and, after a warning glance from Sporborg and some eyebrow Morse from Nick, I reluctantly surrendered them.

Locking them in her briefcase with an array of silks I couldn't spare, she thanked me for trusting her with them (another joke perhaps?), and departed five minutes later to accompany Nick on a tour of the stations.

I subsequently learned from Heffer that she'd christened the silks 'toys' and the coders 'Marks's harem'. He didn't disclose what she'd christened me.

My encounter with her had been a wholly new experience not because she was a Minister's PA but because I'd been supported throughout by an invisible presence.

This wasn't the moment to dwell on who she was, or how I'd been lucky enough to meet her, or any other such trivia. All that mattered to me was that she'd become part of the code war, and that I wanted her beside me for the rest of my life.

Although Selborne relied on the old hands in Baker Street for ammunition to convince the Cabinet that SOE's activities were an asset, it wasn't the Executive Council, the country sections or the Signals directorate which enabled him to make his first breakthrough. It was Flemming Muus of Denmark.

In the nine months since this remarkable agent (the Danish equivalent of Tommy) had taken control of his country's Resistance, he'd not only succeeded in ensuring that SOE continued to receive key information about the rocket sites at Peenemünde; he'd welded his co-patriots into a Secret Army, organized over 900 acts of sabotage, and started a training school at Zeeland for would-be agents. Although reluctant to leave Denmark, he'd been recalled to London in October for consultations with Commander Hollingsworth and the Free Danish Council, and Lord Selborne had decorated him with the DSO on King George VI's behalf.

I'd given him a code-briefing early in November, and he was as hearty and forthcoming as when I'd briefed his Table Top team. He admitted it was hard to concentrate on codes when he had so much else to attend to, and we arranged to meet again before he left, which he estimated would be within two weeks 'at the outsidest.'

On 2 December he was still in London, and accompanied Commander Hollingsworth to a conference convened by Brigadier Mockler-Ferryman (head of the Western directorate). Neither they nor any of the other officers present knew why they'd been summoned.

They were informed by Mockler-Ferryman that SOE had been instructed by the War Office to cease all operations in Denmark, Holland and Belgium until further notice. They were also told that the War Office required an acknowledgement of the order by ten o'clock next morning, and wanted draft plans to be submitted for the recalling of SOE personnel.

On 3 December an enraged Muus descended on Whitehall, accompanied by Mockler-Ferryman and Hollingsworth, who soon found themselves redundant.

Determined to prove with the plain-speaking for which he was famous that there was no danger of his country becoming another Holland, he bombarded the War Office and Air Ministry with facts about the Danish Resistance of which they were completely unaware.

The War Office withdrew its embargo, and the Air Ministry agreed to resume sorties over Denmark – with the exception of certain areas which Muus pointed out were too well protected for the aircrews' safety.

He was due to return to Denmark on 11 December to attend to his lesser duties, and on 9 December I gave him his final code-briefing. The invisible presence sat next to him throughout, and when he thanked me for the WOKs and LOPs he was taking home with him, she kissed him goodbye on his invaluable forehead.

Her name was Ruth, and she lived with her parents in a flat in Park West, and we'd met two months ago in unpromising circumstances. She enjoyed the swimming pool, and early one morning she'd caught me swinging across the rings in my bowler hat, which I'd doffed to her without falling in, and even that hadn't prevented her from seeing me again.

Although we were able to meet for only a few hours a week, every sked with her taught me that there were forms of communication which I didn't know existed. I learned that she had a Jewish mother and a Catholic father, which meant that I could safely take her home to my parents as she was half a nice Jewish girl.

I'd persuaded her that I worked in an admin office in Baker Street and she wondered if it was the 'funny outfit' which used to be run by her godfather. She then informed me that he lived in Park West – 'His name's Charles Hambro and he's a merchant banker.'

I told her that he'd need to be as he was a customer of my father's.

I did my best not to think about her in Baker Street (if agents could cut away their silk life-lines, so could I) but my best wasn't good enough, and I could think of little else. I'd been worried about going to bed with her in case I talked in my sleep but soon discovered that she *was* my sleep.

We both tried to forget that she was returning to Canada shortly before Christmas to resume training at an air-ambulance base.

On 10 December Sporborg warned Gubbins in his strongest telegram yet that C and the Air Ministry were broadening the scope of their attack and were trying to force an enquiry into 'every aspect' of SOE's activities. (He'd underlined 'every aspect' in red ink, for which there was no cipher equivalent, so we repeated the phrase in case eagle-eye missed it.)

The warning had the desired effect, and on 11 December Gubbins flew to Algiers *en route* to London.

By the Mighty Atom's standards, he'd failed to accomplish his Middle East master plan. By anyone else's, his successes were phenomenal. Ignoring the climatic conditions (and possibly causing them), he'd not only established SOE's future role in the Balkans, which the Americans were trying to diminish; he'd reorganized Cairo and Massingham, sorted out the chaos in Greece, and sold SOE's potential to a general named Eisenhower. He'd even found time to convince Marshal Tito of Yugoslavia that SOE would send his partisans the arms and supplies they needed, though the same assurances had been given to his rival Mihailovič.

He arrived in Baker Street on 16 December, and at once composed a memorandum for the Cabinet and Chiefs of Staff which Nick described to Heffer as 'a masterpiece', a term he usually reserved for Signals equipment.

With the Mighty Atom now in control of the Whitehall conflict, it was possible to concentrate on SOE's other little war.

On 18 December Dourlein and Ubbrinck (the Dutch escapees) sent a message from Spain amplifying their warnings that all Dutch radio links were in enemy hands, and identifying the WT operators they'd encountered in Haaren prison (the two agents had been smuggled out of Switzerland by MI6).

On 22 December Flemming Muus reported from Copenhagen that

the decisions reached in London had been fully implemented, and Denmark had been divided into six military districts, each supervised by a regional committee on which SOE was represented. All this in a tiny country infested with Germans.

It was a very different situation for the Free French and Buckmaster. On 23 December messages from France warned both Duke Street and F section that shortage of supplies was forcing agents to take unnecessary risks in order to survive, and that many of them had been caught by the Gestapo or the Vichy police. The messages urged SOE to resume dropping operations.

On Christmas Eve I learned from Ruth's father that she'd been killed in a plane crash in Canada. I went up to the roof of Norgeby House, which was the closest I could get to her.

Someone called out, 'There's an idiot on the roof.'

There was a quick way down from it, but she wouldn't have approved. Looking up at God's pavement for signs of new pedestrians, I transmitted a message to her which I'd failed to deliver when I'd had the chance:

> The life that I have
> Is all that I have
> And the life that I have
> Is yours.
>
> The love that I have
> Of the life that I have
> Is yours and yours and yours.
>
> A sleep I shall have
> A rest I shall have
> Yet death will be but a pause.
>
> For the peace of my years
> In the long green grass
> Will be yours and yours and yours.

End of sked.

I went downstairs and wished the girls a Happy Christmas.

SIXTY

Fumigated

'It's impossible to share premises with the country
stations. They don't bother to make appointments,
hold endless conferences in corridors, and take the
lot of us for granted. Well, it's damn well got to
stop.'

(Heffer, when he'd been interrupted from his
newspaper once too often)

The Signals directorate began the New Year by seeking self-
containment, and on 1 January 1944 Nick and his department heads
left Norgeby House and occupied the whole of Montagu Mansions,
a block of flats off Baker Street where we'd be cut off from the rest
of SOE yet within easy reach (the Guru thought too easy) of the
country sections. The Signals Office, teleprinter rooms and distribution departments remained in situ for practical reasons. Nor did
we disturb the WOK-makers as some of them could no longer see
straight, and mightn't have found the new premises.

Our departure enabled Gubbins to reshuffle Norgeby House. He'd
long wanted all the country sections under one roof, and he at once
ordered Tommy and Co. to leave Dorset Square and occupy the space
we'd vacated, a decision which gave the Free French the illusion of
parity with Buckmaster.

I learned from Tommy (who disliked sharing premises with
'Maurice's lot') that my old office was to be used by the head of RF
section, 'once it had been fumigated'.

My new one was soon in need of similar treatment. It was twice
the size of my previous office, and I had it entirely to myself. The

455

windows were heavily barred, in keeping with my chest, and I kept the curtains drawn as the room was at street level and there was no longer anything I wanted to look out on.

Muriel had covered the walls with silks, which were concealed behind drapes. Fluorescent lights shone on to them whenever I could find the switch, and although it was against the rules for low-levels like me to have carpets in their offices, she'd found one which matched the drapes. But my most unexpected acquisition was a FANY sergeant named Penelope Wyvol-Thompson. Formerly a coder, then a WOK-maker, she'd become Muriel's assistant and now spent most of her time ensuring that 'no-one interfered with the little man's privacy'. As a bodyguard she was worth her weight in WOKs.

Unable to settle down, I spent the first day inspecting the premises, and spotted a slender young secretary named Anne Turner struggling to carry a large typewriter down the corridor.

To her astonishment and mine I took the machine from her and carried it to the typing pool's office, where she thanked me profusely in front of her awestruck colleagues. Although to my regret she never worked for the code department, she was destined to make a contribution to it of which at the time she was mercifully unaware.*

I returned to my office and tried to make a home of it.

By mid-January the demands for silks had become impossible to meet. The Free French wanted 1,000 more copies of the FFI code-book, country sections had doubled their D-Day estimates (if only half of their operations were mounted, the invasion would be superfluous), and Italy, Cairo and India had increased their orders by 50 per cent.

But our greatest problems were caused not by SOE's expansion but by Pat Hornsby-Smith.

The sledgehammer had phoned three times to demand more 'toys' for the minister, and on Nick's instructions I'd supplied them immediately. But it wasn't the handfuls of silks she required which put us under pressure; it was the use Selborne made of them.

---

* Some fifty years later Anne typed the whole of this book, probably on the same machine.

I'd no idea whom he showed them to, but within hours of the last delivery 'outside organizations' (including C) began bombarding Nick with requests to call at Baker Street to inspect our codes. He agreed to every request, except C's (he was discussing it with The Executive Council), and by the middle of January my office had become London's leading toyshop.

Most of the visitors seemed impressed by the silks, but to my relief none of them tried to place any orders.

Nick had twice warned me (once in writing to stress that he meant it) that if any organizations made direct contact with me I must refer them to him for screening before agreeing to an appointment. It wasn't long before this contingency arose.

On 18 January Muriel informed me that a Captain Astor was in her office. She added that he was a member of the SAS, and that he'd called on the off-chance that I'd see him without an appointment! Liking the sound of a captain who took off-chances, I told her that I'd give him a quarter of an hour as soon as she'd checked his credentials.

Five minutes later a fair-haired young captain appeared on the threshold, but at once turned to leave when he saw that I was on the phone. Unaccustomed to such consideration, I beckoned him to a chair whilst I finished talking to the Grendon supervisor in shorthand. He spent the time staring apprehensively at the blackboard, on which I'd written a famous quotation from Frances Croft Cornford for the coders to reconstruct at my next lecture (I'd produced no poems of my own since Xmas Eve):

> O fat white woman whom nobody loves,
> Why do you walk through the fields in gloves,
> Missing so much and so much?

Replacing the receiver, I asked Captain Astor how I could help him.

He replied that the SAS needed an expert to advise them on codes, and if possible to supply them, and he'd reason to believe he'd come to the right person.

I knew nothing about the SAS except that they operated behind enemy lines and had been founded by a maverick young officer named David Stirling, who sounded as if he were SOE-minded.

So did Captain Astor, but before I could allow him to proceed there was one formality which had to be disposed of.

'Sorry to have to ask you this, Captain, but who gave you the authority to approach SOE?'

'Sorry to have to tell you this, Mr Marks, but I forgot to ask for it! Here's my CO's number if you want it.'

'I don't think it'll be necessary.' His reply had ensured that he'd get all the help I could give him.

'What sort of traffic are you likely to pass?'

He produced a bundle of specimen messages (the first visitor who'd done so) but they were so carefully phrased I suspected they'd been composed especially for the occasion. Pressed for detail, he estimated that the average message would be fifty letters long and that most of the D-Day traffic would be between France and London, though in certain areas two-way communication between SAS units would save 'a lot of to-ing and fro-ing.'

We to-ed and fro-ed between ourselves for several minutes, and I decided that they could most safely pass their paramilitary-type messages in code-books and letter one-time pads. We'd also have to supply them with WOKs for emergencies, of which I imagined there'd be plenty. Providing them with two-way communication as well meant that we'd have to dig into the last of our reserves. But so would the SAS when they reached the field. It was time to demonstrate the merchandise.

Pulling back the curtains (I knew by now where the light switch was), I explained the various systems and added that if the SAS proved to be temperamentally unsuited to code-books they could encode their messages directly on to pads.

Captain Astor had only one question for me: 'How soon can we have some for training purposes?'

'Would tomorrow be soon enough?'

The smile which parachuted from his eyes to his lips reminded me of Tommy's when he was still able to smile.

I then explained that I'd need an informed estimate of the quantities they'd require, and that he'd better leave the formalities to me as his approach had been somewhat irregular.

He shook my hand in silence.

Five minutes later he took a final glance at the 'fat white woman whom nobody loves' and hurried away, probably to drop in on the Chiefs of Staff without an appointment.

The following morning I was assembling Astor's training codes when Heffer strolled in.

'Prepare yourself for a shock.' he said, an innovation which was a shock in itself.

He waited till his cigarette was aglow with excitement before making his announcement. 'We've been asked by the War Office to supply codes for *all* Special Forces.'

I had just enough strength to enquire what quantities this would involve.

'It'll make no difference! Nick's agreed that we'll do it.'

He watched my face slither (it hadn't the vitality to fall), and smiled. 'There's a bright side to it – you'll have the authority to supply Captain Astor with the codes you'd agreed to send him anyway. His CO took the trouble to phone Nick to tell him in detail how helpful you'd been. But you needn't worry about the consequences . . .' He assured me that I was reasonably popular with SOE at the moment because the request couldn't have come at a better moment for Gubbins and Selborne, and was a kick in the balls for C.

'But Heff, we can't even cope with our own requirements, let alone the whole of Special Forces.'

'Try telling that to Nick – he's waiting to see you.'

I reached his office in twenty-five seconds, an in-house record.

Nick was far too elated by his directorate's popularity (WT sets, signal-plans and variable call-signs were also in demand) to be disturbed by trivia such as shortage of silk. He pointed out that I'd solved previous production problems without much difficulty by talking to George Courtauld and Tommy Davies (the 'hard men'.), and instructed me to approach them immediately. He added that they already knew of the War Office's request as Davies was on the Executive Council, which had endorsed his decision to supply Special Forces with everything they needed.

The 'hard men' weren't at all pleased to see me. They listened with growing impatience as I explained that we'd get no help with the new commitment from our present printers and photographers as they were already pushed to their outer limits.

'So are we,' snapped Tommy Davies.

'Indeed we are,' echoed George Courtauld.

I assured them that I didn't take their help for granted, and knew how difficult it would be for them to find new firms for us. I added that it wasn't just the codes themselves which had caused them to catch on but the quality of the printing and photography for which they alone were responsible. I then admitted that I'd recommended to my colleagues that signal-plans and variable call-signs should also be printed on silk, which would increase the work-load still further.

Davies stared out of the window as if wondering if it would be a suitable exit for me. 'We'll do what we can, but I don't hold out much hope.'

'Very little indeed.' echoed Courtauld.

Three days later four new firms of printers and photographers were put at SOE's disposal. They began work at once with silk supplied by the 'hard men', and made far fewer than the usual quota of beginners' mistakes.

The War Office's first demands arrived a day later. They wanted 500 LOPs on silk or waterproof paper, and 300 WOKs.

We promised to supply them within a fortnight at the latest, and delivered them in less than a week.

Only one thing marred our new role in the code war.

No one was able to press a magic button for Tommy – not even Gubbins, Selborne or the 'hard men'.

Tommy's friends Brossolette and Bollaert had never been in greater jeopardy. They'd been waiting since December to be picked up from France, but the first Lysander which had been sent to collect them had been forced to turn back due to bad weather, and the replacement had been shot down. Since then no further aircraft had been available to SOE, and the two agents were still hiding in a Breton sea-port.

Tommy had urged them to wait for the January moon, when another attempt would be made to pick them up by Lysander. But the RAF had been unable (or unwilling) to mount a third operation, and Tommy was convinced that his friends wouldn't wait any longer and would risk boarding a ship.

The latest news from the field caused him even greater anxiety. Dozens of Free French agents were being arrested daily, and he was convinced that the Secret Army and the Maquis would be wiped out if they didn't receive the arms and supplies he'd promised them (the Maquisards had one rifle to every eighteen men, and were equally short of food and clothing). He'd besieged the Whitehall ministries, but had emerged with nothing but promises or outright rejection, and his failure to keep his word to those who trusted him had made him unapproachable; I had to telephone Kay Moore to ask how he was.

She was concerned about his state of mind and puzzled by his recent behaviour.

He'd begun spending whole days away from the office without saying where he'd gone and had warned her that at the beginning of February he was likely to be completely unavailable but hadn't explained why.

She was convinced that he was up to something but had no idea what. She wondered how the strain was affecting Barbara.

From 20 January onwards the Rabbit (now more grey than white) began calling at my new office as he had at my old, and I knew then that it was officially open.

On 25 January he came in at midnight as he 'just happened to be passing' and sat in silence, clutching an unlit cigar. More out of habit than inclination, he picked up one of Mother's sandwiches and allowed it to nibble away at him.

We spent a few minutes discussing the Free French code-book but for once his mind was elsewhere, and I knew that there was nothing I could say to him which would ease his sense of failure.

Turning towards the window, he stared at the iron bars (the room's brightest feature) and spoke to himself (and the Maquisards?) as if there were no one else present: 'It's the only step left open to me . . .'

He turned sharply towards me but I pretended not to have heard him, and offered him a match for his cigar.

Two days later the Rabbit took that 'only step'. He went to Downing Street and had a meeting with Churchill.

SIXTY-ONE

A Mere Squadron Leader

'I don't put much beyond our Tommy if it helps the
Free French. But to have gone all the way to the Prime
Minister on his own initiative defies belief.... The
whole of SOE is in his debt.'

(Nick to author, 3 February '44)

A student of human nature, provided it wasn't his own, Nick spent
several minutes trying to determine how a mere squadron leader had
managed to gain access to England's most sought-after ear – despite
the high-level competition for it and despite its owner's antipathy to
de Gaulle. The quality which eluded him was chutzpah.

Using his own contacts to bypass official channels, our Tommy
had stated the case for supporting the Free French to the only man
in the country in a position to sanction it. Their encounter gave SOE's
grapevine its busiest time since Hambro's resignation.

Some believed it had lasted ten minutes; others all day. Some were
convinced that Churchill had treated him coldly, others that he'd
listened carefully to his account of the Secret Army's potential, and
had assured him that he wouldn't be penalized for bringing it to
his attention by unorthodox means. But there was no disputing the
outcome of their meeting.

The Air Ministry had been instructed by Churchill to supply SOE
with 100 aircraft capable of flying 250 sorties over France every
moon period, and had already put twelve Liberators, two Halifaxes
and sixteen Stirlings at RF section's disposal. The other recalcitrant
ministries had been given similar instructions, and large quantities of

463

weapons, equipment and clothing had also been delivered, with the promise of more by the end of the month.

I waited for the announcement that Tommy was now Prime Minister and that Churchill had joined the Maquis.

I also waited for the sound of Tommy's footsteps and, as soon as I heard them a few midnights later, hastily concealed an *aide-mémoire* marked NQAC (no questions about Churchill).

I expected him to be elated by his shopping expedition, but he'd seldom been more truculent as he advanced towards me brandishing two small artefacts for concealing silks. Slamming them on the desk, he pointed out that no attempt had been made to age them, and that they'd be dangerous for agents to carry as leather goods of this type were no longer obtainable in France. Or hadn't I heard there was a war on?

His complaints were justified (they usually were), but I suspected that he was venting his anxieties about Brossolette and Bollaert, and that he'd been scouring the Signals Office for news of their whereabouts. (I knew that there was none.)

Accepting one of Dad's cigars (I was hoping he'd brief me about Churchill's), he instructed me to give the Camouflage Station 'a real bollocking' unless I preferred him to do it for me, an offer I declined with thanks.

Finally sitting down, he suggested it was time I got off my arse and gave the poor bastards who relied on me for codes a bit of service.

'Oui, mon général. Vous avez raison.'

'Translate that! I don't speak German!' His eyes hardened as he uttered the word, but a new thought seemed to occur to him and he looked at me intently.

I waited for another bollocking, but his expression had changed and I thought I glimpsed a hint of concern.

'Is anything wrong? I don't mean with your work, there always is! . . . I mean with you personally . . .'

'I'm a bit tired, that's all. Too many Free French indecipherables.'

'You're sure it's nothing else? Are your parents all right?'

I assured him that they were, and that I was simply a bit tired.

'Then pack up and go home to them – or to whoever else is waiting for you.'

Sensing my reluctance, he stood up abruptly and switched off the lights. 'If I come back in ten minutes and you're still here, there'll be hell to pay. Is that understood?'

'Ja, mein Kommandant.'

In the silence which followed I wondered what else the squadron leader had to do before they promoted him – arrest Hitler in person?

He glanced back at me as he reached the door, and once again took me by surprise. 'I was shit-scared of meeting him. . . . Never encountered such a mind. Every word was pure Havana. Tell you more when you've obeyed doctor's orders . . . thanks for asking no questions.' He closed the door quietly.

I obeyed his instructions ten minutes later, and had my worst nightmare since Christmas Eve.

I dreamed that Churchill was in danger of dying, and that Tommy was stating his case to God. Tommy offered the Lord a WOK, and then a LOP, and then himself, if Churchill could be spared. Christ and Moses were present as members of the Executive Council. Barbara was taking notes, and I was holding a copy of the FFI code-book in case Jehovah wanted that too. 'No,' said Barbara, 'Tommy's life will be enough,' and a tear fell on her notebook. A heavenly choir began chanting 'Hosanna' in Morse.

Twenty-four hours later a message from Brittany reported that Brossolette and Bollaert had been arrested. No details were known except that they'd tried to escape by sea.

A subsequent message reported that on 3 February their boat had been shipwrecked off the coast of Brittany. They'd managed to reach shore but had aroused the suspicions of a Feldgendarme as they tried to make their way inland. They were now in a local prison being questioned by the Germans.

It was the worst news for RF section and Duke Street since the death of Jean Moulin. But it was even worse for Tommy.

He knew that the dye which disguised Brossolette's famous white forelock would soon wear off, and that when it did the Germans would identify him immediately and his torture would begin. (His own already had.) He also knew that he was the only person in SOE in a position to continue his joint mission with Brossolette, on which they'd spent eight weeks together establishing a new chain of command and preparing the Resistance groups for D-Day.

He informed his colleagues that he intended to return to France in the next moon period. He also informed them (though he had no need to) that he would try to rescue Brossolette before his dye wore off.

Dismore did his best to remind him that his own security was blown as the Gestapo had circulated a detailed description of Shelley (his field-name) and had put a high price on his head. He also pointed out that he mustn't feel responsible for Brossolette's capture as he'd been warned not to attempt to escape by sea.

Passy used much the same arguments on behalf of Duke Street, but had no more success than his Baker Street counterpart.

The grapevine once again went into action.

I learned from Charlotte (our in-house expert on French affairs) that Dismore and Passy had met privately to discuss Tommy's return. They agreed that his presence in France would be invaluable as he was so widely trusted, and that he'd soon restore morale. Their overriding problem was the extent of his knowledge, and the possibility that he'd crack under torture, though they hadn't said so to him. They finally decided that his capture was a risk that had to be taken, and that they should give him all the help they could.

Churchill (who'd written to Selborne, 'Pray keep me informed about Yeo-Thomas') was reported to have exhaled the view that he shouldn't yet return to France but should be prevailed upon to take whatever decision 'would best enable him to serve his country the longest', but he declined to intervene.

So did Gubbins, and it seemed to RF section and Duke Street that the final decision was being left entirely to them, in accordance with standard procedure.

But they'd reckoned without the Signals directorate.

The only person in SOE capable of blocking Tommy's return was Nick. Since joining the Executive Council, he'd constantly maintained that country section officers who had a detailed knowledge of their agents' operations shouldn't be allowed to go into the field. (His prime target had been Bodington, who made frequent trips to France and then returned to Baker Street to resume his duties as Buckmaster's deputy before going in again. Bodington had since been sent on indefinite leave.) Although convinced that the malpractice must cease, in the debates that followed Nick reluctantly conceded that country section heads were in the best position to evaluate the information they were putting at risk, but on one point he was adamant.

He absolutely insisted that country section officers who had a detailed knowledge of their agents' codes, security checks and WT conventions should *under no circumstances* be allowed to go into the field without the express consent of the Signals directorate. He made clear that unless this happened immediately, he'd no longer accept responsibility for the security of SOE's traffic. The council had unanimously agreed to his embargo, but expressed the hope that he'd use it sparingly.

The Rabbit not only fell into Nick's forbidden category, he was also deputy head of RF section, and Nick informed the council that, much as he admired Tommy, he would categorically oppose his return to France! He was setting a precedent to prevent one from being set.

Faced with Tommy's wrath if they agreed and Nick's resignation if they didn't, the council asked Nick to put his reasons in writing in the hope that Dismore and Duke Street would accept their validity, and his green ink had already covered three pages.

I was anxious to have no part in opposing Tommy's return, but Nick instructed me to prepare a list of all the poems and security checks which he'd seen when accompanying me to briefings, as well as a detailed report on everything he'd learned about codes from his visits to my office.

Nick had given me twenty-four hours in which to complete it.

Twenty-two of these had already elapsed, and I hadn't begun.

In mid-February a new message from France reported that Brossolette had been taken to Rennes prison but hadn't yet been identified (he was posing as a Monsieur Bourdet).

The moon period was imminent, and Tommy knew that it would be his last chance to mount a rescue operation. But he also knew (like most rabbits, he kept his ears close to the ground) that the Signals directorate was trying to block his return, and he came storming into my office twenty minutes before I was due to meet Nick.

I reached for my cigar case, but he was in no mood for peace pipes and greeted me with a simple announcement: 'If you try to stop me from going in I shall never speak to you again.'

Since further conversation was unlikely if he did go in, the threat was academic and I looked at him in silence.

'I know bloody well what's going on so don't play the innocent with me. Do you people in Signals think I'm completely irresponsible and haven't thought the risks through? Christ Almighty, do you think I'm not prepared for what might happen, and don't know my limitations? I trust your judgement – have some respect for mine. Enough said?'

Taking for granted that it was, he announced that he'd be leaving in a week.

I made no comment.

'You'll be pleased to hear I don't expect to pass much traffic.'

I didn't think he would either.

Glancing at a pile of silks, he said I should start preparing his codes immediately and let him have a morning with a briefing officer as he was 'probably a bit rusty'; '. . . how long will you need for my final briefing?'

'An hour if you're in the right mood – for ever if you're not.'

He then asked how many agents I met in the course of a week – ten? – twenty?

'None at all in a good week.'

'Do you remember one named Brossolette?' His timing was pure Tommy.

I pretended to be thinking it over. 'The name seems familiar . . . Didn't you once tell me he owns a bookshop in Paris?'

'I'd like him to continue running it.' He leaned across the desk. 'Just you remember that I know sod-all about codes when you write that report . . .'

I was already late in delivering it, and glanced at my watch.

Tommy took this personally. 'Sorry to take up so much of your time. Shan't for much longer.'

He left without his cigar.

Nick was studying a lengthy document, which I suspected was his report to the council. Heffer was studying the ash on his cigarette.

I apologized for being late, and advanced towards them clutching a single sheet of foolscap.

Nick's eyebrows arched as I proffered it for inspection. 'Is this the complete list – down to the last detail?'

I assured him that it was, and laid the piece of paper in front of him. It was headed 'Yeo-Thomas'. The rest of the page was blank.

'What the devil's this?'

'A summary of his knowledge, sir. He knows nothing about codes – he can hardly remember his own poems, let alone other people's. His mind's always on something else.' I hastily added that he had no head for security checks either.

Nick controlled himself admirably. But then he'd had plenty of practice. 'I distinctly remember you telling me that he regularly attended briefings with you –'

'Attended's the wrong word, sir. He sat on the telephone while I did the briefings – he didn't even look at the agents' conventions. I still don't know why he bothered to come.'

Heffer's cigarette sighed, and ash fell like a tear on the empty page.

Nick leaned towards me, and I hoped that apoplexy wasn't infectious. 'I've lost count of the times you've told me about the indecipherables he's helped you to break – *including those of other country sections because "it's all one war to Tommy."* If you're now saying that he helped you without seeing the code conventions I'll recommend him to Bletchley.'

I looked at him in what I hoped was astonishment. 'That wasn't Tommy, sir. The most he ever did to help was make fresh coffee to keep me awake. It was one of the supervisors who lent a hand, sir, and she's gone to Massingham, I'm sorry to say.'

Heffer began lighting a new cigarette, possibly from his thoughts.

Nick put down his pen and spoke very quietly. 'Leo, I share your respect for him – but there's a limit to the torture anyone can take, and God knows how many agents we'd lose if Tommy reached breaking point. I'm going to repeat my question for the last time –'

'May I ask you one first, sir?'

He nodded.

'Didn't you say that the whole of SOE was in his debt?'

He nodded again.

'Isn't the Signals directorate part of SOE?'

'Come to the point.'

'If we're in his debt, is this the way to repay him? Stopping him from doing what he's convinced he must because he might reach breaking-point?'

I feared my words were dropping blind over enemy territory, and pulled the ripcord: 'There's only one person in the world who can crack Yeo-Thomas – and that's you, sir, if you try to prevent him from rescuing Brossolette.'

There was a long silence, especially inside me.

Nick turned towards Heffer as if he alone could break it.

The Guru obliged in mid-puff. 'There's only one solution from a Signals standpoint. Send Marks in with him to do the coding.'

'Don't tempt me,' said Nick. He closed his eyes, and I prayed that the Lord would open them.

A few seconds later he picked up my blank sheet of paper. 'In the presence of Captain Heffer I now ask you formally on behalf of the Executive Council – *whose poems does Yeo-Thomas know, whose security checks?*'

'His own, and possibly Passy's old ones. No one else's, to the best of my knowledge and belief.'

'I question your knowledge,' said Nick, 'but share your belief.'

He picked up his pen. 'I shall withdraw my objections on the grounds that I was misinformed about his knowledge. You can go.'

The least one could do for a friend was help him to kill himself.

SIXTY-TWO

Without Precedent

On 12 February I was asked by Muriel if I would accept a phone call from Commandant Manuel. Knowing that he was a senior member of the Free French hierarchy and was alleged to be Signals-minded, I took it at once.

He informed me in excellent English that he would be obliged if I would call on him at Duke Street 'at my quickest convenience'. He added that no appointment would be necessary.

Convinced it was about Tommy, I was there twenty minutes later.

He greeted me warmly, though I sensed a hint of unease. He finally said that he had some rather bad news for me: much as he admired the new silk codes, he was no longer sure that they were suitable for Free French traffic. He then produced a telegram from Archiduc stating that Circonference had been unable to decipher any of London's messages as her code (a one-time pad) had not been in her possession.

Looking at me apologetically, Manuel said that messages mustn't be delayed because the right codes were unavailable due to the danger of street searches, and he was writing to Dismore recommending that agents should abandon their silks and use only their poems until it was safer for them to carry them or they could do their coding in safe-houses.

'I wanted you to hear this from myself as you have done so much to help us, and you must not think we are not grateful.'

I thanked him for his courtesy and said I shared his concern. (I didn't tell him that a week ago the same situation had arisen with two F section agents, as Buckmaster and Duke Street didn't compare notes.)

Manuel gave his first sigh of the meeting (by Duke Street standards it was late in arriving) and said that one-time pads had been issued to so many agents that he felt the letter must be sent.

'Of course.'

I noticed a few WOKs on his desk which seemed to be winking up at me, and asked if the same objection applied to them.

He said he didn't think so because they contained enough for 200 messages on only two sheets of silk. But 200 messages on one-time pads needed twelve sheets plus a substitution square, which made them far more dangerous to carry . . . perhaps in future his agents could be given worked-out keys only?

The WOKs on his desk nodded, but I pointed out that the system had one disadvantage. Every WOK message had to contain at least 100 letters for security reasons. But one-time pads were so safe that they need contain only ten letters and the agents could then get off the air. I added that the enemy's direction-finding units cost almost as many lives as their cryptographers, and that WT operators had the most dangerous job in the field.

Manuel gave another sigh, this time garlic-flavoured, then silently handed me a sheet of paper. It was a message to Archiduc instructing him to tell Circonference that she must use her poem from now on, and that London would do the same.

'As it concerns your department, I need your agreement to send it.'

I reluctantly gave it.

'You are not happy about this?'

I tried to imitate his sigh but it came out like a hiccup. 'Commandant Manuel, nothing to do with the poem-code makes me happy. The damn thing should be used only in emergencies – and bloody great ones at that.'

He looked at me thoughtfully. 'May I be allowed to ask a stupid question?'

I was convinced he was incapable of it, but encouraged him to try.

'Why has it not been possible for you to give us a better system?'

Delighted that he'd asked (no one else had), I rattled off a few hundred reasons why it was technically difficult to produce a *safe* code which had to a) be memorized, b) be used frequently, and c) pass messages which enemy cryptographers could not anticipate. 'I've been trying for two years to find a solution.'

'But you have not given up.' It was a statement rather than a question.

'It's just possible I'm in sight of one. I'm still working on it.'

'I am sure you will succeed. But is there any chance it will be ready for our friend? It may be dangerous for him to carry silks.'

I didn't know the French for knife, though the one which sliced through my intestines was in a universal language. 'No, mon commandant – it will not be ready for Tommy.'

I decided to ease the ache of failure by admitting the extent of it, and hoped that the novelty would help: 'We have great trouble teaching agents double-transposition, though it's basically quite simple. But this new code's so damn complicated it would be easier to teach 'em calculus. In its present form I'm not even sure that I understand it myself.'

Manuel smiled sympathetically. 'I am sure you will find a way to simplify it. Would it be a help to your instructors if we allowed our agents to have longer code-training periods?'

This was an extraordinary offer – most country sections did their best to reduce them.

'It would be a very great help indeed.'

'You have only to ask me.'

There was a finality to his tone, and I realized that I'd been with him for an hour and there was nothing more to be said.

He stood up and thanked me for coming at such short notice and for being so understanding about his letter. He then held out his hand in silence, and we both shook Tommy's.

I hurried back to my office to make the new system simpler, but soon put down my pen.

I couldn't stop thinking about Tommy.

Five minutes later I made my first contribution to the ditty-box since Christmas eve:

Make the most of it
A coast to coast
Toast of it
For what you think
Has been God-sent to you
Has only been lent to you.*

The country sections never informed the Signals directorate of agents' cover-stories, rightly regarding them as strictly their business, but a grateful Dismore set a precedent and told Nick of the precautions Tommy had devised to reduce the risk of identification and torture. They were unique in the history of SOE.

He'd decided to tell the Gestapo that he was entitled to be treated as a prisoner of war as he was a member of the crew of a British aircraft which had been shot down over France! Knowing that the Germans had a copy of the air force list and could check the names of all air-crews, he'd asked the Air Ministry to put him in touch with any RAF officer who'd a) baled out over France in the past six months, b) returned to England, and c) been excluded from further operations, and they'd quickly produced one.

His name was Squadron Leader Dodkin, and Tommy visited him to learn his serial number, the operations he'd taken part in and his personal history. He then acquired a duplicate disc bearing Dodkin's name, which he intended to keep 'suitably concealed about his person' to confirm his identity in case he was searched.

But Tommy's cover-story was no more unique than his new terms of reference. He was the first Englishman to be allowed to go into France on Duke Street's behalf without being accompanied by a Free French officer. He would also be representing SOE's interests, and was virtually an Anglo-French mission of one.

He'd been code-named Asymptote (a line that continually approaches a curve but never meets it), and his brief caused no more than a hint of dissension between Dismore and Manuel, who'd jointly prepared it. The far-sighted commandant warned Dismore in writing

---

* Issued in February 1944 to Denise Bloch (Ambroise), an F section WT operator. She was executed at Ravensbruck in 1945.

that Asymptote's *ordres de mission* must in no way be regarded as a precedent as the Free French had only agreed to them because of Asymptote's 'exceptional personality'.

In the short time remaining to him, all the exceptional personality had to do was absorb the details of his new mission, learn his new cover-stories (Dodkin was only one of them), and ensure that he remembered how to jump. I knew he hadn't forgotten his coding but he spent several hours with a FANY instructress.

He telephoned me shortly afterwards to thank me for choosing such a patient one (she wished it could have lasted a week), and added that he wasn't going to wait for the next moon period but would leave for France as soon as the weather permitted. 'I'll drop in this evening for my final briefing, if that suits you?'

I assured him that his codes and cigars were ready for him.

I wished that the same could be said of me.

Tommy sat opposite me with a cigar in one hand, a pencil in the other, and a plate of Mother's finest beside him. Pushing the plate aside, he instructed me to treat him 'like any other agent', and I spent the next twenty minutes making him practise his conventions, though it was only a formality.

He was to use a LOP to keep his messages short, with a WOK in reserve. The LOP was to be concealed in a chess-set, but he hadn't yet decided where to hide his WOK (next to Dodkin's disc, perhaps?). Conceding the possibility that his silks might not always be available, he asked if 'just for luck' he could use his old Sea-horse poem in emergencies, and since he'd need all the 'merde alors' he could get, I raised no objections. Nor did I ask him to repeat it.

'That's it then.'

He lit his cigar, helped himself to a sandwich, and I knew that he'd made time for a chat.

Looking at me quizzically, he said he understood from Manuel that I'd finally produced a system which was safer than the poem-code.

'Tommy, it's still in its infancy –'

'Then it's in the right hands. Show me how it works.'

'I'm not sure that it does . . .' I wanted to change the subject but knew that if I did so the godfather of WOKs would almost certainly conclude that I no longer trusted him with the details of new codes.

'It's called a MOP.'

He looked at me in astonishment.

'Short for mental one-time pad.'

'It's also short for Marks is an old piss-pot.'

He asked for further details.

I warned him that agents would go mental if I couldn't find a way to simplify it, and began outlining its principles, but he soon held up his hand.

'Thank God I won't be around to use it.'

I noticed that he was wearing a signet-ring which I hadn't seen before, and was about to comment on it when I realized that it was a receptacle for his L-tablet.

He caught me looking at it. 'That reminds me, I have a question for you! What mustn't I tell them if I crack?'

No other agent had asked me this, and it stunned me.

'Well?' he said impatiently. 'What mustn't I tell them?'

'Where I get my cigars and your security checks – in that order.'

He glanced at the pile of WOKs and LOPs on the desk. 'Nothing else about codes? They can be very inquisitive.'

'You can tell them whatever you like about codes – they know it all anyway. Besides, nobody's going to catch you except Barbara, and the sooner she does the better.'

His face clouded over, and I'd have bitten my tongue out if I'd known where to find it.

'I hope my friends will keep her informed of whatever news comes in.' He stressed the word 'whatever'.

'You know bloody well they will.'

He glanced at his watch, and I realized that it was time for the closing ceremony.

I took one of Father's finest Corona Coronas from my cigar-case and held it up for his inspection. 'It'll be here when you get back. Unless Buckmaster takes up smoking.'

'The most he can do is smoulder. Thanks, it's a beauty . . . and I'd like to say thanks to your father. Does he still think that you work at the Labour Exchange?'

'Yes. He thinks I use 'em to bribe a supervisor.'

'So you do.'

To my surprise, he glanced at the ditty-box. 'If I do pass any traffic, would it be safer if I scrapped my Sea-horse poem and memorized one of those damn things?'

'Yes.'

'Then why haven't you tried to persuade me?'

'I did for your Arquebus mission. You weren't exactly receptive.'

'I am now. Have you got one you'd like me to use?'

I opened the ditty-box, extracted my last entry and held it out to him. 'This might do.'

He made no attempt to take it. 'Poets enjoy reading their works. Say it.'

'I'm not a poet.'

'And put that card down. If you don't know the bloody lot by heart, then my name's Buckmaster!'

'I'm sorry to say this, Maurice, but I have no heart. You sods have broken it.'

He looked at me in amusement. 'There's no need to be bashful. I'm not expecting Shakespeare.'

'Neither was Anne Hathaway.'

'Who's she – one of your coders?'

He repeated his request, this time more firmly.

I held the card in both hands as it was suddenly very heavy, and pretended to be reading from it:

> They cannot know
> What makes you as you are
> Nor can they hear
> Those voices from afar
> Which whisper to you
> You are not alone.
>
> They cannot reach
> That inner core of you
> The long before of you
> The child inside
> Deep deep inside

Which gives the man his pride.
What you are
They can never be
And what they are
Will soon be history.

He took the card from me and read it carefully. 'Can I have a copy of this?'

'You can keep that card – we have a duplicate.'

'I'll let you know if I have time to remember it. To be on the safe side I'll continue to use my Sea-horse poem, but if I ever send a message in this one you'll know I've been caught. . . . Would it need a special prefix?'

'Your Sea-horse prefix would do.'

He nodded the card in his briefcase and closed it abruptly. He then took a final glance at the pile of WOKs and LOPs waiting to be dispatched. 'Keep 'em coming, and merde alors with MOPs – but for God's sake keep 'em simple.'

'I'll tailor them for you.'

We both stood up. He put his hand on my shoulder, and looked at me in silence.

I couldn't read what his eyes were saying as mine weren't altogether in focus.

On 24 February he dropped into France.

SIXTY-THREE

Open Arrest

'Stop taking their imprisonment personally. The way
they're being handled is no concern of yours . . . it's
Holland's future that's at stake.'
(Nick to author, 1 March 1944)

We'd been discussing SOE's treatment of Ubbrinck and Dourlein,
the Dutch agents who'd escaped from Haaren prison and reported
the collapse of the Dutch Resistance to the British embassy in Berne
when they'd reached Switzerland in November.

IS YOUR JOURNEY REALLY NECESSARY? was one of London's
most widely displayed posters.

Although fair play in SOE was rare and usually the result of a
lapse in concentration, I was hoping that both men would be given
the benefits of whatever doubts existed in the minds of those purblind
enough to have any. I should have known better.

They'd arrived in London on 1 February and amplified their
accounts of the German penetration, but their N section interrogators
preferred to believe the warnings from Holland that the Gestapo had
'turned' them and allowed them to escape to spread disinformation;
they'd been sent to a holding camp in Guildford under open arrest.
By early March they were still incarcerated, and were likely to remain
so until Giskes lost his creative flow. Nor did yet another change of
leadership in N section enhance their chances of being released.

Bingham had been dispatched to Australia (hopefully to the Out-
back), and Major Dobson of the Belgian section had taken his place.
Whereas Bingham believed everything, Dobson believed nothing, and
his responses to Ubbinck and Dourlein were as guarded as 84's to

the Revenue. (Three more agents had escaped from Haaren in November but Dobson was so suspicious of alleged escapees that none of them had been allowed to return to England.)

Having been given the most unenviable job in SOE (with the possible exception of mine.), Dobson inevitably approached his new directorate with an eye to damage control. He was as suspicious of the traffic from Holland as he was of the escapees, and the Dutch situation was deadlocked, with the emphasis on the dead.

German aircraft were dropping bombs on London as if they were mounting a blanket attack on an indecipherable which had to be broken. It was clear that these raids were little more than target practice and that far worse was to come. As a precaution, all code records had been duplicated and stored in the country.

RF section and Duke Street had also taken action. Knowing that Tommy listened avidly to news bulletins from London and would be worried about Barbara's welfare, they sent weekly messages to him over the BBC assuring him of her safety.

They had even more reason to be concerned about his. He'd landed at night near Clermont-Ferrand with a saboteur named Trieur, and within twenty-four hours they'd left the area and boarded a train for Paris (200 miles away). As soon as they'd reached the capital, he'd found a safe flat for Trieur, and spent his first days questioning Resistance Movement leaders about the latest situation in Paris, Tours and Brittany. Finding their morale low (SOE's expanded dropping operations had only recently begun), he assured them that large quantities of arms and supplies were on their way to all parts of France, that more would be following, and that the invasion *would* take place.

He'd discovered through his trusted friend Maud (who was on 'friendly terms' with a German official) that Brossolette and Bollaert were in Rennes prison, and that the Gestapo still believed that Brossolette was Pierre Bourdet.

On 1 March he'd left Paris with Maud, and was now in Rennes reconnoitring the prison and finalizing his plans. The entire Brittany organization had been put at his disposal for the rescue attempt.

Manuel believed it would be another two weeks before Brossolette's dye wore off. Less of an optimist, Dismore thought it might last another one.

I accompanied Tommy on his journey to Rennes, and then embarked on a rescue operation which could no longer be postponed.

The last promise I'd made him was to simplify MOPs.

The fundamental purpose of a mental one-time pad was to make its code-groups so closely resemble those of a real LOP that the enemy wouldn't attempt to break them. And even if they learned of the subterfuge from a captured agent they would still find the code-groups troublesome to break.

If the mechanics of MOPs could be simplified, they'd be stable-companions to our other deception scheme (Gift-horse), which made WOK-messages look as if they'd been passed in poems to tempt enemy cryptographers to waste their precious time attacking them. The difference was that MOP messages were designed to deter them from trying.

But there was one technical problem, which was the cryptographic equivalent of getting Brossolette out of Rennes. Enemy cryptographers could identify genuine LOP code-groups at a glance because of the preponderance of consonants. And those same deadly eyes could just as easily identify transposition traffic because of the preponderance of vowels. Since MOPs were based on transposition, a way had to be found to make their code-groups contain the requisite number of uncommon consonants.

To achieve this, an agent would have to memorize two poems, and be taught how to make a substitution square, without which no one-time pad could function. His nightmare would then begin.

He'd have to choose five words from poem A, and obtain a transposition-key in the normal way. But instead of encoding a message in it, he'd encode the whole of poem B and use the resulting code-group as his one-time pad! Suppose his message were:

WHOEVER DEVISED THIS FUCKING SYSTEM SHOULD BE SHOT.

If he encoded it in a poem or WOK his code-groups would be:

SEOLI CTIBN SEFEI WOVEH DDTEU SEDGS UDEOH TRSEU VUKHH.

But if he used a MOP the code-groups would be:

ZVKML PDYYQ XRRUV FXLLT KZPNT DSWLD APPLZ ORTTY PKHGW.

(If the latter didn't convince the Germans that he'd used a one-time pad then I deserved to be shot.)

Putting aside the 'deceptive element', the system was secure enough to allow short messages to be passed in it (the shorter the better), but even twenty letters could take more than an hour to encode. I stumbled on a way to cut the time in half, but it still remained a laborious process even in ideal working conditions with no Gestapo but Nick prowling outside.

Anxious to test it on some suitable victims, I explained the system to six expert coders and three renowned plodders, and asked them to encode a lengthy MOP message.

The six experts included the phenomenal Ensign Hornung, who found nothing too difficult except being at ease. But even she had to agree with her fellow-experts that the system was far too complicated and would cause endless indecipherables (including their own), and that the average coder would take for ever to learn it. They then retired to their less taxing duties.

I suddenly realized that the three plodders were still ploughing on. Although I was convinced that they had no idea what they were doing, the least I could do was wait for them to finish, and I spent the next thirty minutes pretending to be breaking an indecipherable while I watched them in silence. They finished simultaneously (a knack of plodders), and handed me their messages as if reluctant to part with them. I checked them in their presence (making three mistakes in the process), and to my astonishment discovered that every message had been flawlessly encoded.

But the miracle didn't end there. They all volunteered to try another MOP message 'as it was really rather fun reaching the end'.

I was tempted to hug them but consulted Heffer instead.

The Guru had no difficulty in explaining the phenomenon as he was one himself. Using the analogy of the tortoise and the hare (which he probably originated), he said that in his experience plodders were able to cope with complex processes like MOPs because their minds didn't race ahead, and each step gave them a feeling of accomplishment, whereas experts needed to find short cuts to prove that they were experts. He added that he'd sooner be operated on by a plodding surgeon than an expert, which made me wonder which part of his anatomy had been.

Still doubting the system's practical value, I decided to test it on a group of briefing officers and training-school instructors, giving them no warning of what to expect.

I wasn't surprised when they pronounced MOPs far too cumbersome to be taught to average agents in the limited time at their disposal, if at all. But one of the instructresses reluctantly agreed to try them on her present batch of pupils, who'd finished their training and were filling in time.

I wanted to sit at the back of the room to monitor her presentation but decided that my presence might put her off, and that I could well be identified as the creator of the system.

She telephoned two days later to ask if I'd like her to come to London to tell me the results in person, and I at once agreed, though I suspected she fancied a shopping expedition.

Of the six agents she'd Mopped, two had given up in despair and one had gone to bed with a headache from which he had yet to recover. But the other three had decided that although it was extremely hard work, they'd like to practise the system as they wanted to use it in the field.

Astounded, I saw the agents long before I was due to in the hope of discovering what had prompted their decision.

They had no hesitation in telling me. They felt that one-time pads were so simple to use that they couldn't possibly be safe, whereas MOPs were so complicated that no one could break them.

Recovering from my astonishment, I disabused them, and they promised to use MOPs only in emergencies. But their answer made me realize that other agents might be under the same misapprehension, and I made a mental note that in future no agents were to be considered fully briefed until they understood why one-time pads were unbreakable, with WOKs a second-best.

I also decided that MOPs should be taught to carefully selected agents once their normal training was finished, and that the ultimate decision as to whether to use them must be theirs.

I sensed that MOPs would have some place in the code war, if only for the wrong reasons.

On 8 March Nick left for India on a tour of inspection, and Heffer took his place. Nick's last instruction was to keep him informed about Tommy's progress.

Messages from France reported that in mid-March Brossolette had been identified by the Germans, and had been transferred from Rennes prison to Gestapo headquarters in the Avenue Foch. He'd tried to escape by jumping through a window, but had fallen five storeys and was dead. (Duke Street believed he'd committed suicide to escape further torture.)

Reports about Tommy arrived shortly afterwards. He'd returned to Paris to complete his plans for rescuing Brossolette from Rennes. Unaware that his friend was lying on a slab only a few streets away from him, he'd gone to the Paris Métro on the morning of the 21st to meet a contact, and had been arrested by the Germans. He was now in the hands of the Gestapo in the Rue des Saussailes.

I prayed that he'd swallow his L-tablet before they realized who he was.

Barbara had been told of his capture.

Duke Street had informed de Gaulle.

Selborne had notified Churchill.

Merde alors, Tommy.

> They cannot know
> What makes you as you are
> Nor can they hear
> Those voices from afar
> Which whisper to you
> You are not alone.

SIXTY-FOUR

Misgivings

A captured agent's first task, and frequently his last, was to withstand forty-eight hours of interrogation in all its forms to allow the rest of his circuit time to go underground. Tommy always warned agents that if they were caught, 'those first forty-eight hours' would be the hardest to endure.

He'd been in the hands of the Gestapo for seventy-two.

RF section and Duke Street suspected that he'd been betrayed by a fellow-agent. They also feared that he'd been identified as Shelley.

On 10 March Delhi HQ informed Heffer that he was to remain in charge of Signals for at least a fortnight while Nick completed his inspection of India's WT stations.

The Guru took his new responsibilities in his stroll, arriving even later than usual, leaving even earlier, and exuding even more smoke rings.

His first official act was to call a meeting of all department heads to discuss our preparations for the invasion of France. The first few hours were taken up with technical wireless problems, including the allocation of new frequencies, the introduction of new signal-plans, and the distribution of D-Day traffic between our three stations.

I was the last to be called upon as it was believed that all was well with the code department.

Unfortunately it wasn't.

I'd realized, hopefully in time, that there were major flaws in our contribution to Overlord, and was obliged to tell my colleagues that we now had to discuss two problems which not only affected our D-Day traffic but could have repercussions far beyond it.

I was convinced that unless we took immediate precautions, the huge increase in our French traffic between now and D-Day couldn't fail to alert the enemy that we were organizing mass uprisings all over France, and might even blow the imminence of Overlord.

My second worry was the use of BBC messages to agents in the field.

Taking first things first, if only for the novelty, I suggested that one way to disguise the growth of our traffic would be to start flooding the air with dummy messages which would be transmitted round the clock to every part of Europe. Each message would be encoded in a WOK, LOP or poem, and would be indistinguishable from our genuine traffic.

This minor undertaking was enthusiastically received, and Heffer allowed me forty-eight hours in which to present him with the details.

I then disclosed at length why I believed that the BBC's *en clair* messages to agents had become a major security risk (responsibility for vetting them was vested in our liaison officer with the BBC).

They agreed that my misgivings were thoroughly justified, and that a solution must be found as soon as possible.

Since I was the one who'd raised the problem, Heffer allowed me the same forty-eight hours in which to solve it, and I asked if I could be excused from the rest of the meeting (it seemed likely to last until well after D-Day).

Someone whispered, 'Lucky sod' as I hurried from the room.

But then he didn't know the extent of the problem I'd just talked myself into.

The idea of BBC announcers reading short *en clair* messages to agents in the field had been conceived in 1941 by George Bégué, the first SOE agent to be parachuted into France.

Bégué (who'd escaped from a Vichy prison in '42 and was now Captain Noble of F section) had been given a poem-code and an elementary WT set, and dropped into the Châteauroux area to communicate with London. He'd soon discovered that the Germans were jamming his traffic, that their direction-finding vans were scouring the vicinity, and that he was risking his life every time he came on the air. He'd also realized that many of London's messages consisted of instructions to carry out orders he'd already been given. Anxious not to use his set if he could possibly avoid it, he'd suggested to London that their last-minute instructions to him could safely be conveyed in short prearranged phrases, whose meaning only he and F section would know. If London agreed, he would listen every night to the BBC's foreign service until these phrases were broadcast.

His concept of 'personal messages' was at once adopted, and rapidly spread to every country section in SOE. Since then, short plain-language messages had become an integral part of agents' communications, and were currently being used to confirm safe-houses, passwords and dropping operations, substantially reducing an operator's air-time.

They also fulfilled a function which Noble hadn't foreseen. They enabled agents in the field to say to those whose help they badly needed but who doubted their bona fides, 'Make up a short message – it doesn't matter what – and I'll arrange for it to be broadcast a week from now on the BBC's foreign service.' The results of this offer never failed to produce the desired effects, and often enabled agents to borrow large sums of money on the lender's assumption (not always well founded) that London would repay the advance when the war was over.

These all-important phrases had been christened 'iodoforms' by someone in Baker Street with a classical education, though it was hard to guess his identity.

A typical iodoform was 'Je ne regrette rien', and a typical Signals problem was that the agent it was intended for had to be aware of its significance; the only way London could convey it to him was through WT messages which he'd then have to acknowledge.

There was no danger in this if WOKs and LOPs had been used, but if the details were transmitted to him in a poem-code (as so many iodoforms were) the agent was likely to have beaucoup to regret. If the enemy had broken his poem, they'd know the meaning of his 'personal messages' and be in a position to take appropriate action.

And there was another danger: even if they hadn't broken his code, if they scoured his traffic for the words of iodoforms they suspected were his, their anagrammers would have a field-day, and the life of the poem would soon be over. And the agent's with it.

But an even greater nightmare was rapidly taking shape.

I'd been told by Nick that shortly before D-Day SOE intended to use iodoforms to instruct Secret Armies and agents that it was time to break cover and cause maximum havoc in every way they could. I'd been too preoccupied with recruitment problems to point out that a) even on D-Day dozens of agents would still be using poem-codes, either because we'd failed to deliver silks to them or because they'd mislaid them, and that b) if the D-Day iodoforms had been pre-arranged in broken poems, the enemy would not only know that Overlord was imminent, they might be able to pinpoint where the landings would take place.

I didn't need forty-eight hours to decide what had to be done.

But I wondered what else we experts had missed.

Seated at Nick's desk as if he were there for the duration, the Guru began the most important conversation we were ever likely to have by instructing me to present my ideas as succinctly as possible as he had to leave the office early.

Trying to sound casual, I said that the code department's contribution to concealing the spiralling volume of our traffic would be to supply the stations with 10,000 dummy code-groups a week for transmission round the clock to all parts of Europe. I then reminded him (not because he needed to be reminded but because I liked saying it) that each message would be encoded in a WOK, LOP or poem, and would be indistinguishable from our genuine traffic, and stressed that the sooner these dummy transmissions started the better.

The Guru expressed concern about the extra work dummy traffic would cause coders and WT operators.

I replied that I couldn't answer for the WT operators but I could for the coders and pointed out that to simulate LOP-traffic, the girls had only to copy out the code-groups of a one-time pad, and hand them over for transmission.

But I conceded that simulating WOK and poem-code traffic would be a very different matter: all such messages were the product of double-transposition, and if their code-groups didn't contain the correct proportion of vowels and consonants they'd be recognized as counterfeit. Since we couldn't devise the texts ourselves, we'd have to rely on the country sections to compose large numbers of dummy messages as if they were genuine, but I doubted if they'd agree to this request without considerable pressure.

The Guru expressed his gratification at the prospect of applying it, and undertook to call a meeting of the country section heads to explain what was required of them.

Glancing at his watch, he announced with a sigh that it was time we dealt with iodoforms. He agreed that it was impossible to dispense with them, and was relieved when I admitted that the only suggestion I could make about concealing their growth was to introduce dummy iodoforms immediately.

I added that even though the BBC surrounded our iodoforms with other 'personal messages' (some genuine, the rest dummy), there weren't nearly enough of them, and their quantity must be doubled, though it would mean asking for extra air-time.

He immediately undertook to contact Major Buxton (our liaison officer with the BBC) to ensure that we got it. He then glanced at his overflowing in-tray, and silently conveyed that the meeting was over.

But I had bad news for him. 'There's just one more problem . . .'

'There always is with you. Well? What is it?'

'A lot of the dummy traffic would have to be Free French.'

'Well? What of it?'

'Valois may not like the idea of dummy messages, and his word is law in Duke Street – just as yours is with us. What can we do if he won't co-operate?'

'I shall leave Valois to you,' he announced magnanimously.

He had just enough energy to point to the door.

Passy, Manuel and Valois were all convinced of Valois's brilliance, and for once I agreed with them completely.

The French wizard and I had had no further disputes since he'd stopped needing secret code prefixes, though he still believed that the outcome of the Signals war depended on radios and signal-plans, with codes bringing up the rear, preferably someone else's. It would be the first time we'd met without Kay Moore having to act as our interpreter (his English was on a par with my French) but I knew that if we didn't speak the same language now we never would.

He rose from behind a desk even more cluttered than mine, and I had no difficulty in understanding his opening remark. 'Ah, Tommee.' he said, and shook his head sadly.

I accepted a cup of his atrocious coffee, and thanked him for seeing me at such short notice but we had a 'très important problem que the deux of us must discutez'.

He appeared to get the drift of this. 'Problème, Monsieur Marks? Quel problème? What is it?'

I expounded 'le problème de our growing traffic et le need pour dummy messages' as succinctly as I could, but five minutes later caught him looking at me in such total bewilderment that I was about to telephone Kay Moore for assistance when something in his eyes stopped me.

Shaking his head as if to remove the droppings of my pigeon-French, he explained in Valois-English that he'd been thinking of telephoning me to suggest dummy traffic but wasn't sure how I'd respond.

I accepted another cup of coffee because it was suddenly delicious, and we spent the next hour discussing 'le problème', which we approached from completely different viewpoints.

Many of his ideas for misleading the enemy, such as using variable frequencies at irregular intervals with identical call-signs, were completely beyond me, and mine for making some messages look easy to break meant little to him. But one thing was clear to both of us: we were speaking the same language. We were both convinced that the dummy traffic should start as soon as possible, and he promised that his Duke Street colleagues would provide suitable texts.

I didn't know the French for 'keep stumm' but had no difficulty in convincing him that the less we said to our respective chiefs about our little tricks the better. He also agreed that to facilitate our phone-calls we should give the dummy traffic a code-name only he and I would know. I tried to persuade him to choose one but he insisted on leaving the code-name to me.

I remembered his opening remark. 'How about calling it "R. Tommee"?' I suggested.

It was unanimously adopted.

On 26 March we learned that Tommy had been transferred to Fresnes prison.

Perhaps it was coincidence, but later that night we transmitted our first batch of 'R. Tommee' messages.

SIXTY-FIVE

'The Life that I Have'

One of the most novel experiences in SOE was to receive a phone call from a country section head admitting he was wrong, but Maurice Buckmaster phoned on 23 March and apologized to me for 'making another gaffe'.

He admitted that he'd mistakenly believed that one of his trainee agents, who'd been taught codes at training school, would have no use for them whatever when she reached the field, and he'd excluded her from the list of agents due for refresher courses in London. Her code-name was Louise, and she was to have been dropped into France in mid-march with Maurice Southgate to act as his courier, but their drop had been postponed until April because of the weather.

He and Southgate had since decided it might be useful if Louise could use encoded messages in an emergency. Could she possibly be given a refresher course immediately, and would I give her a final code-briefing as soon as I could?

I agreed to send an instructress to Orchard Court within the next ten minutes, and to give Louise a final briefing later in the week.

He phoned again the next morning to thank me for the instructress, and to say he'd made another mistake. Louise might not be in London for more than a couple of days. Could I possibly give her a final briefing at once?

Although I was used to briefing his women agents (they included Noor, Odette and an Australian boomerang named Nancy Wake), I was still uneasy in their presence and needed adequate warning to practise growing-up, but Maurice pressed me for an answer and I reluctantly agreed to see Louise in an hour.

I then remembered that most women agents seemed slightly more approachable when I addressed them by their real names, and I asked him what hers was.

'Violette Szabo,' he said, and hung up to take another call.

According to her instructress's report, Violette had no problems with her WOK but was careless with her poem-code, and seemed unable to number her transposition keys without making mistakes. More practice was recommended.

I stood outside Orchard Court for ten minutes to sharpen my inner ear and convince myself that the code war's only problem was helping Louise, then opened the door of the briefing room.

A dark-haired slip of mischief rose from behind a desk which Noor had once occupied, held out her hand, and smiled.

It seemed inappropriate for the head of Codes to mark the occasion by singing 'Every little breeze seems to whisper Louise', so I shook her hand in silence.*

Resuming her seat, she picked up a WOK which was lying in front of her and declared the proceedings open. 'I like this code,' she said, 'but Colonel Buckmaster thinks it won't be safe for me to carry it. I had such a good place to hide it, too.' She had a cockney accent, which added to her impishness.

Professor Higgins instructed Eliza Doolittle to encode a WOK message at least 200 letters long.

She complied at once (everything about her was immediate, especially her impact) and I watched her covertly, though I suspected she knew it.

She was the first agent whose exact age I wanted to know (she was clearly in her early twenties), and I wondered what this had to do with the job in hand, and what my inner ear was up to.

She finished encoding her message in under twenty minutes (which put her in Knut Haugland's class if she'd enciphered it correctly), and I picked it up to check it.

'Oops sorry,' she said. She then snatched it back and inserted her

---

* This song, which Maurice Chevalier made famous in the early thirties, was Archambault's reserve poem. Several other agents had asked permission to use it, but it was a case of first come, first disserved.

security checks (she had to change her printed indicator-groups by adding one to every first letter and four to every third).

Our hands touched as she returned the message, and I was tempted to say, 'Oops sorry' for what I was thinking. I tried to concentrate on her message.

It was flawlessly encoded, and contained 200 letters instead of the minimum of 100 I'd stipulated (the only other agent to have enciphered more letters than strictly necessary was Knut Haugland). It was also in a mixture of English and French, a security precaution most trainees forgot, and she'd signed off 'that's all for now' (even experienced agents still clung to 'message ends'). Her dummy letters didn't contain a single 'x' or 'z', and seemed on the verge of spelling a swear-word. I realized that she was intelligent as well as quick-witted and said a silent prayer that she wasn't also telepathic.

I warned her that she must cut away the keys from her silk as soon as she'd used them.

'I don't think I could – silk is so expensive.'

'So is a captured agent if her back traffic can be read.'

She promised that she'd will herself to do it.

I then asked her to encode a message in her poem, and to make sure it contained at least 200 letters.

She took a deep breath, then wrote out five words from her poem as if each one soiled the paper, and proceeded to number them.

I glanced at her code-card. Her poem was in French, and seemed to be a nursery rhyme based on 'Three Blind Mice'.

She certainly behaved like one as she scurried from letter to letter trying to number her key-phrase. She finally succeeded, and thirty minutes later handed me her message for checking. It was exactly 200 letters long.

I handed it back without making contact, and asked her to decode it herself. I knew it was indecipherable long before I heard her muttering something in French which was considerably more substantial than 'Oops sorry'.

'It won't come out.' She looked at me in despair. 'Why do I keep making mistakes?'

She thumped her forehead: 'Pourquoi, pourquoi, pourquoi?'

I asked her to encode a second message while I tried to find out pourquoi.

'But I'm taking up so much of your time.'

'I've got all day,' I said. And hoped that I'd need it.

'If I get it wrong this time I'll ...' She finished the sentence in French, then snatched up her pencil and began her new assault while I examined the indecipherable.

She'd misspelt one of the five words she'd chosen from her poem, which threw out the whole of her transposition-key. I waited until Little Miss Skinnarland had finished her new message, and pointed out what she'd done.

'But the code's so easy. Why can't I get it right?' She thrust her new effort at me without waiting for an answer, but I again insisted that she decoded it herself.

A pounding on the desk announced the result. 'I've done it again. It won't come out.'

Her pencil snapped in two, and her face snapped with it from the weight of self-disgust.

I took the message from her before she could tear it up, and rapidly checked it. 'You've misspelt your poem again. 'Trois' should have an 's' on it.'

She muttered something like 'C'est pas possible', and looked at me despairingly. 'If Colonel Buckmaster hears about this he may not let me go in.'

'He won't hear about it because we're going to get it right.'

'But how?'

A sensible question. Her only mistakes had been to misspell the words of her poem, and she'd done this consistently. Since Freud believed that all mistakes were unconsciously motivated and I believed Freud, I wondered if she were reacting against the poem because it had unconscious associations for her.

Professor Dr Sigmund Marks asked whether she'd chosen it herself or whether the training school had issued it to her.

'I chose it. It's a nursery rhyme I learned at school and I know it backwards. Why?'

I explained that some agents who were otherwise good coders often made spelling mistakes in their key-phrases, and we'd found that they weren't really happy with their poems, though they didn't always know why.

She considered the matter carefully. 'I hadn't thought of it that way.' Her expression was troubled, and she seemed to have left Orchard Court for some childhood briefing room.

She returned a few moments later to the poem-bound present. 'I shouldn't have chosen it. I couldn't spell it as a child, and I still can't . . . I'd like to change it but I suppose it's too late.'

'Do you know any others?'

'They're all nursery rhymes, and I'd feel so stupid if I used one – I know I would. . . . Look, let me try another message . . .'

'How about trying another poem?'

'*Could I?*'

'Are you a quick learner?'

'I am at some things, but they're nothing to do with codes.'

The imp was back, and looked at me appealingly. 'Do you know a poem you'd like me to try?'

For the first time since Xmas Eve I thought of the words which had occurred to me on the roof of Norgeby House. I wrote them in block capitals on a sheet of squared paper, and checked the spelling before handing them over.

I then did what I could to descend from the roof.

An aircrash or two later I heard a tiny intake of breath, and turned to look at her. She was speaking the words to herself, and I felt I was intruding on her privacy.

She finally looked up at me. 'I could learn this in a few minutes. I promise you I could.'

'You're sure you want to?'

'Oh yes. Oh yes. I almost know it now.'

'Well then . . . take those few minutes, then encode two messages in it. I'll come back this time tomorrow and go through them with you.'

She promised she'd be ready.

At least I had a good reason for seeing her again.

She stood up when I entered the briefing room, waiting until I was seated opposite her, then made a simple statement of fact:

The life that I have
Is all that I have
And the life that I have
Is yours.

The love that I have
Of the life that I have
Is yours and yours and yours.

A sleep I shall have
A rest I shall have
Yet death will be but a pause.

For the peace of my years
In the long green grass
Will be yours and yours and yours.

It was she who broke the silence. 'Who wrote this?'

'I'll check up, and let you know when you come back.'

I had a gut feeling that she wasn't going to, and busied myself checking the two messages she'd encoded. Each was 300 letters long, and there wasn't a single mistake in either.

Not knowing if she'd been up all night encoding them, I asked her to encode another message in front of me. '200 letters will be enough.'

She set to work at once, and produced a 200-letter message in under fifteen minutes. It was perfectly encoded.

I congratulated her, finalized her security checks, and reminded her to cut away the keys of her silk. I wasn't sure how to say 'that's all for now' because for me it certainly wasn't, but she solved the problem.

'I've got a present for you.' She fumbled in her handbag and produced a miniature chess-set which she said she'd won at a shooting-gallery.* Holding it out shyly, she said she thought that people who

---

* I also discovered that she was the deadliest shot her training school had yet encountered. Since she rarely had enough money to buy cigarettes she used to win them at shooting galleries.

invented codes were sure to play chess and she'd like me to have it for all the help I'd given her.

I tried to thank her for giving me a first edition of Caxton's *Game and Playe of Chesse* (which was how it felt), but she gently interrupted to say that she was late for an appointment with Vera Atkins, who wanted to check everything she was taking in with her.

I told her I looked forward to playing chess with her when she returned from France, and she said she'd like that too as it would give her time to learn it.

I unlocked the special drawer in my desk and put her chess-set between my other prize possessions: Rabinovitch's photograph of Joe Louis's left hook and Tommy's cigar.

I then surrendered the words of the poem to Muriel as they'd formally become a code.

I didn't think Ruth would mind.

SIXTY-SIX

April Fool's Day

Like all organizations riddled with the stress which they were trying to inflict on others, SOE was full of practical jokers (some of them aware of it) and on 1 April I was relieved to discover that I was sufficiently well regarded to be targeted as an April fool.

That was my first impression when I received an urgent call on the scrambler from Ken Howell (chief signalmaster at 53b), who was anxious to read a message to me which had just been received from Holland in plain language over the Heck/Blue set.

By the end of the first sentence I realized that the catch in his voice was unlikely to be confected as he was neither an actor nor a politician, and I listened in silence till he'd finished.

I then asked him to read it again and teleprint the message to London.

MESSRS BLUNT,* BINGHAM AND SUCCS LTD., LONDON.
IN THE LAST TIME YOU ARE TRYING TO MAKE BUSINESS IN THE NETHERLANDS WITHOUT OUR ASSISTANCE STOP WE THINK THIS RATHER UNFAIR IN VIEW OUR LONG AND SUCCESSFUL CO-OPERATION AS YOUR SOLE AGENTS STOP BUT NEVER MIND WHENEVER YOU WILL COME TO PAY A VISIT TO THE CONTINENT YOU MAY BE ASSURED THAT YOU WILL BE RECEIVED WITH SAME CARE AND RESULT AS ALL THOSE YOU SENT US BEFORE STOP SO LONG
1 April 1944, sent on HECK/BLUE set.

---

* The name Blunt had been used by Major Blizzard as a pseudonym when he was head of N section.

The identical message had been transmitted by ten other agents, including Ebenezer, Parsnip, Turnip and Beetroot. 53b had acknowledged four of them but on Heffer's instructions had ignored the rest.

I learned from Muriel (queen of the grapevine) that Nick had walked into his office and that a copy of Giskes's message (he had no need to sign it) was waiting on his desk.

I realized what a bastard I was for feeling even a moment's elation at being proved right, but this wasn't the moment to dwell on my more endearing characteristics. It was time to concentrate on Giskes's, and I compiled a list of questions, knowing that only he could answer most of them.

What did he gain by confirming over ten channels that we were kaput in Holland when he must know that even we would realize that our Belgian escape routes must also be blown, and that many Belgian agents were under arrest?

Had he decided that London was so suspicious of him that there was no longer any point in trying to deceive us? If so, what had caused him to make this decision?

Was it the cessation of dropping operations? Or the arrival in London of Ubbrinck and Dourlein? Or the impossibility of answering N section's questions?

Was his message designed to discredit SOE with the Chiefs of Staff? Or had he sent it for career considerations? Was it better for him in the eyes of his superiors to cease contact with us before we broke it off with him?

As for Signals, had he learned of the existence of WOKs and LOPs and realized that London's indecipherable to Boni (Plan Giskes) was a trap he'd walked into?

Had he learned of the exchange of 'Heil Hitler' call-signs?

I looked up to find Nick watching me from the doorway. He said that he wanted to talk to me as soon as he'd finished a council meeting. Although his eyes watered so frequently that we referred to him as Niagara Nick, I was certain that the liquid trickling down his nose was caused by defective vision concerning Holland.

I realized that the more time I wasted, the greater Giskes's triumph would be, and resumed my efforts to prepare for D-Day.

*   *   *

On the night of 5 April, Violette and Philippe Leiwer (Southgate) boarded an aircraft and were dropped near Chatêau Dun.

It would be Ruth's first trip to France.

SIXTY-SEVEN

The New Boys

By mid-April the Americans were communicating so freely with us, and we with them, that it was hard to believe we were allies. Until exposed to them in bulk, all I really knew about their mother-country was that it contained many of 84's best customers, and that Spencer Tracy (the finest actor I'd seen apart from Heffer in a hurry) was born there.

But the OSS were a nostalgic lot, and after a series of late-night sessions with them I could have gone shopping in New York, or brothel-hunting in LA, and knew where to find an honest game of bridge in Washington.

On less serious matters, they were appalled to learn of our acute shortage of silk, and had promised to deliver large quantities from the States, 'even if it meant stripping Mae West's tits'. The first consignment had already arrived.

An even more welcome surprise was their ability to run their own wireless station (53c), with Americans manning the radio sets and a FANY-staffed room from which was controlled by an assiduous young captain named Phoenix.

None of us believed that the new boys would be capable of taking over the Scandinavian traffic from 53b without serious consequences, but throughout the two months in which they'd been handling it not a single SOE agent had suffered from their inexperience. Nor had any of the FANYs who'd queued up to be exposed to it.

Our joint Jedburgh operations would be their ultimate test as the traffic would be handled entirely by them, and they'd have only their own mistakes to learn from.

One of our few remaining reservations was their concept of

security. They may have been teasing us (one of their favourite relax-ations) but a rumour had reached Nick that they'd invited *Time Magazine* to visit 53c and photograph its interior. Believing them capable of any indiscretion provided it was great enough, he'd gently informed them that although he had nothing against the magazine he was a little concerned about its circulation and its effect on General Gubbins's.

No matter what differences arose between us, they were promptly settled by Commander Graveson (their head of Signals), usually in our favour.

'Gravy' held frequent meetings with Nick, and I had to attend several of them. They were arduous affairs: Gravy found it hard to believe that when Nick closed his eyes it wasn't because he'd dozed off out of boredom, or had given up in despair at the Americans' stupidity, but because he was communing with his private WT stations.

It was at Gravy's instigation that I was invited to give a lecture at his sacrosanct Grosvenor Square headquarters for the benefit (he hoped) of the main-line coders who knew 'damn-all' about agents' traffic. It would also be attended by some OSS staff officers, who knew even less.

I was admitted the following day to a building so innocuous that only the enemy would suspect what it contained, and escorted to a large lecture room, where fifty or so of our unfortunate saviours awaited whatever was about to be inflicted on them in the name of Anglo-American relations. Gravy explained my credentials, which didn't take long, and seated himself in the front row next to an officer whom I subsequently identified as William Casey.*

Nick, who'd recently lectured the OSS on signals and had been strangely subdued for the rest of the week, had warned me that they were a 'hard lot to talk to', and I decided to be strictly factual and make no attempt to sell myself, an altogether new departure.

I wrote out two messages of equal length on the blackboard, and invited them to help me break them.

Their responses to the parlour-game were so immediate, and their

---

* Head of the CIA during Nixon's regime but a major asset when we knew him.

guesses (even when wrong) so imaginative, that half an hour later I wanted to head-hunt the lot of them, Gravy included. They were the sharpest bunch I'd yet encountered, and had no difficulty in reconstructing the key-phrase 'Yankee Doodle Dandy'. They gazed respectfully at the silk panaceas (including the Jedburgh code-book) which I brandished aloft, but I sensed that the code war's artifacts didn't interest them as much as its humanities, and I described the FANYs' round-the-clock dedication to breaking indecipherables. There was a gasp or two when I announced that their success rate was over 90 per cent. Our briefing techniques and selection procedure were also box-office.

They kept their real perceptiveness for question-time. They were particularly interested to know what instructions I gave the girls when they aroused agents late at night to help them practise their coding. I replied that they weren't expected to give them the wrong kind of arousal, though I suspected that there would be no finer mnemonic than pussy.

A giant sergeant with a striking resemblance to Joe Louis then raised his hand and asked who was the most difficult agent I'd ever briefed personally, and to my surprise his question met with widespread approval.

'If you really want the answer, it's the hell of a long one.'

They insisted that they did.

I told them that his code-name was Lemur (his real name was Raoul Latimer), and that besides being highly intelligent and exceptionally resourceful he had the added distinction of being one of the few agents in the SOE who was both an organizer and a WT operator, which required attributes rarely found in the same individual.

He'd been taught to use a poem-code (the only system in use at the time) and dropped into Belgium in November '42 to report on the progress of the Belgian Secret Army which he was helping its zone commanders to form.

He was recalled to London in late '43 after transmitting a series of flawlessly encoded messages, and was scheduled to return to Belgium a month ago with the code-name Pandarus. His new mission was to teach untrained partisans to use codes and WT sets, start a radio network with London, and communicate with each other on D-Day. It would be a difficult enough task for an entire training school, let alone for an agent in the field.

Our problems with him began when he returned to his training school for a refresher course. His despairing instructor couldn't understand why anyone of his intelligence was unable to use a one-time pad without making mistakes which 'even the biggest idiots managed to avoid'. (I broke off to explain that even Commander Graveson had mastered a LOP in under ten minutes. I also explained that Pandarus had made an equally spectacular balls-up when he tried to use a WOK.)

I'd spent a whole morning with him making him practise both systems, but for every mistake I pointed out he made two new ones. It was a magnificent performance of sustained imbecility.* I finally gave up explaining the advances of WOKs and LOPs and asked why he was determined not to use them.

'They're too fucking dangerous to carry. Besides, they're too diffi-cult . . . I've come this far with the poem-code, and I'm bloody well going to stick with it.' He then recited three new poems, all of them in French (he was bilingual), which he already knew by heart and intended to use for his future traffic.

I reminded him that his mission was to teach codes to the partisans, and asked if he proposed to memorize all their poems.

'If I have to.'

He finally conceded that he might take a batch of microfilmed poems with him but under no circumstances would he carry silk codes, even if they were camouflaged. The Germans weren't the cunts London seemed to think they were, and he had enough trouble hiding his radio sets without walking about with half a ton of silk stuck up his arse.

I assured him that I didn't want to damage his Low Countries, and undertook to provide him with microfilmed poems on waterproof paper and leave it at that.

---

* Like many of our best agents, he had the makings of an actor, though most of our actors, with the exception of Anthony Quayle, were poor agents.

The suspicious bastard then wanted to know why I'd changed my mind so quickly.

Praying that my timing was right, because nothing else was, I admitted to him that although I'd reserved a batch of WOKs and LOPs for his partisans, I was relieved that they wouldn't be needed because they were in very short supply, and the Belgian section's priority wasn't as high as some other country sections . . .

'If you gentlemen were in your offices that morning and heard an explosion from the direction of Baker Street, it was Pandarus fighting for the rights of the Belgian partisans.'

As soon as he'd quietened down to a frenzy, he announced that I wasn't the only one who could change his mind, and that on thinking things over he'd decided that silk codes *did* keep messages shorter and *were* more secure, and he intended to take some with him just as an experiment.

I reminded him that he'd found them difficult to use.

'*Who, me?*'

He then encoded two WOK/LOP messages in close to record time without a single mistake, and half an hour later we finalized his security checks.

On 3 March he parachuted into Belgium to start a Signals course for the Secret Army. He took camouflaged silk codes with him as well as microfilmed poems, WT sets, signal-plans and crystals.

'And that, gentlemen, is the most difficult individual I've ever had to brief with the exception of a certain naval commander whose name I needn't mention.' I was convinced that they'd heard enough about Pandarus but I'd forgotten whom I was dealing with.

Three of them (including Bill Casey) wanted to know what he'd achieved in the field, and I was delighted to tell them that he'd taught over 100 freedom fighters to use WOKs and LOPs, and given them their security checks. He'd also taught them to use microfilmed poems in case of emergencies. Their first LOP messages had already reached London, and were perfectly encoded. The one-man Signals directorate had also recruited some WT operators, and was training them in a flat in Brussels. Satisfied with their progress, he'd begun issuing them with WT sets (which he'd hidden in a safe-house in Verlaine until they were needed, though I didn't say so for security reasons). He'd also given them signal-plans, crystals and codes.

There was a chorus of approval. Although I'd exceeded my scheduled time by twenty minutes (which they probably expected from an Englishman), they hadn't finished with me yet and asked a score of other questions about SOE generally. The final one came from a bemedalled major, who I ultimately discovered was head of a psychiatric unit. He wanted to know what the agents were most frightened of.

I replied that above all else they were scared of a lady dentist who had to make sure that none of their fillings were of English origin. She had also to change the impressions of their teeth before they left for the field in case the Germans had records of them. And she used continental-style Platarcke to hollow out their teeth and make cavities for L-tablets.* We had learned never to brief agents within a week either side of their appointments with her. There were a number of open mouths as I described how she did it, but I wasn't asked for her address.

I left Grosvenor Square with only one disappointment.

I'd counted on somebody spotting a serious flaw in what I'd said and questioning me about it, but no one had.

It concerned Pandarus. I'd carefully planted that he had to give security checks to other agents. But how safely could they use these checks if Pandarus was aware of them and might himself be caught? Was this SOE's idea of good security?

The day after my visit I was sent for by Nick. He held out a piece of paper in silence (never a good sign) and waited impatiently while I read it.

It was a memo from Hardy Amies (head of the Belgian section) to a senior member of the government-in-exile, whose confidence in SOE was waning:

---

* Her name was Beryl Murray-Davies, and Buckmaster made sure that his agents were taken to her Wimpole Street consulting rooms by car to ensure their arrival.

EHA/1274   M.O.1. (S.P.)

Major Hardy Amies   21st April 1944

Colonel J. Marissal,
40 Eaton Square,
S.W.1.

My dear Colonel,

PANDARUS

I thought you would be interested in the following information volunteered by our coding and signal department.

'PANDARUS has done extremely well from the signals point of view. Before he left he was briefed by signals to give MANELAUS an identity check. This was in such a form that PANDARUS himself, *if caught later by the enemy, would be unable to remember it*. The position now is that MANELAUS is using the check.

'This is the first time in SOE history that an agent recruited in the field has been given an identity check without anything passing in writing!'

The same system of identity check will, in due course, be used by the Zone Commanders when they use their own codes.

Yours sincerely,

Nick reminded me as head of Signals that he was *my* zone commander, and asked if I'd kindly tell him the secret of Pandarus's ability to forget the security checks which he had to pass on.

Astonished by its simplicity, he stared at the ceiling and muttered, 'Jesus.' (Pandarus, who'd blasphemed so frequently I was convinced he was devout, said he'd try the system out. He was the first agent to use it but unless I could find a way to vary it, was likely to be the last.)*

I hurried back to my office and wrote a UFA (unsuitable for agents) for the girls to reconstruct:

---

* I have been advised that for security reasons I must forget how it worked! Has nothing changed in fifty years except Britain's prestige?

508

She liked smiling
At strangers
And the last one
Who smiled back at her
Took her to some woods
And she was still smiling
When they found her.

She liked black horses
And would have fondled them
If she could
When they drove her to her rest
Aged eight

Will one of your staff
Please explain to her
Why you were out of your office
That day

She calls you Mister Goddy
And will smile at you too

If given the chance.

I realized that April was almost over but I might still have time to
contribute something useful.
If given the chance.

SIXTY-EIGHT

Inexcusable

On 30 April five Dutch agents (including Cricket and Swale) were dropped blind into Holland, each taking with him a LOP and a WOK with a poem in reserve.

On the same night Violette Szabo was picked up by Lysander and returned to England.

Also on the same night I realized how unlucky agents were to depend on me for their safety. I'd made a mistake which could have cost many of them their lives, and while the rest of SOE welcomed May as their last chance to prepare for D-Day (it was expected in June) I relived that mistake in case I could learn from it.

It concerned a Buckmaster agent code-named Bricklayer, whose real name was France Antelme, field-name Renault, and who, according to Charlotte, was an 'agent extraordinaire'. It was easier (and still is) to dwell on what made him extraordinary than on what I'd done to make him extinct.

In his early forties and exceedingly rich (he'd inherited sugar, tobacco and coconut plantations in Mauritius), he was an astute businessman with a large number of high-level financial, industrial and political contacts, especially in Paris. He'd been dropped into France in November '42, and returned to London in March '43. He was dropped again in May '43 and returned in July '43. In the course of these missions he'd persuaded bankers and industrialists to make substantial contributions to Resistance activities (and to set aside vast sums of currency for the invading forces), reported the collapse of Prosper to London, and been a great help to Bodington. He'd also found a safe-house for Noor Inayat Khan (Madeleine). But to Buckmaster the most important part of Antelme's activities was his efforts

510

to persuade Edouard Herriot (the former Prime Minister, and France's 'Grand Old Man') to return to England with him. If he could achieve this, it would be a major coup for F section, especially as Herriot was in close touch with the new Premier, Paul Reynaud. But Herriot had so far resisted on grounds of old age.

Determined to try again, Antelme was due to return to France in February '44. And this was the start of the code department's nightmare.

A hard man to dissuade once his mind was made up (and an awkward customer at the best of times), Anthelme had decided that he would return to a dropping ground and reception committee organized by the highly suspect Phono circuit, of which Noor was an active member. Although Buckmaster and George Noble tried to convince him that Noor was caught, and showed him the two-way traffic they'd exchanged with her in an effort to prolong her life, he refused to believe them. Nor would he accept that Phono was blown. Noble then explained that Noor had a 'special' security check which she must use only if she were caught, and showed him how it worked. But Antelme maintained that she'd used it by accident or hadn't understood the check in the first place.

Buckmaster tried to persuade him to 'drop blind' but he refused to consider it; and Maurice (anxious not to antagonize him and perhaps not quite as convinced of Noor's capture as Noble and I were) finally agreed to instruct the Phono circuit to prepare to receive Bricklayer and two other agents during the next moon period. They must also be prepared to receive fourteen containers.

Maurice then took the precaution (as he saw it) of sending in four young agents on 8 February to prepare for Bricklayer's arrival. They included an American WT operator named Robert Byerley, to whom I'd given an 'extended briefing' in the use of his one-time pad and checks. On 10 February he sent a message in his LOP confirming his safe arrival, but his security checks were wrong. Noble at once asked him a test question, to which he should have answered 'Merry Xmas'. The following day he replied, 'Happy New Year'.

Although there was no doubt that Byerley (and presumably his three companions) had been caught, Bricklayer insisted on proceeding with his plans, and on 29 February he was dropped near Chartres accompanied by his WT operator, Daks (Lionel Lee), and a young Frenchwoman (Madeleine Damerment), who was to act as his courier.

On 2 March Noor sent a message confirming that arms, radio equipment and money had been successfully dropped but that Bricklayer had severely damaged his head on landing. She amplified this a few days later by saying he'd been taken to hospital, that he was in a coma, and that according to his doctors his condition was critical.

Nothing had yet been heard from Daks, and London demanded to know why he hadn't reported the accident himself.

After another week of radio silence (an awesome sound) Daks sent a message in his one-time pad explaining that his WT set had been damaged on landing, and this accounted for the delay. He confirmed that Bricklayer had been taken to hospital and was still in a coma.

So were Daks's security checks: the code room supervisor had marked his message 'security checks incorrect' but hadn't given the details.

Knowing that he was an erratic coder who'd frequently omitted his security checks in training or substituted those of his own making, I sent for the code-groups so that I could examine them myself. Like all WOK/LOP users, he'd been taught never to transmit the indicator-groups exactly as they were printed but to change them by prearranged numbers. He was to add 4 to the second letter and 3 to the third. If he changed them by any other numbers we'd know that he'd been caught. The indicator in his first message was DBOPR, and he should have changed it to DFRPR to tell us he was safe. But instead he'd inverted the last two letters of DBOPR and transmitted DBORP.

I immediately informed Noble that we must assume Daks was under duress, but warned him he'd made exactly the same inversions in two of his training messages, and that there was an outside chance that he was having one of his lapses. Noble hoped that he was but didn't think it likely and undertook to ask him some personal questions immediately. He added that Bricklayer and Daks had been instructed to cut contact with the Phono circuit as soon as they'd landed, but he was convinced that they hadn't done so.

On 8 April Daks transmitted two more messages, and the supervisor at 53a telephoned me to report that she'd decoded them herself, and that he'd used his security checks correctly. Since she was the most reliable of all our supervisors, I didn't ask her to teleprint the code-groups to London so that I could double-check them. Instead I informed Noble that Daks was now using his security checks correctly, though there must still be a question-mark against him.

Noble phoned me soon afterwards with an even larger one. Was I certain that Daks's security checks were correct? He'd made no attempt to answer his personal questions.

Ten minutes later I did the double-checking I should have done in the first place. Daks had again inverted the last two letters of his indicator group, but had made no attempt to change the second and third letters by the requisite numbers. Yet the supervisor had told me that his checks were correct. I telephoned to ask her what she thought they were, unaware that the Decline and Fall of the Holy Coding Empire was only seconds away.

According to the station's code-card, Daks hadn't been given any secret numbers. All he had to do to tell us he was safe was insert three sets of dummy letters at the beginning, middle and end of every message. He'd failed to do so in his first message but had inserted them correctly in the two we'd just received.

We'd sent the station the wrong code-card. The one she believed to be Daks's was a copy of the conventions he'd used at training school before his checks had been finalized. He'd been taught to insert three sets of dummy letters as an additional check, and this was all that he'd remembered. I asked what significance she'd attached to the inversion of his indicator-groups.

She replied, 'None at all.' She then reminded me that I'd warned the girls that many agents found their silks difficult to read, and that their indicators were often Morse-mutilated, and she'd assumed that either or both of these factors accounted for Daks's inversions. She also thought I'd given him a 'special check' as I had to Noor, and that it consisted only of inserting dummy letters.

But the Daks disaster didn't end there. I discovered that his real code-card was nestling in his training file and had never been dispatched. I also discovered that a trusted member of the typing pool had misspelt two words of his poem.

However, the real mistakes were mine. I'd neglected to examine his code-groups myself, and if Noble hadn't questioned my assurances about his security checks, the cost to F section's agents would have been unquantifiable.

I felt equally guilty about the typing errors and our failure to send the right code-card as I'd chosen the girls responsible and should have realized that their limitations were almost as great as mine.

I tried to confess the balls-up to Noble but Buckmaster took the call. I explained what had happened, admitted that the mistake was entirely my fault, and said that there could no longer be any doubt that Daks had been caught.

There was a moment's silence, the longest I'd known in a conversation with Buckmaster. 'Ah well,' he said, 'it's only agents' lives which are at stake . . .'

On 20 April Daks regretted to inform London that Bricklayer had died in hospital without recovering consciousness.

On the 21st Noor sent a similar message, and asked whether London would be sending a replacement.

If there'd been any justice, I'd have volunteered.

On 5 May we received our first message from Holland in a one-time pad. It was in Cricket's code, and had been transmitted by Swale. Cricket reported that the RVV (the clandestine organization he'd been ordered to contact) didn't want a liaison officer; it needed a bloody nursemaid. His security checks were correct.

On 8 May Swale reported that he was transmitting from an attic which wasn't properly earthed, and wanted to know whether his key-clicks would disturb other radios. He also enquired about the dangers of DF-ing in Amsterdam, which he feared were considerable. His security checks were correct.

For the next ten days the agents kept in regular contact with London. Cricket reported that he was trying to arrange a dropping point so that the RVV could receive arms and explosives. He was also trying to put them in radio contact with London so that they could receive instructions from the Allied High Command when they'd established their bridgeheads. (He'd been authorized to give the RVV 50,000 florins when he considered it appropriate.)

Swale reported that German troop-trains were moving soldiers from Holland to Paris, and asked if he could be told the date of the invasion a few days in advance as half Amsterdam's police force would go into hiding to avoid being sent to Germany.

On 19 May he reported that he was training a new WT operator to take over his skeds on alternate weeks, and asked permission to show him his signal-plan. He also repeated his request to be told the date of the invasion as it was very important. But, for the first time in nine messages, he'd used the wrong security checks. He should have added 2 to the second letter of his indicator-group and 4 to the fourth. Instead he'd added 19 to the second letter and 20 to the fourth.

I informed Dobson (head of N section) that Swale had been caught.

On 20 May Dobson asked him for the full name of his new WT operator, and regretted that he was unable to give him the date of the invasion.

On 21 May Swale supplied the name of his new operator, and repeated his request to be allowed to show him his signal-plan. This time he added 21 to the second letter of his indicator-group and 22 to the fourth, and I wondered what his pattern was.

On 22 May Dobson authorized him to share his signal-plan with the new operator, and then asked him a test question: 'What do you know?' If he was safe, he'd reply, 'American soldier.'

On 23 May he replied, 'American sailor.' He also reported that he'd been unable to deliver London's messages to Faro as his cut-out had disappeared. This time he'd added 23 to the second letter of his indicator-group, and 24 to the fourth, and I realized that he'd told the Germans he had to alter his indicator-group according to the date!

On the 24th London informed him that Cricket had been instructed to cut contact with Faro as he might be in danger, and advised him for his sake to do the same.

On 22 May Cricket sent a message giving London a dropping point. For the first time in fourteen messages his security checks were incorrect. He should have added 2 to the second letter of his indicator-group and 3 to the third. Instead he'd added 4 to the fourth letter and 5 to the fifth. He'd also numbered his message 14 when it should have been 15.

I told Dobson that Cricket had also been caught and offered to show him the checks if he had any doubts. But he'd already suspected it.

On 24 May he informed Cricket that his dropping ground couldn't be accepted, and reminded him that for his own safety he should cut contact with Faro. The two-way bluff traffic showed no signs of abating, and I didn't envy Dobson the onus of sustaining it.

But May's losses weren't confined to France and Holland. Pandarus had been in regular contact since his return to Belgium, and all his messages had been perfectly encoded with their security checks correct. Six of his pupils had also started using their one-time pads with the checks that he'd given them. We'd received no traffic from Pandarus for a fortnight.

On 30 May Hardy Amies telephoned to say that he'd learned 'from a reliable source' that Pandarus had been caught. Hardy, who trusted people completely on the rare occasions when he trusted them at all, said that he continued to believe that Pandarus would be unable to remember the checks he'd passed on to other agents, though I still hadn't told him how the system worked.

But I wasn't properly earthed myself, and the moment he rang off I began wondering if my 'bright idea' had flaws in it which I hadn't foreseen. If it did, the security of countless Belgian partisans would be in jeopardy.

I also wondered what else could go wrong in the run-up to D-Day. There was no invasion quite as deadly as self-doubt.

SIXTY-NINE

For Your Ears Only

By 1 June (referred to as 'D-Day minus five' by the cognoscenti) Nick was still endeavouring to weld his collection of freak talents into a Morse-minded entity, and it wouldn't be his fault if we failed our entrance exam to maturity.

As a result of the support he'd given to technicians he trusted, WT operators were no longer forced to come on the air at fixed times and on the same frequencies. They were now using variable signal-plans, which enabled them to pass their traffic at irregular intervals and on different channels. Nor did they any longer have to carry camouflaged WT sets weighing almost forty pounds from safe-house to safe-house – often the last journeys they made. Instead they were given portable wireless sets, each equipped with a power-pack which made the operators independent of mains and ensured that their consumption of electricity could no longer be detected. Other life-savers sponsored by him included S-phones and Eurekas, which enabled agents to talk to aircraft, and squirt transmitters, which could send 100 letters in a matter of seconds.

But he shared my anxiety about the number of agents who'd been told in poem-codes which BBC messages they must listen out for, and what they signified. He'd warned the country sections that the meaning of the prearranged phrases could only safely be transmitted to agents who were using WOKs or LOPs but on the night of 1 June the BBC broadcast over 300 'stand by' messages alerting the Resistance that D-Day was imminent. The significance of at least thirty of them had been conveyed in poem-codes.

On 3 June Nick instructed me to report to him in advance of yet

517

another meeting with Gravy as he had something to tell me which the OSS mustn't hear.

He disclosed that although Eisenhower continued to have confidence in SOE, the Chiefs of Staff were worried about our role on D-Day, and feared that our Dutch débâcle would be repeated in France. They didn't trust our communications either as they believed that our technical improvements had come too late, and that some of our traffic would blow the date of Overlord. They'd also concluded (with a little help from C) that the French Resistance 'had been penetrated to such a significant extent' that the most the partisans could contribute to D-Day was 'a nuisance value'. Because of these and numerous other reservations (especially about de Gaulle) they'd decided that the Secret Armies 'and SOE's other odds and sods' mustn't be alerted to the imminence of Overlord till the last possible moment.

Nick was about to amplify these misgivings when he was informed by his secretary that Commander Graveson had arrived, and he reluctantly told her to show him in at once.

This reluctance was a new factor because by now Gravy had become 'one of us', but we could no longer talk freely in front of him as the OSS had begun a joint operation with C. We knew that its code-name was Sussex, and that it was an Intelligence-gathering operation taking place in France, but that was the extent of our knowledge, and we hoped that the Germans were equally ill-informed.

Gravy had called in to report on his recent inspection of Milton Hall, the Jedburgh training school which was staffed by British and American instructors (by mutual consent, for once genuine, it was under the overall command of the British). He dealt first with the Americans' reaction to the Jedburgh code-book.

Careful to stress his admiration for the way in which it reduced the effects of Morse mutilation, he said that many Americans had complained that looking up the phrases they needed and then copying the code-groups on to one-time pads was 'one hell of a performance', and they wanted to encode their messages straight on to one-time pads without using the code-books. Did we agree?

I replied that it would be perfectly safe for them to do this, but if they had long messages to transmit the code-book would greatly reduce their length and allow them to get off the air quickly, a major consideration at all times, especially on D-Day. We agreed that they should be given the option.

He then said that 'all Jedburghs, not just the Americans' found double-transposition 'heavy going' and that most of them questioned if they'd ever need to use it.

I pointed out that if they didn't know how to, they'd be unable to use WOKs, which would enable them to pass another 200 messages safely. Nor could they use poems, which would be their last chance of communicating if they lost their silks. Heavy going or not, there could be no compromise on this.

He at once changed the subject, and shot a series of questions at Nick which seemed so unrelated to Signals problems that I indulged in an iodoform-brood.

He wanted to know why British instructors placed so much emphasis on the cutting of telephone wires. Surely it was equally important to destroy bridges and railway lines, attack ammunition dumps and make roads impassable? So why was absolute priority given to telephone wires?

I could tell from the silence which followed that he'd asked a key question and Nick's answer was the biggest compliment I'd heard him pay anyone. He told us that the explanation was known to very few people but he was prepared to give it on the understanding that it mustn't be discussed outside this room.

I stood up to leave, partly to save Nick from having to ask me to but mainly because I still couldn't see the relevance of Gravy's question.

Nick waved me back, and took a deep breath. He then told Gravy that twelve months ago 'someone highly placed' (it turned out to be Tiltman the Great) had asked Gubbins to continue to ensure that agents gave absolute priority to cutting telephone lines because it forced the Germans to communicate by radio, and gave Bletchley an opportunity to break their codes. He then explained to the now silent commander and the open-mouthed small boy seated beside him that the Germans didn't realize the extent to which Bletchley had penetrated their traffic – 'God forbid they ever do because they'd change

519

their codes at once, which would be a major setback for the entire war effort.'

Without going into details, he added that the contributions made by Bletchley and Y (the interception service) towards shortening the war would one day be recognized, but at this crucial stage they were known only to Churchill and his trusted advisers. And so it must remain.

The commander shook Nick's hand and promised that what he'd just learned wouldn't be repeated.

The small boy tried to look as if he'd known it all the time.

SEVENTY

Neptune's Trident

Despite intense competition from air-raids, the ugliest sounds in June were the voices of the BBC announcers.

They stopped reading 'Stand by' messages on the 4th, and began broadcasting 'Action' messages on the 5th. The prearranged phrases lasted for eight hours, and I learned that it was possible to grow hoarse through listening. The significance of at least fifty iodoforms had been conveyed in poem-codes.

The D-Day uprisings were timed to take place simultaneously right across France to conceal where the Allies intended to land, and above all to divert attention from Neptune. The purpose of this key-operation was to land sea and airborne forces near the mouth of the Seine, and the Resistance was to act as Neptune's trident by attacking enemy troops, disrupting communications and blocking reinforcements.

Nick warned us that Neptune's traffic would be 'somewhere between heavy and crippling', and squads of coders stood by to deal with the holocaust of coding mistakes which the 'Action' calls seemed certain to engender. But on D-Day only one indecipherable was received from the whole of France, and that was the result of Morse mutilation. 'Decipherability-Day' (as 6 June was henceforth known) had other surprises.

The traffic was far lighter than expected, there were no queries from the country sections, and my phone didn't ring until one o'clock. The signalmaster at 53a wanted me to listen to a message from France which had been transmitted *en clair* over the Butler circuit.

The message was addressed to Colonel Buckmaster, and was similar to Giskes's on April Fool's day:

WE THANK YOU FOR THE LARGE DELIVERIES OF ARMS AND
AMMUNITIONS WHICH YOU HAVE BEEN KIND ENOUGH TO SEND
US. WE ALSO APPRECIATE THE MANY TIPS YOU HAVE GIVEN US
REGARDING YOUR PLANS AND INTENTIONS WHICH WE HAVE
CAREFULLY NOTED. IN CASE YOU ARE CONCERNED ABOUT THE
HEALTH OF SOME OF THE VISITORS YOU HAVE SENT US YOU
MAY REST ASSURED THEY WILL BE TREATED WITH THE CON-
SIDERATION THEY DESERVE.

I telephoned Maurice at once, hoping that I'd be in time to cushion
the shock.

I received one when he chuckled. 'They're trying to shake our
confidence,' he said, and rang off to draft a reply.

Noble and I suspected that he'd never completely shared our conviction that his Butler circuits were blown, and he'd continued to
drop stores, explosives and money to them, ostensibly to deceive the
Gestapo. But he'd dropped agents as well, and I wondered what his
true feelings were.

I also wondered if I were about to receive a similar communication:

WE THANK YOU FOR THE LARGE QUANTITIES OF WOKS AND
LOPS YOU HAVE SENT US WHICH WE HAVE HAD MUCH PLEA-
SURE IN BREAKING. WE MUST ALSO THANK YOU FOR YOUR R.
TOMMEE TRAFFIC WHICH HAS GIVEN US HOURS OF AMUSE-
MENT. HOWEVER, WE HAVE LEARNED FROM A RELIABLE
SOURCE THAT YOUR FATHER REFUSES TO STOCK MEIN KAMPF,
AND REGRET TO INFORM YOU THAT HIS SHOP WILL BE
TARGETED AT OUR EARLIEST OPPORTUNITY.

Expecting an influx of visitors on D-Day (not one of whom had
appeared), the only appointment I'd made was with Valois. He'd
never seen my workshop and I'd invited him to call in for a tête-à-tête,
confident his tête would be clearer than mine.

But it wasn't the Valois I'd learned to like and respect who stood
in the doorway. His hostility was even more apparent than in the
days of our mutual antagonism over de Gaulle's secret code, and I

grabbed his hand as there seemed a distinct possibility that he was about to return to Duke Street.

Refusing the refreshments I'd prepared in readiness for the invasion which hadn't taken place, he sat glumly at my desk and looked sharply away when he spotted a copy of the FFI code-book. But he couldn't resist examining its next-door neighbour: a code-book on silk which was being widely used in guerrilla warfare against the Japanese (the Far Eastern conflict was of great concern to Duke Street). He looked closely at the code-groups, which minimized the effects of Morse mutilation, and gave a curt nod of approval.

I then showed him the only item which might break his silence: the cigar I was keeping for Tommy (he was still in Fresnes prison).

Leaving his own cell for a moment, Valois told me that the Free French had arranged for groups of cyclists to call out the latest BBC bulletins as they rode past the prison courtyard, and that some of them shouted out messages from Barbara. He then returned to his solitary confinement.

Wondering if the Free French had heard bad news which I knew nothing about, I finally asked what had happened to upset him.

He looked at me reproachfully as if convinced I knew the answer. It was only when I told him that I regarded us as friends and would repeat nothing he said to me that he began speaking in rapid French; to my astonishment I understood every word of it.

The Free French were outraged at the way France's Allies ('particulièrement les Anglais') had treated de Gaulle. He hadn't been allowed to return from Algiers until 3 June, and had been excluded from all discussions about Overlord. He hadn't even been told the date of the invasion until Churchill sent for him on the night of the 4th. But the greatest of all insults was that his troops in the 3rd SAS regiment had received their orders before he'd been allowed to know what they were.

I nodded sympathetically (the best exercise I'd had in months), and was about to ask why he thought I was one of the Anglais responsible for such disgraceful behaviour when he spat out the subject of communications.

The general was anxious to exchange messages with his followers in France and North Africa but had been forbidden to use his own codes. He even had to communicate with his committees in codes which the British had provided. Valois hastened to add that our 'systèmes de codage' were safe and excellent, but the British could read them and I must understand that this was no longer acceptable as the committees had proclaimed themselves the provisional government of France.

I explained that the provisional governor of SOE's code room wasn't consulted on such matters, and that what he'd said was complete news to me. I added that as far as I knew SHAEF (the Supreme HQ Allied Expeditionary Force) had decided that only the British, Americans and Russians could use their own codes while the invasion was in progress, and that General de Gaulle hadn't been singled out for special treatment. I then assured him that not even Nick could reverse SHAEF's decision, much as he'd want to.

The little wizard nodded his head. He then looked at me sadly and said that the war leaders, 'especially Mr Churchill', had treated General de Gaulle as if he were . . . He struggled for the word.

I didn't know the French for 'outsider' and nearly said 'Juif', but that might have been too great an insult.

'Il est tout seul' ('He is quite alone'), he said finally.

He then began to do justice to a bottle of Father's wine and a plate of mother's finest.

At this point Jerry Parker (head of Signal-planning) waddled in, and was astonished to see his Free French opposite number seated beside me toasting the success of the invasion. They immediately began a discussion in English, French and Signalese, and left shortly afterwards for Gerry's office.

General de Marks was left tout seul with his thoughts.

Shortly before midnight the Signals Office supervisor read me Buckmaster's reply to the Germans' message, which he'd instructed the station to transmit *en clair*:

SORRY TO SEE YOUR PATIENCE IS EXHAUSTED AND YOUR NERVES NOT AS GOOD AS OURS BUT IF IT IS ANY CONSOLATION YOU WILL BE PUT OUT OF YOUR MISERY IN THE NEAR FUTURE. PLEASE GIVE US DROPPING GROUNDS NEAR BERLIN FOR

RECEPTION ORGANIZER AND W.T. OPERATOR BUT BE CAREFUL
NOT TO UPSET OUR RUSSIAN FRIENDS WHO TAKE OFFENCE
MORE QUICKLY THAN WE DO. WE SHALL DELIVER FURTHER
COMMUNICATIONS PERSONALLY.

I thought about all the agents who were in no position to share
the joke. One in particular.

I then thought about Tommy's idol, Winston Churchill, who'd
emerged from his wilderness to lead us out of ours. Was the person
yet born who could replace him if we needed his like again?

For the first time on D-Day I found my pen in my hand:

> Are you tomorrow's Winnie
> Though still in your pinny?
> Tomorrow's war-leader
> Though still a breast-feeder?
> Tomorrow's saviour
> Learning potty behaviour?
>
> Little one
> Little one
> All snot-and-spittle one
> Is our D-Day
> Your three times a pee day?
>
> And when you're a giant
> On whom the free world is reliant
> As well as a gallon of whisky man
> Whom lesser mortals
> Call a House of Commons risky man
> Will you please spare a nod
> For every poor sod
> Who today met his God
> And make sure that Overlord
> Really is over, Lord.

A few minutes later it was D-Day plus one.

SEVENTY-ONE

Staying Power

'If Christ were alive today they wouldn't crucify him.
They'd make him a member of the Signals directorate.'

(Nick to author, D-Day plus four)

Why the 'if'?

I hadn't the slightest doubt that *He* was alive as our codes and
coders were withstanding the strain of the invasion traffic, and there
was no sign that the enemy had penetrated the BBC's iodoforms.

But there was every sign that Nick, whose religion was signals,
was carrying the heaviest Morse-cross of his long career. He was
answerable to the High Command for the security of SOE's traffic,
and as if that weren't burden enough the War Office had asked him
to supply the codes for all Special Forces. His confidence that we'd
delivered the 'right goods' was greater than mine as we'd had little
experience of paramilitary traffic, and the SAS were the main recipi-
ents of our first venture into it. We would soon know if they regretted
zooming along Baker Street for 'a spot of advice'.

One op. which the SAS mounted on D-Day required such audacity
– even by their standards – that Gubbins had found time to monitor
its progress.

Two three-man teams from the 1st SAS regiment were dropped
near the Cherbourg peninsula to convince the Germans that the Normandy landings were only a diversion, and that the main assault was
taking place in the Pas-de-Calais.

They were cogs in Fortitude, a deception scheme to persuade the enemy to send reinforcements to the wrong beach-heads. But even six members of the SAS couldn't be mistaken for an army of invaders, and hundreds of dummies had been dropped with them to give the impression of a major landing. To heighten the illusion, each team had been issued with gramophones, Very pistols and an assortment of flares. The gramophones played records of intensive small-arms fire with soldiers' voices in the background, and the Very pistols and flares turned the skies into an illuminated manuscript with an unmistakable text.

The Germans immediately rushed troops to the area to repel the invaders, and partisans harassed them en route to add verisimilitude to their journey. One SAS operator sent a message to base, 'The buggers have fallen for it,' but as no such phrase was included in his code-book's vocabulary he'd had to spell it out on his one-time pad.

Gubbins wanted the Resistance to take a far greater part in Fortitude but the Deception Committee didn't trust SOE's competence. Nor did they have much faith in the SAS's, and three of their deception drops were cancelled without notice, a rejection which they took in their inexhaustible stride.

The SAS rarely sought help from other organizations; they preferred to be left alone 'to do things their way' (an attitude which only the enemy had cause to regret), but they'd allowed me to brief a group of their instructors and to meet some of their troops. They regarded the invasion as a night out on the town, especially if it were in enemy hands. Two thousand of them were now standing by to cause their special brand of havoc, and three advance parties had been dropped behind enemy lines to demolish fortifications and link up with the Resistance.

The Jedburghs were also in action, but wouldn't be for long if their luck didn't change. The three-man teams had made a disastrous start.

Quinine and Ammonia (some humorist in authority had decided to code-name Jedburghs after patent medicines) were the first teams to be launched from Algiers. They set off for France on 5 June, but missed D-Day altogether as their pilots couldn't find the dropping grounds and had to return to base. The ops. were remounted; Quinine and Veganin were landed on the 9th and Ammonia on the 10th. But one member of the Veganin team was killed whilst jumping as he hadn't hooked up the static line of his parachute, which so upset his team-leader that he had to be withdrawn from the field. Half the

Quinine and Ammonia teams were also out of action due to appalling stomach cramps, diarrhoea and raging fever, maladies which were reported to London in the Lord's Prayer as the WT operator had mislaid his silk codes. (He'd used 'Hallowed be Thy name' as his key-phrase but spelt 'hallowed' with three 'l's, and it took 4,000 attempts to decipher his message.)

By 11 June fever of another kind (no less insidious because it was psychological) had infected the Jedburghs at Milton Hall who'd been waiting for weeks (and in some instances, months) to go into action. They'd been promised a key role on D-Day, and were angry at their exclusion. They were even angrier that they still hadn't been given a firm departure date, and according to their coding instructress had lost confidence in their briefing officers, felt neglected and deceived, and were in a state of near mutiny.

Choosing her words carefully, which was rare amongst FANY sergeants, she advised me to stay away from Milton Hall.

I'd arranged with Colonel Musgrove (the station's CO) to go there on the 14th but he phoned me on the 11th and urged me not to come as the last two lecturers had been given a 'very rough reception' and had had to leave the platform in a hurry. He added that the Jedburghs 'knew their bloody codes backwards' as he'd made them practise them for hours 'to help pass the time', and I'd no need to brief them: 'Marks, I must say this to you frankly. The last thing they want is another lecture, least of all on codes, and if you insist on coming down here I shan't be answerable for the consequences.'

He clearly feared that a know-it-all civilian of unmistakably Semitic origin would start a riot of unquantifiable proportions.

Nick and Heffer also urged me to stay away as the timing was wrong. But it wasn't for me.

I hadn't faced a lynch-mob since admitting to the Free French that I'd broken de Gaulle's secret code, and badly needed the illusion of courage. I also wanted to inspect Milton Hall's library, most of which had come from 84.

I decided to arrive on the 14th wearing a bullet-proof vest, and returned to the lesser heroics of the invasion.

The traffic made clear that the extent of SOE's contribution to Overlord had come to the attention of the British as well as the

Germans. Although the High Command still had reservations about the Resistance Movement's staying-power and SOE's competence, SHAEF headquarters in France sent a telegram to Gubbins confirming that the landings in Normandy and Brittany owed much of their success to the widespread uprisings, and even more to the number of troop-carrying trains derailed and sabotaged by the Pimento organization.

This remarkable group consisted entirely of railway workers, and was controlled by an express-train of an agent named Tony Brooks (code name Alphonse), who'd been dropped into France in June '42 when he was a locomotive of twenty – the youngest agent Buckmaster had yet dispatched to the field.

Knowing little about trains but a great deal about passengers, he spent the next two years preparing Pimento for D-Day, and his efforts achieved the historic result of surpassing Buckmaster's expectations. Since receiving their first 'Action' messages, Pimento had derailed over 1,000 trains, and the crack Das Reich division, which had been ordered to rush to Normandy to repel the invasion, was forced to travel by road, giving the Allies the time they needed to consolidate their beach-heads. Pimento had also paralysed scores of railway yards, brought all the traffic in the Rhône valley to a standstill, and ensured that every train leaving Marseilles for Lyons was derailed at least once in the course of its journey. Of the dozens of messages reporting Pimento's progress, only three had themselves been derailed, but the mishaps had been caused by Morse mutilation and not by mistakes in coding.

Pimentos were Mother's favourite vegetable.

On 11 June her favourite only child began preparing his address to the Milton Hall mutineers so that it would sound spontaneous in three days' time but I was unable to get beyond my opening sentence ('Listen, you bastards, if you can remember how to') as I couldn't stop brooding about the Polish government-in-exile.

An important Polish operation, code-named Bardsea, which was supposed to have taken place on D-Day, had been abandoned because of political in-fighting amongst the Polish authorities, an art at which they had no equal.

SOE's relationship with the Polish government-in-exile was as hard to understand as a mental one-time pad. Its complexity not only caused problems for everyone but the enemy, it made reality fight for its life.

SOE's Polish directorate (known as MP) was run by Colonel Perkins, and was responsible for recruiting Polish expatriates, turning them into agents, and dropping them into France and Poland to work for SOE. But the Polish government-in-exile also recruited expatriates, though in far larger numbers, and dispatched them to the same territories, usually on missions of which we knew nothing.

Foreseeing most of this and realizing that some semblance of co-ordination would be helpful, Gubbins had a conference in 1940 with General Sikorski (the Polish prime minister whom SOE had smuggled into England), and agreed to create a special department in the Polish directorate known as EU/P.

As I understood it, EU/P's function was to liaise with the Polish authorities to prepare Bardsea for D-Day, to ensure that their operations into France weren't duplicated, and to start a free exchange of information. The ministries agreed to the arrangement, and honoured it whenever it suited them. The head of EU/P was Major Hazell, who'd been doing the job since 1941 but had little to show for it except premature old age and the prospect of monitoring Bardsea after spending three years discussing it. His unofficial remit was to find out as much as he could about the government-in-exile's independent operations. But the Polish authorities found a use for Hazell which SOE hadn't foreseen.

By D-Day the Polish Ministry of the Interior and their Ministry of National Defence were no longer on speaking terms, and insisted on using Hazell's EU/P section as their sole means of communication, which may not have helped the war effort but guaranteed him full employment.

Bardsea's traffic did as much for me. The Polish agents were to use LOPs and WOKs for their messages, which they'd been instructed to keep to a minimum (a near guarantee that they wouldn't). But it wasn't the agents' traffic which was taking up so much brooding-time. It was the government-in-exile's.

Despite a recent Foreign Office ruling that until further notice all governments-in-exile must pass the whole of their traffic (including diplomatic) in British, American or Russian ciphers, the Polish government-in-exile was still allowed to use its own codes. I'd no idea what they were, and Nick warned me that under no circumstances must I attempt to find out as they were none of SOE's business: 'The decision's been taken at the highest level. Don't even think of questioning it.'

I wasn't able to stop. Nick may have forgotten (his memory had become an Overlord casualty) that on the eve of Tiltman-the-Great's visit to Baker Street he'd told me that both Bletchley and the Germans had been reading Russian codes for years, and that it was only when the Germans declared war on the Soviet Union that the Foreign Office warned the Russians to change them immediately. I found this aspect of the code war completely indecipherable as it must have cost tens of thousands of Russian lives.

It seemed certain that the Polish authorities in London would want to report Bardsea's progress to their ministries abroad, which would cause unquantifiable damage if the codes weren't high-grade.

Had the Foreign Office vetted them? It was such an obvious precaution that it couldn't be taken for granted. And why had the Poles been made an exception to the rule? Above all, had the Foreign Office been properly briefed about Bardsea?

Its importance had begun filtering through to the Signals directorate.

It was to be a joint operation: the Poles were to supply the agents; SOE was to drop them. Its purpose was to land 100 highly trained agents near Lille, where they'd link up with the half million Polish expatriates who lived and worked in the area. Amongst their other Resistance activities, these expatriates had formed a Secret Army called Monica.

SOE had been told little about Monica apart from its code-name, but in February Chalmers-Wright (a former member of the Political Warfare Executive) had crossed the Pyrenees on a tour of inspection, and strolled back two months later by the same route to report to Perkins and Hazell that, if Monica could be supplied with arms and explosives and given the proper targets, it could mount and maintain a major uprising and would have an enormous D-Day potential.

Without disclosing what he knew, Hazell tried to persuade the

Poles to clarify Monica's role on D-Day while there was still time to exploit its potential, but they were reluctant to discuss Monica's activities, and all EU/P section had so far discovered was that Bardsea agents were to be dropped to Monica's reception committees.

End of brood, and the start of my efforts to find out what I could about the government-in-exile's codes.

I manufactured an excuse to visit Hazell, and casually mentioned that it would be a pity if the Germans learned about Monica through the government-in-exile's traffic, and he equally casually mentioned to their chief signals officer that SOE had a good line in codes. The signals officer replied that he was familiar with our systems and thought they were excellent, but perhaps we'd come up with some new ones he hadn't been shown, in which case he'd be glad if Hazell could produce a few specimens.

I invited him to my office, and gave him freedom of the walls after removing the Free French and SAS code-books (I left the Jedburgh code-books intact as the Poles were aware of their activities).

It may have been Mother's sandwiches, Muriel's red hair, or the effect of the lighting, but just when I was wondering how to introduce the subject of the code which mattered most to me he asked if we could possibly supply him with 200 LOPs immediately as he needed them 'for a most important purpose'.

Although we couldn't afford to part with them, I promised that they'd be delivered to his office within the next two hours, hoping that the government-in-exile would start using them at once.

He then asked if I'd like to accompany him to meet the 100 Bardsea agents in training. I was due to visit them anyway, but accepted his invitation. Two days later, he turned up at the wheel of a jeep, and I soon learned how Chalmers-Wright felt crossing the Pyrenees.

A few mountain peaks later he thanked me for the LOPs, then immediately began discussing the route, so I still don't know what their 'urgent purpose' was. Our dropping zone was a holding school near Horsham, where the Bardsea agents had been incarcerated for months, waiting for D-Day.

Reluctant to surrender the driving seat to me, the signals officer insisted on acting as interpreter.

They understood their LOPs perfectly but had to struggle a bit with their WOKs, and I sensed from the extra weight in their eyes that the Bardseas had been taught to use other codes about which we knew nothing. Although some of them had almost certainly taken part in the national sport of confining Polish jews to ghettos, they were a magnificent bunch, highly trained, counting the seconds to go, and excellent pupils. Mass briefings like this were usually two-way traffic pogroms, but the Bardseas has a special quality, and several hours later I felt almost ready to drop with them to Monica.

On D-Day the entire Bardsea operation was cancelled due to another bout of in-fighting. None of us doubted the Poles' courage, or their determination to attack the common enemy, or how much the Allies owed to General Sikorski's leadership (he'd died in '43).

But what a fuck-up. What a waste of 100 first-class agents, of Monica's potential, of LOPs wc couldn't spare.

Hazell asked if they could be returned to us but the signals officer replied that the Poles 'would find very good use for them'.

Knowing their macabre sense of humour, I didn't ask what it was.

On the morning of the 12th I learned that Violette Szabo had been captured by the Germans.

She'd been dropped back into France on the 7th with Staunton to re-establish his Salesman circuit, but three days later she and one of his assistants (Anastasie) were trying to reach Limoges by car when they were spotted by an advance party of the Das Reich division. She held up the Germans with her sten-gun for as long as she could to give Anastasie the chance to escape and complete his mission but was caught when her ammunition ran out.

I hadn't seen her since she'd returned by Lysander in April as her coding instructress had told me that all Violette needed was a new WOK. She hadn't yet used her poem, and was anxious not to change it.

Since I couldn't justify a visit, I'd sent her a note saying that I hadn't lost a single game of chess with the set that she'd given me, which was true as I hadn't yet used it.

She sent a note back promising if she had to use her poem she wouldn't make a single spelling mistake.

I left for Milton Hall with her chess-set in my briefcase.

SEVENTY-TWO

'They Also Serve . . .'

Built in the seventeenth century, Milton Hall was a few miles from Peterborough but managed to live it down, and everything about it was sepulchral except for its present inhabitants, who were waiting for me in the lecture room, all of them wearing British, American or French uniforms.

I'd asked Colonel Musgrove not to introduce me and strode to the platform unannounced. Someone laughed, and someone else blew a raspberry (or worse) as I turned to face them, and I knew that if I didn't establish a beach-head with my first sentence, there wouldn't be a second.

I remembered the approach I'd selected on the night of the Bardsea brood: 'Listen, you bastards, if you can remember how to . . .'

Beach-head established.

'. . . while we're scoring points off each other, an agent in France has only one hope of not being caught, and that's to be picked up by Lysander in the next few hours . . . would it bore you to know what's stopping us?'

This is the most important talk I've ever given.

'. . . he's lost his silks, and had to use his poem to give us his pick-up points, but the silly sod's made a mistake in his coding and the bloody thing's indecipherable, indéchiffrable, impossible to read . . .'

Is it the shock of Violette's capture that's made me realize what I must say?

'. . . two hundred girls are working the clock round to break it, and I should be up there trying to help them instead of pissing around with Jedburghs who've forgotten how to learn . . .'

Concentrate on the girls.

'. . . they've already made ten thousand attempts to crack it, and they're on their second ten now, and you might like to know that when you're in France, as you bloody soon will be, we'll do the same for you because we happen to be cunts enough to believe that you're worth it . . .'

Shoulders back, change tone, the next bit's critical.

'. . . you've been told that because you'll be wearing uniform, you'll be treated as prisoners of war if you're caught. I don't think you should bank on it . . .'

Colonel Musgrove stiffened at this because I'd no right to say it. But I'd even less right not to. The first thing they'd be tortured for would be their codes and security checks.

'. . . if you're caught, you could lie to them about your one-time pads and WOKs, provided you've had the sense to destroy the used portions, but poems are a different matter.'

Stop dreading the next stage or the bastards will pick it up.

'. . . I'm going to risk turning my back on you because there's something I want you to have a good look at, and I don't mean my arse.'

I took the cover off the blackboard, on which the coding instructress had written two messages of equal length, one on top of the other. 'These are two messages in the same poem-code. I want you to see how the Boche would break them, and they're a bloody sight better at it than I am . . .'

I'd been dreading this moment because I hadn't shown anyone what I was about to show them. Until now I'd made a parlour-game of poem-cracking, which most audiences enjoyed as much as I did. But these audiences had never included agents, who'd had to make do with warnings as I was afraid that the extra anxiety would make them send even more indecipherables.

Christ, how wrong I was, and how late to find it out.

More and more agents were using their poems because their silks weren't to hand, or because it was more convenient. But we didn't know how the Jedburghs would behave, though the signs were ominous. Their traffic would be equally new to the Germans, who would take great interest in it.

But it would be no good warning this bunch to keep their poems for emergencies; they'd go out of their way to create them. Nor would it be enough to play the parlour-game with them. I had to make brave men *frightened* to use their poems and risk the indecipherables they'd send us. And the only way to frighten them would be to make them watch the mathematics involved, and show them the technical tricks of the trade, even though they were unlikely to understand them.

Herr von Marks began breaking the two messages without any concessions to the Jedburghs, hoping they'd let him finish. But in the middle of playing a German cryptographer I had a lapse of concentration, and found myself thinking about 'The Life That I Have', and for the first time wished I hadn't written it.

But that wasn't my only lapse. The room was so full of death I began thinking about a conversation I'd heard in the Signals Office concerning a young man who was about to be hanged for murder, and the girls had asked what I thought about capital punishment.

I hadn't answered them then but a poem spurted out now:

> It's agreed
> That a good preventative
> Must be neither weak nor tentative
> And that the vicious and aberrant
> Are in need of a deterrent
> But while millions are going under
> By design or blunder
> Must we claim one more
> Just to settle the score?
> Shall we really feel safer
> When he snaps like a wafer?
> Will there never be enough breath about
> While there's breath about?*

Glancing at my mental watch, I found I'd overrun by six minutes. I spared them the interval counts (they'd never know how lucky they

---

* Photographed on to soluble paper, and issued to one of those present as a reserve poem.

were) and five minutes later the code-groups surrendered their texts.

I turned round to see the effect. They were staring at the blackboard as if they'd just discovered holes in their bullet-proof vests.

This is the moment for the parlour-game.

I showed them how the Boche reconstructed poems from transposition-keys, and invited them to have a go at the key I'd just broken. They were the noisiest cryptographers I'd met, competing with each other to roar out their suggestions, some of them right.

Keep quiet and let 'em go solo.

They continued Jedburghizing the key for another ten minutes, which was as much as it could take.

I hoped I'd chosen an appropriate quotation: 'They also serve who only stand and wait.' The cheer that went up could have been heard by its author after whom Milton Hall was named (it was the last line of Milton's sonnet on his blindness).

I'll know in the next ten seconds if I've really seen the light.

'Any questions?'

A hand shot up but I couldn't see who owned it.

'Yes, hand?'

'This may be a damn stupid suggestion . . .'

Christ, a shy Jedburgh.

'Mr Marks . . . can we do anything to help you break that agent's message?'

An even louder cheer went up, reducing the others to a whisper.

That's the most important question I've ever been asked.

I mumbled my thanks, and undertook to let them know at once if the girls needed help with the keys. 'Any more questions?'

An authoritative voice called out. 'Get back to that indecipherable. You've told us all we need to know.'

I left for London without inspecting the library.

I returned to a summons from Nick, who told me at once that he'd had a call from Colonel Musgrove; he was 'far from displeased by the results of my visit' but had said something which puzzled him. '. . . the Jedburghs are pestering him to know if the indecipherable's been broken, and he's interested too. Which message are they talking about?'

'It came in from Emile last week. We broke it on Friday, and he was picked up on Saturday. I pretended we were still working on it because they don't like ancient history.'

He seemed about to comment but changed his mind and announced that I was to keep the whole of tomorrow morning free for a 'very important visitor'.

Still thinking about the Jedburghs, I learned that his name was Commander Denniston, and that he'd been in charge of Bletchley until two years ago.

I woke up sharply. 'Then he knows Tiltman?'

'*Knows him?* – He was John's boss.'

'I never knew he had one. What's Denniston doing now?'

'That's not your concern. He'll be here at ten o'clock tomorrow, and you're to answer his questions fully.'

'What's he after?'

'He'll tell you himself.' He looked at me critically. 'The commander has no time to waste, so you'd better be on top form for him. Go home early. That's an order.'

He dismissed me before I could question him further.

I sent a message to the Jedburghs: 'Message out, rescue op. mounted, wish you all merde alors.'

I had a feeling that at ten o'clock tomorrow I'd be needing it myself.

SEVENTY-THREE

Self-Defence

'We all need a centre
A core we can rely on
Our private Mount Zion
Which all can see
But none can spy on.'
(Written on the eve of Commander Denniston's visit)

The most unnerving part of Denniston-Day was its tranquil start – only eight indecipherables were waiting to be broken, only three agents had lost their silks, and only two lots of codes had been sent to the wrong stations. Better still, there were only three messages from Cairo demanding more WOKs and LOPs, only one request from Melbourne for more briefing officers, and only two agents had used the same WOK-keys twice.

By the time I'd persuaded the latter's country sections to remind them of their instructions it was ten o'clock.

Commander Denniston had an open manner, though every hair of his head seemed shampooed with secrets, and I was relieved to find that I could look a Bletchley wizard in the eye with some sense of parity as he was no taller than I was.

Declining my offer of refreshments – an unpromising start – he said that he'd heard a great deal from Nick and others about the codes we were using, and wanted to see them for himself.

Longing to ask who the 'others' were, I pointed to the codes on the wall, which he'd already taken in at a glance. 'There they all are, sir. Please help yourself.'

He nodded his acceptance, and I christened his walk the Bletchley two-step.

He had a unique way of examining the silks. He seemed to inhale them like Father testing a Havana for counterfeit leaf, asking me pertinent questions as he passed from one to the other and nodding at my answers (he turned out to be an expert in nod-language). He seemed particularly interested in the code-books (especially the one I'd delivered to the FFI) and asked if much use had been made of them.

I replied that most agents preferred to encode their messages directly on to one-time pads as it took less time.

'That's disappointing – especially as the code-groups reduce Morse mutilation.'

I hadn't pointed this out.

As he put the code-books aside, I was suddenly convinced that I'd done something wrong, and that it wasn't only codes he was here to examine.

WOKs came next. 'Isn't this the system you showed John Tiltman because you needed his blessing before you could use it?'

'Yes, sir. He's their godfather.'

'You couldn't have a better.'

I realized that he knew about Tiltman's visit, and wondered what other homework he'd done.

I wish to Christ I knew what the little sod's after.

He questioned me closely about WOK-production, and wanted to know why we preferred keys made by hand to the machine-made keys supplied by Bletchley.

I explained that Bletchley hadn't produced them in sufficient quantities, and that the ones which they'd sent us didn't seem to me as random as the keys the girls produced by shuffling counters.

He looked at me doubtfully, so I gave him six sheets of keys produced by the girls, and six by Bletchley. He correctly identified Bletchley's, agreed there was a pattern to them, and asked if I'd drawn their attention to it. When I admitted that I hadn't because we were so grateful to Bletchley he suggested that I did so at once as it might be helpful to them.

Surely these are minor matters for a man with no time to waste?

His next comment made me wonder even more what his new job was, and where the hell this was leading.

He said that he'd heard from Nick that I'd devised a deception scheme called Gift-horse. '. . . I'd like you to explain its function, and then show me some examples.'

I was ready to discuss anything, but Gift-horse was the one subject I wasn't prepared for as Nick rarely enquired about it and I didn't believe that he'd absorbed its technicalities.

'The function of Gift-horse is to make WOK-messages look as if they've been passed in poem-codes to waste the enemy's time, and make our traffic more trouble than it's worth.'

'Method?'

'Without agents knowing it, we repeat the indicator-groups on their WOKs to make it look as if they've used the same keys twice, though they're different every time.'

'Examples?'

I removed twelve Gift-horsed WOKs from the safe and spread them in front of him in silence.

He examined each one carefully, and I could tell from his nod-language that he'd spotted the repeated groups at a glance. I then made the mistake of saying that we also Gift-horsed our dummy traffic.

'*What dummy traffic?*'

I explained that we transmitted dummy messages round the clock to hide the volume of our real traffic, and without being asked showed him six examples.

Nod nod frown frown nod nod. 'I've two questions about Gift-horse.'

He's letting me off lightly.

'You display Top Secret material on the walls of your office, so why do you keep Gift-horsed WOKs in a safe?'

'To stop me from gloating over them.'

'You've good reason to.'

Then why does his voice have an edge to it?

'My second question's this. Have you discussed Gift-horse with John Tiltman or anyone else at Bletchley Park?'

He could tell at a glance that I hadn't.

541

'Did you think it wouldn't interest them – or that it was none of their business?'

He didn't wait for an answer, which was just as well as I'd need a year to find one.

'I'll come back to that later.'

If you must.

'I'm going to ask you a question about letter one-time pads, and I want you to consider your answer carefully.'

Safe ground at last.

'Do you believe they're breakable on a depth of two?'

I dropped my unlit cigar. I couldn't believe that an expert cryptographer was asking me a question which a FANY coder could have answered without the slightest difficulty.

'Take your time.'

'I'm certain they can be. I've done it myself with the help of the FANYs.'

He immediately asked for details, and I became more convinced than ever that I was on some kind of trial.

Still wondering what the hell I'd done wrong apart from being born, I said that despite our warnings that used code-groups must be destroyed at once, agents often used the same ones twice; in order to see how much damage a 'depth of two' caused I'd asked a supervisor to encipher two messages on the same code-groups without telling anyone the texts (which were scabrous), and after feeling our way for twenty-four hours the girls and I had cracked them.

'How?'

What's he expecting – a cryptographic breakthrough?

'Nothing new, sir. I used the system I'd been taught at Bedford but adapted it a bit.' I showed him the adaptation which I'd passed on to the girls, and wondered why he spent so long studying it.

'Has anyone else seen this, apart from you and the coders?'

'No, sir.'

Good God, he can sigh.

'. . . perhaps there's something else I should mention, sir.'

'I've little doubt of it.'

I added that although one-time pads were simple enough to be agent-proof, they'd found so many ways to send indecipherables in them that I'd given the girls nine guidelines on the quickest way to break them.

He studied them in silence, then asked if I'd sent a copy to Tiltman.

He didn't wait for my answer. 'Why not?'

'They're so elementary by Bletchley's standards.'

'I see. I suggest you send them copies of the guidelines and the "adaptation", if possible today. I'd also like copies myself.'

I made a note to dispatch them because I knew I'd want to forget it.

'. . . it's Denniston with two 'n's . . . Nick will know where to send them.'

I looked up to find him studying me intently.

I've been sucked into the inner space of an uncluttered mind.

'I doubt if you confine your deception schemes to WOKs and dummy traffic . . . Do you ever Gift-horse one-time pads?'

Is the bastard telepathic?

'I'm working on a way to do it, but it's still only an itch. I'll be scratching it tonight.'

He asked me to tell him the principle (a word seldom used in SOE).

'It's to make one-time messages look as if they've been enciphered on the same code-groups . . . it could waste a lot of the Boche's time if they fall for it.'

'Keep scratching . . . Which brings me to my next point. I understand you've devised a mental one-time pad.'

Is there anything Nick hasn't told him?

'How's the system work?'

It usually took me an hour to explain the complexities of a MOP, but he nod-nodded his way through them in under five minutes, and had only one question. 'Have you shown this code to Bletchley?'

To which I had only one answer – 'No. I thought it was secure enough not to need vetting.'

'Of course it bloody well is, but that's not the point . . .'

Controlling his anger (but only just) Commander Two Ns abruptly changed the subject. 'A year or so ago you showed Tiltman some charts you'd devised for breaking indecipherables –'

Forestalling him, I said that I'd sent the charts to Bletchley.

'But surely you've amended them since then?'

'Well . . . here and there.'

'What's your current breaking-rate?'

'Ninety per cent in under six hours.'

'Send the amendments to Bletchley.'

He waited impatiently while I made a note, then jerked his finger at the FFI code-book. 'How long after you'd broken the secret French code in front of them did you deliver that code-book to Algiers?'

I was no longer surprised by anything he knew or asked. 'Five or six weeks.'

His next comment was more to himself than to me: 'That code-book's clearly intended for de Gaulle's provisional government.'

Is that why he studied the vocabulary so carefully?

'Do you supply code-books to any governments-in-exile?'

'We supply them to their agents, but I doubt if the vocabularies would be much use to their governments . . .'

Wondering if this were a clue to his job, and wishing he'd go back to it, I suddenly remembered the Bardsea episode. 'We had to send two hundred one-time pads to the Poles for an unspecified purpose.'

'Ah.'

It was then that I saw a new Commander Two Ns. Glancing at his watch as if it had been Gift-horsed, he said with a hint of shyness that he'd be glad of some coffee if the offer were still open.

'Absolutely.'

I pressed the buzzer twice, and a few moments later the sight of Muriel carrying in her tray had its customary effect, even on him. He accepted the coffee gratefully but declined the sandwiches as he'd arranged to have lunch with Nick. But despite his friendliness, something warned me that he was about to make a meal of me.

I hadn't long to wait. 'It's time I spoke to you frankly . . .'

I noticed how bright his eyes were, though they could no longer conceal how long they'd been open.

'You have great responsibilities, and you don't need me to tell you that you've done a damn good job – you started off with poem-codes and ended with all this . . .' He glanced at the silks but seconds later his tone stopped matching them.

'It's not your ability I'm questioning, it's your attitude . . .' He leaned forward until we were only a few miles apart. 'Don't you realize that Bletchley has to deal with all grades of cipher, and needs every bit of help it can get? Hasn't it occurred to you that some of your unorthodoxies would interest them greatly – Gift-horse and MOPs to name only two? But what chance do you give them to judge for themselves? You wait for people like Dudley-Smith to visit you a couple of times a year, and then show them the minimum. Why must you be so damn insular? You don't strike me as being modest, but surely you're aware that your approach to codes is, to say the least, uncommon, and could be of the utmost value to Bletchley and others. I urge you from this moment onwards to pass on new ideas like Gift-horsing one-time pads because SOE isn't the only organization trying to kick the Boche in their cryptographic balls . . . and now, if I may, I'll try one of those sandwiches.'

He tried two but I didn't join him because I knew that he hadn't quite finished with me.

'John tells me that you've still not visited Bletchley.'

'No, sir.'

'Why not?'

'I might want to stay there.'

'They might even let you' – his eyes twinkled – 'if only because you're the one that got away.' He looked slowly round the office. 'Perhaps it's as well that you did.'

He stood up and held out his hand, which was a lot drier than mine. 'You've been more help to me than you can possibly know.' He closed the door quietly.

I still didn't know what he did or why he'd come.

There's a club among senior signals officers and I'll never be admitted to it, and aspects of the code war I'll never understand.*

Ten minutes later I began Gift-horsing LOPs.

---

* Some fifty years later I met Commander Denniston's son Robin and learned that Denniston senior left Bletchley in '42 to take charge of the department which specialized in breaking diplomatic traffic. To this day neither of us knows the purpose of his visit or how I was of help to him (though I do know how much his son has been able to help me throughout the writing of this book).

SEVENTY-FOUR

Taken for Granted

During the past two months, which felt more like centuries, SHAEF had made radical changes to SOE's structure, many of them long overdue.

On 1 May they'd ordained that SOE in London should henceforth be known as Special Forces Headquarters, and that our OSS counterparts should cease calling themselves O/S and adopt the same cover.

In mid-June they insisted on amalgamating our rival French sections, and gave Buckmaster and Passy an outer limit of 1 July in which to place themselves and their resources under the command of General Koenig, head of the EMFII (État-Majeur des Forces Françaises de l'Interior), which had been created for the sole purpose of controlling all Resistance groups which had previously worked for either French section.

SHAEF then implemented a decision which stood the Signals directorate on what remained of its head. They established an SFHQ in France. It was known as Special Forces Advanced Headquarters, and was adjacent to their own Advanced Headquarters. By mid-June it was already in operation and by July many of SOE's finest (including Robin Brook) had left Baker Street to advise SHAEF on what the Resistance could deliver.

There were no communication problems as all messages between Brook and Co. and London were exchanged in one-time pads, but at the beginning of July Special Forces Advanced (though in Signals matters retarded) HQ informed Nick that it was essential for them to be able to exchange messages at short notice with circuits of agents anywhere in France. They also informed him that this same facility was required by SOE's representatives with 21 Army Group and the 1st British and 2nd Canadian armies.

But even that wasn't all. Army commanders needed to order agents anywhere in France to sabotage specific targets at short notice. It was taken for granted that SOE's Signals directorate would provide the solution forthwith.

It took six of us twelve agonizing hours to devise a three-way communication system, though we couldn't be sure it would work.

A week later it was fully operational. All messages for agents were relayed to London by SFHQ, and we then re-enciphered them in the agents' own codes and retransmitted them. Conversely, agents sent their replies to London in WOKs or LOPs and we re-enciphered them in one-time pads, and re-transmitted them to SFHQ. With Nick's backing I'd refused to allow any of the three-way traffic to be retransmitted in the poem-codes which still bedevilled segments of our traffic.

The urgency of the messages was unlike any we'd known, and the code rooms in London and our three WT stations had to pool their resources to minimize delay.

But by 1 July the satisfaction of watching the girls achieve impossible targets was put into perspective by one of the most sickening telegrams ever to pass through the code room.

It was transmitted by Roger (Francis Cammaerts), who'd been appointed head of all Allied missions in south-eastern France, and who'd organized Jockey, a railway-demolition network in the Alpes-Maritimes, which was on a par with Pimento. Cammaerts had repeatedly warned London that without the heavy weapons which the Americans had promised to drop, the freedom fighters at Vercors would have no chance of withstanding a major German counter-attack, and he was convinced that they'd be wiped out if they didn't disperse immediately.

A week later the Germans landed crack SS troops on the Vercors plateau, and overwhelmed the lightly armed Maquis. In the carnage which followed one woman was raped by seventeen men in succession while a German doctor held her pulse, ready to restrain the soldiers if she fainted. Another woman was disembowelled, and left to die with her intestines wound round her neck. A third had the fingers of both hands amputated.

It was no consolation to the girl who decoded the message to learn from subsequent messages that the Americans had broken through in Brittany, that the SAS and the Resistance had secured the Breton countryside, and that the Jedburghs had finally (and successfully) gone into action. She asked to be transferred to other duties, and I put her to work Gift-horsing WOKs.

I escaped from Vercors by spending the next eight hours attacking our first indecipherable from a Jedburgh. It had been transmitted by Andy in his one-time pad, and had already defied three blanket attacks and my so-called guidelines.

Eleven hundred failures later I threw the pad on to the floor in disgust, and discovered that instead of starting on page one of his pad he'd started on page six, a major cryptographic breakthrough. (I subsequently learned that he'd detached page six so that he could always have a sheet of his pad with him, and had decided to use it before it became too crumpled.)

His message made disturbing reading, if anything could be after Vercors. Two members of his team had met with accidents on landing and had broken three legs between them.

Eleven other Jedburgh teams were also operating in France, and their encoding was flawless. (One message stated, 'We're now sitting and waiting', which puzzled the Jedburgh section but which I took to be a reference to our Milton Hall encounter.)

No longer quite so 'damn insular', thanks to Commander Two Ns, I noticed that the attempt to merge our rival French sections under Koenig had only driven them further apart, whereas the fusion of SOE and a branch of the OSS into SFHQ had had the opposite effect.

The Americans were more co-operative than ever, and had supplied us with large quantities of silk, which we badly needed to produce new codes for the Middle East and Burma. Their eagerness to help in every way they could may have been due to the difficulties we suspected them of having with Sussex (their Intelligence-gathering operation with C), though they never referred to them. And under the leadership of Captain Phoenix their code room at Station 53c had quickly mastered the complex re-encipherment drill, and had developed a character of its own, as any good code-room should.

I became totally absorbed in trying to speed up the three-way system, and was surprised when Nick ordered me to report to his office immediately. I was sitting rigidly at his desk with Heffer only a puff or two away. Whatever they'd been discussing had drained the room of air.

'What I have to tell you is highly confidential.' With a quick glance at Heffer, he extracted three documents from a Top Secret folder. 'These mustn't be discussed outside this room . . .'

He seemed uncertain how to proceed or even whether he should, but finally said that three messages in code had been intercepted and the only thing he could tell me about them was that I had to break them as quickly as possible. 'The last message is incomplete,' he added.

So was his summary. He'd said nothing about who'd sent the messages, who'd intercepted them, or why they were in his possession, and Heffer's expression warned me not to ask.

I was finally allowed to look at them. 'It's obviously a substitute code of some kind – any idea what language they're in?'

'Possibly Dutch.'

'From an agent, sir?'

'To one more likely . . . they may have been sent, I repeat *may*, by the Dutch government-in-exile.'

I received another silent warning from Heffer to ask no more questions.

Nick then instructed me to choose six coders from London or the stations to help me break them. They'd work in a room next to the Signals Office to which only he, Heffer and I would have access, but on no account must they know what they were working on. 'You're to tell them that we've been asked to help break some important German messages which they're not to discuss with anyone.'

He seemed to think the meeting was over, but I suggested that a

Dutch linguist might be useful and was sharply informed that he or she would have to be a member of the Signals directorate as no one else in SOE must know what we were doing.

Heffer then made his first vocal contribution. 'The messages may contain place names, so a few maps might be handy . . .'

His face was the only map I could rely on, and it warned me to 'get cracking'.

I chose three coders from London and three from the stations, and a rumour spread throughout the Signals Office that Mr Marks was forming a team to break Hitler's secret diary.

But before putting the girls to work, there were some questions to be answered.

Why did Nick suspect that the messages were from the Dutch government-in-exile? He was in touch with his former colleagues in Y, who'd almost certainly intercepted them. Could it be they who'd told him? And had the government-in-exile got SHAEF's permission to send messages abroad, and been allotted special frequencies?

The person who'd know all about the frequencies, and who was also in touch with Y, was Jerry Parker, the head of Signal-planning. I questioned him without disclosing my reasons or mentioning the government-in-exile, but Gerry had his own antennae and seemed to sense what I was after. Or perhaps he already knew.

He told me that the 'Dutch bastards' (with him a term of endearment) could communicate with the Netherlands any time they wanted to by getting messages to their fleet, which would have no trouble transmitting them according to instructions. He was convinced that they'd frequently been in touch with Philips of Eindhoven, who could easily receive their messages because of the huge quantity of radio equipment they were manufacturing. He had no doubt about their objectives: 'They've got millions of guilders at stake, and want to protect 'em. They're more concerned with playing politics than winning the war, like the rest of the bastards.'

He left to continue playing them himself.

I still didn't know why the messages were important, or why Nick didn't send them to Bletchley, or why he wouldn't tell me who'd intercepted them.

But of one thing I could be certain. It was time to 'get cracking'.

The first message was fifty letters long, the second fifty-five, and the third (which Nick had said was incomplete) only twenty. The first step was to take a frequency count of the individual letters, then of the bigrams (or pairs of letters), and finally of the three-letter combinations.

The girls, some of whom had come armed with German dictionaries, set about the tedious task (which Bletchley probably did by machine) as if they were embarking on an early morning run. It became increasingly uphill.

The frequency count confirmed that a substitution code had been used, and it seemed safe to assume that with millions of guilders at stake, government-in-exile, would use one-time pads, and I proceeded on that basis. And got nowhere.

After three days of trying every permutation I could think of, the girls had lost all confidence in me, and I was pleased with their good judgement.

There was no sign that the messages had been enciphered on the same code-groups, which would be our only hope of breaking them, and I was more than ever convinced that this was a job for Bletchley, whose cryptographers didn't need to drop one-time pads on the floor to achieve their results.

I was now on the floor myself, with my self-esteem more crumpled than page six of Andy's LOP. The only other time I'd felt as low as this was when I'd failed to find a way to set a trap for Herr Giskes, and I suddenly remembered how the solution had finally come.

I'd gone to 84 and sat in the chair once occupied by Freud when he was writing *Moses and Monotheism*, and the idea of sending Giskes a deliberate indecipherable had popped up from the unconscious, the greatest of all code rooms. Hoping that 84 would provide another miracle, I returned to Freud's chair without leaving my office, and remembered what else had happened.

He'd been shown every book on Moses that Marks and Co. had in stock, and I'd read one which had particularly interested him. I hadn't thought about it since, but closed my eyes and did so now . . .

When Moses was rescued from the bulrushes by his adoptive mother, she was forced by law to take him in front of Pharaoh, who was determined to find the infant King of the Jews and kill him. To test the baby's credentials, the high priest held out the crown jewels of Egypt to Moses with one hand, and a brazier of burning coals with the other.

The infant stretched out his hand towards the jewels, but the Angel of the Lord guided it to the brazier, and he put the burning coals in his mouth.

Pharaoh was convinced that no King of the Jews would make such a mistake and allowed the infant's adoptive mother to remove him, but Moses spoke with a stammer for the rest of his life.

According to George Plummer, Freud interpreted the incident as a symbol of oral penetration, and used it to develop his theory that Moses and Aaron had a homosexual relationship.

I opened my eyes, and discovered that my hand was resting on something. *Had it been guided there by the Angel of the Lord?*

It was a copy of an agent's Playfair code, an elementary system suitable for concealing brief messages in 'innocent letters' but for very little else. It was marginally more secure than invisible ink, and even Duke Street knew better than to use it for WT traffic.

Only a novice angel would suggest that Playfair was my burning coals. Yet was I being the novice? . . . *Could* Playfair be the answer? It would explain the lack of indicators, the frequency of the consonants and the repetition of the bigrams. And it was possible that the three messages had been enciphered on the same Playfair phrase.

I hurried in to the girls, who were less than pleased to see me. Doing my best not to stammer, I said that there was one last thing to be tried.

'Our patience,' one of them whispered.

I showed them how to break Playfair (it was just tricky enough to interest them) and then hurried away to see what else the Angel could do for us.

But no miracles occurred, and after slogging away for twenty-four hours without the slightest success I began cursing 84, Freud and those poofters Moses and Aaron. I was about to tell Nick that he needed to consult Tiltman when the telephone rang.

It was the team supervisor, but I could hardly hear what she was saying above the babble in the background. One of the girls thought she'd found a German word, but the linguist was convinced it was Dutch.

She was right.

Two hours later the messages were *en clair*, and the cheer that went up in the code room could have been heard in the Netherlands.

I marched the jubilant code-busters into Nick's office and carried the broken messages aloft as if they were the Torah.   His face blessed us. As we left he was reaching for the telephone.

I still didn't know what the messages contained as my Dutch was on a par with my Egyptian, and the girls were too elated to care. But it was Heffer who was responsible for the breakthrough: the messages contained several place names, as the Guru had suggested.

All of them were new to me, and I looked them up on the map in case they cropped up again.

One of them was a town called Arnhem.

SEVENTY-FIVE

The Day of Reckoning

By mid-August the outcome of Overlord was no longer in doubt, least of all to the Germans. The Allies had begun pushing them back towards the frontiers of their Fatherland, the French had ensured that entire divisions never reached it and showed them what was meant by a National Uprising, and de Gaulle was expected to arrive in Paris within the next few weeks.

The code department had also made an advance or two. We'd produced over 20 million one-time pad groups, over 750,000 transposition-keys and over 8,000 code-books. We'd also re-enciphered over 4,000 three-way messages.

But despite all this (and perhaps a little more) there was one country section which had made no demands on us whatsoever, whose traffic (if it passed any) we hadn't handled, and whose plans were completely unknown to us. Yet it was potentially the most important country section in the whole of SOE: it was responsible for the infiltration of agents into Germany, and was known as X section.

It was run by a major named Field-Robinson with the help of two assistants, but I knew them only by their symbols (AD/X, AD/X PA and AD/X1 respectively). I knew even less about their activities, which appeared to be non-existent, yet if they intended to operate inside Germany they'd need WT sets, signal-plans and codes unless they proposed to send their messages by carrier-pigeon.

I raised the question with Nick, who'd been unusually forthcoming since the breaking of the three Playfair messages and he explained the mystery of X section's silence at greater length than I'd expected.

The decision not to infiltrate agents into Germany had been taken by Hambro when he was CD. He was convinced that security in the

Fatherland was so tight that large-scale operations would end in disaster, and that the infiltration of individual agents would achieve nothing.

Gubbins had agreed with this view, much to C's relief as many of their peacetime agents were still operating in Germany and Austria and they didn't want SOE's saboteurs to cause even tighter security measures and thus blow their established agents (one of their principal complaints against us in the rest of Europe). But the OSS took a completely different view, and had the power to enforce it. They planned to infiltrate agents into Germany and Austria via Switzerland, Italy and Yugoslavia. X section's function would be limited to supplying them with contacts and the benefit of their inexperience.

Nick added that their first join-op was code-named Downend and was already being mounted. It was on a very small scale, and no WT communications were involved.

I'd listened in silence until now. 'Won't SOE ever operate inside Germany?'

He looked at me with a trace of his old wariness. 'Not unless the policy changes, but stop worrying. One day your codes will be used inside the Fatherland, I assure you of that.' He smiled at me from the power-base of his secret knowledge, and the briefing was over.

A sure sign that France was about to be liberated was the number of senior officers who were anxious to leave Baker Street and join Special Forces Advanced HQ. They knew that de Gaulle's re-entry into Paris was imminent, and wanted to be there to make him feel at home.

They made a surprising request of the Signals directorate: they wanted to understand the workings of our three-way communications, and had asked Nick and me to brief them. He'd agreed that he'd deal with the WT aspects, and that I'd fill them in about codes.

I certainly intended to fill them in, but not in the way they expected.

I followed my leader into a packed conference room, and the first people who caught my eye and returned most of it were the 'hard men' (George Courtauld and Tommy Davies), without whom we'd have had no silks. They were flanked by Harry Sporborg (Gubbins's right hand) and by Mr Murray (who'd shared my office for a week and was now Gubbins's left hand). Group Captain Venner (head of Finance) was also in the front row totting up expenses.

I wasn't prepared for such a collection of power-houses and sensed that there was more to this meeting than I'd realized, but nothing was going to deflect me from my intention, which I hadn't disclosed to Nick.

He mounted a small platform at the end of the room and, despite his lumbago and his preference for giving lectures on a one-to-one basis, spent the next twenty minutes describing the signal-plans, WT sets and procedures which had made our three-way communications possible. Speaking from notes without looking up, he appeared not to notice that many of his audience had begun producing symptoms of mental lumbago.

But he still wasn't ready to end his sked. Turning his attention to codes, by no means his strongest subject, he spent another five minutes describing the innovations 'Marks has introduced' (some of which I recognized) but suddenly seemed to remember that he hadn't arrived unaccompanied, and turned aside to let me take over.

I'd waited two years for this moment. There were many officers present who'd insisted that agents must re-encode their indecipherables if we'd failed to break them in time, and this was the day of reckoning.

I mounted the platform, and all the girls who'd stayed up night after night trying to break those indecipherables against the clock stood beside me, red eyes, periods and all. I pulled the covers off my customary prop, and those still awake stared with disinterest at the two encoded messages which had been written on the blackboard in my own unfair hand.

But these were no ordinary messages. They were real indecipherables which had arrived from a Buckmaster agent a year ago, and which had taken us over 11,000 attempts to break. They'd been encoded on the same transposition-keys, and the only alteration I'd made was to shorten one of them to make their lengths identical.

Trying to keep the anger out of my deep brown melter, and restraining the impulse to start, 'Listen, you bastards, if you can remember how to', I explained what the messages were and described what the girls had done to break them until all our heads were reeling.

My blanket attack then gathered momentum. 'Nick wants me to explain to you why no poem-code traffic must be passed by SFHQ.'

Nick, who'd asked no such thing, nodded emphatically.

I spent the next ten minutes explaining the weaknesses of the poem-code, probing for theirs by shooting questions at them like a schoolmaster with a recalcitrant class.

'Nick also wants you to understand the gift you make to the Germans when you order agents to re-encode their indecipherables.'

Nick nodded again.

Pointing to the two messages, I explained the anagramming process and challenged them to call out whichever words they thought most likely to appear.

I was convinced that, with less help from me than usual, it would take SOE's intelligentsia hours to find the right phrases. They recovered both clear-texts within twenty minutes and sat back, ready to join Bletchley. But although they'd been unexpectedly patient with me, a few of them (including Nick) began glancing at their watches.

'There's one last thing Nick wants you to see.'

I broke the speed limit trying to explain how the enemy reconstructed poems, then pointed to the transposition-key on the blackboard and invited them to attack it. It would be more difficult than most as the agent's poem was in French.

They were slow at first, but as soon as Sporborg discovered the word 'chanson', a miscreant at the back called out the poem in full.

George Courtauld whispered, 'Well, I'll be buggered.' Tommy Davies spoke very quietly to him, and a few seconds later Courtauld looked at me and nodded.

I'd taken even longer than Nick, and still hadn't discussed the three-way traffic. I turned to the door without waiting for questions.

Tommy moved very quickly considering that he was a member of the Executive Council. Taking my arm, he asked if I'd accompany him to his office as there was something important he wished to discuss with me in private.

I couldn't imagine what.

Looking hard at me, he confided that Courtauld's (of which he was a director) spent substantial sums of money in peacetime sending cables around the world. They used a code-book of some kind which he was sure I could improve on and thus reduce their costs. He didn't know my long-term plans, but would I be interested in running Courtauld's code department when the war was over?

My short-term plan was to kick him in the balls, but I abandoned it for three reasons:

1   He'd been invaluable to us
2   We still needed him
3   It was the best offer I'd had.

I replied that from the moment I'd been conceived my father had been waiting for me to run his rare bookshop and I couldn't disappoint him, but I'd gladly assist Courtauld's in any way I could in my spare time. Meanwhile I'd be grateful if he'd help us with a list of urgent requirements which I happened to have with me.

He made a note of the estimated quantities, reduced them by half and agreed to do his best. He then announced that there was something else he wanted me to do for him, but I must bear with him while he fully explained his reasons. He was seriously concerned about the number of people who'd stopped concentrating on the war effort.

He quickly made clear that it wasn't the Signals directorate he was targeting, especially after this morning. He was worried about the factory workers who assembled WT sets and spare parts for SOE. 'Far too many of 'em are taking victory for granted,' he thundered, 'and their loss of urgency is reflected in their output.'

He blamed the falling-off in production on the 'bloody stupid' campaigns being run by the Ministry of Information to buoy up morale, and on the BBC and the press for giving the public the impression that the war was almost won, instead of stressing how far we had to go and that Hitler wasn't finished yet.

I was wondering what this had to do with me when he suddenly said that a remedy had occurred to him, and that George Courtauld agreed with it.

I remembered their whispered conversation and the way Courtauld had nodded.

When I understood what their remedy entailed, even the Ministry of Information couldn't restore my morale. The 'hard men' were convinced that Nick and I made an excellent double-act, and wanted us to address the workers at four of their factories.

'We've no doubt that you'll increase their output,' Tommy said, 'no doubt at all.' He added that the four factories were within easy reach of London, that the workers were under the Official Secrets Act so there'd be no security problems, and that we needn't overburden them with details. It was the feelings we conveyed that would restore their sense of urgency. 'But the pep-talks must start at once before the rot sets in completely.' He anticipated no other problems.

I foresaw plenty. My own spare parts were beginning to feel worn, and I had to reassemble them every time I played the parlour-game. Sustaining the code department's war effort was difficult enough without trying to pep up other people's, a sign of staleness I'd no intention of remedying.

The whole concept appalled me, and my expression must have said so because he snatched up the phone to Nick and explained what he and Courtauld wanted. He added that I'd seemed reluctant to take part.

He listened inscrutably for almost a minute, then said, 'Thanks, Nick,' and replaced the receiver.

Drumming his fingers on my list of requirements, he announced that Nick was prepared to start the talks immediately, if necessary without me. However, he and Courtauld believed it was our contrasting styles which made our act effective.

I was left with a choice: either I could cancel three production meetings, four final briefings and six interviews with coders, or I could risk offending the 'hard men'.

I decided to go on the road with Nick.

SEVENTY-SIX

Pockets of Resistance

Our two-man crusade was launched at a factory near Barnet. Fifty or so girls in overalls were waiting for us in a large canteen and looked up without much interest as we arrived, escorted by the factory manager.

Nick addressed them first, and thirty minutes later I told them what else they needed to know.

In return they taught me the nuts and bolts of communication: to stop making phrases, to leave the jokes to Jack Benny, and to allow the facts to speak for themselves. It was entirely due to them that when I returned to the office I was able to simplify mental one-time pads, Jedburgh code-books and the growing concept of *Peeping Tom*.

At the end of the third lecture we heard from Tommy Davies that production had risen by 60 per cent.

But on the morning of our final sortie I learned from Valois that 'our friend Tommee' had been put on a train to Germany and sent to an extermination camp. Valois believed it was Buchenwald. I found it a little difficult to see the blackboard that morning, and the deep brown melter had developed a croak, but the girls didn't seem to notice.

Since I couldn't share Tommy's suffering I did the next best thing by producing a series of abscesses in the axilla which had to be lanced each morning by a doctor who warned me that if I didn't ease off from whatever I was doing he really wouldn't be responsible.

(I didn't know it at the time, but the RAF bombed Tommy's train and set part of it alight, and a girl in manacles crawled down the corridor to bring him water. It was Violette Szabo, and it was their first and only meeting.)

A few medications later I learned from Buckmaster that Noor Inayat Khan had been sent to Dachau but was thought to be alive.

At this point in the war (late August '44) time was measured in code-groups and 100,000 of these later I was twenty-four (an event of which the code department had been given ample notice). But on the same morning (24 September) news broke through from the outside world that thousands of Allied troops in Holland had had their last birthdays.

According to the Dutch traffic (90 per cent of which was in one-time pads or WOKs), the Germans had massacred the British and American forces who'd been ordered to capture Arnhem, and I remembered that the town had twice been mentioned in the three Playfair messages Nick had given us to break. If the Germans had intercepted them (and others from the same source?) could they have contributed to the disastrous losses? Nick was convinced that they weren't responsible for the massive counter-attacks, which were only to be expected, Heffer wasn't sure, and I was unable to establish any connection.*

The Germans were also counter-attacking at their own frontiers, and the Allies were unable to cross them.

Yet X section still showed no signs of sending agents into Germany, and I still couldn't understand why there was no place for SOE inside the Fatherland, or why the task of harassing them from within should be left to the Americans.

The one thing I did understand was the growing list of SOE's casualties. On 2 November I learned that Rabinovitch had been sent to a concentration camp, and was thought to have been hanged.

By now, time could also be measured in exterminated agents.

I was looking at the photograph Rabinovitch had given me of Louis knocking out Schmeling (which was next to Violette's chess-set and Tommy's cigar) when I received a message to report to Gubbins immediately. It was so long since I'd been to his office that I'd forgotten the ferocity of his 'Come.'

Six crossed swords were pointed at my jugular. Four of them belonged to Gubbins and Nick, but by far the sharpest adorned the shoulders of a general standing by the window.

---

* Nor have I since.

He had eyes which could lance an abscess, a court-martial of a mouth, and an expression which warned me that he'd found his next victim.

Gubbins came straight to the point (he knew no other way).

Five minutes later I learned that SOE was to play a major part in a deception scheme code-named Periwig.

The purpose of Periwig was to convince the Germans that there was a large Resistance Movement inside Germany which was about to be activated. Gubbins stressed that the Germans would expect London to send instructions to these agents, and that dummy traffic would be an essential part of the Periwig op.

'Any ideas?'

'I'm afraid not, sir.'

I took his disappointment as a compliment.

'I know nothing about German traffic . . .'

The unknown general took a step towards me. '*What do you need to know?*'

'This is General Templar,' barked Gubbins.

A razor nicked my ear, and I realized that Templar was still addressing me.

'Kindly answer my question. *What do you need to know?*'

'Whether the bulk of the traffic is passed in letters or figures, whether they're in groups of four or five –'

'Time for that later. Don't you have any ideas?'

I suggested that one way of helping Periwig would be to drop code-books printed in German to all the areas where the Resistance Movement was supposed to be operating.

Gubbins and Templar glanced at each other sharply.

I added that the code-books would contain vocabularies designed for active Resistance Movements, and that they'd be dropped with silk one-time pads. I then began describing how we handled our other dummy traffic but Templar turned impatiently to Gubbins.

'Colin, I think the best thing would be if Marks brought this dummy traffic and the rest of his bumpf to my office at 1700 hours, and I'll have a good look at it.'

Gubbins nodded approvingly.

'Right,' said Templar with a hint of satisfaction, 'that's it then.'

Not quite.

Mindful of military protocol, I addressed Templar through my superior officer. 'Brigadier Nicholls, wouldn't it simplify matters if General Temple were to –'

'*Templar*,' barked Templar.

'I'm sorry, sir . . . wouldn't it be better if General Templar came to my office so that I could show him the whole of our bumph?'

Nick turned to him. 'I think it would, Gerald.'

Templar graciously conceded that he'd call on me at 1700 hours.

I turned again to my superior officer. 'Could the general please make it seventeen thirty hours, sir? . . . I've a lecture to give which I can't cancel, and some agents to brief . . .'

The silence could have been cut with a sword.

'I suppose you need the extra half-hour to come up with all the answers?' suggested Templar.

'He's been known to do it in less,' said Nick, my protector.

Gubbins turned to me abruptly. 'Right, Leo – off you go.'

It was the first Leo of the meeting, so I must have said something which pleased him.

I hurried in to Heffer, who seemed to be expecting me, and described my encounter with Templar. 'Help me, Heff. What can you tell me about him? What's his background? What's he like as a man?'

Never one to refuse an appeal for help even if it meant putting down his newspaper, Heffer said that Templar was an old friend of Gubbins, that he was a senior staff officer with a reputation for unorthodoxy, and that Montgomery thought highly of him. But all he knew about him as a man was that he was supposed to have a command of bad language which was second to none. He urged me to set up a working relationship with him immediately or I'd never recover.

The tone of that relationship was set by Templar the moment he walked in.

'You knew my name was Templar, didn't you?'

'Yes, sir.'

'And you *could* have seen me at seventeen hundred hours, couldn't you?'

'Yes, sir.'

'Right. Well, from this moment onwards, stop playing games.'

He then sat opposite me, glared at my overflowing ashtray, and asked how I wanted to begin.

'I'd like to ask a question if I may, sir.'

'What d'you think I've come for? To smell those stinking cigars?'

'Assuming we get Periwig right, sir, what's our time-scale?'

'*Did I hear you say "assuming"?* – I bloody well hope not.' He thumped the desk, and the inkwell pee'd itself. '*We're going to get Periwig right – and fast.* Starting now . . . and I mean *NOW*. Show me what you've got.'

I produced six different code-books and spread them in front of him.

He examined them carefully, and addressed me without looking up. 'Did you have a hand in these vocabularies?'

'I kept a watching brief, sir. My main job was preparing the code-groups.'

'I'll want you in on every discussion. Periwig's vocabulary has got to be right. I won't tolerate half-arsed concoctions.'

At this moment Muriel entered with Mother's far from half-arsed concoctions, and he stared at them in astonishment. 'What are these – camouflaged code-books?'

'Perhaps you'd prefer something stronger, sir?'

'Yes – a good idea for Periwig.'

Nevertheless he helped himself to coffee, sampled the sandwiches, and then asked where they came from.

For some reason I told him the truth.

'You an only child?'

I nodded.

'I thought as much.'

He then sharply reminded me that the main purpose of Periwig was to bog down 'the Hun's security forces all over Germany' and that I mustn't lose sight of this when preparing the code-groups and the dummy traffic.

'No, sir.'

Glancing at his watch, he asked at what time I usually reported for duty.

'At 0700 hours, unless there's a crisis.'

'Periwig's a crisis. I'll be here at 0600 every morning. Your mother must call you early.'

He then informed me that he intended to take a Jedburgh code-book with him so that he could study it overnight. 'I enjoy a little light reading,' he added.

He slipped one into his briefcase, nodded abruptly and turned to the door.

'Excuse me, sir, but we don't allow code-books to be taken off the premises.'

He halted in mid-stride, then performed an about-turn which would have done credit to a sergeant-major. 'Are you seriously objecting? Or are you playing games again?'

'Both, sir.'

Apparently satisfied with my answer, he replaced the code-book on the desk and walked out in silence.

My self-confidence walked out with him. After working alone for so long I knew I couldn't function under the constant supervision of a military dictator. My only hope was that Templar wouldn't be with us for long.

I learned next morning that he'd been appointed head of X section.

SEVENTY-SEVEN

Operation Periwig

Nineteen forty-five had a miraculous start. Templar went abroad for a few days to an unknown destination (hopefully Berlin), giving all who worked for him the chance to recuperate.

However, he was back all too soon, and discovered that Periwig had made no progress in his absence due to a policy dispute. He asked me to explain why 'this bloody outfit took so long to reach a decision' and was kind enough to supply the answer: '*It's because SOE as a whole is the sum total of its farts – and they'd better not start blowing in Periwig's direction.*'

He was angry with me because although Periwig's vocabulary was finished it couldn't be delivered to the printers as I was bogged down with the code-groups. Although I'd convinced myself that an active Resistance Movement existed in Germany because Tommy was in prison there, I was equally convinced that the code-groups weren't ready to stand up to expert scrutiny.

I was having the utmost difficulty in standing up to Templar's. He'd begun calling on me on his way home to check the day's progress, and seemed to enjoy watching me flounder while he made up for lost sandwiches.

One night he caught me pencilling some code-groups on my copy of the vocabulary.

'*Finished at last?*'

'Getting there, sir. I'm convinced the basic concept's right but I'm trying to improve it . . .'

He gave his 'How long, O Lord' look, and I decided to ask him a question.

'Sir, how sure are you that *any* of the code-books will be captured?'

'Leave that problem to me, *and get on with yours.*'

He was back the next night for a repeat performance, but this time Gubbins came to collect him half an hour later.

Gubbins watched me in silence for as long as he could bear to (roughly ten seconds), then shot a question at me à la Templar. 'What's your problem, Marks?'

'Verisimilitude, sir.'

'Give her my regards,' he said, and took Templar away with him.

An hour later I realized what the code-groups should be.

It took Muriel three hours to type them opposite the 6,000 phrases, and the RAF unit half a day to photograph the now completed code-book on to a single sheet of silk.

The moment I heard Templar marching down the corridor I buried my head in my hands in mock despair.

'*Now what's the hold-up?*'

'You are, sir.' I pointed to the sheet of silk on my desk. '. . . it's waiting for you.'

The way he picked it up, and stared at it in astonishment, was a moment to relish.

'Good God! . . . I'd no idea it would look like this.'

Neither had I till a few hours ago.

K

He examined the code-groups for at least fünf minuten, then looked up at me and nodded his head like Commander Two Ns.

I then asked him to look at the code-groups again, and see if he noticed anything special about them.

He examined the ones printed under F, which I knew by now was his favourite letter, then shook his head irritably. 'Come on, come on! What am I missing?'

I explained that the sum of the first two figures was *always* the same as the sum of the last two:

'Look at 1551, sir [F-wird-zweimal-gefunkelt] . . . 1 and 5 come to 6, and so do 5 and 1. Now look at 1560 . . . 1 and 5 come to 6, so do 6 and 0. Now try 1579 . . . 1 and 5 come to 6, and 7 and 9 come to 6.'

'They came to 16 in my day.'

'You don't carry the tens, sir.'

'All very interesting – *but what's it in aid of?*'

'Reducing Morse mutilation, sir.'

I explained that if one figure in four were mutilated the agent could work out which it was, and invited him to try it for himself, but he preferred to take my word for it. I added that we used a similar system for the Jedburgh, SAS and FFI code-books, and that the Boche must have captured some and would expect us to use nothing less for the Fatherland.

'Had any other ideas for Periwig?'

I told him that I thought iodoforms would be useful.

'Iodo*what*?'

He listened carefully while I explained their function, and then asked who prepared them.

'The country sections, sir.'

'I'll want you to sit in on Periwig's.'

He then produced a handsome fountain pen from his pocket, covered a sheet of foolscap as quickly as Father writing out a bill, and caught me watching him. 'No one can read my writing the right way up! It's safer than a code.'

I hadn't been trying to read his writing because I'd been too busy admiring his fountain pen, though I could have told him that he'd misspelt iodoforms.

He crushed a yawn as if it were a minor rebellion, glanced at his watch, and seemed surprised at how long we'd been Periwigging. He then picked up the code-book with surprising delicacy. 'Any objections if I take this home with me!?'

'None, sir. If the enemy stole it from you it would help Periwig.'

He put the silk into his briefcase, muttered, 'Saucy little sod,' and issued his parting instructions over his shoulder – 'Get a good night's sleep. – *It could be your last for some time.* I'll be here at 0700 hours to discuss something else.' He closed the door more quietly than usual.

I spent most of the night wondering what the something else was.

*   *   *

At 0600 hours he came straight to the coffeeless point.

'You've been told damn all about one aspect of Periwig because it isn't part of your need-to-know. But you're a bright little bugger and may have some ideas on it so I'm going all the way with you – *Don't make me regret it.*'

He then confided that there was a German officer in a prisoner-of-war camp who could be a great help to Periwig. His name was Schiller, and he was a double-agent. '. . . he's worked for both sides, and done a good job for each. But he doesn't know what we've got in mind for him, and bloody well mustn't. *Is that understood?*'

A bewildered 'bright little bugger' nodded his head.

'Ever met a double?'

'Not as far as I know, sir.'

'Well, you're bloody soon going to. I can promise you that.'

He poured himself some coffee, and for the first time put no milk in it. 'I'm going to tell you a few things about him.' He then proceeded to give me the kind of guarded briefing which the military seemed to reserve for civilians.

Schiller had started off by working for the Germans, who'd landed him in Cornwall to report on our D-Day preparations, but we'd captured him and he'd agreed to work for us. He sent a dozen messages back to Germany (he was a first-class WT operator), but realized they'd grow suspicious if he carried on too long, and broke off contact. We then put him in a POW camp but he soon got bored with it, and two weeks ago volunteered to return to Germany to continue working for us.

'And so he's bloody well going to, but not in the way he thinks.'

He paused for only the second time since I'd known him, then seemed to remember that he was 'going all the way'.

'Jumping's a hazardous business, and Schiller might meet with a fatal accident before he's even touched ground. In this unfortunate event the huns would find your code-book on his body . . . Now, then! . . . *What else should they find on him that would lend verisimilitude – your word, I believe – to operation Periwig?*'

I looked at him in silence. He'd gone far enough to make me realize that I was being asked to contribute to a fatal accident which my idea had probably triggered.

'If you've got any qualms about this, he's betrayed as many British agents as he has German – probably more. *What else should be found on him?*'

I asked which British organizations Schiller had worked for.

'What the hell's that to do with it?'

'It would be a help if I knew what codes they'd given him.'

'He worked for C.'

'In that case he understands double-transposition.'

'Yes, yes – answer my question for Christ's sake. *What else should be found on him?*'

I suggested that he should be dropped with a supply of Periwig code-books and one-time pads to be given to other agents and that they should include instructions printed in German. He should also take in our latest WT sets and some specially prepared signal-plans.

'Nick's already taken care of it.'

He brushed a crumb from his tunic as if it were a signals officer and I felt the singe of his number one glare. 'You're going to have to go to that camp and brief Schiller yourself, and you must bloody well do it with complete conviction. Anything less and he'll see right through you. Think you're up to it?'

I nodded.

'Then stand by tomorrow. It'll take you an hour to get there and you'll be provided with an escort, which is more than I am. Departure time later.'

He hurried away to start his day's work.

My escort was a cherubic young captain named Wilson, and we confined our conversation in the car to banalities in case our FANY driver were Himmler in drag, but he finally volunteered that we were on the outskirts of Basingstoke. A few minutes later we reached some tall iron gates and two large military policemen approached the car. Captain Wilson produced his pass, and I noticed that one of the policemen recognized him at once. Seconds later the gates swung back.

It was the first time I'd visited a prisoner-of-war camp other than Baker Street. It was also the first time I'd seen so many Germans gathered together except in news reels or in Fritz Lang's films. They were imprisoned behind wire-netted compounds, some standing, some sprawling, some kicking footballs.

We drove slowly down a long path between the compounds, and I felt our progress being monitored every inch of the way. Although it was impossible to tell which of them were soldiers and which wild animals, I asked the driver to pull up, leapt out of the car and strode towards one of the compounds. I'd spotted a powerfully built six-footer brandishing his fist in the face of a fellow-prisoner who wasn't much bigger than me. I stared at him in silence as if trying to recall where I'd seen him before, and continued to stare at him until I caught a look of fear in his eyes.

I then made some rapid notes ('Hope the bastard wants to pee as badly as I do'), took a final look at him and Templared back to my anxious escort.

'Mr Marks, what in God's name were you up to?'

'I've always wanted to scare the shit out of a German soldier.'

Our stately progress continued until we reached a courtyard without a German in sight, and we drew up outside a small office block.

Two more military policemen approached the car. Again my escort produced his pass, and again one of them recognized him.

Five minutes later we were only a flight of stairs away from 'Operation Fatal Accident'. As we reached the top of the stairs, my escort confided that he knew Schiller, and that General Templar had told him to introduce us, and then leave us alone.

I wondered what other instructions Templar had given him.

I caught my first glimpse of Schiller as he rose from behind a table and greeted Wilson as if they were old friends meeting for a drink. He had Tommy's stocky build but was at least ten years younger, and I searched in vain for his 'double chin' (I needed every joke I could think of).

Wilson introduced me as the coding officer but didn't refer to me by name, and said he'd wait next door but there was absolutely no hurry as he had plenty of work to catch up on. He then left us alone in a small interview room which had bars across its solitary window, and the indefinable smell of protracted interrogations.

Schiller remained standing until I was seated, then resumed his place behind the table, and patiently waited for the proceedings to begin.

I immediately set about killing him by code.

Whoever had briefed him previously had done a good job. He knew how to use a code-book, and studied the Periwig vocabulary with interest. 'So much on one piece of *Seide* – silk – is excellent,' he said.

So was his English, and I had no difficulty in explaining the special feature of the code-groups. He listened in silence until I'd finished, then nodded approvingly.

I then produced a one-time pad and showed him how to use it, though it soon became apparent that he could have shown me. I stressed the importance of cutting away the code-groups after every message and asked him to see for himself how easy it was. I then handed him a pair of scissors, and watched him cut his own throat.

It was WOK-time next and it seemed to come as a welcome surprise to him. 'Makes it very much easy,' he said.

I stressed that WOK-keys must also be destroyed message by message and again asked him to try it for himself.

At this point a large corporal appeared carrying tea and buns. Schiller waited till I'd helped myself, but instead of sampling his 'elevenses' he picked up the scissors and finished cutting away the silk. I had some difficulty in swallowing as I watched him, and he seemed to sense it because he looked at me sharply.

I asked him to listen very carefully to what I now had to tell him, and he sat forward but continued to study me thoughtfully. I explained the advantages of one-time pads over WOKs and of both over poem-codes, which must be used only in emergencies. Did he know how the system worked?

He asked if it was the same as using phrases from a novel (a favourite C system), and I confirmed that it was except for the indicator-groups, which I'd show him later. Was there any particular poem that he'd like to use?

He said that there was, and I told him to write it out for me. He did so in block capitals, and I then asked him to speak it aloud so that I could compare it with what he'd written.

Like so many agents asked to repeat poems, he spoke it in block capitals. The words meant little to me except that they weren't the 'Horst Wessel', and I again warned him that he must use them only in emergencies.

'The most important thing of all is your security checks . . .' I spent ten minutes explaining them to him, but for the first time didn't have it all my own way.

He wanted to change his indicator-groups by 8 and 5, and when I asked why he said that 8 May was his birthday and the 5th his mother's and he wouldn't forget either of them, but I pointed out that many agents used this idea and that the Germans were on to it, and he at once agreed to the figures I'd suggested.

I then produced three coded messages, and asked him to decipher them. He began working as if his life depended on it.

I hoped that someone would engrave 8 May on his headstone, though I doubted if he'd have one. He was having a hard time with the task I'd set him as I'd mutilated the code-groups to make decipherment more difficult, but he remembered what I'd shown him and persevered until he proudly produced the correct clear-text.

The LOP, WOK and poem-code messages gave him no trouble, but at the end of them he sat back exhausted and poured himself some tea.

I then instructed him to encode three messages (one in each system), and to *make sure that he inserted his security checks*. Forty minutes later he'd finished all three, and took a deep breath.

I checked each message carefully, and pointed out a small mistake.

He swore in German and apologized in English, an appropriate arrangement.

We'd already spent more than two hours together, and I enquired if he had any questions.

'Not about codes. But, sir . . . do you know when I am intentioned to go in?'

Sir explained that this wasn't his department, and Schiller appeared to accept it. I added that I was leaving now but if he had any questions after I'd gone I'd gladly come to see him again.

He looked at me with a smile not unlike Tommy's. 'You have taken much trouble with me – very much trouble. And I am just as much grateful.'

I'd intended at this point to wish him 'Hals and Beinbruch.', which I thought was the equivalent of 'merde alors', but I'd discovered that its literal meaning was 'good luck – break a leg'. So I held out my hand, and wished him 'Viel Gluck' instead.

To my astonishment, I found that I meant it.

Templar was waiting for me in my office.

'Well? What did you make of him?'

'I'm sure he'll do a good job for both sides, sir.'

'Wilson tells me you did a bloody good one yourself. He was listening in.'

I remembered Schiller's last question to me. 'He's anxious to know when he's going to be sent in.'

'Have your bumph ready in two days at the latest. He'll be back in his homeland by the end of the week.'

I dispatched the 'bumph' to X section and waited for Templar's next visit, but he suddenly stopped calling on me.

I then learned from Heffer that he was leaving SOE. According to the Guru, Montgomery had something else in mind for him and he'd soon be taking off. 'Don't try to make sense of it, this is SOE,' he said, and returned to his newspaper.

A week later I still hadn't heard from Templar and was wondering whether to call and say goodbye or to wait for the official announcement when in he walked.

I couldn't believe what I saw: he was carrying a small posy of flowers, which he presented to me with great delicacy, and I wondered what the hell he thought I was.

'These are for your mother. Tell her they're from you as they bloody well should be.' He then insisted that Muriel took them away and put them in water as they couldn't survive the whole day in my stink-hole of an office. He then settled down to the less serious business of Periwig.

'You'll be sorry to hear that your friend Schiller has met with a fatal accident – they'll have found the codes on him by now so get a move on with those dummy messages. But that's not what I'm here to talk about.' I felt the singe of his number two glare. 'I suppose you know that I'm leaving this place?' He didn't actually say stink-hole but his expression conveyed it.

'Yes, sir.'

'Of course you do! – damn stupid question. Barry is taking over, and he'll be getting in touch with you. Help him all you can. You'll find him a lot easier to deal with.'

I didn't comment.

'There are two questions I've been meaning to ask you but never got round to . . . *But you're under no obligation to answer them, is that understood?*'

I was too touched by the flowers to do anything but nod.

'The first concerns Holland. I've heard many versions about what went wrong there. I'd like to hear yours. You have my word it'll go no further.'

That was good enough for me.

I began with Ebenezer's stip-step-stapping, explained the significance of the total lack of coding mistakes and ended with Plan Giskes, but made no reference to my battles with SOE as I felt he understood.

He thanked me for making things clear to him, and then said that his other question was personal. 'But I repeat – you don't have to answer it if you don't want to. – *is that understood?*'

I nodded.

'What made you become a cryptographer?'

I had a stock answer for this but it wasn't the moment for it. I described how I'd broken 84's code at the age of eight, and he listened with the hint of a smile while I synopsized the consequences.

He then quietly informed me that all his military books had come from 84, and that he'd probably met my father. 'Short chap. Writes very quickly . . . a bloody good salesman.'

'That's Dad.'

'One of his oldest customers used to be a pal of mine. His name's Clarence Hatry. Don't suppose you've heard of him.?'

I hoped for Periwig's sake that his other suppositions were better founded.

I knew so much about Hatry that even in Templar's presence I could think of little else . . .

Hatry was a financier who'd defrauded the City of London of two million pounds, which in the early thirties was a significant achievement. Most of his vast library had come from 84, and he walked into the shop in the middle of a major slump, told Father that he

576

knew times were difficult, and apologized for having to ask him to make an offer for his library.

Although books for which Dad had paid £1,000 would no longer fetch £100, he knew Hatry needed to raise money for his trial at the Old Bailey, and told him that he had 'a bit of good news for him'. He was able to offer him a profit on his books – 'a small profit mind you, but a profit'. Despite his partner's protestations he bought Hatry's library for three times what it was worth but, being Dad, he didn't leave it at that.

When Hatry was sentenced to a long term of imprisonment, he contacted the prison governor (a fellow Freemason), and Hatry was made the prison librarian. When he was finally released, he bought a well-known bookshop, used it to raise capital for his other operations, and made another million pounds . . .

'Yes, sir – I know a bit about Hatry.'

'He'd have done a damn good job for SOE – especially in the finance department.' He glanced at his watch, and I wondered how to say goodbye to him.

He had his own way of saying it to me. Reaching into his pocket, he took out his fountain pen and carefully laid it on the Periwig code-book. 'I caught you looking at this with more respect than you've ever shown me. Hope you'll make better use of it than I do.'

I was at a loss for the words which I hoped the pen would one day write.

He allowed me a moment to recover. 'I'll say this for you, Leo – you've been a new experience – and I've had a few in my time, I can tell you that.'

I stood up when he did. 'I've enjoyed every minute of it, sir.'

His final words echoed round the room. '*Stop playing games.*'

He played a few himself in the years which followed: by the mid-sixties he was Field Marshal Sir Gerald Templar, head of the Imperial General Staff. His nickname amongst those who understood his achievements in the war against Japan, and the one he most savoured, was the 'Tiger of Malaya'.

To me he would always be Periwig.

I wrote the first draft of *Peeping Tom* with his fountain pen.

SEVENTY-EIGHT

Serial Number 47685

April's good news came first, and could hardly have been better. Hitler had committed suicide, and Tommy had escaped from Buchenwald!

I knew the Führer's destination but had no idea of Tommy's until I learned from Colonel Dismore that though he'd been 'tortured beyond belief and was barely able to walk', he'd reached the American forces at Chemnitz, and was 'hell-bent' on making his way to Paris, regardless of German patrols. He was too choked to say more.

I also learned that Violette Szabo had been executed at Ravensbrück, and Noor Inayat Khan at Dachau.

Vera Atkins subsequently confirmed that neither girl had died alone. Violette had knelt down, holding hands with Lilian Rolfe and Denise Bloch, and been shot in the back of the head. Noor (perhaps remembering her *Jakarta Tales*) had also knelt down, and Yolande Beekman, Madeleine Damerment and Eliane Plewman had crossed the bridge with her. Vera Leigh, Diana Rowden and Andrée Borell had been given lethal injections at Natzweiler, and Yvonne Rudellat had been buried at Belsen.

The list of male agents who'd been executed was still coming in.

So were rumours that the war was 'on its last legs', and that SOE must prepare for dismemberment. Unhappily for some of us, the latter part of this rumour had no foundation.

Although our traffic had been reduced by 80 per cent, so had the girls' vigilance, and I had to remind them that the code war hadn't ended with Hitler's death, and that until the new German supremo, Admiral Doenitz, had signed a promissory note called a peace treaty none of them must relax. The admiral knew better than to keep them waiting.

War-weary Baker Street, dispirited by the losses and aware of its mistakes, was revitalized by the details of Tommy's survival which began coming in.

Despite the torture he'd suffered at the hands of the Gestapo in Paris, he'd maintained his cover-story that he was Squadron Leader Dodkin, serial number 47685, and the Germans knew him as such when he arrived at Buchenwald. He'd escaped from the camp by convincing the German officer in charge of injecting prisoners with typhus that if he allowed him and twenty-one other prisoners to escape he'd testify on his behalf at his war-crimes trial.*

He'd been injected with a harmless liquid instead of the deadly typhus, and was smuggled out of Buchenwald. He was then sent to other camps, but on 16 April escaped from a train bound for Czechoslovakia when it stopped to dispose of the 170 bodies to which his own was about to be added.

When he finally reached Chemnitz (after being captured by a German patrol, and escaping once again) he gave his American interrogators details of all the German troops and battery locations which he'd seen en route, and was disappointed that they wouldn't let him take part in the mopping-up operations.

He set out for Paris in a car driven by two friends, and although they were fired on by German patrols, with typical Tommy timing he arrived there on VE Day.

But that wasn't all he'd achieved. Whilst still in the typhus block expecting to be executed, he'd managed to smuggle three messages out of the camp. Two were farewell letters to Barbara and Dismore, the third was an official report which he'd enciphered in his Sea-horse code with his security checks correct.

The report gave details of the experiments in bacteriological warfare being carried out in Buchenwald, and stated that he and his fellow-prisoners would try to secure records of them until the arrival of airborne forces on or before the German capitulation. He asked for the message to be acknowledged by iodoform 'du moineau au lapin' and sent his love to Barbara.

* A promise which he honoured despite the opposition of the authorities as he'd given the word of a British officer.

579

The report finally reached London via the Americans, by which time he'd escaped.

On 8 May he flew back to England.

Colonel Dismore and Barbara were waiting on the runway. They'd been warned about his appearance.

A few weeks later I was writing a report for Nick when I heard the door open. Thinking it was Muriel, I didn't look up, and then became aware that she'd been silent for far too long.

An old man was watching me from the doorway. I was about to ask if he had an appointment, but realized in time that he'd never needed one.

I knew that sixteen of Tommy's friends had been suspended from hooks in the Buchenwald crematorium, and been killed by slow strangulation. They were hanging from his eyes.

'Fuck 'em,' I said.

'I did my best . . .' His voice was a quaver.

I shook hands with him in the time-honoured way – by producing the cigar which I'd been keeping in my desk.

His smile hadn't changed, though it seemed to hurt his lips. 'Haven't smoked one for a while,' he said. 'Better keep it for the moment.'

I lent him my cigar-case.

'Hope the report I sent came out easily. The light wasn't too good . . .'

'It was up to your usual lousy standards.'

He refused my offer of refreshments as he couldn't stay long, then asked how my parents were.

I told him they'd celebrated VE Day by going to the synagogue for the first time in twenty years, but had forgotten most of the passwords.

'It happens to the best of us.' He glanced at the pile of codes on the desk. 'Still at it, I see. Won't keep you now . . . just looked in to say hello . . . I'll probably call in one night for a chat.'

'I'll be here.'

We shook hands in silence.

I waited until his footsteps had shuffled away, and was then violently sick on behalf of mankind.

SEVENTY-NINE

For Services Rendered

By the end of June the code department had been reduced to a skeleton staff and its head to a skeleton.

I'd made the mistake of trying to say goodbye to each girl individually, and been dismembered in the process. I'd found it impossible to thank them, and was astonished when some of them thanked me. When the question of their decorations arose I suggested to Heffer that they should all be made Dame Commanders of the British Empire.

'They'll be lucky if they get MBEs. Prepare a list but limit it to twelve.'

Before I could protest he said that honours for members of technical departments like Signals were causing SOE problems. The difficulty was that outstanding performers could hardly be given honours higher than those awarded to their superior officers, and that to save embarrassment decorations would be awarded according to rank. He added that it was just possible that one day the question of an honour for me might arise.

I assured him that in that unlikely event there'd be no problem as I'd accept no honour higher than the ones SOE gave the girls. 'Just think what that would make me. I'd be the first male Dame Commander of the British Empire.'

Although I'd have loved to enable my parents to dangle a bit of ribbon in front of the neighbours who'd sent their only child white feathers, I'd already been given the chance to shake hands with agents who'd returned from the field, and no other reward was comparable.

A month later Churchill was ousted as Prime Minister in the July elections and was replaced by Attlee. Nick (a Conservative in everything but Signals) was appalled that the man who'd ordered us to 'Set Europe Ablaze' had himself been extinguished.

Perhaps he identified with him, because he picked up a piece of paper which he'd kept on his desk for the past two months. It was a copy of a message which Eisenhower had sent to Gubbins when SFHQ in France was about to be dispersed. The message praised SOE's 'high achievements' in the battle against Germany, and included a phrase which most of us in Signals knew by heart: 'Particular credit must be due to those responsible for communications with the occupied territories.'

Glancing at the face of the man who most deserved the praise, I wondered what Nick's future would be when SOE closed down.

On 5 August the Americans announced that they'd dropped an atomic bomb on Japan.

On the 9th they dropped another, and a few hours later Heffer dropped one on me.

He said that Japan was certain to surrender within the next few weeks, and that SOE would be disbanded by the end of the year. He then disclosed in confidence that Gambier-Parry (head of C's Signals) had asked Nick to find out whether I'd be prepared to work for C as soon as my present job was over.

I'd sooner go to Hiroshima and my expression must have shown it.

'I'm telling you this now to give you a chance to think it over before Nick puts it to you officially.' He added that at least a dozen senior SOE officers had been invited to join C, and that most of them had agreed.

'Merde alors to the lot of them. I never want to see another code when SOE packs up, but thanks for the warning.' I hurried from his office.

I knew the pressure the bastards were capable of exerting; I had to leave SOE as quickly as I could.

But I had one major job to do before SOE would release me: Gubbins required all department heads to write comprehensive reports of their department's activities. The code department's would be a massive task which would take me several weeks to complete, and I hadn't even begun. I told Muriel I wanted no calls or interruptions and tried to settle down to it.

An hour later a catastrophe occurred. I thought of a code which would be suitable for agents in peacetime.

The idea was so novel that I wanted to rush in to Nick with it, but I realized just in time that it might interest C. I also realized that it might be useful to our enemies in peacetime, if we had any apart from ourselves.

The purpose of the code was to enable agents to communicate freely with each other in any language they chose, even though they didn't speak a single word of it. Suppose two German agents were working in England, and their sole means of communicating with each other was by post. They could write to each other in English, though neither understood a word of it, and every letter they exchanged would contain a secret message of one-time pad security.

They would first write out their secret messages in German, using figure one-time pads and code-books. They then had to turn these figures into colloquial English, of which they understood 'Nichts'. To achieve this they would refer to a sheet of silk which had English phrases printed opposite every number.

Suppose the first number to be concealed were 9: he'd copy out the phrase opposite 9.

0	You'll be glad to know
1	I hope you'll be glad to know
2	You'll be happy to know
3	You'll be very happy to know
4	You'll be pleased to hear
5	You'll be very pleased to hear
6	I'm glad to tell you
7	I'm very glad to tell you
8	I'm delighted to tell you
9	I can't wait to tell you

His letter would therefore begin: 'I can't wait to tell you'.

Suppose the second figure to be encoded were 0. He'd refer to the next column of his silk, and copy out the phrase opposite 0.

0	that after all this time
1	that after such a long time
2	that after all this while
3	that after all this delay
4	that at last
5	that at long last
6	that finally
7	that in God's good time
8	that eventually
9	that despite the difficulties

His letter would therefore begin: 'I can't wait to tell you that after all this time', and he'd continue to chat away about what had happened for as long as the code-groups demanded.

His correspondent's reply must appear to answer this letter. Suppose the first number to be concealed were 5: he'd copy out the phrase opposite 5.

0	Of course I'm glad
1	Of course I'm pleased
2	Naturally I'm glad
3	Naturally I'm pleased
4	I'm glad to hear
5	I'm damn glad to hear
6	I'm delighted to hear
7	I'm relieved to hear
8	I'm thrilled to hear
9	I'm happy to hear

His letter would therefore begin: 'I'm damn glad to hear'.
Suppose the next figure to be concealed were 1:

0	that after trying so hard
1	that after all your efforts
2	that after trying for so long
3	that after trying so hard for so long
4	that you've finally managed to

5   that you've at last managed to
6   that you're now able to
7   that you're finally able to
8   that you've at last managed to
9   that you've finally be able to

His letter would therefore begin: 'I'm damn glad to hear that after all your efforts', and would continue to use as many phrases as he needed (they'd all make sense).

The basic idea could be put to other uses, but I did my best to abort them and tried to start my report. But I was stuck for an opening (a good phrase for a letter?) because 'other uses' kept cropping up, and I made no progress whatever.

On 15 August Japan surrendered and SOE's closure was now a certainty.

I was more determined than ever not to surrender to C but was still only on page one of my report.

I was struggling to abort yet another use for the code when Nick summoned me to his office. He'd recovered from his depression, and asked how the report was progressing.

'I'm halfway through it, sir.'

'Good man – the general's anxious to read it.'

He then reminded me that Gubbins wanted me to write a separate report on Holland, which I was to deliver to him personally; no copies must be taken.

'I've already warned Muriel, sir.'

I noticed that Eisenhower's letter was still on his desk, and looked up to find him watching me. 'You've invented a new code, haven't you?'

I was too astonished to answer.

'If I don't know the symptoms by now, I'm in the wrong job. What sort of code? Who's it intended for?'

'Whoever empties our waste-paper baskets.' I added that it was just a vague idea which would be of no practical use to anyone but had helped with the tedium of the report.

He glared at me in disbelief and immediately asked if I'd considered C's offer.

So he knows Heffer's already discussed it with me.

I gave him much the same answer as I had the Guru and he looked at me just as impatiently. 'We'll come back to that later. Heffer's told you that we're closing down at the end of December?'

'Yes, sir.

Well, there's been a development you should know about.' Obviously hating every word of it, he said that all SOE's records were to be taken over by C.

'But that's like burying Hitler in Westminster Abbey.'

'There's not a damn thing we can do about it.' He then said that both parties had agreed that the hand-over could only succeed if various members of the country sections and the Signals directorate stayed behind to take part in it. 'The Signal records are essential to the hand-over. I don't need to tell you that the code department's are the largest of all, and by far the most important.'

Nor did he need to tell me what was coming next.

'. . . in other words, Leo, General Gubbins and I want you to supervise the handing over of all the coding records, and all cipher traffic. It might take you three months. How about it?'

'I don't have three months, Nick.' I wanted to add that I sometimes felt that I didn't have three minutes.

'I suppose you realize that most of us in SOE will be muzzled for the rest of our lives, and that those records will be all that remain of us? Doesn't that matter a damn to you?'

A frothing brigadier is a terrifying sight.

'As for not wanting to see another code when SOE packs up, don't you realize that Britain will soon be on its own again? . . . that Russia's the new menace, and will be for years? . . . that the Americans are behaving appallingly in Siam, and are no longer the allies they were?'

Neither was Nick.

'We'll need a first-class Intelligence service to keep us in the running, and the whole of our traffic will have to be rethought . . . Who's going to help us with it – the Russians? – the Americans? – General de Gaulle's lot? Hasn't it occurred to you that peacetime agents will need new codes and security checks and as much training as ours? Don't you realize that many of Bletchley's best cryptographers will go back to their old occupations? You're too young to have had one so you've no excuses unless you're too tired to think straight. Just tell me this: doesn't any part of the code war interest you any more?'

I owed him the truth. 'Yes, sir. How to put it behind me.'

His voice took on a new edge. 'Then finish this report, and get on with whatever's more important to you than helping your country.'

Our double-act was now over and I felt more alone than the British.

EIGHTY

Exemplary Conduct

The main problem with finishing the report was knowing what to exclude, and I had to make a major decision. Gubbins had stressed that nothing must be glossed over, and I had to choose whether or not to make a disclosure which I hadn't dared to make previously for fear of instant dismissal. I now decided that I would because it might hasten my departure.

It concerned the 'War Diary', and the way that certain people in SOE (myself in particular) had wilfully misled it.

It was known throughout Baker Street as the 'war diarrhoea', and its far from natural function was to provide Gubbins and the Executive Council with a synopsis of every message to and from the field so that they could absorb our daily traffic at a glance and historians would have a reliable record of our main activities – a laudable enough concept were it not for one thing.

Much of the traffic which passed between the agents and the country sections (and between the agents and Signals) was in shorthand, and when our Pepyses tried to paraphrase it for Gubbins and posterity they often missed the all-important sub-texts.

One of the busiest members of the War Diary was Lionel Hale, a drama critic on the *News Chronicle*, who'd bought most of his theatrical books from 84 but was otherwise intelligent. Hale had represented SOE on a Top Secret committee which specialized in disseminating propaganda in neutral territories, and was considered one of SOE's star performers. But someone in Baker Street must have decided that his ability to sum up complicated plot-points for the *News Chronicle* would be a help to the War Diary, and for a brief period in '43 he was seconded to it.

For most of us it wasn't brief enough.

Used to double-entendres, he quickly realized that much of the traffic contained messages within messages, but instead of telephoning his queries to people like Buckmaster and me (as his more considerate colleagues did), he insisted on bringing them to us personally, and soon became the most lied-to officer in Baker Street, with the possible exception of the head of Finance. Although we told him the truth if it didn't lead to further questions, our preparations for D-Day had to be given slightly greater priority, and we often fobbed him off with whatever explanations would get rid of him most quickly.

To ensure that he left my office with something worth having, I arranged for him to be given a discount at 84. But the idea of making special use of him didn't occur to me until he was rash enough to confide that he often wrote reports on his various visits which he passed on to Gubbins and the Executive Council if he thought they'd be of interest.

I fabricated a series of 'Highly Confidential' reports, ostensibly from me to Heffer, and pretended to be immersed in them whenever he arrived. When he finally enquired what they were, I informed him that they were part of my own 'War Diary', and he immediately asked if he could look at them.

Each report falsified our reserves of silk codes, understating the stocks in hand, overstating the demands for them, and presented him with a picture of a cipher Dunkirk. One of them regretted to inform Heffer that unless our production facilities were increased, no more silks could be sent to the Middle East, and their agents would have to revert to using novels.

Once a reporter, always a reporter . . . within a week of showing him these reports, the code department received unsolicited offers of help from the head of Personnel and the director of Finance, and we won twenty more coders, a dozen more briefing officers, and a new firm of printers. It was a great loss to the code department when he left SOE to resume his old duties.

Our misrepresentations to the War Diary (which certain professional historians would one day take literally in their erudite treatises) were then scaled down.

By the end of November my report was almost finished except for 'the coding habits of agents which never would be', (every one of them deserved a mention). I'd limited my selection to twenty, and it included Patrick Leigh-Fermor (who'd kidnapped a German general but couldn't transpose), Nancy Wake (who'd used a pornographic poem which she'd made even more pornographic by her habit of misspelling it), Brian Stonehouse (a painter who'd brilliantly depicted his fellow-prisoners at three concentration camps, but whose previous indecipherables were even greater works of art) and Yvonne Cormeau code-named Annette, (who'd sent over 400 messages without a single mistake, possibly because I hadn't briefed her). Nor could I resist recording that at Major O'Reilly's instigation 84 Charing Cross Road had been used to give agents practice in picking up messages concealed in books when I was sent for by Nick, who warned me that within the next two weeks military vans would call at night to start collecting whatever records were ready to be handed over, and he hoped that some of mine were.

I assured him that large numbers of files I no longer needed had already been crated up, and he looked at me as if he were about to be crated up himself. 'I'd like to understand your new code before I leave.'

I couldn't resist this and blurted out the whole concept.

A whispered 'Good God' was followed by the longest silence which had ever passed between us. 'You do realize its value in peacetime?'

'It needs a lot of work, Nick.'

'And it bloody well deserves it. I'm going to talk to C.'

'I'm not going to be pressured into working for them.'

'That won't stop me from trying.' He snatched up the receiver, and asked to be put through to Gambier-Parry (C's head of Signals).

I hurried away to finish my report.

The following morning Nick walked in followed by Gambier-Parry and a captain whose name turned out to be Johnson.

I'd met Gambier-Parry nine months ago when he'd asked to examine the codes we were using, and I'd greeted him with a particularly hard handshake for wishing the poem-code on us.

This time he was prepared for it and, after rapidly disengaging, took a quick look round the office. 'I see your desk hasn't got any tidier.' He inspected its contents as if they already belonged to him.

'I want you to show the brigadier how the new code works,' said Nick.

Ten minutes later Gambier-Parry stared incredulously at Nick, then glanced at Captain Johnson, who'd been listening intently.

Johnson asked a number of perceptive questions, and I pretended that I didn't yet know the answers.

Gambier-Parry looked at me sharply. 'How long will it take you to find 'em?'

'Three months at least, sir . . . and then I mightn't succeed.'

'Let's find out, shall we? Come to C for as long as it takes, and you can help us sort out your coding records. Then we'll talk about other things. I'll fix up the details with Nick.'

He took for granted that his offer was accepted, and five minutes later they left.

Two days after their visit Heffer walked in and showed me a report from Bletchley which Nick wanted me to see. The report stated that it was a 'novel, ingenious and highly secure code', which apart from its obvious uses would allow agents to use radio telephony in complete safety, and had similar potential for amateur wireless operators. It would also provide a valuable means of communicating with agents via the BBC, and would replace the extremely weak system of using secret inks for letter communications.

'That shows how wrong even Bletchley can be . . .'

'What have you decided to do about it?'

I told him that before I retired at Xmas I'd hand over a blueprint of the code to Gambier-Parry and leave it to some other cryptographer to finish.

My response didn't seem to surprise him but the length of his puff warned me that something else was worrying him.

'Something's wrong, Heff. What is it?'

Several puffs later he admitted that it was personal. He said that his job in SOE was virtually over, and that he hadn't much to do for the next few months. Trying to make light of it, he told me that he'd been 'quite interested in doing a stint for C', though he hadn't yet been asked.

I realized that the Guru was trying to tell me that he was facing unemployment.

Twenty minutes later I was alone with Nick. I told him that I'd decided to accept Gambier-Parry's offer on two conditions: one was the length of my engagement, which must be limited to three months; the other concerned Heffer.

I explained that I'd be too busy with the new code to spend much time sorting out the records and that Heffer would be the ideal person to help me. He could supervise the rest of the Signals handover, and we might even be able to write a joint report on it.

'That's an excellent idea if you think he'd do it.'

'I feel sure he would.'

'I'll talk to Gambier-Parry at once.' He snatched up the telephone.

It occurred to me after I'd left that he wasn't as surprised as he might have been, and I wondered if there'd been a spot of collusion between him and the Guru.

Two days later he was 'delighted to be able to tell me' that Heff's appointment had been confirmed.

I subsequently learned that it had been settled weeks ago. For reasons which eluded me I loved them all the more for it.

SOE's records had taken far longer to collect than expected, and by Xmas the vans were still drawing up, which gave me time to fill my own mental vans with every important conversation I'd had since joining SOE.

My reports had been finished weeks ago (or as finished as they ever could be). The main one was 300 pages long; the separate report on Holland fifteen (Plan Giskes had been fully documented, and was added as an appendix). I'd delivered my Dutch report to Gubbins personally, but hadn't heard from him since. Perhaps it was because I'd also written an unsolicited paper called 'Ciphers, Signals and Sex'.

This was Dr Sigmund Marks's attempt to borrow Freud's theories on the unconscious 'will to self-destruct' to explain why agents failed to bury their parachutes (a foetal symbol), destroy their silk codes, or take elementary precautions to avoid capture. I also borrowed his more salacious theories to explain certain aspects of the girls' conduct but needed no help from him to explain their periods.

I then learned that Gubbins had a great deal more on his mind than starting reading reports. According to the grapevine, he'd been officially informed that when his present job ended the War Office would have no further use for him.

I asked Heffer why SOE's brilliant, brave, bloody-minded CD had been dismissed like a redundant doorman.

According to the Guru, Gubbins had put a strongly worded case to the Chiefs of Staff and others for the nucleus of an SOE-type organization to continue in peacetime under the auspices of C, but C had responded by convincing all concerned that Gubbins should have no part in it.

I slid morosely into 1946, knowing that I was about to start working for an organization which had no respect for the Mighty Atom.

C had been kind enough to tell me my new workshop's address. It was at the top end of Curzon Street, an area frequented by London's more professional tarts. The terms of my engagement with C had also been settled. They'd agreed to continue paying me my present salary of £45.15s.8d. (gross) per month. They'd also agreed that one member of my present staff could accompany me to Curzon Street, presumably to ward off the tarts.

Much as I wanted Muriel to come, the closure of SOE seemed the least painful break-point for both of us. I chose instead a FANY named Elizabeth Vaughan, a highly intelligent coder with a sense of humour she was likely to need.

Just as we were ready to leave Baker Street, SOE produced its last surprise.

Mindful, perhaps, of Churchill's injunction to 'Set Europe Ablaze', on 17 January parts of Michael House went up in flames, and though 'immediate action was taken' to put them out, many important records were destroyed. A FANY corporal named Barbara Hare was injured in the fire and had to be taken to St Mary's Hospital.

I'd worked too long for SOE to believe it was accidental, and wished the arsonist had chosen Montagu Mansions. Signals officers were used to getting their fingers burnt.

It was time to say goodbye to Nick.

His appointment had ended and the use of his office was a courtesy, but he was unlikely to need another as the army had finished with him just as it had with Gubbins.

I handed him a small parcel which Father had insisted on wrapping himself when he understood its purpose.

Nick unwrapped it just as carefully.

It contained a book with no indication of its contents (I'd left its catalogued description inside the cover with its price deleted). The first page contained two signatures: George V's and Queen Mary's.

It was an autograph-book which had belonged to Kitty Bonar Law, the eight-year-old daughter of the then Prime Minister. Kitty had refused to go to bed until she'd trotted downstairs in her nightdress to collect the autographs of her father's distinguished visitors (they had to be in those days to gain admission to Number 10). Her collection included an original line of music from Paderewski, a self-portrait from H. G. Wells, and a goodwill message from Winston and Clementine Churchill. She'd also obtained messages from dozens of leading statesmen, as well as the signatures of British MPs who could write.

On the last page I'd affixed a letter from Nick to me ('From D/SIGS to D/YCM'), which he'd signed in green ink. It was dated February '43, and authorized me to proceed at once with the production of silk codes.

I'd pinned a note to it which I'd written with Templar's pen. It was 'From D/YCM to D/SIGS', and thanked him on SOE's behalf for 'the most valuable signature of all which is yours'.

He returned to page one, and went through the whole book again as if unable to believe that it belonged to him.

He was still looking at it when I quietly left the room.

The next morning I dipped into my £45.16s.8d. (gross) per month and took a taxi to Curzon Street. But it wasn't my lucky day. The driver knew a quick cut.

I spent several minutes watching the tarts arriving for early-morning duty and thought I recognized Doris, but searched in vain for her dog.

It was time to go in.

EIGHTY-ONE

The Last Mischief

'Vengeance is mine' saith the Lord, and it soon became apparent to SOE's expatriates that someone in C had read the Bible.

None of us expected a civic reception but we were quite unprepared for the torture which was about to be inflicted on us in the name of security.

The moment we arrived at Curzon Street House we were incarcerated in the noxious bowels of a sub-basement where it was as difficult to breathe as to think, and where we were visited once a day by a doctor, though he was himself asphyxiated by the end of his rounds.

My assistant Liza Vaughan had a turkish bath next to mine, and Ann Turner (who had sole charge of SOE's WT records) had an office within choking distance. Heffer didn't need one as he only looked in twice a week 'to see how things were going', and promptly went with them. We rarely saw our country section colleagues but could hear them coughing in the corridor, a reasonable indication that they were still alive.

We were forced to accept that we'd walked out of the fire and into the frying pan, yet there was one compensation.

The sub-basement we occupied had been used by the War Cabinet to protect them from the worst bombing, and at least twice a day I had the privilege of peeing into a toilet once used by Churchill. I put out my cigar on these occasions as its fumes would have spread throughout the building. Heffer, an expert in such matters, said that an early-morning fart in Curzon Street House would be wafted back to its owner by the end of the day.

In deference to his judgement I christened the new code

'Windswept'. An astute colonel named Maltby (who was Gambier-Parry's Heffer) often looked in to examine its progress, and professed himself 'delighted with it'. Which was more than I was.

Although I was convinced by now that there would never be lasting peace as long as governments used codes, I'd devised one which would allow ambassadors to communicate their good intentions *en clair* whilst concealing their real ones with a little help from Windswept. Perhaps I'd finally learned the meaning of SOE-mindedness.

On 12 February Heffer called in, though he'd already done his two days' stint. 'You might like to see this,' he said.

He held out a copy of the *London Gazette* and pointed to a brief announcement: 'The King has been graciously pleased to award the George Cross to Acting Wing Commander Forest Frederick Yeo-Thomas, MC (89215), Royal Air Force Volunteer Reserve.' (The French had their own way of saying 'Merci, Tommee'. They subsequently named a street in Paris 'La rue Yeo-Thomas'.)

I pinned the announcement to the wall to give the room its only natural light, and six weeks later Windswept was finished. Although I'd refused Gambier-Parry's and Maltby's offers to continue in C in whatever capacity suited me best, they'd allowed me the privilege of signing off in their Broadway HQ instead of the building at the top of St James's Street where the ritual normally took place.

I noticed that the door of the code room was kept tightly closed throughout but Gambier-Parry and Maltby were there to shake hands, and Maltby saw me off the premises.

My code war was over, and I stood in the fresh air with nowhere to go.

Twenty minutes later I found myself in Baker Street.

Montagu Mansions was in the hands of the agents, and had a TO LET sign outside it. There was no one in sight, and the front door was open.

I entered my old office. It was even barer than I felt. The walls had been covered in off-white paint which matched my complexion, and the room had been stripped by a demolition expert.

It was impossible to believe that 40 million code-groups had passed through this nothing of a room, or that Tommy and Nick, Gubbins and Templar had once paced up and down it. Or that this was where I'd learned of the capture of Noor and Violette.

Wondering whether the new agents would suffer as much as ours had, and how we'd managed to learn so little from so much, I felt the sudden onset of a poem. Although I'd resolved not to write one in peacetime (poems had killed too many agents), it demanded the same rights of way as 'The Life That I Have'.

I had no paper but found a piece of chalk and wrote it on the wall where the silks had once stood:

> We listen round the clock
> For a code called peacetime
> But will it ever come
> And shall we know it when it does
> And break it once it's here
> This code called peacetime.
>
> Or is its message such
> That it cannot be absorbed
> Unless its text is daubed
> In letters made of lives
> From an alphabet of death
> Each consonant a breath
> Expired before its time.
>
> Signalmaster, Signalmaster
> Whose Commandments were in clear
> Must you speak to us in code
> Once peacetime is here?

I suddenly felt that someone was watching me, and turned round slowly hoping it was Ruth.

A charlady was standing in a doorway with a mop in one hand, a bucket in the other, and a cigarette dangling from her mouth. She looked at me suspiciously. 'You from the agents?' she asked.

'Yes,' I said, 'I suppose I am . . .'

She glared at the defacement on the wall.

I tried to erase it but had no rubber, and asked if I could borrow her mop, which she reluctantly surrendered.

I took a last look round the room, and closed my eyes while I said goodbye to it.

'Lost something?' she enquired.

'Yes,' I said, 'I suppose I have . . .'

And walked out of her office to make what I could of a code called peacetime.

Epilogue

Tommy died in 1964 without knowing that I was going to write this book, which doesn't necessarily mean that he hasn't read it, and there are certain facts he would expect me to disclose.

Ninety per cent of the WT records handed over to C in 1946 have been destroyed, and the code department's records scarcely exist. According to successive archivists (whose assurances I accept), 'intensive efforts' have been made to find my 300-page cipher report, my Dutch report and a long report on Belgium, but 'no trace can be found of them'. Even the ditty-box has been 'mislaid', and there are only two documents in the archive which are directly attributable to me. The first is a lecture I'd given entitled 'Be Near Me When My Light Is Low', and the other is my paper on 'Ciphers, Signals, and Sex'.

To be fair to the Foreign Office, it has retained its sense of humour, whatever else it may have lost, and I was informed by the then curator that 'Ciphers, Signals and Sex' had been graced with a label 'TO BE PRESERVED AS A DOCUMENT OF HISTORICAL IMPORTANCE', but someone had crossed out 'historical' and written 'hysterical'. Having re-read it, I agree with him.

A film was made about Violette Szabo called *Carve Her Name with Pride*, and I allowed its producer, Daniel Angel, to use the poem in his film providing that its author's name wasn't disclosed. Thousands of letters poured in asking who'd written it and the Rank Organization professed not to know but felt they should send me a letter they'd received from the father of an eight-year-old boy.

He said that his son was desperately ill, and could *someone* please answer the enclosed letter, which was written in code.

I managed to break his baby code, and the clear-text read: 'Dear code-master. She was very brave. Please how does the poem work. I'm going to be a spy when I grow up.'

I replied to him in his code (this was essential), saying that as soon as he was better of course I'd show him how it worked. And as soon as he was better he might like to come to the Special Forces Club and meet some of the other agents he might have read about. In the meantime I was sending him a chess-set which Violette once gave me because I knew that she'd like him to have it.

Six weeks later I received a letter from his father saying that his son had rallied for a month, and had died with the chess-set and the poem on his bed.

In 1949 the Dutch government instituted a Commission of Inquiry to establish the truth about Holland. It was particularly anxious to discover whether the disasters had been caused by a traitor in SOE or whether Dutch lives had deliberately been sacrificed as part of a British deception scheme (a theory as prevalent then as it is today).

The tribunal sat for almost a year and, as a gesture of goodwill, and to avoid any suggestion of a cover-up, the Foreign Office gave its chairman a list of SOE officers, from Gubbins downwards, who'd been 'responsible' for the conduct of clandestine operations in the Netherlands, and suggested that he should invite them to have frank discussions with him.

Every one of them, including Gubbins, agreed to meet him, and their conversations took place between 3 and 10 October.

It is doubtful whether a single participant in these 'frank discussions' could have shown the chairman how to break an indecipherable, or assess the significance of a total lack of them.

No member of the Signals directorate was invited to attend, though Nick and I were available at the time.

It is possible that we'd have had something useful to contribute.

APPENDIX ONE

Fingerprinting W.T. Operators

A W.T. operator's touch on the keyboard was as individual as a fingerprint. This didn't deter the enemy's radio experts from trying to simulate it, and from the summer of '43 until S.O.E. stopped passing traffic, detailed recordings were made of every operator's 'fist' before he or she left for the field.

Method. The operators were instructed to transmit every letter of the alphabet at varying speeds, followed by every numeral, but were given no warning that they were being 'fingerprinted' to avoid self-conscious transmissions. Their dots, dashes and morse hesitations were then transferred to a paper tape which moved at 16 feet per minute. This magnified even the smallest morse dots by quarter of an inch, allowing an in-depth study to be made of every operator's style. The details were recorded on square-ruled paper, and lodged with the Chief Signalmasters at the W.T. stations. When the operators reached the field, their 'fists' varied from message to message, responding to the tensions of the moment, but the basic characteristics were always present. Yet the Signalmasters needed no 'fingerprinting' charts to identify these characteristics: their morse-trained ears were attuned to every nuance of an operator's touch, and they recognised it at once. The Funk-Horchdienst (the German interception service) was equally adept. Its radio experts were able to counterfeit our operators' style to perfection if a sufficient number of messages had been intercepted.

The only real value of 'fingerprinting' was that it gave the operators confidence – which in itself was priceless. The concept of 'fingerprinting' had been brought to Nick's attention by a fair-haired WAAF Officer named Kay Cameron whose father had invented it. Nick immediately took her into S.O.E. as she was otherwise homeless. Determined that she should be based in London and posted to the stations only when necessary, he seconded her to the code-department and asked me 'to keep an eye on her'. As a contra-account (not that I needed one) he authorised me to head-hunt young Captain Appleby, a camouflage expert from the Thatched Barn who was a genius at devising new hiding places for WOKs and LOPs.

Shortage of space meant that Kay and Appleby had to share an office. They also shared an urge to help agents and each other in every way they could, and their enthusiasm for their near-impossible tasks turned their tiny office into a suite.

Those close to them sometimes wondered if they indulged in mutual fingerprinting, and though this was a pointless speculation as they were experts at camouflage, it allowed us to forget for a few moments that the average life-expectancy of a W.T. operator in France was at best six weeks.

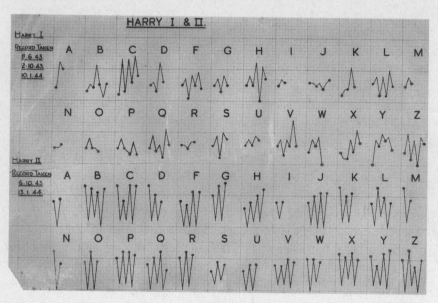

APPENDIX TWO

Minute of 2 November 1943 from L. S. Marks, HQ Security & Planning Office

Indecipherable Messages on Letter One-Time Pads

Owing to the very simple construction of the letter one-time pad code it is most improbable that many indecipherable messages will be received. However, when these indecipherables occur, the following are the lines of attack which should be attempted.

Attempt No 1

Assume that the agent has written his message *beneath his indicator group*. Consequently, all groups will have to be moved one group to the left. If this does prove to be the case, in outward messages the home station should also write beneath the indicator group. There are two points to bear in mind however.

Firstly, if the agent sends a series of messages correctly, and then suddenly makes a mistake by writing his message under the indicator group, the home station should not follow suit, but assume that it is an error on the part of the agent. If the agent sends his first message with the clear text written beneath the indicator group, the home station should reciprocate for his outward traffic until further notice.

Attempt No 2

The outstation may be confused over prefixes, therefore the second, as well as the first group of the message should be eliminated. This gives two attempts, i.e. eliminating the first two groups of the message and writing the third group as it should be written underneath the first group of the pad; and secondly, eliminating the first two groups and writing the third group underneath the indicated group of the one-time pad.

Attempt No 3

Should a message commence by reading sense, and suddenly breaks off into gibberish, the first group from which the gibberish appears should be moved immediately to the right, in case:

a. a group has been omitted in wireless transmission, and
b. the agent has slipped a group of his one-time pad when encoding his message.

Attempt No 4

The Home Station should now try to assume that the agent has written the message on top of the one-time pad groups instead of beneath them. Therefore, in order to decode, they should take the column of large capital letters on the extreme left of the substitution square, and this column should be regarded as the letters of the one-time pad. The small letters running along this line should be regarded as the letters of the cipher message. Letters at the head of the column in which the little letter stands must be regarded as the *en clair* group. For example, assume that the one-time pad group is ZVRBI, and that the agent has encoded the word 'house'. Write the letters HOUSE above ZVRBI and the result is BIPJB.

To encode to agents who are making this error, the first pair of letters for the home station to examine will be B over Z. They will go to B in the column at the extreme left of their substitution square, and glance along until they find the little letter Z. When they have found Z, they must glance up and see in which column it stands. They will find it to stand in column H.

The next pair of letters to examine will be I over V. They will go to column I at the extreme left of their substitution square, and glance along until they find little letter V. When they have found V, they must glance up and see in which column it stands. It will be found to be in column O.

604

Take P over R, J over B, B over I in the same manner, and the word HOUSE will be decoded.

Attempt No 5
It must be assumed now that the agent glances to the wrong side of his substitution square when enciphering, i.e. he will always look to the left of the capital letter instead of the right.

Attempt No 6
Assume that the agent, instead of taking the little letter as the cipher group and the large letter as the *en clair*, reverses the process and takes the little letter as the *en clair* group, and the large capital as the cipher group.

Attempt No 7
In all cases where any great difficulty is experienced and the above methods fail, the home station must concentrate on the end of the message and try to work backwards, as it must never be forgotten that an agent may be passing a message for someone else, and begin by Playfairing without giving us any warning. Caution must be taken, however, with the last group, which may consist of dead letters. The penultimate group is really the key group at this stage of the attack.

Attempt No 8
When you find the agent's indicator, assume that all the one-time pad groups he has used consist of the groups immediately beneath this indicator group, i.e. in the same column instead of running along the same parallel.

Attempt No 9
It must also be assumed that an agent may omit a line, start on the wrong line, or use the same line twice. He may also use the wrong page.

The breaking of this code will depend very greatly on individual observation, as sometimes an agent will be merely a letter out, which means a sliding along to the left of one letter instead of five.

The first attempt of all will therefore be a "fanning out" in both directions, firstly group by group, secondly letter by letter. If this fails, the "fan" must consist of two letters on either side being left out, then three, then four.

In extreme cases, it must be assumed that up to ten groups of the pad may be omitted.

Index